SCOTTISH FAMILY HISTORIES

SCOTTISH

FAMILY

HISTORIES

compiled by

JOAN P. S. FERGUSON

assisted by Dennis Smith and Peter Wellburn

NATIONAL LIBRARY OF SCOTLAND

EDINBURGH

1986

ISBN 0-902220-68-3

British Library Cataloguing in Publication Data

Ferguson, Joan P. S.
Scottish family histories. —— 2nd ed.
1. Scotland —— Genealogy —— Bibliography
I. Title   II. Smith, Dennis, 1945 Mar. 7-
III. Wellburn, Peter   IV. Ferguson, Joan P. S.
Scottish family histories held in Scottish libraries
016.929'2'09411   Z5313.G7S3

PREFACE

IT is with great pleasure that I commend the present revised edition of *Scottish Family Histories*, which extends the scope and content of the earlier edition of 1960, and includes, for the first time, the extensive holdings of the National Library of Scotland.

Thanks are due, first and foremost, to the compiler of *Scottish Family Histories*, Miss Joan P. S. Ferguson, Librarian of the Royal College of Physicians, for her dedicated work. Thanks are also due to Mr Dennis Smith, Editor, Bibliography of Scotland, who undertook the task of incorporating the National Library's holdings, assisted by a team employed under the auspices of the Manpower Services Commission (Miss F Aitken, Miss R Farningham, Mr G Flanagan, Miss J Kirkland and Mr E Lamont); to Mr Peter Wellburn, Head of the Periodicals Unit, who edited the present edition for publication; and to Miss Christian Wright, Superintendent of Lending Services, for advice on library codes. The supervision of the project was carried out by Mr J. R. Seaton, formerly Principal Keeper of Printed Books, and latterly by Dr Ann Matheson, Keeper of Printed Books.

E. F. D. ROBERTS
Librarian
June 1986

INTRODUCTION

MARGARET STUART and Sir James Balfour Paul published their *Scottish Family History* in 1930, and it has become the standard reference tool for Scottish genealogists and family historians. Thirty years later, in 1960, the Scottish Central Library published *Scottish Family Histories held in Scottish Libraries*, compiled from returns of holdings sent in by 76 Scottish libraries, and containing some 2,000 titles and their locations. Its publication coincided with an upsurge of interest in genealogy and family history which, today, shows no sign of waning, but is rather waxing greater both at home and around the world, wherever Scots have emigrated.

Stuart and Paul's work contained not only references to separately printed histories but also to articles in periodicals. It seemed desirable, therefore, to aim for the inclusion of periodical articles from 1930 to date in any future edition of *Scottish Family Histories*. This has been achieved in the present revised edition. It has also been possible to incorporate the extensive holdings of the National Library of Scotland which could not be done in 1960. Once more, Scottish libraries have co-operated in returning up-to-date details of their holdings, including works published since 1960, and the present work contains some 3,200 entries, almost twice the size of the original.

My thanks are due to all colleagues in the co-operating Scottish libraries for their help and, in particular, to the assistance of colleagues in the National Library of Scotland who have brought this edition to publication.

J. P. S. FERGUSON
June 1986

NOTE ON SCOPE AND ARRANGEMENT

USERS of *Scottish Family Histories* are asked to note the following:

1.   The present edition of *Scottish Family Histories* is based on information in the 1960 edition, which was compiled from replies from 76 co-operating libraries, updated by responses from 50 libraries to Questionnaires sent out in 1982. The contributing libraries are listed in the Key to Locations. For the first time the extensive holdings of the National Library of Scotland have been included.

2.   Biographies of individuals have not been included, except where they contain sufficient information about the families to justify inclusion as family histories.

3.   The arrangement of the works is alphabetically by *family name*, subdivided by branches, and with references from titles, e.g.

> **Campbell**
> **Campbell,** Earl of, Marquess of, Duke of Argyll
> **Campbell** of Auchinbreck
>
> **Argyll,** Earl of, Marquess of, Duke of, *see*
> **Campbell,** Earl of, Marquess of, Duke of Argyll

4.   An exception to the foregoing rule is made for *peerage cases*, where titles were disputed, and the works are more conveniently entered under the title, e.g.

> **Mar,** Earldom of

5.   Where ascertainable, the place and date of publication are given. The abbreviations 'n.p.' and 'n.d.' mean that the place or date respectively of the work have not been ascertained from the work itself.

6.   The present edition of *Scottish Family Histories* includes printed books, pamphlets, and articles about Scottish family history excerpted from a range of periodicals. It also includes manuscript Scottish family histories reported by the contributing libraries.

7.   The inclusion of any work in this list does not necessarily imply that it is available for loan. Readers are advised first to check with the individual library whether the item is available for loan.

8.   An asterisk is used to denote an imperfect copy, or an imperfect run of a periodical.

9.   The reorganization of Scottish local government in 1975 allocated responsibility for public libraries (in the majority of cases) to district councils. This led to mergers between existing libraries and to the break-up and re-allocation of some county library stocks. It has not always been possible, with the limited resources available, to verify the present location of copies reported in 1960, and this may have led to omissions.

The National Library will be glad to receive information relating to the holdings of libraries participating in the present edition, either additions or deletions.

June 1986

KEY TO LIBRARY CODES

SCOTTISH Family Histories uses the library codes published in the *Directory of Library Codes*, 1984, issued by the British Library Lending Division, Boston Spa, now renamed the British Library Document Supply Centre. A number of libraries do not lend material in their collections and, consequently, users of *Scottish Family Histories* are advised first to check with the individual library whether the item is available for loan.

CODE	LIBRARY
AD/U-1	See AD/U-3
AD/U-3	ABERDEEN UNIVERSITY LIBRARY Queen Mother Library, Meston Walk, Aberdeen AB9 2UE
DN/U-1	DUNDEE UNIVERSITY LIBRARY Perth Road, Dundee DD1 4HN
ED/M-1	ROYAL COLLEGE OF PHYSICIANS OF EDINBURGH 9 Queen Street, Edinburgh EH2 1JQ
ED/N-1	NATIONAL LIBRARY OF SCOTLAND George IV Bridge, Edinburgh EH1 1EW
ED/N-2	NATIONAL LIBRARY OF SCOTLAND LENDING SERVICES 312-320 Lawnmarket, Edinburgh EH1 2PJ
ED/S10	SIGNET LIBRARY Parliament Square, Edinburgh EH1 1RF
ED/U-1	EDINBURGH UNIVERSITY LIBRARY George Square, Edinburgh EH8 9LJ
ED/U-3	HERIOT-WATT UNIVERSITY LIBRARY Riccarton, Currie, Edinburgh EH14 4AS

CODE	LIBRARY
GL/U-1	GLASGOW UNIVERSITY LIBRARY Hillhead Street, Glasgow G12 8QE
QZ/L37	COURT OF THE LORD LYON HM New Register House, Edinburgh EH1 3YT
QZ/P-1	CITY OF GLASGOW DISTRICT LIBRARIES The Mitchell Library, North Street, Glasgow G3 7DN
QZ/P-3	MONKLANDS DISTRICT LIBRARIES Coatbridge Library, Academy Street, Coatbridge ML5 3AW
QZ/P-4	CLYDEBANK DISTRICT LIBRARIES Central Library, Dumbarton Road, Clydebank G81 1XH
QZ/P-6	RENFREW DISTRICT LIBRARIES Marchfield Avenue, Paisley PA3 2RJ
QZ/P-7	KILMARNOCK AND LOUDOUN DISTRICT LIBRARIES Public Library, Dick Institute, Elmbank Avenue, Kilmarnock KA1 3BU

QZ/P-9	MIDLOTHIAN DISTRICT LIBRARIES 7 Station Road, Roslin, Midlothian EH25 9PF	QZ/P34	EAST LOTHIAN DISTRICT LIBRARY Lodge Street, Haddington EH41 3DX
QZ/P10	DUMFRIES AND GALLOWAY REGIONAL LIBRARY SERVICE Ewart Library, Catherine Street, Dumfries DG1 1JB	QZ/P38	ORKNEY LIBRARY SERVICES Laing Street, Kirkwall, Orkney KW15 1NW
QZ/P11	BORDERS REGIONAL LIBRARY St Mary's Mill, Selkirk TD7 5EW	QZ/P40	HIGHLAND REGIONAL LIBRARY SERVICE 31A Harbour Road, Inverness IV1 1UA
QZ/P13	FALKIRK DISTRICT LIBRARIES Public Library, Hope Street, Falkirk FK1 5AU	QZ/P40(I)	HIGHLAND REGIONAL LIBRARY SERVICE Inverness Library, Margaret Street, Inverness IV1 1LS
QZ/P14	STIRLING DISTRICT LIBRARY Borrowmeadow Road, Springkerse Industrial Estate, Stirling FK7 7TN	QZ/P40(D)	HIGHLAND REGIONAL LIBRARY SERVICE Dingwall Library, Old Academy, Dingwall IV15 9JZ
QZ/P15	CLACKMANNAN DISTRICT LIBRARY 17 Mar Street, Alloa FK10 1HT	QZ/P40(W)	HIGHLAND REGIONAL LIBRARY SERVICE Wick Library, Sinclair Terrace, Wick KW1 5AB
QZ/P16	DUNFERMLINE DISTRICT LIBRARIES Central Library, Abbot Street, Dunfermline KY12 7NW	QZ/P41	SHETLAND LIBRARY Lower Hillhead, Lerwick, Shetland ZE1 0EL
QZ/P18	KIRKCALDY DISTRICT LIBRARIES East Fergus Place, Kirkcaldy KY1 1XT	QZ/P42	WEST LOTHIAN DISTRICT LIBRARIES Wellpark, Marjoribanks Street, Bathgate, West Lothian EH48 1AN
QZ/P20	DUNDEE DISTRICT CENTRAL LIBRARY The Wellgate, Dundee DD1 1DB	QZ/P49	DUMBARTON DISTRICT LIBRARIES Levenford House, Helenslee Road, Dumbarton G82 4AH
QZ/P22	CITY OF ABERDEEN DISTRICT LIBRARIES Central Library, Rosemount Viaduct, Aberdeen AB9 1GU	QZ/P50	MORAY DISTRICT LIBRARIES 21 Tyock, Elgin, Morayshire IV30 1XY
QZ/P26	PERTH AND KINROSS DISTRICT LIBRARIES Shore Road, Perth PH2 8BH	QZ/P52	INVERCLYDE DISTRICT LIBRARIES Central Library, Clyde Square, Greenock, Renfrewshire PA15 1NA
QZ/P27	ARGYLL AND BUTE DISTRICT LIBRARY Hunter Street, Kirn, Dunoon, Argyll PA23 8JR	QZ/P53	HAMILTON DISTRICT LIBRARIES 98 Cadzow Street, Hamilton ML3 6HQ
QZ/P28	ANGUS DISTRICT LIBRARIES Central Services Unit, Municipal Buildings, Bank Street, Brechin DD9 6AX	QZ/P56	MOTHERWELL DISTRICT LIBRARIES Hamilton Road, Motherwell ML1 3BZ
QZ/P30	NORTH EAST SCOTLAND LIBRARY SERVICE 14 Crown Terrace, Aberdeen AB9 2BH	QZ/P99	CITY OF EDINBURGH DISTRICT LIBRARIES Central Library, George IV Bridge, Edinburgh EH1 1EG

QZ/Q17   NORTH EAST FIFE DISTRICT LIBRARY
St Catherine Street, Cupar, Fife
KY15 4TA

QZ/Q41   WESTERN ISLES LIBRARIES
Public Library, Stornoway, Isle of Lewis
PA87 2QG

QZ/Q71   CLYDESDALE DISTRICT LIBRARIES
Lindsay Institute, Hope Street, Lanark
ML11 7NN

QZ/Q76   STRATHKELVIN DISTRICT LIBRARIES
170 Kirkintilloch Road, Bishopbriggs,
Glasgow G64 2LX

QZ/Q78   EASTWOOD DISTRICT LIBRARIES
Eastwood Park, Rouken Glen Road,
Giffnock G46 6UG

QZ/Q81   CUMBERNAULD AND KILSYTH DISTRICT LIBRARY
8 Allander Walk, Cumbernauld,
Glasgow G67 1EE

QZ/Q88   CUMNOCK AND DOON VALLEY DISTRICT LIBRARY
Bank Glen, Cumnock, Ayrshire
KA18 1PQ

QZ/Q91   EAST KILBRIDE DISTRICT LIBRARIES
Civic Centre, East Kilbride G74 1AB

SA/U-1   ST ANDREWS UNIVERSITY LIBRARY
North Street, St Andrews, Fife
KY16 9TR

ST/U-1   STIRLING UNIVERSITY LIBRARY
Stirling FK9 4LA

SCOTTISH FAMILY HISTORIES

Abercorn, Marquess of, Duke of *see* **Hamilton,** Marquess, Duke of Abercorn

Abercrombie
SHEARER, John Elliot
Abercrombies of Fifeshire, Banffshire,
Tullibody and Aboukir. [Stirling, n.d.]
ED/N-1 (6.1890) QZ/P14 QZ/P99

TOD, David A.
The Abercrombies of Fife and Forfar,
1592-1775. [N.p., 19--.]
QZ/P28

Abercrombie of Abercrombie
ROSE, David Murray
The tragic history of the Abercrombies.
[Banff, 1902]. (Reprinted from *Banffshire Journal*,
Oct.-Nov. 1902.)
ED/N-1 (5.4190) QZ/P30 ED/N-2 QZ/P50

Abercrombie in Baltimore
ABERCROMBIE, Ronald Taylor
A genealogical and biographical sketch of the
family of David Abercrombie who settled in
Baltimore, Maryland, in 1848. Baltimore, 1940.
ED/N-1 (R.172.c)

Abercromby
ABERCROMBY, Cavendish Douglas
The family of Abercromby. Aberdeen, 1927.
ED/N-1 (S.122.e) QZ/P30 QZ/P22
AD/U-1 SA/U-1 GL/U-1 QZ/L37
QZ/P50 QZ/P99

HALLEN, Arthur Washington Cornelius *and*
SHEARER, John Elliot
Family of Abercromby of Kersie, Abbotts Kersie,
and Abbots Throsk in the county of Stirling,
Scotland, 1456-1895. Stirling, [n.d.].
ED/N-1 (6.1890) QZ/P14

MACKIE, Mary P.
Three Abercromby families. [N.p.], 1981.
QZ/P15 QZ/P30

Abercromby of Airthrey and Menstrie
FERGUSSON, Robert Menzies
Logie: a parish history. Vol. 2: Lands and
landowners. Paisley, 1905.
ED/N-1 (R.243.a) QZ/P14

Abercromby of Birkenbog
['ACCOUNT of the family of Abercrombie of
Birkenbog'. 1811?]
ED/N-1 (Adv.MS.6.1.17., ff.3-6.)

Abercromby of Glasshaugh
TAYLER, Henrietta
The Abercrombies of Glasshaugh. (In *Transactions of
the Banffshire Field Club*, 7 March 1939, pp. 1-22.)
ED/N-1 (NE.3.g.1)

Abercromby of Tullibody
[PRINTED papers presented to the Court of Session
in the matter of the lands of Tullibody, George
Cumming of Pittulie, trustee for James Ogilvie of
Auchiries, pursuer, Alexander and George
Abercromby of Tullibody, defenders.] [Edinburgh],
1740-3.
ED/N-1 (X.44.h.40)

Aberdeen, Earl of
GORDON, John Campbell, *Earl of Aberdeen*
Case on behalf of the Right Honourable John
Campbell, Earl of Aberdeen in the peerage of
Scotland, claiming a writ of summons to
Parliament as Viscount Gordon of Aberdeen in the
peerage of the United Kingdom. London, 1872.
ED/N-1 (A.19.a; 6.492) ED/S10

Abernethy
ACCOUNT of the family of Abernethy.
[N.p., n.d.]
ED/S10 (Unconfirmed location)

ABERNETHIE, John
Information for John Abernethie of Mayen against
Sir John Gordon of Park. 2 parts. [Edinburgh,
1695.]
ED/N-1 (6.282(28,29))

ADDITIONAL information for John Abernethy of
Mayen against John Gordon of Rothemay.
[Edinburgh, 1695.]
ED/N-1 (6.282(30))

Aboyne, Earl of *see* **Gordon,** Earl of Aboyne

Adair of Kinhilt
ROSE, David Murray
Adairs of Kinhilt. [N.p., n.d.]
AD/U-1

Adam

[A BOOK of notes concerning the family of Adam, 1549-1967. N.p., 19--.]
QZ/P28

[A BOOK of notes concerning the family of Adam, 1600-1916. N.p., n.d.]
QZ/P28

Adam of Blairadam

ADAM, Sir Charles Elphinstone
Sir Charles Elphinstone Adam, bart., of Blair-Adam: [lineage]. Blair-Adam, 1925.
ED/N-2 QZ/P99

PEDIGREE of the Adam family, as certified by the Provost and Bailies of Forfar in 1776. (*Typescript*)
QZ/P99

Adam in Glasgow

BULLOCH, John Malcolm
The Adam family of Glasgow, more particularly Frank Adam. [1937.] (*Press cuttings and miscellaneous letters*)
ED/N-2

Adam Smith

ADAM SMITH, Janet
A family century in the Alpine Club. (In *Alpine Journal*, vol. 87, no. 331, 1982, pp. 142-8.)
ED/N-1 (Y.205)

Adams

PERRY, S. A.
Adams family records. [N.d.]
QZ/P99

Adamson in Edinburgh

INGLIS, John A.
Sir John Hay "the incendiary", 1578-1654. [With genealogical tables.] Glasgow, 1937.
ED/N-1 (R.186.c)

Agnew

AGNEW, Sir Andrew
The Agnews of Lochnaw: a history of the hereditary Sheriffs of Galloway. Edinburgh, 1864.
ED/N-1 (A.113.e) ED/N-2 SA/U-1 GL/U-1
QZ/P16 QZ/L37 QZ/P99

— The hereditary Sheriffs of Galloway. 2nd ed. Edinburgh, 1893. 2v.
ED/N-1 (Hist.S.114.c) QZ/P11 SA/U-1
GL/U-1 QZ/L37 QZ/P99

AGNEW, Sir Crispin
A genealogy of the Agnews of Lochnaw. [N.p.], 1977.
QZ/L37

AGNEW, Douglas
The whites of their eyes. [Edinburgh, 1982.]
ED/N-1 (H2.83.206) QZ/P99

Agnew of Kilumquha

REID, Robert Corsane
Agnew of Kilumquha. (In *Transactions of the Dumfriesshire and Galloway Natural History & Antiquarian Society*, 3rd series, vol.xxiii,1940-4, pp.151-4.)
ED/N-1 (J.187)

Ailsa, Marquess of *see* **Kennedy,** Marquess of Ailsa

Ainslie

FOULIS, William Ainslie
Ainslie family charts. [N.d.] (*MS.*)
QZ/P99

— Ainslie family: miscellaneous papers. [N.d.] (*MS. and typescript papers*)
QZ/P99

— [Ainslie papers.] [N.d.] (*MS. and typescript papers*) 4v.
QZ/99

— The Ainslies of Dolphinston, Falla, Ulliston, etc. in Roxburghshire, and Pilton, Pentland, Hillend etc., Midlothian [N.d.] (*MS.*)
QZ/P99

— [Genealogical chart of the families of Ainslie.] [N.d.] (*MS.*)
QZ/P99

['GENEALOGY and descent of George Ainslie of Pilton and Jean Anstruther his spouse'. 17--.]
ED/N-1 (Adv.MS.20.1.6.,ff.32-41.)

MORDEN, Robert Lyle Price
Border bairns: an Ainslie family history. Woodstock, Ontario, 1978.
QZ/P99

Airlie, Earldom of *see also* **Ogilvy,** Earl of Airlie

Airlie, Earldom of
OGILVIE, Walter
Case of Walter Ogilvie.
QZ/L37

— Additional case of Walter Ogilvie.
QZ/L37

OGILVY, David
Case of David Ogilvy, Esq., claiming the titles etc.
of Earl of Airlie and Lord Ogilvy of Alith and
Lintrathen.
QZ/L37

Airth, Earldom of *see also* **Allardice** of Allardice

Airth, Earldom of
AIRTH papers. [N.p., n.d.]
ED/N-1 (NE.25.h.15)   ED/N-2   QZ/L37

AIRTH peerage: case of Robert Barclay Allardice
Barclay-Allardice, Esquire . . . claiming the
Earldom of Airth in the peerage of Scotland. [With
a genealogical table.] London, 1906.
ED/N-1 (6.274(8))

ALLARDICE, Robert Barclay
Case of Robert Barclay Allardice of Urie and
Allardice with two appendixes of evidences. 1838.
QZ/L37

MINUTES of evidence. 1839.
ED/N-1 (Yule.144.(2))   QZ/L37

MINUTES of evidence taken before the Committee
for Privileges to whom was referred the petition of
Mrs. Margaret Barclay-Allardice . . . that it may be
adjudged and declared that she is entitled to . . . the
Earldom of Airth. [London], 1870.
ED/N-1 (6.274(6))

MINUTES of evidence taken before the Committee
of Privileges in the petition of Nicholas
Donnithorne Bishop and Mary Eleanor Bishop
against the claim of Robert Barclay Allardice to the
Earldom of Airth. [With genealogical tables.]
[London], 1839.
ED/N-1 (6.274(7))

NICOLAS, Sir Nicholas Harris
History of the earldoms of Strathern, Monteith and
Airth; with a report of the proceedings before the
House of Lords on the claim of Robert Barclay
Allardice to the earldom of Airth. London, 1842.
ED/N-1 (A.114.c)   ED/N-2   SA/U-1   AD/U-1
GL/U-1   QZ/P26   QZ/L37   QZ/P99

Aitken of Thornton
RUVIGNY and RAINEVAL, M. A. H. D. H. de la C.
Massue de Ruvigny, *9th Marquis de*
Aitken of Thornton. London, 1901.
ED/N-1 (5.1570)

Aiton *see* Ayton

Albany, Duke of *see* **Stewart,** Duke of Albany

Alexander
ALEXANDER, Helen
Passages in the lives of Helen Alexander and James
Currie of Pentland, and other papers. [With a
genealogical table, with manuscript additions.]
[Belfast], 1869.
ED/N-1 (NC.272.f.8)

ALEXANDER, John E.
A record of the descendants of John Alexander of
Lanarkshire, Scotland and his wife Margaret
Glasson, who emigrated from County Armagh,
Ireland to Chester County, Pennsylvania in 1736.
Philadelphia, 1878.
ED/N-1 (A.120.a)

SONDLEY, F. A.
Descent of the Scottish Alexanders. [N.p., 1912.]
ED/N-1 (1960.10)   ED/N-2

Alexander of Longkerse
FERGUSSON, Robert Menzies
Logie: a parish history. Vol. 2: Lands and
landowners. Paisley, 1905.
ED/N-1 (R.243.a)   QZ/P14

Alexander, Earl of Stirling *see also* **Stirling,**
Earldom of

Alexander, Earl of Stirling
An ACCOUNT of the resumption of the titles by the
present Earl of Stirling . . . with an epitome of the
genealogy of . . . Alexander. London, 1826.
QZ/P99 (Unconfirmed location)

HUMPHRYS, Alexander
Narrative . . . also a genealogical account of the
family of Alexander. Edinburgh, 1836.
ED/N-1 (R.290.b)   QZ/P14   GL/U-1   QZ/P99

MACAULAY, Joseph Babington
The life of the last Earl of Stirling. Paignton, 1906.
ED/N-1 (S.153.f)   QZ/P-1   QZ/P14   QZ/P99

REMARKS on the trial of the Earl of Stirling, at Edinburgh, April 29th, 1839 for forgery. [N.p.], 1839.
QZ/P14   QZ/P99

ROGERS, Charles
Memorials of the Earl of Stirling and of the House of Alexander. Edinburgh, 1877. 2v.
ED/N-1 (Gramp.Club.30)   SA/U-1   GL/U-1   QZ/L37   QZ/P-1   QZ/P-3   QZ/P14   QZ/P16   QZ/P99

SONDLEY, Forster Alexander
Descent of the Scottish Alexanders. [N.p.], 1912.
ED/N-1 (1960.10)   ED/N-2   QZ/P99

TURNBULL, William
The Stirling peerage: trial of Alexander Humphreys or Alexander, styling himself Earl of Stirling before the High Court of Justiciary for forgery on 29th April, 1839. Edinburgh, 1839.
ED/N-1 (Yule Donation No.95)   QZ/P99

Alice

HOMAN, William MacLean
Ancestors and descendants of Andrew Mitchell and Janet Alice his wife. [With a genealogical table.] Glasgow, 1938.
ED/N-1 (6.231)

Alison

MORRISON, Leonard A.
The history of the Alison or Allison family in Europe and America, 1135-1893. Boston, 1893.
ED/N-1 (R.172.e)

Allan

McCALL, Hardy Bertram
Memoirs of my ancestors. Birmingham, 1884.
ED/N-1 (A. 114.a)   QZ/P99

'MATERIAL relating to the lands and lairds of Allan'. [N.p., n.d.]
QZ/P-6

Allan of Easter Crombie

ROSE, P.
A genealogy of the Allans, formerly of Easter Crombie, Banffshire. (In *Transactions of the Banffshire Field Club*, 1903-4, pp. 50-65.)
ED/N-1 (NE.3.g.1)   QZ/L37

Allan in Kirkcaldy

McCALL, Hardy Bertram
Some old families: a contribution to the genealogical history of Scotland. Birmingham, 1890.
ED/N-1 (A.36.a)   QZ/P11   QZ/L37   QZ/P99

Allardice of Allardice *see also* **Airth,** Earldom of

Allardice of Allardice

The DESCENDANTS of the late Mrs Margaret Barclay-Allardice, daughter and heiress of the late Robert Barclay Allardice. London, [1904].
ED/N-1 (S.120.a)

The PEDIGREE of Robert Barclay-Allardice, heir apparent of the line of Prince David Stuart, Earl Palatine of Strathearn, the Earls of Menteith and Airth, Lord Graham of Kilpont and Kilbryde, and the families of Barclay of Mathers and Ury, and Allardice of Allardice. Edinburgh, 1892.
ED/N-1 (S.120.a)   ED/S10

ROSE, David Murray
Allardice of that ilk. [N.d.] (*Xerox-copy*)
QZ/P99

WOOD, John Philp
Memorials of various families. [1830?] (*MS.*)
QZ/P99

Alston

CRESSWELL, Lionel
Stemmata Alstoniana: a collection of genealogical tables and memoranda relating to the ancient family of Alston. [N.p.], 1905.
ED/N-1 (S.122.c)

Ancram, Earl of *see* **Ker,** Earl of Ancram

Anderson

ANDERSON, F. J.
Descent of the family of Anderson of Gracedieu, County Waterford. [A genealogical chart.] [N.p.], 1916.
ED/N-1 (NE.25.a.19)

ANDERSON, William
The Croft House Andersons; with memories of Ceres in the sixties and seventies of last century. Cupar, 1933.
ED/N-1 (R.172.g)   SA/U-1   QZ/P14   QZ/P99

Anderson of Ardbrake
ANDERSON, F. J.
Anderson of Wester Ardbrake, Banffshire. [Chart.]
[N.p.], 1911.
AD/U-1

Anderson of Dumfries
ANDERSON, John
Andersons of Dumfries: record of an old burgh
family. Welshpool, 1961.
ED/N-1 (NE.25.b.19) GL/U-1 QZ/P10

Anderson in Inverness
ANDERSON, Isabel Harriet
An Inverness lawyer and his sons, 1796-1878. [With
a genealogical table.] Aberdeen, 1900.
ED/N-1 (S.147.f) QZ/P40 QZ/P99

Anderson in Peterhead
ANDERSON, John
Records of a family of "Andersons" of Peterhead and
their connections. [N.p.], 1936.
AD/U-1 QZ/L37 QZ/P99

Anderson of Phingask
WOOD, James Mackenzie Anderson
The Andersons in Phingask and their descendants.
Aberdeen, 1910.
QZ/P30 QZ/P22 SA/U-1 QZ/P99

Andrews
ANJOU, Gustave
Andrews family. [N.p., 1910?] (*Typescript*)
ED/N-1 (NE.25.h.23)

Angus *see also* **Douglas**

Angus
MCINTOSH, Mary
Roots and branches: the story of the Angus and
Leybourne families. [With genealogical tables.]
Newcastle, [1958].
ED/N-1 (NE.63.e.12)

WATSON, Angus
The Angus clan (years 1588 to 1950). Gateshead,
1955.
ED/N-1 (NE.25.c.6) SA/U-1 ED/N-2 QZ/P22
QZ/P99 QZ/P40 (D)

Angus, Earl of *see also* **Douglas,** Earl of Angus

Angus, Earl of
NAPIER, Mark
A "memorie" historical and genealogical of my
mother's paternal lineage, namely the Hamiltons of
Innerwick, the Lothian Kerrs, and the Earls of
Angus. Edinburgh, 1872.
ED/N-1 (F.7.d.3) ED/N-2

['NOTES on the genealogy of the Earls of Angus and
their descendants'. 1709.]
ED/N-1 (Adv.MS.34.6.24.,ff.66,67)

Annand of Sauchie
BROWN-MORISON, John Brown
Genealogical notes anent some ancient Scottish
families. Perth, 1884.
QZ/P15

Annandale, Earldom of *see also* **Johnstone,** Earl of
Annandale

Annandale, Earldom of
CASES.
QZ/L37

HOPE, John
[Session papers relating to the claims of John, Lord
Hope, and his mother Henrietta, Countess of
Hopetoun, on the title and estate of George,
Marquis of Annandale. Edinburgh, 1733-37.]
ED/N-1 (R.282.c)

MACDONALD, James Alexander Donald John
The Annandale mystery. Dumfries, [1932].
ED/N-2

— The Annandale peerage: enquiry concerning the
alleged extinction of Captn. the Hon. John
Johnstone of Stapleton, brother of William, Earl
and Marquis of Annandale, 1655-1721 and uncle of
George, last Marquis of Annandale, 1720-1792.
[1925.]
ED/N-1 (S.123.f.1(1))

— The contest with the Hopes and Westerhalls and
the disappearance of the titles of the Johnstones of
Annandale, followed by the Hope Johnstone deed
of entail of 1799. Dumfries, [1925].
ED/N-1 (S.123.f.1(2))

MINUTES of evidence ... petition of John James
Hope Johnstone of Annandale, Esq., ... claiming
the earldom of Annandale and Hartfell. 1825-1838.
QZ/L37

SESSION and appeal papers in the case of the
Annandale peerage; Sir James Johnstone, John J.
Hope Johnstone, the elder and the younger, John H.
Goodinge Johnstone, Sir Frederick G. Johnstone,
Dougal Campbell, Sir Frederick J. W. Johnstone,
and Edward Johnstone of Fulford Hall, claimants.
[With genealogical tables.] Edinburgh and London,
[1792-1881].
ED/N-1 (Yule.161,162(11,15),170; R.282.c)

SPEECHES and judgments. 4v.
QZ/L37

Anstruther

ANSTRUTHER, Arthur Wellesley
History of the family of Anstruther. Edinburgh,
1923.
ED/N-1 (S.122.c) QZ/Q17 SA/U-1 QZ/L37
QZ/P99

['GENEALOGY and descent of George Ainslie of
Pilton and Jean Anstruther his spouse'. 17--.]
ED/N-1 (Adv.MS.20.1.6,ff.32-41)

GREAT BRITAIN. HOUSE OF LORDS
Before the Committee of Privileges: titles of Lord
Newark [assumed by William Anstruther] now
extinct. [With genealogical chart.] [London, 1771?]
ED/N-1 (Yule.168(11))

Anstruther-Thomson of Charleton

['ANSTRUTHER-THOMSON of Charleton, Fife.'
18--.] (MS.)
GL/U-1

Arbuthnot

ARBUTHNOT, Ada Jane P. Stewart-Mackenzie
Memories of the Arbuthnots of Kincardineshire
and Aberdeenshire. London, 1920.
ED/N-1 (S.122.d) QZ/P30 GL/U-1 QZ/P22
ED/U-1 SA/U-1 QZ/P99

ROSE, David Murray
The Lords of Arbuthnot. [N.p., n.d.] (Reprinted
from Stonehaven Journal, 1902-3.)
ED/N-1 (1904.14)

Arbuthnott, Viscount of

GORDON, George
Unto His Grace, His Majesties High Commissioner,
and the . . . Estates of Parliament, the petition of
George, Earl of Southerland [to be appointed a
guardian to his grandson, the Viscount of
Arbuthnott]. [Edinburgh, 1695.]
ED/N-1 (6.282(103))

Archer

ARCHER, James H. L.
Memorials of families of the surname of Archer.
London, 1861.
ED/N-1 (A.35.g.1;A.35.b.1) ED/N-2

Arcus see also Harcus

Arcus

ARCUS, James G.
The Arcus family through ten centuries, including
Harcars of that ilk, and Harcus. Vancouver, 1972.
ED/N-1 (NE.26.d.1) QZ/P41 QZ/P99

Ardincaple of Ardincaple see Macaulay

Argyll, Earl of, Marquess of, Duke of see Campbell, Earl of, Marquess of, Duke of Argyll

Armstrong

ARMSTRONG TRUST LIMITED
The Milnholm cross newsletter: journal of the
Armstrong Trust Limited. Vol.1, no.1- . Edinburgh,
1980- .
ED/N-1 (HP.1a.646)

ARMSTRONG, James Lewis
Chronicles of the Armstrongs. Jamaica, N.Y., 1902.
ED/N-2 QZ/P99

ARMSTRONG, W. A.
The Armstrong borderland: a reassessment of
certain aspects of border history. Galashiels, 1960.
ED/N-1 (NE.25.b.12) GL/U-1 ED/N-2
ED/U-1 QZ/P11 QZ/P99

REID, Robert Corsane
The kinsmen of Kinmont Willie. (In Transactions of
the Dumfriesshire and Galloway Natural History &
Antiquarian Society, 3rd series, vol.xviii, 1931-3,
pp.62-70.)
ED/N-1 (J.187)

Arnot

ARNOTT, James
The House of Arnot and some of its branches.
Edinburgh, 1918.
ED/N-1 (S.121.c) SA/U-1 QZ/L37 GL/U-1
QZ/P99

Arnot in Orkney

CRAVEN, James Brown
Sir John Arnot of Barswick and the family of Arnot
in South Ronaldshay. Kirkwall, 1913.
QZ/P99

Arrott

MACBAIN, James M.
Eminent Arbroathians: being sketches historical,
genealogical, and biographical, 1178-1894.
Arbroath, 1897.
ED/N-1 (250.a)

Arthur of Barshaw

BARCLAY, John F.
Arthur & Company, Limited, Glasgow: one
hundred years of textile distribution. Glasgow,
1953.
ED/N-1 (NF.1174.d.7) QZ/P-6

Atholl, Earl of, Marquess of, Duke of *see* **Murray,**
Earl of, Marquess of, Duke of Atholl

Atholl, Earl of, Marquess of, Duke of *see also*
Stewart-Murray, Duke of Atholl

Atholl, Earldom of

COWAN, Samuel
Three Celtic earldoms: Atholl, Strathearn,
Menteith. Edinburgh, 1909.
ED/N-1 (S.120.e) ED/N-2 QZ/P14 QZ/P22
GL/U-1 QZ/P26 ST/U-1

['NOTES on the genealogy of the Earls of Atholl
and their descendants'. 1709.]
ED/N-1 (Adv.MS.34.6.24,ff.67,68)

PATON, Sir Joseph Noel
Genealogy of the Celtic earls of Atholl, with chart
of the descendants of Conan. [N.p.], 1873.
ED/N-1 (S.307.c;F.6.b.7(9)) ED/N-2 QZ/L37
QZ/P16

Auchincloss

ANJOU, Gustave
Auchincloss. [N.p., 1910?] (*Typescript*)
ED/N-1 (HP1.77.1497)

Auchindoir

PIRIE, Margaret Forbes
The story of the families of two Aberdeenshire
manses: Dyce and Auchindoir. Aberdeen, 1967.
AD/U-1

Auchinleck

MAIDMENT, James
Genealogical fragments relating to the families of . . .
Auchenleck. Berwick, 1855.
ED/N-1 (Ry.II.e.51(1);Y.59.f.2) QZ/P40 GL/U-1
QZ/P99

Auchmuty

TOWNSEND, A.
Auchmuty family of Scotland and America. [N.p.],
1932.
ED/N-1 (NE.25.g.2)

Avery

['ACCOUNT of the Avery family'. 1728.]
ED/N-1 (MS.2094, pp. 101-105)

Ayton, Aytoun, Aiton of Ayton

AITON, William
Enquiry into the origin, pedigree and history of the
family, or clan, of Aitons in Scotland. Hamilton,
1830.
ED/N-1 (Ry.I.3.14) QZ/P53 ED/N-2 QZ/P99

AYTOUN, A.
The Aytons of Ayton in the Merse: an old chapter of
family history derived from the charters of
Coldingham Priory. [N.p.], 1887.
ED/N-1 (S.274.b) QZ/P11 ED/N-2 QZ/L37
QZ/P99

Aytone of Dunmore

['A GENEALOGICAL account of the family of Aytone
of Dunmore'. 1659?] (*MS.*)
ED/N-1 (Adv.MS.33.2.27,f.317)

Aytone of Kinaldey

['A GENEALOGICAL account of the family of Aytone
of Dunmore. 1650?] (*MS.*)
ED/N-1 (Adv.MS.33.2.27,f.319)

Baikie of Burness

[ORIGINAL family papers.]
QZ/P38 (Unconfirmed location)

Baikie of Tankerness

MARWICK, Hugh
The Baikies of Tankerness. (In *Orkney Miscellany*,
vol. 4, 1957, pp. 27-48.)
QZ/P38 QZ/P-1 (Unconfirmed locations)

[ORIGINAL family papers.]
QZ/P38

Baillie

BAILLIE, James William
Lives of the Baillies. Edinburgh, 1872.
ED/N-1 (S.123.f) QZ/P40 SA/U-1 QZ/L37
QZ/P99

BULLOCH, Joseph Gaston Baillie
The family of Baillie of Dunain, Dochfour and
Lamington. Green Bay, Wisc., 1898.
QZ/P40   AD/U-1   QZ/L37

—Genealogical and historical records of the Baillies
of Inverness, Scotland and some of their descendants
in the United States of America. Washington, D.C.,
1923.
ED/N-1(6.307)   QZ/P40

Baillie of Dunain
FRASER-MACKINTOSH, Charles
The Baillies of Dunain. Inverness, 1900.
QZ/P40

Baillie of Jerviswood
BAILLIE, George
Pedigree of George Bailey, Esq. of Jerviswoode.
[N.p., n.d.]
ED/N-1(MS.3421, f.69)

MURRAY, Lady Grisell
Memoirs of the lives and characters of the Right
Honourable George Baillie of Jerviswood and of
Lady Grisell Baillie. Edinburgh, 1822.
ED/N-1(R.231.f)   QZ/P11

— — Edinburgh, 1824.
QZ/P11

Bain *see also* **Bean**
Bain *see also* **McBain**
Bain *see also* **MacBane**
Bain *see also* **Macbean**

Bain
LAWRENCE, A.J.
The Clain Bain with its ancestral and related
Scottish clans. Inverness, 1963.
ED/N-1(NE.25.a.12)   ED/N-2   ED/U-1
SA/U-1   QZ/P22   QZ/P27   QZ/P40(I,D,W)
QZ/P99

ROGERS, Charles
Genealogical chart of the family of Bain, co.
Haddington. [Edinburgh, 1871.]
ED/N-1(Gramp.Club.24)   SA/U-1   QZ/L37
QZ/P99   QZ/P16

Bain in London
BAIN, James Stoddart
A bookseller looks back: the story of the Bains.
London, 1940.
ED/N-1(R.195.a)

Baird

BAIRD, Allan Fullarton
Annals of a Scots family, [Baird], 1691-1936.
Glasgow, 1936.
ED/N-1(R.172.f)   SA/U-1   QZ/P99

BAIRD, William
Dominus fecit: genealogical collections concerning
the sir-name of Baird, and the families of
Auchmedden, Newbyth and Sauchtonhall.
London, 1870.
ED/N-1(A.114.b)   QZ/P-6   QZ/P30   QZ/P22
QZ/P40   SA/U-1   AD/U-1   QZ/P99

BULLOCH, John Malcolm
The Bairds of Auchmedden and Strichen,
Aberdeenshire. Peterhead, 1934.
ED/N-1(6.1821)

—The last Baird laird of Auchmedden and Strichen:
the case of "Mr. Abington". Aberdeen, 1934.
ED/N-1(6.769(32))   QZ/P22   QZ/P99

FRASER, William N.
Account of the surname of Baird—particularly of
the families of Auchmedden, Newbyth, and
Sauchtonhall. Edinburgh, 1857.
ED/N-1(A.114.a)   ED/N-2   QZ/P22   AD/U-1
SA/U-1   GL/U-1   QZ/L37

[GENEALOGICAL collections concerning the name
of Baird. 1770.]
ED/N-1(Adv.MS.32.6.12)

SHAND, Eliza
God is in the generation of the righteous: [a brief
account of the Baird family.] London, 1864.
SA/U-1

Baird of Gartsherrie
BURKE, Sir Bernard
Vicissitudes of families. London, 1860.
ED/N-1(A.14.g)   QZ/P22

MACGEORGE, Andrew
The Bairds of Gartsherrie: some notices of their
origin and history. Glasgow, 1875.
ED/N-1(NE.25.h.4)   QZ/P-3   ED/N-2   QZ/P44
QZ/P99   GL/U-1

Baird of Saughton Hall
WOOD, John Philp
Memorials of various families. [1830?](*MS.*)
QZ/P99

Balbirnie

BALBIRNIE, William
An account, historical and genealogical . . . of the
family of Vance in Ireland, Vans in Scotland. [and an
historical and genealogical account of the family of
Balbirnie.] Cork, 1860.
ED/N-1 (R.172.e)

Baldwin, Stanley *see* **Macdonald**

Balfour

MAC LEAN, J.
Balfour. (In *De Nederlandsche Leeuw*, jaarg.94,
nos. 5/6, mei/juni 1977, cols 146-203.)
ED/N-1 (7.139)

SIBBALD, Sir Robert
Memoria Balfouriana, sive historia rerum pro literis
promovendis, gestarum a clarissimis fratribus
Balfouris, D. D. Jacobo, Barone de Kinaird.
Edinburgh, 1699.
ED/M-1   ED/N-1 (Ry.II.h.44)   QZ/Q17

Balfour, Lord Balfour of Burleigh *see also*
Kilwinning, Lord

Balfour, Lord Balfour of Burleigh

BALFOUR, Francis Walter
Case on behalf of Francis Walter Balfour of Fernie.
QZ/L37

—Pedigree of Francis Walter Balfour of Fernie, heir
male of the Lords Burghly, claiming the title of Lord
Burghly in the peerage of Scotland. [N.p.], 1861.
ED/N-1 (6.249(2);6.249(3);6.249(4))

—Supplemental case.
QZ/L37

BRUCE, Alexander Hugh
Case on behalf of Alexander Hugh Bruce of
Kennet.
QZ/L37

BRUCE, Robert
Case on behalf of Robert Bruce of Kennet, in the co.
of Clackmannan, Esq., claiming the dignities of
Lord Balfour of Burley and Lord Kilwinning in the
peerage of Scotland. [1860.]
QZ/L37

EGLINTON, Archibald William Montgomerie,
14th Earl of
Case . . . Archibald Wm. Montgomerie, Earl of
Eglinton and Winton, Lord Montgomerie and
Kilwinning and Baron Ardrossan.
QZ/L37

[GENEALOGICAL papers concerning the Balfours,
Lords of Burleigh. 18--.]
ED/N-1 (MS.15983)

MINUTES of evidence . . . etc. 1860-64.
QZ/L37

[PROCEEDINGS in the claim of Bruce of Kennet to
the dignities of Lord Balfour of Burley and Lord
Kilwinning in the peerage of Scotland.] London,
1861-9.
ED/N-1 (Yule donation no.153)

Balfour of Denmilne

['ACCOUNT of the family of Balfour of Denmiln'.
1770.]
ED/N-1 (Adv.MS.6.1.17.,ff.81-3)

MACKIE, John Duncan
The Denmilne MSS. in the National Library of
Scotland. Edinburgh, 1928.
ED/N-1 (1959.65)   QZ/L37   QZ/P16

Balfour of Pilrig

BALFOUR, James
A record of family grace: [a short sketch of the
family of Balfour of Pilrig.] [Edinburgh], 1891.
ED/N-1 (1934.35)

BALFOUR-MELVILLE, Barbara
The Balfours of Pilrig: a history for the family.
Edinburgh, 1907.
ED/N-1 (S.120.b)   SA/U-1   AD/U-1   GL/U-1
ED/U-1   QZ/P99

MELVILLE, E. W. M. Balfour
The Balfours of Pilrig and Melvilles of Strathkinnes.
(In *Scottish Genealogist*, vol.viii, no.1, February
1961, pp.17-21.)
ED/N-1 (Gen.7)   QZ/P18

Balfour of Powis

MORRISON, Alexander
An account of the three David Balfour's [*sic.*] of
Powis and their friends. Stirling, 1929.
ED/N-1 (1929.26)   QZ/Q17   QZ/P14   QZ/P99

Baliol, Balliol

ANDREWS, Herbert C.
The Benstede family and its predecessors in
Hertfordshire and Essex, the de Valoignes and
Balliols. [With a genealogical table.] London,
1937.
ED/N-1 (6.198)

CAMERON, Annie Isabella
Two groups of documents relating to John Baliol from the Vatican Archives. [With a genealogical table.] [N.p., n.d.]
ED/N-1 (6.909)

HUYSHE, Wentworth
The Royal manor of Hitchin and its lords; Harold and the Balliols. London, 1906.
ED/N-1 (NE.42.a.13)

MACDOWALL, John Kevan
Carrick Gallovidian: a historical survey ... with genealogical charts and notes. Ayr, 1947.
ED/N-1 (R.241.d)

SINCLAIR, Alexander
Heirs of the royal house of Baliol. Edinburgh, [1870?].
ED/N-1 (B.c.3)   QZ/P-9

—Remarks on the tables of the heirs of the royal house of Baliol. Edinburgh, [1870?].
ED/N-1 (NE.26.d.2(1-4))   QZ/L37

SWEENY, R. Mingo
The House of Baliol. (In *Scottish Genealogical Helper*, part 5, 1975, pp.58-60.)
ED/N-1 (P.la.6393)

Baliol le Scot

BAIN, Joseph
The Baliol le Scot family and their heart stone. (In *Collection of miscellaneous papers*.) [N.d.]
QZ/P-1 (Unconfirmed location)

Ballantyne

BALLANTYNE of Peebles. [With a genealogical table.] Peebles, [n.d.].
ED/N-1 (5.2183)

HENRY Ballantyne and Sons, Limited, Walkerburn. [With a genealogical table.] London, 1929.
ED/N-1 (R.292.g)

Ballingal

BULLOCH, John Malcolm
A notable military family: the Gordons in Griamachany in the parish of Kildonan. [Dingwall], 1907.
QZ/P26

[GENEALOGICAL notes concerning the Ballingal family. 18--.]
ED/N-1 (MS.2110-12)

Balmerino, Lord *see* **Elphinstone,** Lord Balmerino

Balveny

CRAMOND, William
The castle and the lords of Balveny. [N.p.], 1892.
ED/N-2

Bandini, Marchioness *see* **Newburgh,** Earldom of

Bannatyne

WILSON, William. Folklore and genealogies of uppermost Nithsdale. Dumfries, 1904.
ED/N-1 (R.241.h)

Bannerman

MORGAN, Patrick
Annals of Woodside and Newhill, historical and genealogical. Aberdeen, 1886.
ED/N-1 (A.120.a)

Bannerman of Elsick

BANNERMAN, Sir Donald
Bannerman of Elsick: a short family history. [Edinburgh, 1974.]
ED/N-1 (NE.27.h.1)   QZ/L37   QZ/P22

ROSE, David Murray
The Bannermans of Elsick and Watertown. [Aberdeen, 1900?]
QZ/P22

— — (In *Scottish Notes and Queries*, 2nd series, vol.3, no.2, August 1901, pp.17-18.)
ED/N-1 (V.457)

SOME account of the family of Bannerman of Elsick. Aberdeen, 1812.
ED/N-1 (6.1257(17))   QZ/P22   DN/U-1   QZ/L37

Barbour

GORDON, Malcolm
The Barbour tree: the descendants of John Barbour, born Paisley, 1759. 1949. (*MS.*)
QZ/P-6

Barbour of Forehouse

LYLE, William
Some notes on the Barbours of Forehouse, Kilbarchan, and their descendants. 1967. (*MS.*)
QZ/P-6

Barbour of Kilbarchan
LYLE, William
The Barbours of Kilbarchan: a genealogical roll.
(*MS.*)
QZ/P-6

Barclay
ANDERSON, Verily
Friends and relations: three centuries of Quaker
families. London, 1980.
ED/N-1 (H3.80.5649)

BANNERMAN, William
The thanage of Glendowachie. (Reprinted from
Banffshire Journal, November, December 1897.)
ED/N-1 (R.247.h)

BARCLAY, Charles W. *and* BARCLAY, Hubert F.
A history of the Barclay family, 1067-1933. London,
1924-34. 3v.
ED/N-1 (S.122.c) QZ/P30 ED/N-2 QZ/P22
SA/U-1 GL/U-1 QZ/L37* QZ/P99

BARCLAY, John
Relation of the Barclay family in Scotland.
Gothenburg, 1853.
ED/N-2

BARCLAY, Leslie George de Rune
History of the Scottish Barclays. Folkestone,
1915.
ED/N-1 (S.120.g) QZ/P22 QZ/P30 SA/U-1
AD/U-1 GL/U-1 QZ/L37 QZ/P28 QZ/P99

MATERIAL relating to the lands and lairds of
Barclay. [N.p., n.d.]
QZ/P-6

MAULE, Harry
Registrum de Panmure. Edinburgh, 1874. 2v.
ED/N-1 (Gen.8.P) QZ/P28 QZ/P26 SA/U-1
AD/U-1 GL/U-1 QZ/L37 QZ/P99

Barclay of Barclay
WIMBERLEY, Douglas
The Barclays of Barclay of Grantully or Gartly and
of Towie Barclay. Aberdeen, 1903.
ED/N-2 QZ/L37 SA/U-1 QZ/P99

Barclay of Hills
GENEALOGICAL roll of the Barclays of Hills.
[N.p., n.d.]
QZ/P-6

Barclay of Mathers and Ury *see also* **Barclay** of Urie

Barclay of Mathers and Ury
['ANCESTRY of the Barclays of Mathers and Ury.
n.d.]
ED/N-1 (MS.1034.,ff.81-7)

PAPERS from the collection of Sir William Fraser;
edited by J. R. N. Macphail. Edinburgh, 1924.
(Scottish History Society Publications, 3rd series,
vol.v.)
ED/N-1 (Ref.54)

The PEDIGREE of Robert Barclay-Allardice . . . the
Earls of Menteith and Airth, Lord Graham of
Kilpont and Kilbryde: and the families of Barclay of
Mathers and Ury, and Allardice of Allardice.
Edinburgh, 1892.
ED/N-1 (S.120.a)

Barclay of Tollie
PETER, John
The Barclays of Tollie: [genealogical chart] . . .
down to 1877. Edinburgh, 1878.
QZ/P22 QZ/L37 QZ/P99

STEWART, William
The Barclays of Tollie and their descendants. (*MSS.*)
QZ/P22

Barclay of Towiebarclay
MILNE, J.
Barclays of Towiebarclay. (In *Transactions of the
Banffshire Field Club*, 20 August 1887, pp.72-86.)
ED/N-1 (NE.3.g.1)

SOME notes on the Towie-Barclay family. (Reprinted
from *Banffshire Journal*, 1902.)
QZ/P30

Barclay of Urie *see also* **Barclay** of Mathers and Ury

Barclay of Urie
BARCLAY, Robert
A genealogical account of the Barclays of Urie,
formerly of Mathers. [With a genealogical table.]
Aberdeen, 1740.
ED/N-1 (Hall.133.b;BCL.C.2330)

— — London, 1812.
ED/N-1 (A.114.c.9) SA/U-1 GL/U-1
QZ/L37 QZ/P30 QZ/P99

BUDGE, Frances Anne
The Barclays of Ury, and other sketches of the early
Friends. London, 1881.
ED/N-1 (A.113.e) QZ/P22 QZ/P99

Barclay in U.S.A.

MOFFAT, R. Burnham

The Barclays of New York: who they are and who they are not, and some other Barclays. New York, 1904.

ED/N-1 (S.120.c) QZ/L37

Barclay-Allardice *see* **Allardice** of Allardice

Barnard

WILSON, S. C.

The peat moss of Faringdon, Roxburghshire and the Barnard family. (In *Transactions of the Hawick Archaeological Society*, 1935, pp.29-31.)

ED/N-1 (P.220)

Barr of Tradestoun

BARR, Robert

Robert Barr, engineer, of Tradestoun: a genealogical roll. [N.d] (*MS.*)

QZ/P-6

Bayne of Tulloch

MACKINNON, Donald

The Baynes of Tulloch. (In *Scottish Genealogist*, part 1, vol.ii, no.1, January 1955, pp.3-7; part 2, vol.ii, no.2, April 1955, pp.17-23.)

ED/N-1 (Gen.7)

Bean *see also* **Bain**

Bean

PEDIGREE of Bean of Portsoy. [N.p., n.d.]

QZ/P99

Bean in Exeter

BEAN, Bernie

The life and family of John Bean of Exeter and his cousins. Washington, 1970.

QZ/P40 (I) QZ/P99

Beatie *see* **Beatson**

Beaton *see also* **Bethune**

Beaton

BEATONS of Skye. (In *Clan Macleod Magazine*, vol. ii, no.18, 1953, pp.97-100.)

ED/N-1 (NF.1572)

COLLACOTT, R. A.

Hereditary physicians of the Scottish islands. (In *Scottish Medical Journal*, vol.28, no.4, October 1983, pp.377-81.

ED/N-1 (NJ.319/1)

PEEL, Hilary M.

The Beatons could cure it. (In *Scots Magazine*, new series, vol.120, no.1, October 1983, pp.50-3.)

ED/N-1 (HJ3.152)

Beaton of Culnaskea

The BEATONS of Culnaskea in Ferindonald. (Reprinted from *Ross-shire Journal*, 20 July 1979.)

QZ/P99

Beaton of Culnaskiach

MACKINNON, Donald

The Beatons of Culnaskiach. (In *Scottish Genealogist*, vol.iii, no.1, January 1956, pp.8-11.)

ED/N-1 (Gen.7)

Beaton of Islay *see also* **Macbeth**

Beaton of Islay

MACKINNON, Donald

Genealogy of the Macbeths or Beatons of Islay and Mull. (In *Caledonian Medical Journal*, new series, vol.v, 1902/4, pp.141-53.)

ED/N-1 (M.120.d)

Beatson

[BEATSON family pedigree: extracted from the Jackson Collection, Sheffield City Libraries. N.d.]

QZ/P99

BEATSON, Alexander John

Genealogical account of the families of Beatson. 2nd ed. Edinburgh, 1860.

ED/N-1 (A.113.a) QZ/L37 ED/U-1 QZ/P99 QZ/P16

BEATSON, William Burns

Story of the surname of Beatson. (In *Genealogical Magazine*, vol.iii, 1899/1900, pp.94-100, 140-2, 190-3, 236-41, 285-8, 334-8, 394-400, 435-42.)

ED/N-1 (Q.77)

— — (Reprinted from *Genealogical Magazine*, vol.iii, 1899/1900, with revisions.)

SA/U-1 QZ/P99

Belhaven and Stenton, Lord

HAMILTON, James

Case on behalf of James Hamilton . . . claiming . . . Lord of Belhaven and Stenton in the peerage of Scotland. 1874.

ED/N-1 (Yule.154) QZ/L37

—Supplementary case. 1875.

QZ/L37

HAMILTON, Robert William
Case.
QZ/L37

MINUTES and proceedings. 1875.
QZ/L37

PEDIGREE of the Lords Belhaven. [N.p., 1792.]
ED/N-1 (Yule.168(10))

[PROCEEDINGS in the case of the claims to the
Belhaven and Stenton peerage by James Hamilton
and Robert William Hamilton before the
Committee of Privileges of the House of Lords,
1874.] 6pts. London, 1874-5.
ED/N-1 (Yule.154(1-6);Law)

Bell

ALSTEAD, Stanley
The Reverend William Bell's family. (In *Society of
Friends of Dunblane Cathedral* [*Transactions*], vol.xii,
part 4, 1977, pp. 16-20.)
ED/N-1 (Y.176)

BELL, Charles Davidson
Memorial of the clan of the Bells, more particularly
of the Bells of Kirkconnel and Bells of Blackethouse.
Cape Town, 1864.
ED/N-1 (1936.21) QZ/L37 QZ/P99

BELL, Robin
The Bell family of Arkinholm [Langholm]. [1958.]
(*Typescript*)
QZ/P10 (Unconfirmed location)

[GENEALOGY of the Bell family. 18--.]
ED/N-1 (Adv.MS.32.72)

STEUART, James
The Bell family in Dumfriesshire. (*Records of the
Western Marches*, vol.ii.) Dumfries, 1932.
ED/N-1 (R.241.b) QZ/P11 SA/U-1 DN/U-1
QZ/L37 ED/U-1 QZ/P99

Bell of Blacket House

WATSON, Charles Brodie Boog
Alexander Cowan of Moray House and Valleyfield,
his kinsfolk and connections. Perth, 1915, 17. 2v.
ED/N-1 (S.299.b) QZ/P22 SA/U-1 QZ/P99

Bellenden

LEITH, Peter
The Bellendens and the Palace of Steness. (In
Proceedings of the Orkney Antiquarian Society, vol.xiv,
1936/7, pp.41-4.)
ED/N-1 (R.250.a)

Bellenden-Ker *see* **Roxburghe,** Duke of

Bellenden-Ker *see* **Roxburghe,** Lord, Earl of,
Duke of

Benzies

BENZIES, Frank
A Benzies inheritance, 1260-1695. Coupar Angus,
[1977].
ED/N-1 (NE.25.f.27) ED/N-2 QZ/P22
QZ/P26 QZ/P30 QZ/P99

— A Benzies quest, 1435-1972. Coupar Angus,
1972.
QZ/P26 QZ/P22 QZ/P30

Bethune *see also* **Beaton**

Bethune *see also* **Lindsay,** Lord Lindsay of the Byres

Bethune

A SKETCH of the Bethune family. [Bristol?, 18--.]
SA/U-1

WEISSE, John Adam
A history of the Bethune family; translated from
the French of André du Chesne, with additions
from family records and other available sources.
New York, 1884.
SA/U-1

Bethune of Creich

OGILVY-BETHUNE marriage contract, 1566.
[N.p., n.d.] (*Facsimile*)
QZ/P-1 (Unconfirmed location)

Bethune of Gairntilloch

BRODIE, James
A memoir of Annie Mdonald Christie, . . . to which
is now added a brief notice of her grandsons, John
and Alexander Bethune. 3rd ed. Edinburgh, 1849.
ED/N-1 (W.W.7)

POLISHED stones from a highland quarry: a sketch of
the Bethune family. London, 1864.
ED/N-1 (3/2330(12))

Bethune in Skye

WHYTE, Thomas
Historical and genealogical account of the Bethunes
of the island of Sky. Edinburgh, 1778.
ED/N-1 (Abbot.110(14)) GL/U-1 QZ/P99

— — London, 1893.
ED/N-1 (S.122.e) QZ/Q17 ED/N-2 QZ/P40
AD/U-1 SA/U-1 DN/U-1 QZ/L37
QZ/P30 QZ/P27

Beveridge

BEVERIDGE, Erskine
A Beveridge family pedigree and letter. 1918. (*MS.*)
ED/N-2 QZ/P99

BEVERIDGE, Sydney A.
The story of the Beveridge families of England and
Scotland. Melbourne, 1923.
ED/N-1 (S.123.f) QZ/P18 QZ/P99

HALLEN, Arthur Washington Cornelius
An account of the family of Beveridge in
Dunfermline. Edinburgh, 1890.
ED/N-2 QZ/P15 QZ/P99 QZ/P16

MAIR, Philip Beveridge
Shared enthusiasm: the story of Lord and Lady
Beveridge. [With a genealogical table.]
Windlesham, 1982.
ED/N-1 (H3.83.1580)

Biggar

SHIRLEY, George William
The family of Biggar, Stewartry of Kirkcudbright
... 1614-1912: genealogical tables with notes.
Dumfries, 1912.
ED/N-2

Bignold

BIGNOLD, Sir Robert
Five generations of the Bignold family, 1761-1947.
London, 1948.
ED/N-1 (R.158.a) QZ/P40 (W)

Binning of Binning

WOOD, John Philp
Memorials of various families. [1830?] (*MS.*)
QZ/P99

Binning of Wallyford

INGLIS, John A.
The Binnings of Wallyford. (In *Miscellanea
Genealogica et Heraldica*, 5th series, vol.i, 1916,
pp.205-209.)
ED/N-1 (NH.296)

— — (Reprinted from *Miscellanea Genealogica et
Heraldica*, 5th series, vol.i, 1916.)
ED/N-1 (S.121.b)

Birnie

[ACCOUNT of the family of Birnie of Birnie &
Broomhill. 1730.]
ED/N-1 (MS.536)

BIRNIE, John
Account of the families of Birnie and Hamilton of
Broomhill. Edinburgh, 1838.
ED/N-1 (A.124.b) SA/U-1 AD/U-1 GL/U-1
QZ/L37 ED/U-1 QZ/P99

Birnie of Ashgrove, Aberdeenshire

BIRNIE, Joseph Earle
The Earles and the Birnies. [Atlanta], 1974.
ED/N-1 (H3.75.801) QZ/P22

Bishop

MINUTES of evidence taken before the Committee
of Privileges in the petition of Nicholas
Donnithorne Bishop and Mary Eleanor Bishop
against the claim of Robert Barclay Allardice to the
Earldom of Airth. [With genealogical tables.]
[London], 1839.
ED/N-1 (6.274(7))

Bishop of Whitburn

SCOTT, Stanley R. *and* MONTGOMERY, Robert H.
Family history of John Bishop of Whitburn,
Scotland, Robert Hamilton Bishop of Oxford,
Ohio, Ebenezer Bishop of McDonough County
Illinois, John Scott of Ireland. With some account
of related families, etc. Topeka, Kansas, 1951.
ED/N-1 (NE.25.a.1)

Bisset

BATTEN, Edmund Chisholm
The charters of the priory of Beauly, with notices
of the priories of Pluscardine and Ardchattan and
of the family of the founder, John Byset. Edinburgh,
1877. (Grampian Club, 12.)
ED/N-1 (Gramp.Club.12) QZ/L37

Bisset of Lessendrum

BULLOCH, John Malcolm
Maurice George Bisset of Lessendrum, 1757-1821.
[Aberdeen], 1929.
QZ/P30 QZ/P99

Bisset of Lovat

MACDONALD, Archibald
The old lords of Lovat and Beaufort. Inverness,
1934.
ED/N-1 (R.172.d) QZ/P22

Black

ADAM and Charles Black, 1807-1957: some chapters
in the history of a publishing house. London, 1957.
ED/N-1 (NE.110.c.27) QZ/P99

Black of Breich Water

BLACK, John
Melodies and memories with a history of the Blacks of Breich Water district. Glasgow, 1909.
ED/N-1 (NG.1169.h.31)

Black of Over Abington

BLACK, William George
A note on the family of Black of Over Abington, 1694-1924 with memoranda on . . . Willison of Redshaw . . . Steel of Annathill, and Blackie of Glasgow. Glasgow, 1908.
GL/U-1 QZ/L37

— — [2nd ed.] Glasgow, 1924.
ED/N-1 (S.121.e) ED/N-2 QZ/P22 QZ/Q71 QZ/P99

Blackader of Tulliallan

BLACKADER, John
The life and diary of Colonel John Blackader. Edinburgh, 1824.
ED/N-1 (A.108.f) QZ/P14 QZ/P16

— Select passages from the diary and letters of the late John Blackader . . . to which is prefixed an account of the life and parentage of the writer [by Charles Stuart of Dunearn]. Edinburgh, 1806.
ED/N-1 (Jac.V.7/2) QZ/P14

CRICHTON, Andrew
Memoirs of the Rev. John Blackader. Edinburgh, 1823.
QZ/P16

Blackford

JONES, Nora E. S. and BRANT, N. E.
Blackford genealogy, 1702-1935. [N.p.], 1935.
ED/N-1 (Mf.4(13))

Blackhall

MORISON, Alexander
The Blackhalls of that ilk and Barra, hereditary coroners and foresters of the Garioch. Aberdeen, 1905. (New Spalding Club, 29.)
ED/N-1 (New Spald.Club.29) QZ/Q41 QZ/P30 ED/N-2 QZ/P28 QZ/P40 QZ/P22 DN/U-1 GL/U-1 QZ/L37 ED/M-1 QZ/P99

Blackie

BLACK, William George
A note on the family of Black of Over Abington . . . with memoranda on . . . Blackie of Glasgow. Glasgow, 1908.
GL/U-1 QZ/L37 QZ/P99

— — [2nd ed.] Glasgow, 1924.
ED/N-1 (S.121.e) ED/N-2 QZ/P22 QZ/Q71 QZ/P99

BLACKIE, Agnes C.
Blackie and Son, 1809-1959: a short history of the firm. [N.p.], 1959.
ED/N-2 QZ/P99

BLACKIE, Walter G.
Sketch of the origin and progress of the firm of Blackie & Son, publishers, Glasgow, from its foundation in 1809 to the decease of its founder in 1874. Glasgow, 1897.
ED/N-1 (T.462.e) QZ/P99

Blackwood

OLIPHANT, Margaret Oliphant Wilson
Annals of a publishing house: Wm. Blackwood and his sons. Edinburgh, 1897-8. 3v.
ED/N-1 (X.175.a) QZ/P34 QZ/P11 QZ/P-9 QZ/P99

TREDREY, Frank D.
The House of Blackwood, 1804-1954: the history of a publishing house. Edinburgh, 1954.
ED/N-1 (X.175.a) QZ/P99

Blackwood of West Fife

BLACKWOOD, Isabella C.
The early House of Blackwood. Edinburgh, 1900.
ED/N-1 (4.166(4)) QZ/P22 QZ/P99 QZ/P16

Blaikie of Aberdeen

YOUNG, Amy Helen Hathorn
Blaikie of Aberdeen. [Pietermaritzburg, S.A., 1971.]
ED/N-1 (NE.25.f.14) QZ/P22 AD/U-1 ED/N-2

Blair

[MATERIAL relating to the lands and lairds of Blair.]
QZ/P-6

MITCHELL, Arthur T.
Five generations of the family of Blair, from the counties of Perth and Forfar. Exeter, 1895.
ED/N-2 QZ/P99

MURRAY, Archibald
William Scott Blair *v*. Hamilton Blair . . . appellants case and respondents case to be heard at the Bar of the House of Lords . . . 4th April, 1739. [Edinburgh, 1739.]
QZ/P99

Blair of Balthayock
ANDERSON, William
The family of Blair of Balthayock, Perthshire. [N.p., n.d.]
ED/N-1 (5.1081(18)) QZ/P26 ED/N-2

BAETCKE, Adolph Julius
Die Schottische Abstammung der Lothringer de Blair. Hamburg, [n.d.].
ED/N-1 (4.208(2)) QZ/L37

Blair of Carsehall
[MATERIAL relating to the lands and lairds of Blair of Carsehall. N.d.]
QZ/P-6

Blane in Ayrshire
BAILEY, William Henry
A chronicle of the family of Gairdner of Ayrshire, Edinburgh and Glasgow, and their connections from the 17th century. Taunton, 1947.
ED/N-1 (R.159.i) QZ/P-1 SA/U-1 AD/U-1 GL/U-1 QZ/P99

Blaw of Castlehill
JOHNSTON, Christopher Nicholson, *Lord Sands*
Blaw of Castlehill, Jacobite and criminal. Edinburgh, 1916.
ED/N-1 (S.170.i) QZ/P14 QZ/P99

Blyth
BLYTH, Edward Lawrence Ireland
Notes on the pedigree of the family of Blythe or Blyth of Norton and Birchet. [With a genealogical table.] Edinburgh, 1893.
ED/N-1 (NE.63.a.23)

Boase *see also* **Bowes**

Boase
An ACCOUNT of the families of Boase or Bowes, originally residing at Paul and Madron in Cornwall; and of other families connected with them by marriage, etc. [Exeter], 1876.
ED/N-1 (A.23.c)

Bogle
HARLE, John Innes
The Bogle family history. [N.p.], 1977.
QZ/L37

MINUTES of evidence taken before the Committee of Privileges in the petition of Nicholas Donnithorne Bishop and Mary Eleanor Bishop against the claim of Robert Barclay Allardice to the Earldom of Airth. [With genealogical tables.] [London], 1839.
ED/N-1 (6.274(7))

RICHARDSON, H. E.
George Bogle and his children. (In *Scottish Genealogist*, vol.xxix, no.3, September 1982, pp.73-83.)
ED/N-1 (Gen.7)

Bogle of Hutchiston
GRAHAM, Elizabeth
Documents regarding the extinction of Lady Elizabeth Graham, daughter of John Lord Kilpont, and wife of Sir John Graham of Gartmore, and her descendants. Edinburgh, [n.d.].
ED/N-1 (Ry.III.a.25)

Bogue
BOGUE, Virgil T.
Bogue and allied families. Geneva, Ohio, 1944.
ED/N-1 (R.272.e) QZ/P11 QZ/P99

LILLIE, William
Bogues in Berwickshire. (In *Scottish Genealogist*, vol.xxii, no.3, September 1973, pp.69-76.)
ED/N-1 (Gen.7)

Boog
WATSON, Charles Brodie Boog
Traditions and genealogies of some members of the families of Boog, Heron, Leishman, Ross, Watson. Perth, 1908.
ED/N-1 (S.120.d) QZ/P18 ED/N-2 SA/U-1 QZ/P99 QZ/L37

Booth of Aberdeen
MILNE, Marcus K.
[Family of Booth of Aberdeen. 1960?] (*MS. and typescript*)
QZ/P22

Borthwick

HARRISON, Godfrey
Borthwicks: a century in the meat trade, 1863-1963.
London, 1963.
ED/N-1 (NG.1297.h.29)

Borthwick, Lord Borthwick

BORTHWICK peerage: pedigree of the Lords
Borthwick. [London, 1869.]
ED/N-1 (Yule.157(6))

BORTHWICK, Archibald
Case of Archibald Borthwick, Esq., claiming the
title of Lord Borthwick. [1808.]
QZ/L37

—Case . . . with reference to the objection to that
claim made by John Borthwick of Crookston.
QZ/L37

—Minutes of the evidence given before the
Committee of Privileges, to whom the petition of
Archibald Borthwick . . . claiming the title and
dignity of Lord Borthwick, was referred. [London],
1812.
ED/N-1 (Yule.157(2))

BORTHWICK, Cunninghame
Borthwick peerage: proofs of the pedigree of
Cunninghame Borthwick . . . connecting him with
Henry, Lord Borthwick through their common
ancestor William Borthwick, third of Soltray.
[London], 1869.
ED/N-1 (Yule.157(5))

—Case on behalf of Cunninghame Borthwick, Esq.,
on his claim to . . . Lord Borthwick in the peerage
of Scotland. 1868.
ED/N-1 (Yule.157(1)) QZ/L37

—House of Lords: proceedings on the Borthwick
peerage claim. [With a genealogical table.]
[London, 1869.]
ED/N-1 (Yule.157(3))

—House of Lords: speeches of counsel on the
Borthwick peerage claim, Monday, 12th July 1869.
[London, 1869.]
ED/N-1 (Yule.157(4))

—In the House of Lords. Case on behalf of
Cunninghame, Lord Borthwick, on his claim to
precedency. [London, 1871?]
ED/N-1 (Yule.157(12))

—In the House of Lords: petition of Cunninghame,
Lord Borthwick, praying to be placed in his proper
precedency on the roll of the peers of Scotland.
London, 1871.
ED/N-1 (Yule.148(2))

—Minutes of evidence taken before the Committee
for Privileges, to whom was referred the petition of
Cunninghame Borthwick . . . praying Her
Majesty . . . to declare him entitled to the . . . dignity
of Lord Borthwick in the peerage of Scotland, etc.
[London, 1869.]
ED/N-1 (Yule.157(10)) ED/S10

—MINUTES of evidence taken before the Committee
for Privileges to whom was referred the petition of
Cunninghame, Lord Borthwick . . . that the dignity
of Lord Borthwick may be placed . . . immediately
after the dignity of Lord Cathcart, etc. [London],
1871.
ED/N-1 (6.1439(1))

BORTHWICK, Henry
Case of Henry Borthwick . . . claiming . . . Lord
Borthwick . . . 1762. Reprinted. 1868.
ED/N-1 (3.5) QZ/L37

BORTHWICK, John
Case of John Borthwick of Crookston. 1764.
Reprinted. 1868.
QZ/L37

—Case of John Borthwick of Crookston objecting
to the claim of Mr. Archd. Borthwick to the title of
Lord Borthwick. 1809.
QZ/L37

—Additional case of above. 1774. Reprinted. 1868.
QZ/L37

—Case of John Borthwick . . . 181- . Reprinted.
1868.
QZ/L37

—Additional case of above.
QZ/L37

[FACSIMILES of letters and documents relating to the
barony of Borthwick. N.p., n.d.]
ED/N-1 (Yule.157(8))

MINUTES of evidence . . . [With appendix.]
1812-1814.
QZ/L37

PEDIGREE of the family of Borthwick.
QZ/L37

Boston

BOSTON, Thomas
A general account of my life. Edinburgh, 1908.
ED/N-1 (S.156.a) QZ/P99

Bosville of New Hall *see* **Macdonald** of the Isles

Boswell

BOSWELL, Jaspar John
History and genealogical tables of the Boswells.
London, [1906].
ED/N-1 (Mf.6(7)) ED/N-2 QZ/P99

CAMPBELL, Jane *and* CAMPBELL, Mary
A family chronicle: [the family of Robert Campbell
of Alloway]. Edinburgh, 1925.
QZ/P99

Boswell of Auchinleck

BOSWELL, James
Boswelliana: the commonplace book of James
Boswell. London, 1876. (Grampian Club.)
ED/N-1 (Gramp.Club.7)

BUCHANAN, David
The treasures of Auchinleck: the story of the
Boswell papers. [With a genealogical table.]
London, 1975.
ED/N-1 (H3.75.1595) QZ/P-7

Bower

BOWER, Sir Alfred Louis
History of the Bower family, 1066-1930.
[N.p., 1935?]
QZ/L37

Bowes *see also* **Boase**

Bowes(-Lyon), Earl of Strathmore *see also* **Lyon,**
Earl of Strathmore

Bowes(-Lyon), Earl of Strathmore *see also*
Strathmore, Earldom of

Bowes(-Lyon), Earl of Strathmore

ARNOLD, Ralph
The unhappy countess and her grandson John
Bowes. London, 1957.
ED/N-1 (NF.1313.b.9)

DAY, James Wentworth
The Queen Mother's family story. [London], 1967.
ED/N-1 (NE.25.f.3) QZ/P56 QZ/P28
QZ/P30 QZ/P99

— — 2nd ed. Bath, 1981.
ED/N-1 (H3.81.4534)

WILLIAM Laing *v.* George Callandar: summons of
maills and duties, Laing against Callandar. 1826.
QZ/P99

Bowie

ELLIS, Leola B.
George Bowie of Stirlingshire, Scotland and Boston
and Truro, Massachusetts: his ancestry and
descendants. [Portland, 1962.]
ED/N-1 (6.2685)

Boyd

BOYD, Frederick Tilghman
History of the Boyd clan and related families.
Ft. Lauderdale, 1962.
ED/N-1 (1975.87) QZ/P-7

['GENEALOGICAL notes concerning the Boyd family'.
19--.]
ED/N-1 (MS.9298.,ff.1-33)

PEDIGREE of the House of Boyd; compiled from
authentic documents. [N.p., 1904.]
ED/N-1 (6.1560) QZ/P-7 SA/U-1 QZ/P99

Boyd of Badenheath and Blairlin

CLELAND, Harry
Blairlin district and the Clelands. Kirkintilloch,
1934.
ED/N-1 (NE.25.d.4) ED/N-2 QZ/P-3

Boyd, Earl of Kilmarnock

CAMERON, Florence
Annals of the House and family of Boyd, Earls of
Kilmarnock and lairds of Penkill Castle and
Tochrogue, A.D. 1153-A.D. 1963. [Edinburgh], 1963.
ED/N-1 (NE.25.a.16) GL/U-1

CLARKE, Seymour
Dean castle, Kilmarnock, and the family of Boyd
(1263-1746). 1918. (*MS.*)
ED/N-2 QZ/P99

CORBETT, Cunningham
Boyds of Kilmarnock, Porterfields of Porterfield
and Corbetts of Tolcross. [N.p., n.d.]
ED/N-2

['GENEALOGY of the Earls of Kilmarnock'. N.d.]
ED/N-1 (Adv.MS.34.6.10.,ff.254-8)

KILMARNOCK AND DISTRICT HISTORY GROUP
The Boyds of Kilmarnock. Kilmarnock, [1980].
ED/N-1 (HP3.80.1591) QZ/Q88

MAIDMENT, James
Selection from papers of the family of Boyd of
Kilmarnock, 1468-1590. Edinburgh, 1837.
(Abbotsford Club, vol.11.)
ED/N-1(Abbot.11) AD/U-1 QZ/P-7

MEMOIRS of the lives and families of the Lords
Kilmarnock, Cromartie and Balmerino. London,
1746.
ED/N-1(Blk.442)

ROBERTSON, William
Ayrshire, its history and historic families.
Kilmarnock, 1908. 2v.
ED/N-1(Hist.S.91.A)

Boyd of Kipps
INGLIS, John A.
The Monros of Auchinbowie and cognate families.
Edinburgh, 1911.
ED/M-1 ED/N-1(S.121.d)

Boyd of Penkill and Trochrig
CLARKE, Seymour
The Boyds of Penkill and Trochrig. Edinburgh,
1909.
ED/N-1(S.120.d) ED/N-2 QZ/P44 SA/U-1
AD/U-1 GL/U-1 ED/U-1 QZ/P99

Boyd in U.S.A.
HILL, William B.
The Boyds of Boydton. Clarkesville, [1967].
ED/N-1(5.3488)

Boyle of Kelburne, Earl of Glasgow
BOYLE, Robert Elphinstone
Genealogical account of the Boyles of Kelburne,
Earls of Glasgow. [N.p.], 1904.
ED/N-1(R.172.b) ED/N-2 SA/U-1 GL/U-1
QZ/L37 QZ/P99

ROBERTSON, William
An account of the family of Boyle of Kelburn,
adapted and abridged from an unpublished memoir
by Col. the Hon. Robert Boyle, and inc. in vol.II of
his History of Ayrshire. Kilmarnock, 1908.
ED/N-1(Hist.S.91.A)

Brandon, Duke of *see* **Hamilton,** Duke of Hamilton

Breadalbane, Earldom of *see also* **Campbell** of
Breadalbane

Breadalbane, Earldom of
BREADALBANE, John, *Earl of*
Case of John, Earl of Breadalbane in the peerage
of Scotland. 1872.
ED/N-2 QZ/L37

CAMPBELL, Gavin
Case on behalf of Gavin Campbell claiming to be
Earl of Breadalbane etc., on his claim to . . . Earl of
Breadalbane, etc. in the peerage of Scotland.
ED/N-1(Yule.146(1)) QZ/L37

CAMPBELL, John
Case on behalf of John Campbell, Esq., claiming . . .
Earl of Breadalbane, etc. [1867.]
QZ/L37

CAMPBELL, John Alexander Gavin
Petition of John Alexander Gavin Campbell of
Glenfalloch claiming the title. [1867.]
QZ/L37

MINUTES of evidence. 1872.
ED/N-1(Yule.146(5)) QZ/L37

MINUTES of proceedings on the Breadalbane peerage
claim of Gavin Campbell and of John MacCullum
. . . 21st June, 25th July 1872. 2pts. London, 1872.
ED/N-1(Yule.146(3,4))

PATERSON, James
The Breadalbane case. Edinburgh, 1863.
ED/N-1(3.1625;Ry.I.3.137) QZ/P26

PROCEEDINGS. 1867.
ED/N-1(Yule.146(6)) QZ/L37

[PROCEEDINGS in the competition for the
Breadalbane estates between John A. G. Campbell
of Glenfalloch and Charles W. Campbell of
Borland.][Edinburgh], 1864-7. 4v.
ED/N-1(Yule.139-142)

SINCLAIR, Alexander
Statement of the Breadalbane case. Glasgow, 1866.
ED/N-1(Alex.I.6) QZ/P26 ED/N-2 GL/U-1
QZ/P99

Brechin
MAULE, Harry
Registrum de Panmure. Edinburgh, 1874. 2v.
ED/N-1(Gen.8.P) QZ/P28 AD/U-1 QZ/P26
SA/U-1 QZ/L37 QZ/P99

Breingan of Clackmannanshire
BREINGAN, Stanley R.
  The Breingans of Clackmannanshire. (In *Scottish Genealogist*, vol.xxvii, no.1, March 1980, pp.5-14.)
  ED/N-1 (Gen.7) QZ/P15

Brisbane
['PRINTED genealogical table showing descent and connexions of Anna Maria Makdougall Brisbane, Lady of Makerstoun'. 1840.]
  ED/N-1 (Adv.MS.25.8.18)

Brisbane of Bishoptoun
FRASER, Sir William
  Genealogical table of the families of Brisbane of Bishoptoun and Brisbane, Makdougall of Makerstoun, and Hay of Alderstoun, etc. Edinburgh, 1840. (*Xerox copy*)
  ED/N-2

Brisbane of Brisbane
BRISBANE, Sir Thomas Makdougall
  Reminiscences of General Sir Thomas Makdougall Brisbane. Edinburgh, 1860.
  ED/N-1 (A.114.b)

Broatch
REID, Robert Corsane
  Castlemains papers (Lochmaben): papers relating to the families of Broatch, Hightae, and calendared. [N.d.] (*MSS. and typescript*)
  QZ/P10 (Unconfirmed location)

Brodie
LAWRANCE, Robert Murdoch
  Brodie family history. Glasgow, 1915.
  ED/N-1 (LC.3345(15)) ED/N-2 QZ/P22
  QZ/P50 QZ/P99

LESLIE,
  A family history: [a short acount of the families of Brodie, Dunbar, Farquhar and Davidson.] [Brighton, 1891?]
  ED/N-1 (6.2484)

WOOD, James Alexander Fraser
  The Brodies. (In *Scotland's Magazine*, vol.65, no.11, November 1969, pp.42-7.)
  ED/N-1 (Y.31)

Brodie of Brodie
BRODIE, William
  The genealogy of the Brodie family from Malcolm Thane of Brodie, 1249-85, to 1862. Eastbourne, 1862.
  ED/N-1 (J.135.b) ED/N-2 QZ/L37 QZ/P50

HISTORY of the family of Brodie of Brodie. [N.p., 1881?]
  ED/N-2 QZ/P50 QZ/P99

INNES, Sir Thomas
  The Brodie family: Alexander Brodie of Brodie, 1697-1754. 1930. (Reprinted from *Transactions of the Banffshire Field Club*.)
  QZ/P22

Brodie of Kerse
[MATERIAL relating to the lands and lairds of Brodie of Kerse. N.d.]
  QZ/P-6

Brodie of Maine
CRAMOND, William
  Extracts from the diary of Alexander Brodie of Maine, 1671-1676. Elgin, 1903.
  ED/N-1 (1903.45(8))

Brooker
BROOKER, J. G.
  The Brooker family, showing lines of descent through many Cumberland families from the ancient Saxon, Scottish and Irish kings. [N.p., 19--.] (*Typescript*)
  QZ/P22

Broun
BROUN, Robert J.
  History of the Broun family and related families. [Tequesta, Florida, 1971?]
  ED/N-1 (S.314.b)

Broun of Colstoun
BAIRD, John George Alexander
  Papers of an old Scots family: Broun of Colstoun. [Edinburgh], 1907. (Reprinted from *Blackwood's Magazine*, July 1907.)
  ED/N-1 (Ry.I.3.336)

BROWN-MORISON, John Brown
  Genealogical notes anent some ancient Scottish families. Perth, 1884.
  ED/N-2 QZ/P15 QZ/L37

—A monograph on the notice of the ancient family of Broun of Colstoun in Crawford's MS. Baronage. [N.p.], 1881.
ED/N-1(S.122.g) QZ/L37 QZ/P26

HAUCH-FAUSBØLL, Theodor
Af slaegten Browns historie. [With genealogical tables.] Kjøbenhavn, 1918.
ED/N-1(R.291.b)

— — Copenhagen, 1930.
SA/U-1 GL/U-1

LINDSAY, Edith C. Broun
Colstoun: story of a Scots barony. (In *Transactions of the East Lothian Antiquarian and Field Naturalists Society*, vol.4, 1948, pp.19-33.)
ED/N-1(Hist.S.91.E)

Broun of Sauchie, Balquarne and Finderlie

BROWN-MORISON, John Brown
Genealogical notes anent some ancient Scottish families. Perth, 1884.
ED/N-2 QZ/P15 QZ/L37

Broun-Morison of Finderlie and Murie

BROWN-MORISON, John Brown *and* BROWN, James
The progress of titles of Finderlie during the 16th century. [N.p., n.d.]
ED/N-1(S.122.c) QZ/P99

Brown

['GENEALOGICAL material concerning the Brown family'. 1746-1915.]
ED/N-1(MS.Acc.6134)

[A GENEALOGICAL table showing the antecedents of Robert Shortreed. N.p., 1844.]
ED/N-1(7.106(66-9))

THOMSON, Elizabeth M.
The Browns. [N.d.] (*MS.*)
QZ/P-6

Brown of Colstoun *see* Broun of Colstoun

Brown of Cultermains

The BROWNS of Cultermains: being an historical sketch of that old Clydesdale family. Chiefly extracted from *Biggar and the House of Fleming*. Edinburgh, 1866.
ED/N-1(Ry.II.e.51(3);1882.43(3);NE.25.f.11(1))

Brown of Dolphinton

MACKENZIE, Alice Ann
Dolphinton. [N.p.], 1888.
QZ/L37

Brown of Fordell

BROWN, Marguerite Willette
Genealogy of John Brown of Hampton, New Hampshire. Massachusetts, 1977.
QZ/P22

STODART, Robert Riddle
Memorials of the Browns of Fordell, Finmount and Vicarsgrange. Edinburgh, 1887.
ED/N-1(R.272.a) QZ/P22 QZ/P18 QZ/P26
QZ/P99 ED/N-2 QZ/P11 SA/U-1 AD/U-1
GL/U-1 QZ/L37

Brown of Haddington

BROWN, Delyse
[Letter, 4th April 1982 to the District Librarian, East Lothian District Library, concerning descendants of the Reverend John Brown of Haddington.] (*MS.*)
QZ/P34

BROWN, Rachel *and* NOBBS, E. A.
The family tree of the Rev. John Brown of Haddington. [1952-4.] (*Typescript*)
ED/N-2 QZ/P99

Brown of Newburgh, Fife

CRAMER, Sydney
[Inscriptions in three Bibles. Dundee, n.d.]
ED/N-1(Mf.25(12[4]))

Brown of Newhall

['GENEALOGICAL notes concerning the Brown family of Newhall'. 18--, 19--.]
ED/N-1(MS.9298,ff.34-41)

Brown of Newmilns

BROWN, Alexander Taylor
Genealogical tree of the Browns of Newmilns, Ayrshire, and their descendants. [N.p.], 1930.
QZ/P99

Brownlee

CARVEL, John L.
One hundred years in timber: the history of the city saw mills, 1849-1949. [With a genealogical table.] Glasgow, 1950.
ED/N-1(R.154.c)

Bruce

ARMSTRONG, William Bruce
Collectanea Bruceana: two ... MS. volumes presented ... by the compiler. 1898.
QZ/L37

—[Genealogical papers on the Bruces. 18--.]
ED/N-1 (MS.15982-8)

BOREL D'HAUTERIVE, André François Joseph
Notice généalogique sur la maison de Bruce en
Angleterre, en Ecosse et en France. Paris, 1865.
ED/N-1 (6.1734(16)) ED/N-2 QZ/P99

BRUCE, Sir Charles
Milestone on my long journey: notes relative to my
family: the Bruces of Blairhall, Kinross and Arnot.
[N.p.], 1917.
QZ/P26

BRUCE, Mary Elizabeth Cumming
Family records of the Bruces and the Cumyns.
Edinburgh, 1870.
ED/N-1 (Gen.8.B;A.113.a;R.172.b) ED/N-2
QZ/P22 QZ/P11 QZ/P40 AD/U-1 QZ/P14
SA/U-1 GL/U-1 QZ/L37 QZ/P50 QZ/P49
QZ/P41 QZ/P99

CARRICK, Andrew
Some account of the ancient Earldom of Carrick; to
which are prefixed notices of the Earldom after it
came into the families of De Bruce and Stewart, by
James Maidment. Edinburgh, 1857.
ED/N-1 (Ry.II.e.31) QZ/P-1

CLARK, John
Genealogy, records and intermarriages of the
Fordyce, Bruce and Clark families at Unst,
Shetland. 2nd ed. Falkirk, 1902.
ED/N-1 (R.172.h) ED/N-2 QZ/P99

— — Falkirk, 1902.
ED/N-1 (H2.80.1076)

GENEALOGY of the branch of the Bruce family
settled in Ireland, heirs male of the Bruces of
Newtoune and eldest cadets of Airth. [With a
genealogical table.] [N.p., 1877?]
ED/N-1 (7.95)

HEWISON, J. K.
Robert the Bruce: a family romance. (In *Transactions
of the Dumfriesshire and Galloway Natural History &
Antiquarian Society*, 3rd series, vol.xvii, 1930-1,
pp.162-8.)
ED/N-1 (J.187)

HISTORIES of nobles families; edited by Henry
Drummond. London, 1846. 2v.
ED/N-1 (S.300.a) GL/U-1 QZ/P99

MACDOWALL, John Kevan
Carrick Gallovidian: a historical survey . . . with
genealogical charts and notes . . . Ayr, 1947.
ED/N-1 (R.241.d)

SINCLAIR, Alexander
Genealogical descent of the royal line of Bruce.
Edinburgh, 1860.
QZ/L37 QZ/P16

SURENNE, Gabriel
Prospectus of the history of the Royal Scottish
House of Bruce, in three volumes. [Edinburgh?],
1856.
ED/N-1 (3.1369;4.36(12)) QZ/L37

WALLACE, James
Wallace-Bruce and closely related families.
Minnesota, 1930.
QZ/P14 GL/U-1

Bruce of Airth
ARMSTRONG, William Bruce
The Bruces of Airth and their cadets. Edinburgh,
1892.
ED/N-1 (A.58.a) QZ/P14 ED/N-2 QZ/P15
SA/U-1 QZ/P22 QZ/L37 GL/U-1 QZ/P13
ED/U-1 QZ/P99

—Notes on the origin of the baronial house of Bruce
of Airth. London, 1888.
ED/N-1 (1970.317(14)) ED/N-2

McGROUTHER, Thomas
Airth problems. Stirling, 1926.
QZ/P14

—The Bruces of Airth and their barony. Stirling,
1928.
AD/U-1

Bruce of Annandale
HORNBY, Charles
Three letters containing remarks on some of the
numberless errors and defects in Dugdale's
'Baronage'; and occasionally on some other authors.
[With genealogical tables.] London, 1738.
ED/N-1 (A.37.e.15)

Bruce, Earl of Carrick *see* **Carrick,** Earldom of

Bruce of Clackmannan
BRUCE, William Downing
Collections towards a history of the county of
Clackmannan. Part 1: Parish of Clackmannan.
[Alloa, 1868?]
ED/N-1 (5.22(17));NE.9.d.2) ED/N-2

GORDON, Thomas C.
The tower of Clackmannan, the ancient seat of the Bruces. Clackmannan, 1959.
ED/N-1 (5.2161)

[MS. volume of copies of charters relating to the Bruces from 1330 to 1829.]
ED/S10 (Unconfirmed location)

Bruce of Cultmalundie
ARMSTRONG, William Bruce
Bruces of Cultmalundie in Perthshire, of Muness, Sumburgh, Symbister in Shetland. [N.p., n.d.]
QZ/P41 QZ/P99

Bruce of Earlshall
FAMILY of Bruce of Earlshall in the parish of Leuchars, Co. Fife. [N.p.], 1880.
QZ/Q17

['A GENEALOGICAL account of the family of Bruce of Earlshall'. 1635?]
ED/N-1 (Adv.MS.33.2.27.,f.315)

STODART, Robert Riddle
Bruce of Earlshall in the parish of Leuchars, Co. Fife. (In *The Genealogist*, vol.7, 1883, pp.131-142.)
ED/N-1 (Y.215)

Bruce of Inverurie
[DOCUMENTS, letters, day books and account books relating to the Bruce family of Heatherwick farm. 1845-1936?] (*MSS.*)
QZ/P22

Bruce of Kennet *see* **Balfour,** Lord Balfour of Burleigh

Bruce, Baron Bruce of Kinloss *see also* **Kinloss,** Lord

Bruce, Baron Bruce of Kinloss
BRUCE, James Ernest Brudenell
Remarks on Scottish peerages: their limitations by patent or otherwise, particularly with reference to the barony of Bruce, of Kinloss, now enjoyed by the Earl of Elgin and Kincardine, but claimed by the Duke of Buckingham and Chandos. London, 1868.
ED/N-1 (Law) SA/U-1 QZ/P16

PEDIGREE of the Bruces, Barons Bruce of Kinloss, showing the heirs of line and the collateral heirs male. [N.p., 1867.]
QZ/P22 QZ/P99

Bruce of Kinnaird
GIBSON, John C.
Lands and lairds of Larbert and Dunipace parishes. [With genealogical tables.] Glasgow, 1908.
ED/N-1 (R.243.c) QZ/P14

Bruce of Muness *see* **Bruce** of Cultmalundie

Bruce of Newtown
An ACCOUNT of the Bruces of Newtoune and of the Irish branch of that house and now representing it in the male line. [N.p., n.d.]
QZ/L37

Bruce of Stenhouse
GIBSON, John C.
Lands and lairds of Larbert and Dunipace parishes. [With genealogical tables.] Glasgow, 1908.
ED/N-1 (R.243.c) QZ/P14

Bruce of Sumburgh *see* **Bruce** of Cultmalundie

Bruce of Symbister *see* **Bruce** of Cultmalundie

Bruce in Tottenham
ADAMS, William M.
Wolfhall and Tottenham: the homes of the Seymour and the Bruce. London, 1907.
ED/N-1 (R.88.h;R.88.h.1(2))

COURT rolls of the manors of Bruces, Dawbeneys, Pembrokes—Tottenham—1 Richard II to 1 Henry IV, 1377-1399; prepared for publication, with an introduction by E.H. Fenton. Tottenham, 1961.
ED/N-1 (S.311.c)

Bruce of Uyeasound, Shetland
CLARK, John
Genealogy, records and intermarriages of the Fordyce, Bruce and Clark families at Uyeasound, Unst, Shetland. 2nd ed. Falkirk, 1899.
ED/N-1 (R.172.h) ED/N-2

— — Falkirk, 1902.
ED/N-1 (H2.80.1076) QZ/P99

— Index to Fordyce, Bruce and Clark families at Uyeasound, Unst, Shetland, 2nd ed., 1902. Prepared with some additional information from the Unst marriage registers 1797-1863 or concerning the Sandison family by Alexander Sandison. Cambridge, 1955.
ED/N-1 (NE.25.f.4) QZ/P22

Brudenell
> WAKE, Joan
> The Brudenells of Deene. London, 1953.
> ED/N-1 (NE.63.b.9) DN/U-1

Brunton
> ADAM, Alastair T.
> Bruntons, 1876-1962. Edinburgh, 1962.
> ED/N-1 (NG.1297.c.25)

Brydone of Selkirk
> BRYDONE, James Marr
> Mungo Park and the Brydones of Selkirk. London, [1963].
> ED/N-2 SA/U-1 QZ/P99

Buccleuch, Earl of, Duke of *see* **Scott,** Earl of, Duke of Buccleuch

Buchan, Earl of *see* **Comyn,** Earl of Buchan

Buchan, Earldom of
> MACKENZIE, Sir Colin
> Case of Sir Colin Mackenzie of Kilcoy, Bt., on his claim to the title and dignity of Earl of Buchan and Lord Auchterhouse. [N.p., 18--.]
> ED/N-1 (Yule.162(9)) SA/U-1 QZ/L37

Buchan of Auchmacoy
> WOOD, John Philp
> Memorials of various families. [1830?] (*MS.*)
> QZ/P99

Buchanan
> The BUCHANAN Society. Glasgow, 1927.
> ED/N-1 (NE.13.b.17) QZ/P99

> BUCHANAN, Alice Lilian
> A memoir of the Buchanan family, and in particular of George Buchanan, Kt., 1831-1895. Aberdeen, 1941.
> ED/N-1 (R.272.f) QZ/P14 QZ/P22 ED/N-2
> SA/U-1 QZ/P99

> BUCHANAN, Arthur William Patrick
> The Buchanan book: the life of Alex. Buchanan, Q.C., of Montreal, followed by an account of the family of Buchanan. Montreal, 1911.
> ED/N-1 (R.172.d) QZ/P99 QZ/L37 GL/U-1

> —Later leaves of the Buchanan book. Montreal, 1929.
> ED/N-1 (R.172.d) QZ/L37 QZ/P99

> BUCHANAN, Barbara Isabella
> Buchanan family records: James Buchanan and his descendants. Capetown, 1923.
> ED/N-1 (NE.25.g.1)

> BUCHANAN, R. M.
> Notes on the members of the Buchanan Society, nos. 1-366 (1725-1829). Glasgow, 1931.
> QZ/P-1 (Unconfirmed location)

> BUCHANAN, William
> A historical and genealogical essay upon the family and surname of Buchanan. Glasgow, 1723.
> ED/N-1 (A.114.d;Nha.A163(4)) GL/U-1
> ED/N-2

> — — Edinburgh, 1775.
> ED/N-1 (Hall.199.f.26) QZ/L37

> — — Glasgow, 1793.
> ED/N-1 (Hall.197.g.1) QZ/P27 QZ/P49

> — — Glasgow, 1820.
> ED/N-1 (Alex.1.6) ED/N-2 GL/U-1 QZ/P99

> —An inquiry into the genealogy and present state of Scottish surnames. With the origin and descent of the . . . family of Buchanan. (In *Miscellanea Scotica*, vol.iv, 1820.)
> ED/N-1 (NE.20.c.12;NE.22.d.14(5)) ED/U-1

> ['GENEALOGICAL material concerning the family of Buchanan'. 17--.]
> ED/N-1 (Adv.MS.20.1.6.,ff.97-118)

> ['MEMOIR of the Buchanans of Drumpellier, Auchuitoylie and Ardenconnell'. 1827?]
> ED/N-1 (Adv.MS.19.2.17.,ff.32-7)

> SMITH, John Guthrie
> Strathendrick and its inhabitants. Glasgow, 1896.
> ED/N-1 (A.58.a) QZ/P14 ED/N-2

Buchanan of Ardoch
> ['DRAFT genealogical account of the Buchanan family of Ardoch'. 1827?]
> ED/N-1 (Adv.MS.19.2.17.,ff.38-43)

> PARKES-BUCHANAN, John
> The family book of the Buchanans of Ardoch, commonly called the Ardoch Register. Glasgow, 1894.
> ED/N-1 (A.57.a) QZ/L37 QZ/P49

Buchanan of Spittal

HAMILTON, Francis
Claim of Dr. Francis Hamilton Buchanan of Spittal
[to be considered chief of the name]. Edinburgh,
1826.
ED/N-1 (S.122.e.1(1))

— Second claim of Dr. Francis Hamilton Buchanan
of Spittal. Edinburgh, 1828.
ED/S10

Buchanan of Wester Cameron

BUCHANAN, John
Additional particulars relating to Buchanan of
Wester Cameron. [N.p., 1862?]
ED/N-1 (Hall.197.g.1(2))

Budge

BUDGE, Eleanor M.
The genealogy of the Budges. (In *Scottish
Genealogist*, part 1, vol.iv, no.3, July 1957, pp.63-9;
part 2, vol.iv, no.4, October 1957, pp.92-6.)
ED/N-1 (Gen.7)

Budge of Trotternish

BUDGE, Eleanor M.
The history and genealogy of the Budge family
of Trotternish, Skye. Inverness, [1975].
ED/N-1 (5.6410) QZ/P40 (I) ED/N-2 QZ/P99

Bulloch

BULLOCH, Joseph Gaston Baillie
The family of Baillie of Dunain, etc. Green Bay,
Wisc., 1898.
QZ/P40 AD/U-1

—History and genealogy of the families of Bulloch
and Stobo and Irvine of Cults. Washington, D.C.,
1911.
QZ/P22 QZ/L37

Buncle

BUNCLE, Peter A.
The story of the Buncle family in Scotland. Revised
ed. Worthing, 1979.
ED/N-1 (H9.79.193)

Burden

STODART, R. R.
Burden of Auchingarrich and Feddal. [N.d.]
QZ/P99

Burn-Murdoch

FORSYTH, Dorothea
A family memoir. Malton, 1939.
ED/N-1 (R.172.g)

Burnes *see also* **Burns**

Burnes

BURNES, James
Notes on the name and family of James Burnes,
K.H., F.R.S. Edinburgh, 1851.
ED/N-1 (Hall.149.c) QZ/P22 QZ/P99

BURNESS, Lawrence Ruxton
The family of Burnes. [1875-1969.] (*MSS.*)
ED/N-1 (Mf.100)

Burness

[GENEALOGICAL table of the family of Burness,
1700-1834: ancestors and relatives of Robert Burns.
N.p., 1928.]
QZ/P28

Burnett

BURNETT, Charles Howard
The Burnett family, with collateral branches. Also
historical and genealogical notes on allied families,
and biographical sketches of various eminent
Burnetts. Los Angeles, Calif., 1950.
AD/U-1 QZ/P99

POWIS papers, 1507-1894, edited by John George
Burnett. Aberdeen, 1951. (3rd Spalding Club.)
ED/N-1 (3rd Spald.Club.16) QZ/P14 QZ/P28
QZ/P99

Burnett of Burnetland and Barns

BURNETT, Montgomery
Genealogical account of the family of Burnett of
Burnetland and Barns. 2nd ed. Edinburgh, 1880.
ED/N-1 (NE.25.h.21) ED/N-2 QZ/P11
AD/U-1 QZ/P99 SA/U-1

— — Edinburgh, 1882.
ED/N-1 (S.122.d) QZ/L37 QZ/P99

Burnett of Gadgirth
The CHALMERSES and Burnetts of Gadgirth.
[N.p., n.d.]
QZ/P44 (Unconfirmed location)

Burnett of Leys

BURNETT, George
The family of Burnett of Leys, with collateral branches; from the MS. of the late G. Burnett; edited by J. Allardyce. Aberdeen, 1901. (New Spalding Club, 22.)
ED/N-1 (Ref.47) ED/N-2 DN/U-1 GL/U-1
ST/U-1 QZ/L37 QZ/P22 QZ/P30 QZ/P40
QZ/P99

BURNETT, William Kendall
Genealogical tree of the family of Burnett of Leys. Aberdeen, 1893.
ED/N-1 (3.2597(12)) ED/N-2 QZ/P40
QZ/P30 QZ/P99

RAMSAY, Elizabeth Maule
Legends of Leys; collected from oral traditions of the Burnett family, etc. Aberdeen, 1856.
ED/N-1 (3.2597(12)) QZ/P22 QZ/P99

Burns *see also* **Burnes**

Burns

BALLANTINE, James
Chronicle of the hundredth birthday of Robert Burns. Edinburgh, 1859.
ED/N-1 (X.170.c) QZ/P-7 QZ/P14 QZ/P22
GL/U-1 QZ/P49 QZ/Q88 QZ/P99

BOLD, Alan
Robert Burns. London, 1973.
QZ/L37

BURNS, J. G.
The Burne, Burn, or Burns family, now Burns: notes. [1956.]
QZ/P99

CHALMERS and Burns roll of honour. Edinburgh, 1915. [Contains names of 96 descendants of James Chalmers, printer . . . Aberdeen, 1741-1810 . . . and John Burns . . . H.M. Customs, Borrowstounness, 1730-1817, etc.]
QZ/P99

DOBSON, Peter
Robert Burns and his East Lothian connections. Prestonpans, 1974.
QZ/P34

DUTHIE, Robert
Ancestors, descendants and collateral relatives of Robert Burns. Stonehaven, 1859.
QZ/P22

McCRORIE, Tom
The family tree of Robert Burns from the framed parchment in Burns' house, Dumfries; compiled from parish records and authentic sources. Dumfries, 1963.
ED/N-1 (1964.101) ED/N-2 QZ/P22 QZ/P99

ROBERTSON, James
A history of Burns' forefathers, his travels in Scotland and his masonic affairs. Aberdeen, 1950.
ED/N-1 (5.1961)

ROGERS, Charles
Book of Robert Burns: genealogical and historical memoirs of the poet, his associates, etc. Edinburgh, 1889-91. 3v. (Grampian Club.)
ED/N-1 (Gramp.Club.23) QZ/P-7 QZ/P-6
GL/U-1 QZ/Q88 QZ/P99 QZ/P16

—Genealogical memoirs of the family of Robert Burns and of the Scottish house of Burnes. London, 1877.
ED/N-1 (S.121.e) QZ/Q17 QZ/P-7 ED/N-2
QZ/P22 QZ/P40 QZ/P14 SA/U-1 AD/U-1
GL/U-1 QZ/L37 QZ/P16 QZ/P99
QZ/P52 (Unconfirmed location)

SMITH, Grant F. O.
The man Robert Burns. [With genealogical tables.] Toronto, 1940.
ED/N-1 (1967.128) QZ/P99

WATSON, James
Genealogical sketch of the descendants of Robert Burns in Kincardineshire. Aberdeen, [n.d.]. (*Typescript*)
QZ/P22

Bute, Marquess of *see* **Crichton-Stuart,** Marquess of Bute

Butter

BUTTER, C. A. J.
Notes on the Butter family. [N.p., 1962.]
ED/N-1 (7.152) ED/N-2

Butter of Faskally

BUTTER, Archibald Edward
Family history of the Butters of Faskally. 1895. (*Newscutting*)
QZ/P26

Byres

GILL, Andrew J. Mitchell
The families of Moir and Byres. Edinburgh,
1885.
ED/N-1 (A.23.c) ED/N-2 QZ/P22 GL/U-1
SA/U-1 QZ/L37 QZ/P99

Byres of Coates

MEMOIR of the family of Sir John Byres of Coates,
now of Tonley in the county of Aberdeen. (In
*Memoir and genealogy of the family of Sandilands of
Crabstone & Cotton in Aberdeenshire*) [N.p.], 1863.
ED/N-2 ED/S10

Byset, Bysset *see* Bisset

Cadell

CADELL, Patrick
The industrial associates of the Cadell family in the
eighteenth century. (In *Scottish Genealogist*, vol.xxiii,
no.3, September 1976, pp.69-76.)
ED/N-1 (Gen.7)

STEVENSON, John Horne
The Cadells of Banton, Grange, Tranent and
Cockenzie, etc., 1668-1890. Edinburgh, 1890.
ED/N-1 (FB.el.99) QZ/P99

Cadenhead

CADENHEAD, George
The family of Cadenhead. Aberdeen, 1887.
ED/N-1 (A.113.b) QZ/P30 ED/N-2 QZ/P22
SA/U-1 QZ/P99 ED/S10 GL/U-1 QZ/P28

CADENHEAD, William George
Memoirs of an ordinary man. Fareham, 1969.
QZ/P22

Caird

CAIRD, Rennie Alexander
A history of, or notes upon family of Caird
(Scotland). 2pts in 1. Leicester, 1913,15.
ED/N-1 (NE.26.d.6) ED/N-2

SNODDY, Thomas G.
Caird & Company, shipbuilders, Greenock, and
James Tennant Caird. [With a genealogical table.]
Kirkcaldy, 1938.
ED/N-1 (1968.15)

Cairncross

CAIRNCROSS, A. F.
History of a Forfarshire family. [N.p.], 1920.
ED/N-2

CAIRNCROSS, A. F. *and* CAIRNCROSS, B. L.
Cairncross: the history of a Scottish family. [With
genealogical tables.] George, Cape Province,
1959.
ED/N-1 (NE.25.b.20)

Cairns

IRVINE, Lyn
Alison Cairns and her family. [With a genealogical
table.] Cambridge, 1967.
ED/N-1 (NF.1364.a.2) QZ/P22

LAWLOR, Henry Cairnes
A history of the family of Cairnes or Cairns and
its connections. London, 1906.
ED/N-1 (S.120.c) GL/U-1 AD/U-1 SA/U-1
QZ/P99 QZ/L37

RICHMOND, Keith *and* CRAGO, Maureen
A genealogical study: Richmond, Campbell, Cairns
and Croft. [Armidale, N.S.W.], 1975.
ED/N-1 (6.2868)

Caithness, Earldom of

SINCLAIR, James
Information for James Sinclair in Reiss against
William Sinclair of Ratter. [N.p.], 1769.
QZ/P99

Calder *see also* Campbell of Cawdor or Calder

Calder

[An ACCOUNT of the family of Calder. 1773?]
ED/N-1 (MS.9982)

The ANCIENT and honourable family of Calder: the
book of Calder. [N.d.] (*MS. with watercolour
illustrations*)
ED/N-2 QZ/P40

DEUCHAR, A.
Genealogical collections relative to the family of
Calder. [N.d.] (*MS.*)
QZ/P-1 (Unconfirmed location)

GENEALOGICAL tree of the family of Calder. [N.d.]
(*MS.*)
ED/N-2 QZ/P40

SHAW, Lauchlan
A succinct account of the family of Calder.
Edinburgh, 1914. (In *Highland papers*; edited by
J. R. N. MacPhail, Vol.1 (Scottish History Society
Publications, 2nd series, vol.v.), pp.117-39.)
ED/N-1 (Ref.54) QZ/P-1 QZ/P22 QZ/P27
ED/N-2

['A SUCCINCT account of the family of Calder'.
18--.]
ED/N-1 (Adv.MS.34.3.21.,ff.29-33)

Calderwood

TAYLOR, Albert A.
The Calderwood families of Scotland, Ireland and
America. London, 1965.
ED/N-1 (NE.25.b.24) ED/N-2 QZ/P-9
QZ/P99

Calderwood of Polton

The COLTNESS collections, MDCVIII-
MDCCCXL; edited by James Dennistoun. [With
a genealogical table.] Edinburgh, 1842. (Maitland
Club.)
ED/N-1 (Mait.Club.58) ED/U-1 GL/U-1
QZ/L37 QZ/P-1 QZ/P40 QZ/P56 QZ/P99

Caldwell

GORDON, L. A.
The Caldwells of that ilk & associated branches.
(In *Scottish Genealogist*, vol.xxviii, no.4, December
1981, pp.185-9.)
ED/N-1 (Gen.7)

JAMIESON, E. L.
Caldwells of Lanark and other stories. [Lanark,
Ont.], 1973.
ED/N-1 (HP2.76.4)

Callendar of Callendar

MEIKLE, John
Callendar House: its place in Scottish history.
Falkirk, 1925. (Reprinted from *Falkirk Herald*,
1878/9.)
ED/N-1 (R.243.g) ED/N-2 QZ/P14

Cameron

ARBUTHNOT, Archibald
A brief account of the life and family of Miss Jenny
Cameron, the reputed mistress of the Pretender's
eldest son. London, 1746.
ED/N-1 (Blk.340) QZ/P40

CAMERON, Barbara Cheyne
Some family memories. [N.p.], 1978.
ED/N-1 (HP2.78.1147)

CAMERON, George Henry
John Cameron, non-juror, his ancestors and
descendants; with special reference to the Camerons
of Worcester. 4pts. Oxford, 1919-23.
ED/N-1 (NE.63.a.14) SA/U-1 QZ/L37

CAMERON, John
The Clan Cameron . . . with short notices of
eminent clansmen. Kirkintilloch, 1894.
ED/N-1 (A.124.d) QZ/P27 QZ/P22 QZ/P40
SA/U-1 QZ/Q76 ED/U-1 QZ/P99

EAST, Sir Ronald
The Kiel family and related Scottish pioneers:
Findlays, Hossacks, Gilberts, Camerons, Stewarts,
McAlpins, McCallums, McDonalds. [Victoria,
1974.] (*A Family Who's Who*, vol.2.)
ED/N-1 (NE.26.d.3) ED/N-2 GL/U-1 QZ/P50

FRASER, Charles Ian
Clan Cameron: a patriarchy beset. Edinburgh,
1953.
ED/N-1 (Gen.7;Hist.S.111) QZ/P26 QZ/P27
QZ/P40 SA/U-1 QZ/P22 QZ/P-6 QZ/P11
QZ/L37 QZ/P30 QZ/P49 ED/U-1 QZ/P99

— — 3rd ed. Edinburgh, 1979.
ED/N-1 (HP1.80.2916) QZ/P56 QZ/P99

The LIFE of Dr. Archibald Cameron . . .: containing
. . . the reasons which induced the doctor to list
himself among the rebels . . . the genealogy of the
Camerons. London, 1753.
ED/N-1 (Hall.195.f.3(6))

MACKENZIE, Alexander
History of the Camerons; with genealogies of the
principal families of the name. Inverness, 1884.
ED/N-1 (Gen.8.c;Hist.S.111.c) QZ/P27 ED/N-2
QZ/P22 QZ/P40 QZ/P14 AD/U-1 SA/U-1
GL/U-1 QZ/L37 QZ/P30 QZ/P41 ED/U-1
QZ/P99

STEWART, John
The Camerons: a history of Clan Cameron.
Stirling, 1974.
ED/N-1 (Gen.8.c;H4.80.617) ED/N-2 SA/U-1
ST/U-1 ED/S10 QZ/P14 QZ/P34
QZ/P40(I,D) QZ/P53 QZ/P56 QZ/Q41
QZ/P99

Cameron of Glendessary

CAMERON, Alastair
Some stray notes on the Camerons of Glendeshary
(In *Transactions of the Gaelic Society of Inverness*,
vol.xxxviii, 1937-41, pp.278-87.)
ED/N-1 (NF.1559) QZ/Q41

MACLEAN, James N. M.
The Camerons of Glendessary and Dungallon: cadets of Lochiel. (In *Scottish Genealogist*, part 1, vol.xviii, no.4, December 1971, pp.74-88; part 2, vol.xix, no.2, June 1972, pp.51-60.)
ED/N-1 (Gen.7)

Cameron of Letterfinlay

FRASER-MACKINTOSH, Charles
The Camerons of Letterfinlay, styled "Macmartin". (In *Transactions of the Gaelic Society of Inverness*, vol.xvii, 1890-91, pp.31-45.)
ED/N-1 (NF.1559)

Cameron of Lochiel

CAMERON, John, *20th of Lochiel*
Answers for His Majesty's Advocate, in behalf of His Majesty; to the claim of John Cameron, son of the deceased Donald Cameron of Lochiel [to his father's forfeited estate. (Dec. 12, 1749)]. [Edinburgh, 1749.]
ED/N-1 (Ry.II.b.19(33))

DEWAR, John
The Dewar manuscripts: Scottish West Highland folk tales. [With genealogical tables.] Vol.1. Glasgow, 1964.
ED/N-1 (Lit.S.62)

DRUMMOND, John
Memoirs of Sir Ewen Cameron of Lochiel, with an introductory account of the history and antiquities of that family and the neighbouring clans. Edinburgh, 1842. (Abbotsford Club.)
ED/N-1 (Abbot.Club.24) GL/U-1 QZ/P40 QZ/P99

GORDON, Cosmo George
Unto the Lords of Council and Session, the claim of Cosmo George, Duke of Gordon ... upon the forfeited estate of Donald Cameron, late of Lochiel. [1749.]
ED/N-1 (Ry.II.b.19(37))

Campbell

Ane ACCOMPT of the genealogie of the Campbells. Edinburgh, 1916. (In *Highland Papers*; edited by J. R. N. MacPhail. Vol.2 (Scottish History Society Publications, 2nd series, vol.xii.), pp.69-111.)
ED/N-1 (Ref.54) ED/N-2 QZ/P-1 QZ/P41 ED/U-1 QZ/P40

[ACCOUNT of the Campbell family. 1700?]
ED/N-1 (MS.2124)

Ane ACCOUNT of the depredations committed on the Clan Campbell and their followers during the years 1685 and 1686, with the names of the sufferers. [Edinburgh], 1816.
ED/N-1 (A.112.b) ED/N-2

BALFOUR, Lady Frances
Lady Victoria Campbell. 2nd ed. London, [1911].
ED/N-1 (S.163.b) QZ/P99

BALFOUR-MELVILLE, J. L.
Descendants of Dr Alexander James Campbell and Mary Turner Wedderburn Maitland-Heriot. [Mount Waverley, Victoria?], 1970.
ED/N-2

BEDE, Cuthbert
Argyll's Highlanders, or MacCailein Mor and the Lords of Lorne. Glasgow, 1902.
ED/N-1 (R.249.a) QZ/P27 QZ/P40

BORTHWICK, John Douglas
Borthwick Castle: or, sketches of Scottish history. With biographical notices of the chiefs of the House of Argyll. Montreal, 1880.
ED/N-1 (R.232.c)

BRADLEY, Edward
Argyll's Highlands: or, MacCailein Mor and the Lords of Lorne; with traditionary tales and legends of ... the Campbells and Macdonalds ... Glasgow, 1902.
ED/N-1 (R.249.a) QZ/P-1

CAMPBELL ASSOCIATION OF AMERICA
The Highlander, Nos. 1, 2. 1930-9.
QZ/P99* QZ/P-1*

CAMPBELL, Colin
Mackerlich Campbells in the Breadalbane court books. Part 1 (In *Scottish Genealogist*, vol.xxvii, no.1, March 1980, pp.20-1. 24-33.)
ED/N-1 (Gen.7)

— Recent Campbell matriculations and grants. (Reprinted from *Coat of Arms*.) 6pts. Salisbury, [1957-8].
ED/N-1 (1970.266)

CAMPBELL, Sir Duncan
The Clan Campbell ... from the Campbell collection formed by Sir D. Campbell of Barcaldine and Glenure ...; edited by H. Paton. 8v. Edinburgh, 1913-22.
ED/N-1 (Gen.8.c; Hist.S.111.c) ED/N-2*
AD/U-1 ED/U-1 SA/U-1 QZ/L37* QZ/P27
QZ/P40* QZ/P99 QZ/Q17 QZ/P30

—Records of the Clan Campbell in the military service of the Hon. East India Co., 1600-1858. London, 1925.
ED/N-1 (S.121.f) QZ/Q17 AD/U-1 QZ/P22 GL/U-1 ED/U-1 QZ/P99

CAMPBELL, Gavin
In the House of Lords . . . minutes of proceedings on the Breadalbane peerage claim of Gavin Campbell and of Sir John MacCullum . . . 21st June (25th July) 1872. 2pts. London, 1872.
ED/N-1 (Yule.146(3,4))

CAMPBELL, Glenn Harold
The Campbells are coming. New York, 1947.
ED/N-1 (R.233.d) ED/N-2

CHRISTIE, John
The lairds and lands of Loch Tayside. Aberfeldy, 1892.
ED/N-1 (A.120.c) DN/U-1 QZ/L37 QZ/P99

COWAN, Edward J.
Clanship, kinship and the Campbell acquisition of Islay. (In *Scottish Historical Review*, vol.58, no.2 (no.166), October 1979, pp.132-57.)
ED/N-1 (Ref.53)

DESCENT of Campbell of Shian from Egbert, King of England; Malcolm, King of Scotland and Gillespie Campbell. [N.p., n.d.] (*Typescript*)
QZ/P99

DEWAR, John
The Dewar manuscripts: Scottish West Highland folk tales. [With genealogical tables.] Vol.1. Glasgow, 1964.
ED/N-1 (Lit.S.62)

[GENEALOGICAL notes concerning the family of Campbell. N.p., 1916.]
QZ/P28

['GENEALOGICAL notes on the Campbells'. 18--.]
ED/N-1 (MS.2114)

['GENEALOGICAL papers of the Campbells. ca. 1617-1873'. 18--.]
ED/N-1 (MS.Acc.8168.Box.1)

GILLIES, William
Some aspects of Campbell history. (In *Transactions of the Gaelic Society of Inverness*, vol.1, 1976-8, pp.256-95.)
ED/N-1 (NF.1559)

INFORMATION for the Countess of Argyle. [With reference to her claim for aliment from her husband.] [N.p., 1695.]
ED/N-1 (Ry.II.a.22(46))

JOHNSTON, George Harvey
The heraldry of the Campbells, with notes on all males of the family, etc. Edinburgh, 1920,21. 2v.
ED/N-1 (S.121.b) QZ/P27 QZ/P99

— — Inveraray, 1977.
ED/N-1 (Her.31) QZ/P40 (I,D) QZ/P-6 ED/N-2

McKERRAL, Andrew
Clan Campbell (Clan Diarmid): a record of service by a race of statesmen. Edinburgh, 1953.
ED/N-1 (Gen.7;S.111) QZ/P26 QZ/P27 ED/N-2 QZ/P40 QZ/P11 QZ/P22 QZ/L37 QZ/P-6 SA/U-1 QZ/P30 QZ/P49 QZ/P16 QZ/P99

— — 2nd ed. Edinburgh, 1979.
ED/N-1 (HP1.80.2919) ED/N-2 QZ/P22 QZ/P56 QZ/P99

RICHMOND, Keith *and* CRAGO, Maureen
A genealogical study: Richmond, Campbell, Cairns and Croft. [Armidale, N.S.W.], 1975.
ED/N-1 (6.2868)

SINTON, Thomas
Family and genealogical sketches. Inverness, 1911.
ED/N-1 (R.172.b) AD/U-1 DN/U-1 QZ/P-1 QZ/P22 QZ/P40 QZ/P99

Campbell of Aberuchill
['ACCOUNT of the family of Campbell of Aberuchill'. 1811?]
ED/N-1 (Adv.MS.6.1.17,ff.53-7)

Campbell of Aird
['ACCOUNT of the family of Campbell of Aird'. 1811?]
ED/N-1 (Adv.MS.6.1.17,ff.100-105)

Campbell of Alloway
CAMPBELL, Jane *and* CAMPBELL, Mary
A family chronicle: the family of Robert Campbell of Alloway. Edinburgh, 1925.
ED/N-1 (S.120.i;R.172.g) ED/N-2 QZ/P99

Campbell in Angus
COWAN, Edward J.
The Angus Campbells and the origin of the
Campbell-Ogilvie feud. (In *Scottish Studies*, vol.25,
1981, pp.25-38.)
ED/N-1 (NH.317)

Campbell, Earl of, Marquess of, Duke of Argyll
ARGYLL, John G. E. H. D. S. Campbell, *9th Duke of*
Joint print of documents in causa His Grace the
Duke of Argyll, against Angus John Campbell of
Dunstaffnage and another. Edinburgh, 1910.
QZ/P99

CAMPBELL, Robert
Life of the most illustrious Prince John, Duke of
Argyle and Greenwich, containing a . . .
genealogical account of His Grace's family and
ancestors. London, 1745.
ED/N-1 (A.114.d) QZ/P27 QZ/P22 GL/U-1
QZ/P99

GRANT, Neil
The Campbells of Argyll. London, 1975.
ED/N-1 (NE.25.a.18) QZ/P22 QZ/P56
QZ/Q88 QZ/P27 ED/N-2 QZ/P99

A HISTORY of the Campbells, Dukes of Argyle . . . to
1776. [1776.] (*MS.*)
QZ/P99

HOGG, John
The Clan Campbell and the Marquis of Lorne: an
epitome of the story of the House of Argyle.
London, [1871].
ED/N-1 (Ry.IV.e.26(14)) QZ/P22 QZ/P40

The HOUSE of Argyll and the collateral branches of
Clan Campbell. Glasgow, 1871.
ED/N-1 (A.113.d) QZ/P27 QZ/P-6 ED/N-2
SA/U-1 QZ/P40 AD/U-1 GL/U-1
QZ/L37 ST/U-1 ED/U-1 QZ/P99 QZ/P52
(Unconfirmed location)

LETTERS to the Argyll family from Elizabeth, Queen
of England, Mary, Queen of Scots, King James VI,
King Charles I, King Charles II and others.
Edinburgh, 1839. (Maitland Club, 50.)
ED/N-1 (Mait.Club.50) QZ/P27 GL/U-1
QZ/P99

MAIDMENT, James
The Argyle papers, 1640-1723. Edinburgh, 1834.
ED/N-1 (L.C.1210;A.114.c.2) QZ/L37 SA/U-1
ST/U-1 ED/U-1 QZ/P99

['NOTES on the genealogy of the Earls of Argyle and
their descendants'. 1709.]
ED/N-1 (Adv.MS.34.6.24,f.65)

SKAE, Hilda T.
The Campbells of Argyll. London, [1913].
ED/N-1 (S.120.g) QZ/P27 QZ/P99

SMITH, Hely Hutchinson Augusta
The MacCallum-More: a history of the Argyll
family. London, 1871.
QZ/Q17 QZ/P27 QZ/P26 QZ/P27 ED/N-2
AD/U-1 QZ/P22 QZ/P40 SA/U-1 QZ/P99

STUART, Lady Louisa
Some account of John, Duke of Argyll, and his
family, by his great-niece. London, 1863.
ED/N-1 (S.121.g) QZ/P11 QZ/L37

Campbell of Asknish
ALLARDICE, W. P.
Observations on a publication by Duncan
Campbell-MacIver of Asknish entitled "Remarks
on writings of the Rev. P. C. Campbell, etc."
Edinburgh, 1870.
QZ/L37

Campbell of Auchinbreck
The CAMPBELLS of Auchinbreck. Edinburgh, 1934.
(In *Highland Papers*; edited by J. R. N. MacPhail.
Vol.4 (Scottish History Society Publications, 3rd
series, vol.xxii.), pp.57-90.)
ED/N-1 (Ref.54) QZ/P14 QZ/P27

['GENEALOGICAL notes on the Campbells of
Auchinbreck'. 1932?]
ED/N-1 (MS.810)

['GENEALOGY of the cadets of the family of
Auchinbreck'. 1741.]
ED/N-1 (Adv.MS.34.6.19.,ff.24-40)

Campbell of Auchindarroch
CAMPBELL, Julia Beatrice
A few words borrowed from the past . . .. [Glasgow,
n.d.] (Auchindarroch Miscellany, part ii.)
ED/N-1 (Hall.210.g.1(4))

Campbell of Barbreck
A LETTER to Mrs. Campbell of Barbreck containing
an account of the Campbells of Barbreck from their
first ancestor to the present time. Ipswich, 1830.
QZ/L37

Campbell of Barcaldine
  FRASER, Alexander Campbell
    The book of Barcaldine: three centuries in the West
    Highlands. London, 1936.
    ED/N-1 (R.172.g) QZ/P14 QZ/P26 ED/N-2
    QZ/P-6 QZ/P30 QZ/P11 AD/U-1 QZ/P22
    DN/U-1 QZ/P49 QZ/P99

Campbell of Blythswood
  EASTON, W.J.
    Family of Blythswood. Paisley, 1876.
    QZ/P-6

Campbell of Bragleen
  ['GENEALOGY of the family of Campbell of
    Bragleen'. 1904.]
    ED/N-1 (MS.10260)

Campbell of Breadalbane *see also* **Breadalbane,**
  Earldom of

Campbell of Breadalbane
  The BLACK book of Taymouth; edited by Cosmo
    Innes. Edinburgh, 1855. (Bannatyne Club, 100)
    ED/N-1 (Bann.Club.100) QZ/P27 QZ/P40
    GL/U-1 QZ/L37 QZ/P99
  CAMPBELL, Donald Draper
    File concerning John Breadalbane Campbell in
    Florida, U.S.A. [N.p.], 1975.
    QZ/L37
  GIBB, Sir George Duncan
    Pedigree of James Reid Campbell of Inverardine,
    Cornwall and Canada, head of the Canadian branch
    of the Breadalbane Campbell family. London, 1872.
    ED/N-1 (5.14(3)) QZ/P99

Campbell of Cawdor or Calder *see also* **Calder**

Campbell of Cawdor or Calder
  CAWDOR [guidebook. With a genealogical table.]
    Aberdeen, [197-].
    ED/N-2
  ['The HISTORY of the family of Calder of the
    surname of Campbell'. 18--.]
    ED/N-1 (Adv.MS.34.3.21.,ff.33-8.]
  INNES, Cosmo
    The book of the thanes of Cawdor: a series of papers
    selected from the Charter Room, Cawdor,
    1236-1742. Edinburgh, 1859. (Spalding Club, 30.)
    ED/N-1 (Spald.Club.30) ED/N-2 GL/U-1
    QZ/P40 QZ/L37 QZ/P50 QZ/P99

SMITH, G. Gregory
    The book of Islay. [With genealogical tables.]
    Edinburgh, 1895.
    ED/N-1 (A.58.a)

Campbell of Craignish and Lagganlochan
  CAMPBELL, Alexander
    The manuscript history of Craignish. Edinburgh,
    1926. (In *Miscellany of the Scottish History Society*,
    vol.4 (Scottish History Society Publications,
    3rd series, vol.ix.), pp.175-299.)
    ED/N-1 (Ref.54) QZ/L37
  CAMPBELL, T. Hay
    Craignish and Lagganlochan: a genealogical sketch.
    [N.p.], 1890.
    ED/N-1 (6.676) QZ/L37
  GENEALOGICAL and historical account of the family
    of Craignish, with genealogical chart and other
    MS. papers. 2pts. [N.p., n.d.] (*Typescript*)
    QZ/P-1 (Unconfirmed location)

Campbell of Dunstaffanage
  MEMORIAL for Colin Campbell of Ederline ...
    pursuer, against Mrs Isabel Macneil, relict of Neil
    Campbell of Dunstaffanage, and Lilias and
    Margaret Campbell, their daughters, defenders,
    August 24, 1765. [Edinburgh], 1765.
    ED/N-1 (X.44.h.7(1))
  MEMORIAL for Colin Campbell of Ederline, trustee
    for Angus Campbell of Dunstaffanage against Mrs
    Isabel Macneil, Lilias and Margaret Campbell.
    (July 5, 1766.) [Edinburgh], 1766.
    ED/N-1 (X.44.h.7(2))

Campbell of Duntroon
  CAMPBELL, Herbert
    The Campbells of Duntroon and their cadets. 2pts.
    Exeter, 1913-21. (Reprinted from *Genealogist*.)
    ED/N-2 QZ/L37

Campbell in Garth
  CAMPBELL, Duncan
    The book of Garth and Fortingall. Inverness, 1888.
    ED/N-1 (R.246.f) ED/N-2 QZ/P99

Campbell of Glenfalloch *see* **Breadalbane,**
  Earldom of

Campbell of Glenlyon

CAMPBELL, Duncan
The lairds of Glenlyon: historical sketches of Appin, Glenlyon and Breadalbane. Perth, 1886.
ED/N-1 (A.113.b) ED/N-2 QZ/P99

GILFILLAN, George, *and others*
The massacre of Glencoe and the Campbells of Glenlyon. Stirling, 1912.
ED/N-1 (R.249.1) QZ/P14

Campbell of Glenorchy

The BLACK book of Taymouth; edited by Cosmo Innes. Edinburgh, 1855. (Bannatyne Club, 100.)
ED/N-1 (Bann.Club.100) GL/U-1 QZ/P27 QZ/P40 QZ/P99

GILLIES, William A.
In famed Breadalbane. Perth, 1938.
ED/N-1 (R.246.f)

— — 2nd ed. Strathtay, 1980.
ED/N-1 (H3.82.1269) QZ/P22

Campbell in Gothenburg

CORMACK, Alexander Allan
Colin Campbell, 1686-1757, merchant, Gothenburg, Sweden: his will annotated. [Aberdeen], 1960.
ED/N-1 (5.2322)

Campbell of Inverardine

GIBB, Sir George Duncan
Pedigree of James Reid Campbell of Inverardine, Cornwall, Canada. London, 1872.
ED/N-1 (5.14(3)) GL/U-1 QZ/P99

Campbell of Inverawe *see also* **Campbell** of Kilmartin

Campbell of Inverawe

CAMPBELL, Ian MacLeod
Notes on the Campbells of Inverawe. Edinburgh, 1951.
ED/N-1 (R.272.f) QZ/P27 ED/N-2 SA/U-1 QZ/P30 QZ/P99

Campbell of Jura

BUDGE, Eleanor N.
The Campbells of Jura. (In *Scottish Genealogist*, vol.iv, no.1, January 1957, pp.3-9.)
ED/N-1 (Gen.7)

Campbell of Killin

CAMPBELL, Colin
Statement of Isabel Campbell in Killin, 1802. (In *Scottish Genealogist*, vol.viii, no.1, February 1961, pp.1-16.)
ED/N-1 (Gen.7)

Campbell of Kilmartin

WIMBERLEY, Douglas
Memorials of four old families. Inverness, 1894.
ED/N-1 (Y.59.a.23) QZ/P40 DN/U-1 QZ/P-1 QZ/P22 QZ/P99

— Memorials of the family of Kilmartin, and some notes on the family of Campbell of Inverawe. Inverness, 1894.
QZ/P30 QZ/P27 SA/U-1 AD/U-1

Campbell of Kiltearn

MACGREGOR, Duncan
Campbell of Kiltearn. Edinburgh, 1874.
ED/N-1 (Hall.252.g) QZ/P40

Campbell of Kinloch

LOGIN, Edith Dalhousie
The story of the Campbells of Kinloch. London, 1924.
ED/N-1 (S.120.g) QZ/P27 QZ/P26 QZ/P22 SA/U-1 AD/U-1 QZ/L37 GL/U-1 ED/U-1 QZ/P99

Campbell of Knapdale

MACMILLAN, Somerled
Families of Knapdale: their history and their place names. Paisley, [1960].
ED/N-1 (1936.29) ED/N-2 QZ/P18 QZ/P27

Campbell of Lagganlochan

CAMPBELL, Thomas Fraser
The Campbells of Lagganlochan: a chapter in Scottish family history. [1929.] (*Typescript*)
QZ/L37 QZ/P99

— — Edinburgh, [1930].
ED/N-1 (S.120.b) QZ/P27

Campbell of Lawers

STODART, R. R.
Campbell of Lawers. [N.d.]
QZ/P99

Campbell of Lix
CAMPBELL, Colin
A note on the Campbells of Lix. (In *Scottish Genealogist*, part 1, vol.x, no.2, 1963, pp.2-5; part 2, vol.x, no.3, 1963, pp.1-4.)
ED/N-1 (Gen.7)

Campbell of Lochdochart
PATERSON, James
Scottish surnames: a contribution to genealogy. Edinburgh, 1866.
ED/N-1 (K.115.a) QZ/P28 QZ/P22 DN/U-1

Campbell of Lochnell
['GENEALOGY of the Campbell family of Lochnell'. 1830, 1966?]
ED/N-1 (MS.10260)

Campbell in London
CAMPBELL, Dougal
Memorial for the daughters of the deceast Dougal Campbell, portioner of Monktounhall, against George Campbell, surgeon, brother to the said Dougal. [In the litigation concerning the will of Captain D. Campbell of London.][Edinburgh, n.d.]
ED/N-1 (Ry.III.c.35(16))

Campbell of Loudoun
[PAPERS concerning the genealogy of the Campbells of Loudoun. 1760.]
ED/N-1 (Adv.MS.20.1.9.,ff.32-51)

ROBERTSON, William
Ayrshire: its history and historic families. Kilmarnock, 1908. 2v.
ED/N-1 (Hist.S.91.A)

Campbell of Melfort
CAMPBELL, Margaret Olympia
A memorial history of the Campbells of Melfort, Argyllshire; which includes records of the different highland and other families with whom they have intermarried. London, 1882.
ED/N-1 (A.116.a) QZ/Q17 QZ/P27 GL/U-1
QZ/L37 SA/U-1 ED/U-1 QZ/P99

— — Supplement. London, 1894.
QZ/P27 SA/U-1 GL/U-1 QZ/L37

Campbell in Norway
CAMPBELL, Johan H. S.
Stamtavler over familien Campbell i Norge, samt slaegterne Megeland, Sebben, Harrje, Halthaus og Kling. Bergen, 1877.
ED/N-1 (5.2555)

Campbell of Racheane and Peatoun
['A GENEALOGICAL account of the Campbells of Racheane and Peatoun'. 1828.]
ED/N-1 (Adv.MS.19.2.17,ff.73-8)

Campbell of Strachur
The CAMPBELLS of Strachur. (In *Scottish Genealogist*, vol.xviii, no.1, March 1971, pp.1-9.)
ED/N-1 (Gen.7)

Campbell of Succouth
['A GENEALOGICAL account of the Campbells of Succouth. 1826?)
ED/N-1 (Adv.MS.19.2.17,ff. 79-83)

Campbell in Sydney
NEWMAN, Charles E. T.
The spirit of Wharf House: Campbell enterprise from Calcutta to Canberra, 1788-1930. [Sydney], 1961.
ED/N-1 (NF.1340.b.1)

Campbell of Tuerarchan
CAMPBELL, Colin
Statement of Isabel Campbell in Killin, 1802. (In *Scottish Genealogist*, vol.viii, no.1, February 1961, pp.1-16.)
ED/N-1 (Gen.7)

Campbell-Maclachlan
CAMPBELL-MACLACHLAN, A. N.
Memorial history of the family of Campbell Maclachlan. London, 1883.
ED/S10 (Unconfirmed location)

Cannan
CANNON, D. V.
The Cannan family in Galloway: [typed notes in connexion with the article on the family in *Transactions of the Dumfriesshire and Galloway Natural History & Antiquarian Society*, vol.xxxi].
QZ/P10 (Unconfirmed location)

CANNON, D. V. *and* REID, Robert Corsane
The Cannan family in Galloway. (In *Transactions of the Dumfriesshire and Galloway Natural History & Antiquarian Society*, vol.xxxi, 1952-3, pp.78-120.)
ED/N-1 (J.187) QZ/L37

REID, Robert Corsane
[Cannan notes: extracts from register of deeds, sasines, testaments, etc.] (*MSS.*)
QZ/P10 (Unconfirmed location)

Caraher
JOURNAL of the Caraher Family History Society.
No. 1- . Muthill, by Crieff, 1980- .
ED/N-1 (P.1a.8896)

Cargill
CARGILL, John
Cargill of Haltoun of Rattray: notes, on the history
of the family. 1930. 4v. (*MS.*)
SA/U-1

Carlaw
HOUSE, Jack
A family affair: the story of David Carlaw & Sons,
Ltd. of Glasgow. Edinburgh, [1960].
ED/N-1 (NG.1297.f.13)

Carlisle
CARLILE, J. W., *and others*
History of the Paisley branch of the Carlisle, or
Carlile family. Winchester, 1909.
ED/N-1 (S.121.a) QZ/P-6 QZ/L37 QZ/P99

CARLISLE, Nicholas
Collection for a history of the ancient family of
Carlisle. 1822. (*MS.*)
QZ/P99

CARLYLE, T. J.
Review of N. Carlisle's History of the family of
Carlisle. Dumfries, 1881.
QZ/L37 ED/N-2

WOOD, John Philp
Memorials of various families. [1830?] (*MS.*)
QZ/P99

Carlyle of Waterbeck
The CARLYLES of Waterbeck. 1914.
QZ/P10 (Unconfirmed location)

Carmichael
DONALD,
Carmichael and his descendants. [1924.]
QZ/P99

Carmichell of Balmedie
['A GENEALOGICAL account of the family of
Carmichell of Balmedie'. 1650?]
ED/N-1 (Adv.MS.33.2.27.f.320)

Carnegie of Lour
GRAHAM pedigree connecting Montrose and
Carnegies of Lour. [N.p., 18--.]
QZ/P28

Carnegie of Pitarrow
CORMACK, A. A.
Echo from the 1745 rebellion. (Reprinted from
Montrose Review, 25 May 1961.) [N.p., n.d.]
QZ/P22

—Montrosian who made good in Sweden. (In
Montrose Review, vol.cliii, no.7819, 25 May 1961,
p.7.)
ED/N-1 (Annexe 216)

Carnegie of Skibo
GRAY, Peter
Skibo: its lairds and history. Edinburgh, 1906.
ED/N-1 (R.250.g) ED/N-2 AD/U-1 QZ/P22
QZ/P40 QZ/P16 QZ/L37 QZ/P99

Carnegie, Earl of Southesk *see also* **Southesk,**
Earldom of

Carnegie, Earl of Southesk
FRASER, Sir William
History of the Carnegies, Earls of Southesk, and of
their kindred. Edinburgh, 1867. 2v.
ED/N-1 (Gen.8.c) QZ/P28 AD/U-1 GL/U-1
QZ/L37 ED/U-1 QZ/P99

SOUTHESK,   , *Lord*
Genealogical note concerning the Carnegie family
of Southesk, 1400-1855. [N.p.], 1866.
QZ/P28

Carnegie in Sweden
ATTMAN, Linus A.
D. Carnegie & Co., 1803-1953: en hundrafemtioarg
merkantil och industriell verksamhet. [With
genealogical tables.] Goteborg, 1953.
ED/N-1 (NE.69.h.2)

CORMACK, Alexander Allan
The Carnegie family in Gothenburg. Montrose,
1942.
QZ/P28

— — Montrose, 1947.
ED/N-1 (5.1159) QZ/P30 ED/U-1

Carr-Harris
CARR-HARRIS, Grant
Supplementary notes of Carr-Harris history and
genealogy. [N.p., 1973.]
ED/N-1 (5.5491) QZ/L37

Carrick, Earldom of *see also* **Neilson,** of Craigcaffie

Carrick, Earldom of

CARRICK, Andrew
Some account of the ancient earldom of Carric.
Edinburgh, 1857.
ED/N-1 (Ry.II.e.31) GL/U-1 QZ/L37 QZ/P99
QZ/P-1

Carruthers

CARRUTHERS *v.* Clyde: Carruthers family history.
1980.
QZ/P99

CARRUTHERS, Arthur Stanley
A collection of records setting forth the history of
the Carruthers family. Purley, 1925.
ED/N-1 (S.122.e)

CARRUTHERS, Arthur Stanley *and* REID, Robert
Corsane
Records of the Carruthers family. London, 1934.
ED/N-1 (R.172.d) QZ/L37 QZ/P99

— — Supplement. London, 1958.
ED/S10

GILLESPIE, John
The Carruthers family: an interesting record.
[N.p., n.d.]
QZ/P10 (Unconfirmed location)

REID, Robert Corsane
Calendar of the Holmains writs. [N.p., 1931.]
QZ/P10 (Unconfirmed location)

— Carruthers notes: abstracts from the general
register of sasines, 1617-1720 and in particular the
register of sasines, 1617-1732 and 1732-1840, and
Dumfries testaments. 2v. [N.p., n.d.]
QZ/P10 (Unconfirmed location)

Carruthers of Brydegill

CARRUTHERS, A. Stanley
The descendants of George Carruthers of Brydegill.
(In *Transactions of the Dumfriesshire and Galloway
Natural History & Antiquarian Society*, 3rd series,
vol.xxxv, 1956-7, pp.122-6.)
ED/N-1 (J.187)

Carruthers of Holmains

CARRUTHERS, Hugh Warde
The Inverness branch of the family of Carruthers of
Holmains. [N.p.], 1972.
QZ/L37

Cassells

CASSELLS, Robert
Records of the family of Cassells and connexions.
Edinburgh, 1870.
ED/N-1 (A.114.b) QZ/L37 QZ/P99

— — Supplement, by D. K. Cassels and F. K. Cassels.
Great Barford, 1980.
ED/N-1 (HP4.81.842) QZ/L37

CHART of the Royal descent. [N.p.], 1962.
ED/N-2

Cassie

CASSIE, George M.
The Cassie family: an interim report. [Huntsville,
Ontario], 1976.
ED/N-1 (HP.1.77.2170)

— The Cassie family: a revised report. [Huntsville,
Ontario?], 1980.
ED/N-1 (H3.81.470) QZ/P22

CASSIE, R. L.
The Cassies. Banff, 1932.
ED/N-1 (R.172.g) QZ/P22 DN/U-1 QZ/P99

SMITH, James
Genealogies of an Aberdeen family, 1540-1913.
Aberdeen, 1913.
ED/N-1 (S.121.d)

Cassillis, Earldom of *see also* **Kennedy,** Earl of Cassillis

Cassillis, Earldom of

DOUGLAS, William
The case of William, Earl of Ruglen and March,
claiming the title and dignities of Earl of Cassillis
and Lord Kennedy. [N.p., 1762.]
ED/N-1 (1.5(95))

GORDON, John
Copies of the summons and of the printed papers . . .
in the process of declarator of precedency . . . and
the cases of William, the Earl of Ruglen and March,
and of Sir Thomas Kennedy of Culzean both
claiming the titles and dignities of Earl of Cassillis
. . . 27th January 1762. Edinburgh, 1766.
ED/N-1 (Yule.79)

KENNEDY, Sir Thomas
The case of Sir Thomas Kennedy, (claiming the title,
honour and dignity of) Earl of Cassillis. 1761.
ED/N-1 (1.5(98))

—The Cassillis peerage, 1760-4. [N.p., 1764.]
ED/N-1 (Yule.78)

MAIDMENT, James
The Cassillis peerage, 1760-64, with folding
pedigree by W. B. Turnbull. [Edinburgh, 1840.]
AD/U-1

—Reports of claims . . . to the House of Lords . . . of
the Cassillis, Sutherland, Spynie and Glencairn
peerages, 1760-1797. Edinburgh, 1840.
ED/N-1 (Yule.94) QZ/L37

— — Reprinted. Edinburgh, 1882.
ED/N-1 (Law) DN/U-1 GL/U-1 QZ/P-1
QZ/P99

Cathcart of Carleton and Killochan
FERGUSSON, Sir James
The Cathcarts of Carleton and Killochan. (In
*Ayrshire Archaeological & Natural History Society
Collections*, 2nd series, vol.4, 1955-7, pp.133-42.)
ED/N-1 (R.241.b)

Cathcart, Earl Cathcart
GRAHAM, Ethel Maxtone
The beautiful Mrs. Graham and the Cathcart circle.
London, 1927.
ED/N-1 (S.124.c) QZ/P99

Catto of Cairncatto
CATTO, Thomas Sivewright
Thomas Sivewright Catto, Baron Catto of
Cairncatto . . . 1879-1959. [With genealogical
tables.] Edinburgh, 1962.
ED/N-1 (NF.1359.a.2)

Cawdor *see* **Campbell** of Cawdor or Calder

Chalmers
CHALMERS and Burns roll of honour. Edinburgh,
1915. [Contains names of 96 descendants of James
Chalmers, printer . . . Aberdeen, 1741-1810 . . . and
John Burns . . . H.M. Customs, Borrowstounness,
1730-1817, etc.]
QZ/P99

CHALMERS, Patrick H.
Memorandum as to branch of family from which
Principal George Chalmers, D.D., was descended.
[Aberdeen, 1885.]
QZ/L37

CORMACK, Alexander Allan
The Chalmers family and Aberdeen newspapers:
links between Aberdeen and Gothenburg.
[Aberdeen], 1958.
ED/N-1 (5.2054) QZ/P22 QZ/P30 QZ/P99

['GENEALOGICAL material concerning the family of
Chalmers'. 1845?]
ED/N-1 (MS.15478,ff.87,99,115,156-207)

GRANT, A. Thomson
MSS. notes on family of Chalmers. [N.d.]
QZ/P28

GUTHRIE, Charles John
Genealogy of the descendants of the Rev. Thomas
Guthrie . . . connected chiefly with the families of
Chalmers and Trail . . . Edinburgh, 1902.
ED/N-1 (S.120.a) QZ/P28 QZ/P22 SA/U-1
GL/U-1 QZ/P99 QZ/P-1

['NOTICES of families in Aberdeenshire of the name
of Chalmers from various registers'. 1840?]
ED/N-1 (MS.15479)

Chalmers of Balnacraig
MUNRO, Alexander
Genealogical history of the family of Chalmers of
Balnacraig and cadet branches. Aberdeen, 1901.
(*Typescript*)
QZ/P22

Chalmers of Gadgirth
The CHALMERSES and Burnetts of Gadgirth.
[N.p., n.d.]
QZ/P44 (Unconfirmed location)

Chalmers of Mouse
RATTRAY, Thomas
The story of the ghaist of Mouse. [Blairgowrie,
1905.]
ED/N-2

Chalmers in Poland
PAPERS relating to the Scots in Poland, 1576-1793;
edited with an introduction by A. F. Steuart.
Edinburgh, 1915. (Scottish History Society
Publications, vol.59.)
ED/N-1 (Ref.54;NE.21.d.12)

Chambers
WRIGHT, Marcus Stults
Our family ties: some ancestral lines of Marcus S.
Wright, Jr. and Alice Olden Wright. [With
genealogical tables.] South River, N.J., 1960.
ED/N-1 (NF.1373.a.4)

Charles in East Lothian
CHARLES, J. H.
Our family history. Bournemouth, 1935.
QZ/P99

Charteris
REID, Robert Corsane
[Extracts from registers of sasines, etc. . . . with index.][N.p., n.d.] 2v.
QZ/P10 (Unconfirmed location)

Charteris of Amisfield *see also* **Wemyss,** Earl of Wemyss

Charteris of Amisfield
REID, Robert Corsane
The family of Charteris of Amisfield. [With genealogical tables.] Dumfries, 1921.
QZ/L37
— — Dumfries, 1936.
ED/N-1 (R.241.e) AD/U-1 SA/U-1 QZ/P26 QZ/P99

Charters
WATSON, Charles Brodie Boog
Traditions and genealogies of some members of the families of Boog, Heron, Leishman, Ross and Watson. Perth, 1908.
ED/N-1 (S.120.d) SA/U-1 QZ/P99

Chatelherault, Duke of *see also* **Hamilton,** Duke of Hamilton

Chatelherault, Duke of
ABERCORN, James Hamilton, *2nd Duke of*
Consultation pour J. H., Marquis d'Abercorn . . . contre le Duc d'Hamilton. (Maintien et confirmation du titre héréditaire de Duc de Chatellerault concédé à James Hamilton par Henri II, Roi de France, en 1548.) Paris, 1865.
QZ/P53 ED/N-2 QZ/L37

DEFENSE pour S. A. Mme. Marie Cardine de Bade Duchesse d'Hamilton . . . contre M. James Hamilton, Marquis d'Abercorn, etc. [1864.]
QZ/L37

PIÈCES touchant le Duché de Chastellerault. [N.p., n.d.]
ED/N-1 (Hall.295.f.22)

TEULET, Jean Baptiste Alex. Theodore
Mémoire justificatif du droit qui appartient à M. le duc d'Hamilton de porter le titre de Duc de Chatellerault. Paris, [1864].
ED/N-1 (Hall.197.a) QZ/P53 GL/U-1 QZ/P99

TITRES et pièces justificatives des legitimes prétentions de la maison de Hamilton. 1713.
QZ/L37

TURNBULL, William Barclay David Donald
Factum of the Earl of Arran touching the restitution of the Duchy of Chatelherault, 1685. Edinburgh, 1843.
QZ/P53 ED/N-2 QZ/L37 QZ/P99

Chattan, Clan *see* **Mackintosh**

Chene
ROSE, David Murray
Knightly Chenes. [N.p., n.d.]
AD/U-1

Cheyne
CAMERON, Barbara Cheyne
Some family memories. Aberdeen, 1978.
QZ/P22

CHEYNE, Archibald Ythan
The Cheyne family in Scotland. Eastbourne, 1931.
ED/N-1 (R.172.b) QZ/P53 QZ/P30 QZ/P26 QZ/P56 QZ/P28 QZ/P18 QZ/P40 QZ/P22 QZ/P11 QZ/P14 SA/U-1 AD/U-1 QZ/P38 GL/U-1 QZ/L37 QZ/P13 QZ/P41 QZ/P49 ED/U-1 QZ/P99 QZ/P16

CHEYNE-MACPHERSON, W. D.
Cheynes of Inverugie, Esslemont and Arnage, and their descendants. Kirkwall, 1943.
ED/N-1 (5.1031) QZ/P40 SA/U-1 AD/U-1 QZ/L37 QZ/P99

YOUNG, Robert
Notes on Burghead . . . containing notices of families connected with the place, [those of De Moravia, Cheyne, etc.] Elgin, 1867.
ED/N-1 (Hall.197.a)

Chirnside
RONALD, Heather B.
Wool past the winning post: a history of the Chirnside family. South Yarra, Victoria, 1978.
QZ/P11

Chisholm

ANDERSON, James Stuart Murray
Memoir of the Chisholm, late M.P. for Inverness-shire. London, 1842.
ED/N-1 (Stirton.c.20) GL/U-1 QZ/L37
QZ/P40 QZ/P99

CLAN Chisholm Journal. No.1- . Glasgow, 1960- .
ED/N-1 (7367 PER)

DUNLOP, Jean
The Clan Chisholm. Edinburgh, 1953.
ED/N-1 (Gen.8.c;Gen.7;NE.35.c.4) QZ/P26
QZ/P40 QZ/P99 QZ/L37 SA/U-1 QZ/P30
QZ/P49

— — Connel, 1968.
ED/N-1 (H1.78.236)

['A HISTORY of the Chisholm family'. 1840.]
ED/N-1 (MS.3570)

MACKENZIE, Alexander
History of the Chisholms, with genealogies of the
principal families of that name. Inverness, 1891.
ED/N-1 (Gen.8.c) DN/U-1 ED/N-2 QZ/P22
QZ/P11 QZ/P40 SA/U-1 AD/U-1 GL/U-1
QZ/L37 QZ/P30 ED/U-1 QZ/P99

MUNRO, Jean
Strathglass: home of the Clan Chisholm. [N.p.,
1970?]
ED/N-1 (IIP1.78.5228)

STIRTON, John
A day that is dead. [Memoir of Mrs Chisholm,
Glassburn House, Strathglass.] Forfar, 1913.
ED/N-1 (S.166.b)

— — 2nd ed. Forfar, [1929].
ED/N-1 (MS.3065. Author's copy with MS. notes)
QZ/P30 QZ/P22 QZ/P40 QZ/P99 QZ/L37

Christie

BROWN, Elisabeth Christie
The Kildrummy Christies. Aberdeen, 1948.
ED/N-1 (R.272.f) SA/U-1 QZ/Q17 QZ/P30
ED/N-2 QZ/P22 QZ/P99

GERARD, Robert
Letter containing note on Christie family including
a Provost of Montrose. [N.p., 1771.]
QZ/P28

ROGERS, Charles
Genealogical memoirs of the Scottish House of
Christie. London, 1878.
ED/N-1 (Y.59.c.21;RB.s.327;L.C.1007) ED/N-2
QZ/P14 AD/U-1 SA/U-1 QZ/P50 QZ/P16
QZ/P99

Christie of Cornton

FERGUSSON, Robert Menzies
Logie: a parish history. Vol.2: Lands and landowners.
Paisley, 1905.
ED/N-1 (R.243.a) QZ/P14

Christie of Ferrybank

RICHARDSON, Ralph
Family tree of Christie of Ferrybank, Fifeshire.
[Edinburgh, 1902.]
QZ/Q17 SA/U-1

Christie in Montrose

CHRISTIE, Richard Copley
Selected essays and papers of Richard Copley
Christie . . . [With genealogical tables.] London,
1902.
ED/N-1 (S.144.a)

Christie in Norway

CHRISTIE, Helga
Slekten Christie i Norge. [With a genealogical
table.] Oslo, 1964.
ED/N-1 (6.1084)

Christison of Glenesk

LOW, James G.
Letter concerning Christison family of Glenesk,
17--. [N.p., 1936.]
QZ/P28

Clark

GENEALOGICAL roll of the Clark family. [N.p., n.d.]
QZ/P-6

Clark in Aberdeenshire *see* **Thomson** in Aberdeenshire

Clark of Paisley

CLARK family tree: a genealogical roll. [N.d.] (*MS.*)
QZ/P-6

Clark of Uyeasound, Shetland

CLARK, John
Genealogy, records and intermarriages of the
Fordyce, Bruce and Clark families at Uyeasound,
Unst, Shetland. 2nd ed. Falkirk, 1899.
ED/N-1 (R.172.h) ED/N-2

— — Falkirk, 1902.
ED/N-1 (H2.80.1076)   QZ/P99

— Index to Fordyce, Bruce and Clark families at
Uyeasound, Unst, Shetland, 2nd ed. 1902. Prepared
with some additional information from the Unst
marriage registers 1797-1863 or concerning the
Sandison family by Alexander Sandison.
Cambridge, 1955.
ED/N-1 (NE.25.f.4)   QZ/P22

CLARKE, Seymour Spender Somerset
The genealogy of the Martins of Ross. [N.p., n.d.]
ED/N-2

Cleland

CLELAND, Harry
Blairlin district and the Clelands. Kirkintilloch,
1934.
ED/N-1 (NE.25.d.4)   QZ/P-3   ED/N-2

NISBETT, Hamilton More *and* AGNEW, Stair
Carnegie
Cairnhill. Edinburgh, 1949.
ED/N-1 (R.272.f)   QZ/P-3

Cleland of Cleland

CLELAND, John Burton
The ancient family of Cleland: an account of the
Clelands of that ilk, in the county of Lanark; of the
branches of Faskine, Monkland, etc., and of others
of the name. London, 1905.
ED/N-1 (S.120.f)   ED/N-2   QZ/P-3

GROSSART, William
Historic notices and domestic history of the parish
of Shotts. Glasgow, 1880.
ED/N-1 (A.118.d)

SIMPSON, R. R.
Pedigree of the Linlithgowshire Simpsons, including
pedigrees of the families of Cleland of Cleland,
Jervies, Russells and Raleighs. Edinburgh, 1895.
ED/U-1

Clerk

[The FAMILIES of Gill, Clerk … N.d.] (*MS.*)
QZ/P99

Clouston

CLOUSTON, J. Storer
The family of Clouston. Kirkwall, 1948.
QZ/L37   AD/U-1

Clunies-Ross

HUGHES, John Scott
Kings of the Cocos: the family of John Clunies-Ross
who settled in Keeling-Cocos. London, 1950.
ED/N-1 (S.43.a)

Coats

COATS, A.
From the cottage to the castle. [N.d.] (*MS.*)
ED/N-1 (R.272.e)   QZ/P26   QZ/P-6

Coats of Paisley

COATS family tree: a genealogical roll. [N.d.] (*MS.*)
QZ/P-6

COATS, George Holms
Rambling recollections. Paisley, 1920.
ED/N-1 (R.183.i)

Cochran

CALLENDER, James Hodge
History and genealogy of the Cochran family of
Kirkcudbright and New York. [New York], 1932.
ED/N-1 (NE.25.g.3;H4.81.289)

HAUGHTON, Ida Clara Cochran
Chronicles of the Cochrans, etc. Columbus, Ohio,
1915.
QZ/P-1 (Unconfirmed location)

Cochran of Kilmoss

[GENEALOGICAL roll of the Kilmoss Cochrans.
N.p., n.d.]
QZ/P-6

Cochran of Ladyland

[GENEALOGICAL roll of the Ladyland Cochrans.
N.p., n.d.]
QZ/P-6

Cochran of Linthills

[GENEALOGICAL roll of the Linthills Cochrans.
N.p., n.d.]
QZ/P-6

Cochran of Muirsheil

[GENEALOGICAL roll of the Muirsheil Cochrans.
N.p., n.d.]
QZ/P-6

Cochrane

COCHRANE family tree: a genealogical roll. [N.d.]
(*MS.*)
QZ/P-6

COCHRANE, Alexander
The fighting Cochranes: a Scottish clan. London,
1983.
ED/N-1 (H3.84.1036)   QZ/P99

Cochrane in Brasil
AZEVEDO, Aroldo de
Cochranes do Brasil: a vida e a obra de Thomas
Cochrane e Ignacio Cochrane. [With genealogical
tables.] Saõ Paolo, 1965.
ED/N-1 (1966.176)

Cochrane of Clippens
THOMPSON, Margaret D. W. *and* MACKIE,
Alexander
A fortune unfolded. (In *Scottish Genealogist*, vol.xxiv,
no.1, March 1977, pp.23-8.)
ED/N-1 (Gen.7)

Cochrane of Cochrane *see also* **Dundonald,**
Earldom of

Cochrane of Cochrane
GRANT, Sir Francis James
Inventory of the charter chest of the Earldom of
Dundonald, 1219-1672. Edinburgh, 1910. (Scottish
Record Society, 36.)
ED/N-1 (Ref.55)   DN/U-1   QZ/P99

PARKER, Katherine
Pedigree of the Cochranes of Cochrane, Lord
Cochrane of Dundonald; Earls of Dundonald,
Lords Cochrane of Paisley and Ochiltree. London,
[1908].
ED/N-1 (S.120.a)   SA/U-1   AD/U-1   QZ/L37
ED/U-1   QZ/P99

ROBERTSON, William
Ayrshire: its history and historic families.
Kilmarnock, 1908. 2v.
ED/N-1 (Hist.S.91.A)

THOMSON, Elizabeth M.
Dundonalds/Cochranes. [N.d.] (*MSS.*)
QZ/P-6

Cochrane, Earl of Dundonald *see* **Cochrane** of
Cochrane

Cochrane in U.S.A.
WATKINS, Walter Kendall
The Cochranes of Renfrewshire, Scotland: the
ancestry of Alex. Cochrane of Billerica and Malden,
Mass., U.S.A. Boston, Mass, 1904.
ED/N-2   QZ/L37   QZ/P99

Cochrane-Inglis *see also* **Inglis**

Cochrane-Inglis in Nova Scotia
EATON, Arthur Wentworth Hamilton
The Cochrane-Inglis family of Halifax. Halifax,
N.S., 1899.
ED/N-1 (S.120.d)

Cockburn
COCKBURN, Sir Robert *and* COCKBURN, Henry A.
The records of the Cockburn family. Edinburgh,
1913.
ED/N-1 (S.121.c)   QZ/P34   QZ/P11   AD/U-1
QZ/L37   SA/U-1   QZ/P-9   QZ/P99

COCKBURN-HOOD, Thomas H.
House of Cockburn of that ilk, and the cadets
thereof. Edinburgh, 1888.
ED/N-1 (R.272.a)   QZ/P34   ED/N-2   QZ/P11
SA/U-1   AD/U-1   DN/U-1   GL/U-1   QZ/L37
QZ/P-9   QZ/P99

[GENEALOGICAL material concerning the family of
Cockburn. N.d.]
ED/N-1 (MS.Dep.235, Box 3)

Cockburn of Langton
['ACCOUNT of the family of Cockburn of Langton'.
1811?]
ED/N-1 (Adv.MS.6.1.17,ff.154-7)

Coghill
COGHILL, James Henry
The family of Coghill, 1377 to 1879. Cambridge,
Mass., 1879.
ED/N-1 (A.22.e)

Colden
DUNCAN, Angus
Cadwallader Colden, 1688-1776, Scots Lieutenant
Governor of New York. [Edinburgh, 1966.]
ED/N-1 (5.3074)

Collie
COLLIE, George F.
The Collie family tree. Cults, 1957.
QZ/P22

Collins
COLLINS, Edward
An account of the information gained in the course
of research regarding the pedigree of the family of
Collins of Glasgow. [N.p.], 1928.
QZ/P-1 (Unconfirmed location)

KEIR, David
The House of Collins: the story of a Scottish family
of publishers from 1789. London, 1952.
ED/N-1 (NE.25.b.3) ED/N-2 QZ/P22
GL/U-1 QZ/P99

Colquhoun

BIRRELL, James
Annals of the Cowan family. [N.p.], 1896.
(*Typescript*)
ED/N-2

COLQUHOUN, F. Mary *and* COLQUHOUN, Neil
Campbell
The Clan Colquhoun Society, constitution, office-
bearers . . .; also traditions . . . of the clan. [Glasgow,
1897.]
ED/N-1 (1897.28(4)) QZ/P27 QZ/P49

FRASER, Sir William
Cartulary of Colquhoun of Colquhoun and Luss.
Edinburgh, 1873.
ED/N-2 QZ/P49 QZ/P99

— The Chiefs of Colquhoun and their country.
Edinburgh, 1869. 2v.
ED/N-1 (Gen.8.c) QZ/P56 ED/N-2 SA/U-1
AD/U-1 GL/U-1 QZ/L37 QZ/P-4 QZ/P49
ED/U-1 QZ/P99

[PAMPHLET relating to Colquhouns and their
connection with the Falconers, etc.] Bath, [185-?].
QZ/L37

Colquhoun of Camstradden

['DRAFT genealogical account of the family of
Colquhoun of Camstradden'. 1830?]
ED/N-1 (Adv.MS.19.2.17,ff.141-3)

Colquhoun of Garscadden and Killermont

['DRAFT genealogical account of the Colquhouns of
Garscadden & Killermont'. 1829?]
ED/N-1 (Adv.MS.19.2.17,ff.151-6)

Colquhoun of Luss

DONALD, T. F.
The Colquhouns of Luss. (Reprinted from *Glasgow
Herald*, 13, 20 November 1909.)
ED/N-1 (1909.35)

['DRAFT genealogical account of and transcripts of
charters and other papers concerning the
Colquhouns of Luss'. 1831?]
ED/N-1 (Adv.MS.19.2.17,ff.84-136)

GENEALOGICAL tree of family of Colquhoun of
Luss. [N.p.], 1873. (Compiled from *Chiefs of
Colquhoun* by Wm Fraser, and from other sources.)
QZ/P40

IRVING, Joseph
The book of Dumbartonshire. Edinburgh, 1879.
ED/N-1 (R.286.c)

MACLEOD, Donald
A nonogenarian's reminiscences of Garelochside
and Helensburgh and the people who dwelt thereon
and therein. Helensburgh, 1883.
ED/N-1 (A.122.e)

Colt

COLT, George Frederick Russell
History and genealogy of the Colts of that ilk and
Gartsherrie and of the English and American
branches of the family. Edinburgh, 1887.
ED/N-1 (R.272.e) QZ/P-3 ED/N-2 GL/U-1
QZ/P99 QZ/L37 SA/U-1 ST/U-1 QZ/Q76
QZ/P-9

ROGERS, Charles
Genealogical memoirs of the families of Colt and
Coutts. London, 1879. (Cottonian Soc.)
ED/N-1 (S.120.e) QZ/P28 QZ/P22 QZ/P40
QZ/P26 QZ/P14 SA/U-1 AD/U-1 DN/U-1
QZ/P20 QZ/P-6 QZ/P16 QZ/P99

Colville, Lord, Viscount Colville of Culross

COLVILLE, Georgiana M.
The ancestry of Lord Colville of Culross. London,
1887.
ED/N-2 QZ/L37 QZ/P16

PAYNTER, R.
Colville, Culross & Ochiltree. London, 1872.
ED/N-1 (APS.1.76.23)

PEMBER, Francis W.
The Lord Calvin. [N.p.], 1929.
ED/N-1 (1929.30)

Colyer-Fergusson *see* Fergusson

Comyn, Earl of Buchan

[A HISTORY of the Comyns, Earls of Buchan. 18--.]
ED/N-1 (MS.2099)

STUART, Gordon
The Comyns. (In *Scotland's Magazine*, vol.66, no.11,
November 1970, pp.34-9.)
ED/N-1 (Y.31)

Coningsburgh

REID, Robert Corsane
Notes on the family of Coningsburgh. (In
*Transactions of the Dumfriesshire and Galloway Natural
History & Antiquarian Society*, 3rd series, vol.xx,
1935-6, pp.133-9.)
ED/N-1 (J.187)   QZ/L37

Connal

MITCHELL, John Oswald
Two old Glasgow firms: William Connal & Co.,
and the Crums of Thornliebank. Glasgow, 1894.
ED/N-1 (1894.23(12))

OAKLEY, Charles Allen
Connal & Co., Ltd. [of Glasgow], 1722-1946.
[Glasgow, 1947.]
QZ/P44   QZ/P-1 (Unconfirmed locations)

Constable

ROGERS, Charles
Four Perthshire families: Roger, Playfair, Constable
and Haldane of Barmony. Edinburgh, 1887.
ED/N-1 (Gramp.Club.35)   QZ/P26   ED/N-2
QZ/P14   GL/U-1   SA/U-1   QZ/L37   QZ/P16

Constable-Maxwell, Lord Herries *see* Herries,

Lord Herries of Terregles

Cook

COOK, George Milne
A family history. Aberdeen, 1951. (*Typescript*)
QZ/P22

Copland

KING, Norman
The Copland family in Galloway and
Dumfriesshire. 1954. (*Typescript*)
ED/N-2

Corbet

The FAMILY of Corbet. London, [1915-19]. 2v.
ED/N-1 (S.121.a)

Corbett

CORBETT, Cunningham
The families of Boyd of Kilmarnock, Porterfield of
Porterfield and Corbett of Tolcross. [N.p., n.d.]
ED/N-2

Cormack of Eday

CORMACK, Maribelle
[Typescript family history of the Cormacks of Eday
(Orkney). With family crests and genealogical
tables.]
QZ/P99

Cornwall of Bonhard

STODART, Robert Riddle
Genealogy of the family of Cornwall of Bonhard,
co. Linlithgow. Edinburgh, 1877.
ED/N-1 (6.887)   AD/U-1   QZ/L37

Corrie

CORRIE, Jessie Elizabeth
Records of the Corrie family, 802-1899. London,
1899. 2v.
ED/N-1 (S.120.a)   ED/N-2   SA/U-1   QZ/P99

Corsane of Meikle Knox

EDGAR, Robert
An introduction to the history of Dumfries. [With
genealogical tables.] Dumfries, 1915.
ED/N-1 (R.241.b;L.C.1922)

[PAPER on the origins of the Corsanes of
Meikleknox. 18--.]
ED/N-1 (Adv.MS.81.2.9)

Coulthart

CHEYNE, Alexander *and* KNOWLES, George Parker
Coulthart of Coulthart, Collyn, and Ashton under
Lyne. [N.p., n.d.]
ED/N-1 (R.172.d.1(3))

The COULTHARTS of Coulthart. (Reprinted from
the *Herald and Genealogist*, vol.iii, part xiii, March
1865, pp.17-24.)
ED/N-1 (R.172.d.1(4))

KNOWLES, George Parker
A genealogical and heraldic account of the
Coultharts of Coulthart and Collyn, chiefs of the
name. London, 1855.
ED/N-1 (R.172.d(1))   ED/N-2   QZ/L37
QZ/P99

Couper

OSLER, James Couper
Osler tree: [chart pedigree], with some
supplementary notes on . . . Coupers. [Dundee],
1924.
QZ/L37   ED/N-2

THOMSON, David Couper
Some supplemental notes on Oslers . . . [Dundee],
1924.
ED/N-1 (HP1.77.4104)

— Thomson, Couper, Yule, Sinclair genealogical
chart. Dundee, [1936].
QZ/L37   QZ/P20   QZ/P99

Couper of Glasgow
COUPER of Glasgow 1850, through the Craigends
and the Hows: a genealogical roll. [N.d.] (*MS.*)
QZ/P-6

Couper of Gogar
['GENEALOGICAL papers relating to the claim to the
baronetcy of Gogar'. 1773-75.]
ED/N-1 (MS.5390.,ff.1-95)

STODART, R. R.
Cooper of Gogar. [N.d.].
QZ/P99

Coutts
FORBES, Sir William
Memoirs of a banking house. London, 1860.
ED/N-1 (L.C.2652)   QZ/P99

— — Edinburgh, 1860.
ED/N-1 (N.8.a;L.C.2653-4)   ED/N-2   QZ/P22
GL/U-1

RICHARDSON, Ralph
Coutts and Co., bankers, Edinburgh and London:
memoirs of a family distinguished for its public
services in England and Scotland. London, 1900.
ED/N-1 (S.147.d)   QZ/P22   QZ/P28   QZ/P99

— — 2nd ed. London, 1901.
DN/U-1   QZ/P28

ROBINSON, Ralph Mosley
Coutts': the history of a banking house. London,
1929.
ED/N-1 (R.113.c)   QZ/P28   ED/N-2

ROGERS, Charles
Genealogical memoirs of the families of Colt and
Coutts. London, 1879. (Cottonian Soc.)
ED/N-1 (S.120.e)   GL/U-1   QZ/P22   QZ/P40
QZ/P14   SA/U-1   AD/U-1   QZ/P28   QZ/P-6
DN/U-1   QZ/L37   QZ/P16   QZ/P99

STOKES, M. Veronica
Notes on the origin and history of Coutts &
Company. [London, 1964.]
ED/N-1 (5.3562)

Coutts in Montrose
LOW, James G.
John Coutts, or notes on an eminent Montrose
family. Montrose, 1892.
ED/N-1 (Hist.252.c)   QZ/P28   QZ/P22
QZ/P99

Cowan
BIRRELL, James
Annals of the Cowan family. 1896. (*Typescript*)
ED/N-2   QZ/P99

COWAN, Robert L.
A history of the Cowan family in Scotland. [N.p.],
1967.
QZ/L37   QZ/P99

FORSYTH, Mary
The Cowans at Moray House. Edinburgh, 1932.
ED/N-1 (R.172.f)   SA/U-1   QZ/P-9

JOURNALS of the family of Cowan, 1830-44.
Edinburgh, 1845.
ED/N-2   QZ/P99

WATSON, Charles Brodie Boog
Alexander Cowan of Moray House and Valleyfield,
his kinsfolk and connections. Perth, 1915-17. 2v.
ED/N-1 (S.299.b)   QZ/P22   SA/U-1   QZ/L37
QZ/P-9   QZ/P99

Cowan of Valleyfield
MENZIES, Helen
Family memorials. [With MS. notes on the Cowan
family. 1827.]
ED/N-1 (MSS.Acc.5265)

Cowen
TRIMBLE, William Tennant
The Trimbles and Cowens of Dalston,
Cumberland. Carlisle, 1935-7. 2v.
ED/N-1 (R.172.c)

Cowper, Earl of
['GENEALOGICAL account of the Earls of Cowper'.
1802?]
ED/N-1 (Adv.MS.33.5.9,ff.545-50)

Cowper, Lord Dingwall *see* **Dingwall,** Lord

Cox
COX, William Henry
The family of Cox in Angus and Perthshire. [Perth,
1961.]
ED/N-1 (NE.26.g.1)   DN/U-1   ED/N-2

Craig

CRAIG, Margaret
Genealogical chart of Craig-Brechin, Canada,
Chicago. Aberdeen, [1925?].
ED/N-2 QZ/P22

LANG, Patrick Sellar
The Langs of Selkirk, with some notes on the
Sibbalds of Whitelaw.... Melbourne, 1910.
ED/N-2 QZ/P99 QZ/P11

Craig of Newbattle and New Monkland

A CENTURY of paper-making, 1820-1920: [a history
of R. and R. Craig Ltd]. Edinburgh, 1920.
ED/N-1 (NE.12.a.2) QZ/P99

Craigmyle, Baron *see* Shaw, Baron Craigmyle

Cran

CRAN, John Duncan
Family tree of the family and lineal descendants of
Robert Cran of Belhinny and Lesmoir. [N.p.], 1912.
QZ/P22

Cran in Strathbogie

NOTABLE men and women of Strathbogie: the Cran
family. (Reprinted from the *Huntly Express*,
12 June 1980.)
QZ/P22

Cranna

CRANNA, William H.
The surnames of Cranna and Vass. Aberdeen, 1926.
(*Typescript*)
QZ/P22

Cranston

GOVETT, Bryan M.
Arms across the Atlantic: Cranston from Scotland
to Rhode Island. (In *Coat of Arms*, new series, vol. v,
no. 122, summer 1982, pp. 37-9.)
ED/N-1 (NJ.689)

Cranstoun

CRANSTOUN papers MSS.: a collection of papers
relative to the Cranstoun family, household
accounts, receipts, letters, etc. [1800?] (*MSS.*)
QZ/P99

Craufurd of Auchenames and Crosbie

FERGUSSON, Sir James
Lowland lairds. London, 1949.
ED/N-1 (R.232.d) ED/N-2 QZ/P13 QZ/P49
QZ/P99

Craufurd of Kilbirnie

WILLIAMSON, George
Old Cartsburn: a history of the estate from ... 1699
... with notices of the families of Kilbirnie,
Jordanhill and Cartsburn. Paisley, 1894.
ED/N-1 (R.290.c)

Craven, Cravie

CRAVEN, J. B.
Genealogical collections relating to the family of
Cravie or Craven in Scotland, with notes and
documents illustrative of their family connections.
Kirkwall, 1910.
ED/N-1 (S.120.f) QZ/P99

Crawford

CRAWFORD, Fred E.
The early ancestors of the Crawfords in America.
Cambridge, Mass., 1940.
ED/N-1 (NE.815.a.4)

CRAWFORD, J. H.
Crawford: an historic Scottish family. [N.p.], 1963.
QZ/P-7

[FAMILY papers, documents, letters, etc.]
QZ/P52 (Unconfirmed location)

MACDOWALL, John Kevan
Carrick Gallovidian: a historical survey ... with
genealogical charts and notes. Ayr, 1947.
ED/N-1 (R.241.d)

SEAVER, Jesse M.
Crawford genealogical data. Texas, 1966.
ED/N-2

Crawford, Earldom of

ADAMS, Alexander Maxwell
The Crawfurd peerage: with other original
genealogical, historical and biographical particulars
relating to the illustrious houses of Crawfurd and
Kilbirnie; including, also, a succinct account of the
persecutions and abuses to which John Lindsay
Crawfurd has been subjected. Edinburgh, 1829.
ED/N-1 (A.114.b.2) QZ/P26 ED/N-2 QZ/P40
QZ/P22 GL/U-1 QZ/P99

—A sketch of the case of John Lindsay Crawford.
Edinburgh, 1834.
ED/S10 (Unconfirmed location)

CRAUFURD, John Lindsay
Sketch of the life of John Lindsay Craufurd, Esq., containing a full . . . account of his claim to the title and estates of George, Earl of Craufurd & Lindsay . . . written by himself. 2nd ed. Dalry, 1812.
GL/U-1

CRAWFURD, John Lindsay
An epitome of the history of the claim of John Lindsay Crawfurd, esq. to the titles and estates of the Earls of that name and of the evidence upon which his claims are founded. [N.p.], 1835.
ED/N-1 (Yule.163(1))

—In the House of Lords before the Lords Committee of Privileges case of John Lindsay Crawfurd, Esq., claimant of the titles, honours, and dignities of Earl of Crawfurd and Lindsay. London, 1845.
ED/N-1 (Yule.163(3))

—Memoir of the claim of Mr. John Lindsay Crawfurd to the titles and estates of Crawfurd and Kilbirnie. Paisley, 1819.
ED/N-1 (5.125(9))

—Pedigree of John Lindsay Crawfurd Esq. claiming to be Earl of Crawfurd and Lindsay. [N.p., 1835.]
ED/N-1 (Yule.163(2))

DOBIE, James
Examination of the claim of John Lindsay Crawfurd to the titles and estates of Crawfurd and Lindsay. Edinburgh, 1831.
ED/N-1 (A.114.b) QZ/P-6 ED/N-2 GL/U-1 QZ/L37 QZ/P-7 QZ/P99

['GENEALOGY of the Lindsays, Earls of Crawford'. 1713.]
ED/N-1 (Adv.MS.23.3.27,ff.39-50)

INFORMATION for the Earl of Crawfurd and the Earl Marischall against the Earl of Sutherland. Edinburgh, 1706.
ED/N-1 (A.114.e.28(8-11))

INFORMATION for the Earl of Sutherland against the Earl of Crawfurd. Edinburgh, 1706.
ED/N-1 (Λ.114.e.28(1-7);A.114.e.27;Yule.17; Ry.I.2.127(13))

LINDSAY, James, *24th Earl of Crawford and 7th Earl of Balcarres*
Analysis of the objections started by the Crown and of the replies furnished by John Riddell, in the matter of the evidence adduced by the Earl of Balcarres claiming the Earldom of Crawford. [N.p., n.d.]
ED/N-1 (Yule.35(2))

—Case of James, Earl of Balcarres, etc. claiming titles, honours and dignities of the Earldom of Crawford and older Barony of Lindsay. Edinburgh, [1845].
ED/N-1 (Yule.181;A.12.a) QZ/L37 QZ/P99

—Crawford and Lindsay peerage: speeches of counsel and judgment. [London, 1845-8.]
ED/N-1 (Yule.181)

—In the House of Lords . . . summary or abstract of the chief deeds and evidence founded upon by James Earl of Balcarres in his claim to the Earldom of Crawford and older barony of Lindsay; with the reasons and pleas of law. [London, 1845.]
ED/N-1 (Yule.180)

—Petitions, evidence, &c., presented to the House of Lords, 1850-53, by James, Earl of Crawford and Balcarres, supporting his claim to the Dukedom of Montrose, and by James, Duke of Montrose, opposing the claim, including material relating to the case of the Earl of Eglinton versus the Earl of Glencairn in 1648. London, [1850-3.] 2v.
ED/N-1 (Yule.182-3)

—Summary or abstract of the chief deeds and evidence founded upon James, Earl of Balcarres, etc. etc. in his claim to the Earldom of Crawford and older Barony of Lindsay. . . . [N.d.]
QZ/P-1 (Unconfirmed location)

MINUTES of evidence taken before the Committee for Privileges . . . the petition of James, Earl of Balcarres . . . and also the petition of Robert Lindsay Crawfurd, Esq. 1845.
ED/N-1 (Yule.179-180) ED/N-2 QZ/L37

RIDDELL, John
Abstract of the claim of James, Earl of Balcarres, to the honours of Earl of Crawford and Lord Lindsay; abridged from the case drawn up by John Riddell. [N.p., n.d.]
ED/N-1 (Yule.35(1))

—Analysis of objections . . . and of the replies furnished by John Riddell in the matter of the evidence adduced by the Earl of Balcarres, claiming the Earldom of Crawford and Barony of Lindsay. [N.p.], 1847.
ED/N-1 (Yule.35(2)) QZ/P22 QZ/L37

SHORT biographical sketches of the Earls of Crawford from the earliest times to the present. Wigan, 1885.
QZ/P22

SPEECHES of counsel, and judgement. [1845-8.]
QZ/L37

Crawford in Donegal, Ireland
CRAWFORD, Robert
The Crawfords of Donegal. [N.p.], 1886.
ED/N-2

Crawfurd of Cartsburn
WILLIAMSON, George
Old Cartsburn: a history of the estate from the year 1669 . . . with notices of the families of Kilbirnie, Jordanhill and Cartsburn. Paisley, 1894.
ED/N-1 (R.290.c;L.C.1263) ED/N-2 QZ/P99

Crawfurd of Jordanhill *see* **Crawfurd** of Cartsburn

Crawfurd of Kilburnie *see* **Crawfurd** of Cartsburn

Crichton
CRICHTON, Douglas
Sanquhar and the Crichtons. Dumfries, 1907.
ED/N-1 (R.241.h) ED/N-2 AD/U-1 QZ/L37
QZ/P99

SINTON, Thomas
Family and genealogical sketches. Inverness, 1911.
ED/N-1 (R.172.b) AD/U-1 DN/U-1 QZ/P-1
QZ/P22 QZ/P30 QZ/P40 QZ/P99

STEELE, John Haughton
Genealogy of the Earls of Erne. Edinburgh, 1910.
ED/N-1 (S.120.d) SA/U-1 QZ/P99

WILSON, William
Folklore and genealogies of uppermost Nithsdale. Dumfries, 1904.
ED/N-1 (R.241.h)

Crichton, Lord Frendraught *see* **Frendraught,** Lord

Crichton-Stuart, Marquess of Bute
DAVIES, John
Cardiff and the Marquesses of Bute. Cardiff, 1981.
ED/N-1 (H3.81.1133) QZ/Q88

[GENEALOGICAL account of the Stuarts, Marquesses of Bute. 1802?]
ED/N-1 (Adv.MS.33.5.9,pp.191-9)

Croft
RICHMOND, Keith *and* CRAGO, Maureen
A genealogical study: Richmond, Campbell, Cairns and Croft. [Armidale, N.S.W.], 1975.
ED/N-1 (6.2868)

Crogo
PROOFS of the descent of the family of Crogo in the Stewartry of Kirkcudbright. [N.d.]
QZ/P10 (Unconfirmed location)

Cromartie
CROMARTIE, William
The William Cromartie family: a pamphlet arranged from data purchased from Miss E. J. Black concerning an Orkney family who moved to the U.S. Elizabethtown, N.C., [n.d.].
QZ/P38 (Unconfirmed location)

Cromartie, Earl of *see* **Mackenzie,** Earl of Cromartie

Crombie
ALLAN, John R.
Crombies of Grandholm and Cothal, 1805-1960: records of an Aberdeenshire enterprise. Aberdeen, 1960.
ED/N-1 (NE.25.a.11) QZ/P30

Crookshank of Aberdeen
GEDDES, David
'David Geddes whom you pronounced dunce': typescript family history of the families of John Johnston (of Stromness and Quebec), Dr. Andrew Crookshank (of Aberdeen) and David Geddes (of Orkney). [N.p., 1970.]
QZ/P38 (Unconfirmed location)

Crosbie
CROSBIE HISTORICAL COMMITTEE
Our ain folk: the story of William and Margaret Crosbie, pioneers of Waikawa Valley. Waikawa Valley, N.Z., 1977.
ED/N-1 (H4.82.319)

Crosbie of Oulcottis and Holm
EDGAR, Robert
An introduction to the history of Dumfries. [With genealogical tables.] Dumfries, 1915.
ED/N-1 (R.241.b)

Crozier

CROZIER, F. H.
Memorials of the family of Crozier. Lymington, 1881.
ED/S10   ED/N-2   QZ/P-1 (Unconfirmed location)

Cruickshank

CRUICKSHANK, E. G. G.
Pedigree of the Cruickshanks of Strathcathro. [N.p.], 1847.
ED/N-2

CRUICKSHANK, E. G. G. *and* GORDON, W.
Cruickshank in Strathspey and of Stracathro. Elgin, 1847.
QZ/P22   ED/N-2

Cruikshank

JOHNSTON, William
A genealogical account of the descendants of James Young, merchant burgess of Aberdeen, and Rachel Cruikshank, his wife, 1697-1893. Aberdeen, 1894.
ED/N-1 (A.57.a)

Crum of Thornliebank

CRUM, Frederic Maurice
Alexander Crum of Thornliebank, 1828-1893. [N.p.], 1954.
ED/N-1 (NC.266.d.2)

MITCHELL, John Oswald
Two old Glasgow firms: William Connal & Co. and the Crums of Thornliebank. Glasgow, 1894.
ED/N-1 (1894.23(12))

Cumine of Rattray

DICKIE, Julie
The Cumines of Rattray. (In *Transactions of the Buchan Field Club*, vol.xviii, part 1, March 1958, pp.31-8.)
ED/N-1 (M.145)

Cuming, Cumming of Culter

TOMKINS, Henry Barr
A table showing the families descended from Sir Alexander Cumming of Coulter created a Scots baronet in 1695. [N.p., 1877.]
ED/N-1 (6.529)   QZ/L37

Cuming, Cumming of Lochtervandich

CUMINE, James
History of the Cumins of Lochtervandech. [N.p., 1900?]
QZ/P22   QZ/P30   AD/U-1

Cumming

DUNLOP, Annie Isabella Cameron *and* POLACZEK, Helena
Diploma of nobility of Thomas Cumming, 1727. (Reprinted from the *Juridical Review*, March 1938.)
ED/N-1 (6.908)   QZ/P99

Cumyn

BRUCE, Mary Elizabeth Cumming
Family records of the Bruces and the Cumyns. Edinburgh, 1870.
ED/N-1 (Gen.8.B;A.113.a)   ED/N-2   QZ/P22
QZ/P11   QZ/P40   QZ/P14   GL/U-1   SA/U-1
AD/U-1   QZ/L37   QZ/P50   QZ/P41   QZ/P99

Cuninghame

PATERSON, James
Scottish surnames: a contribution to genealogy. Edinburgh, 1866.
ED/N-1 (K.115.a)   QZ/P28   QZ/P22   DN/U-1

Cuninghame of Auchenharvie

SELECTIONS from the papers: in memoriam W. D. Kerr. (In *Ayrshire Archaeological & Natural History Collections*, 2nd series, vol.6, 1958-60, pp.175-92.)
ED/N-1 (R.241.b)

Cunningham

[GENEALOGY of various branches of Cunninghams. 16--.]
ED/N-1 (MS.3033)

PRINDLE, Paul Wesley
Descendants of John and Mary Jane (Cunningham) Gillespie. [N.p.], 1973.
ED/N-1 (H3.77.3012)

Cunningham of Glencairn

[GENEALOGICAL account of the Cunninghame family of Glencairn.]
ED/N-1 (MS.5266)

Cunningham, Earl of Glencairn *see* Glencairn, Earldom of

Cunninghame of Craigend

MCKENZIE, R. D.
Notes on Cunninghames of Craigend. [*c.* 1900.] (*MS.*)
QZ/P-6

Cunninghame of Kilmaurs
LANDSBOROUGH, Drew McClamroch
Our Galloway ancestors revisited: a genealogical
and historical investigation . . . of the Laird of
Lamrochton, c.1400, cadet of the Cunninghames of
Kilmaurs, Ayrshire, the Lords Kilmaurs and Earls of
Glencairn. Thornton Heath, 1978.
ED/N-1 (HP3.80.1823) QZ/P-1 QZ/P10

Cunynghame
CUNYNGHAME, Robert Myrton
Robert Myrton Cunynghame, second son of Sir
Wm. Augustus Cunynghame of Livingston, Bt . . .
appellant. David Cunynghame . . . respondent.
[N.p., 1777.]
QZ/P99

Cunynghame of Conheath, Woodhall and Dumfries
EDGAR, Robert
An introduction to the history of Dumfries. [With
genealogical tables.] Dumfries, 1915.
ED/N-1 (R.241.b)

Currie
ALEXANDER, Helen
Passages in the lives of Helen Anderson and James
Currie of Pentland, and other papers. [With a
genealogical table, with manuscript additions.]
[Belfast], 1869.
ED/N-1 (NC.272.f.8)

CURRIE, W. M.
With sword and harp: Clan Mhurrich (Currie), the
warrior poets. Milngavie, 1977.
ED/N-1 (HP1.78.3855) QZ/P22 QZ/P27
QZ/P56 ED/N-2 QZ/P99

THORNTON, Robert Donald
James Currie: the entire stranger and Robert Burns.
[With genealogical tables.] Edinburgh, 1963.
ED/N-1 (Lit.S.18) QZ/P14

Currie of Cowal
CURRIE, William
The Curries of Cowal: a history of the district.
Dunoon, 1975.
QZ/P27

Currie of Howford
LANG, Patrick Sellar
The Langs of Selkirk, with some notes on the
Sibbalds of Whitelaw. . . . Melbourne, 1910.
ED/N-2 QZ/P99 QZ/P11

Cursiter
CLOUSTON, John Storer
A note on an odal family. (In *Orkney & Shetland
Miscellany of the Viking Club*, vol.1, 1907/8,
pp.135-6.)
ED/N-1 (R.250.f)

Curwen
CURWEN, John F.
History of the ancient house of Curwen of
Workington in Cumberland and its various
branches. Kendal, 1928.
ED/N-1 (S.122.f)

Cuthbert
BULLOCH, Joseph Gaston Baillie
The Cuthberts of Castlehill and their descendants in
South Carolina and Georgia. Washington, 1908.
QZ/P40 QZ/L37

['CORRESPONDENCE and papers concerning the
genealogy of the Cuthbert family'. 1871-91.]
ED/N-1 (MS.17941-2)

Cuthbert of Castlehill
FRASER-MACINTOSH, Charles
The Cuthberts of Castlehill styled "MacSheorais".
Inverness, 1899.
QZ/P40

Dalgleish of Tinnygask
RUVIGNY and RAINEVAL, M. A. H. D. H. de la C.
Massue de Ruvigny, *9th Marquis de*
Dalgleish of Tinnygask. London, 1902.
QZ/L37 QZ/P16

Dalhousie, Earl of *see* **Ramsay,** Earl of Dalhousie

Dallas
DALLAS, James
A history of the family of Dallas. Edinburgh, 1921.
ED/N-1 (S.121.c) QZ/Q17 QZ/P40 SA/U-1
AD/U-1 QZ/P22 QZ/L37 GL/U-1 QZ/P30
ST/U-1 QZ/P50 QZ/P99

Dallas in Oslo, Norway
SCHWABE-HANSEN, G.
Dallas-Glad-Lie-Bull (Saertrykk av *Norsk
Slektshistorisk Tidsskrift*, vol.14, 1954, pp. 198-214.)
[Oslo, 1954.]
ED/N-1 (6.652)

Dalmahoy

FALCONER, Thomas
The family of Dalmahoy of Dalmahoy, Ratho,
county of Edinburgh. [London, 1870?]
ED/N-1 (A.113.b) ED/N-2 SA/U-1 QZ/L37
ED/S10 QZ/P99

Dalrymple

DALRYMPLE, Christian
Private annals of my own time, 1765-1812.
Edinburgh, 1914.
QZ/P99

PARSONS, Coleman O.
The Dalrymple legend in the Bride of
Lammermoor. (Reprinted from *Review of English
Studies*, vol.xix, no.73, January 1943, pp. 51-8.)
London, 1943.
ED/N-1 (1973.241)

SETON, George
Memoir of Alexander Seton . . . with an appendix
cont. . . . genealogical tables of the legal families of
Erskine, Hope, Dalrymple and Dundas. Edinburgh,
1882.
ED/N-1 (R.181.f) QZ/P-1 QZ/P16 QZ/P99
— — Edinburgh, 1883.
ED/N-1 (L.C.1915)

Dalrymple of Langlands

SHAW, John
The Dalrymples of Langlands. Bath, [1868].
ED/N-1 (R.172.g) ED/N-2 QZ/P-7 QZ/P99

Dalrymple, Earl of Stair

DALRYMPLE, Hew Hamilton
Genealogical account of the Dalrymples of Stair,
Earls of Stair. [N.p.], 1909.
ED/N-1 (NE.25.h.14) SA/U-1 QZ/L37

— Pedigree of the Macgills of Oxfuird, showing
descent of Stair family. [1893.]
ED/N-1 (MS.3421,f.1)

DALRYMPLE, John
The case of John, claiming the title, honour, and
dignity of, Earl of Stair, Viscount Dalrymple, Lord
Newliston, Glenluce, and Stranraer. London, 1748.
ED/N-1 (Yule.171(9))

GRAHAM, John Murray
Annals and correspondence of the Viscount and the
1st and 2nd Earls of Stair. Edinburgh, 1875. 2v.
ED/N-1 (A.113.e;L.C.1911,1912) QZ/P-7
ED/N-2 QZ/P11 GL/U-1 ST/U-1 QZ/P99

MASSON, Rosalind
The secret marriage of Lady Primrose and John,
second Earl of Stair. (In *Chambers's Journal*, 7th
series, vol.ii, 1911/12, pp. 731-5.)
ED/N-1 (P.31)

STAIR, , *Earl of*
[Portraits and plates dealing with the Stair family.]
ED/U-1

Dalrymple of Waterside

McCALL, Hardy Bertram
Some old families: a contribution to the
genealogical history of Scotland. Birmingham,
1890.
ED/N-1 (A.36.a) QZ/P99

Dalyell of Binns

DALYELL, Sir James Bruce Wilkie *and* BEVERIDGE,
James
The Binns papers, 1320-1864. Edinburgh, 1938.
(Scottish Record Society, 70.)
ED/N-1 (Ref.55) DN/U-1 GL/U-1 ED/U-1
QZ/P99

Dalzell

BURGH OF MOTHERWELL AND WISHAW PUBLIC
LIBRARIES
The Barony of Dalzell. Motherwell, 1970.
ED/N-1 (5.4959)

DALZELL, J. B.
Concerning an old Scottish surname. (Reprinted
from the *Christian Leader*, 6 September 1883.)
[N.p., 1883.]
ED/N-1 (4.68(1))

Dalziel

WILSON, William
Folklore and genealogies of uppermost Nithsdale.
Dumfries, 1904.
ED/N-1 (R.241.h)

Darleith of Darleith

['DRAFT genealogical account of the Darleiths of
Darleith'. 1828.]
ED/N-1 (Adv.MS.19.2.17,ff.157-61)

Darnley, Earl of *see* Lennox, Duke of

Davidson

DAVIDSON, James D. G.
The Davidsons. (In *Clan Chattan*, vol.viii, no.1,
1982, pp.35-40.)
ED/N-1 (Y.130)

DAVIDSON, William Harold
An account of the life of William Davidson, otherwise John Godsman of Banffshire and Aberdeenshire in Scotland and Miramichi in British North America. [With a genealogical table.] Saint John, New Brunswick, 1947.
ED/N-1 (1915.19)

LESLIE,
A family history: [a short account of the families of Brodie, Farquhar and Davidson]. [Brighton, 1891?]
ED/N-1 (6.2484)

WOOD, James Alexander Fraser
The Davidsons. (In *Scotland's Magazine*, vol.66, no.12, December 1970, pp.29-31.)
ED/N-1 (Y.31)

Davidson of Muirhouse
PHILIP, Adam
The ancestry of Randall Thomas Davidson, Archbishop of Canterbury. London, 1903.
ED/N-1 (S.120.d;L.C.1135) QZ/P14 QZ/P26 QZ/P99 QZ/P22 DN/U-1

Dawson
ADAMS, Percy Walter Lewis
A brief history of a branch of the Dawson family of Dysart and Kirkcaldy, Fife (1690-1840) and their descendants of Madras, Rangoon and Pyapon, Burma and Long Stanton, Cambridgeshire. Stoke-on-Trent, 1952.
ED/N-1 (NE.63.b.5) QZ/P18 ED/N-2 QZ/P99

De Hawick
VERNON, Joshua John
St. Mary's Church, Hawick, and its associations prior to the Reformation, and concerning the surname De Hawick. (Reprinted from the *Hawick Express*, 1898.) [Hawick, 1898.]
QZ/P11

De Maria
STIRTON, John
Notes on the family of De Maria. Aberdeen, 1920.
ED/N-1 (MS.3066: author's copy with *MS.* notes.)
QZ/P22

De Mundeville *see also* **Mundeville**

De Mundeville
REID, Robert Corsane
The Mundevilles in Scotland. (In *Transactions of the Dumfriesshire and Galloway Natural History & Antiquarian Society*, 3rd series, vol.xxxiv, 1955/6, pp.78-83.)
ED/N-1 (J.187)

De Quincy
BAIN, Joseph
The Scottish De Quencys of Fawside and Leuchars. (In *Proceedings of the Society of Antiquaries of Scotland*, vol.xxxiv, 1900, pp.124-8.)
ED/N-1 (Ref.52) QZ/P34

IRELAND, William W.
Notes on the Scottish de Quencys of Fawsyde and Leuchars. (Reprinted from *Proceedings of the Society of Antiquaries of Scotland*, 1898-1900.) Edinburgh, 1898.
QZ/P34 QZ/L37

—Supplementary notes on the Scottish De Quencys. (In *Proceedings of the Society of Antiquaries of Scotland*, vol.xxxiv, 1900, pp.241-5.)
ED/N-1 (Ref.52) QZ/P34

De Soulis
M'MICHAEL, Thomas
The feudal family of de Soulis. (In *Transactions of the Dumfriesshire and Galloway Natural History & Antiquarian Society*, 3rd series, vol.xxvi, 1947/8, pp.163-93.)
ED/N-1 (J.187)

— — (Reprinted from *Transactions of the Dumfriesshire and Galloway Natural History & Antiquarian Society*, 3rd series, vol.xxvi, 1947/8.)
QZ/P-7

REID, Robert Corsane
Some early de Soulis charters. (In *Transactions of the Dumfriesshire and Galloway Natural History & Antiquarian Society*, 3rd series, vol.xxvi, 1947/8, pp.150-62.)
ED/N-1 (J.187)

— — (Reprinted from *Transactions of the Dumfriesshire and Galloway Natural History & Antiquarian Society*, 3rd series, vol.xxvi, 1947/8.)
QZ/P-7

De Valoniis

MAULE, Harry
Registrum de Panmure. Edinburgh, 1874. 2v.
ED/N-1 (Gen.8.P)   QZ/P28   QZ/P26   SA/U-1
AD/U-1   GL/U-1   QZ/L37   QZ/P99

De Vaux

DOUGLAS, William
The owners of Dirleton. (In *History of the Berwickshire Naturalists' Club*, vol.xxvii, 1929/31, pp.75-92.)
ED/N-1 (Y.210)   QZ/P34

De Veteripont, Vipont

REID, Robert Corsane
De Veteripont. (In *Transactions of the Dumfriesshire and Galloway Natural History & Antiquarian Society*, 3rd series, vol.xxxiii, 1954/5, pp.91-106.)
ED/N-1 (J.187)

— — (Reprinted from *Transactions of the Dumfriesshire and Galloway Natural History & Antiquarian Society*, 3rd series, vol.xxxiii, 1956.)
QZ/L37   QZ/P99

Dempster

DEMPSTER, George
Letters of George Dempster to Sir Adam Fergusson, 1756-1813, with some account of his life. [With genealogical tables.] London, 1934.
ED/N-1 (Hist.S.115.D)

[GENEALOGY and correspondence of the family of Dempster.]
ED/N-1 (MS.15481,f.26)

Denham of Westshield

The COLTNESS collections, MDCVIII-MDCCCXL; edited by James Dennistoun. [With a genealogical table.] Edinburgh, 1842. (Maitland Club)
ED/N-1 (Mait.Club.58)   ED/U-1   GL/U-1
QZ/L37   QZ/P-1   QZ/P40   QZ/P56   QZ/P99

Dennistoun

['DRAFT genealogical account of the Dennistoun families of Dalvair and Tullichewan'. 1828.]
ED/N-1 (Adv.MS.19.2.17,ff.162-5)

Dennistoun of Colgrain

DENNISTOUN, James Wallis
Some account of the family of Dennistoun of Colgrain. [With genealogical tables.] Dumbarton, 1859.
ED/N-1 (NE.25.a.25)

— — Glasgow, 1906.
ED/N-1 (6.215)   SA/U-1

IRVING, Joseph
The book of Dumbartonshire. Edinburgh, 1879. 3v.
ED/N-1 (R.286.c)

[GENEALOGICAL account of the Dennistouns of Colgrain. 1859.]
ED/N-1 (MS.Acc.5525(4))

Dennistoun of Dennistoun

DONALD, Thomas F.
The Dennistouns of Dennistoun. Glasgow, 1918.
QZ/P-1 (Unconfirmed location)

Denny of Dumbarton

DENNY, Dumbarton, 1844-1932. [With a genealogical table.] London, [1933.]
ED/N-1 (T.459.g)

Deuchar

DEUCHAR, J. C. A.
Pedigree of the Deuchar family. [N.d.]
QZ/P-1 (Unconfirmed location)

Dewar

ANDERSON, Joseph
The Dewars, or hereditary keepers of relics of the Celtic Church in Scotland. (In *Highland Monthly*, vol.ii, 1890/91, pp.84-96.)
ED/N-1 (Q.106)

— — (Reprinted from *Highland Monthly*, vol.ii, 1890/91.)
QZ/P-1 (Unconfirmed location)   QZ/P99

DEWAR, Peter de Vere Beauclerk
The Dewars formerly of King's Park and Craigniven. [N.p.], 1966.
ED/N-1 (6.1345)   QZ/L37

Dick

PLAYFAIR, William
Antiquity of the family of Dick. Reading, 1826.
ED/N-1 (5.1236(12))

Dick of Braid

[HISTORY of the family of Dick of Braid. 18--,19--.]
ED/N-1 (MS.1995,f.3)

SIR William Dick of Braid, Knight, and the pretensions of his descendants to a baronetcy. (In *Herald and Genealogist*, vol.8, 1974, pp.257-69.)
ED/N-1 (Q.103)

—(Reprinted from *Herald and Genealogist*, vol.8, 1974.)
QZ/P99

Dick of Prestonfield

FORBES, Mrs Atholl
Curiosities of a Scots charta chest, 1600-1800. Edinburgh, 1897.
ED/N-1 (A.58.a) ED/N-2 GL/U-1 QZ/P99

Dick-Lauder *see also* Lauder

Dick-Lauder

SMITH, J. Stewart
The Grange of St. Giles, the Bass and other baronial homes of the Dick-Lauder family. Edinburgh, 1898.
QZ/P34 ED/N-2 QZ/P40 QZ/P22 QZ/P99

Dickson

DICKSON, Mora
The aunts. [With a genealogical table.] Edinburgh, 1981.
ED/N-1 (H3.81.4612)

DIXON, Bernard Homer
The border, or riding clans . . . a history of the clan Dickson. Albany, N.Y., 1889.
ED/N-1 (Y.59.c.9) ED/N-2 QZ/P99

—Scotch border clan Dickson, the family of B. Homer Dixon and of the family of De Homere or Homer. Toronto, 1884.
ED/N-1 (APS.1.78.5) ED/N-2 QZ/P99

FLAGLER, Lyla D.
The story of a Scottish family. Falmouth, Mass., 1958.
ED/N-1 (NE.25.f.22)

M'CREADY, Christopher Teeling
Dickson genealogy. Dublin, 1868.
ED/N-2

SMITH, Austin Wheeler
The Dickson-McEwen and allied families genealogy. 2nd ed. Cookeville, Tenn., 1975.
ED/N-1 (H3.79.978)

Dingwall

The DINGWALLS of Kildun: a genealogy. (In *Clan Munro Magazine*, no.11, 1969, pp.34-40.)
ED/N-1 (P.med.1307)

Dingwall, Lord

COWPER, Francis Thomas de Grey, *Earl*
Case on behalf of . . . on his claim to . . . Lord Dingwall.
QZ/L37

—Supplementary case of above.
QZ/L37

—[Lords and session papers relating to the claim of Francis Thomas de Grey, Earl Cowper to the dignities of Lord Dingwall.] [London, 1870-71.]
ED/N-1 (Yule.143)

MINUTES of evidence . . . to whom were referred the petitions of . . . Francis Thomas de Grey, Earl Cowper, Viscount Fordwich & Baron Cowper, K.G., . . . to declare he is entitled to . . . barony of Dingwall in the peerage of Scotland. 1870.
QZ/L37

Dingwall-Fordyce

FORDYCE, Alexander Dingwall
Epitome, or who, what, where, when respecting the family of Dingwall-Fordyce and connections, 1655-1884. [Fergus, Ont.], 1884.
ED/N-1 (5.3251(22)) AD/U-1 QZ/P99

— — Family record of the name of Dingwall-Fordyce, including relatives of both names and connections. Toronto, 1885,88. 2v.
ED/N-1 (Y.59.d.21) QZ/P22 QZ/P99

Dinsmoor

MORRISON, Leonard Allison
Among the Scotch-Irish. With history of Dinsmoor family. Boston, Mass., 1891.
ED/N-1 (NE.57.g.8)

Dinwiddie

HOLLADAY, Elizabeth Dinwiddie
Dinwiddie family records; with special attention to the line of William W. Dinwiddie, 1804-1882. Charlottesville, Va., 1957.
QZ/P99

Dinwiddie in Virginia, U.S.A.

DINWIDDIE, Robert
The official records of Robert Dinwiddie, Lieutenant-Governor of the colony of Virginia, 1751-1758. [With a genealogical table.] Richmond, Va., 1883, 84. 2v.
ED/N-1 (S.75.a)

Dirom

BULLOCH, John Malcolm
The Dirom family. 1935.
QZ/P22

—Provost Dirom of Banff and his descendants. (In
Transactions of the Banffshire Field Club, 10 December
1935, pp. 131-48.)
ED/N-1 (NE.3.g.1)

Diven

MANNING, Doreen Caraher
From Scotland to the U.S.A.: a civil war diary, the
McRobbie/Divan migration and transition. (In
Scottish Genealogist, vol.xxviii, no.4, December
1981, pp.177-80.)
ED/N-1 (Gen.7)

Dixon

The DIXON family and their connection with
Glasgow. (Excerpts from *Memoirs and portraits of one
hundred Glasgow men*, by J. O. Mitchell [and others].
1886. 2v.
QZ/P-1 (Unconfirmed location)

Don in Angus

DON, William Gerard
Memoirs of the Don family in Angus: with a
general survey of the etymology of the name.
London, 1897.
ED/N-1 (A.120.b) QZ/P28 SA/U-1 QZ/P99

Donald *see* Macdonald

Donaldson

DONALDSON, Alexander
A history of the Donaldson family and its
connections. Pittsburgh, Pa., 1878.
ED/N-1 (5.3098(37))

DUNNETT, Alastair MacTavish
The Donaldson Line: a century of shipping,
1854-1954. [With a genealogical table.] Glasgow,
1960.
ED/N-1 (NG.1297.h.10)

SKINNER, Robert T.
A notable family of Scots printers. Edinburgh,
1927.
ED/N-1 (Birk.167;S.122.e) QZ/P22 GL/U-1
QZ/P99

Donnachaidh *see* Robertson

Dougall *see also* MacDougall

Dougall

DOUGALL, Richardson
James Dougall of Glasgow (1699-1760) and his
descendants through Dougall and McDougall lines
in the United States and Canada. Ann Arbor, Mich.,
1973.
ED/N-1 (H8.80.166)

Douglas *see also* Angus

Douglas

The BROKEN cross: a legend of Douglas; with
chronicles of the Black Douglas and an appendix.
Glasgow, 1859.
ED/N-1 (T.7.c) QZ/P53 QZ/P11 GL/U-1
QZ/P99

CARRE, Walter Riddell
Border memories. Edinburgh, 1876.
QZ/P11

DOUGLAS, Charles Henry James
A collection of family records . . . of various families
and individuals bearing the name Douglas.
Providence, R.I., 1879.
QZ/P-1 (Unconfirmed location)

FRASER, Sir William
The Douglas book: memoirs of the house of
Douglas and Angus. Edinburgh, 1885. 4v.
ED/N-1 (Gen.8.d) QZ/P56 ED/N-2 QZ/P11
SA/U-1 AD/U-1 GL/U-1 QZ/L37 ED/U-1
QZ/P99

HERD, James
The martial achievements of the Houses of Douglas,
Angus and Queensberry. Edinburgh, 1769.
QZ/L37

HUME, David
The history of the House and race of Douglas and
Angus. 1643.
QZ/P10 (Unconfirmed location)

—History of the House of Douglas and Angus.
Edinburgh, 1644.
ED/N-1 (A.114.b;Ry.III.c.26;F.6.e.13;F.5.c.23)
ED/N-2 QZ/P28

— — Edinburgh, 1648.
ED/N-1 (Ferg.190) AD/U-1 ED/U-1

— — London, 1657.
ED/N-1 (A.114.b;ABS.5.78.8) SA/U-1

— — Edinburgh, 1743. 2v.
ED/N-1 (A.114.e) QZ/P26 AD/U-1 GL/U-1
QZ/P99

— — [Edinburgh], 1748. 2v.
QZ/L37

— — Aberdeen, 1820.
ED/U-1 AD/U-1 QZ/P-7 QZ/P11 QZ/P22
QZ/P20 QZ/P99

— — London, 1820.
ED/N-1(A.114.d) QZ/Q17

— The lyves of the illustrious familie and name of
Douglas. [Edinburgh, 1633?]
ED/N-1(H.25.b.20)

JOHNSTON, George Harvey
The heraldry of the Douglases, with notes on all the
males of the family. Edinburgh, 1905.
QZ/P99

— — Edinburgh, 1907.
ED/N-1(S.120.c;Hall.139.b) QZ/P99 QZ/P11
QZ/P30

LETTERS etc. relating to the family of Douglas.
1802-5.
QZ/P-1 (Unconfirmed location)

MACDOWALL, John Kevan
Carrick Gallovidian: a historical survey ... with
genealogical charts and notes. ... Ayr, 1947.
ED/N-1(R.241.d)

MCINTOSH, Mary
Roots and branches: the story of the Angus and
Leybourne families. [With genealogical tables.]
Newcastle, [1958].
ED/N-1(NE.63.e.12)

MCMASTER, Jane Harvey *and* WOOD, Marguerite
Supplementary report on the manuscripts of His
Grace the Duke of Hamilton, [1583-1789].
[London], 1932.
ED/N-1(GRH.5/21)

MAXWELL, Sir Herbert Eustace
A history of the House of Douglas from the earliest
times down to the legislative union of England and
Scotland. London, 1902. 2v.
ED/N-1(S.120.e) QZ/P53 QZ/P28 QZ/Z17
QZ/P40 QZ/P11 DN/U-1 QZ/P26 QZ/P27
QZ/P56 QZ/P99 ED/N-2 QZ/P22 QZ/P14
SA/U-1 GL/U-1 QZ/P49 QZ/P-6 QZ/L37
QZ/P30 ST/U-1 QZ/P13

[MS. notes and press cuttings on the family of
Douglas. N.d.]
QZ/P99

['PAPERS concerning the genealogy of the Douglas
family'. 17--.]
ED/N-1(Adv.MS.20.1.7,ff.6-13)

PINEDA, Peter
A synopsis of the genealogy ... of the family of the
Brigantes or Douglas. London, 1754.
ED/N-1(A.114.e) GL/U-1 QZ/L37 SA/U-1
ED/U-1 QZ/P99

QUEENSBERRY, Francis Archibald Kelhead Douglas,
10th Marquess of
The sporting Queensberrys. London, 1942.
ED/N-1(R.197.d) QZ/P14 ED/N-2 QZ/P-7

RAMAGE, Craufurd Tait
Drumlanrig Castle and the Douglases. Dumfries,
1876.
ED/N-1(Hist.S.91.D) ED/N-2 QZ/P11
QZ/P22 GL/U-1 QZ/L37 QZ/P99

RIACH, Charles C.
Douglas and the Douglas family. Hamilton, 1927.
ED/N-1(NE.12.a.3) ED/N-2 QZ/P99

ROBERTS, Brian
The mad bad line: the family of Lord Alfred
Douglas. London, 1981.
ED/N-1(H3.81.3225) QZ/P14 QZ/P99

STEDMAN, Douglas C.
The Black Douglases. London, 1913.
ED/N-1(S.120.g)

STOCQUART, Émile
Les flamands en Écosse au moyen âge et l'origine des
comtes de Douglas. Bruxelles, 1900.
ED/N-1(5.184)

WIGTOWNSHIRE charters; edited by R. C. Reid.
Edinburgh, 1960. (Scottish History Society
Publications, 3rd series, vol.51.)
ED/N-1(Ref.54)

Douglas, Marquess of *see also* **Hamilton,** Duke of
Hamilton

Douglas, Marquess of
ANDERSON, William
Speeches and judgements ... George James, Duke
of Hamilton ... against Archibald Douglas.
Edinburgh, 1768.
ED/N-1(Law) QZ/P53 QZ/P56 QZ/P40
GL/U-1 QZ/P99

BOSWELL, James
Dorando: a Spanish tale. [A satire on the Douglas cause.] London, 1767.
ED/N-1 (F.7.b.3)

— The essence of the Douglas cause . . . London, 1767.
ED/N-1 (Ry.1.4.62)   QZ/P99

— The speeches, arguments and determinations of . . . the Lords of Council and Session . . . upon that important cause. 1767.
QZ/P99

— A summary of the speeches, arguments and determinations of . . . the Lords of Council and Session . . . upon that important cause. 1767.
QZ/P99

COLVILL, Robert
Fate of Julia, an epic poem in two cantos, sacred to the memory of L - dy J - n D - - g - -s [i.e. Lady Jane Douglas aft. Stewart]. 2nd ed. [N.p.], 1769.
ED/N-1 (1.825.(9))

— The merry wives of Douglas; or the Douglas garland . . . written by a young gentleman. Edinburgh, 1769.
QZ/P-1 (Unconfirmed location)

CONSIDERATIONS on the Douglas Cause, in a letter from a gentleman in Scotland to his friend in London. London, 1767.
ED/N-1 (1969.289(16))

DALRYMPLE, David
Replies for George James, Duke of Hamilton, Lord Douglas Hamilton, and their tutors, and Sir Hugh Dalrymple of North Berwick, Baronet, pursuers, to the answers made in the name of 'Archibald Douglas of Douglas, Esq., and his curators.' [N.p.], 1764.
QZ/P53

— — Edinburgh, 1776.
ED/N-1 (Ry.I.1.130(3))

DE LA TORRE, Lillian
The heir of Douglas. London, 1953.
ED/N-1 (NF.1174.a.30)   QZ/P53   QZ/P40   QZ/P11   QZ/P28   QZ/P22   QZ/P99

DOUGLAS, Archibald James Edward
Answers for Archibald Douglas of Douglas esq.; and his curators. [N.p., n.d.]
ED/N-1 (5.3975(3))

— Archibald Douglas of Douglas, Esq.; an infant, and his guardians . . . appellants, his Grace the Duke of Hamilton, Lord Douglas Hamilton, and their guardians, Sir Hew Dalrymple, Bart. and others, respondents, et e contra, case of Archibald Douglas. 2pts. [N.p., 1764.]
ED/N-1 (6.1734(7))

— Archibald James Edward Stewart, alias Douglas under the assumed character of son of the deceased Lady Jane Douglas, appellant . . . George James Duke of Hamilton and Brandon . . . and Lord Douglas Hamilton, and their guardians, Sir Hew Dalrymple . . . respondents: case of the respondents. [Edinburgh, 1768?]
ED/N-1 (L.C.Folio 57 A;Law;X.212.a)

— Case of Archibald Douglas against the Duke of Hamilton and others. [Edinburgh], 1769.
ED/N-1 (Law)   QZ/P34   QZ/P53   QZ/P40   QZ/P99

— Interlocutor upon advising reclaiming petition for Archibald Douglas, and answers for the Duke of Hamilton, &c. . . . 10th August, 1764. Edinburgh, 1764.
ED/N-1 (6.1734(3))

— Memorial for A. Douglas . . . defender, against the Duke of Hamilton, pursuer. (June 28. 1763.) Edinburgh, 1763.
ED/N-1 (5.3975(15))

— Memorial for Archibald Douglas of Douglas, Esq., and for Margaret Dutchess of Douglas, etc. . . . against George James, Duke of Hamilton . . . [Signed Ilay Campbell]. [Edinburgh], 1766.
ED/N-1 (Law)   QZ/P34   QZ/P53   ED/M-1   QZ/P99

— Minutes of hearing on the 19th of July, 1769, in the cause of Archibald Douglas, of Douglas, Esquire against Dunbar, Earl of Selkirk. [N.p., 1769.]
ED/N-1 (6.1734(10))

— Proof for Archibald Douglas of Douglas, Esq., defender; in the reduction, the Duke of Hamilton, Lord Douglas Hamilton, and Sir Hew Dalrymple, against him. [Edinburgh?], 1766.
ED/N-1 (Law)

— Unto the . . . Lords of Council and Session, the petition of Archibald Douglas . . . and his curators. (December 6th, 1746, 1764.) [Edinburgh, 1764.]
ED/N-1 (6.1877(13))

—Unto the . . . Lords of Council and Session, the petition of Archibald Douglas . . . and his curators. (November 11th, 1766.) Edinburgh, [1766].
ED/N-1 (5.4720(3))

DOUGLAS, Francis
A letter to a noble lord: or, a faithful representation of the Douglas Cause. London, 1769.
QZ/P20   QZ/P-1 (Unconfirmed locations)

FITZGERALD, Percy Hetherington
Lady Jean: the romance of the great Douglas cause. London, 1904.
ED/N-1 (S.171.d)   SA/U-1   QZ/P99

FRAZER, Sir William
Lady Jane Douglas and the Douglas cause. (Reprinted from the *Douglas Book*.) Edinburgh, 1886.
ED/N-1 (NF.1355.a.5)   QZ/P56

HAMILTON, Douglas
His grace Douglas, Duke of Hamilton and Brandon . . . nearest and lawful heir male of Archibald, Duke of Douglas, deceased, appellant. Dunbar Earl of Selkirk, and Archibald Douglas . . . respondents. The appellant's case. (To be heard at the Bar of the House of Lords, on . . . 30th day of March, 1778.) [N.p., 1778.]
ED/N-1 (7.112(32))

HAMILTON, James George, *7th Duke of*
Archibald James Edward Stewart alias Douglas . . . appellant and George James, Duke of Hamilton, and others, respondents. Case of the respondents, the Duke of Hamilton, etc. [N.p., n.d.]
ED/N-1 (Law)

—Case, George-James, Duke of Hamilton, etc. against the person pretending to be Archibald Douglas. [Signed Alex. Lockhart.] [N.p., 1766.]
QZ/P20   QZ/P-1 (Unconfirmed locations)

—[A collection of papers relating to the Douglas cause, in which the Duke of Hamilton claimed the estates of the Duke of Douglas by reason of the illegitimacy of A. J. E. Douglas.] Edinburgh, [1763-7].
ED/N-1 (NC.304.b.3)

—Information for George-James, Duke of Hamilton . . . against Dunbar, Earl of Selkirk, and Archibald Stewart, Esq., [signed Alex. Lockhart.] [Edinburgh, 1762.]
QZ/P20 (Unconfirmed location)

—Mémoir abregé pour M. de Douglas . . .: observations servant de réponse à un écrit anonime . . . avec l'articulation des faits de supposition de part et les quatre lettres du prétendu accoucheur Pier Lamarr. Paris, 1763.
ED/N-1 (Law)

—Memorial for George-James, Duke of Hamilton and Brandon . . . against Archibald Stewart, Esq. (April 15, 1762.) [N.p.], 1762.
ED/N-1 (5.3975(5))

—Memorial for George-James, Duke of Hamilton, Marquis of Douglas etc. . . . against a person pretending to be Archibald Stewart alias Douglas. [Edinburgh], 1767.
ED/N-1 (Law)   QZ/P40   ED/M-1

—Minutes in the process of reduction, the Duke of Hamilton, and others, against Archibald Douglas, Esq., containing some facts and arguments stated to the court by both parties before pronouncing the interlocutor 10th August 1764. (August 10. 1764.) [N.p.], 1764.
ED/N-1 (6.1734(4))

—Observations for the Duke of Hamilton, Lord Douglas Hamilton, and Sir Hew Dalrymple, upon the answers for Archibald Douglas of Douglas . . . dated June 30, 1764. (July 4. 1764.) [N.p., 1764.]
ED/N-1 (7.87)

—Procedure et preuve faites en France dans la contestation, pour le Duc d'Hamilton, le Lord Douglas Hamilton, et le Chevalier Dalrymple, poursuivans contre la personne se prétendant être Archibald Douglas de Douglas . . . défendeur. Paris, 1764.
ED/N-1 (Law)

—Proof in the conjoined processes, George-James, Duke of Hamilton . . . against the person pretending to be Archibald Stewart alias Douglas . . . Dec. 19, 1765 and Feb. 5, 1766. [Edinburgh?, 1766.]
ED/N-1 (NC.304.b.4)   QZ/P53   ED/M-1

—Trial of George-James, Duke of Hamilton and others and Archibald Douglas. Edinburgh, 1768.
QZ/P40

HAMILTON, James George, *7th Duke of, and others*
The cases given to the Court of Session previous to the pleadings in the important cause of *suppositio portus*, George-James, Duke of Hamilton and others, pursuers; against Archibald Douglas, Esq., defender. Edinburgh, 1768.
QZ/P-1 (Unconfirmed location)

HENDERSON, Andrew
A letter to a noble lord: or a faithful representation of the Douglas cause. London, 1769.
ED/N-1 (F.7.b.5(1))

HIS Grace Douglas, Duke of Hamilton and Brandon, Marquis of Douglas, appellant, Dunbar, Earl of Selkirk, and Archibald Douglas, Esq., respondents: the appellant's case, to be heard ... 30th day of March, 1778. [N.p., 1778.]
ED/N-1 (7.112(32))

[LEGAL papers relating to the Douglas cause.] 1761-3.
QZ/P-1 (Unconfirmed location)

MONITOIRE important du neuf juillet, mil sept cent soixante trois. [concerning the birth of A. Douglas in 1748.] Paris, 1763.
ED/N-1 (Law)

PAPERS on the Douglas peerage case. 11v.
QZ/L37

PRATT, Charles
A second letter to a noble lord: or, the speeches of the Lord Chancellor, and of Lord Mansfield, on ... the Douglas cause. London, [1769].
ED/N-1 (F.7.b.5(2))

RECUEIL des pièces présentées à sa Majesté ... 1763, au sujet de la contestation entre le Duc d'Hamilton, et le Chevalier Dalrymple d'une part; et de l'autre part, Archibald Stewart Douglas, qui prétend être fils de Milady Jeanne Douglas & du Chevalier Jean Stewart. Paris, 1763.
ED/N-1 (Law)

RICHARDSON, Robert
A state of the evidence in the [Douglas] cause. London, 1769.
ED/N-1 (NF.1540.b.1)

SPEECHES, arguments and determinations of the ... Lords of Council and Session in Scotland, upon that important cause. London, 1767.
ED/N-1 (Newb.2167;Law) QZ/P53

STATE of the facts etc. in the Douglas cause. 1766-7. 2v.
QZ/P40

STEUART, Archibald Francis
The Douglas cause. Glasgow, 1909.
ED/N-1 (Law) QZ/P34 ED/N-2 QZ/P22
GL/U-1 QZ/P99

STEWART, Lady Jane
Letters of the Right Hon. Lady Jane Douglas. London, 1767.
ED/N-1 (Bh.5/1)

STEWART, John
Articulation des faits de supposition de part, admis par la Cour Souveraine d'Ecosse contre le pretendu fils du Chevalier Stewart et de Milady Jeanne Douglas. Paris, 1763.
ED/N-1 (DC.1.96(3);Law)

STUART, Andrew
Letters to the Rt. Hon. Lord Mansfield from Andrew Stuart. London, 1773.
ED/N-1 (NC.304.g.8;1945.11(13);L.218.e;Law)
QZ/P99

A SUMMARY of the speeches ... of the right honourable the Lords of Council and Session in Scotland upon that important cause wherein his Grace the Duke of Hamilton and others were plaintiffs and Archibald Douglas of Douglas, Esq., defendant. Edinburgh, 1767.
ED/N-1 (NC.304.d.2) QZ/P53

The WEEKLY Magazine, or, Edinburgh amusement, Thursday, May 25, 1769.
QZ/P-1 QZ/P99 (Unconfirmed locations)

Douglas, Earl of Angus
KELLEY, Michael Garhart Roosevelt
The Douglas Earls of Angus. [N.p.], 1973. 2v.
ED/U-1

NAPIER, Mark
A "memorie" historical and genealogical of my mother's paternal lineage, namely the Hamiltons of Innerwick, the Lothian Kerrs and the Earls of Angus. Edinburgh, 1872.
ED/N-1 (F.7.d.3) ED/N-2

Douglas of Baads
THOMAS, Kenneth Bryn
James Douglas of the pouch and his pupil William Hunter. [With a genealogical table.] London, 1964.
ED/N-1 (NF.1344.c.11)

Douglas of Brigton

SACRED to the memory of David and Graham
Douglas, sons of William Douglas of Brigton.
Rochester, 1814.
ED/N-1 (NC.274.i.8)

Douglas of Douglasdale

HUTCHISON, J. D.
Douglasdale, its history and traditions. [With a
genealogical table.] Glasgow, 1940.
ED/N-1 (R.243.g)

Douglas of Kelhead *see* **Queensberry,** Marquessate of

Douglas of Mains

['DRAFT genealogical account of the family of
Douglas of Mains'. 1828?]
ED/N-1 (Adv.MS.19.2.17,ff.213-7)

Douglas of Morton

ADAMS, Percy Walter Lewis
A history of the Douglas family of Morton in
Nithsdale and Fingland, and their descendants.
Bedford, 1921.
ED/N-1 (S.122.d) ED/N-2 QZ/P11 SA/U-1
QZ/P22 GL/U-1 QZ/L37 QZ/Q71 ED/U-1
QZ/P99

DOUGLAS, James
Papers relating to the Earl of Morton's case. [N.p.,
1702.]
ED/N-1 (Ry.II.a.22(53))

['GENEALOGICAL notes concerning the family of the
Earls of Morton'. 1709.]
ED/N-1 (Adv.MS.34.6.24,ff.83-5)

INNES, Sir Thomas
The heraldry of Douglas of Morton. (In *Transactions
of the Dumfriesshire and Galloway Natural History &
Antiquarian Society*, 3rd series, vol.xxix, 1950/51,
pp.66-80.)
ED/N-1 (J.187)

REGISTRUM honoris de Morton: a series of ancient
charters of the Earldom of Morton with other
original papers. Edinburgh, 1853. 2v. (Bannatyne
Club, 94)
ED/N-1 (Bann. Club.94) GL/U-1 QZ/L37
QZ/P-1 QZ/P99

Douglas of Mulderg

AIRD, Gustavus
Genealogy of the families of Douglas of Mulderg
and Robertson of Kindeace with their descendants.
Dingwall, 1895.
ED/N-1 (A.113.e) ED/N-2 QZ/P40 SA/U-1
AD/U-1 QZ/P22 GL/U-1 ED/U-1 QZ/P99

Douglas, Earl of Ruglen *see* **Cassillis,** Earldom of

Douglas in Sweden

DOUGLAS, Archibald
Robert Douglas: en krigargestalt, från vår storhetstid.
Stockholm, 1957.
ED/N-1 (NE.528.c.7)

Douglas of Threave Castle

ROBISON, Joseph
The Black Douglasses and Threave Castle. [Castle
Douglas], 1911.
ED/N-1 (5.1917) ED/N-2

— — 2nd ed. [Castle Douglas], 1924.
ED/N-1 (5.2233)

Douglas of Tilquhilly

HOME, James
History of the family of Douglass of Tilwhilly or
Tilliqhuilly. Bath, 1800.
ED/N-1 (1968.211(13))

— — Bath, [1874].
SA/U-1 AD/U-1 DN/U-1 QZ/P22

PEDIGREE of Douglas of Tilquhilly, or Tilwhilly,
co. Kincardine. [N.p., 1881?]
ED/N-1 (A.124.c) QZ/P99

Douglas of Timpendean

WATSON, George
Timpendean Castle. (In *History of the Berwickshire
Naturalists' Club*, vol.xxx, 1938, pp.23-32.)
ED/N-1 (Y.210)

Douglas in U.S.A.

DOUGLASS, Hiram Kennedy
My southern families. [With genealogical tables.]
Gillingham, 1967.
ED/N-1 (NF.1372.b.18)

Douglas of Whiteriggs

MAIDMENT, James
Genealogical fragments relating to the families of . . .
Douglas. Berwick, 1855.
ED/N-1 (Y.59.f.2;Ry.II.e.S1(1)) QZ/P40 GL/U-1
QZ/P99

Douglass

WATKINS, Walter Kendall
The life and ancestry of Francis Douglass, bookseller and author, of Aberdeen and Paisley. Boston, Mass., 1903.
QZ/P22 QZ/L37 QZ/P99

Drever

DREVER, Dorothy
Typescript family history of William Drever and James Harcus of Faray (or Pharay) in Orkney, who emigrated to the U.S. [N.p., 1956.]
QZ/P38 (Unconfirmed location)

Drummond

['COPY of part of William Drummond's Genealogy of the family of Drummond'. 16--.]
ED/N-1 (Adv.MS.34.3.14,ff.70-5)

DRUMMOND, Adelaide
The honourable Adelaide Drummond: retrospect and memoir. [With a genealogical table.] London, 1915.
ED/N-1 (S.168.g)

DRUMMOND, Charles Edward
The detection of infamy. London, 1816.
ED/N-1 (Ry.I.4.242)

DRUMMOND, George
Historical facts and explanations regarding the succession to the Lordships, Baronies and free regality of Drummond and Earldom of Perth. Paris, 1866.
ED/N-1 (1945.5(6))

DRUMMOND, James
The female rebels: being some remarkable incidents of the lives, characters and families of the titular Duke and Dutchess of Perth. Dublin, 1747.
ED/N-1 (Ry.IV.f.47)

DRUMMOND, P. R.
Perthshire in bygone days: one hundred biographical essays. [Section 6: The Perthshire Drummond ballads. With a genealogical table.] London, 1879.
ED/N-1 (A.113.d)

DRUMMOND, Thomas
An interesting statement of the claims of Thomas Drummond . . . to the . . . Earldom of Perth; interspersed with copious memoirs of the most noble house of Drummond. Newcastle, 1830.
ED/N-1 (Yule.84(1)) QZ/P40 SA/U-1 QZ/P99

['GENEALOGY of the families of Gordon, Drummond and Maule'. 16--,17--.]
ED/N-1 (Adv.MS.23.3.24,ff.1-81)

HAY, George
Memorial of George, Earl of Kinnoull, for himself, and of Robert Hay-Drummond, his second son. Edinburgh, [1720].
ED/N-1 (Mf.9(8[9]))

HISTORIES of noble British families; edited by Henry Drummond. London, 1846. 2v.
ED/N-1 (S.300.a) GL/U-1 QZ/P99

MALCOLM, David
A genealogical memoir of the most noble and ancient House of Drummond, and of the several branches. Edinburgh, 1808.
ED/N-1 (A.114.e) QZ/P26 SA/U-1 AD/U-1 DN/U-1 GL/U-1 QZ/L37 ED/U-1 QZ/P99

STRATHALLAN, William Drummond, *1st Viscount*
The genealogy of the most noble and ancient House of Drummond. Edinburgh, 1831.
ED/N-1 (A.114.a) QZ/P26 QZ/P27 AD/U-1 QZ/L37 QZ/P-9 ED/U-1

— — Glasgow, 1889.
ED/N-1 (Gen.8.D;NE.25.h.6) SA/U-1 QZ/P99

VITON DE SAINT ALLAIS, Nicolas
Généalogie historique des branches ainées de l'ancienne et illustre maison de Drummond. [With a genealogical table.] Paris, 1840.
ED/N-1 (R.272.f)

Drummond of Biddick *see* Perth, Earldom of

Drummond of Colquhalzie

FITTIS, Robert Scott
An ancient Perthshire family: the Drummonds of Colquhalzie. (*Miscellanea Perthensis*, 1853-1861, newspaper cutting no.67.)
QZ/P26

Drummond of Hawthornden

ERICKSON, Rica
The Drummonds of Hawthornden. [With a genealogical table.] Nedlands, Western Australia, 1975.
ED/N-1 (H3.84.79)

Drummond of Logiealmond *see also* **Perth,**
Earldom of
DRUMMOND, Thomas
Case of Thomas Drummond of Logy-almond,
claimant against His Majesty's advocate, in behalf of
His Majesty, respondent, 1750.
ED/N-1 (Ry.II.b.19(52)) ED/N-2

FORRESTER, David Marshall
Logiealmond. Edinburgh, 1944.
QZ/P-1 (Unconfirmed location)

Drummond in London
BOLITHO, Henry Hector *and* PEEL, Derek
The Drummonds of Charing Cross. [With a
genealogical table.] London, 1967.
ED/N-1 (NG.1296.c.12) QZ/P26

Drummond, Earl of Perth *see also* **Perth,** Earldom of

Drummond, Earl of Perth
EARL of Perth & Melfort *v.* the Lord Elphinstone
[case in the House of Lords]. 1871.
GL/U-1 QZ/P99

HISTORICAL facts and explanations regarding the
succession to the Lordships, Baronies and Regality
of Drummond and Earldom of Perth. Paris, 1866.
ED/N-1 (1945.5(6)) ED/N-2 QZ/L37 QZ/P99

Drummond in Portugal and Brazil
MENEZES DRUMMOND, Antonio A. de
A heraldica da Casa de Drummond: brazões de
armas concedidos em Portugal e Brasil aos
descendentes de D. João Escocio de Drummond.
São Paulo, 1937.
ED/N-1 (5.884)

Drummond, Viscount of Strathallan
DRUMMOND, Andrew
The case of Andrew Drummond . . . claiming the
titles and dignity of Viscount of Strathallan.
[Edinburgh, 1790.]
ED/N-1 (5.3010(4))

DRUMMOND, William H.
[Reproductions from an old family album of
photographs including family groups, taken by the
Hon. W. H. Drummond, 1844-64.]
ED/N-1 (L.232)

Dryden
TAYLOR, Earl J.
The Drydens of Teviotdale. [N.p., 196-?]
(*Typescript*)
QZ/P11

Ducat
NOTES concerning the family of Ducat.
[N.p., 1916.]
QZ/P28

Dudhope, Viscount
GREAT BRITAIN. Parliament. House of Lords.
Dudhope peerage: proceedings before the
Committee for privileges and judgement. London,
1953.
QZ/L37

SKINNER, William Cumming
The Barronie of Hilltowne, Dundee: its industrial,
social and religious life. Dundee, 1927.
ED/N-1 (R.246.f)

Duff
BAIRD, William
Genealogical memoirs of the Duffs. Aberdeen,
1869.
ED/N-1 (A.114.f) QZ/P30 SA/U-1 QZ/L37
QZ/P50 QZ/P99

BULLOCH, John Malcolm
The Duffs and the Gordons: a table bringing out
the literary instincts of the two. [N.d.] (*MS.*)
QZ/P99

— The "Lucky Duffs", showing how they rose to a
dukedom and became allied with the Royal Family.
[N.p., n.d.]
ED/N-1 (Blk.715) QZ/P50

TAYLER, Alistair *and* TAYLER, Henrietta
The book of the Duffs. Edinburgh, 1914. 2v.
ED/N-1 (S.121.b) SA/U-1 QZ/P30 GL/U-1
QZ/P22 QZ/P40 AD/U-1 QZ/L37 QZ/P50
QZ/P99

Duff, Duke of Fife
CRAMOND, William
The genealogy of the Duke of Fife. Edinburgh,
[1889].
ED/N-1 (5.22(15)) QZ/P22

WOOD, William
A short account of the Earls of Fife, compiled from documents relating to Scotland preserved in the Record Offices in London and Edinburgh, and other authentic sources. Kirkcaldy, 1896.
ED/N-1 (5.5691)

Duff of Muirtown
['GENEALOGICAL account of the Duffs of Muirtown'. 1833.]
ED/N-1 (MS.9854,ff.177-80)

Duff of Premnay
IRVINE, Alexander
[Papers in the case of Alexander Irvine of Drum, and his tutors, pursuers, against George, Earl of Aberdeen, and Margaret Duff, relict and representative of the deceased Patrick Duff of Premnay and others, defenders. Edinburgh, 1767-9.]
ED/N-1 (Yule.97)

Duffus
TRANTER, Nigel
The lost lordship of Duffus. (In *Scots Magazine*, vol.89, no.4, July 1968, pp.352-9.)
ED/N-1 (U.424)

Duguid
MAIDMENT, James
Genealogical fragments relating to the families of . . . Duguid. Berwick, 1855.
ED/N-1 (Ry.II.e.51(1);Y.59.f.2)   QZ/P40   GL/U-1   QZ/P99

Duke of Brechin
GENEALOGICAL papers concerning the family of Duke of Brechin, 1832-1935. [N.p., n.d.]
QZ/P28

Dun
JACOB, Violet
The lairds of Dun. London, 1931.
ED/N-1 (R.172.e)   ST/U-1

Dunbar
DRUMMOND, Henry
Histories of noble British families. Vol. 2: Dunbar, Hume, Dundas. London, 1846.
ED/N-1 (S.300.a)   GL/U-1   QZ/P99

DUNBAR, William
Life, letters and papers of William Dunbar of Elgin, Morayshire, Scotland and Natchez, Mississippi; compiled by Mrs Dunbar Rowland. [With a genealogical table.] Jackson, Mississippi, 1930.
ED/N-1 (NE.815.e.12)

DUNBAR, William
A short record of the ancient family of Dunbar. Herne Bay, [1982?].
ED/N-1 (H2.82.1056)   QZ/P99   QZ/P34

[GENEALOGY of the family of Dunbar. 1554, 1744.]
ED/N-1 (Adv.MS.32.3.2)

JAGGARD, William
Dunbar pedigrees: a biographical chart . . . of the Dunbar family through fourteen centuries. Stratford, 1910.
ED/N-1 (S.121.b)   QZ/P34   ED/N-2   AD/U-1   QZ/P99

MURRAY, James G.
The book of Burgie. 1933.
ED/N-1 (R.247.f)

['PAPERS concerning the genealogy of the family of Dunbar'. 17--.]
ED/N-1 (Adv.MS.20.1.7,ff.21-34)

Dunbar, Earldom of
WOOD, John Philip
Memorials of various families. [1830?] (*MS.*)
QZ/P99

Dunbar of Grangehill
LESLIE,
A family history: [a short account of the families of Brodie, Dunbar and Davidson.] [Brighton, 1891?]
ED/N-1 (6.2484)

MURRAY, James G.
The Dunbars of Grangehill. Rafford, [n.d.].
QZ/P50

Dunbar of Mochrum
REID, Robert Corsane
Mochrum notes: calendar of Mochrum papers. 3v. (*MSS.*)
QZ/P10 (Unconfirmed location)

Duncan
CEDERBERG, A. R.
Some notes on the Duncan family. (In *Scottish Genealogist*, vol.i, no.4, September 1954, pp.3-9.)
ED/N-1 (Gen.7)

DUNCAN, James Alexander *and* DUNCAN, Robert
Some family leaves. Edinburgh, 1911.
ED/N-1 (X.171.c) QZ/P22 ED/N-2 SA/U-1
GL/U-1 QZ/P99

FORBES, Alexander
Memorials of the family of Forbes of Forbesfield.
[With notes on connected ... Duncans.] Aberdeen,
1905.
ED/N-1 (S.120.c) QZ/P22 SA/U-1 GL/U-1
QZ/P99

GENEALOGICAL notes concerning the family of
Duncan. [N.p., n.d.]
QZ/P28

THORNTON, Robert Donald
James Currie: the entire stranger and Robert Burns.
[With genealogical tables.] Edinburgh, 1963.
ED/N-1 (Lit.S.18) QZ/P14

Dundas

DRUMMOND, Henry
Histories of noble British families. Vol.2: Dunbar,
Hume, Dundas. London, 1846.
ED/N-1 (S.300.a) GL/U-1 QZ/P99

DUNDAS, Francis De Sales
The Dundas genealogy. 2nd ed. Staunton, Va.,
[1954].
QZ/L37

[MS. notes and press cuttings on the family of
Dundas. N.d.]
QZ/P99

McCALL, Hardy B.
Memoirs of my ancestors. Birmingham, 1884.
ED/N-1 (A.114.a) QZ/P99

WHAT have the Dundases done for Orkney and
Shetland? In a letter to the constituency, by an
Orkney elector. Kirkwall, 1846.
ED/N-1 (1933.17)

Dundas of Arniston

FORBES, Louisa Lillias
[Genealogy of Dundas of Arniston, 1570-1880.]
[N.p., 1880.]
ED/N-1 (S.120.a) ED/N-2 SA/U-1 QZ/L37
QZ/P99

['GENEALOGICAL notes concerning the Dundas
family of Arniston'. 17--.]
ED/N-1 (Adv.MS.19.1.21,ff.170-182)

OMOND, George William Thomson
The Arniston memoirs: three centuries of a Scottish
house, 1571-1838. Edinburgh, 1887.
ED/N-1 (Hall.242.c) ED/N-2 GL/U-1 SA/U-1
QZ/P22 QZ/L37 QZ/P99

Dundas of Breastmill

WHYTE, Donald
Dundas of Breastmill. (In *Scottish Genealogist*; part 1,
vol.vi, no.2, April 1959, pp.14-15; part 2, vol.viii,
February 1961, pp.22-5.)
ED/N-1 (Gen.7)

Dundas of Duddingston

WHYTE, Donald
Dundas of Duddingston. (In *Scottish Genealogist*,
vol.v, no.1, 1958, pp.16-20.)
ED/N-1 (Gen.7)

Dundas of Dundas

MACLEOD, Walter
Royal letters and other historical documents selected
from the family papers of Dundas of Dundas.
Edinburgh, 1897.
ED/N-1 (A.58.b) QZ/Q17 ED/N-2 QZ/P40
GL/U-1 SA/U-1 QZ/L37 QZ/P99

SETON, George
Memoir of Alexander Seton ... with an appendix
cont. ... genealogical tables of the legal families of
Erskine, Hope, Dalrymple and Dundas. Edinburgh,
1882.
ED/N-1 (R.181.f) QZ/P-1 QZ/P16 QZ/P99

— — Edinburgh, 1883.
ED/N-1 (L.C.1915)

Dundas of Fingask

DUNDAS, Margaret Isabella
Dundas of Fingask: some memorials of the family.
Edinburgh, 1891.
ED/N-1 (Hall.232.a) QZ/P26 QZ/L37 SA/U-1
QZ/P99

Dundas of Kingscavil and Blair

WHYTE, Donald
Dundas of Kingscavil and Blair. (In *Scottish
Genealogist*, vol.viii, no.2, August 1961, pp.2-4.)
ED/N-1 (Gen.7)

Dundas of Manor

FERGUSSON, Robert Menzies
Logie: a parish history. Vol.2: Lands and landowners.
Paisley, 1905.
ED/N-1 (R.243.a) QZ/P14

Dundas of Morton
WHYTE, Donald
Dundas of Morton. (In *Scottish Genealogist*, vol.vi, no.1, 1959, pp.12-13.)
ED/N-1 (Gen.7)

Dundas of Newliston and Craigton
WHYTE, Donald
Dundas of Newliston and Craigton. (In *Scottish Genealogist*; part 1, vol.v, no.2, 1948, pp.35-7; part 2, vol.v, no.3, 1958, pp.47-50.)
ED/N-1 (Gen.7)

Dundas of Ochtertyre
LETTERS of John Ramsay of Ochtertyre, 1799-1812; edited by Barbara L. H. Horn [With a genealogical table.] Edinburgh, 1966. (Scottish History Society Publications, 4th series, vol.3.)
ED/N-1 (Ref.54)

Dundas of Philipstoun
WHYTE, Donald
Dundas of Philpstoun. (In *Scottish Genealogist*, vol.v, no.4, 1958, pp.65-7.)
ED/N-1 (Gen.7)

Dundee, Earldom of
GREAT BRITAIN. Parliament. House of Lords. Earldom of Dundee. Proceedings before the Committee for privileges and judgement. London, 1953.
QZ/L37

Dundonald, Earldom of *see also* **Cochrane** of Cochrane

Dundonald, Earldom of
CHARTER chest of the earldom of Dundonald, 1219-1672; edited by Francis J. Grant. Edinburgh, 1910. (Scottish Record Society Publications.)
ED/N-1 (Ref.55)

DUNDONALD, Thomas Barnes, *Earl of*
Case on behalf of Thomas Barnes, Earl of Dundonald. [1861.]
QZ/L37

MINUTES of evidence taken ... to whom was referred the petition of Thomas Barnes, Earl of Dundonald, etc. ... to declare he is of right entitled to titles of Earl of Dundonald and Lord Cochrane and Paisley & Ochiltrie in the peerage of Scotland. 1861-3.
QZ/L37

Dunfermline, Earl of *see* **Seton,** Earl of Dunfermline

Dunkeld, Lord *see* **Galloway**

Dunlap
HANNA, J. A. M.
The House of Dunlap. 1956.
QZ/P99

Dunlop
DUNLOP, Archibald
Dunlop of that ilk: memorabilia of the families of Dunlop. Glasgow, 1898.
ED/N-1 (A.118.b) QZ/P-7 QZ/P53 ED/N-2
SA/U-1 GL/U-1 QZ/P-6 QZ/P99

—Dunlops of Dunlop and of Auchenskaith, Keppoch and Gairbraid. (Dunlop papers, vol. 2.) Frome, 1939.
ED/N-1 (R.172.g) QZ/P-7 GL/U-1 QZ/L37
ED/U-1 QZ/P99
QZ/P52 (Unconfirmed location)

—Letters and journals, 1663-1889: selected and annotated by J. G. Dunlop. (Dunlop papers, vol. 3.) London, 1953.
ED/N-1 (R.172.g) QZ/P-6 SA/U-1 AD/U-1
ED/U-1 QZ/P99

DUNLOP, J. G.
Autobiography of John Dunlop. London, 1932. (Dunlop papers, vol. 1.)
ED/N-1 (R.172.g) AD/U-1

[MATERIAL relating to the lands and lairds of Dunlop.]
QZ/P-6

REID, Robert
Records of the Dunlops of Dunlop. Dunmow, 1900.
ED/N-1 (NE.25.h.19) SA/U-1 GL/U-1
QZ/P99

— — Dunmow, 1912.
ED/N-1 (NE.25.h.20) QZ/P-7

TAYLOR, G. Rankin
Thomas Dunlop & Sons, shipowners, 1851-1951. [Glasgow, 1952.]
ED/N-1 (NE.1178.f.6)

Durie of Craigluscar
DURIE, Charles
History of the Duries of Craigluscar from 1100-1768. (*Typescript*)
QZ/P16

Dyce of Aberdeen
GENEALOGICAL tree of the family of Dyce: tracing the Dyss or Dyce family from 1457. (*MSS.*)
QZ/P22

Dyce-Ochterlony
BULLOCH, John Malcolm
Lieutenant John Gordon of the Dundurcus family, massacred at Patna, 1763. [With a genealogical table.] Keith, 1908.
ED/N-1 (1908.2)

Dysart, Earldom of
DYSART, William John Manners, *Earl of*
Case of William John Manners, Earl of Dysart ... to admit his succession to the dignities of Earl of Dysart and Lord Huntingtower in the peerage of Scotland. 1880.
QZ/L37

MINUTES of evidence ... 1880-1.
QZ/L37

TOLLEMACHE, Albert Edwin
Case on behalf of Albert Edwin Tollemache in opposition to the claim of William John Manners claiming ... Earl of Dysart.
QZ/L37

Earle
BIRNIE, Joseph Earle
The Earles and the Birnies. [Atlanta], 1974.
ED/N-1 (H3.75.801)

Easson
OSLER, James Couper
Osler tree: [chart pedigree], with some supplementary notes on ... Eassons. [Dundee], 1924.
ED/N-2   QZ/L37

THOMSON, David Couper
Some supplemental notes on Oslers.... [Dundee], 1924.
ED/N-1 (HP1.77.4104)

Eaton
EATON, Arthur Wentworth Hamilton
Families of Eaton-Sutherland, Layton-Hill. New York, 1899.
ED/N-1 (S.120.e)

Echlin(e)
CRAWFURD, George
Memoirs of the ancient familie of the Echlins of Pittadro, in the County of Fyfe, in Scotland, now transplanted to Ireland. Dated, Glasgow, 18th August, 1747. [N.p., n.d.].
SA/U-1   QZ/L37

ECHLIN, John R.
Genealogical memoirs of the Echlin family, compiled from various authentic sources, with extracts from a MS. memorial composed by George Crawfurd, Esq. in the year 1747. 2nd ed., rev. and enl. Edinburgh, [n.d.].
ED/N-1 (Hall.195.g)   QZ/Z17   SA/U-1
QZ/L37   QZ/P99

Edgar
EDGAR, Andrew *and* ROGERS, C.
Genealogical collections concerning the Scottish house of Edgar. London, 1873. (Grampian Club, 5.)
ED/N-1 (Gramp.Club.5)   ED/N-2   QZ/P-7
QZ/P22   QZ/L37   QZ/P26   QZ/P11   QZ/P40
GL/U-1   QZ/P-6   QZ/P49   QZ/P28   QZ/P16
QZ/P99

EDGAR, Ralph W.
Edgar. Eau Claire, 1975.
ED/N-1 (6.2635)

Edgar of Wedderlie
LAWRENCE-ARCHER, James Henry
An account of the sirname Edgar, and particularly of the family of Wedderlie in Berwickshire. London, 1873.
ED/N-1 (A.114.a)   ED/N-2   QZ/P99

Edgecumbe of Laneast *see* **Livingston** of Callendar

Edmondstone of Ednem and Duntreath
EDMONSTONE, Sir Archibald
Genealogical account of the family of Edmonstone of Duntreath. Edinburgh, 1875.
ED/N-1 (A.114.b)   ED/N-2   AD/U-1   SA/U-1
GL/U-1   QZ/L37   ED/U-1   QZ/P99

GENEALOGY of the lairds of Ednem and Duntreath, 1063-1699. Glasgow, 1699.
ED/N-1 (2.74(11))   QZ/P40   ED/U-1

—Edited by J. Maidment. Edinburgh, 1834.
ED/N-1 (2.589)   ED/N-2   QZ/L37   QZ/P99

Edward of Auchinblae
[FAMILY papers of Archibald Edward, farmer of
Nether Coullie and later Upper Coullie,
Auchinblae, Fordoun. 1823-1884?] (*MSS.*)
QZ/P22

Eglinton, Earl of *see also* **Montgomery,**
Earl of Eglinton

Eglinton, Earl of
['GENEALOGICAL notes concerning the Earls of
Eglinton and their descendants'. 1709.]
ED/N-1 (Adv.MS.34.6.24,ff.71,72)

Eliot *see also* **Elliot**

Eliot
ELIOT, Walter Graeme
A sketch of the Eliot family. [N.p.], 1887.
ED/N-2

Eliot of Lostwithiel *see* **Livingston** of Callendar

Ellice
[GENEALOGICAL papers concerning the family of
Ellice. 1875?]
ED/N-1 (MS.15176)

Ellice of Aberdeenshire
ELLICE, E. C.
The family of Ellice in Aberdeenshire. [N.d.]
QZ/P99

Elliot *see also* **Eliot**

Elliot
CARRE, Walter Riddell
Border memories. Edinburgh, 1876.
ED/N-1 (A.118.g)   QZ/P11

ELIOTT, Lady Dora *and* ELIOTT, Sir Arthur
The Elliots: the story of a border clan. London,
1974.
ED/N-1 (Gen.8.E)   QZ/P53   SA/U-1   QZ/P34
QZ/L37   QZ/P99   QZ/P22   QZ/P11   ED/S10
QZ/P10   ED/N-2

ELLIOT, Fitzwilliam
Elliot traditions, also family anecdotes. Edinburgh,
1922.
ED/N-1 (S.120.h)   SA/U-1   QZ/P99

ELLIOT, George Francis Stewart
The Border Elliots and the family of Minto.
Edinburgh, 1897.
ED/N-1 (Gen.8.E; S.122.f; A.58.a)   SA/U-1
QZ/P11   GL/U-1   QZ/L37   ED/U-1   QZ/P99

ELLIOT, William
The Elliots of Brugh and Wells. London, 1925.
QZ/L37

[GENEALOGICAL papers concerning the family of
Elliot. 1700?]
ED/N-1 (MS.13095)

[A GENEALOGICAL table showing the antecedents of
Robert Shortreed.] [N.p., 1844.]
ED/N-1 (7.106(66-9))

MCINTOSH, Mary
Roots and branches: the story of the Angus and
Leybourne families. [With genealogical tables.]
Newcastle, [1958].
ED/N-1 (NE.63.e.12)

SCOT, Walter
Metrical history of the honourable families of the
name of Scot and Elliot in the shires of Roxburgh
and Selkirk. Edinburgh, 1892.
ED/N-1 (F.5.d.1)   ED/N-2   QZ/P11   GL/U-1
QZ/P99   QZ/P-1

Elliot of Binks
GENEALOGY of Elliot of Binks. Edinburgh, 1906.
QZ/P11

Elliot of Larriston
BARTON, E.
The Elliots of Larriston. (In *Transactions of the
Hawick Archaeological Society*, 1944, pp.10-19.)
ED/N-1 (P.220)

— — (Reprinted from *Transactions of the Hawick
Archaeological Society*, 1944.) Hawick, 1944.
QZ/L37

Elliot of Minto
ELLIOT-MURRAY-KYNYNMOUND, Nina Helen
Notes from Minto manuscripts. [Being a selection
from letters written by and to the Elliots of Minto
from 1762-1758.] Edinburgh, 1862.
SA/U-1

OLIVER, James Rutherford
Border sketches, historical and biographical.
Hawick, 1904.
ED/N-1 (NE.15.a.5)

SCOTT, Matthew
The Elliots of Minto: historical review of a great
border family. (In *Transactions of the Hawick
Archaeological Society*, 1938, pp.71-8.)
ED/N-1 (P.220)

Ellis

ELLIS, William Smith
Notices of the Ellises of England, Scotland and
Ireland, including the families of Alis, Fitz Elys,
Hellis. London, 1857-66.
ED/N-1 (NE.63.g.35)

Elphinstone

BROWN, John
Historical and genealogical tree of the ancient and
noble house of Elphinstone, from John de
Elphinstone [1263] . . . until the present time, 1808.
Edinburgh, [1808].
ED/N-1 (P.r.1.b.4) AD/U-1

[COLLECTION of photographs, newscuttings, etc.,
formerly in the possession of the Elphinstone family
at Carberry Tower, Musselburgh. 1930?]
QZ/P99

FRASER, Sir William
The Elphinstone family book of the Lords
Elphinstone, Balmerino and Coupar. Edinburgh,
1897. 2v.
ED/N-1 (Gen.8.e) ED/N-2 AD/U-1 SA/U-1
GL/U-1 QZ/L37 ED/U-1 QZ/P99

McCLINTOCK, Mary Howard
The Queen thanks Sir Howard: the life of Major
General Sir Howard Elphinstone. [With a
genealogical table.] London, 1945.
ED/N-1 (S.154.f)

PICTURES at Carberry Tower. [N.d.]
QZ/P99

Elphinstone, Lord Balmerino

MEMOIRS of the lives and families of the Lords
Kilmarnock, Cromartie and Balmerino. London,
1746.
ED/N-2

WHITEFIELD, C.
The life of Arthur, Lord Balmerino from the time
of his birth to that of his execution. London, 1746.
QZ/P-7

Erne, Earl of see Crichton

Erroll, Earl of see Hay of Erroll

Erskine

The ERSKINES. [MSS. notes on the Erskine family.]
QZ/P28 (Unconfirmed location)

FERGUSSON, Alexander
The Hon. Henry Erskine, Lord Advocate for
Scotland, with notices of certain of his kinfolk.
Edinburgh, 1882.
ED/N-1 (NE.25.a.5) GL/U-1 QZ/L37 QZ/P99

KELLIE,   , Earl of
Brief account of the titled family of Erskine of
Scotland. Alloa, [n.d.].
ED/N-2 QZ/L37

MACEWEN, Alexander Robertson
The Erskines. Edinburgh, 1900.
ED/N-1 (Hall.238.f) QZ/P-6 QZ/P15

The ORIGIN, increase, branches and alliances of the
family of Erskine of that ilk. [Cardiff, 1896.]
ED/N-1 (K.117.a)

SINCLAIR, Alexander
Remarks upon the petition of the Earl of Kellie as
being in many points delusive. [N.p., n.d.]
ED/N-1 (Hall.199.e.1(6))

— — Edinburgh, 1883.
ED/N-1 (L.C.1915)

SETON, George
Memoir of Alexander Seton . . . with an appendix
cont. . . . genealogical tables of the legal families
of Erskine, Hope, Dalrymple and Dundas.
Edinburgh, 1882.
ED/N-1 (R.181.f) QZ/P16 QZ/P 1

Erskine of Cardross

The BARONY of Cardross. (In *Gentleman's Magazine*,
new series, 1866, pp.76, 228-9, 362-5, 525-9.)
ED/N-1 (Reading Room)

The BARONY of Cardross and summary of the case
for the most ancient Earldom of Mar. (Reprinted
from *Gentleman's Magazine*, 4th series, 1 April
1866.)
QZ/P-1 ED/S10 (Unconfirmed location)

DUN, P.
Summer at the Lake of Menteith. Glasgow, 1866.
ED/N-1 (A.118.e) QZ/P14

ERSKINE, Sir David
The memoirs of Sir David Erskine of Cardross.
London, 1926.
QZ/Q17

Erskine of Dun

BOWICK, James
Life of John Erskine, Baron of Dun. Edinburgh,
1828.
ED/N-1 (S.145.j)

JACOB, Violet
The lairds of Dun. London, 1931.
ED/N-1 (R.172.e) QZ/P34 QZ/Q17 QZ/P14
DN/U-1 QZ/P22 QZ/P40 QZ/P28 SA/U-1
AD/U-1 GL/U-1 ED/S10 ED/N-2 ED/U-1
QZ/P99

PAPERS from the charter chest at Dun, 1451-1703.
Aberdeen, 1849. (In *Miscellany of the Spalding Club*,
vol.4, pp.1-112.)
ED/N-1 (Spald.Club.3) ED/N-2 QZ/P22
QZ/P28

SINCLAIR, Alexander
Genealogical tree of the ancient family of Erskine
of Dun. [N.p., n.d.]
ED/N-1 (S.120.b)

Erskine of Dunfermline

SCOTT, Ebenezer Erskine
The Erskine-Halcro genealogy: the ancestors and
descendants of Henry Erskine, minister of
Chirnside, his wife, Margaret Halcro of Orkney,
and their sons, Ebenezer and Ralph Erskine.
London, 1890.
ED/N-1 (A.38.d) QZ/P40 SA/U-1 ED/N-2
QZ/P16

— — 2nd ed. Edinburgh, 1895.
ED/N-1 (A.124.d) QZ/Q17 QZ/P14 ED/N-2
QZ/P28 QZ/P11 QZ/P40 SA/U-1 QZ/P22
GL/U-1 QZ/P-6 QZ/P16 QZ/P99

Erskine, Lord Garioch *see* **Garioch,** Earldom of

Erskine, Earl of Kellie *see* **Kellie,** Earldom of

Erskine of Linlathen

HENDERSON, Henry Frank Hornby
Erskine of Linlathen. Edinburgh, 1899.
ED/N-1 (S.147.g) QZ/P28

Erskine, Earl of Mar *see* **Mar,** Earldom of

Erskine of Pittodrie

ERSKINE, Henry William Knight
Royal descent of Henry William Knight Erskine, of
Pittodrie, co. Aberdeen ... from Alfred the Great,
King of England. [N.p., n.d.]
QZ/P99

Eunson

EUNSON, Jerry
A pioneer of the fishing industry: William Strong
Eunson of Fair Isle, "Old Bill" of Aberdeen. [With a
genealogical table.] [Glasgow], 1959.
ED/N-1 (NF.1322.c.4)

Ewart

[PAMPHLETS and miscellaneous material.]
QZ/P10 (Unconfirmed location)

Ewen *see* **MacEwen**

Ewing

EWING, Elbert W. R.
Clan Ewing of Scotland: early history and
contributions to America. Ballston, Va., 1922.
ED/N-1 (Mf.52(5))

EWING, Presley K. *and* EWING, M. A.
The Ewing genealogy with cognate branches.
Houston, [1919].
ED/N-1 (NF.1373.a.13)

Faed

McKERROW, Mary
The Faeds: a biography. Edinburgh, 1982.
ED/N-1 (H8.82.329) QZ/P10

Fairlie

FAIRLIE family: genealogical material. [N.d.]
QZ/P99

MARSHALL, G. F. L.
The Muir book. [N.p.], 1930.
ED/N-2

Fairrie

FAIRRIE, Geoffrey
The sugar refining families of Great Britain. [With
genealogical tables.] London, 1951.
ED/N-1 (NE.63.b.3)

Fairweather

FAIRWEATHER, Alexander
Memorandum regarding the Fairweathers of
Menmuir parish, Forfarshire, and others of the
surname. London, 1898.
ED/N-1 (A.113.e) AD/U-1 QZ/P99

HALIBURTON, Gordon
The descendants of David Fairweather of West
River and River John, Pictou County. (In *Nova
Scotia Historical Quarterly*, vol.9, no.4, December
1979, pp.363-77.)
ED/N-1 (NB.114)

Falconer

FALCONER, Thomas
An account of the family of Dalmahoy of that ilk
and of the family of Falconer. London, [n.d.].
ED/N-2 QZ/L37

—[Miscellaneous items concerning the family of
Falconer. 1870?]
ED/S10

[PAMPHLET relating to Colquhouns and their
connection with the Falconers.] Bath, [185-?].
QZ/L37

Fall

FALL, Freda *and* FALL, Geoffrey
In search of a family called Fall. [Boston Spa, 1975.]
ED/N-1 (6.2767) ED/N-2

GRAY, William Forbes
The Falls of Dunbar. Haddington, [1938].
QZ/P99

— The Falls of Dunbar: a notable Scots family. (In
Transactions of the East Lothian Antiquarian Society,
vol. iii, 1938, pp.120-41.)
ED/N-1 (Hist.S.91.E)

Farmer

The FARMERS: an East Fife agricultural family.
[N.p.], 1973.
QZ/L37

Farquhar

LESLIE,
A family history: [a short account of the families of
Brodie, Dunbar, Ogilvie . . . and Farquhar].
[Brighton, 1891?]
ED/N-1 (6.2484)

Farquhar in New Zealand

FARQUHAR, I. J.
Highcliff pioneers, George and Isabella Farquhar: a
typescript relating to the descendants of George
Farquhar born in Alford, Aberdeenshire, in 1849.
[New Zealand, 1970?]
QZ/P22

Farquharson

DONALD Farquharson of Castleton, etc. Founder of
the Clan Farquharson. (MS. article and cuttings
from *Scottish Notes & Queries* relative to the Clan
Farquharson.)
ED/N-2 QZ/P40

FARQUHARSON, Francis
Case of Mr. John Farquharson, the only surviving
son of the late Francis Farquharson, Esq., of Finzean.
Glasgow, 1819.
ED/N-2 QZ/P40

MACKINTOSH, A. M.
Farquharson genealogies from the Brouch dearg
MSS. of 1773. Nairn, 1913-18. 3v.
ED/N-1 (S.120.h) SA/U-1 QZ/P22 QZ/P40
AD/U-1 QZ/L37 QZ/P99

MEACHER, A. J.
History of the lands of Kinloch. Edinburgh, 1956.
ED/N-1 (NE.6.a.1) QZ/P18

MICHIE, John Grant
Records of Invercauld, 1547-1828. Aberdeen, 1901.
(New Spalding Club, 23.)
ED/N-1 (New Spald.Club.23) QZ/P22
DN/U-1 GL/U-1 ED/N-2 QZ/P40 QZ/P99

Farquharson of Invercauld

['GENEALOGICAL account of the Farquharsons of
Invercauld'. 1833.]
ED/N-1 (MS.9854, ff.115-21)

Fasken

FASKEN, William Henry
The family of Fasken. Stroud, 1931.
ED/N-1 (S.122.d) QZ/L37 QZ/P50 ED/U-1
QZ/P99

Fea

FEA, Peggy
An Orkney family saga, or history does not repeat
itself. [N.p., 1970?]
ED/N-1 (6.2848)

Fea of Clestrain

FEA, Allan
The real Captain Cleveland. London, 1912.
ED/N-1 (S.164.a)

MARWICK, Hugh
The Feas of Clestran. (In *Proceedings of the Orkney
Antiquarian Society*, vol.11, 1933, pp.31-43.)
ED/N-1 (R.250.a)

Fedderet

YOUNG, Robert
Notes on Burghead, ancient and modern; with an
appendix containing notices of families connected
with the place. Elgin, 1867.
ED/N-1 (Hall.197.a)

Fenton of Baikie

OSLER, James Couper
Osler tree: [chart pedigree], with some supplementary notes on . . . Fentons . . . [Dundee], 1924.
ED/N-2 QZ/L37

THOMSON, David Couper
Some supplemental notes on Oslers . . . [Dundee], 1924.
ED/N-1 (HP1.77.4104)

Fergus *see* **Fergusson**

Ferguson *see* **Fergusson**

Fergusson

COOPER, D. Aldred
[Ferguson family tree showing the descendants of Adam Ferguson to 1956.] 1956. (*MS.*)
QZ/P22

—MacGregor, Fergusson pedigree. [N.p., n.d.].
ED/N-2

The FERGUSON family and Inverurie. (In *The Royal burgh of Inverurie in the Coronation year*. 1902.)
QZ/P22

FERGUSON, James
The clan and name of Ferguson: an address delivered 14 April, 1892. Glasgow, 1892.
ED/N-1 (A.124.c) QZ/P30 QZ/P22 QZ/L37
QZ/P99

—History of the Ferguson family in Scotland. [N.p.], 1905.
QZ/P26

FERGUSON, James *and* FERGUSSON, Robert Menzies
Records of the clan and name of Fergusson, Ferguson and Fergus. (And Supplement.) Edinburgh, 1895, 99. 2v.
ED/N-1 (A.124.c) QZ/P22 QZ/P40 QZ/P14
SA/U-1 AD/U-1 GL/U-1 QZ/L37 QZ/P99

FERGUSSON, Sir James
The Fergussons: their lowland and highland branches. Edinburgh, 1956.
ED/N-1 (Gen.8) QZ/Q17 QZ/P53 QZ/P14
QZ/P27 QZ/P56 ED/N-2 QZ/P40 QZ/P11
QZ/L37 SA/U-1 QZ/Q88 QZ/P49 ED/U-1
QZ/P99

— — Edinburgh, [1973].
ED/N-2

GENEALOGICAL memoranda relating to the families of Fergusson and Colyer-Fergusson. [N.p.], 1897.
ED/N-1 (R.172.c)

MACDOWALL, John Kevan
Carrick Gallovidian: a historical survey . . . with genealogical charts and notes. Ayr, 1947.
ED/N-1 (R.241.d)

Fergusson of Badifurrow

FORBES, Alexander
Memorials of the family of Forbes of Forbesfield. [With notes on connected . . . Fergusons.] Aberdeen, 1905.
ED/N-1 (S.120.c) QZ/P22 QZ/P30 SA/U-1
GL/U-1 QZ/P99

Fergusson of Dunfallandy

[PEDIGREE showing the connection with the Robertsons of Struan and Stewarts of Garth.] (*MS.*)
QZ/P22

Fergusson of Kilkerran *see also* **Glencairn,** Earldom of

Fergusson of Kilkerran

DEMPSTER, George
Letters of George Dempster to Sir Adam Fergusson, 1756-1813, with some account of his life. [With genealogical tables.] London, 1934.
ED/N-1 (Hist.S.115.D)

FERGUSSON, Sir James
Lowland lairds. London, 1949.
ED/N-1 (R.232.d) ED/N-2 QZ/P14 QZ/P49
ED/U-1

ROBERTSON, William
Ayrshire, its history and historic families. Kilmarnock, 1908. 2v.
ED/N-1 (Hist.S.91.A)

Fergusson of Kinmundy

The FERGUSONS of Kinmundy, and their kinsfolk. [N.d.] 3v. (*MS.*)
QZ/P99

Fergusson of Pitfour

[COPIES of Pitfour papers, transcribed by James and William Ferguson of Kinmundy, 31 December, 1896.] (*MS.*)
QZ/P99

Fernie

PATERSON, James
Scottish surnames: a contribution to genealogy.
Edinburgh, 1866.
ED/N-1 (K.115.a) QZ/P28 QZ/P22 DN/U-1

Ferrier

GENEALOGY of the Ferriers of Kirklands. [N.p., n.d.]
QZ/P-6 SA/U-1

Fife, Duke of see Duff, Duke of Fife

Fife, Earldom of

WOOD, William
A short account of the Earls of Fife. [Edinburgh?],
1896.
ED/N-1 (5.5691(6)) QZ/Z17 AD/U-1

Findlater

FINDLATER, W.
Genealogical tree of Findlater family. Dublin, 1921.
AD/U-1 QZ/P99

MAIDMENT, James
Genealogical fragments. Berwick, 1855.
ED/N-1 (Y.59.f.2;Ry.II.e.51(1)) GL/U-1 QZ/P40
QZ/P99

Findlater, Earl of see Ogilvy, Earl of Findlater

Findlay

EAST, Sir Ronald
The Kiel family and related Scottish pioneers:
Findlays, Hossacks, Gilberts, Camerons, Stewarts,
McAlpins, McCallums, McDonalds. [Victoria,
1974.] (*A Family Who's Who*, vol.2.)
ED/N-1 (NE.26.d.3) ED/N-2 GL/U-1
QZ/P50

Findlay of Boturich

FINDLAY, James
A copy of most of the "Red Book"; with 1966
Findlay tree appended. [N.p., n.d.]
QZ/L37

Findlay of Coltfield

MEMORANDUM of the family of the Findlays of
Coltfield, in the parish of West Alves, co. Elgin,
Scotland, extracted from the parish register prior to
the year 1800. [N.p.], 1874.
QZ/P99

Findlay in Pretoria, South Africa

FINDLAY, Joan
The Findlay letters, 1806-1807. [With a genealogical
table.] Pretoria, 1954.
ED/N-1 (NE.835.c.5)

Finlay

JAMES Finlay & Company Limited, manufacturers
and East India merchants, 1750-1950. Glasgow,
1951.
ED/N-1 (NF.1169.a.5) QZ/Q88

Finlayson of Aucorn

HALLIDAY, Clarence
The Aucorn Finlaysons in Canada. [Toronto?],
1973.
ED/N-1 (6.2389)

Fitz-Gerald

MACKENZIE, George
Proposals for printing the genealogical history of
the Fitz-Geralds and Mackenzies. [26 October
1725.] [N.p., 1925.]
ED/N-1 (1.5(49))

Fitz-Simon see Fraser

Fitzwalter,

Scotland's lost royal line: the descendants of Duncan
II. (Reprinted from *Dumfries & Galloway Standard*,
20 February, 23 March 1957.) Dumfries, 1957.
ED/N-1 (1955.6)

Fleming

FLEMING, John Arnold
Flemish influence in Britain. Glasgow, 1930. 2v.
ED/N-1 (R.18.b) QZ/P34 QZ/P26 ED/N-2
QZ/Q76 QZ/P49 QZ/Q76

HUNTER, William
Biggar and the house of Fleming. Biggar, 1862.
QZ/P11 GL/U-1 ED/U-1 QZ/L37 QZ/P99

— — 2nd ed. Edinburgh, 1867.
ED/N-1 (A.118.c.3) QZ/P53 ED/N-2 QZ/P15
QZ/P11 QZ/P40 QZ/P22 GL/U-1 QZ/P-6
QZ/L37 QZ/Q76 QZ/Q91 QZ/Q71
QZ/P99

TOD, Donald A.
The Flemings of Athol and Glen Shee, 1500-1800.
[N.p.], 1927. (*Typescript*)
DN/U-1

Fleming in U.S.A.
UHRBROCK, Richard S.
Flemings of Fleming, Ohio, U.S.A. (In *Scottish Genealogist*, vol. xxi, no.1, March 1974, pp.1-6.)
ED/N-1 (Gen.7)

Fleming, Earl of Wigtown
GRANT, Francis James
Charter chest of the Earldom of Wigtown, 1214-1681. Edinburgh, 1910. (Scottish Record Soc., 36.)
ED/N-1 (Ref.55) QZ/P-6 ED/N-2 DN/U-1 QZ/P14

WIGTOWNSHIRE charters; edited by R. C. Reid. Edinburgh, 1960. (Scottish History Society Publications, 3rd series, vol.51.)
ED/N-1 (Ref.54)

Fletcher of Auchallader
FLETCHER, John
The Fletchers of Auchallader. (Reprinted from the *Celtic Monthly*, May 1916.) [Stirling, 1917.]
ED/N-1 (1917.1) QZ/P14

Fletcher of Glenorchy
MASON, Margaret F. P.
An ancient Scottish clan: the Fletchers of Glenorchy. Wimborne, 1973.
ED/N-1 (1973.256) SA/U-1 QZ/P40 (I) DN/U-1 QZ/P27 QZ/P26 QZ/P49 QZ/P99

Fletcher of Saltoun
[GENEALOGICAL material concerning the Fletcher family.]
ED/N-1 (MS.17858-60)

RECOLLECTIONS respecting the family of the Fletchers of Salton. Edinburgh, 1803.
ED/N-1 (6.1081(14)) ED/N-2 QZ/L37 QZ/P99

Forbes
FORBES, A.
Who was Kenneth, first King of Scots? Aberdeen, 1911.
ED/N-1 (1937.8) QZ/P22 QZ/P30 QZ/P99

LUMSDEN, Matthew
Genealogy of the family of Forbes . . . 1580; edited by W. Forbes. Inverness, 1819.
ED/N-1 (2.371) SA/U-1 QZ/P30 QZ/P22 QZ/P40 GL/U-1 QZ/L37 QZ/P50 QZ/P99

— — Reprinted. Inverness, 1883.
ED/N-1 (A.114.d) QZ/P26 QZ/P99

['PAPERS concerning the genealogy of the family of Forbes'. 17--.]
ED/N-1 (Adv.MS.20.1.7,ff.82-94)

TAYLER, Alistair *and* TAYLER, Henrietta
The House of Forbes. Aberdeen, 1937. (Third Spalding Club.)
ED/N-1 (Third.Spald.Club.7) QZ/P30 QZ/P27 ED/N-2 QZ/P22 QZ/P40 QZ/P28 DN/U-1 GL/U-1 QZ/P14 ST/U-1 QZ/P50 QZ/P13 ED/U-1 QZ/P99

WOOD, James Alexander Fraser
The Forbes. (In *Scotland's Magazine*, vol.65, no.7, July 1969, pp. 16-20.)
ED/N-1 (Y.31)

Forbes of Blackton
FERGUSON, James
Two Scottish soldiers of fortune . . . and a Jacobite laird and his forbears. Aberdeen, 1888.
ED/N-1 (Hall.244.a) ED/N-2 QZ/P22 QZ/P99

MILNE, J.
Forbeses of Blackton. (In *Transactions of the Banffshire Field Club*, 6 October 1886, pp.87-9.)
ED/N-1 (NE.3.g.1)

Forbes of Corse and Craigievar
FORBES, John
Memoirs of the Earls of Granard. London, 1868.
SA/U-1 QZ/P99

Forbes of Echt
BROWNE, George Forrest
Echt-Forbes family charters, 1345-1727: records of the Forest of Birse. Edinburgh, 1923.
ED/N-1 (S.122.a) QZ/P30 ED/N-2 QZ/P22 SA/U-1 QZ/P-1 ED/U-1 QZ/P99

Forbes of Forbesfield
FORBES, Alexander
Memorials of the family of Forbes of Forbesfield. [With notes on connected Morgans, Duncans and Fergusons.] Aberdeen, 1905.
ED/N-1 (S.120.c) QZ/P30 ED/N-2 QZ/P22 SA/U-1 GL/U-1 QZ/L37 QZ/P99

Forbes of Monymusk

FORBES, Louisa Lillias
Circular genealogical table of the Forbes family of Monymusk and Pitsligo, 1460-1880. [N.p.], 1880.
ED/N-1 (S.120.a) QZ/P22 SA/U-1 QZ/L37
QZ/P99

FORBES, Sir William
Narrative of the last sickness and death of Dame Christian Forbes. Edinburgh, 1875.
ED/N-1 (H.22.b) QZ/P99

['GENEALOGICAL notes concerning the Forbes family of Monymusk'. 17--.]
ED/N-1 (Adv.MS.19.1.21,ff.185-8)

Forbes of Pitsligo

FORBES, John Stuart
In the House of Lords: the case of Sir John Stuart Forbes of Pitsligo and Fettercairn, baronet, claiming the title and dignity of Baron Forbes of Pitsligo. [London, n.d.]
ED/N-1 (Yule.162(10))

[NOTES on the collateral families of Forbes of Pitsligo.] 1938. (*Typescript*)
QZ/P22

Forbes of Schivas

BURR, Helen Alexander
Forbes family of Schivas. [1931?] (*Typescript*)
QZ/L37

Forbes of Skellater

NEIL, James
Ian Roy of Skellater, a Scottish soldier of fortune. Aberdeen, 1902.
ED/N-1 (S.150.g) QZ/L37 ED/N-2

Forbes of Tolquhoun

DAVIDSON, J.
The genealogy of the House of Tolquhon. Aberdeen, 1839.
ED/N-1 (1938.19(6)) ED/N-2 QZ/L37
QZ/P99

Forbes in U.S.A.

FORBES, Arthur Carroll
The descendants of William Forbes: a genealogical and biographical history of the branch of the family of Forbes as descended from Wm. Forbes of Aberdeen, Scotland. [N.p.], 1955.
ED/N-1 (H3.79.984) QZ/P22

Forbes of Watertoun

FORBES, John
Memoranda relating to the family of Forbes of Waterton. Aberdeen, 1857.
ED/N-1 (R.172.b) QZ/P30 GL/U-1 QZ/P22
SA/U-1 QZ/P99 ED/S10

Forbes-Leith

STIRLING, Anna Maria D. W. Pickering
Fyvie Castle: its lairds and their times. London, 1928.
ED/N-1 (R.247.e) ED/N-2 QZ/P30 QZ/P49

Forbes-Mitchell

MITCHELL, William Forbes
Genealogy of the family of William Forbes-Mitchell. [Seepore, 1881.]
ED/N-1 (R.272.g)

Forbes-Morison

MORISON, Mary Anne Cushnie
An outline of the genealogy of the House of Forbes-Morison. 1869. (*MS.*)
ED/M-1

Forbes-Robertson of Hazlehead

BULLOCH, John Malcolm
The Forbes-Robertson family of Hazlehead. Aberdeen, 1927. (Extract from *The Tiger and the Sphinx: the journal of the Gordon Highlanders*.)
QZ/P22

—The picturesque ancestry of Sir Johnston Forbes-Robertson. Aberdeen, 1926.
ED/N-1 (1926.2) QZ/P22 ED/U-1

Fordyce

FORDYCE, Alexander Dingwall
Epitome, or who, what, where, when respecting the family of Dingwall-Fordyce and connections, 1655-1884. [Fergus, Ont.], 1884.
ED/N-1 (5.3251(22)) AD/U-1 QZ/P99

—Family record of the name of Dingwall-Fordyce, including relatives of both names and connections. Toronto, 1885,88. 2v.
ED/N-1 (Y.59.d.21) QZ/P30 GL/U-1 QZ/P22
SA/U-1 ED/N-2 QZ/P99

FORDYCE, Andrew G. *and* WILSON, Laura Elizabeth
The family tree of the Fordyces of Knightsmill in Drumblade and Comisty in Forgue, Aberdeenshire. [Orpington, 1977?]
ED/N-1 (P.r.2.c.6)

KEITH, Alexander
Provost George Fordyce and his family. (In
Aberdeen Chamber of Commerce Journal, spring 1957,
pp.120-2.)
ED/N-1 (U.450) QZ/P22

Fordyce of Uyeasound, Shetland
CLARK, John
Genealogy, records and intermarriages of the
Fordyce, Bruce and Clark families at Uyeasound,
Unst, Shetland. 2nd ed. Falkirk, 1902.
ED/N-1 (R.172.h; H2.80.1076) ED/N-2 QZ/P99
—Index to Fordyce, Bruce and Clark families at
Uyeasound, Unst, Shetland, 2nd ed. Prepared with
some additional information from the Unst
marriage registers 1797-1863 or concerning the
Sandison family by Alexander Sandison.
Cambridge, 1955.
ED/N-1 (NE.25.f.4) QZ/P22

Forrest
CARVEL, John L.
One hundred years in timber: the history of the city
saw mills, 1849-1949. [With a genealogical table.]
Glasgow, 1950.
ED/N-1 (R.154.c)

Forrest of Gimmers Mills
MONTGOMERIE, A.
The Forrests of Gimmers Mills and their charter
chest. (In *Transactions of the East Lothian Antiquarian
Society*, vol.v, 1952, pp.39-49.)
ED/N-1 (Hist.S.91.E)

Forrester
BULLOCH, John Malcolm
The House of Gordon . . .: genealogical tree; with
the descendants of James Hutchison and Mary
Forrester added and brought down to date.
Peterhead, 1908.
ED/N-1 (5.174)

FORRESTER, Colin D. I. G.
Le Forestier in Normandy: cadets of the Forresters
of Corstorphine. (In *Scottish Genealogist*, vol.xxx,
no.3, September 1983, pp.83-8.)
ED/N-1 (Gen.7)
—The Forresters of Strathendry and Gibliston. (In
Scottish Genealogist, vol.xxx, no.2, June 1983,
pp.37-46.)
ED/N-1 (Gen.7)

Forrester of Corstorphine
PEDIGREE of Thomson and Forrester of
Corstorphine. [N.p., 1926.]
ED/N-1 (Portfolio II; J.138.c)

POTTINGER, Don
The families of Forrester and Thomson of
Corstorphine, showing the succession of the Lords
Forrester of Corstorphine. 1961. (*Xerox-copy*)
QZ/P99

WOOD, John Philp
Manuscript draft for a history of Corstorphine
parish. [Edinburgh], 1955.
ED/N-1 (NE.11.a.3)

Forrester of Denovan
GIBSON, John C.
Lands and lairds of Larbert and Dunipace parishes.
[With genealogical tables.] Glasgow, 1908.
ED/N-1 (R.243.c) QZ/P14

Forrester of Logie
FERGUSSON, Robert Menzies
Logie: a parish history. Vol.2: Lands and
landowners. Paisley, 1905.
ED/N-1 (R.243.a) QZ/P14

Forrester of Torwood
FERGUSSON, Sir James
Lowland lairds. London, 1949.
ED/N-1 (R.232.d) ED/N-2 QZ/P14 QZ/P49
ED/U-1
GIBSON, John C.
Lands and lairds of Larbert and Dunipace parishes.
[With genealogical tables.] Glasgow, 1908.
ED/N-1 (R.243.c) QZ/P14

Forsyth
FORSYTH, Alistair Charles William
Short notices of the family of Forsyth. Arbroath,
1977.
ED/N-1 (HP2.78.1724)

FORSYTH, W. H.
Forsythiana. [1969?]
QZ/P99

Forsyth of Dykes
FORSYTHS of Dykes. (In *Clan Forsyth Society
Newsletter*, no.2, February 1979.)
ED/N-1 (P.med.31)

Forsyth of Failzerton
FORSYTH, W. H.
Forsyths of Failzerton. [1969?]
QZ/P99

Forsyth of Nydie
The FORSYTHS of Nydie. (In *Clan Forsyth Society Newsletter*, no.1, January 1978.)
ED/N-1 (P.med.31)

Foster
FOSTER, William Edward
The royal descent of the Fosters of Moulton and the Mathesons of Shinness and Lochalsh. [N.p.], 1912.
ED/N-2

Foulis
FOULIS, William Ainslie
Foulis family: miscellaneous papers. [N.d.] (*MS. and typescript*)
QZ/P99

—Genealogical chart of the families of Foulis. [N.d.] (*MS.*)
QZ/P99

Foulis of Dunipace
GIBSON, John C.
The lands and lairds of Dunipace. [With genealogical tables.] Stirling, 1903.
ED/N-1 (R.248.f)   QZ/P14   QZ/P99

—Lands and lairds of Larbert and Dunipace parishes. [With genealogical tables.] Glasgow, 1908.
ED/N-1 (R.243.c)   QZ/P14

Foulis of Ravelston
ANSWERS for His Majesty's Advocate, on behalf of His Majesty to the claim of John Foulis, brother-german to the deceast Sir Archibald Primrose of Dunipace. (3d January, 1751.) [Edinburgh, 1751.]
ED/N-1 (Ry.II.b.19(61))

FOULIS, John
Unto the . . . Lords of Council and Session, the claim of John Foulis, brother-german to the deceast Sir Archibald Primrose of Dunipace. (January 4, 1751.) [Edinburgh, 1751.]
ED/N-1 (Ry.II.b.19(60))

Foullarton *see also* **Fullarton**

Foullarton
LOW, James G.
Galraw: the home of the Foullartons. Montrose, 1937.
ED/N-1 (HP1.82.3277)   QZ/P28

Franceis *see* **French**

Francis *see* **French**

Francus *see* **French**

Fraser
DAVIDSON, Arthur Aitken
A highland family. London, 1924.
AD/U-1

FRASER, Alexander
The Clan Fraser in Canada: a souvenir of the first annual gathering of the clan in Toronto in 1894. Toronto, 1895.
ED/N-1 (NF.1372.d.11)   QZ/P40   GL/U-1

FRASER, James
Chronicles of the Frasers: the Wardlaw MS. . . . or the true genealogy of the Frasers. Edinburgh, 1905. (Scottish History Soc., vol.47.)
ED/N-1 (Ref.54)   QZ/P-6   ED/N-2   QZ/P40
QZ/P22   DN/U-1   GL/U-1   QZ/P13
QZ/P99

FRASER, R. J.
As others see us: Scots of the Seaway Valley. 1959.
QZ/P99

[The HISTORY of the Fraser family. 1749.]
ED/N-1 (Adv.MS.36.6.13)

KELLY, Bernard W.
The fighting Frasers of the Forty-Five and Quebec. London, 1908.
ED/N-1 (1924.6)   AD/U-1   QZ/P99

MACKENZIE, Alexander
History of the Frasers of Lovat, with genealogies of the principal families of the name, to which is added those of Dunballoch and Phopachy. Inverness, 1896.
ED/N-1 (Gen.8.f)   QZ/P27   ED/N-2   QZ/P30
QZ/P22   QZ/P40   SA/U-1   AD/U-1
DN/U-1   GL/U-1   QZ/P41   ED/U-1   QZ/P99

MACLAREN, Moray David Shaw
The House of Neill, 1749-1949. [With a genealogical table.] Edinburgh, 1949.
ED/N-1 (R.251.a)

MAXWELL, Alice Constable
Avenue of ancestors. [With genealogical tables.]
Dumfries, 1965.
ED/N-1 (NE.25.e.1) ED/N-2 QZ/P-1 QZ/P14
QZ/P34 QZ/P99

SIMSON, Archibald
Annals of such patriots of the distinguished family
of Fraser, Frysell, Sim-son or Fitz-Simon, as have
signalised themselves in the public service of
Scotland. Edinburgh, 1795.
ED/N-1 (A.114.d.8;6.769(11)) QZ/P40 QZ/P99

— — 2nd ed., edited by A. Fraser of Lovat.
Edinburgh, 1805.
QZ/P30 QZ/P11 QZ/P40 SA/U-1 QZ/L37

[WARDLAW MS. history of the Fraser family. 17--.]
ED/N-1 (MS.3658)

WARRAND, Duncan
Some Fraser pedigrees. Inverness, 1934.
ED/N-1 (Gen.8.f) ED/N-2 GL/U-1 QZ/P22
QZ/P40 QZ/L37 SA/U-1 ED/U-1 QZ/P99

Fraser of Ardachy
CAMBPELL, Thomas Fraser
The Frasers of Ardachy. [N.d.] (*Typescript*)
ED/N-1 (6.202) QZ/P40 QZ/L37

Fraser of Balnain
['GENEALOGICAL account of the Frasers of Balnain'.
1833.]
ED/N-1 (MS.9854,ff.141-7.)

Fraser of Durris
FRASER, Sir William
Memorial of the family of the Frasers [of Durris].
[Edinburgh, 1904.]
AD/U-1 QZ/P30

Fraser of Fairfield
FRASER-MACKINTOSH, Charles
The Frasers of Fairfield, Inverness. (In *Celtic
Magazine*, vol.x, 1885, pp.336-40.)
ED/N-1 (J.183) QZ/Q41

Fraser of Foyers
FRASER-MACKINTOSH, Charles
The Frasers of Foyers "Sliochd Huistean
Fhrangaich". (In *Transactions of the Gaelic Society of
Inverness*, vol.xviii, 1891-2, pp. 17-32.)
ED/N-1 (NF.1559) QZ/Q41

Fraser of Fraserfield
SOME account of the family of Fraserfield or
Balgownie. [N.p., 1870?]
AD/U-1

Fraser in Glengarry, Canada
FRASER, Robert James
The Frasers of Glengarry. (In *Glengarry News*,
19 July 1956.)
QZ/P22

Fraser of Guisachan
FRASER-MACKINTOSH, Charles
The Frasers of Guisachan (Culbokie), styled
"MacHuistean". (In *Transactions of the Gaelic Society
of Inverness*, vol.xviii, 1891-2, pp.309-25.)
ED/N-1 (NF.1559) QZ/Q41

GENEALOGY of Fraser of Guisachan and Culbockie.
1867. (*MS.*)
QZ/P40

Fraser in Ireland
FRASER, Thomas
Recollections with reflections: a memoir of a
Scottish soldier family in Ireland from the
seventeenth century. [With a genealogical table.]
Edinburgh, 1914.
ED/N-1 (S.168.a)

Fraser of Ledeclune and Morar
PEDIGREE of the family of Fraser of Ledeclune and
Morar, Baronet. [N.p., n.d.]
ED/N-1 (J.132.a)

Fraser, Lord Fraser of Lovat *see* Lovat, Lord Fraser of

Fraser of Lovat
ANDERSON, John
Historical account of the family of Frisel or Fraser,
particularly Fraser of Lovat. Edinburgh, 1825.
ED/N-1 (A.114.b) QZ/P-7 QZ/P27 QZ/P30
QZ/P22 QZ/P40 AD/U-1 SA/U-1 GL/U-1
QZ/L37 QZ/P99

FRASER, Charles Ian
The Clan Fraser of Lovat: a highland response to a
lowland stimulus. Edinburgh, 1952.
ED/N-1 (Gen.7) QZ/P14 QZ/P27 QZ/P26
QZ/P20 QZ/P40 QZ/P22 QZ/P11 QZ/L37
QZ/P-6 SA/U-1 QZ/P30 QZ/P49 ED/U-1
QZ/P99

— — 2nd ed. [N.p.], 1966.
ED/N-1 (Gen.7)

FRASER, Hugh
Historical account of the family of Fraser or Frizel
of Lovat. Inverness, 1850. 2v. (*MSS.*)
QZ/P40

GENEALOGICAL tree of the family of Lovat,
1416-1823. 1867. (*MS.*)
QZ/P40

HISTORY of the most ancient, noble and illustrious
family of Fraser, particularly of the family of Lovat.
[1749.] 3v. (*MSS.*)
QZ/P40

MACDONALD, Archibald
The old Lords of Lovat and Beaufort. Inverness,
1934.
ED/N-1 (R.172.d) QZ/P40 (D) QZ/P30
QZ/P22 SA/U-1 DN/U-1 QZ/L37 QZ/P99

[PAMPHLETS, feu charters, circular letters, public
notices and other printed papers relating to the
family of Fraser of Lovat.] [N.p.,1792-1814.]
ED/N-1 (S.273.b)

Fraser of Philorth
SALTOUN, Alexander Fraser, *17th Baron*
The Frasers of Philorth. Edinburgh, 1879. 3v.
ED/N-1 (Gen.8.f) QZ/P30 QZ/P56 ED/N-2
QZ/P22 QZ/P40 SA/U-1 AD/U-1 GL/U-1
QZ/L37 ED/U-1 QZ/P99

SHORT genealogical account of Fraser of Philorth
or Saltoun. 1867. (*MS.*)
QZ/P40

Fraser of Powis
POWIS papers, 1507-1894; edited by John George
Burnett. Aberdeen, 1951. (3rd Spalding Club).
ED/N-1 (3rd.Spald.Club.16) QZ/P14 QZ/P99
QZ/P28

Fraser of Strichen
MAXWELL, Alice Constable
Avenue of ancestors. [With genealogical tables.]
Dumfries, 1965.
ED/N-1 (NE.25.e.1) QZ/P34 QZ/P14
ED/N-2

Fraser of Touch
GIBSON, John C.
The lands and lairds of Touch. Stirling, 1929.
ED/N-1 (1929.5) QZ/P14 QZ/P99

French
FRENCH, A. D. Weld
Index armorial to an emblazoned MS. of the
surname of French, Franc, Francois, Frenc, and
others, both British and foreign. Boston, Mass.,
1892.
ED/N-1 (E.116.b) QZ/P11

—Notes on the surnames of Francus, Franceis,
French, etc. in Scotland, with an account of the
Frenches of Thorndykes. Boston, Mass., 1893.
ED/N-1 (A.38.d) QZ/P11 QZ/P14 SA/U-1
QZ/P22 GL/U-1 QZ/L37 QZ/P99

Frendraught, Lord
ABSTRACT of the evidence on the claim of David
Maitland Makgill of Rankeilour to be served heir of
line in general of James Crichton, first Viscount
Frendraught. [1839.]
ED/N-2 QZ/L37

Freskyn, Earls of Sutherland *see also* **Sutherland,**
Earldom of

Freskyn, Earls of Sutherland
GRAY, James
Sutherland and Caithness in saga-time: or, the Jarls
and the Freskyns. Edinburgh, 1922.
ED/N-1 (R.250.e)

Frisel *see* **Fraser** of Lovat

Frysell *see* **Fraser**

Fullarton *see also* **Foullarton**

Fullarton *see also* **Spynie,** Lord Spynie

Fullarton
CAMERON, Lolita Jean
The broad canvas: a history of my mother's family.
Chesham, 1974.
ED/N-1 (6.2749) QZ/P-7

Fullarton of Kirrilaw
GENEALOGICAL roll of Gavin Fullarton of Kirrilaw.
[N.p., n.d.]
QZ/P-6

Fulton of Lisburn
HOPE, Sir Theodore C.
Memoirs of the Fultons of Lisburn. [With
genealogical tables.] London, 1903.
ED/N-1 (R.172.b)

Fyfe

PATTERSON, Betty
Robert and Margaret (Fyfe) Pirie and their
descendants. [Madison, Wis., 1980.]
ED/N-1 (HP3.81.1551)

Fyvie, Lord *see* **Seton,** Lord Fyvie

Gade/Gadie *see* **Goudie**

Gair

GAYRE, George Robert *and* GAIR, R. L.
Gayre's book: being a history of the family of Gayre.
London, 1948-59. 4v.
ED/N-1 (R.272.a) QZ/L37 ED/U-1* QZ/P99

GAYRE, Robert
The House of Gayre and an account of Minard
Castle. Edinburgh, [197-].
ED/N-1 (HP2.80.2077)

— Who is who in the Clan Gayre? Edinburgh, 1962.
ED/N-1 (NE.25.b.21) ED/N-2 QZ/P22

Gairdner

BAILEY, William Henry
A chronicle of the family of Gairdner of Ayrshire,
Edinburgh and Glasgow, and their connections
from the 17th century. Taunton, 1947.
ED/N-1 (R.159.i) SA/U-1 AD/U-1 GL/U-1
QZ/P-1 QZ/P99

Galbraith

GALBRAITH, Edwin A. S.
Galbraith settlers in 19th century Ontario,
Canada. Weston, Ont., 1978.
ED/N-1 (HP4.80.134)

SMITH, John Guthrie
Strathendrick and its inhabitants. Glasgow, 1896.
ED/N-1 (A.58.a) ED/N-2

Galbreath

GALBREATH, Joseph William
Galbreath family genealogy. Fairfield, Ill., 1976.
ED/N-1 (HP3.78.1428)

Galloway

The GALLOWAYS of Lipnoch, Co. Perth and the
Galloways, Barons Dunkeld. [N.p., 1964?]
ED/N-1 (6.1413) QZ/P-6 QZ/P14 QZ/P18
QZ/P22 ED/N-2 QZ/P15 QZ/P28 ED/U-1
QZ/P26 QZ/P99

Galloway, Earl of *see* **Stewart,** Earl of Galloway

Garden

GARDEN, William
Notes with reference to a branch of the Garden
family. Edinburgh, 1887.
ED/N-1 (R.272.f) AD/U-1 QZ/P22

THORNTON-KEMSLEY, Colin
Bonnet lairds. Montrose, 1972.
ED/N-1 (NE.25.f.17) QZ/P22 ED/N-2
QZ/L37 QZ/P14 QZ/P56 QZ/P-1

Garden of Troup

TAYLER, Alistair N.
The Gardens of Troup. (In *Transactions of the
Banffshire Field Club*, 23 March 1937, pp.2-26.)
ED/N-1 (NE.3.g.1)

Gardner

MAIDMENT, James
Genealogical fragments relating to the families
of . . . Gardner. Berwick, 1855.
ED/N-1 (Y.52.f.2;Ry.II.e.51(1)) QZ/P40 GL/U-1
QZ/P99

Garioch, Earldom of

DAVIDSON, John
Inverurie and the earldom of the Garioch.
Edinburgh, 1878.
ED/N-1 (R.247.a) QZ/P27 ED/N-2

Garland in Fordoun

MAXWELL, A. S.
The descendants of Robert Garland and his son
John of Craighall of Criggie and Cairnton, parish
of Fordoun from the late 1600's to 1974. [N.p.,
1975.]
QZ/P22

Gaudie, Gawdie, Gawdy *see* **Goudie**

Gayre *see* **Gair**

Geddes

[GENEALOGICAL material concerning the Geddes
family. 18--, 19--.]
ED/N-1 (MS.10607)

GEDDES, Auckland Campbell Geddes, *1st Baron*
The forging of a family. London, 1952.
ED/N-1 (NF.1188.b.19) QZ/P30 ED/N-2
QZ/P22 QZ/P-6 QZ/P13 QZ/P49 ED/U-1
QZ/P99

Geddes of Glass

GEDDES, William Duguid
Memorials of John Geddes, 1797-1881. [With a genealogical table.] Banff, 1899.
ED/N-1 (R.183.b)

Geddes in Orkney

GEDDES, David
'David Geddes whom you pronounced dunce': typescript family history of the families of John Johnston of Stromness and Quebec, Dr. Andrew Crookshank of Aberdeen and David Geddes of Orkney. [N.p., 1970.]
QZ/P38 (Unconfirmed location)

Geddes in U.S.A.

STEVENS, John Grier
The descendants of John Grier, with histories of allied families. Baltimore, Md., 1964.
ED/N-1 (NF.1372.a.4)

Geddie

GEDDIE, Jack
Colfax: [history of the Geddie, McPhail and other families in the U.S.A.] [N.p.], 1963.
ED/N-1 (NF.1250.b.18)

—The families Geddie and McPhail. Fort Worth, Tex., 1959.
ED/N-1 (NE.25.d.2) ED/N-2 QZ/P50
QZ/P18 SA/U-1 QZ/P-1 QZ/P99 QZ/P16

Gemmell, Gemmill

GEMMILL, J. Leiper
Notes on the probable origin of the name Gemmell or Gemmill, with a genealogical account of the family of Gemmill of Raithmuir, Fenwick, from *c.* 1518. Glasgow, 1909.
ED/N-1 (S.120.d) SA/U-1 QZ/P-7 ED/U-1
QZ/P99

GEMMILL, John Alexander
Note on the probable origin of the Scottish surname of Gemmill or Gemmell, with a genealogical account of the family of Gemmill of Templehouse, Scotland. Montreal, 1898.
ED/N-1 (NE.25.a.14) QZ/P53 ED/N-2

— — Ottawa, 1901.
QZ/L37 QZ/P99

Gerard

HARROWER, Rachel Blanche
The Gerard family. (In *Aberdeen University Review*, vol.10, 1922/3, pp.114-29.)
ED/N-1 (Y.237)

— — (Reprinted from *Aberdeen University Review*, vol.10, 1922/3.)
ED/N-2 QZ/P22 QZ/P99

Gibb

RAE, Lettice Milne
The story of the Gibbs. [With a genealogical table.] Edinburgh, 1961.
ED/N-1 (NE.25.b.15) AD/U-1 QZ/P22
QZ/P99

TYTLER, Sarah
Three generations: the story of a middle-class Scottish family. London, 1911.
ED/N-1 (S.168.f) QZ/P18 QZ/P22 QZ/P-1
QZ/P99

Gibb of Aberdeen

KEITH, Alexander
Five generations of engineering Gibbs. (In *Aberdeen Chamber of Commerce Journal*, vol.40, no.1, autumn 1958, pp.234-7.)
ED/N-1 (U.450) QZ/P22

Gibb of Carriber

GIBB, Sir George Duncan
Life and times of Robert Gib, lord of Carriber ... with notices of his descendants. London, 1874. 2v.
ED/N-1 (YY.2/1) GL/U-1 QZ/L37 QZ/P-1
QZ/P99

Gibb of Falkland

GIBB, Sir George Duncan
Pedigree of J. R. Campbell and Sir G. D. Gibb. London, 1872.
ED/N-1 (5.14(3)) ED/N-2 QZ/P99

—Pedigree of the family of Gibb ... of Falkland. Guildford, 1874.
ED/N-1 (5.14(4)) SA/U-1 AD/U-1 GL/U-1
QZ/P99

Gibbon of Lonmay

GIBBON, Geoffrey
Gibbon of Lonmay: the descendants of Charles Gibbon, minister of Lonmay and his wife, Ann Duff. [N.p.], 1976. (*Typescript*)
QZ/P22

Gibson

['ACCOUNT of the Gibson family history'. 1811?]
ED/N-1 (Adv.MS.6.1.17,ff.44-52)

Gibson of Arbroath

CORMACK, Alexander A.
Arbroath Gibsons in Sweden: the romantic saga of a
Scandinavian family with its roots in Angus. (In
Arbroath Herald, Christmas 1950.)
QZ/P28

Gibson of Glencrosh

FALLOW, T. M.
Some notes on the family of Gibson of Glencrosh.
Dumfries, [1905].
ED/N-2

Gibson in Göteborg, Sweden

WILLIAM Gibson och hans barn. Göteborg, 1962.
QZ/P28

Gifford

CHARLES-EDWARDS, G.
The descent of James Gifford of West Linton,
sculptor, from John, the brother of James Gifford of
Sheriffhall, 1445. (In *Scottish Genealogist*, vol.xxvi,
no.4, December 1979, pp.112-20.)
ED/N-1 (Gen.7)

—The origin of the Gifford family in Scotland. (In
Scottish Genealogist, vol.xxvii, no.4, December
1980, pp.152-61.)
ED/N-1 (Gen.7)

Gifford of Busta, Shetland

GREIG, P. W.
Annals of a Shetland parish: Delting. Lerwick,
1892.
ED/N-1 (A.122.d)   QZ/P41   QZ/P-1

SCOTT, Francis
The true romance of Busta. Edinburgh, 1934.
ED/N-1 (5.556)   QZ/P41

Gilbert

EAST, Sir Ronald
The Kiel family and related Scottish pioneers:
Findlays, Hossacks, Gilberts, Camerons, Stewarts,
McAlpins, McCallums, McDonalds. [Victoria,
1974.] (*A Family Who's Who*, vol.2.)
ED/N-1 (NE.26.d.3)   ED/N-2   GL/U-1
QZ/P50

Gilchrist

CORMACK, Alexander Allan
A Scoto-Swedish study: the Rev. John Gilchrist . . .
his grandsons in Sweden. Peterculter, 1969.
ED/N-1 (1970.10)   QZ/P30   QZ/P28

Gilfillan

WOOD, Charles G.
John Alexander Gilfillan, 1793-1864. [Glasgow],
1980
ED/N-1 (HP4.82.716)

Gill

[The FAMILIES of Gill, etc. N.d.] (*MS.*)
QZ/P99

Gill of Blairythan and Savock

GILL, Andrew J. Mitchell
Gill of Blairythan and Savock. [N.p.], 1882.
QZ/P22   QZ/L37

Gillespie

JAMES, Henry E. M. *and* JAMES, William A.
Extracts from the pedigrees of James of Barrock
containing the descent of . . . Gillespie. Exeter,
1913.
ED/N-1 (NF.1373.e.5)

PRINDLE, Paul Wesley
Ancestry of Elizabeth Barrett Gillespie (Mrs
William Sperry Beinecke). [N.p.], 1976.
ED/N-1 (H4.77.780)

—Descendants of John and Mary Jane
(Cunningham) Gillespie. [N.p.], 1973.
ED/N-1 (H3.77.3012)

Gillespie of Wiston

BOOMHOUR, W. H.
A Gillespie family. (In *Clan Chattan: Journal of the
Clan Chattan Association*, vol.vii, no.2, 1978,
pp.79-82.)
ED/N-1 (Y.130)

Gilmore in U.S.A

GILMORE, Pascal Pearl
Gilmore ancestry, or the direct line of descent from
John Gilmore. [Bucksport, Ma., 1925.]
ED/N-1 (1929.8)

Gilmour

GILMOUR, Henry F.
Genealogical tables giving the descendants of John Gilmour of "Dockanyfauld", Gorbals, Glasgow, dating from 1737 to 1902. [N.p., n.d.]
QZ/P-1

HARVIE, Barry J.
The history and family tree of John Harvie, 1810-1889, and his wife, Margaret née Gilmour, 1820-1902, and their descendants. Adelaide, 1975.
QZ/P-7

IRELAND, Kingsley
For generations yet unborn: the Jamieson family 1747-1978, the history and family tree of Alexander Jamieson 1816-1912 and his wife Janet, née Gilmour, and their descendants. [Adelaide, 1978.]
ED/N-1 (H4.79.784) ED/N-2

JAMIESON, Alan
The Jamieson and Gilmour families in Scotland: supplement to "For generations yet unborn". [Angaston, South Australia?, 1982.]
ED/N-1 (H4.79.784)

Gladstain see also Gledstone

Gladstain

HAINING, James H.
The local Gladstains down to the present time. (In *Transactions of the Hawick Archaeological Society*, 1937, pp.34-42.)
ED/N-1 (P.220)

Gladstone

CHECKLAND, S. G.
The Gladstones: a family biography, 1764-1851. Cambridge, 1971.
ED/N-1 (NC.273.c.10) QZ/P34 SA/U-1
QZ/P99

MILLAR, Alexander Hastie
The Gladstones and their connection with Dundee. (Reprinted from *Dundee Advertiser*, 21 August 1890.)
QZ/P20 (Unconfirmed location)

Gladstone of Edinburgh see Gledstane of Edinburgh

Glaister

GLAISTER, John
The Glaisters of Scotland and Cumberland. (In *Transactions of the Cumberland and Westmoreland Antiquarian and Archaeological Society*, new series, vol.20, 1920, pp.188-231.)
ED/N-1 (U.408)

— — (Reprinted from *Transactions of the Cumberland and Westmoreland Antiquarian and Archaeological Society*, new series, vol.20, 1920.)
QZ/L37

Glas

GIBSON, John C.
The baronies and owners of Sauchie and Bannockburn. Stirling, 1934.
ED/N-1 (NE.25.f.24(1)) QZ/P14

Glasfurd

GLASFURD, Alec
The Glasfurd family, 1550-1972. Edinburgh, [1972].
ED/N-1 (1972.314) QZ/Q17 SA/U-1 AD/U-1

Glasgow, Earl of see Boyle of Kelburne, Earl of Glasgow

Glasgow of Kilbirnie

The GLASGOWS of Kilbirnie who have royal blood: a genealogical roll. [N.d.] (*MS.*)
QZ/P-6

Glassell

HAYDEN, Horace Edwin
Virginia genealogies: a genealogy of the Glassell family of Scotland and Virginia, also of the families of Ball . . . and others, of Virginia and Maryland. Baltimore, 1979.
ED/N-1 (H3.81.3660) ED/N-2 QZ/P-1

Gledstane of Edinburgh

NATIONAL TRUST FOR SCOTLAND
A companion to Gladstone's Land, Lawnmarket, Edinburgh. [With genealogical tables.] Edinburgh, [1979].
ED/N-1 (P.1a.2927)

Gledstane of Over Kelwood and Craigs

EDGAR, Robert
An introduction to the history of Dumfries. [With genealogical tables.] Dumfries, 1915.
ED/N-1 (R.241.b)

Gledstone

OLIVER,
The Gledstones and the siege of Coklaw. Edinburgh, 1878.
ED/N-1 (LC.748) ED/N-2 QZ/P11 AD/U-1
QZ/P-1 QZ/P99

OLIVER, James Rutherford
Border sketches, historical and biographical.
Hawick, 1904.
ED/N-1 (NE.15.a.5)

WATSON, David McB.
The family of Gledstanes: their connection with
Hawick. Hawick, [1897?].
QZ/P11

Glen

CAMPBELL, Marion
A dynasty of stonemasons. (In *Notes & Queries of
the Society of West Highland Historical Research*, no.1,
30 November 1972, p.4.)
ED/N-1 (P.med.3574)

GLEN, Mifflin G.
Extracts of genealogies of Scottish and American
Glens. [N.p.], 1977.
QZ/L37

ROGERS, Charles
Memorials of the Scottish family of Glen.
Edinburgh, 1888.
ED/N-1 (NE.25.g.6) QZ/P14 GL/U-1
QZ/L37 QZ/P-1 QZ/P16 QZ/P99

Glencairn, Earldom of *see also* Fergusson of
Kilkerran

Glencairn, Earldom of

FERGUSSON, Adam
In the House of Lords, before the Lords Committee
of Privileges: the case of Sir Adam Fergusson of
Kilkerran, Baronet, claiming the title and dignity of
Earl of Glencairn and Lord Kilmaurs. London,
[1797].
ED/N-1 (6.365(78))

GLENCAIRN peerage: [speech of Lord
Loughborough]. 1839.
QZ/P99

MAIDMENT, James
Reports of claims . . . to the House of Lords . . . of
the Cassillis, Sutherland, Spynie and Glencairn
peerages, 1760-1797. Edinburgh, 1840.
ED/N-1 (Yule.94) QZ/L37

— — Reprinted. Edinburgh, 1882.
ED/N-1 (Law) DN/U-1 GL/U-1 QZ/P-1
QZ/P99

SINCLAIR, Alexander
A succinct account of the long feud between the
Earls of Glencairn and Eglinton on account of the
Bailliary of Kilwinning. [N.p., n.d.]
ED/N-1 (Hall.199.e.1(2)) QZ/P-9

Glendinning

CLINDENING, Gerald Talbot
The House of Glendonwyn: a record of its
progenitors, members and descendants for a
thousand years. 12pts. Adelaide, 1933-43.
ED/N-1 (1971.155) QZ/L37 QZ/P-1 QZ/P16

GLENDINNING, P.
House of Glendinning. Edinburgh, 1879.
(Reprinted from the *Eskdale & Liddesdale Advertiser*.)
ED/N-1 (S.120.e) QZ/P11 ED/N-2 GL/U-1
QZ/P-1 QZ/P99

Glendonyng

REID, Robert Corsane
The family of Glendonyng. (In *Transactions of the
Dumfriesshire and Galloway Natural History &
Antiquarian Society*, 3rd series, vol.xxii, 1938-40,
pp.10-17.)
ED/N-1 (J.187)

Glenfield

HISTORY of the lairds of Glenfield. Paisley, 1860.
QZ/P-6

Godsman of Mains of Birness

DAVIDSON, William Harold
An account of the life of William Davidson,
otherwise John Godsman of Banffshire and
Aberdeenshire in Scotland and Miramichi in British
North America. [With a genealogical table.] Saint
John, New Brunswick, 1947.
ED/N-1 (1915.19)

Goldman of Dundee

WEDDERBURNE, David
The compt buik of David Wedderburne, merchant
of Dundee, 1587-1630; edited by A. H. Millar.
Edinburgh, 1898. (Scottish History Society
Publications, vol.28.)
ED/N-1 (Ref.54)

Goodsir

ROBERTSON, John
The Ross of Glencalvie and Ross of Kindeace:
pedigree of the families of Ross of Kindeace and
Goodsir of Pitcruvie. [N.p., n.d.]
QZ/P40 (D) ED/N-2 QZ/P99

Gordon

ACCOUNT of the Dukes of Gordon. [N.p., n.d.]
ED/L37

BULLOCH, John Malcolm
Bibliography of the Gordons. Section I. (A to
Augusta—1924. "Chinese Gordon"—Lord
George Gordon.) Aberdeen, 1924.
ED/N-1 (R.255.f) GL/U-1 QZ/P-1 ED/U-1

—The Caterans of Inveraven. (In *Proceedings of the
Society of Antiquaries of Scotland*, vol.lxi (6th series,
vol.i), 1926/7, pp.210-22.)
ED/N-1 (Ref.52)

— — (Reprinted from *Proceedings of the Society of
Antiquaries of Scotland*, vol.lxi (6th series, vol.i),
1926/7.)
QZ/P-1 QZ/P22 QZ/P30 QZ/P99

—"Chinese" Gordon's family origins. Aberdeen,
1933.
QZ/P22

—The Duffs and the Gordons: a table bringing out
the literary instincts of the two. [N.d.] (*MS.*)
QZ/P99

—The families of Gordon at Invergordon, Newhall,
also Ardoch, Ross-shire and Carroll, Sutherland.
Dingwall, 1906.
ED/N-1 (5.4551) QZ/P40 (D) QZ/P30

—The first duke of Gordon. Huntly, 1908.
ED/N-1 (1909.4) QZ/P22 QZ/P-1 QZ/P99

—The fourth duke of Gordon's third regiment:
muster roll of the Northern Fencibles. 1793-9.
[N.p., n.d.]
QZ/P22 QZ/P99

—The gay adventures of Sir Alexander Gordon,
Knight, of Navidale. Dingwall, 1925.
ED/N-1 (1925.5) QZ/P-1 QZ/P99

—The Gay Gordons: some strange adventures of a
famous Scots family. London, 1908.
ED/N-1 (S.121.e) DN/U-1 QZ/P30 GL/U-1
QZ/P40 QZ/P22 QZ/P-3 QZ/P15 SA/U-1
QZ/P-7 QZ/P-1 ED/U-1 QZ/P99

—The Gordon book. Aberdeen, 1902.
ED/N-1 (NE.25.g.7) QZ/P30 QZ/P22
QZ/P50 QZ/P99

—Gordons in Germany, the Brandenburg line.
Aberdeen, 1932.
ED/N-1 (1932.32) QZ/P22 QZ/P-1 ED/U-1
QZ/P99

—Gordons in Perthshire: as pioneers to Canada.
Perth, 1930.
ED/N-1 (1930.33) QZ/P26 QZ/P99 QZ/P22

—The Gordons in Poland. "Marquises of Huntly"
with a line in Saxony. Peterhead, 1932.
ED/N-1 (5.476) QZ/P22 QZ/P-1 ED/U-1

—The House of Gordon . . .: genealogical tree
extracted from "The House of Gordon". Peterhead,
1908.
ED/N-1 (5.174) QZ/P30

—The making of the West Indies: the Gordons as
colonists. Buckie, [1915].
ED/N-1 (1915.1) QZ/P-1 QZ/P22 QZ/P30

—The name of Gordon. Huntly, 1906.
ED/N-1 (1906.11) QZ/P22 QZ/P-1 QZ/P99

—The second duke of Gordon and the part he
played at the battle of Sheriffmuir. Huntly, 1911.
ED/N-1 (1911.19) QZ/P22

—Sporting visitors to Badenoch. Inverness, 1931.
ED/N-1 (1931.29)

—The strange adventures of Lewis Gordon. Elgin,
1908.
ED/N-1 (1908.27) QZ/P22

—The strange adventures of the Reverend James
Gordon, sensualist, spy, strategist (?) and soothsayer.
Buckie, 1911.
ED/N-1 (1911.18)

—Thomas Gordon: the independent Whig.
Aberdeen, 1918.
ED/N-1 (1918.24) GL/U-1 QZ/P99

DUNLOP, Jean
The Clan Gordon: "Cock o' the North".
Edinburgh, 1955.
ED/N-1 (Gen.7) QZ/P26 QZ/P30 QZ/P40
QZ/P22 QZ/P11 QZ/L37 QZ/P-6 GL/U-1
SA/U-1 QZ/P-1 ED/U-1 QZ/P99

— — 2nd ed. Edinburgh, 1965.
ED/N-1 (Gen.7)

GAFFNEY, James V.
The lordship of Strathavon: Tomintoul under
the Gordons. Aberdeen, 1960. (3rd Spalding Club.)
ED/N-1 (3rd.Spald.Club.20)

['GENEALOGY of the families of Gordon,
Drummond and Maule'. 16--, 17--.]
ED/N-1 (Adv.MS.23.3.24,ff.1-81)

GORDON, Duke of Gordon in Scotland, and Earl of Norwich in England. [N.p., 185-.]
ED/N-1 (X.225.a)

GORDON, Armistead C.
Gordons in Virginia; with notes on Gordons of Scotland and Ireland. Hackensack, 1918.
ED/N-1 (6.2054)

GORDON, C. Andrew
Concise history of the ancient and illustrious House of Gordon. Aberdeen, 1754.
ED/N-1 (A.114.f) SA/U-1 QZ/P99

— — 2nd ed. with additions by A. M. Mackintosh. Aberdeen, 1890.
ED/N-1 (A.114.e) QZ/P30 QZ/P22 QZ/P40 SA/U-1 GL/U-1 QZ/P50 QZ/P-1 QZ/P99

GORDON, Cosmo George
Answers and defences for his Majesty's advocate . . . to the claim of Cosmo George, Duke of Gordon . . . upon the forfeited estate of Donald Cameron late of Lochiel, (January 16th 1750). [Edinburgh, 1750.]
ED/N-1 (Ry.II.b.19(38))

— Answers and defences for his Majesty's advocate . . . to the claim of Cosmo George, Duke of Gordon . . . upon the forfeited estate of Evan Macpherson late of Clunie, (January 5th 1750). [Edinburgh, 1750.]
ED/N-1 (Ry.II.b.19(36))

— Unto the . . . Lords of Council and Session, the claim of Cosmo George, Duke of Gordon . . . upon the forfeited estate of Donald Cameron, late of Lochiel. [Edinburgh, 1749.]
ED/N-1 (Ry.II.b.19(37))

— Unto the . . . Lords of Council and Session, the claim of Cosmo George, Duke of Gordon . . . upon the forfeited estate of Evan Macpherson of Cluny. [Edinburgh, 1749.]
ED/N-1 (Ry.II.b.19(35))

GORDON, George
The last Dukes of Gordon and their consorts, 1743-1864. Aberdeen, 1981.
AD/U-1 QZ/P30 QZ/P50

GORDON, Sir Henry William
Gordon memoirs, 1745-1887. Edinburgh, 1895.
AD/U-1

GORDON, Spencer
Our Gordon family. [With genealogical tables.] [N.p.], 1941.
ED/N-1 (R.272.e)

GORDON, William
The history of Scotland, from the beginning of King Robert I to the year 1690 . . . and also a particular account of the antient, noble . . . family of Gordon, from their first arrival in Scotland in the reign of King Malcolm III. London, 1732. 2v.
QZ/P22

— History of the ancient, noble and illustrious family of Gordon, from their first arrival in Scotland in Malcolm III's time to 1690. Edinburgh, 1726, 27. 2v.
ED/N-1 (NE.25.c.8) QZ/P-1 QZ/P22 QZ/P30* QZ/P50 QZ/P99

— Tables of pedigree of the family of Gordon in Scotland from . . . 1057 to . . . 1784. [N.p., 1784.]
ED/N-1 (R.291.b) QZ/P30

GORDONS who were parish ministers. [N.p., n.d.] (*Typescript*)
QZ/P99

GREEN, James
The history of Scotland: from the death of Queen Margaret . . . to the accession of James II . . . [to which is prefixed "An historical and genealogical account of the noble family of Gordon"]. Edinburgh, 1802.
QZ/P-1 QZ/P99

HENDERSON, Janet
The Gordon-Henderson story. [N.p.], 1961. (*Typescript*)
QZ/P22 QZ/P99

The HOUSE of Gordon; edited by John Malcolm Bulloch. Aberdeen, 1903-12. 3v. (New Spalding Club.)
ED/N-1 (New.Spald.Club.26,33,39) ED/N-2 GL/U-1 QZ/L37 QZ/P-1 QZ/P22 QZ/P30 QZ/P40 QZ/P50 QZ/P99

HUNTLY and Gordon families: a genealogical discussion. [N.p., 1870?]
ED/N-1 (NE.26.d.2(2))

HUNTLY, Charles Gordon, *11th Marquess of*
The Cock o' the North. London, 1935.
ED/N-1 (R.172.f) QZ/P30 ED/N-2 QZ/P40 SA/U-1 QZ/Q88 QZ/P13 QZ/P-1 QZ/P99

HUNTLY, George W. Mitchell
Huntly and the Gordons. (In *Transactions of the Buchan Club*, vol.xviii, part 1, 1964, pp.11-16.)
ED/N-1 (M.145)

IRVINE, Alexander
[Papers in the case of Alexander Irvine of Drum,
and his tutors, pursuers, against George, Earl of
Aberdeen, and Margaret Duff, relict and
representative of the deceased Patrick Duff of
Premnay, and others, defenders. Edinburgh,
1767-9.]
ED/N-1 (Yule.97)

LAWRANCE, Robert Murdoch
The Gordons of Aberdour, Auchlunies, Cairnbulg,
etc.; extracted from the ancient registers in St. Peter's
Church, Fraserburgh. [1912.]
QZ/P99

STUART, Alexander Moody
Life and letters of Elizabeth, last Duchess of
Gordon. 3rd ed. [N.p.], 1865.
QZ/P-1

VON GORDON, Eduard
Gordon family: a German family of Gordon from
Aberdeenshire: a letter written in 1874 to Charles,
11th Marquess of Huntly. (*MS.*)
QZ/P22

WRIGHT, Marcus Stults
Our family ties: some ancestral lines of Marcus S.
Wright, Jr. and Alice Olden Wright. [With
genealogical tables.] South River, N.J., 1960.
ED/N-1 (NE.1373.a.4)

Gordon, Viscount of Aberdeen *see* **Aberdeen,** Earl of

Gordon of Aberdour
BULLOCH, John Malcolm
The Gordons of Aberdour. Peterhead, 1913.
QZ/P30   QZ/P22   QZ/P99

LAWRANCE, Robert Murdoch
The Gordons of Aberdour, Auchlunies, Cairnbulg,
etc. (Reprinted from *Fraserburgh Herald and Northern
Counties Advertiser*, 19 March 1912.)
ED/N-1 (L.C.3345(14);1912.7)   DN/U-1
QZ/P22   QZ/P30

Gordon, Earl of Aboyne *see also* **Gordon,** Earl,
Marquess of Huntly

Gordon, Earl of Aboyne
BULLOCH, John Malcolm
The Earls of Aboyne. Huntly, 1908.
ED/N-1 (1908.4)   QZ/P30   QZ/P22   QZ/L37
QZ/P-1   QZ/P99

Gordon of Aikenhead
BULLOCH, John Malcolm
The Gordons of Aikenhead. Aberdeen, 1930.
QZ/P22

LEWIS Gordon of Aikenhead. [N.d.] (*MS.*)
QZ/P22

Gordon of Airds *see* **Gordon** of Earlston and Afton

Gordon of Auchanchy
BULLOCH, John Malcolm
Elizabeth Gordon, the long-lost heiress of
Auchanchie... (In *Transactions of the Banffshire
Field Club*, 13 December 1928, pp.57-76.)
ED/N-1 (NE.3.g.1)

— — (Reprinted from *Transactions of the Banffshire
Field Club*, 13 December 1928.)
QZ/P-1   QZ/P99

Gordon of Beldorney *see also* **Gordon** of Wardhouse

Gordon of Beldorney
WIMBERLEY, Douglas
A short family history of the later Gordons of
Beldorney, and of Beldornie, Kildrummie and
Wardhouse. Banff, 1904.
ED/N-1 (1933.37)   QZ/P99

Gordon of Birkenburn
GEORGE, James
The Gordons of Birkenburn, near Keith: their
ancestry, connections and descendants. [Chart]
Keith, 1912.
AD/U-1

Gordon of Cairnfield
BULLOCH, John Malcolm
The Gordons of Cairnfield and Rosieburn. (In
Transactions of the Banffshire Field Club, 5 May 1910,
pp.28-63.)
ED/N-1 (NE.3.g.1)

— Gordons of Cairnfield, and their hold on the lands
of Echres, Auchinhalrig... and Rosieburn. Keith,
1910.
ED/N-1 (1910.33)   QZ/P99   QZ/P-1   QZ/P30

— — 1937.
QZ/P22

— A Rosieburn pilgrim. (In *Transactions of the
Banffshire Field Club*, 20 January 1937, pp.90-8.)
ED/N-1 (NE.3.g.1)

Gordon of Cluny

BULLOCH, John Malcolm

The Gordons of Cluny from the early years of the 18th century down to the present time. [Buckie], 1911.

ED/N-1 (S.120.g) ED/N-2 SA/U-1 QZ/P22 QZ/P50 QZ/P99

Gordon of Coldwells

BULLOCH, John Malcolm

The Gordons of Coldwells, Ellon. Peterhead, 1914.

ED/N-1 (1914.1) QZ/P30 QZ/P22 GL/U-1 QZ/P-1 QZ/P99

Gordon of Craichlaw

MACMATH, William

The Gordons of Craichlaw. Dalbeattie, 1924.

ED/N-1 (S.122.d) QZ/Q17 QZ/P30 ED/N-2 AD/U-1 SA/U-1 DN/U-1 GL/U-1 QZ/P-1 ED/U-1 QZ/P99

Gordon of Craig

BULLOCH, John Malcolm

The Gordons of Craig. (In *Proceedings of the Society of Antiquaries of Scotland*, vol.lxiv (6th series, vol.iv), 1929/30, pp.96-106.)

ED/N-1 (Ref.52)

— — (Reprinted from *Proceedings of the Society of Antiquaries of Scotland*, vol.lxiv (6th series, vol.iv), 1929/30.)

ED/N-1 (5.452) QZ/P-1 QZ/P22 QZ/P30 QZ/P99

WIMBERLEY, Douglas

Memorials of the family of Gordon of Craig. Banff, 1904.

ED/N-1 (1933.37;1934.19) QZ/P30 ED/N-2 SA/U-1 QZ/P-1 QZ/P99

Gordon of Croughly

GORDON, George Huntly Blair

The Croughly book. [London], 1895.

ED/N-1 (R.172.g) QZ/P22 SA/U-1

Gordon of Culvennan

GORDON, William *and* GORDON, William

Gordon of Culvennan family history. 7v. (*MSS.*)

QZ/P10 (Unconfirmed location)

REID, Robert Corsane

The Culvennan writs. (In *Transactions of the Dumfriesshire and Galloway Natural History & Antiquarian Society*, 3rd series, vol.x, 1922/3, pp.20-80.)

ED/N-1 (J.187)

— — (Reprinted from *Transactions of the Dumfriesshire and Galloway Natural History & Antiquarian Society*, January 1923.)

QZ/L37 QZ/P-1

Gordon of Dundurcus

BULLOCH, John Malcolm *and* SKELTON, Constance Oliver

Lieutenant John Gordon of the Dundurcus family massacred at Patna, 1763. [With genealogical table.] Keith, 1908.

ED/N-1 (1908.2) QZ/P30

Gordon of Earlston and Afton

GORDON, Sir John

[Earlston MSS.] A short and concise abridgement of the origin of the name and illustrious family of Kenmore with their no less renowned descendants. (*Inc.* Airds, Afton and Earlston.) [179- .] (*MSS.*)

QZ/L37

REID, Robert Corsane

The Earlston charters. (*MSS.*)

QZ/P10 (Unconfirmed location)

Gordon of Ellon

BULLOCH, John Malcolm

A grim Edinburgh murder: the genealogy of a legend about the Gordons of Ellon. Inverness, 1932.

ED/N-1 (1932.30) QZ/P22   QZ/P-1 ED/U-1

Gordon of Embo

BULLOCH, John Malcolm

The Gordons of Embo. Dingwall, 1908.

ED/N-1 (1909.19) QZ/P30

Gordon in Forfarshire

BULLOCH, John Malcolm

The Gordons in Forfarshire. Brechin, 1909.

ED/N-1 (HP1.82.3284) QZ/P22 QZ/P99

Gordon of Fyvie

STIRLING, Anna Maria D. W. Pickering

Fyvie Castle: its lairds and their times. London, 1928.

ED/N-1 (R.247.e) QZ/P30 ED/N-2 QZ/P-1

Gordon in Germany

BULLOCH, John Malcolm
    Gordons in Germany: from Pomerania to
    Pennsylvania. (In *Scottish Notes & Queries*, 3rd series,
    vol.xiii, 1935, pp.88-91, 98-101, 121-3.)
    ED/N-1 (V.457)

    — — (Reprinted from *Scottish Notes & Queries*,
    3rd series, vol.xiii, 1935.)
    QZ/P99

Gordon of Gight

BULLOCH, John Malcolm
    The Gordons of Gight. (In *Transactions of the Buchan
    Club*, vol.xiii, 1924/8, pp.149-54.)
    ED/N-1 (M.145)

    — — (Reprinted from *Transactions of the Buchan Club*,
    vol.xiii, 1924/8.)
    QZ/P-1 QZ/P99

SPENCE, James
    The Gordons of Gight. (In *Transactions of the
    Banffshire Field Club*, 13 August 1892, pp.48-51.)
    ED/N-1 (NE.3.g.1)

Gordon of Glenbuchat

The BOOK of Glenbuchat; edited by W. Douglas
    Simpson. Aberdeen, 1952. (3rd Spalding Club.)
    ED/N-1 (3rd Spald.Club.11)

BULLOCH, John Malcolm
    Gordons of Glenbuchat and their connection with
    Stirlinghill and Peterhead. (In *Transactions of the
    Buchan Club*, vol.xiii, 1924/8, pp.47-53.)
    ED/N-1 (M.145)

    — — (Reprinted from *Transactions of the Buchan Club*,
    vol.xiii, 1924/8.)
    QZ/P99

    —A missing Glenbuchat Gordon. Aberdeen, 1924.
    (*Newspaper cuttings*)
    ED/N-2 QZ/P22

Gordon, Lord Gordon

G.B. Parliament. House of Lords. Gordon peerage:
    speeches delivered by counsel before the Committee
    for Privileges and Judgements to whom was referred
    the petition of Sir Bruce Gordon Seton, Bt., C.B.,
    to His Majesty claiming the title, honour and
    dignity of Lord Gordon in the peerage of Scotland,
    1928. London, 1929.
    ED/N-1 (S.123.f) GL/U-1 QZ/P99

HUNTLY, Charles, *Marquis of*
    Case of Charles, Marquis of Huntly.
    QZ/L37

    —Additional case of the above. . . .
    QZ/L37

SETON, Sir Bruce Gordon
    Case on behalf of Sir Bruce Gordon Seton, Bt., of
    Abercorn . . . his claim . . . Lord Gordon in the
    peerage of Scotland.
    QZ/L37

    —Supplemental case . . . in reply to the case for . . .
    Charles, Marquis of Huntly in opposition to his
    claim to the title . . . of Lord Gordon.
    QZ/L37

PEDIGREE of Sir Bruce Gordon Seton.
    QZ/L37

Gordon of Gordonstoun *see also* **Sutherland,**
Earldom of

Gordon of Gordonstoun

['PAPERS concerning the genealogy of the family of
    Gordon of Gordonstoun'. 17--.]
    ED/N-1 (Adv.MS.20.1.7,ff.97-127)

WYNESS, Fenton
    The Gordons of Gordonstoun. (In *Scotland's
    Magazine*, vol.58, no.7, July 1962, pp.8-11.)
    ED/N-1 (Y.31)

    —Spots from the Leopard. Aberdeen, 1971.
    ED/N-1 (NE.3.e.6)

Gordon in Griamachary

BULLOCH, John Malcolm
    The family of Gordon in Griamachary in the parish
    of Kildonan. [Dingwall], 1907.
    ED/N-1 (HP1.79.2658) QZ/P30 QZ/P22
    QZ/P26 GL/U-1 QZ/P99

BULLOCH, John Malcolm *and* SKELTON, Constance
Oliver
    A notable military family: the Gordons in
    Griamachary, in the parish of Kildonan. Huntly,
    1907.
    ED/N-1 (1907.21) QZ/P-1 QZ/P22

Gordon of Haddo

TEMPLE, William
    Gordon of Haddo and Methlick. (In *Transactions of
    the Banffshire Field Club*, 15 November 1888,
    pp.3-16.)
    ED/N-1 (NE.3.g.1)

Gordon, Earl, Marquess of Huntly

The CASE of George Marquis of Huntly, K.T. to be added to the Scottish union roll as Marquis of Huntly, and in reference to the titles of Earl of Enzie, Lord Gordon, and Badenoch. [N.p.], 1838.
ED/N-1 (Yule no.162(6)) ED/S10

CHRONOLOGICAL abstract of the charters of Huntly. [N.p., n.d.]
ED/N-1 (1948.4(3[1]))

EARL and Marquis of Huntly and Duke of Gordon. [N.p., n.d.]
ED/N-1 (1948.4(3[2]))

GENEALOGIE de l'illustre & ancienne maison de haut et puissant prince Mylord duc de Gourdon, marquis de Huntly . . . . [France, 1699.]
ED/N-1 (BCL.D1349(15))

MINUTES of evidence taken before the Lords Committees to whom was referred the petition of George, Earl of Aboyne, stating his right to the titles, honours and dignities of Marquess of Huntly. . . . [London], 1838. (House of Lords. Session Papers, 1837/8, no.197.)
ED/N-1 (House of Lords. PP.XIX. 1837/38, Session paper 197) ED/S10

PAPERS from the charter chest of the Duke of Richmond at Gordon Castle. Abedeen, 1849. (In *Miscellany of the Spalding Club*, vol.4, pp.123-319.)
ED/N-1 (Spald.Club.3) ED/N-2 QZ/P-1

The RECORDS of Aboyne, MCCXXX-MDCLXXXI; edited by Charles, 11th Marquis of Huntly. Aberdeen, 1894. (New Spalding Club.)
ED/N-1 (New Spald.Club.13) ED/N-2 QZ/L37
QZ/P-1 QZ/P14

SINCLAIR, Alexander
Historical, genealogical and miscellaneous tracts. [N.p., n.d.]
QZ/P10 (Unconfirmed location)

Gordon of Invergordon

BULLOCH, John Malcolm
The families of Gordon of Invergordon, Newhall, also Ardoch, Ross-shire and Carroll, Sutherland. [Dingwall], 1906.
ED/N-1 (5.4551) ED/N-2 QZ/P22 QZ/P40
QZ/P30 QZ/P99

Gordon of Kildrummie *see* **Gordon** of Beldorney

Gordon of Kirkhill

BULLOCH, John Malcolm
The Gordons of Kirkhill. Huntly, 1927.
ED/N-1 (1928.18) QZ/P30 QZ/P22 QZ/P-1
ED/U-1 QZ/P99

Gordon of Knockespoch

BULLOCH, John Malcolm
Knockespoch Gordon's connection with America. 1934.
QZ/P22

FELLOWES-GORDON, Ian
The Gordons of Knockespoch. (In *Leopard*, no.87, March 1983, pp.20-3.)
ED/N-1 (HJ8.30)

WIMBERLEY, Douglas
A genealogical account of the family of Gordon of Knockespoch. (Reprinted from the *Banffshire Journal*.) [Banff], 1903.
ED/N-1 (NE.25.b.29) QZ/P22 ED/N-2
SA/U-1 QZ/P-1 QZ/P99

Gordon of Laggan

BULLOCH, John Malcolm
The Gordons of Laggan. (In *Transactions of the Banffshire Field Club*, 31 January 1907, pp.3-54.)
ED/N-1 (NE.3.g.1) QZ/P-1

Gordon of Lesmoir

BULLOCH, John Malcolm
The Gordons of Lesmoir claim to the baronetcy in 1887. 1936.
QZ/P22

PEDIGREE of the Gordons of Lesmoir. [N.p., 1900?]
ED/N-1 (S.120.g)

WIMBERLEY, Douglas
Gordons of Lesmoir. [Aberdeen, 1907.]
DN/U-1

—Memorials of the family of Gordon of Lesmoir in the county of Aberdeen. Inverness, 1893.
QZ/P30 GL/U-1 AD/U-1 QZ/L37

—Memorials of four old families. Inverness, 1894.
ED/N-1 (Y.59.a.23) QZ/P22 QZ/P40 DN/U-1
QZ/P-1 QZ/P99

Gordon of Letterfourie

BULLOCH, John Malcolm
The Gordons of Letterfourie. (In *Transactions of the Banffshire Field Club*, 17 December 1929, pp.76-86.)
ED/N-1 (NE.3.g.1)

Gordon of Minmore

BULLOCH, John Malcolm
The Gordons and Smiths at Minmore,
Auchorachan and Upper Drumin in Glenlivet.
Huntly, 1910.
ED/N-1 (R.172.e)   QZ/P22   QZ/P50

Gordon of Mosstown

BULLOCH, John Malcolm
A Logie-Buchan laird and his loans: the Gordons of
Mosstown. Aberdeen, [n.d.].
QZ/P99

Gordon of Myrieton

BULLOCH, John Malcolm
The Gordons of Myrieton. (In *Transactions of the
Banffshire Field Club*, 5 December 1933, pp.67-75.)
ED/N-1 (NE.3.g.1)

Gordon of Nethermuir

BULLOCH, John Malcolm
The Gordons of Nethermuir. Peterhead, 1913.
ED/N-1 (1913.14)   QZ/P30   QZ/P22   QZ/P-1
QZ/P99

Gordon of Park

ABERNETHIE, John
Information for John Abernethie of Mayen against
Sir John Gordon of Park. 2 parts. [Edinburgh,
1695.]
ED/N-1 (6.282(28,29))

ANSWERS or defences for His Majesty's Advocate on
behalf of His Majesty to the claim of John
Gordon . . . to the lands and barony of Park, which
. . . belonged to Sir William Gordon of Park,
(25 June, 1750). [Edinburgh, 1750.]
ED/N-1 (Ry.II.b.19(48))

BULLOCH, John Malcolm
Sir John Bury Gordon, Fifth and last baronet of
Park. (In *Transactions of the Banffshire Field Club*,
23 May 1907, pp.70-89.)
ED/N-1 (NE.3.g.1)

GORDON, John
Information for His Majesty's advocate on behalf of
His Majesty, respondent against John Gordon . . .
claimant, in virtue of a tailzie of the lands and
barony of Park. (1st November 1750.) Edinburgh,
1750.
ED/N-1 (Ry.II.b.19(50))

—Unto the . . . Lord of Council and Session the claim
of John Gordon . . . of the lands and barony of Park.
(December 5, 1748.) [Edinburgh, 1748.]
ED/N-1 (Ry.II.b.19(47))

GORDON, Sir John
Information for Sir John Gordon of Park for
himself, and as assigney constitute be John Gordon
of Rothemay against the representatives of
Alexander and James Abernethies and Isobel
Halket, relict of the said Alexander, and Arthur
Forbes of Balveny. [Edinburgh, 1695.]
ED/N-1 (7.70(18))

Gordon of Pitlurg

GORDON, Margaret Maria
John Gordon of Pitlurg and Parkhill. London, 1885.
ED/N-1 (Hall.230.f)

Gordon of Rothemay

ABERNETHIE, John
Additional information for John Abernethy of
Mayen against John Gordon of Rothemay.
[Edinburgh, 1695.]
ED/N-1 (6.282(30))

Gordon of Salterhill

BULLOCH, John Malcolm
The Gordons of Salterhill, and their Irish
descendants. Keith, 1910.
ED/N-1 (1910.41)   QZ/P22   QZ/P50   QZ/P99

Gordon of Sheelagreen

BULLOCH, John Malcolm
The "Mutiny" of the Atholl Highlanders and an
account of the Sheelagreen Gordons. Buckie, 1911.
ED/N-1 (1911.36)   QZ/P22

Gordon, Duke of Sutherland

SINCLAIR, Alexander
Right of the Duke of Sutherland to a higher place
as the Earl of Sutherland than he now has on the
roll of the Scotch Earls since 1606. [N.p., n.d.]
ED/N-1 (Hall.199.e.1(1))

Gordon, Earl of Sutherland *see* **Sutherland,**
Earldom of

Gordon in Sutherland

BULLOCH, John Malcolm
The Gordons in Sutherland. Dingwall, 1907.
ED/N-1 (1909.19)   QZ/P30   QZ/P22   QZ/P99
QZ/P50   QZ/P-1

— — Dingwall, 1908.
QZ/P40

Gordon of Techmuiry
BULLOCH, John Malcolm
The Gordons of Techmuiry. Peterhead, 1933.
QZ/P30 QZ/P99

Gordon of Terpersie
WIMBERLEY, Douglas
Notes on the family of Gordon of Terpersie.
Inverness, 1900.
ED/N-1 (S.120.b) QZ/P30 QZ/P22 QZ/P-1
QZ/P99

Gordon in U.S.A.
GORDON, Frank N.
The descendants of Rev. Edward Clifford Gordon,
D.D., of Missouri, 1842-1923. Kingsville, Tex.,
1952.
QZ/P22

Gordon of Wardhouse *see also* **Gordon** of Beldorney

Gordon of Wardhouse
BULLOCH, John Malcolm
Gay Gordons as Spaniards: the story of the
Wardhouse family. 1933.
QZ/P22

—Gordons of Wardhouse and Beldorney. Banff,
1909.
ED/N-2 QZ/P99

Gordon of Westhall
LETTER to the 11th Marquis of Huntly from Colonel
Edward von Gordon. [1874.] (*MSS.*)
QZ/P22

Gordon-Lennox, Duke of Richmond *and* Gordon
KENT, John
Records and reminiscences of Goodwood and the
Dukes of Richmond, 1672-1896. London, 1896.
ED/N-1 (I.32.d) SA/U-1 QZ/P-1

MARCH, *Earl of*
A duke and his friends: the life and letters of the
second Duke of Richmond. [N.p.], 1911. 2v.
ED/N-1 (S.164.c)

Gorrie
GORRIE, R. M.
The siol Gorrie. 1968.
QZ/P99

Gorthy of Gorthy
FITTIS, Robert Scott
The Barony of Gorthy. (Reprinted from *Perthshire
Constitutional and Journal*, August, September 1878.)
ED/N-1 (Hall.191.j)

Goudie
GOWDY, Mahlon M.
A family history comprising the surnames of Gade,
Gadie, Gaudie, Gawdie, Gawdy, Gowdy, Goudy,
Goudey and Gowdey. Lewiston, Maine, 1919.
QZ/P41

JAMESON, Andrew
Jamesons and Goudies in Channerwick, Shetland.
1980.
QZ/P99

Gourlay
ROGERS, Charles
Memorials of the Scottish House of Gourlay.
Edinburgh, 1888.
ED/N-1 (Gramp.Club.37;A.113.b) QZ/L37
QZ/P18 QZ/P14 SA/U-1 AD/U-1 GL/U-1
QZ/P16 QZ/P99

Gourlay of Dundee
LYTHE, S. G. E.
Gourlays of Dundee: the rise and fall of a Scottish
shipbuilding firm. Dundee, 1964.
ED/N-1 (P.sm.2056) ST/U-1 QZ/P99

— — Dundee, 1969.
QZ/P28

Gow
LINDSAY, Maurice
The fiddling Gows: a Scots musical family. (In
*Selections from the B.B.C. programme "Music
Magazine"* by Anna Instone, 1953, pp. 83-7.)
QZ/P26

Gower *see* **Sutherland,** Earldom of

Graeme
FAMILY letters, 1745-1793: [letters of the Graeme
family]. Edinburgh, 1857.
ED/N-1 (Hall.199.b)

GRAEME, Patrick Sutherland
Pateas amicis: the story of the house of Graemeshall
in Orkney. Kirkwall, 1936.
ED/N-1 (NE.1.c.12) QZ/P40 QZ/P99

Graham, Earl of Airth *see* **Airth,** Earldom of

Graham *see also* **MacIlvernock**

Graham

BAKER,
Graham of Limekilns. 1832.
QZ/P99

FFORDE, Lady Jean
Castles in the air: the memories of a childhood in
two castles. Brodick, 1982.
ED/N-1 (H3.82.2084) QZ/P99

GRAEME, Louisa Grace
Or and sable: a book of the Graemes and Grahams.
Edinburgh, 1903.
ED/N-1 (S.120.c) QZ/P53 QZ/P-6 QZ/P26
QZ/P14 SA/U-1 AD/U-1 QZ/P22 GL/U-1
QZ/L37 QZ/P-1 QZ/P99

GRAHAM pedigree connecting Montrose and
Carnegies of Lour. [N.p., 18--.]
QZ/P28

GRAHAM, Lady Helen
The Grahams. [N.p.], 1920.
ED/N-2

GRAHAM, James
The Grahams of Wallacetown, Knockdolian,
Grugar, Auchenbowie, Auchencloich, Tamrawer,
Dougalston, Kilmannan and Kilmardinny.
Glasgow, 1887.
ED/N-2 QZ/L37 QZ/P-1

The PEDIGREE of Robert Barclay-Allardice . . ., the
Earls of Menteith and Airth, Lord Graham of
Kilpont and Kilbryde: and the families of Barclay of
Mathers and Ury, and Allardice of Allardice.
Edinburgh, 1892.
ED/N-1 (S.120.a)

SMITH, John Guthrie
Strathendrick and its inhabitants. Glasgow, 1896.
ED/N-1 (A.58.a) ED/N-2 QZ/P49

STEWART, John
The Grahams, with tartans and arms in colour, and
a map. Edinburgh, 1958.
ED/N-1 (Hist.S.111;Gen.7) QZ/P14 QZ/P-6
QZ/P26 ED/N-2 QZ/P40 QZ/P11 GL/U-1
SA/U-1 QZ/P49 QZ/P-1 ED/U-1 QZ/P99

— — Reprinted. Edinburgh, [1973].
ED/N-2

Graham of Airth
['GENEALOGICAL papers concerning the family of
Grahams of Airth' 1861-88.]
ED/N-1 (MS.10962)

Graham of Auchencloich *see also* **Graham** of
Tamrawer

Graham of Auchencloich
GRAHAM, John St John Noble
The Grahams of Auchencloich and Tamrawer: a
record of seven centuries. Lisbon, 1952.
ED/N-2 QZ/L37 QZ/P-1 QZ/P99

Graham on the Borders
BAIN, Joseph
The Grahams or Graemes of the debateable land:
their traditional origin considered. (In *Archaeological
Journal*, vol.xliii, 1886, pp.116-23.)
ED/N-1 (J.187,188)

— — (Reprinted from *Archaeological Journal*, vol.xliii,
1886.)
QZ/L37 QZ/P-1 QZ/P99

GRAHAM, John
Condition of the Border at the Union: destruction
of the Graham clan. Glasgow, 1905.
ED/N-1 (R.240.g) QZ/P11

— — 2nd ed. London, 1907.
ED/N-1 (R.240.g) ED/N-2 QZ/P-1 QZ/P11
QZ/P22

REID, Robert Corsane
The Border Grahams: their origin and distribution.
(In *Transactions of the Dumfriesshire and Galloway
Natural History & Antiquarian Society*, 3rd series,
vol.xxxvii, 1959/60, pp.85-113.)
ED/N-1 (J.187)

— — (Reprinted from *Transactions of the Dumfriesshire
and Galloway Natural History & Antiquarian Society*,
3rd series, vol.xxxvii, 1959/60.)
QZ/P11

Graham of Breckness
[ORIGINAL family papers.]
QZ/P38 (Unconfirmed location)

Graham of Claverhouse
FITTIS, Robert Scott
[The Grahams of Claverhouse and Duntrune. (In
Scottish Miscellanies, vol.3, 1894-1900, newspaper
cutting no.19.)]
QZ/P26

TAYLER, Alistair Norwich *and* TAYLER, Helen
Agnes Henrietta
John Graham of Claverhouse. [With a genealogical
table.] London, 1939.
ED/N-1 (R.194.i)

Graham of Fintry
COOK, William Bowie
[The Stirling antiquary. Stirling, 1893-1912.] (*MSS.*)
QZ/P14

MUDIE, Sir Robert Francis
Pedigree of the Grahams of Fintry. Dundee, 1962.
QZ/P20 (Unconfirmed location)

MUDIE, Sir Robert Francis *and* WALKER, David M.
Mains Castle and the Grahams of Fintry. Dundee,
1964.
ED/N-1 (P.sm.2056) QZ/P30 QZ/P26 ST/U-1
ED/U-1 QZ/P99

Graham of Gartmore
MCINTYRE, Alex. C.
The Grahams of Gartmore. Glasgow, 1885.
ED/N-1 (NE.25.e.2(1)) QZ/P14 QZ/P49
QZ/P-1

Graham in Knapdale
MACMILLAN, Somerled
Families of Knapdale: their history and their place-
names. Being a compendium of information . . . on
the MacIlvernocks, or Grahams and others of
Knapdale. Paisley, [1960].
ED/N-1 (1936.29)

Graham, Earl of Menteith *see also* **Menteith,**
Earldom of

Graham, Earl of Menteith
BURNETT, George
The "Red book of Menteith" reviewed: in reply to
charges of literary discourtesy made against the
reviewer in a letter to the author of that work.
Edinburgh, 1881.
ED/N-1 (S.122.e) SA/U-1 AD/U-1 QZ/P22
QZ/L37 QZ/P14 QZ/P13 ED/U-1 QZ/P-1
QZ/P99

COWAN, Samuel
Three Celtic earldoms: Atholl, Strathearn,
Menteith, with facsimile of Foundation Charter of
Inchaffray. Edinburgh, 1909.
ED/N-1 (S.120.e) QZ/P14 QZ/P22

FRASER, Sir William
The Red book of Menteith. Edinburgh, 1880. 2v.
ED/N-1 (Gen.8.m) ED/N-2 QZ/P14 AD/U-1
GL/U-1 SA/U-1 QZ/L37 QZ/P56 QZ/P49
ED/U-1 QZ/P-1 QZ/P99

['PAPERS concerning the genealogy of the Grahams,
Earls of Menteith.' 17--.]
ED/N-1 (Adv.MS.20.1.9,ff.74-81)

STEWART, John Alexander
Inchmahome and the Lake of Menteith.
Edinburgh, 1933.
ED/N-1 (R.290.e)

Graham, Duke of Montrose *see* **Montrose,**
Dukedom of

Graham of Tamrawer *see also* **Graham** of
Auchencloich

Graham of Tamrawer
GRAHAM, James Edward
The Grahams of Tamrawer: a short account of their
history. Edinburgh, 1895.
ED/N-1 (A.113.d) SA/U-1 GL/U-1 QZ/L37
QZ/P-1 QZ/P99

Graham-Patterson *see* **Patterson**

Granard, Earl of *see* **Forbes** of Corse and Craigievar

Grant *see also* **Ogilvie-Grant,** Earl of Seafield

Grant
ANDERSON, Peter John
Major Alpin's ancestors and descendants. Aberdeen,
1904.
ED/N-1 (S.120.d) QZ/P22 QZ/P40 SA/U-1
GL/U-1 AD/U-1 QZ/P-1 QZ/P99

A BRIEF account of the family of the Grants; with
the life of Sir Francis Grant, Lord Cullen. [N.p.,
n.d.]
ED/N-1 (4.55(8)) QZ/P22 QZ/P-1

CASSILLIS, Archibald Kennedy, *Earl of*
The rulers of Strathspey: a history of the lairds of
Grant and Earls of Seafield. Inverness, 1911.
ED/N-1 (S.161.e) ED/N-2 QZ/P40 SA/U-1
AD/U-1 QZ/P22 DN/U-1 QZ/P50 QZ/P-1
ED/U-1 QZ/P99

CLAN GRANT SOCIETY (U.K. Branch)
Stand fast!: newsletter of the Clan Grant Society
(U.K. Branch). Vol.1, no.1- . [1982- .]
ED/N-1 (483/A PER)

ELLIOT, William Hume
The story of the "Cheeryble" Grants, from the Spey to the Irwell. Manchester, 1906.
ED/N-1 (S.120.h) SA/U-1

FAMILY of Grants. Edinburgh, 1883.
AD/U-1

FRASER, Sir William
The Chiefs of Grant. Edinburgh, 1883. 3v.
ED/N-1 (Hist.S.112.G) QZ/P56 ED/N-2
QZ/P40 SA/U-1 AD/U-1 QZ/P22 GL/U-1
QZ/L37 QZ/P50 QZ/P-1 ED/U-1 QZ/P99

A FULL and correct genealogy of the honourable family of Grant of Grant, brought down to the year 1826. Elgin, 1826.
ED/N-2

['GENEALOGICAL notes concerning the family of Grant'. 1729.]
ED/N-1 (Adv.MS.20.1.7,ff.131-65)

GRANT, Sir A.
Account of the root, rise and offspring of the clan Grant. 1872. (*MS.*)
QZ/P40

—Anc account of the rise and offspring of the name of Grant. Aberdeen, 1876.
ED/N-1 (R.172.g) QZ/P22 AD/U-1 QZ/L37
QZ/P50 QZ/P-1 QZ/P99

GRANT, Charles
Mémoires . . . de la Maison de Grant. London, 1796.
ED/N-1 (A.114.d) QZ/P40 AD/U-1 GL/U-1
QZ/L37

— — 1806.
QZ/P99

GRANT, Isabel Frances
The Clan Grant: the development of a clan. Edinburgh, 1955.
ED/N-1 (Gen.7) QZ/P26 ED/N-2 QZ/P40
QZ/P22 QZ/P-6 QZ/P11 QZ/L37
GL/U-1 SA/U-1 QZ/P30 QZ/P49
QZ/P-1 ED/U-1 QZ/P99

— — Reprinted. Edinburgh, [1972].
ED/N-2

GRANT, Maria M.
Notes on clan Grant. 1903. (*Typescript*)
AD/U-1

[HISTORY of the family of Grant. 1782.]
ED/N-1 (MS.3568)

MACKINNON, Charles
The Clan Alpin confederation: MacGregor, MacKinnon, MacNab, MacQuarrie, MacAulay, Grant and MacFie. (In *The Augustan*, book 1, 1973, pp.39-46.)
ED/N-1 (P.173)

MEMORIAL of the majority of the Rt. Hon. Viscount Reidhaven, Master of Grant. Banff, 1872. (Reprinted from the *Banffshire Journal*, 8 October 1872.)
QZ/P99

[MSS. notes and newspaper cutings relating to the Grants, Leiths, MacKintoshes of Blervie. N.d.]
QZ/P40

STRATHSPEY, *Lord*
A history of Clan Grant. Chichester, 1983.
QZ/P99

Grant of Aberlour
ABERLOUR succession: [newspaper cuttings on the disputed succession to the estate of Margaret G. Macpherson Grant of Aberlour. 1877-79].
ED/N-1 (Hall.210.g.3(2))

Grant of Corrimony
GRANT, Sir Francis James
The Grants of Corrimony. Lerwick, 1895.
ED/N-1 (A.58.a) ED/N-2 GL/U-1 QZ/P40
SA/U-1 AD/U-1 QZ/L37 QZ/P-1 QZ/P99

Grant of Glenmoriston
SINCLAIR, Allan
Reminiscences, historical and traditional of the Grants of Glenmoriston. Edinburgh, 1887.
ED/N-1 (A.124.f) SA/U-1 QZ/P40 QZ/P22
AD/U-1 QZ/P50 QZ/P-1 ED/U-1 QZ/P99

Grant in Manitoba, Canada
MACLEOD, Margaret A. *and* MORTON, William L.
Cuthbert Grant of Grantown, warden of the plains of Red River. [With a genealogical table.] Toronto, 1963.
ED/N-1 (NF.1340.b.11)

Gray
[The FAMILIES of Gill . . . Gray etc. N.d.] (*MS.*)
QZ/P99

GENEALOGICAL notes concerning the family of Gray. [N.p., 1916.]
QZ/P28

GRAY, Patrick
Kalendar showing descent of the Gray family from Fergus the Scoto-Irish King, A.D. 503-1892. [N.d.]
QZ/P20 (Unconfirmed location)

GRAY, Peter
The descent and kinship of Patrick, Master of Gray. Dundee, 1903.
ED/N-1 (S.149.i) QZ/P26 ED/N-2 ED/N-2 QZ/P28 QZ/P22 QZ/L37 QZ/P-1 QZ/P99

— The House of Gray: pedigree of Patrick Gray of Southfield. [Dundee, 1908.]
QZ/P20 (Unconfirmed location)

SCOTT, Earl
Genealogy of the Pirie-Gray family, 1836-1977. 1977. (*MS.*)
QZ/P-1

The SCOTTISH family of Gray. Genealogical chart. [1914.]
ED/N-2 QZ/P-1

URQUHART, Edward Alexander
Castle Huntly: its development and history. [Dundee], 1956. (Abertay Historical Society Publications, no.4.)
ED/N-1 (P.sm.2056) ED/N-2

Gray, Lord Gray
GRAY, Alexander
Case of Alexander Gray, with the pedigree of Gray, Lord Gray. [N.p., 1880.]
ED/N-2 QZ/L37

MINUTES of evidence ... Mrs Eveleen Smith ... claiming to be Baroness Gray. 1896.
ED/N-2 QZ/L37

SMITH, Eveleen
Case on behalf of Mrs Eveleen Smith. 1896.
ED/N-2 QZ/L37

Gray of Skibo
GRAY, Peter
Skibo: its lairds and history. Edinburgh, 1906.
ED/N-1 (R.250.g) ED/N-2 AD/U-1 QZ/P22 QZ/P40 QZ/L37 QZ/P-1 QZ/P16 QZ/P99

Gregor *see* **MacGregor**

Gregory
ANDERSON, P. J.
The Gregories. (In *Deeside Field*, no.2, 1924, pp.48-53.)
ED/N-1 (6.589)

GREGORY, Georgina
A short account of the family of Gregorie, from the time they gave up the name of Macgregor. [N.p.], 1873.
ED/N-2 QZ/L37 SA/U-1 GL/U-1 QZ/P99

GREGORY, Philip Spencer
Records of the family of Gregory. Edinburgh, 1886.
ED/N-1 (R.172.b) AD/U-1 QZ/P99

STEWART, Agnes Grainger
The academic Gregories. Edinburgh, 1901.
ED/N-1 (Hall.238.f) QZ/Q17 QZ/P14 QZ/P30 ED/N-2 QZ/P-7 QZ/P15 SA/U-1 GL/U-1 ST/U-1 QZ/P-1 ED/U-1 QZ/P99

SURLES, Flora B.
Surnamed Gregorie: eight generations in profile, *c*. 1510-1852. Charleston, S.C., 1966.
ED/N-1 (1967.113) SA/U-1

Gregory of Kinnairdy
BEACH, S. E. Hicks
The yesterdays behind the door. Liverpool, 1956.
ED/N-1 (NF.1180.f.15)

JAMES Gregory tercentary memorial volume; edited by Herbert Westren Turnbull. [With a genealogical table.] London, 1939.
ED/N-1 (X.153.c)

Greig
['GENEALOGICAL material concerning the family of Greig'.]
ED/N-1 (MS.Dep.190, Box 1)

Grier *see also* **MacGregor**

Grier in U.S.A.
STEVENS, John Grier
The descendants of John Grier with histories of allied families. Baltimore, Md., 1964.
ED/N-1 (NF.1372.a.4)

Grierson *see also* **MacGregor**

Grierson of Lag
FERGUSSON, Alexander
The Laird of Lag: a life sketch. Edinburgh, 1886.
ED/N-1 (Hall.238.b) QZ/P11 QZ/P-1

HAMILTON-GRIERSON, Sir Philip James
The Lag charters, 1400-1720. Edinburgh, 1958. (Scottish Record Society.)
ED/N-1 (Ref.55) QZ/P99 QZ/P22 DN/U-1 QZ/P-1 ED/U-1 ED/N-2 QZ/L37

REID, Robert Corsane
The Lag charters. (*Typescript*)
QZ/P10 (Unconfirmed location)

Grierson of Marwhirn
CORRESPONDENCE re Grierson of Marquhirn
(Glencairn) and their descendants. [N.d.] (*MSS.*)
QZ/P10 (Unconfirmed location)

Grierson of Quendale
DICKINS, Molly
A wealth of relations: Aberdeen and Shetland.
Oxford, 1972.
ED/N-1 (6.2228) QZ/P41

Grieve
BONSOR, James C.
Borthwick's Wa's: a lonely border churchyard. (In
Transactions of the Hawick Archaeological Society,
1938, pp.79-86.)
ED/N-1 (P.220)

Groat
TRAILL, H. L. Norton
The family of Groat. (In *Old-lore Miscellany of the
Viking Club*, vol.9, 1933, pp.148-51.)
ED/N-1 (R.250.f) QZ/P22

Grossett
GROSETT, Walter
An account of the family of the Muirheads of
Lachop. [N.p., n.d.]
ED/N-1 (1937.24(4)) QZ/P99

Groundwater
GROUNDWATER, Henrietta
Memories of an Orkney family. Kirkwall, 1967.
ED/N-1 (6.1451) QZ/P99

Gunn
CLAN GUNN SOCIETY
Clan Gunn Society Magazine. No.1- . [Glasgow?],
1961- .
ED/N-1 (2606 PER)

GUNN, Mark Rugg
History of the Clan Gunn. Glasgow, [1969].
ED/N-1 (Gen.8.G) ED/N-2 SA/U-1 QZ/P-1
QZ/P22 QZ/P30 QZ/P34

GUNN, Michael James
The Clan Gunn and the office of Crowner of
Caithness. (In *Clan Gunn Society Magazine*, no.16,
1980/81, pp.33-9.)
ED/N-1 (2606 PER)

SINCLAIR, Thomas
The Gunns. Wick, 1890.
ED/N-1 (A.113.b) ED/N-2 SA/U-1 QZ/P40
QZ/P14 AD/U-1 QZ/L37 ST/U-1 QZ/P-1
QZ/P99

Gunn of Braemore
GUNN, Mark Rugg
Braemore Estate, 1818. (In *Clan Gunn Society
Magazine*, no.10, 1974, pp.24-7.)
ED/N-1 (2606 PER)

Gunther *see* **MacIntosh** in St Andrews

Guthrie
EDWARDS, David Herschell
The Auld Neuk house . . . the birthplace of the
Guthries. Brechin, 1916.
ED/N-1 (R.246.g) QZ/P99

GUTHRIE, Charles John
Genealogy of the descendants of Rev. Thomas
Guthrie, D.D., and Mrs Anne Burns, or Guthrie,
connected chiefly with the families of Chalmers and
Traill. Edinburgh, 1902.
ED/N-1 (S.120.a) QZ/P28 QZ/P22 SA/U-1
GL/U-1 QZ/P-1 QZ/P99

GUTHRIE, David Charles
The Guthrie family, 1178-1900. Northampton,
1906.
ED/N-1 (R.291.c) ED/N-2

GUTHRIE, Laurence Rawlin
American Guthrie and allied families . . . with some
post-revolution emigrants and some allied families.
Chambersburg, Penn., 1933.
QZ/P28

WRIGHT, C. E. Guthrie
Gideon Guthrie, 1800. [With genealogical tables.]
[N.p., n.d.]
QZ/P-1

Hadden
FAMILY tree of the descendants of Alexander Hadden
of Aberdeen, 1720-1788 and his wife, Elspeth Young
[compiled by D. J. Hadden]. (*Xerox copy, with family
documents and letters*)
QZ/P22

KEITH, Alexander
The Haddens and the extension of the Burgh of
Aberdeen. (In *Aberdeen Chamber of Commerce
Journal*, vol.38, summer 1957, pp.168-71.)
ED/N-1 (U.450) QZ/P22

MORGAN, Patrick
Annals of Woodside and Newhill, historical and genealogical. Aberdeen, 1886.
ED/N-1 (A.120.a)

SOME account of the Hadden family for upwards of one hundred years and their connections in marriage. [Aberdeen, 18--.]
QZ/P22   QZ/P30

TOUGH, J. D.
A short narrative of the life of an Aberdonian; to which is added "An account of the Hadden family". Aberdeen, 1848.
QZ/P22   QZ/P-1   QZ/P99

Haddington, Earl of *see* **Hamilton,** Earl of Haddington

Hadow

HADOW, Arthur Lovell
[The pedigree of the Hadow family descended from Principal James Hadow.] Kemsing, 1953. 2v. (*Typescript*)
QZ/Q17   SA/U-1

Haig

LAVER, James
The House of Haig. Markinch, 1958.
ED/N-1 (NG.1297.c.9)

Haig of Bemersyde

HAIG, Charles Edwin
Haig of Bemersyde, co. Berwick. (Genealogical table.) [Edinburgh, 1907.]
ED/N-1 (K.117.a)   ED/N-2   SA/U-1   QZ/L37

— — 2nd ed. 1907.
QZ/P99

RUSSELL, John
The Haigs of Bemersyde: a family history. Edinburgh, 1881.
ED/N-1 (R.240.e)   ED/N-2   QZ/P22   QZ/P11
QZ/P40   QZ/P15   QZ/P28   SA/U-1   AD/U-1
GL/U-1   QZ/L37   QZ/P-1   ED/U-1   QZ/P99

TYDE what may: [a Haig family magazine]. Edinburgh, 1894-1900. 5 parts.
ED/N-1 (S.120.b)   QZ/L37*   QZ/P99

Haig of Stirlingshire

HAIG, Charles Edwin
Robert Haig of St Ninians. [N.p., 1895.]
QZ/P99

Hair

WILSON, William
Folklore and genealogies of uppermost Nithsdale. Dumfries, 1904.
ED/N-1 (R.241.h)

Hairstanes of Craigs

EDGAR, Robert
An introduction to the history of Dumfries. [With genealogical tables.] Dumfries, 1915.
ED/N-1 (R.241.b)

Haitlie of Mellerstain

HARDY, Dr
Mellerstain and the Haitlies thereof: appendix of notes. (In *History of the Berwickshire Naturalists' Club*, vol.xv, 1894/5, pp.134-43.)
ED/N-1 (Y.210)

LITHGOW, S. A.
Mellerstain and the Haitlies thereof. (In *History of the Berwickshire Naturalists' Club*, vol.xv, 1894/5, pp.122-33, 194.)
ED/N-1 (Y.210)

PATON, Henry
Mellerstain: its owners, especially the Haitlies. (In *History of the Berwickshire Naturalists' Club*, vol.xxvii, 1929/31, pp.210-17.)
ED/N-1 (Y.210)

Halcro

CLOUSTON, J. Storer
The origin of the Halcros. (In *Proceedings of the Orkney Antiquarian Society*, vol.11, 1933, pp.59-65.)
ED/N-1 (R.250.a)   QZ/P-1

SCOTT, Ebenezer Erskine
The Erskine-Halcro genealogy. London, 1890.
ED/N-1 (A.37.d)   ED/N-2   QZ/P40   QZ/P16

— — New ed. Edinburgh, 1895.
QZ/P14   ED/N-2   QZ/P28   QZ/P22   QZ/P-6
GL/U-1   QZ/L37   QZ/P11   QZ/P40   SA/U-1
QZ/P-1   QZ/P-16   QZ/P99

Haldane

GENEALOGICAL history with the armorial bearings of the family of Haldane of Gleneagles in Perthshire and of the collateral branches of the family. Abergavenny, [1867].
ED/N-1 (MS.20004,f.54)

HALDANE, Louisa Kathleen
Friends and kindred: memoirs of Louisa Kathleen
Haldane. [With genealogical tables.] London, 1961.
ED/N-1 (NF.1334.b.8)

Haldane of Airthrey

HALDANE, Alexander
The lives of Robert Haldane of Airthrey and of his
brother, James Alexander Haldane. Edinburgh,
1855.
ED/N-1 (XX.4) QZ/P14

Haldane of Barmony

ROGERS, Charles
Four Perthshire families: Roger, Playfair, Constable
and Haldane of Barmony. Edinburgh, 1887.
ED/N-1 (Gramp.Club.35) QZ/Q17 QZ/P26
ED/N-2 QZ/P14 GL/U-1 SA/U-1 QZ/L37
QZ/P-1 QZ/P16

— The Scottish House of Roger, with notes
respecting the families of Playfair and Haldane of
Barmony. 2nd ed. Edinburgh, 1875.
ED/N-1 (Gramp.Club.28) ED/N-2 QZ/P-1
QZ/P16 QZ/P99 QZ/L37

Haldane of Gleneagles

HALDANE, Alexander
Memoranda relating to the family of Haldane of
Gleneagles. London, 1880.
ED/N-1 (6.274(3)) ED/N-2 QZ/L37 QZ/P-1
QZ/P99

HALDANE, Sir James Aylmer Lowthorpe
The Haldanes of Gleneagles. Edinburgh, 1929.
ED/N-1 (R.272.a) QZ/P26 ED/N-2 QZ/P14
SA/U-1 QZ/L37 GL/U-1 ST/U-1 QZ/P-1
ED/U-1 QZ/P99

Haliburton *see also* **Halliburton**

Haliburton

DOUGLAS, William
The owners of Dirleton. (In *History of the
Berwickshire Naturalists' Club*, vol.xxvii, 1929/31,
pp.75-92.)
ED/N-1 (Y.210)

— — (Reprinted from *History of the Berwickshire
Naturalists' Club*, vol.xxvii, 1929/31.)
QZ/P34

ROGERS, Charles
Genealogical memoirs of the family of Sir Walter
Scott of Abbotsford; with a reprint of his
"Memorials of the Haliburtons". London, 1877.
(Grampian Club, 13.)
ED/N-1 (Gramp.Club.13) QZ/P-6 QZ/P22
ED/N-2 QZ/P11 QZ/P40 QZ/P14 DN/U-1
GL/U-1 QZ/L37 QZ/P-7 QZ/P-1 QZ/P16
QZ/P99

SCOTT, Sir Walter
Memorials of the Haliburtons. Edinburgh, 1820.
ED/N-1 (F.5.c.12)

— — Edinburgh, 1824.
ED/N-1 (Ry.III.c.13) QZ/P-1 QZ/P22 GL/U-1
QZ/P99

Halkerston

[FAMILY of Halkerston of that ilk. N.p., n.d.]
ED/N-1 (A.114.d)

MCCALL, Hardy Bertram
Memoirs of my ancestors. Birmingham, 1884.
ED/N-1 (A.114.a) QZ/P99

Halkerston of Halkerston Beath

MCCALL, Hardy Bertram
Some old families: contribution to the genealogical
history of Scotland. Birmingham, 1890.
ED/N-1 (A.36.a) QZ/P11 QZ/L37 ED/N-2
QZ/P99

Halkerston of Rathillet

HALKERSTON, Helenus
An appeal to reason: [history of the entail of the
lands of Rathillet in Fife]. 2nd ed. Edinburgh, 1778.
ED/N-1 (ABS.2.79.9) QZ/P18

Halkett of Pitfirrane

['ACCOUNT of the descent of Alexander, 1st Earl of
Rosslyn, and genealogical papers concerning the
Halketts of Pitfirrane. 17--, 1798, 1840.]
ED/N-1 (MS.6503,ff.28-51)

ANGUS, William
Inventory of Pitfirrane writs. 1230-1794.
Edinburgh, 1932. (Scottish Record Society, 67.)
ED/N-1 (Ref.55) ED/N-2 QZ/P-1 QZ/P14

LEEMANS, W. F.
De Schotse officierenfamilie Halkett. The Hague,
1960.
QZ/P16

McNAUGHTON, Duncan
The Halketts of Pitfirrane. [N.p.], 1961.
QZ/Q17 QZ/P18

— The Halketts of Pitfirrane. (In *Scottish Genealogist*,
vol.viii, no.3, July 1961, pp.1-16.)
ED/N-1 (Gen.7)

Hall

WATSON, Charles Brodie Boog
Traditions and genealogies of some members of the
families of Boog, Heron, Leishman, Ross, Watson.
Perth, 1908.
ED/N-1 (S.120.d) SA/U-1 QZ/P99

Halliburton

RUTHERFORD, William K. *and* RUTHERFORD, A. C.
Genealogical history of the Halliburton family.
Revised ed. [Lexington, Miss.], 1972.
ED/N-1 (NE.25.e.7)

Halliday of Ontario, Canada

HALLIDAY, Clarence
A Halliday family tree. [Cobourg, Ont., 1963.]
ED/N-1 (5.2629) QZ/P99

— John Holliday, a forthright man. [With a
genealogical table.] [N.p.], 1962.
ED/N-1 (5.229) QZ/P99

Halyday of Tullieboyle

EDGAR, Robert
An introduction to the history of Dumfries. [With
genealogical tables.] Dumfries, 1915.
ED/N-1 (R.241.b)

Hamilton

['ACCOUNT of the Hamilton family history'. 1750?]
ED/N-1 (Adv.MS.36.6.19,ff.41-65)

AITON, William
An inquiry into the pedigree, descent, and public
transactions of the chiefs of the Hamilton family,
and showing how they acquired their estates.
Glasgow, 1827.
ED/N-1 (Abbot.104(14);A.114.c) QZ/P53
ED/N-2 GL/U-1 SA/U-1 QZ/P-1 QZ/P99

ANDERSON, John
Historical and genealogical memoirs of the House
of Hamilton; with genealogical memoirs of the
several branches of the family. Edinburgh, 1825.
ED/N-1 (A.114.b.1(1)) QZ/P53 QZ/P34
SA/U-1 GL/U-1 QZ/P-6 QZ/P-3 QZ/L37
QZ/P56 QZ/P-1 ED/U-1 QZ/P99

— — Supplement. 1827.
ED/N-1 (A.114.b.1(1)) QZ/P-1

"AUDI alteram partem": pedigree of the Hamilton
family. London, 1867.
QZ/P99

BURNET, Gilbert
The memoires of the lives and actions of James and
William, Dukes of Hamilton and Castleherald.
(*History of the Church and State of Scotland*. Part 2.)
London, 1677.
QZ/P53 QZ/P40 QZ/L37 QZ/P-1

CLARK, Ruth
Anthony Hamilton, Count Grammont: his life and
works, and his family. London, 1921.
ED/N-1 (NF.1338.e.15)

['GENEALOGY of the family of Hamilton'. 1646?]
ED/N-1 (MS.7114)

HAMILTON, Charles William
Index tables to the families of Hamilton. Dublin,
1863.
QZ/P99 QZ/P56 QZ/L37

HAMILTON, Francis
Memoirs of the House of Hamilton, corrected with
an addition. Edinburgh, 1828.
ED/N-1 (A.114.b.1(1)) QZ/P53 GL/U-1
SA/U-1 QZ/P-6 QZ/P-3 QZ/L37 QZ/P-1
QZ/P99

HAMILTON, George
A history of the House of Hamilton. Edinburgh,
1933.
ED/N-1 (Hist.S.112.H) QZ/P53 QZ/P56
AD/U-1 GL/U-1 QZ/L37 QZ/P-1 ED/U-1
QZ/P99

HAMILTON, James
Answers for . . . the Duke of Hamilton and Brandon
to the petition of John, Earl of Selkirk and Ruglen,
heir of line, and William, Lord Daer, sole executor
to the deceast Charles, Earl of Selkirk. (January 24.
1740). Edinburgh, 1740.
ED/N-1 (6.1877(20))

— Memoirs of the life and family of . . . James,
late Duke of Hamilton. London, 1742.
ED/N-1 (Mf.15(14[1]))

HILL, C. H. W.
Statement of facts re Thomas Hamilton, called Ilive, afterwards Ayliffe, and his family, the late Earl of Egremont, and the Wyndham-Ilive family. London, 1889.
ED/N-1 (Dur.405)

JOHNSTON, George Harvey
The heraldry of the Hamiltons: with notes on all the males of the family, and description of the arms, plates and pedigrees. Edinburgh, 1909.
ED/N-1 (S.120.c) QZ/P53 QZ/L37 QZ/Q91 QZ/P-1 QZ/P99

MCMASTER, Jane Harvey *and* WOOD, Marguerite
Supplementary report on the manuscripts of His Grace the Duke of Hamilton. [London], 1932.
ED/N-1 (GRH.5/21)

[MATERIAL relating to the lands and lairds of Hamilton. N.p., n.d.].
QZ/P-6

MEMOIRS of the House of Hamilton, corrected with an addition. Edinburgh, 1828.
QZ/P53

MILLER, Alfred G.
The Hamilton family. [Hamilton, 1897.]
ED/N-1 (NE.25.g.14(2))

—The House of Hamilton: a historical sketch, and other local papers. 1895. (Reprinted from the *Hamilton Advertiser*.)
QZ/P53

—The House of Hamilton. [N.d.] (*Typescript*)
ED/N-1 (Mf.50(17)) ED/N-2 QZ/P53

RIDDELL, John
Reply to the misstatements of Dr. Hamilton of Bardowie, in his late "Memoirs of the house of Hamilton, corrected", respecting the descent of his family; with an appendix of original matter, partly affecting the Hamiltons, and the Stewarts, and representation of the old Earls of Lennox. Edinburgh, 1828.
ED/N-1 (A.114.b.1(3)) QZ/P53 SA/U-1 QZ/P99 GL/U-1 QZ/P-6 QZ/P-3 QZ/L37 QZ/Q76 QZ/P-1

TAYLOR, Wilfred
A few notes on the Hamilton family. [N.p.], 1910.
QZ/P53

Hamilton, Marquess, Duke of Abercorn
ABERCORN, James Hamilton, *1st Duke of*
Consultation pour James Hamilton, Marquis d'Abercorn … contre le duc d'Hamilton … Paris, 1865.
ED/N-1 (5.582(37)) QZ/P99

['GENEALOGICAL account of the Hamiltons, Earls of Abercorn'. 1802?]
ED/N-1 (Adv.MS.35.5.9,ff.165-75)

MEMOIR of James, Duke of Abercorn, K.G. (Reprinted from *Dublin University Magazine*, September 1874.)
ED/N-1 (S.126.a)

Hamilton of Aikenhead
NISBETT, Hamilton More *and* AGNEW, Stair Carnegie
Cairnhill. Edinburgh, 1949.
ED/N-1 (R.272.f) QZ/P-3

Hamilton of Bargany
DALRYMPLE, Hew Hamilton
Hamilton, Lord Bargany. [N.p., 1907.]
ED/N-1 (NE.25.h.2)

—A short account of the Hamiltons of Bargany. Edinburgh, 1897.
ED/N-1 (NE.25.h.3) ED/N-2 QZ/L37 QZ/P99

ROBERTSON, William
Ayrshire, its history and historic families. Kilmarnock, 1908. 2v.
ED/N-1 (Hist.S.91.A)

Hamilton of Barns
['DRAFT genealogical account of the Hamilton family of Barns'. 1828.]
ED/N-1 (Adv.MS.19.2.17,ff.249-57)

Hamilton of Bathgate
EATON, Arthur Wentworth Hamilton
David Dick Hamilton of the Bathgate family and some of his descendants. [N.p., 1905.]
ED/N-1 (5.159)

Hamilton, Lord Belhaven *see* **Belhaven** and Stenton, Lord

Hamilton of Broomhill
[ACCOUNT of the Hamiltons of Broomhill. 1730.]
ED/N-1 (MS.536)

BIRNIE, John
Account of the families of Birnie and Hamilton of Broomhill. Edinburgh, 1838.
ED/N-1 (A.124.b) QZ/L37 ED/N-2 QZ/P-1 QZ/P99

Hamilton of Dalzell
[LETTERS to the family of Hamilton of Orbiston and Dalzell; collected by John Glencairn Carter Hamilton. 1644-1805. 17v.]
QZ/P56

Hamilton of Fala
DALRYMPLE, Hew Hamilton
A short account of the Hamiltons of Fala and of Fala House. [N.p.], 1907.
ED/N-1 (NE.25.h.2) SA/U-1 QZ/P99

Hamilton, Earl of Haddington
FRASER, Sir William
Memorials of the Earls of Haddington. Edinburgh, 1889. 2v.
ED/N-1 (Gen.8.h) QZ/P34 QZ/P56 ED/N-2 QZ/P11 SA/U-1 AD/U-1 GL/U-1 QZ/L37 QZ/P-1 ED/U-1 QZ/P99

Hamilton, Duke of Hamilton *see also* **Chatelherault,** Duke of

Hamilton, Duke of Hamilton *see also* **Douglas,** Marquess of

Hamilton, Duke of Hamilton
HAMILTON, Douglas
The case of the most noble Douglas, Duke of Hamilton and Brandon, touching the peerage of Brandon. [N.p., 1782].
ED/N-1 (Yule.162(1))

HAMILTON, James
Memoirs of the life and family of the most illustrious James, late Duke of Hamilton. London, 1717.
ED/N-1 (R.232.h)

— — [N.p.], 1742.
QZ/P-1

HAMILTON, James G.
Mémoire et consultation sur une question du droit du gens: pour les tuteurs de M. le Duc d'Hamilton et du Lord Douglas Hamilton. Paris, 1763.
ED/N-1 (Law)

HAMILTON, William Alexander Louis Stephen, *12th Duke of*
Memorial for the Duke of Hamilton touching his right to the Duchy of Chatelherault. Edinburgh, 1866.
QZ/P56

NEEDHAM, Marchamont
The manifold practises and attempts of the Hamiltons, and particularly of the present Duke of Hamilton . . . to get the crown of Scotland. 1648.
ED/N-1 (Ry.I.2.64(1)) ED/N-2 QZ/P99

NOEL, William F. P.
[The Dukedom of Hamilton]. 1901. (*Typescript*)
QZ/P-1

RICHARDSON, J.
Examination of the evidence. Edinburgh, 1769.
ED/M-1

TEULET, Jean B. A. T.
Mémoire justicatif du droit qui appartient a M. le Duc d'Hamilton de porter le titre de Duc de Chatellerault. Paris, 1864.
ED/N-1 (A.112.b.5;Hall.197.a) QZ/P53

Hamilton of Innerwick
NAPIER, Mark
A "memorie" historical and genealogical of my mother's paternal lineage, namely the Hamiltons of Innerwick, the Lothian Kerrs, and the Earls of Angus. Edinburgh, 1872.
ED/N-1 (F.7.d.3) ED/N-2

Hamilton in Ireland
HAMILTON, Everard
Hamilton memoirs: being genealogical notices of a branch of that family which settled in Ireland in the reign of King James I. London, 1891.
ED/N-1 (S.122.f)

HAMILTON, Sir James
The Hamilton manuscripts: containing some account of the settlement of the territories of the upper Clandeboye, Great Ardes, and Dufferin in the county of Down. Belfast, 1867.
ED/N-1 (NF.802.d.7) QZ/P-1 QZ/P99

MARSHALL, John J.
Vestry book of the parish of Aghalow, Caledon, Co. Tyrone, with an account of the family of Hamilton of Caldon, 1691-1807. Dungannon, 1935.
ED/N-1 (6.674)

Hamilton in Lexington, U.S.A.

GOODHART, Leander M.
Genealogical tables of the descendants of John
Hamilton of Locust Hill, Lexington, Virginia.
[Strasburg, Va.], 1933.
ED/N-1 (S.122.g)

Hamilton of Murdoston

GROSSART, William
Historic notices and domestic history of the parish
of Shotts. Glasgow, 1880.
ED/N-1 (A.118.d)

Hamilton of Olivestob

EATON, Arthur Wentworth Hamilton
Lt.Col. Otho Hamilton of Olivestob. Halifax,
Nova Scotia, 1899.
ED/N-1 (S.144.b)

— The Olivestob Hamiltons. New York, 1893.
ED/N-1 (A.38.c) QZ/P34 QZ/L37 QZ/P-1
QZ/P99

Hamilton of Orbiston

[LETTERS to the family of Hamilton of Orbiston and
Dalzell; collected by John Glencairn Carter
Hamilton. 1644-1805. 17v.]
QZ/P56

Hamilton of Redhouse

FINLAYSON, J. D.
Redhouse and its owners. (In *Transactions of the East
Lothian Antiquarian Society*, vol.iii, 1938, pp.28-39.)
ED/N-1 (Hist.S.91.E)

Hamilton in Sweden

De SVENSKA atterna Hamilton: en släktkronika;
Arkebiskopen Malcolm Hamiltons attlingar genom
hans sonsoner Malcolm och Hugo Hamilton af
Hageby. [With genealogical tables.] Stockholm,
1936.
ED/N-1 (R.272.a)

Hamilton in U.S.A.

BASKERVILL, Patrick Hamilton
The Hamiltons of Burnside, North Carolina, and
their ancestors and descendants. Richmond, Va.,
1916.
ED/N-1 (S.121.e) QZ/P-1

HAMILTON, Harlan Bernhardt
The Hamiltons of South Berwick, Maine,
1651-1966. New York, 1966.
ED/N-1 (6.1261)

— Some American descendants of David Hamilton
of Hamilton, Scotland, down to the present day,
1620-1961. [N.p.], 1961.
QZ/P53

Hamilton of Waterborough

HAMILTON, Samuel King
The Hamiltons of Waterborough: their ancestors
and descendants. Boston, 1912.
QZ/P14

Hannay

[The FAMILY of Hannay, Hannah or Hanna.]
QZ/P22

FRANCIS, Stewart F. B.
Notes on the Hannay family. 1960. 3v. (*Typescript*)
QZ/P99

HANNA, James Arthur McClellan *and* HANNA,
Alexander
The Clan Hanna, Hannay, Hannah: an ecclesiastical
family. Ohio, 1966.
ED/N-1 (5.3939) QZ/P99

HANNAY, William V.
The genealogy of the Hannay family. New York,
1913.
QZ/P10 (Unconfirmed location)

Hannay of Sorbie

FRANCIS, Stewart F. B.
The Hannays of Sorbie. London, 1961.
ED/N-1 (NE.25.b.16) GL/U-1 QZ/P11
QZ/P10 QZ/P99

— — Revised ed. [N.p.], 1977.
ED/N-1 (NE.25.f.26) ED/N-2 QZ/L37
QZ/P-1 QZ/P10 QZ/P99

HANNA, James Arthur MacClannahan
Hanna of Castle Sorbie, Scotland, and descendants.
Vol.1. Ann Arbor, Mich., 1959.
ED/N-1 (H8.79.176) QZ/P10 QZ/P99

Harcar *see* **Harcus**

Harcus *see also* **Arcus**

Harcus

ARCUS, James G.
The Arcus family through ten centuries, including
Harcars of that ilk, and Harcus. Vancouver, 1972.
ED/N-1 (NE.26.d.1) QZ/P41

DREVER, Dorothy
[Family history of William Drever and James
Harcus of Faray, or Pharay, in Orkney, who
emigrated to the U.S. N.p., 1956.] (*Typescript*)
QZ/P38 (Unconfirmed location)

Hardy

MCCALL, Hardy Bertram
Memoirs of my ancestors: genealogical memoranda.
[Hardy and McCall.] Birmingham, 1884.
ED/N-1 (A.114.a)   QZ/P-1   QZ/P99

—Some old families: contribution to the
genealogical history of Scotland. Birmingham,
1890.
ED/N-1 (A.36.a)   QZ/P11   QZ/L37   ED/N-2
QZ/P99

Harkness

HEWISON, James King
Dalgarnoc: its saints and heroes: a history of
Morton, Thornhill and the Harknesses. Dumfries,
1935.
ED/N-1 (R.241.e)   QZ/P22   ED/N-2   QZ/P-1
QZ/P99

Harris *see* Carr-Harris

Hart

HART, Samuel Richardson
Hart family diary, 1842-1966.
QZ/P28

Harvey *see* Macmillan

Harvie

HARVIE, Barry J.
The history and family tree of John Harvie,
1810-1889, and his wife, Margaret née Gilmour,
1820-1902, and their descendants. Adelaide, 1975.
QZ/P-7

Hastings

HASTINGS, Charles Cummins
[Manuscript of genealogical records covering the
period 1300 B.C. to 1604 A.D. and containing
references to Scottish ancestries. California, 1982.]
ED/N-1 (7.196)

Haws

HAWS, George W.
The Haws family and their seafaring kin.
Dunfermline, 1932.
ED/N-1 (R.172.g)   DN/U-1   QZ/P-1   QZ/P16

Hay

ALLAN, John Hay
Genealogical table of the Hays . . . 1170 to 1840.
[N.p.], 1840.
ED/N-1 (R.287.c;R.289.c)   ED/N-2   QZ/P99

BARON court book of Urie; edited by D. G. Barron.
Edinburgh, 1892. (Scottish History Society
Publications, vol.12.)
ED/N-1 (Ref.54)

CLAN HAY SOCIETY Newsletter. No.10- . Turriff,
[1953?-].
ED/N-1 (P.la.2012)   QZ/P-1   QZ/P99

COLCOCK, Charles J.
The family of Hay: a history of the progenitors and
some South Carolina descendants of Col. Ann
Hawkes Hay. New Orleans, 1959.
ED/N-1 (H3.83.3423)

FORBES, Louisa Lillias
Genealogy of the family of Hay of Smithfield and
Haystoun. [N.p.], 1879.
ED/N-1 (S.120.a)

—Hay of Smithfield and Haystoun, 1712-1880. 1879.
ED/N-1 (S.120.a)   ED/N-2   QZ/L37   QZ/P99

HAY, Isabella
The simple story of a Scotch grandfather, written
for his grandchildren. [With genealogical tables.]
[Edinburgh, 1935?]
ED/N-1 (NC.270.h.27)

HAY, Kenneth McLennan
The story of the Hays. Edinburgh, [1977].
ED/N-1 (HP2.80.2840)   ED/N-2

The HAYS in Normandy and England. (In *Clan Hay
Magazine*, vol.1, no.2, 1952, pp.7-13.)
ED/N-1 (1964.36)

NISBETT, Hamilton More *and* AGNEW, Stair
Carnegie
Cairnhill. Edinburgh, 1949.
ED/N-1 (R.272.f)   QZ/P-3

ROSS, James
Origio gentis Hayorum: seu, Danorum ad vicum
Loncartem excidii, virtute cujusdam Hayii . . .
historico-poetica narratio. [Edinburgh], 1700.
ED/N-1 (Ry.III.f.20;F.7.g.18(1);5.2051(33);H.31.e)

Hay of Alderstoun

FRASER, Sir William
Genealogical table of the families of Brisbane of Bishoptoun and Brisbane, Makdougall of Makerstoun, and Hay of Alderstoun. Edinburgh, 1840. (*Xerox-copy*)
ED/N-2

Hay of Barro

INGLIS, John A.
Sir John Hay, "the Incendiary", 1578-1654. [With genealogical tables.] Glasgow, 1937.
ED/N-1 (R.186.c)

Hay of Belton

The HAYS of Belton. (In *Clan Hay Magazine*, vol.1, no.6, [1959], pp.13-15.)
ED/N-1 (1964.36)

Hay of Craignethan

HAY, Andrew
The diary of Andrew Hay of Craignethan, 1659-1660; edited by Alexander George Reid. Edinburgh, 1901. (Scottish History Society Publications, vol.39.)
ED/N-1 (Ref.54)

Hay of Delgaty

INNES, Sir Thomas
Hays of Delgaty. (In *Transactions of the Banffshire Field Club*, 16 April 1936, pp.25-43.)
ED/N-1 (NE.3.g.1)

— — (Reprinted from *Transactions of the Banffshire Field Club*, 16 April 1936.)
ED/N-2   QZ/P-1   QZ/P50   QZ/L37

Hay of Duns Castle

HAY, Francis Stewart
Family of Hay of Duns Castle. Edinburgh, [n.d.].
ED/N-1 (1928.15)   ED/N-2   QZ/P11   QZ/P99

Hay of Erroll

DRUMMOND, John
The mistletoe and the oak: [a family history of the Errolls]. (In *Scots Magazine*, vol.108, no.1, October 1977, pp.10-17.)
ED/N-1 (HJ3.152)

The ERROLL papers, 1188-1727. Aberdeen, 1842. (In *Miscellany of the Spalding Club*, vol.2, pp.209-349.)
ED/N-1 (Spald.Club.3)   ED/N-2   QZ/P-1   QZ/P22

['GENEALOGY of the Hays of Erroll'. 17--.]
ED/N-1 (Adv.MS.20.1.7,ff.60-75)

The HOUSE of Erroll.(In *Clan Hay Society Newsletter* Christmas 1980, p.6.)
ED/N-1 (Pla.2012)

MELVILLE, Lawrence
Errol: its legends, lands and people. Perth, 1935.
ED/N-1 (R.246.a)   QZ/P22   QZ/P-1

SLAINS and the Errolls. Peterhead, 1973.
QZ/P30

WAGNER, Anthony R.
The origin of the Hays of Erroll. (In *Genealogists' Magazine;* part 1, vol.xi, no.16, December 1954, pp.535-40; part 2, vol.xii, no.1, March 1955, pp.1-6.)
ED/N-1 (Y.173)

Hay, Earl of Kinnoull

[FAMILY tree and life histoy of the Earls of Kinnoull. N.p., n.d.]
QZ/P26

Hay of Leys

DEUCHAR, Alexander
Genealogy of the family of Hay of Leys. [N.p., n.d.]
ED/N-1 (J.138.d,Portfolio I)

HISTORICAL account of the family of Hay of Leys. [With genealogical tables.] Edinburgh, 1832.
ED/N-1 (A.114.a.10)

Hay of Rannes

CRAMOND, William
Genealogy of the Hays of Rannes. (In *Transactions of the Banffshire Field Club*, 7 February 1889, pp.27-35.)
ED/N-1 (NE.3.g.1)

The GENEALOGY of the Hays of Rannes. Banff, 1889.
QZ/Q17

HARVEY, C. Cleland. The Hays of Rannes. (In *Transactions of the Banffshire Field Club*, 3 December 1914, pp.14-15.)
ED/N-1 (NE.3.g.1)

Hay of Seaton

WILLIAMS, Georgiana C.
The ancestral home of the Hays of Seaton. (In *Aberdeen University Review*, vol.xlii, no.138, autumn 1967, pp.133-5.)
ED/N-1 (Y.237)

Hay of Spott

LOWE, C. James
[Letter 7th October 1974 to George Murray, Secretary, East Lothian Antiquarian and Field Naturalists' Society concerning the family of Hay of Spott.] (*MSS.*)
QZ/P34

NOTES of the family of Hay of Spott. [N.d.]
QZ/P99

Hay of Tweeddale

HAY, Richard Augustin
Genealogie of the Hayes of Tweeddale. Edinburgh, 1835.
ED/N-1 (H.19.c) QZ/Q17 ED/N-2 QZ/P11 SA/U-1 AD/U-1 QZ/L37 QZ/P-1 ED/U-1 QZ/P99 QZ/P52 (Unconfirmed location)

Hay in U.S.A.

HAY, Anna
Genealogical sketches of the Hay, Suppes and allied families. Johnstown, Pa., [1923].
ED/N-1 (H4.77.347) ED/N-2

Hay of Yester

['GENEALOGICAL papers concerning the Hays of Yester'. 18--, 19--].
ED/N-1 (MS.14826,f.83-207)

['GENEALOGY, ca.970-ca.1730, of the Hays of Yester'. 16--, 17--.]
ED/N-1 (MS.14500,f.117-30)

[GENEALOGY of the family of Hay of Yester. 1688?]
ED/N-1 (MS.7113)

[GENEALOGY of the Hays of Yester. 17--.]
ED/N-1 (MS.7110)

HARVEY, Charles C. H. *and* MACLEOD, John
Calendar of writs preserved at Yester House, 1166-1625. Edinburgh, 1930. (Scottish Record Society, vol.55.)
ED/N-1 (Ref.55) ED/N-2 DN/U-1 QZ/P-1 QZ/P14 QZ/P34

Hector

[A GENEALOGICAL deduction of the family of Hector: descendants of George Hector, weaver in Old Aberdeen and his wife Marjory Walker.] (*MSS.*)
QZ/P22

Henderson

HENDERSON, Janet
The Gordon-Henderson story. [N.p.], 1961 (*Typescript*)
QZ/P22

HENDERSON, Ralph
Records of my family. Carlisle, 1926.
ED/N-2 QZ/P99

HENDERSON, Vivian
The story of a family: the history and connections of the Hendersons of the "Anchor Line", descendants of Alexander Henderson of Pittenweem. [London], 1958.
QZ/P22

[The HENDERSONS in Scotland; taken from various historical publications. 1917, 21.] 2v. (*MSS.*)
QZ/P-1

Henderson of Beith

GENEALOGICAL roll of the family of Mrs. Henderson of Beith. [N.p., n.d.]
QZ/P-6

Henderson of Borrowstounness

GENEALOGICAL chart of the Hendersons of Borrowstounness. [N.p.], 1892.
ED/N-2

Henderson in Canada

CARR, David Henderson
A history of the descendants of George Henderson of Banffshire, Scotland, 1790-1975. London, Ont., 1976.
QZ/P30 QZ/P22

— — Reprinted. London, Ont., 1978.
ED/N-1 (HP3.80.250)

Henderson of Caskieben

CORMACK, Alexander Allan
The Hendersons of Caskieben: four medical practitioners. Aberdeen, 1963.
ED/N-1 (1969.136) QZ/P22 QZ/P30 QZ/P14 QZ/P99

Henderson in Virginia, U.S.A.

MILLER, Joseph Lyon
Ancestry and descendants of Lieut. John Henderson of Greenbrier County, Virginia, 1650-1900. Richmond, 1902.
ED/N-1 (S.120.e)

Henderson of Westerton
FERGUSSON, Robert Menzies
Logie: a parish history. Vol.2: Lands and
landowners. Paisley, 1905.
ED/N-1 (R.243.a) QZ/P14

Hepburn,
DUNCAN, James Alexander *and* DUNCAN, Robert
Some family leaves. Edinburgh, 1911.
ED/N-1 (X.171.c) ED/N-2 QZ/P22

['NOTES concerning the genealogy of the Hepburn
family'. 17--.]
ED/N-1 (Adv.MS.20.18,ff.11-17)

Hepburn of Monkrig
DUNCAN, James Alexander
Descent of the Hepburns of Monkrig. Edinburgh,
1911.
ED/N-1 (S.120.g) DN/U-1 QZ/P-1 QZ/P99

Hepburn in Smeaton, Australia
QUINLAN, Lucille M.
Here my home: the life and times of Captain John
Stuart Hepburn, 1803-1860. [With a genealogical
table.] Melbourne, 1967.
ED/N-1 (NF.1371.d.12)

Hepburn of Urr
SMITH, A. Cameron
The family of Mr. John Hepburn of Urr. (In
*Transactions of the Dumfriesshire and Galloway
Natural History & Antiquarian Society*, 3rd series,
vol.xxiii, 1940/44, pp.151-4.)
ED/N-1 (J.187)

Hepburn of Wauchton
HEPBURN, Edward
Genealogical notes of the Hepburn family. London,
1925.
ED/N-2 QZ/L37 QZ/P-1 QZ/P34

Heriot
STEVEN, William
History of George Heriot's Hospital, with a memoir
of the founder. 3rd ed. [With a genealogical table.]
Edinburgh, 1872.
ED/N-1 (Hist.S.98.B)

Heriot of Ramornie
REID, Robert Corsane
The Heriots of Ramornie from the 15th to 18th
centuries. Dumfries, 1931.
ED/N-1 (NE.25.a.2) QZ/Q17 ED/N-2
SA/U-1 QZ/P99 ED/S10 QZ/L37 QZ/P18
QZ/P-1 ED/U-1

Heriot of Trabroun
BALLINGALL, G. W.
Collections and notes, historical and genealogical
regarding the Heriots of Trabroun, Scotland.
[N.p.], 1878.
ED/N-1 (S.120.g) QZ/P34 QZ/P99

— Selections from old records regarding the Heriots
of Trabroun. Haddington, 1894.
ED/N-1 (S.120.g;Ry.I.3.180) SA/U-1 ED/N-2
QZ/P-1

Heron
ROGERS, Julian C.
A history of our family (Rogers). [N.p.], 1902.
ED/N-2

WATSON, Charles Brodie Boog
Traditions and genealogies of some members of the
families of Boog, Heron, Leishman, Ross and
Watson. Perth, 1908.
ED/N-1 (S.120.d) QZ/P18 ED/N-2 SA/U-1
QZ/P99 QZ/L37

Herries of Hartwood
HERIES, David C.
Herries of Hartwood. (In *Transactions of the
Dumfriesshire and Galloway Natural History &
Antiquarian Society*, 3rd series, vol.xxii, 1938/40,
pp.35-50.)
ED/N-1 (J.187)

Herries, Lord Herries
HERRIES-CROSBIE, Charles Howard
The story and pedigree of the Lords Herries of
Herries in the male line. Wexford, [19--].
ED/N-1 (6.183(18))

Herries of Maidenpaup
HERRIES, David C. Herries of Maidenpaup
(In *Transactions of the Dumfriesshire and Galloway
Natural History & Antiquarian Society*, 3rd series,
vol.xxi, 1936/38, pp.342-59.)
ED/N-1 (J.187)

Herries, Lord Herries of Terregles

CLARK MAXWELL, Prebendaly
Carruchan and its owners. (In *Transactions of the
Dumfriesshire and Galloway Natural History &
Antiquarian Society*, 3rd series, vol.xix, 1933/35,
pp.123-32.)
ED/N-1 (J.187)

CONSTABLE-MAXWELL, William
Case on behalf of William Constable Maxwell of
Nithsdale . . . claiming to be Lord Herries of
Terregles. London, 1849-1858.
ED/N-1 (Yule.152(1,3))   QZ/P99

FRASER, Sir William
Inventories of the muniments of the families of
Maxwell, Herries and Nithsdale in the charter-room
at Terregles. [N.p.], 1865.
QZ/P-1

MAXWELL, William
Case for William Maxwell of Carruchan, Esq.,
claiming to be Earl of Nithsdale, Lord Maxwell,
Eskdale and Carlyle, and Lord Herries. 1848.
QZ/L37

— — 1857.
ED/N-1 (6.249(1))   QZ/L37

— Case of William Maxwell of Carruchan . . . in
opposition to the petition of William Constable
Maxwell . . . claiming to be Lord Herries of
Terregles. 2pts. [London, 1848], 53.
ED/N-1 (Yule.152(2,4))

— Supplemental case for William Maxwell of
Carruchan . . . in opposition to the case of William
Constable Maxwell, Esq., claiming the title, honour
and dignity of Lord Herries of Terregles. 1853.
ED/N-1 (Yule.152(2,4))   QZ/P-1   QZ/P10

MAXWELL, William Constable
Speeches delivered by Counsel upon the claim to
the Barony of Herries of Terregles, with the Lord
Advocate's reply. [London], 1854.
ED/N-1 (Yule.152(7))

MINUTES of evidence taken before the Committee
for privileges to whom the petition of William
Constable Maxwell . . . claiming as of right to be
Lord Herries of Terregles . . . was referred.
[London], 1849.
ED/N-1 (Yule.152(6))

Hill

DEUCHAR, A.
[General collections relating to the Hill family. N.d.]
(*MS.*)
ED/N-2   QZ/P-1

['GENEALOGICAL notes concening the Hill family'.
18--.]
ED/N-1 (MS.9298,ff.66-96)

HILL, William Henry
Early records of an old Glasgow family, 1520-1791.
Glasgow, 1902.
ED/N-1 (R.172.a)   QZ/P-6   ED/N-2   QZ/P-1
QZ/P99

Hog *see also* **Hogg**

Hog

WHYTE, Donald
The Hogs of Newliston and Kellie; with notes on
some other Hogs, Hoges, Hoggs, Hogges and
Hoogs. Edinburgh, 1981.
ED/N-1 (HP2.82.76)   QZ/L37   QZ/P99

Hog of Harcarse and Bogend

WHYTE, Donald
Hog of Harcarse and Bogend. (In *Scottish
Genealogist*, vol.xiv, no.1, April 1967, pp.21-4.)
ED/N-1 (Gen.7)

Hogarth

CHRISTIE, John
The ancestry of Catherine Thomson Hogarth.
1912.
QZ/P99

Hogg

WHYTE, Donald
American links with the Ettrick shepherd. (In
Scottish Genealogist, vol.xii, no.4, pp.69-85; vol.xiii,
no.3/4, pp.35-8.)
ED/N-1 (Gen.7)

Holland

BULLOCH, John Malcolm
Broadford Works and the Hollands. Aberdeen,
1930. (Cuttings taken from the *Bon-Accord and
Northern Pictorial*.)
QZ/P22

Home *see also* **Hume**

Home

BARTY, Alexander Boyd
Argaty: its lairds and its barony book. Stirling, 1929.
ED/N-1 (R.246.h) QZ/P99

CLARK, Jacobina
Mrs. Jacobina Clark, appellant, and the Rt. Hon.
William, Earl of Home, respondent . . . Edinburgh,
1753.
QZ/P99

WOOD, John Philp
Memorials of various families. [1830?] (*MS.*)
QZ/P99

Home of Broomhouse

LOGAN-HOME, George John Ninian
Historical notes on Broomhouse and the Home
family. (In *History of the Berwickshire Naturalists' Club*,
vol.xxv, part 3, 1925, pp.381-98.)
ED/N-1 (Y.210)

— — (Reprinted from *History of the Berwickshire
Naturalists' Club*, vol.xxv, part 3, 1925.)
QZ/L37

Home of Renton *see* Dunbar, Earldom of

Home of Whitfield and Ninewells

HOME, Eugene A.
[Family history of the Homes. 1927.]
ED/N-1 (MS.Acc.6976)

Honeyman

HONEYMAN, Abraham van Doren
The Honeyman family in Scotland and America
from 1548-1908. Plainfield, N.J., 1909.
ED/N-2

Hope

SETON, George
Memoir of Alexander Seton . . . with an appendix
containing . . . genealogical tables of the legal
families of Erskine, Hope, Dalrymple and Dundas.
Edinburgh, 1882.
ED/N-1 (R.181.f) QZ/P-1 QZ/P16

— — Edinburgh, 1883
ED/N-1 (L.C.1915)

SKINNER, Basil C.
The Hope family in East Lothian (In *Transactions of
the East Lothian Antiquarian and Field Naturalists'
Society*, vol.xviii, 1982, pp.29-36.)
ED/N-1 (Hist.S.91.E)

Hope, Lord Hope of Hopetoun *see* Annandale, Marquessate of

Hope of Hopetoun

HOPES of Hopetoun. (Reprinted from *Edinburgh
Courant*, September 1881.)
QZ/P99

Hopper

MCINTOSH, Mary
Roots and branches: the story of the Angus and
Leybourne families. [With genealogical tables.]
Newcastle, [1958].
ED/N-1 (NE.63.e.12)

Horsburgh

WILLINS, A.
Innerleithen and Traquair, past and present.
Innerleithen, 1863.
ED/N-1 (NE.16.f.2)

Hossack

EAST, Sir Ronald
The Kiel family and related Scottish pioneers:
Findlays, Hossacks, Gilberts, Camerons, Stewarts,
McAlpins, McCallums, McDonalds. Victoria, 1974.
(*A Family Who's Who*, vol.2.)
ED/N-1 (NE.26.d.3) ED/N-2 GL/U-1
QZ/P50

Houldsworth

MACLEOD, William Houldsworth *and*
HOULDSWORTH, Sir Henry Hamilton
Beginnings of the Houldsworths of Coltness.
Glasgow, 1937.
ED/N-1 (R.172.c) QZ/P-3 ED/N-2 QZ/P56
QZ/P13 QZ/P-1 QZ/P99

Houston

[GENEALOGICAL roll pertaining to the Houstouns.
N.p., n.d.]
QZ/P-6

HOUSTON, James
Houstoun: an historical and genealogical account
of the chiefs of the names and arms of Houston,
and some of their branches, also a biographical
description of large numbers of Houston and
Huston families throughhout the world.
Palmerston North, N.Z., 1976.
ED/N-1 (1978.43) QZ/P-6

RODGERS, John
  The common bond. Paisley, 1980.
  ED/N-1 (HP2.81.524) QZ/P99

STEVENSON,
  Houstoniana. [N.p.], 1864.
  ED/N-2

WHYTE, Donald
  The Houstons of Houston. (In *Scottish Genealogist*,
  vol.xv, no.2, 1968, pp.86-91.)
  ED/N-1 (Gen.7)

Houstoun in Georgia, U.S.A.
  JOHNSTON, Edith Duncan
  The Houstouns of Georgia. Athens, Ga., 1950.
  ED/N-1 (NF.1373.a.2) QZ/P-6

Howie of Lochgoin
  FLEMING, David Hay
  John Howie of Lochgoin, his forbears and his
  works. [Princeton, N.J., 1909]. (Reprinted from
  Princeton Theological Review, vol.vii, no.1, January
  1909.)
  ED/N-1 (Ry.I.3.347)

  HOWIE, John
  Memoirs of the life of John Howie, who lived in
  Lochgoin, parish of Fenwick, and died January 5
  1793. Glasgow, 1796.
  ED/N-1 (ii.6/1.22)

Howison of Braehead
  WOOD, John Philp
  The antient and modern state of the parish of
  Cramond. [With genealogical tables.] Edinburgh,
  1794.
  ED/N-1 (A.115.a.16)

Hume *see also* **Home**

Hume
  DRUMMOND, Henry
  Histories of noble British families. Vol. 2: Dunbar,
  Hume, Dundas. London, 1846.
  ED/N-1 (S.330.a) GL/U-1 QZ/P99

  MILNE-HOME, David
  Biographical memoranda of the persons whose
  portraits hang in the dining-room at Milne-Graden
  (Berwickshire). Edinburgh, 1862.
  ED/N-1 (R.172.f) QZ/P11 QZ/P99 QZ/P-1

Hume, Earl of Marchmont *see also* **Marchmont,**
  Earldom of

Hume, Earl of Marchmont
  LOW, David
  Report relative to the Lordship and estate of
  Marchmont, the barony of Hume &c. [N.p.],
  1819.
  ED/N-1 (R.290.c) ED/N-2

  A SELECTION from the papers of the Earls of
  Marchmont, in the possession of the Rt. Hon. Sir
  George Henry Rose, 1685-1750. London, 1831. 3v.
  ED/N-1 (A.114.c) QZ/P11 GL/U-1
  QZ/P-1 QZ/P40 (I) QZ/P99

Hume of Ninewells
  MONTAGUE-SMITH, Patrick W.
  Ancestry of David Hume the philosopher. (In
  Genealogists' Magazine, vol.13, no.9, March 1961,
  pp.274-9.)
  ED/N-1 (Y.173)

  MOSSNER, Ernest C.
  The life of David Hume. [With a genealogical
  table.] Edinburgh, 1954.
  ED/N-1 (H3.75.1014)

Hume of Polwarth
  HUME, Roland Cunningham
  Historia dos familias. [With genealogical tables.]
  Buenos Aires, 1976.
  ED/N-1 (1977.97)

  WARRENDER, Margaret
  Marchmont and the Humes of Polwarth.
  Edinburgh, 1894.
  ED/N-1 (A.124.b) QZ/Q17 QZ/P11 SA/U-1
  AD/U-1 GL/U-1 QZ/L37 QZ/P-1 QZ/P99

Hume of Wedderburn
  HUME, David
  Davidis Humii de familia Humia Wedderburnensi
  liber. Edinburgh, 1839. (Abbotsford Club.)
  ED/N-1 (Abbot.Club.15) ED/N-2 GL/U-1
  QZ/P-1 QZ/P99

  HUME, Edgar Erskine
  A colonial Scottish Jacobite family: the
  establishment in Virginia of a branch of the Humes
  of Wedderburn. Richmond, Va., 1931.
  QZ/P99

  HUME, Roland Cunningham
  Historia de dos familias. [With genealogical tables.]
  Buenos Aires, 1976.
  ED/N-1 (1977.97)

Humphrys *see* **Stirling,** Earldom of

Hunter

HUNTER, Andrew Alexander
The pedigree of Hunter of Abbotshill and Barjarg and cadet families, Hunter of Bonnytoun and Doonholm, Hunter-Blair of Blairquhan, Hunter of Auchterarder, Hunter of Thurston. London, 1905.
ED/N-1 (S.120.a) ED/N-2 SA/U-1 AD/U-1
QZ/L37 QZ/P-1

Hunter in Forfarshire

GUTHRIE, G. G. Hunter
Hunters of Forfarshire, 1528-1928. [N.p., n.d.]
QZ/P28

Hunter of Hunterston

['GENEALOGIES of the Hunters of Hunterstoun'. 17--.]
ED/N-1 (Adv.MS.20.1.9,ff.2-9)

The PEDIGREE of Hunter of Hunterston. [N.p., n.d.]
ED/N-1 (H.22.d) ED/N-2

SOME family papers of the Hunters of Hunterstoun; edited by M. S. Shaw. Edinburgh, 1925. (Scottish Record Society, vol.58.)
ED/N-1 (Ref.55;S.122.d) ED/N-2 DN/U-1
ED/U-1 GL/U-2 QZ/L37 QZ/P-1 QZ/P99

STODART, R. R.
Notice of a recent case in the Court of Session, as to the surname and arms of Hunter of Hunterston. [N.d.]
QZ/P99

Hunter of Knap

FRANKLYN, Charles
A genealogical history of the families of Montgomerie of Garboldisham, Hunter of Knap and Montgomerie of Fittleworth. Ditchling, 1967.
ED/N-1 (L.187.d) QZ/L37 GL/U-1 QZ/P-1
QZ/P26 QZ/P99

Hunter-Blair of Blairquhan *see* **Hunter**

Huntly, Earl of, Marquess of *see* **Gordon,** Earl, Marquess of Huntly

Hutcheson of Lambhill

HILL, Laurence
Huchesoniana, giving the story of Partick Castle, and an account of the Founders of Hutcheson's Hospital. Edinburgh, 1855.
ED/N-1 (Ry.I.3.121)

HILL, William Henry
History of the hospital and school in Glasgow founded by George and Thomas Hutcheson of Lambhill, A.D. 1639-41; with notices of the founders and of their family, properties and affairs. Glasgow, 1881.
ED/N-1 (R.291.c) QZ/L37 QZ/P-1

Hutchison

BULLOCH, John Malcolm
The House of Gordon: genealogical tree, with the descendants of James Hutchison and Mary Forrester added and brought down to date. Peterhead, 1908.
ED/N-1 (5.174)

DEUCHAR, A.
Genealogical collections relative to the family of Hutchison. [N.d.] (*MS.*)
QZ/P-1

Hutchison in Peterhead

HUTCHISON, Thomas
[Pedigree of the Hutchison family of Peterhead, 1668-1900.] (*MSS.*)
QZ/P22

Imbrie

IMBRIE, Addison Murray
Genealogy of the Imbrie family of Western Pennsylvania, descendants of James Imbrie, pioneer settler, and his wife Euphemia Smart. Pittsburgh, Penn., 1953.
ED/N-2 QZ/P16

Imrie of Lunan

BLAIR-IMRIE, William
A record of Lunan: its descent and transmission, 1189-1849. Edinburgh, 1902.
ED/N-1 (R.290.a) QZ/P28

Inglis *see also* **Cochrane-Inglis**

Inglis

['GENEALOGICAL account of the family of Inglis of Manorhead'. 19--.]
ED/N-1 (MS.3581,ff.181-94)

[A GENEALOGICAL table showing the antecedents of Robert Shortreed. N.p., 1844.]
ED/N-1 (7.106(66-9))

INGLIS, James
Oor ain folk: being memories of manse life in the
Mearns and a crack aboot auld times. Edinburgh,
1894.
ED/N-1 (A.122.e)

WILSON, Jean
Inglis family history. [Crystal Brook, S. Australia],
1983.
ED/N-1 (H4.83.1506)

Inglis of Auchindinny

INGLIS, John Alexander
The family of Inglis of Auchindinny and Redhall.
Edinburgh, 1914.
ED/N-1 (S.121.b) ED/N-2 SA/U-1 AD/U-1
GL/U-1 QZ/P22 QZ/L37 QZ/P-1 ED/U-1
QZ/P99

—Inglis of Auchindinny and Redhall: the family tree.
[Edinburgh, 1903.]
ED/N-1 (S.305.c) QZ/L37 QZ/P99

—Sir John Hay "the Incendiary", 1578-1654. [with
genealogical tables.] Glasgow, 1937.
ED/N-1 (R.186.c)

Inglis of Cramond

WOOD, John Philp
The antient and modern state of the parish of
Cramond. [With genealogical tables.] Edinburgh,
1794.
—Memorials of various families. [1830?] (*MS.*)
QZ/P99

Inglis of Edzell

INGLIS Memorial Hall, Edzell, N. B.: proceedings at
the opening ceremony on Friday, the 22nd July,
1898.
QZ/P-1

Inglis of Murdoston

GROSSART, William
Historic notices and domestic history of the parish
of Shotts. Glasgow, 1880.
ED/N-1 (A.118.d)

Inglis of Tarvit

['PAPERS concerning the genealogy of the Inglis
family of Tarvit'. 17--.]
ED/N-1 (Adv.MS.20.1.8,ff.20-5)

Innes

['ACCOUNT of the Innes family'. 1942.]
ED/N-1 (MS.3068-9)

FORBES, Duncan
Ane account of the familie of Innes, compiled . . .
1698. Aberdeen, 1864. (Spalding Club.)
ED/N-1 (Spald.Club.34) ED/N-2 GL/U-1
QZ/L37 QZ/P-1 QZ/P22 QZ/P30 QZ/P40
QZ/P50 QZ/P99

GREGORY, Margaret Innes
A complete record of the family of George and
Jessie MacQueen-Innes, immigrants to Maine, 1873.
[N.p.], 1965.
QZ/P22 QZ/P30 QZ/P40 (I)

HISTORICALL account of the origine and succession
of the family of Innes. Edinburgh, 1820.
ED/N-1 (A.114.a.8) AD/U-1 QZ/L37 QZ/P50
QZ/P-1 QZ/P99

INNES, Frances Marsh
The ancestry and kin of Robert Stewart Innes.
Atlanta, Ga., 1963.
QZ/L37

INNES, Sir Thomas
The Inneses of Benwall and Blairton and collateral
branches. Edinburgh, 1955.
ED/N-1 (5.1994) QZ/P22 AD/U-1 QZ/P50
ED/U-1 QZ/P99

The LAIRDS of Innes. (In *Elgin Literary Magazine*,
no.ii, August 1829, pp.73-9.)
ED/N-1 (Bm.10/1)

['PAPERS concerning the genealogy of the family of
Innes'. 17--.]
ED/N-1 (Adv.MS.20.1.9,ff.12-29)

Innes of Ballogie

STIRTON, John
Relics of the family of Innes of Balnacraig and
Ballogie, Aberdeenshire. (In *Proceedings of the Society
of Antiquaries of Scotland*, 5th series, vol.vii, 1920/21,
pp.100-7.)
ED/N-1 (Ref.52)

Innes of Balnacraig

INNES, Thomas
The Inneses of Balnacraig. (In *Deeside Field*, no.5,
1930, pp.76-83.)
ED/N-1 (6.589)

STIRTON, John
A day that is dead. Forfar, 1913.
ED/N-1 (S.166.b)

— — 2nd ed. Forfar, [1929].
ED/N-1 (MS.3065. Author's copy with MS. notes)
QZ/P22 QZ/P30 QZ/P40 QZ/P99 QZ/L37

— Relics of the family of Innes of Balnacraig and
Ballogie, Aberdeenshire. (In *Proceedings of the Society
of Antiquaries of Scotland*, 5th series, vol.vii, 1920/1,
pp.100-7.)
ED/N-1 (Ref.52)

Innes of Balveny *see* **Innes** of Edingight

Innes in Caithness
SINCLAIR, Thomas
The Innesses of Caithness. [Press-cuttings collected
and bound by John Mowat, of Caithness.]
QZ/P40

— — (From *Northern Ensign*, 5 July, 7 October 1902.)
QZ/P99

Innes of Coxton
The GENEALOGY of the family of Innes of Coxtown.
[N.p., 1819.]
AD/U-1

Innes of Crommey
INNES, Sir Thomas
The barony of Crommey. (In *Transactions of the
Banffshire Field Club*, 17 April 1934, pp.69-107.)
ED/N-1 (NE..3.g.1)

— Innes of Cromcy. (Reprinted from *Transactions of
the Banffshire Field Club*, 1934.)
QZ/L37 QZ/P-1

Innes of Eastraw
MEMORIALS of a faithful servant, William Innes.
[Edinburgh], 1876.
ED/N-1 (3.2673(7))

Innes of Edingight
INNES, Sir Thomas
The chronicles of the family of Innes of Edingight
and Balveny. Aberdeen, 1898.
ED/N-1 (A.58.a) ED/N-2 QZ/P22 QZ/P40
ED/U-1 QZ/P99 SA/U-1 GL/U-1 QZ/L37
QZ/P50 ED/U-1

— The old mansion house of Edingight. (In
Transactions of the Banffshire Field Club, 22 April
1937, pp.27-42.)
ED/N-1 (NE.3.g.1)

Innes of Innes
['COPY of eighteenth century account of the history
of the family of Innes of Innes'. 1698.]
ED/N-1 (Adv.MS.34.6.19, ff.86-109)

Innes of Learney
INVENTORY of the principal progress-writs of the
Barony of Innes, 1225-1767; edited by Sir
Thomas Innes. Edinburgh, 1948. (Scottish Record
Society, part 153.)
ED/N-1 (Ref.55) QZ/P50

Innes of Mathiemill
INNES, Colin W.
Innes of Mathiemill. New York, 1958.
ED/N-2 QZ/L37

Innes of Newseat of Scurdargue
INNES, A. N.
Notes on the family of Innes of Newseat of
Scurdargue from records both public and private,
and family letters. London, 1931.
ED/N-1 (R.172.f) QZ/P22 SA/U-1 AD/U-1
QZ/L37 QZ/P99 QZ/P50 QZ/P-1

Innes of Pethnick
INNES, Sir Thoms
Innes of Pethnick. (Reprinted from *Transactions of
the Banffshire Field Club*, 1935.)
QZ/P-1 QZ/L37

— The regality of Strathisla. (In *Transactions of the
Banffshire Field Club*, 15 May 1935, pp.69-100.)
ED/N-1 (NE.3.g.1)

Ireland of Milnhole
DRUMMOND, P. R.
The Irelands of Milnhole in Perthshire in bygone
days: one hundred biographical essays. [N.p.], 1879.
QZ/P26

Irvine *see also* **Irving**

Irvine
BOYD, Lucinda
The Irvines and their kin. Chicago, 1908.
ED/N-1 (H4.78.1159) ED/N-2

IRVINE, C.
The original of the family of the Irvines or
Erinvines . . . [1828?]
QZ/P99

MIDBRAKE papers: MS. relating to Irvine family of Midbrake, North Yell, miscellaneous Shetland documents, and notes on genealogies and land-holdings. [N.p., n.d.]
QZ/P41

THOM, Robert W.
Wyseby: a legend of the first Irvings. Edinburgh, 1844.
ED/N-1 (Hall.197.d)   QZ/P-1

Irvine of Brucklay

MUNRO, Alexander Macdonald
A note on the Irvines of Brucklay in the parish of New Deer, Aberdeenshire. [With a genealogical table.][N.p., n.d.]
ED/N-1 (NE.25.g.8)

Irvine of Cults

BULLOCH, Joseph Gaston Baillie
History and genealogy of the families of Bulloch and Stobo, and Irvine of Cults. Washington, 1892.
QZ/P22

— — Washington, 1911.
ED/S10 (Unconfirmed location)

Irvine of Drum

ANDERSON, Robert
The Irvines of Drum. Peterhead, 1920.
QZ/P22

IRVINE, Alexander
[Papers in the case of Alexander Irvine of Drum, and his tutors, pursuers, against George, Earl of Aberdeen, and Margaret Duff, relict and representative of the deceased Patrick Duff of Premnay, and others, defenders. Edinburgh, 1767-9.]
ED/N-1 (Yule.97)

IRVING, Edward J. B.
The Irvings of Bonshaw and the Irvines of Drum. (In *Scottish Genealogical Helper*, no.3, 1974, pp.36-7.)
ED/N-1 (P.la.6393)

LESLIE, Jonathan Forbes
The Irvines of Drum and collateral branches. Aberdeen, 1909.
ED/N-1 (S.120.d)   QZ/P30   QZ/P22   SA/U-1   AD/U-1   QZ/L37   GL/U-1   ED/U-1   QZ/P99

WIMBERLEY, Douglas
Memorials of four old families. Inverness, 1894.
ED/N-1 (Y.59.a.23)   DN/U-1   QZ/P-1   QZ/P22   QZ/P40   QZ/P99

— Pedigree of Irvine of Drum. Inverness, 1894.
QZ/P30   QZ/P-1

— A short account of the family of Irvine of Drum in the county of Aberdeen. Inverness, 1893.
ED/N-1 (Y.59.a.23)   SA/U-1   AD/U-1   QZ/P22   QZ/L37   QZ/P30

Irvine in Fermanagh, Ireland

IRVINE, John
A brief account of the Irvine Family, County Fermanagh. [With a genealogical table.] Dublin, [1828].
ED/N-1 (S.120.i)

Irvine of Kingcausie

IRVINE-FORTESQUE, James
Kingcausie. (In *Deeside Field*, no.17, 1981, pp.18-31)
ED/N-1 (P.la.10,166)

Irvine of Monboddo

PAPERS from the collection of Sir William Fraser; edited by J. R. N. Macphail. Edinburgh, 1924. (Scottish History Society Publications, 3rd series, vol.v.)
ED/N-1 (Ref.54)

Irvine in New Zealand

SANDISON, Alexander
Sandisons of Shetland. Part 1: The Delting family, with Poles of Greenbank & Irvines of Dunsandel, N.Z. [South Croydon], 1971.
ED/N-1 (6.1982)   QZ/P41

Irving

HOSMER, Ralph Sheldon *and* FIELDER, M. T. I.
Genealogy of that branch of the Irwin family in New York founded in the Hudson River Valley, 1700-1787. Ithaca, N.Y., 1938.
ED/N-1 (R.172.e)   ED/N-2   QZ/P22

IRVING, John Beaufin
[The book of the Irvings]. The Irvings, Irwins, Irvines or Erinveines or any other spelling of the name: an old Scots border clan. Aberdeen, 1907.
ED/N-1 (S.295.a)   QZ/P22   AD/U-1   QZ/L37   QZ/P-1   QZ/P99

Irving of Bonshaw

FITZMAURICE, Frances Rhoda
Bonshaw Tower: the Irvings and some of their kinsfolk. Dumfries, [1898].
ED/N-1 (Hall.191.d)

IRVING, Edward J. B.
  The Irvings of Bonshaw. (In *Scottish Genealogist*, vol.xviii, no.4, December 1971, pp.64-72.)
  ED/N-1 (Gen.7)

— The Irvings of Bonshaw and the Irvines of Drum. (In *Scottish Genealogical Helper*, no. 3, 1974, pp. 36-8.)
  ED/N-1 (P.la.6393)

MAXWELL-IRVING, Alastair Michael Tivey
  The Irvings of Bonshaw, chiefs of the noble and ancient Scots border family of Irving. [Bletchley], 1968.
  ED/N-1 (NE.25.e.11)   QZ/L37   QZ/P22
  ED/N-2   SA/U-1   QZ/P-1   QZ/P99

Irving in Dumfries
MAXWELL-IRVING, Alastair Michael Tivey
  Genealogy of the Irvings of Dumfries; extracted from his 3 vol. MS., "The Irvings of Dumfries". [N.p.], 1965.
  ED/N-1 (NE.25.h.18)   ED/N-2   QZ/L37

Irving of Hoddom
IRVING, George
  The Irvings of Hoddom. (In *Transactions of the Dumfriesshire and Galloway Natural History & Antiquarian Society*, vol.xvii, 1900-05, pp.175-201.)
  ED/N-1 (J.187)

Irving of Ironshore
IRVING, Aemilius
  James Irving of Ironshore and his descendants, 1713-1918. Toronto, 1918.
  ED/N-1 (R.272.b)

Irving of Newton
IRVING, Miles
  The Irvings of Newton: an appendix to the "Book of the Irvings". [Aberdeen, n.d.]
  ED/N-1 (S.295.a)   ED/N-2   AD/U-1   QZ/L37

Irwin *see* **Irving**

Iver *see* **Maciver**

Jaffray
JAFFRAY, Alexander
  Diary: edited by John Barclay. London, 1833.
  ED/N-1 (A.114.a)   QZ/P22

— — 2nd ed. London, 1834.
  QZ/P-1

— — 3rd ed. Aberdeen, 1856.
  QZ/P-1

JAFFRAY, Robert
  Jaffray genealogy, being an account of a branch of this family which was particularly associated with Stirlingshire. New York, 1926.
  ED/N-1 (NE.25.a.15)   SA/U-1

Jameson
JAMESON, Andrew
  Jamesons and Goudies in Channerwick, Shetland. 1980.
  QZ/P99

SWEET, Jessie M.
  Robert Jameson and Shetland: a family history. (In *Scottish Genealogist*, vol.xvi, no.1, March 1969, pp.1-15.)
  ED/N-1 (Gen.7)   QZ/P41

Jamesone
BULLOCH, John
  George Jamesone, the Scottish 'Vandyck'. [With a genealogical table.] Edinburgh, 1885.
  ED/N-1 (Ca.4/2)

Jamieson
IRELAND, Kingsley
  For generations yet unborn: the Jamieson family 1747-1978, the history and family tree of Alexander Jamieson, 1816-1912, and his wife, Janet née Gilmour, and their descendants. [Adelaide, 1978.]
  ED/N-1 (H4.79.784)   ED/N-2

JAMIESON, Alan
  The Jamieson and Gilmour families in Scotland: supplement to "For generations yet unborn". [Angaston, South Australia?, 1982.]
  ED/N-1 (H4.79.784)

Jarvie
SPENCER, C.L.
  Some notes on the Spencers, Jarvies, and Rintouls in Glasgow, compiled from family tradition and public records. 1935. (*Typescript*)
  QZ/P-1

Jarvie of Pollokshaws
FAMILY history and genealogy of the descendants of William Jarvie of Pollokshaws (d. 1767) and Angus McGhie of Berryknowe, Govan, down to *c.* 1839. (*MSS.*)
  QZ/P-1

Jervie

SIMPSON, R. R.
Pedigree of the Linlithgowshire Simpsons,
including pedigrees of the families of Cleland of
Cleland, Jervies, Russells and Raleighs. Edinburgh,
1895.
ED/U-1

Johnson

JOHNSON, Lorand V.
Scotch-English Johnsons. (In *Scottish-American
Genealogist*, no.17/20, 1980, pp.75-9.)
ED/N-1 (P.la.6393)

Johnson in U.S.A.

JOHNSON, Donald W.
[Pedigree chart. N.p., n.d.]
QZ/P22

CUTHBERT, Alexander A.
Genealogical chart of the Johnston family, Bathgate.
[N.p., 1908.]
ED/N-1 (1908.33)   QZ/L37   QZ/P-1

Johnston

GENEALOGICAL chart of the Johnston family.
[1730-1887.] [N.p., n.d.]
ED/L37 (Unconfirmed location)

JOHNSTON, Francis Alexander
A Johnston family record. [N.p.], 1938.
QZ/P10 (Unconfirmed location)

JOHNSTON, George Harvey
Heraldry of the Johnstons. Edinburgh, 1905.
ED/N-1 (Hall.139.b)   ED/N-2   QZ/P-1
QZ/P99

JOHNSTON, Lorand V.
Selected references relating to Johnston of
Caskieben, Crimond and Caiesmill, with reference
to Alderman Robert Johnson. Shaker Heights,
Ohio, [197-?].
ED/N-1 (H8.79.171)

—Selected references relating to the ancestry of
William and John Johnston, colonial friends
(Quakers) of Virginia: an account of the connections
of the family of Johnston of Caskieben, and of that
ilk, of the Garioch, Aberdeenshire, Scotland.
Shaker Heights, Ohio], 1972.
ED/N-1 (NE.25.f.23)   SA/U-1   QZ/P22
QZ/P30

JOHNSTONE, Catherine Laura
The Johnstons in Edinburgh. [N.d.] (Reprinted
mainly from her *History of the Johnstones*.)
QZ/P-1   QZ/P99

REID, Robert Corsane
Cadets of Johnston. [N.p., n.d.] 2v.
QZ/P10 (Unconfirmed location)

Johnston of Bathgate

CUTHBERT, Alexander A.
Genealogical chart of the Johnston family, Bathgate.
[N.p., 1909.]
ED/N-1 (1964.75)

Johnston of Caskieben

JOHNSTON, Alexander
Genealogical account of the family of Johnston of
that ilk, formerly of Caskieben in the shire of
Aberdeen. Edinburgh, 1832.
ED/N-1 (A.114.b)   SA/U-1   QZ/P22   QZ/L37
QZ/P-1

—Short memoir of James Young, merchant burgess
of Aberdeen, and Rachel Cruickshank his spouse,
and of their descendants. Aberdeen, 1861.
ED/N-1 (Hall.230.a)   QZ/P22   QZ/L37
QZ/P99

— — [New ed.] edited by W. Johnston. Aberdeen,
1894.
QZ/P22   QZ/L37   QZ/P99

Johnston of Craigieburn

JOHNSTON-RATHEN, Max von
Stamm-Tafel der Familie von Johnston und
Kroegeborn. [N.p.], 1886.
ED/N-1 (6.283(33))

—Urkunden und Regesten zur Geschichte der
Familie von Johnston und Kroegeborn. Breslau,
1895.
ED/N-1 (6.212)

Johnston of Kirkhill

[GENEALOGICAL table of the family of Johnston of
Kirkhill.] [N.p., 1890?]
ED/N-1 (NE.25.f.18)

Johnston of Stromness

GEDDES, David
'David Geddes whom you pronounced dunce';
typescript family history of the families of John
Johnston (of Stromness and Quebec), Dr. Andrew
Crookshank (of Aberdeen) and David Geddes (of
Orkney). [N.p., 1970.]
QZ/P38 (Unconfirmed location)

Johnstone

JOHNSTONE and Ruddiman pedigree. [1910?]
ED/N-1 (MS.Acc.5811,no.9a)

JOHNSTONE, Catherine Laura
History of the Johnstones, 1191-1909, with
descriptions of Border life. (And Supplement.)
Edinburgh, Glasgow, 1909-1925. 2v.
ED/N-1 (S.121.d) SA/U-1 QZ/P22 AD/U-1
QZ/P-1 QZ/P99

— — [Supplement only.] Glasgow, 1925.
QZ/P53 QZ/P27 QZ/P26 QZ/P28 QZ/P-7
QZ/P52 QZ/P11 QZ/P16

The JOHNSTONES show supremacy. [N.p., n.d.]
ED/N-1 (5.2294)

REID, Robert Corsane
Johnstone MSS: [extracts from deeds, registers of
sasines, decreets, testaments etc. covering a period,
1413-1885, but more particularly the 17th and 18th
centuries]. [N.p., n.d.]
QZ/P10 (Unconfirmed location)

Johnstone, Earl of Annandale *see also* **Annandale,**
Earldom of

Johnstone, Earl of Annandale

FRASER, Sir William
The Annandale family book of the Johnstones.
Edinburgh, 1894. 2v.
ED/N-1 (Hist.S.112.J;Gen.8.J) ED/N-2 QZ/P11
SA/U-1 AD/U-1 GL/U-1 QZ/L37 QZ/P-1
ED/U-1 QZ/P99

— A century of romance of the Annandale peerages,
with letters of Henry, Lord Brougham. [N.p.], 1894.
(Reprinted from *The Annandale family book*.)
ED/N-2 SA/U-1 AD/U-1 ED/U-1

The JOHNSTONES of Annandale. [With a
genealogical table.] London, 1853. (*Typescript*)
ED/N-1 (R.282.c)

MACDONALD, James Alexander Donald John
The contest with the Hopes and Westerhalls and
the disappearance of the titles of the Johnstones of
Annandale, followed by the Hope Johnstone deed
of entail of 1799. Dumfries, [1925].
ED/N-1 (S.123.f.1(2))

Johnstone of Elphinstone

BULLOCH, James
The Johnstones of Elphinstone (In *Scottish
Genealogist*, vol.xi, no.2, 1964, pp.1-5.)
ED/N-1 (Gen.7)

BULLOCH, James B. P.
The Johnstones of Elphinstone. (In *Transactions of
the East Lothian Antiquarian and Field Naturalists'
Society*, vol.4, 1948, pp.34-50.)
ED/N-1 (Hist.S.91.E)

— — (Reprinted from *Transactions of the East Lothian
Antiquarian and Field Naturalists' Society*, vol.4, 1948.)
QZ/P-1 QZ/P34 QZ/P99

Johnstone of Elschieshields

EDGAR, Robert
An introduction to the history of Dumfries. [With
genealogical tables.] Dumfries, 1915.
ED/N-1 (R.241.b)

Johnstone of Lochwood

REID, Robert Corsane
Lochwood tower. (In *Transactions of the Dumfriesshire
and Galloway Natural History & Antiquarian Society*,
3rd series, vol.xiii, 1925/6, pp.187-93.)
ED/N-1 (J.187)

— — (Reprinted from *Transactions of the Dumfriesshire
and Galloway Natural History & Antiquarian Society*,
3rd series, vol.xiii, 1925/6.)
QZ/L37 QZ/P-1

Jones, John Paul *see* **Paul**

Keddie

TYTLER, Sarah
Three generations: the story of a middle-class
Scottish family. London, 1911.
ED/N-1 (S.168.f) QZ/P-1 QZ/P18 QZ/P22
QZ/P99

Kedie

HAINING, James H.
Genealogical tree of the Kedie family. (In *Transactions
of the Hawick Archaeoogical Society*, 1951, pp.37-8.)
ED/N-1 (P.220)

Keir

CAMPBELL, Julia Beatrice
A few words about an old Highland family.
Glasgow, [1894]. (*Auchindarroch Miscellany*, vol.I.)
QZ/P-1

MOILLIET, Amelia
Sketch of the life of James Keir, Esq., F.R.S.... [with
a genealogy of the family of James Keir]. London,
[1859].
ED/N-1 (Hall.244.b) QZ/P99

Keith

GIBB, Andrew
The Keith family: a history notebook with sketches.
[N.d.] (*MSS.*)
QZ/P22

MERRILL, Adelaide
The Keith book. Minneapolis, Minn., 1934.
ED/N-1 (Gen.8.K) QZ/P30

MS. notes and press cuttings on the family of Keith.
[N.d.]
GL/U-1 QZ/P99

Keith, Earl Marischal

ANDERSON, Robert
Field Marshal Keith. Peterhead, 1910.
QZ/P22

BUCHAN, Peter
Account of the ancient and noble family of Keith,
Earls Marischal of Scotland. Peterhead, 1820.
ED/N-1 (L.C.282) QZ/P30 QZ/P26 ED/N-2
QZ/P22 QZ/P40 GL/U-1 QZ/P28
QZ/L37 QZ/P-1 QZ/P99

EARL-MARISCHAL and Field Marshal: some letters
of the last Earl-Marischal. (In *Scottish Review*,
vol.xxxii, October 1898, pp.316-33.)
ED/N-1 (NH.301) QZ/P99

MCLEAN, Neil N.
Memoir of Marshal Keith, with a sketch of the
Keith family. Peterhead, 1869.
ED/N-1 (Λ.114.f.7) QZ/P22 QZ/P30 QZ/P-1
QZ/P99

NAPIER, James
Stonehaven and its historical associations; with a
biographical sketch of the Keiths, Earls Marischall
of Scotland, and other families. Stonehaven, [1870].
ED/N-1 (NE.3.c.12)

Keith in U.S.A.

KING, Larry
Keith kinfolks: descendants of James Keith, Sr.
from 1720 to 1979. Hendersonville, Tenn., 1979.
ED/N-1 (H4.82.38)

Keith of Whiteriggs

MAIDMENT, James
Genealogical fragments relating to the families of...
Keith... Berwick, 1855.
ED/N-1 (Y.59.f.2;Ry.II.e.51(1)) QZ/P40 GL/U-1
QZ/P-1 QZ/P99

Kellie, Earldom of *see also* Mar, Earldom of

Kellie, Earldom of

MAR, John Francis Miller Erskine, *9th Earl of*
In the House of Lords before the Lords Committees
of Privileges case of John Francis Miller Erskine,
Earl of Mar, Lord Erskine, Garioch, and Alloa,
claiming the titles, honours and dignities of Earl of
Kellie, Viscount Fenton, the Premier Viscount of
Scotland... and Lord Dirltoun. [With a
genealogical table.] [London, 1829?]
ED/N-1 (Yule.162(7))

—Minutes of evidence... 1832-35.
QZ/L37

REPORT of the manuscripts of the Earl of Mar and
Kellie preserved at Alloa House, N.B. London,
1904. 2v.
ED/N-1 (GRH.5/60) QZ/P-1 QZ/P15

Kelso

KELSO family record: a genealogical roll.
[N.d.] (*MSS.*)
QZ/P-6

Kemp

HITCHIN-KEMP, Fred, and others
A general history of the Kemp and Kempe families
of Great Britain and the colonies. London, [1902].
ED/N-1 (S.120.b) ED/N-2 GL/U-1

Kennedy

DOUGLASS, Hiram Kennedy
My Southern families. [With genealogical tables.]
Gillingham, 1967.
ED/N-1 (NF.1372.b.18)

FERGUSSON, Sir James
The Kennedys "twixt Wigton and the town of
Ayr"; with tartan and chief's arms in colour, and a
map. Edinburgh, 1958.
ED/N-1 (Gen.7) QZ/P22 QZ/P40 QZ/P11
GL/U-1 SA/U-1 QZ/Q88 QZ/P49 QZ/P-1
ED/U-1 QZ/P99

GENEALOGICAL chart of the family of Kennedy,
1100-1903. [N.d.] (*MS.*)
SA/U-1

MACDOWALL, John Kevan
Carrick Gallovidian: a historical survey . . . with
genealogical charts and notes. . . . Ayr, 1947.
ED/N-1 (R.241.d) QZ/P-1

MS. notes and press cuttings on the family of
Kennedy. [N.d.]
QZ/P99

MAXWELL, Sir Herbert Eustace
A Scottish vendetta (Kennedy family). 1894.
(Excerpt from the *Nineteenth Century*, 1984.)
QZ/P-1 QZ/P99

MOONEY, John
Kennedys in Orkney and Caithness.
(In *Proceedings of the Orkney Antiquarian Society*;
part 1, vol.x, 1931/2, pp.17-20; part 2, vol.xi, 1932/3,
pp.19-26.)
ED/N-1 (R.250.a)

— — (Reprinted from *Proceedings of the Orkney
Antiquarian Society*, vol.x, 1931/2, vol.xi, 1932/3.)
ED/N-1 (5.471; 5.483) QZ/P-1 QZ/P40 (W)
QZ/L37

PITCAIRN, Robert
Historical and genealogical account of the principal
families of the name of Kennedy. Edinburgh, 1830.
ED/N-1 (A.114.b.15) QZ/P40 SA/U-1
GL/U-1 AD/U-1 QZ/L37 QZ/P-1 QZ/P99

Kennedy, Marquess of Ailsa
PEDIGREE of . . . Archibald Kennedy, Marquess of
Ailsa . . . born 25th August, 1816. Edinburgh, 1849.
ED/N-2 QZ/P99

Kennedy of Auchtyfardle
GOURLAY, James
The Kennedys of Auchtyfardle, and other papers.
[N.p.],1936.
ED/N-2 QZ/P99 QZ/P-1

Kennedy in Ayrshire
ROBERTSON, William
The Kings of Carrick: a historical romance of the
Kennedys of Ayrshire. London, 1890.
ED/N-1 (U.83.a) QZ/P15 QZ/P-1

Kennedy, Earl of Cassillis *see also* **Cassillis,** Earldom of

Kennedy, Earl of Cassillis
COWAN,
Historical account of the noble family of Kennedy,
Marquess of Ailsa and Earl of Cassillis, with notices
of some of the principal cadets thereof. Edinburgh,
1849.
ED/N-1 (A.114.b) QZ/P44 GL/U-1 QZ/L37
QZ/P-1 QZ/P99

ROBERTSON, William
Ayrshire, its history and historic families.
Kilmarnock, 1908. 2v.
ED/N-1 (Hist.S.91.A)

Kennedy of Dunure
TAYLOR, Henrietta
The seven sons of the provost. London, 1949.
ED/N-1 (R.157.i) QZ/P-7 QZ/P14 QZ/P22
ED/N-2 QZ/P40 GL/U-1 QZ/P-6 SA/U-1
QZ/Q88 QZ/P49 QZ/P-1 ED/U-1 QZ/P99

Kennedy of Foss
KENNEDY, James
Our ancestors. [With a genealogical table.]
[N.p.], 1928.
ED/N-1 (1937.26)

Kennedy in Ireland
KENNEDY, Francis M. E.
A family of Kennedy of Clogher and Londonderry,
c.1600-1938. [With genealogical tables.] 3 parts.
Taunton, 1938.
ED/N-1 (6.222)

Kennedy of Knocknalling
KENNEDY, J. Douglas
Kennedy, 1142-1883, Knocknalling branch.
[N.p.], 1884.
QZ/P10 (unconfirmed location)

Kennedy of Uchterlure
WIGTOWNSHIRE charters; edited by R. C. Reid.
Edinburgh, 1960. (Scottish History Society
Publications, 3rd series, vol.51.)
ED/N-1 (Ref.54)

Kenneth *see* **Mackenzie** of Kintail

Kennoway

STEUART, Katherine
Richard Kennoway and his friends. London, 1908.
ED/N-1 (S.156.c; R.159.f) QZ/P18

Ker

CARRE, Walter Riddell
Border memories. Edinburgh, 1876.
QZ/P11

KERR, Robert
"Cunningham" Kers; Triorne, Crummock,
Kersland, and Auchengree, Ayrshire. [N.p.], 1896.
ED/N-1 (6.719) ED/N-2 QZ/P99

NEWCASTLE silversmiths (In *Clan Donnachaidh
Annual*, 1972, pp.36-7.)
ED/N-1 (NB.43)

REID, Christian Leopold
Pedigree of the family of Ker of Cessford,
Greenhead, and Prymsideloch, and later of
Hoselaw, Roxburghshire, etc. Newcastle, 1914.
ED/N-1 (S.121.b) QZ/P11 QZ/L37 QZ/P99

RENILSON, John
Ferniehurst Castle and the Keirs. (In *History of the
Berwickshire Naturalists' Club*, vol.31, 1949, pp.208-20.)
ED/N-1 (Y210)

STODART, R. R.
Notes on the family of Ker, Kerr, or Carre in
Scotland. [N.d.]
QZ/P99

WELLS MABOR, W.
The story of Cessford Castle. (In *History of
Berwickshire Naturalists' Club*, vol.28, 1933,
pp.145-53.)
ED/N-1 (Y.210)

Ker, Earl of Ancram

CORRESPONDENCE of Sir Robert Kerr, 1st Earl of
Ancram, and his son, William, 3rd Earl of Lothian,
1616-1667; edited by David Laing. Edinburgh,
1875. 2v. (Bannatyne Club)
ED/N-1 (Bann.Club.122) ED/N-2 GL/U-1
QZ/L37 QZ/P-1 QZ/P-9 QZ/P11 QZ/P20
QZ/P99

Ker of Cessford

[PAPERS concerning the genealogy of the Ker family
of Cessford. 17--.]
ED/N-1 (Adv.MS.20.1.8, ff.94-112)

Ker of Corbethouse

STODART, Robert Riddle
Kerr of Gateshaw, [Kerr of Corbethouse and Moir
of Otterburn]. (In *The Genealogist*, vol.iii, 1879.)
pp.246-50.)
ED/N-1 (Y.215)

— — (Reprinted from *The Genealogist*, vol.iii, 1879.)
GL/U-1 QZ/L37

Ker of Ferniehurst

[NOTES on the genealogy of the family Ker of
Ferniehurst. 1661.]
ED/N-1 (MS.5447)

Ker of Gateshaw *see* **Ker** of Corbethouse

Ker of Greenhead *see* **Ker**

Ker of Kersland

KERR, Robert Malcolm
Notices of the families of Kerr of Kerrisland. . . .
London, 1880.
SA/U-1 QZ/P-7 QZ/P-1 QZ/L37 QZ/P99

— — 1892.
QZ/P99

Ker, Earl, Marquess of Lothian

BORDER story: the name and house of Kerr at
Monteviot, Jedburgh, Scotland. [Jedburgh], 1980.
ED/N-1 (HP.180.3246) QZ/P99

JEFFREY, Alexander
Memorials of the Marquis of Lothian's majority,
12th August, 1853, with an introductory notice of
the family. Jedburgh, 1853.
ED/N-1 (NE.15.e.9(2)) ED/N-2

NAPIER, Mark
A memorie of my mother's lineage. [N.p.], 1872.
ED/N-2 ED/N-1 (F.7.d.3)

SINCLAIR, Alexander
Brief statement of the dispute for precedency,
which lasted thirty years, between the rival families
of the Kers, Earls of Lothian and Roxburgh.
[N.p.,n.d.]
ED/N-1 (Hall.199.e.1(3)) QZ/P-9

Ker of Prymsideloch *see* **Ker**

Ker, Lord, Duke, etc. Roxburghe *see* **Roxburghe,**
Lord, Earl of, Duke of

Ker of Yair
The GENEALOGY of the families of Karr of Yair and of Kippielaw. [N.d.] (*MSS.*)
ED/N-2 QZ/P-9

Ker-Reid of Hoselaw
REID, Christian Leopold
Pedigree of the family of Ker of Cessford . . . Ker-Reid of Hoselaw, Roxburghshire . . . of Newcastle upon Tyne and London . . . Australia and U.S.A. Newcastle, 1914.
ED/N-1 (S.121.b) QZ/P11 QZ/L37 QZ/P99

Kerr
FAIRRIE, Geoffrey
The sugar refining families of Great Britain. [With genealogical tables.] London, 1951.
ED/N-1 (NE.63.b.3)

[A GENEALOGICAL table showing the antecedents of Robert Shortreed. N.p., 1844.]
ED/N-1 (7.106(66-69))

KERR, W. Hogarth
Lands and lairds of Kerse, Lochwinnoch parish, Renfrewshire. 1970. (*Typescript*)
QZ/P-6

[MATERIAL relating to the lands and lairds of Kerse, Lochwinnoch parish, Renfrewshire. N.d.] (*MSS.*)
QZ/P-6

STODART, R. R.
Carre of Cavers-Carre. [N.d.]
QZ/P99

— Sir Thomas Kerr of Redden and his descendants. [N.d.]
QZ/P99

Kerr in Dunipace
KERR, Wilfred Brenton
From Scotland to Huron: a history of the Kerr family. Seaforth, Canada, 1949.
ED/N-1 (6.423) GL/U-1 QZ/P-1

Kevan
MACDOWELL, John Kevan
Carrick Gallovidian: a historical survey . . . with genealogical charts and notes. . . . Ayr, 1947.
ED/N-1 (R.241.d) QZ/P-1

Kidd
CRAMER, Sydney
[Inscriptions in three Bibles.] Dundee, [n.d.].
ED/N-1 (Mf.25(12[4]))

Kidston of Logie
FERGUSSON, Robert Menzies
Logie: a parish history. Vol.2: Lands and landowners. Paisley, 1905.
ED/N-1 (R.243.a) QZ/P14

Kiel
EAST, Sir Ronald
The Kiel family and related Scottish pioneers: Findlays, Hossacks, Gilberts, Camerons, Stewarts, McAlpins, McCallums, McDonalds. (*A Family Who's Who*, Vol. 2) [Victoria, 1974.]
ED/N-1 (NE.26.d.3) GL/U-1 ED/N-2 QZ/P50

Kilmarnock, Earl of *see* **Boyd,** Earl of Kilmarnock

Kilmaurs, Lord *see* **Cunninghame** of Kilmaurs

Kilpatrick in U.S.A.
KILPATRICK, Marion D.J.
The Kilpatrick family: ancestors of Marion Douglas Jones and Robert Jackson Kilpatrick with related families. [N.p.], 1930.
ED/N-1 (NE.63.c.14)

Kilwinning, Lord *see also* **Balfour,** Lord Balfour of Burleigh

Kilwinning, Lord
BALFOUR, Francis Walter
Case on behalf of Francis Walter Balfour of Fernie. . . . 1862.
QZ/L37

— Supplemental case on behalf of the above. . . . 1864.
QZ/L37

BRUCE, Alexander Hugh
Case on behalf of Alexander Hugh Bruce of Kennet, only son of the late Robert Bruce. . . . [N.p., n.d.]
QZ/L37

BRUCE, Robert
Case on behalf of Robert Bruce of Kennet, claiming to be Lord Balfour of Burley and Lord Kilwinning in the peerage of Scotland. [1860.]
QZ/L37

— [Proceedings in the claim of Bruce of Kennet to the dignities of Lord Balfour of Burley and Lord Kilwinning in the peerage of Scotland. London, 1861-9.]
ED/N-1 (Yule no.153)

— Supplemental case on behalf of the above . . . 1864.
QZ/L37

CASE on behalf of Robert Bruce of Kennet, in the
county of Clackmannan, Esquire, claiming the
dignities of Lord Balfour of Burley and Lord
Kilwinning in the peerage of Scotland. [N.p.,1861.]
ED/N-1 (Yule no.153)

FRASER, William
Case for the Earl of Eglinton.
QZ/L37

— Remarks for the Earl of Eglinton.
QZ/L37

MINUTES of evidence . . . 1861-64.
QZ/L37

MONTGOMERIE, Archibald W.
Remarks for the Earl of Eglinton and Winton,
Lord Montgomerie and Kilwinning, on the claim
of Robert Bruce, Esq. of Kennet, to the title of Lord
Kilwinning. (17th June 1862) [Edinburgh], 1862.
ED/N-1 (6.249(5))

PROCEEDINGS . . . 1864.
QZ/L37

King
[MATERIAL relating to the lands and lairds of King.
N.d.] (*MSS.*)
QZ/P-6

King of Aberdeen
[DOCUMENTS relating to the lives and business
activities of George, Robert and Arthur King. N.d.]
(*MSS.*)
QZ/P22

King of Newmill
YOUNG, Robert
Memoir of the family of Kings of Newmill. Banff,
1904.
ED/N-1 (5.4510; 1904.27)   QZ/P22   QZ/P50

King of Plewlands
CRAMOND, William
Cramondiana. Elgin, 1965.
ED/N-1 (NE.3.a.9)

Kingston-Blair-Oliphant of Ardblair *see* **Maxtone**

Kinloch
KINLOCH, G. R.
Papers relating to the families of Kinloch of that ilk
and of Aberbothrie. [N.p., n.d.]
ED/N-2   QZ/P99

WAYNE, Eve T.
Kinloch of that ilk: a short account of that family.
[N.p.], 1923.
ED/N-1 (6.193)   QZ/P26   DN/U-1   QZ/P99

Kinloch of Dysart
[NOTES on the genealogy of the Kinloch family of
Dysart. 1823.]
ED/N-1 (MS.5060, f.159v)

Kinloch of Gilmerton
WOOD, John Philp
Memorials of various families. [1830?] (*MS*).
QZ/P99

Kinloss, Lord *see also* **Bruce,** Baron Bruce of Kinloss

Kinloss, Lord
AILESBURY, George William Frederick Brudenell,
Marquis of
Case of George William Frederick Brudenell,
Marquis of Ailesbury in opposition to [claim of
Richard Plantagenet]. [N.p., n.d.]
QZ/L37

BUCKINGHAM AND CHANDOS, Richard
Plantagenet, *3rd Duke of*
Case on behalf of Richard Plantagenet, Duke of
Buckingham and Chandos on his claim to Lord
Kinloss in the peerage of Scotland.
QZ/L37

— Supplemental case. . . .
QZ/L37

MINUTES of evidence. . . .
QZ/L37

Kinnaird
KINNAIRD, Harry
A short history of the Scots name Kinnaird, with
heraldic arms and seals. [Glasgow], 1982.
ED/N-1 (HP4.83.617)   QZ/P-1   QZ/P20
QZ/P50

MACLAUCHLAN, John
The silver wedding of Lord and Lady Kinnaird,
and the coming of age of the Master of Kinnaird,
August, 1900, with a sketch of the history of the
Barons of Kinnaird. Dundee, 1900.
ED/N-1 (S.25.i)   QZ/P26   ED/N-2   QZ/P28
DN/U-1   QZ/P-1   QZ/P99

Kinnaird of Culbin
MURRAY, James G.
The Kinnairds of Culbin. Inverness, [1938].
ED/N-1 (HP.1.79.608)   ED/N-2   QZ/P50

Kinniburgh
TOD, Donald A.
The Kinniburgh family, 1150-1919. [N.p.], 1933.
(*Typescript*)
DN/U-1

Kinnisburgh
KINNIBURGH, T. C.
The Kinnisburghs brought from their obscurity.
(In *Scottish Genealogist*, vol.ix, no.4, 1962, pp.1-11.)
ED/N-1 (Gen.7)

Kinnoull, Earl of *see* **Hay,** Earl of Kinnoull

Kirkcaldy of Grange
GRANT, James
Memoirs and adventures of Sir William Kirkaldy of
Grange. Edinburgh, 1849.
ED/N-1 (R.178.g)   QZ/P-1

KIRKALDY, James
A short history of the family of Kirkaldy of
Grange. London, 1903.
QZ/P18

Kirkness
SMITH, William
The knights of Stove in Kirkness, Sandwick,
Orkney. (In *Old lore Miscellany of Orkney, Shetland,
Caithness and Sutherland*, vol.5, 1912, pp.120-21.)
ED/N-1 (R.250.f)   QZ/P-1

Kirko
HAMILTON-GRIERSON, Sir Philip J.
The Kirkos of Glenesland, Bogrie, Chapel and
Sundaywell (In *Transactions of the Dumfriesshire and
Galloway Natural History & Antiquarian Society*,
3rd series, vol.iii, 1914-15, pp.222-41.)
ED/N-1 (J.187)

Kirkpatrick
BULLOCH, John Malcolm
The curious career of the Kirkpatricks. [N.p.], 1898.
ED/N-2

— The curious career of the Kirkpatricks and how
they begat Eugene. (In *San Francisco Weekly
Bulletin*, 12 April 1898.)
QZ/P22

KIRKPATRICK, Alexander de Lapère
Chronicles of the Kirkpatrick family. London, 1897.
AD/U-1   QZ/L37

REID, Robert Corsane
The early Kirkpatricks. (In *Transactions of the
Dumfriesshire and Galloway Natural History &
Antiquarian Society*, 3rd series, vol.xxx, 1951/2,
pp.61-109.)
ED/N-1 (J.187)

Kirkpatrick of Capenoch
GLADSTONE, John
The Kirkpatricks at Capenoch, 1727-1846. (In
*Transactions of the Dumfriesshire and Galloway
Natural History & Antiquarian Society*, 3rd series,
vol.xv, 1928/9, pp.85-94.)
ED/N-1 (J.187)

— — (Reprinted from *Transactions of the Dumfriesshire
and Galloway Natural History & Antiquarian Society*,
3rd series, vol.xv, 1928/9.)
QZ/P-1   QZ/P10 (Unconfirmed location)

Kirkpatrick of Closeburn
ANSWERS for Sir Thomas Kirkpatrick of Closeburn,
to the petition of Hugh Blair of Dunrod, and
Andrew Houston of Calderhall, his cedent, January
24, 1737. 1737.
QZ/P-1 (Unconfirmed location)

KIRKPATRICK, Charles
Records of the Closeburn Kirkpatricks. 1953.
(*Typescript*)
ED/N-1 (NE.63.h.4)   QZ/L37

KIRKPATRICK, Richard Godman
Kirkpatrick of Closeburn. [With a genealogical
table.] London, 1858.
ED/N-1 (R.172.c)   ED/N-2

Kirkpatrick of Killilung
KIRKPATRICK, Harold
The Killilung Kirkpatricks: some episodes relating
to them. (In *Scottish Genealogist*, vol.xxvi, no.4,
December 1979, pp.103-08.)
ED/N-1 (Gen.7)

Kirkwood
[MATERIAL relating to the lands and lairds of
Kirkwood. N.d.] (*MSS*).
QZ/P-6

Knox

CRAWFORD, William
Knox genealogy: descendants of William Knox
and John Knox, the Reformer. Edinburgh, 1896.
ED/N-1 (A.124.c) QZ/R17 QZ/P34 QZ/P22
SA/U-1 QZ/L37 QZ/P99 QZ/P16

GENEALOGICAL tree of the Knoxes, John Knox, the
reformer. . . . Edinburgh, [1858].
ED/N-1 (Ry.I.3.127)

ROGERS, Charles
Genealogical memoirs of John Knox and of the
family of Knox. London, 1879. (Grampian Club, 16.)
ED/N-1 (Gramp.Club.16) QZ/Z17 QZ/P-6
QZ/P40 QZ/P14 AD/U-1 QZ/P22 DN/U-1
GL/U-1 QZ/P99 QZ/L37 QZ/P-7 QZ/P16

SCOTT, Violet Redpath
William Knox, father of John Knox and William
Knox. [N.d.]
QZ/P99

Knox of Ranfurly

MINNEY, Rubeigh J.
Fanny [Knox] and the Regent of Siam. [With a
genealogical table.] London, 1962.
ED/N-1 (NF.1337.b.6)

Kyle

WILSON, William
Folklore and genealogies of uppermost Nithsdale.
Dumfries, 1904.
ED/N-1 (R.241.h)

Laing of Redhouse

FINLAYSON, J. D.
Redhouse and its owners. (In *Transactions of the East
Lothian Antiquarian Society*, vol.iii, 1938, pp.28-39.)
ED/N-1 (Hist.S.91.E)

Lamb

LAMB, Mabel
Some annals of the Lambs: a border family.
London, 1926.
ED/N-1 (R.272.a) GL/U-1 QZ/P99

Lamberton

LANDSBOROUGH, Drew McClamroch
Our Galloway ancestors revisited: a genealogical
and historical investigation . . . of the Laird of
Lamrochton, c.1400, cadet of the Cunninghames of
Kilmaurs, Ayrshire, the Lords Kilmaurs and Earls of
Glencairn. Thornton Heath, 1978.
ED/N-1 (HP3.80.1832) QZ/P-1 QZ/P10

Lamont

CLAN LAMONT SOCIETY
Clan Lamont Journal. Vol.i, no.1 (October 1912)-
vol.iii, no.36 (July 1925). Hereford, 1912-25.
ED/N-1 (R.272.a) QZ/L37 QZ/P99

— Constitution, office-bearers . . . ; also . . . history
of the clan . . . and chiefs of the clan by Norman
Lamont and J. K. Lamont. Oban, 1899.
QZ/P99

— Report of the first General Meeting . . . 22nd
February 1897. Glasgow, 1897.
ED/N-1 (A.113.e) QZ/L37

— Report of the General Meeting . . . 3rd February
1899. Glasgow, 1899.
QZ/L37

LAMONT, Augusta
Records and recollections of Sir James Lamont of
Knockdow. [N.p., 1950.]
ED/N-1 (6.462;Wordie.1446(8)) QZ/P27

LAMONT, Sir Norman
An inventory of Lamont papers, 1231-1897.
Edinburgh, 1914. (Scottish Records Society, 54.)
ED/N-1 (Ref.55) QZ/P27 ED/N-2 QZ/P22
GL/U-1 QZ/P-1 ED/U-1 QZ/P99

— Sketches of the history of Clan Lamont. Dunoon,
[1977].
SA/U-1

LAMONT, Thomas, and others
The Thomas Lamont family. New York, 1962.
ED/N-1 (NC.260.c.22)

LAMONT, William
The Lamont tartan: an address delivered to the Clan
Lamont Society. Glasgow, 1910.
ED/N-1 (5.199) QZ/P-1

— The Lamont tartan: two papers addressed to the
Clan Lamont Society. Glasgow, 1924.
ED/N-1 (5.388; 5.1408) QZ/P-1

MCKECHNIE, Hector
The Lamont clan, 1235-1935: seven centuries of
clan history from record evidence. Edinburgh, 1938.
ED/N-1 (Gen.8.L) QZ/P27 ED/N-2 SA/U-1
AD/U-1 QZ/L37 GL/U-1 QZ/P-7 ST/U-1
QZ/P-1 QZ/P99

Landless

WHITTAKER, Gladys
The family of Landless. [N.p.], 1970.
QZ/L37

Landrum in U.S.A.
SHEDD, Joel P.
The Landrum family. Washington, D.C., 1972.
QZ/P22

Landsborough *see* **M'Clamroch**

Landsborough *see also* **McLandsborough**

Landsborough
LANDSBOROUGH, Drew McClamroch
Our Galloway ancestors revisited: a genealogical
and historical investigation . . . of the Laird of
Lamrochton, c.1400, cadet of the Cunninghames of
Kilmaurs, Ayrshire, the Lords Kilmaurs and Earls of
Glencairn. Thornton Heath, 1978.
ED/N-1 (HP3.80.1823) QZ/P-1 QZ/P10

Lang of Selkirk
GENEALOGICAL chart of the family of Langs of
Selkirk. [N.p., n.d.]
ED/N-1 (7.16)

LANG, Patrick Sellar
The Langs of Selkirk, with some notes on the
Sibbalds of Whitelaw. . . . Melbourne, 1910.
ED/N-2 QZ/P99 QZ/P11

Langland
LANGLAND, Eric
The Langlands of that ilk, Roxburgh, 1290-1790.
[N.p., 1976.] (*Typescript*)
ED/N-2

Lauder *see also* **Dick-Lauder**

Lauder
NISBETT, Hamilton More *and* AGNEW, Stair
Carnegie
Cairnhill. Edinburgh, 1949.
ED/N-1 (R.272.f) QZ/P-3

SHAW, Duncan
The ecclesiastical members of the Lauder family in
the fifteenth century. (In *Records of the Scottish
Church History Society*, vol.xi, 1955, pp.160-75.)
ED/N-1 (NE.30.f)

YOUNG, James
Notes on historical references to the Scottish family
of Lauder. Glasgow, 1884.
ED/N-1 (A.113.a) ED/N-2 SA/U-1 GL/U-1
QZ/P-1 QZ/P99 QZ/P16

— — Glasgow, 1886.
ED/N-1 (NE.25.h.7)

Lauder of the Bass
LAWDER, Charles A. B.
The Lawders of the Bass and their descendants.
[Belfast], 1914.
ED/N-1 (Mf.52(2)) ED/N-2 QZ/P99

Lauder of Hatton
FINDLAY, John Ritchie
Hatton House. Edinburgh, [n.d.].
ED/N-1 (Y.59.b.14)

Lauderdale, Earldom of *see also* **Maitland,** Earl of
Lauderdale

Lauderdale, Earldom of
MAITLAND, Frederick Henry
Case of Major Frederick Henry Maitland . . . 1885.
QZ/L37

MAITLAND, Sir James Ramsay Gibson
Case of Sir James Ramsay Gibson Maitland, Bt.,
[claiming titles] Earl of Lauderdale, Viscount of
Lauderdale, Viscount Maitland, Lord Maitland of
Thirlestane and Lord Thirlestane and Boltoun in
the peerage of Scotland. 1885.
QZ/L37

MINUTES of evidence, etc. 1885.
QZ/L37

Laurie
GLADSTONE, Isabel Olive Joan
The Lauries of Maxwelton and other Laurie
families. London, 1972.
ED/N-1 (NE.25.g.12) SA/U-1 ED/N-2 ED/S10
QZ/L37 QZ/P-1 QZ/P10 QZ/P14 QZ/P99

LAURIE, Peter G.
Sir Peter Laurie: a family memoir. Brentwood, 1901.
ED/N-1 (R.161.g) ED/N-2 SA/U-1 QZ/P99

Laurin
MACLAREN, Margaret
The Maclarens: a history of Clan Labhran. Stirling,
1960.
ED/N-1 (NE.25.b.13) ED/N-2 GL/U-1 SA/U-1
ST/U-1 QZ/P-1 QZ/P13 QZ/P14 QZ/P26
QZ/P27 QZ/P99

MACLAURIN, Daniel
History in memoriam of the Clan Laurin . . . to
1558. London [n.d.].
ED/N-2

Law

[MATERIAL relating to the lands and lairds of Law.
N.p., n.d.]
QZ/P-6

Law of Lauriston

FAIRLEY, John Alexander
Lauriston Castle: the estate and its owners.
Edinburgh, 1925.
ED/N-1 (K.R.28.a;L.C.1147) GL/U-1 QZ/L37
QZ/P-1 QZ/P22 QZ/P99

LAW, Barons de Lauriston en Ecosse et en France.
Blois, 1886.
ED/N-1 (L.C.1859(1))

MICHEL, Francisque Xavier
Les Ecossais en France. [N.p.], 1862.
ED/N-1 (L.C.1859(4))

[REFERENCES to the family of Law of Lauriston
contained in *Notes and Queries*, 3rd series, vols
iii, iv, 1863.] London, 1863. 2v.
ED/N-1 (L.C.3209,3210)

WOOD, John Philp
Memoirs of the life of John Law of Lauriston....
Edinburgh, 1824.
ED/N-1 (Claud.5.18) QZ/P-1

Lawrance

LAWRANCE, Robert Murdoch
A branch of the Aberdeenshire Lawrances.
Aberdeen, 1925.
ED/N-1 (S.122.e) QZ/P30 QZ/P22 AD/U-1
QZ/L37 QZ/P-1 QZ/P99

—The pedigree of the Aberdeenshire Lawrances.
Aberdeen, 1912.
ED/N-1 (L.C.1250) QZ/P30 QZ/P22 QZ/L37

Lawrance of Peterhead

LAWRANCE, Robert Murdoch
Lawrances in Peterhead, 1672-1854. [Aberdeen?,
1912.]
ED/N-1 (L.C.1104)

Lawson

LAWSON-Chester genealogy. [With genealogical
tables.] Boston, 1946.
ED/N-1 (S.121.e)

Lay

LAY, Arthur Croall Hyde
Four generations in China, Japan and Korea.
Edinburgh, 1952.
ED/N-1 (NE.92.c.5) QZ/P-1

Learmonth

['GENEALOGIES of the Learmonth family'. 17--.]
ED/N-1 (Adv.MS.20.1.10,ff.2-15)

Learmonth of Balcomie

['A GENEALOGICAL account of the family of
Learmonth of Balcomie'. 1547?]
ED/N-1 (Adv.MS.33.2.27,f.315)

Leask

CLAN Leask newsletter. Autumn 1981- . Stirling,
1981- .
ED/N-1 (HP.sm.193)

LEASK, Anne
The Leasks. (In *Clan Hay Society Newsletter*,
June 1980, pp.4-6.)
ED/N-1 (P.la.2012)

—The Leasks: historical notes on the Aberdeenshire,
Orkney and Shetland families. Sheringham, 1980.
ED/N-1 (HP1.83.930)

ORKNEY COUNTY LIBRARY
Orcadian families: Leask genealogy. [N.p., n.d.]
ED/N-2

Leatham *see* Letham

Leckie

COOK, William B.
Lairds of Leckie. Stirling, 1906. (Reprinted from
Stirlingshire Sentinel.)
QZ/P14 QZ/P-1 QZ/P99

LECKIE, Robert Gilmour Edwards
Leckie of Leckie. Vancouver, 1913.
QZ/P14 QZ/P99

—Leckie of that ilk. Vancouver, 1913.
ED/N-1 (NE.63.e.20) QZ/P14 ED/N-2
QZ/L37

Ledingham

LEDINGHAM, Alex.
A historic Aberdeen family and its branches.
Peterhead, 1924.
QZ/P22

Leighton

DAVIDSON, Godfray
Robert Leighton: his family and his library. (In
Society of Friends of Dunblane Cathedral [*Transactions*],
vol.viii, part 1, 1958, pp.44-50.)
ED/N-1 (Y.176)

Leighton of Usan
LEIGHTON, Clarence F.
Memorials of the Leightons of Ulishaven (Usan),
Angus, and other Scottish families of the name. A.D.
1260-1931. London, 1931.
ED/N-1 (NE.25.a.17) ED/N-2 QZ/P28
QZ/P-1

Leishman
LEISHMAN, James Fleming
Matthew Leishman of Govan. . . . Paisley, 1921.
ED/N-1 (S.140.e) QZ/P-1

LEISHMAN, Matthew
[Letter books containing copies of his letters written
between 1855 and 1874 with digest of letters and
index.] 3v. (MSS.)
QZ/P-1

WATSON, Charles Brodie Boog
Traditions and genealogies of some members of the
families of Boog, Heron, Leishman, Ross, Watson.
Perth, 1908.
ED/N-1 (S.120.d)   QZ/P18 ED/N-2 SA/U-1
QZ/L37 QZ/P99

Leith
McDERMOTT, Muriel M.
The Leiths of Berwick-upon-Tweed: the story of a
family. [N.p.], 1982.
ED/N-1 (HP2.83.270)

[MSS. notes and newspaper cuttings relating to
the Grants, Leiths, MacKintoshes of Blervie. N.d.]
QZ/P40

Leith of Fyvie
STIRLING, Anna Maria D. W. Pickering
Fyvie Castle: its lairds and their times. London,
1928.
ED/N-1 (R.247.e) QZ/P30 QZ/P-1

Leith of Harthill
BICKLEY, Francis Lawrance
The Leiths of Harthill. London, 1937.
ED/N-1 (S.120.i) QZ/Q17 QZ/P30 ED/N-2
GL/U-1 QZ/P22 SA/U-1 QZ/P-1 QZ/P99

Leith of Leith-Hall
LEITH-HAY, Henrietta and LOCHHEAD, Marion
Trustie to the end: the story of the Leith Hall family.
Edinburgh, 1957.
ED/N-1 (NE.25.b.8) QZ/P34 QZ/P22
QZ/P30 ED/N-2 QZ/P40 SA/U-1 ST/U-1
QZ/P-1 ED/U-1 QZ/P99

Lendrum see also **Landrum**

Lendrum
WILKEN, J.
Extracts from "Ellon in bygone days": a lecture.
Peterhead, 1921. (Typescript)
ED/N-1 (1968.151)

Lennox see also **Gordon-Lennox**

Lennox, Duke of
DARNLEY, John Bligh, Earl of
Case of John, Earl of Darnley, . . . claiming the titles,
honours, and dignities of Duke of Lennox, Earl of
Darnley, Lord Aubigny, Torbolton and Dalkeith.
[N.p., 1830.]
ED/N-1 (Yule.162(5)) SA/U-1 QZ/L37

Lennox, Earldom of see also **Napier**

Lennox, Earldom of see also **Stewart,** Earl of Lennox

Lennox, Earldom of
CARTULARIUM comitatus de Levenax; edited by
James Dennistoun. Edinburgh, 1833. (Maitland
Club.)
ED/N-1 (Mait.Club.24) GL/U-1 QZ/L37
QZ/P-1 QZ/P-4 QZ/P99

FRASER, Sir William
The Lennox. Edinburgh, 1874. 2v.
ED/N-1 (Gen.8.L) ED/N-2 AD/U-1 SA/U-1
QZ/L37 QZ/P-4 QZ/P49 QZ/P-1 ED/U-1
QZ/P99

['GENEALOGICAL notes concerning the Earls of
Lennox and their descendants'. 1709.]
ED/N-1 (Adv.MS.34.6.24,ff.74,75)

HAMILTON, Robert
Case of Margaret Lennox of Woodhead, in relation
to the title, honours and dignity of the ancient Earls
of Lennox, with genealogical tree. Edinburgh,
1813.
ED/N-1 (A.111.c;Yule.104) GL/U-1 QZ/L37
QZ/Q76 QZ/P49 QZ/P-1 QZ/P99

IRVING, Joseph
The book of Dumbartonshire: a history of the
county . . . memoirs of families, and notices of
industries carried on in the Lennox district.
Edinburgh, 1879. 3v.
ED/N-1 (R.286.c)

MACFARLANE, James
  The honour of Lennox. London, 1933.
  ED/N-1 (Vts.154.f.19)

MEMORIAL relative to the succession to the ancient
  Earls of Levenax. [With a genealogical table.]
  [N.p., n.d.]
  ED/N-1 (6.274(5))

NAPIER, Mark
  History of the partition of the Lennox. Edinburgh,
  1835.
  ED/N-1 (A.114.c) QZ/Q17 ED/N-2 QZ/P22
  DN/U-1 GL/U-1 QZ/P-6 QZ/L37 ST/U-1
  QZ/P-4 QZ/P49 QZ/P-1 ED/U-1 QZ/P99
  QZ/P52 (Unconfirmed location)

— The Lannox of auld: an epistolary review of "The
  Lennox" by William Fraser. Edinburgh, 1880.
  ED/N-1 (A.113.a) SA/U-1 GL/U-1 QZ/L37
  QZ/P-4 QZ/P49 QZ/P-1 ED/U-1 QZ/P99

RIDDELL, John
  Additional remarks upon the question of the
  Lennox or Rusky representation, and other topics,
  in answer to the author [i.e. M. Napier] of "History
  of the partition of the Lennox", etc. Edinburgh,
  1835.
  ED/N-1 (A.114.c) ED/N-2 SA/U-1 QZ/L37
  QZ/P-1 ED/U-1 QZ/P99

— Tracts, legal and historical, etc. Edinburgh, 1835.
  ED/N-1 (L.C.758;A.114.c) ED/N-2 QZ/P-1

RIDDELL, John, and others
  The pedigree of Her Royal and Most Serene
  Highness the Duchess of Mantua . . . her descent
  from . . . the Houses of . . . Lennox, Napier, etc.
  New ed. London, 1885.
  ED/N-1 (R.172.c) QZ/L37 QZ/P99

TYTLER, Patrick Fraser
  Historical notes on the Lennox or Darnley jewel:
  the property of the Queen. [London], 1843.
  ED/N-1 (H.35.c.32) GL/U-1 QZ/P99

Lennox of Woodhead *see* **Lennox,** Earldom of

Leslie

LAURUS Leslaeana explicata, sive clarior enumeratio
  personarum utriusque sexus cognominis Leslie,
  unacum affinibus, titulis, officiis, dominiis, gestisque
  celebrioribus breviter indicatis . . . Graecii, 1692.
  ED/N-1 (R.288.b) SA/U-1

LESLIE, Charles
  Historical records of the family of Leslie, 1067-1869.
  Edinburgh, 1869. 3v.
  ED/N-1 (A.113.c) QZ/Q17 QZ/P30 QZ/P18
  QZ/P27 ED/N-2 AD/U-1 QZ/P22
  QZ/P40 SA/U-1 DN/U-1 GL/U-1 QZ/P99
  QZ/L37 QZ/P50 QZ/P-1

LESLIE, Percy C.
  The family of Leslie. (From the records compiled
  by Charles Leslie.) [N.p.], 1953.
  AD/U-1

['PAPERS concerning the genealogy of the Leslie
  family'. 17--.]
  ED/N-1 (Adv.MS.20.1.10,ff.18-62)

PIELOU, P. Leslie
  The Leslies of Tarbert, Co. Kerry, and their
  forebears. Dublin, 1935.
  ED/N-1 (R.172.c) QZ/P-1

Leslie of Balquhain
  LESLIE, Charles
  Pedigree of the family of Leslie of Balquhain . . .
  from 1067 to 1861. Bakewell, 1861.
  ED/N-1 (A.37.d) QZ/P22 QZ/L37 QZ/P-1
  QZ/P99

Leslie of Findrassie
  NISBET, Alexander
  Genealogical memoirs of the Leslies of Findrassie.
  Edinburgh, 1797.
  ED/N-1 (BCL.B5579a)

Leslie, Earl of Leven
  FRASER, Sir William
  The Leven and Melville peerages. 1857. (*MSS.*)
  QZ/L37

— The Melvilles, Earls of Melville, and the Leslies,
  Earls of Leven. Edinburgh, 1890. 3v.
  ED/N-1 (Gen.8.M) QZ/P18 ED/N-2 QZ/P18
  QZ/P56 SA/U-1 QZ/L37 QZ/P-1 QZ/P99

Leslie, Lord Lindores
  HAY, George
  Case of George Marquis of Tweeddale . . . objecting
  to the votes given at the late election under the title
  of Lord Lindores. [With a genealogical table.]
  [N.p., 1793.]
  ED/N-1 (Yule.168(1))

Leslie, Lord Newark
GREAT BRITAIN. House of Lords Before the
Committee of Privileges: title of Lord Newark
[assumed by William Anstruther] now extinct.
[London, 1771?]
ED/N-1 (Yule.168(11))

Leslie of Pitcaple
DOCUMENTS relating to the family of Leslie of
Pitcaple, 1692-1741.
QZ/P22

Leslie of Powis
POWIS papers, 1507-1894; edited by John George
Burnett. Aberdeen, 1951. (3rd Spalding Club.)
ED/N-1 (3rd Spald.Club.16)   QZ/P-1   QZ/P99

Leslie of Warthill, Wartle
LESLIE,
A family history: [a short account of the families of
Brodie, Farquhar, Leslie and Davidson.] [Brighton,
1891?]
ED/N-1 (6.2484)

PEDIGREE of William Leslie of Warthill, tracing
direct descent from at least twelve distinct
nationalities before the Norman Conquest, 1066.
Aberdeen, [n.d.].
QZ/P22   QZ/P99

Letham
DONALDSON-HUDSON, R.
Anglo-Scottish Lords of Leitholm and Strickland.
(In *History of the Berwickshire Naturalists' Club*, vol.36,
part 1, 1962, pp.65-9.)
ED/N-1 (Y.210)

—The lairds of Leitholm in the 14th and 15th
centuries. (In *History of the Berwickshire Naturalists'
Club*, vol.37, part 1, 1965, pp.44-9.)
ED/N-1 (Y.210)

LEATHAM, Louis Salisbury
The Letham or Leatham family book of
remembrance; the story of Robert Letham and his
wife Janet Urquhart, with . . . data on their
ancestry and descendants. Ann Arbor, Mich., 1955.
ED/N-1 (NE.63.h.7)   QZ/P30   QZ/P40
QZ/P-1   QZ/P99

WASHINGTON, G. H. S. L.
The Anglo-Scottish Lords of Leitholme and Great
Strickland. (In *History of the Berwickshire Naturalists'
Club*, vol.35, part 1, 1959, pp.121-5.)
ED/N-1 (Y.210)

Leven, Earl of *see* **Leslie,** Earl of Leven

Leveson-Gower, Duke of Sutherland
FRASER, Sir William
The Sutherland book. Edinburgh, 1892. 3v.
ED/N-1 (Gen.8.S)   GL/U-1   QZ/P-1   QZ/P99

MAIDMENT, James
Reports of claims . . . to the House of Lords . . . of the
Cassillis, Sutherland, Spynie, and Glencairn
peerages, 1760-1797. [N.p.], 1882.
QZ/P-1   QZ/P99

Leybourne
MCINTOSH, Mary
Roots and branches: the story of the Angus and
Leybourne families. [With genealogical tables.]
Newcastle, [1958].
ED/N-1 (NE.63.e.12)

Light
STEUART, M.
History of the family. [N.d.] (*MS.*)
ED/S10 (Unconfirmed location)

Lightbody
LIGHTBODY, William
Lightbody records, 1550-1930, Scotland and abroad.
Farnham, 1932.
ED/N-1 (1933.12)   QZ/L37

Lillie
LILLIE, William
A Lillie link between Setons and McInroys. (In
Scottish Genealogist, vol.xxvii, no.3, September
1980, pp.85-9.)
ED/N-1 (Gen.7)

Lind
DOUGLAS, Sir Robert
The genealogy of the family of Lind, and the
Montgomeries of Smithton. [N.p., 1795.]
ED/N-1 (A.120.a)

Lindesay of Loughry, Ireland
GODFREY, Ernest H.
The Lindesays of Loughry, county Tyrone: a
genealogical history. [With a genealogical table.]
London, 1949.
ED/N-1 (R.272.f)

Lindores, Lord *see* **Leslie,** Lord Lindores

Lindsay

CLAN Lindsay and its chiefs. [N.p.], 1915.
QZ/Q17

CLAN LINDSAY SOCIETY
Publications. Vol.i, no.1-vol.v, no.19. Edinburgh,
1901-50.
ED/N-1 (S.120.f) ED/N-2 QZ/P-1 QZ/P99
QZ/L37 GL/U-1

CRAWFORD, Alexander William Crawford Lindsay,
25th Earl of
Lives of the Lindsays: or, a memoir of the Houses of
Crawford and Balcarres. [With a genealogical
table.] Wigan, 1840. 4v.
ED/N-1 (NE.25.a.20) QZ/P22 QZ/P28
QZ/Q17

— — London, 1849. 3v.
ED/N-1 (Gen.8.L) ED/N-2 SA/U-1 GL/U-1
QZ/P-1 QZ/P27 QZ/P28 QZ/Q17

— — 2nd ed. London, 1858. 3v.
ED/N-1 (L.C.1893-5) GL/U-1 QZ/P-1
QZ/P18 QZ/P22 QZ/P28 QZ/P40 QZ/P56
QZ/P99 QZ/L37 QZ/P16
QZ/P52* (Unconfirmed location)

FOLKARD, Henry T.
A Lindsay record: a handlist of books written by or
relating to the Clan Lindsay . . . in the Wigan Free
Public Library. Wigan, [1899].
ED/N-1 (Hall.201.e) QZ/P22

JERVISE, Andrew
History and traditions of the land of the Lindsays in
Angus and Mearns. Edinburgh, 1853.
ED/N-1 (A.114.d) DN/U-1 QZ/P26 QZ/P28
QZ/P22 QZ/P-1 QZ/L37

— — 2nd ed. rev. by James Gammack. Edinburgh,
1882.
ED/N-1 (R.249.a) DN/U-1 QZ/P26 QZ/P30
QZ/P28 QZ/P22 GL/U-1 QZ/P99 QZ/P52
(Unconfirmed location)

LINDSAY, Daryl
The leafy tree: my family. [With a genealogical
table.] London, 1965.
ED/N-1 (NF.1361.e.2)

— — London, 1967.
ED/N-1 (NF.1362.c.2)

LINDSAY, Margaret Isabella
The Lindsays of America: a genealogical narrative
and family record. Albany, N.Y., 1889.
ED/N-1 (ABS.2.79.120)

LINDSAY, Michael K.
Lindsays in Scotland, 1625-1660. [N.p., n.d.]
QZ/P28

LINDSAY, Sydenham B.
Bishops of the Lindsay Clan. [Montreal], 1957.
ED/N-1 (6.767)

LINDSAY, William
Six generations of ancestors of William Lindsay.
[N.p., n.d.]
QZ/Q17

LINZEE, John William
The Lindesie and Limesi families of Great Britain . . .
Boston, Mass., 1917. 2v.
QZ/P-1

MATHESON, Glenis A. *and* TAYLOR, Frank
Hand-list of personal papers from the muniments
of the Earl of Crawford and Balcarres deposited in
the John Rylands Library of Manchester.
Manchester, 1976.
ED/N-1 (SRR)

THOMSON, Elizabeth M.
Notes re Egidia Stewart [sister of King Robert II]
regarding the Lindsays. [N.d.] (*MSS.*)
QZ/P-6

Lindsay, Earl of *see* **Lindsay,** Lord Lindsay of the Byres

Lindsay of Almerieclose, Arbroath
TURNBULL, G. O.
Our Lindsay forbears. [N.d.] (*Typescript*)
QZ/P28

Lindsay of Belstane
LINDSAY, John
The Lindsays of Belstane. (In *Publications of the Clan
Lindsay Society*, vol.iv, no.14, 1933, pp.87-102.)
ED/N-1 (S.120.f)

Lindsay of Brechin
NOTICE of the family of Smith, Smyth or Smytht,
properly Lindsay of Brechin, Co. Forfar. [With a
genealogical table.] [N.p., n.d.]
ED/N-1 (S.121.g)

Lindsay, Lord Lindsay of the Byres

BETHUNE, Sir John Trotter
Case on behalf of Sir John Trotter Bethune on his claim to the honours and dignities of Lord Lindsay of the Byres. Edinburgh, 1877.
ED/N-1 (6.249(6-18)) QZ/P18 QZ/P22 QZ/L37 QZ/P52 (Unconfirmed location)

—Minutes of evidence . . . the petition of Sir J. T. Bethune of Kilconquair . . . to declare him entitled to . . . Lord Lindsay of the Byres, and of Earl Lindsay and Lord Parbroath, and of Viscount of Garnock and Lord Kilbirny, Kingsburn & Drumry. Edinburgh, 1877.
QZ/L37 QZ/P-1 QZ/P52 (Unconfirmed location)

EXTRACTS from the minutes of evidence given upon the Crawford peerage claim, 1845-48. Edinburgh, 1877.
QZ/L37

['NOTES on the genealogy of the Lords Lindsay of the Byres'. 1714.]
ED/N-1 (Adv.MS.34.6.24,ff.196-9.)

Lindsay of Covington

LINDSAY, John
The lairds of Covington. (In *Publications of the Clan Lindsay Society*, vol.i, no.4, 1907, pp.3-48.)
ED/N-1 (S.120.f)

Lindsay, Earl of Crawford *see* **Crawford,** Earldom of

Lindsay of Dowhill and Kinloch

LINDSAY, John
The Laird of Dowhill (In *Publications of the Clan Lindsay Society*, vol.ii, no.8, 1920, pp.235-78.)
ED/N-1 (S.120.f)

MEACHER, A.J.
History of the lands of Kinloch. Edinburgh, 1956.
ED/N-1 (NE.6.a.1) QZ/P18

Lindsay of Dunrod

LINDSAY, John
The House of Dunrod. (In *Publications of the Clan Lindsay Society*, vol.ii, no.5, 1908, pp.9-63.)
ED/N-1 (S.120.f)

Lindsay of Edzell *see* **Lindsay** of Glenesk

Lindsay of Evelick

LINDSAY, John
The Lindsays of Evelick. (In *Publications of the Clan Lindsay Society*, vol.iii, no.9, 1924, pp.3-51.)
ED/N-1 (S.120.f)

SINTON, Thomas
Family and genealogical sketches. Inverness, 1911.
ED/N-1 (R.172.b) QZ/P-1 QZ/P40

Lindsay of Fairgirth

LINDSAY, John
The House of Fairgirth. (In *Publications of the Clan Lindsay Society*, vol.ii, no.6, 1911, pp.84-125.)
ED/N-1 (S.120.f)

Lindsay of Glenesk

MORTON, Peter Douglas
The Lindsay family of Glenesk and Edzell: an old Forfarshire family. (From *Arbroath Guide*, 2/12/1922-21/4/1923.)
QZ/P28

Lindsay of Kinnettles

LINDSAY, John
The Lindsays of Kinnettles. (In *Publications of the Clan Lindsay Society*, vol.iii, no.11, 1928, pp.137-43.)
ED/N-1 (S.120.f)

Lindsay, Duke of Montrose *see* **Montrose,** Dukedom of

Lindsay of the Mount

AGNEW, Crispin
The Mount-Lord Lyon. (In *Coat of Arms*, new series, vol.11, no.100, Winter 1976/7, pp.87-92.)
ED/N-1 (NJ.689)

Lindsay of Pitairlie

LINDSAY, John
The Lindsays of Pitairlie. (In *Publications of the Clan Lindsay Society*, vol.iii, no.10, 1926, pp.114-26.)
ED/N-1 (S.120.f)

Lindsay, Lord Spynie *see* **Spynie,** Lord Spynie

Lister

DENNY, Sir Henry Lyttleton Lyster
Memorials of an ancient house: a history of the family of Lister or Lyster. Edinburgh, 1913.
ED/N-1 (M.99.e)

Liston

McCall, Hardy Bertram
Memoirs of my ancestors. Birmingham, 1884.
ED/N-1 (A.114.a) QZ/P99

—Some old families: a contribution to the
genealogical history of Scotland. Birmingham,
1890.
ED/N-1 (A.36.a) QZ/P11 QZ/L37 ED/N-2
QZ/P99

Lithgow

Knock, Georgius Marcus
[An extract from the session records of Lanark,
containing a letter of Georgius Marcus Knock of
Dantzig, enquiring about the genealogy of certain
members of the Lithgow family, and the Lanark
Session's reply. Lanark, 1730.]
ED/N-1 (Ry.III.d.3(5))

Little

Little, Margaret
Fragmentary memories of bygone days, modes and
manners. 1913.
QZ/P99

Livingston

MS. notes and press cuttings on the family of
Livingston. [N.d.]
QZ/P99

Van Rensselaer, Florence
The Livingston family in America and its Scottish
origins. New York, 1949.
ED/N-1 (NE.63.f.1)

Livingston of Callendar

Edgecumbe, Edward Robert Pearce
Family records relating to the families of Pearce of
Holsworthy, Edgcumbe of Laneast, Eliot of
Lostwithiel, Livingstone of Calendar. . . . Exeter,
1895.
ED/N-1 (A.37.a)

Livingston, Edwin Brockholst
The Captain of Stirling Castle. Paisley, 1927.
ED/N-1 (T.51.e) QZ/P14

—The Livingstons of Callendar, and their principal
cadets. Edinburgh, 1920.
ED/N-1 (S.121.b) GL/U-1 QZ/L37 SA/U-1
QZ/P13 QZ/P-1 QZ/P99

Livingston, Earl of Callendar

Livingstone, Sir Thomas
Abstract of the written evidence . . . for proving Sir
Thomas Livingstone of Ogilface and Bedlormie,
nearest and lawful heir of James, 1st Earl of
Calander [sic]. [N.p.], 1821.
ED/N-1 (6.2201(53) QZ/L37 QZ/P-1 QZ/P99

Livingston of Dunipace

Gibson, John C.
Lands and lairds of Dunipace. Stirling, 1903.
ED/N-1 (R.243.f) QZ/P14 QZ/P-1 QZ/P99

—Lands and lairds of Larbert and Dunipace parishes.
[With genealogical tables.] Glasgow, 1908.
ED/N-1 (R.243.c) QZ/P14

Livingston of Kilsyth

Anton, Peter
Kilsyth: a parish history. Glasgow, 1893.
ED/N-1 (A.124.f) QZ/P14

Livingston of Lismore

The Bachul or pastoral staff of St. Malouaig. [N.d.]
(MS.)
QZ/P99

Livingston of Livingston Manor

Livingston, Edwin Brockholst
The Livingstons of Livingston Manor. New York,
1910.
ED/N-1 (NE.25.a.7) QZ/P99

Livingston, Earl of Newburgh see Newburgh, Earldom of

Livingstone

Linlithgow Academy History Society
Emblems of mortality: an investigation into the
family of Livingstone and their burial tomb in
Linlithgow. [Linlithgow, 1982?]
ED/N-1 (HP2.82.646) QZ/P99

Livingstone of Lanark

Clark, David Saunders
Notes on the Livingstone family of Lanark,
Scotland and Detroit, Michigan and related families.
Washington, 1966.
ED/N-1 (6.1320) QZ/P-1 QZ/P99

Loch

Loch, Gordon
The family of Loch. Edinburgh, 1934.
ED/N-1 (R.172.b) GL/U-1 QZ/P11 SA/U-1
QZ/L37 QZ/P-1 ED/U-1 QZ/P99

Loch of Drylaw
GRAY, W. Forbes
The Lochs of Drylaw. Edinburgh, 1949. (In *Book of the Old Edinburgh Club*, vol.xxvii, 1949, pp.175-80.)
ED/N-1 (Hist.S.93)

WOOD, John Philp
The antient and modern state of the parish of Cramond . . . [With genealogical tables.] Edinburgh, 1794.
ED/N-1 (A.115.a.16)

Lochhead
LOCHHEAD, John
A reach of the river: a family chronicle, 1880-1954. Gillingham, Dorset, 1955.
ED/N-1 (NE.1180.a.6) QZ/P-6 QZ/P-1
ED/U-1 QZ/P99

Lockhart
NINIAN Lockhart & Sons, Ltd.: textile manufacturers, Linktown Works, Kirkcaldy, Scotland, 1797-1947. [Kirkcaldy, 1947.]
QZ/P18

Lockhart of Carnwath
DICKSON, David
David Dickson, son of William Dickson of Kilbucho . . . appellant . . . George Lockhart, respondent. Edinburgh, 1748.
QZ/P99

Lockhart of Lee
['GENEALOGICAL notes concerning the Lockhart family of Lee'. 1740?]
ED/N-1 (MS.8107,ff.1-8)

LOCKHART, Simon Macdonald
Seven centuries: a history of the Lockharts of Lee and Carnwath. Carnwath, 1976.
ED/N-1 (NE.25.e.12) SA/U-1 QZ/P53
QZ/L37 ED/N-2 QZ/P99 QZ/P-56
QZ/Q71 ED/S10 QZ/P-1

SIR Norman Macdonald Lockhart of Lee and Carnwath, appellant . . . Mary Jane Lockhart Macdonald [and others] respondents. 1837.
QZ/P99

Logan
LOGAN, William
History of the Logans, and clan songs. 1922.
QZ/P-1

LOGAN-HOME, George John Ninian
History of the Logan family. Edinburgh, 1934.
ED/N-1 (R.172.d) ED/N-2 QZ/P11 SA/U-1
QZ/L37 QZ/P-1 ED/U-1 QZ/P99

REID, Robert Corsane
Calendar of the Logan charters, Wigtownshire, now deposited at the Register House. 1944. (*MSS.*)
QZ/P10 (Unconfirmed location)

Logan of Knockshinnoch
H., J. M.
Logans of Knockshinnoch. Edinburgh, 1885.
ED/N-1 (S.120.e) GL/U-1 QZ/Q88 QZ/P-1
QZ/P99

REID, Lesley
The Logans. London, 1979.
ED/N-1 (WP3.79.168) QZ/Q88

Logie
FORRESTER, David Marshall
Logiealmond. Edinburgh, 1944.
ED/N-1 (R.246.e) QZ/P26 ED/N-2 QZ/P-1

MORRIS, Thomas
The lands and lairds of Logie. (*Perthshire Popular Rhymes and Ballad Fragments,* [1872?], newscutting no.18.)
QZ/P26

Lorimer
The LORIMERS: a family of the arts in Fife. St. Andrews, [1983].
ED/N-1 (HP3.83.391)

STODART, Robert Riddle
Genealogy of the Lorimers of Scotland. [N.p., n.d.]
AD/U-1 QZ/L37

Loudon, Earldom of *see* **Campbell**

Louttit
LOUTTIT, Tom J.
The Louttit saga. [Australia?, 1970?] (*Xerox-copy*)
ED/N-1 (HP4.83.543)

Lovat, Lord Fraser of Lovat
FRASER, A. G.
Case of Rev. A. G. Fraser . . . 1845.
QZ/L37

FRASER, Alexander
Answers or defences for His Majesty's Advocate, on behalf of His Majesty to the claim of Alexander Fraser, second son, and Archibald Fraser, third son, of the deceased Simon, late Lord Fraser of Lovat, upon a tailzie made by the said late Lord Lovat. (29th June, 1750.) [Edinburgh, 1750.]
ED/N-1 (Ry.II.b.19(55))

—Information for Alexander Fraser, second son, and Archibald Fraser, third son, to Simon, late Lord Fraser of Lovat, deceas'd, claimants of the estate of Lovat against His Majesty's Advocate, respondent. (November 12. 1750.) [Edinburgh, 1750.]
ED/N-1 (Ry.II.b.19(56))

—Information for His Majesty's Advocate, on behalf of His Majesty, respondent to the claim of Alexander Fraser, second son, and Archibald Fraser, third son, of the deceast Simon, late Lord Fraser of Lovat, to the estate of Lovat, upon a tailzie made by the said late Lord Lovat. (November 7th, 1749.) [Edinburgh, 1749.]
ED/N-1 (Ry.II.b.19(57))

—Unto the . . . Lords of Council and Session, the claim of Alexander Fraser, second son, and Archibald Fraser, third son, to the late Lord Fraser of Lovat, deceased for the estate of Lovat . . . (September 20, 1749.) [Edinburgh, 1749.]
ED/N-1 (Ry.II.b.19(54))

FRASER, John
Case of John Fraser of Carnarvon . . . 1885.
ED/N-2   QZ/L37

—The Lovat peerage. (Reprinted from *Life*, 7 May 1885.)
ED/N-1 (J.133.e.1(42))

—The Lovat peerage and estates. [With genealogical tables.] London, 1885.
ED/N-1 (5.519)

FRASER, Simon
Case of Simon, Lord Lovat in opposition thereto. 1885.
QZ/L37

—Memorial for those of the surname of Fraser. [Edinburgh, 1729.]
ED/N-1 (Yule.88(2))

—Memorials for Simon, Lord Fraser of Lovat, and other documents bearing on his claim to the title. [Edinburgh], 1729.
ED/N-1 (Yule.88(1))   QZ/P40   QZ/P99

FRASER, Thomas
His Majesty's Advocate for Scotland in behalf of His Majesty, appellant Thomas Fraser, younger of Gortuleg, a claimant on the forfeited estate of Simon, late Lord Lovat, respondent: the appellant's case. [N.p., 1757.]
ED/N-1 (7.87)

FRASER, Thomas Alexander
Case of Thomas Alexander Fraser of Lovat . . .
QZ/L37

—Additional case . . . 1854.
QZ/L37

FRASER, William
Memorial for His Majesty's Advocate . . . against W. Fraser . . . claimant upon the forfeited estate of the late Lord Lovat, July 20, 1756. [N.p.], 1756.
ED/N-1 (L.C.1279(15))

The LOVAT peerage and estates: a short history of the case, with evidence in the support of the claim of John Fraser. Edinburgh, 1885.
ED/N-1 (5.519)   QZ/L37   QZ/P40

MACDONALD, Archibald
The old lords of Lovat and Beaufort. Inverness, 1934.
ED/N-1 (R.172.d)   ST/U-1

MINUTES of evidence . . . 1826 and 1855.
QZ/L37

MINUTES of evidence . . . 1856-57.
QZ/L37

MINUTES of evidence and other papers. 1885.
QZ/L37

REPORT of evidence. 1826.
QZ/L37

CANDID and impartial account of the behaviour of Simon, Lord Lovat from the time his death-warrant was deliver'd to the day of his execution. 1747.
QZ/P99

Love
[MATERIAL relating to the lands and lairds of Love. N.p., n.d.]
QZ/P-6

Lovell

WILSON, S. C.
The Barony of Hawick and the Lovell family. (In
Transactions of the Hawick Archaeological Society, 1932,
pp.34-9.)
ED/N-1 (P.220)

Lowis

LOWIS, Charles von
The augmentation of the arms of Lowis of Menar
(Manor) by marks of cadency. Selkirk, 1898.
QZ/P11

Lumsden

DENNISTOUN, James
Memoirs of Sir Robert Strange, Knt., engraver . . .
and of his brother-in-law, Andrew Lumisden,
private secretary to the Stuart princes. London,
1855. 2v.
ED/N-1 (X.X.4)

[The FAMILIES of Gill . . . Lumsden etc. N.d.] (*MS.*)
QZ/P99

LUMSDEN, H. W.
Memorials of the families of Lumsdaine, Lumisden,
or Lumsden. Edinburgh, 1889.
ED/N-1 (A.120.a)   QZ/P22   SA/U-1   GL/U-1
QZ/P99

Lundin of Lundin

DRUMMOND, James
Answers for His Majesty's Advocate on behalf of
His Majesty to the claim of James Lundin, Esq. of
Lundin [to the Earldom of Perth and the Lordship
of Drummond] . . . (December 4, 1750).
[Edinburgh], 1750.
ED/N-1 (Ry.II.b.19(58))

Lyle

FAIRRIE, Geoffrey
The sugar refining families of Great Britain. [With
genealogical tables.] London, 1951.
ED/N-1 (NE.63.b.3)

Lyle of Renfrewshire

LYLE, William
"De insula": or, the Lyles of Renfrewshire. Glasgow,
1936.
QZ/P-6   ED/U-1   QZ/P-1

Lyon

LYON, Walter F.
The genealogical tree of the family of Lyon.
London, [18--].
SA/U-1

ROSS, Andrew
The Lyons of Cossins and Wester Ogil, cadets of
Glamis. Edinburgh, 1901.
ED/N-1 (S.120.b)   QZ/P28   ED/N-2   QZ/P22
SA/U-1   QZ/P99   QZ/L37   QZ/P-1   ED/U-1

Lyon of Glamis

SCOTT-MONCRIEFF, David
A souvenir of Glamis: being a brief history of the
Lyon family and of the castle. Forfar, [1950?].
ED/N-1 (1906.31)   QZ/P26

STIRTON, John
Glamis: a parish history. Forfar, 1913.
ED/N-1 (R.246.a)   QZ/P26

URQUHART, Edward Alexander
Castle Huntly: its development and history.
[Dundee],1956. (*Abertay Historical Society
Publications*, no.4.)
ED/N-1 (P.sm.2056)   ED/N-2

Lyon of Ogil

LYON, William
Lyon of Ogil. London, [1869?].
ED/N-2   QZ/P99

Lyon, Earl of Strathmore *see also* **Bowes(-Lyon),**
Earl of Strathmore

Lyon, Earl of Strathmore

ROSS, Andrew
Lyon, Earl of Strathmore and Kinghorne. [1911].
ED/N-1 (Stirton.b.12)   ED/U-1   QZ/P28

Lyster *see* **Lister**

MacAllister *see also* **Macdonald**

MacAllister

MACMILLAN, Somerled
Families of Knapdale: their history and their place-
names. Paisley, [1960].
ED/N-1 (1936.29)   ED/N-2   QZ/P18   QZ/P27

MacAlpin, McAlpin

EAST, Sir Ronald
> The Kiel family and related Scottish pioneers: Findlays, Hossacks, Gilberts, Camerons, Stewarts, McAlpins, McCallums, McDonalds. [Victoria, 1974]. (*A Family Who's Who*, vol.2.)
> ED/N-1 (NE.26.d.3)   ED/N-2   GL/U-1   QZ/P50

MACKINNON, Charles
> The Clan Alpin confederation: Macgregor, MacKinnon, MacNab, MacQuarrie, MacAulay, Grant and Macfie. (In *Scottish-American Genealogist*, no.17/20, 1980, pp.91-8.)
> ED/N-1 (P.la.6393)

MacArthur, McArthur

CAMPBELL, Alastair
> "But whence comes forth MacArthur?". (In *Notes and Queries of the Society of West Highland and Island Historical Research*, no.xxii, December 1983, pp.3-10.)
> ED/N-1 (P.med.3574)

ENGLISH, Mary Shelton
> The origin of Clan MacArthur. [Waldorf, Md.], 1983. (*History of Clan MacArthur*, vol.1, no.1.)
> ED/N-1 (HP2.83.1164)   QZ/P99

NISBETT, Hamilton More *and* AGNEW, Stair Carnegie
> Cairnhill. Edinburgh, 1949.
> ED/N-1 (R.272.f)   QZ/P-3

SELLAR, W. D. H.
> The lairds of Ardincaple and Darleith: Macarthurs and Macaulays. (In *Scottish Genealogist*, vol.xxi, no.2, June 1974, pp.46-53.)
> ED/N-1 (Gen.7)

MacAskill

WATT, Eilidh
> Euchdan mora a dh'aom: criomagan bho eachdraidh Chloinn MhicAsgaill. (In *Gairm*, air.124, foghar 1983, pp.347-52.)
> ED/N-1 (P.65)

MacAskill of Rudha an Dunain

MACASKILLS of Rudha an Dunain. (In *Clan MacLeod Magazine*, vol.2, no.16, 1951, pp.22-7.)
> ED/N-1 (NF.1572)

Macaulay

MACAULAY,
> Memoirs of the clan "Aulay" . . . Carmarthen, 1881.
> ED/S10 (Unconfirmed location)

MACKINNON, Charles
> The Clan Alpin confederation: MacGregor, MacKinnon, MacNab, MacQuarrie, MacAulay, Grant and MacFie. (In *The Augustan*, book 1, 1973, pp.39-46.)
> ED/N-1 (P.173)

MACKINNON, Donald
> The MacAulays of Bracadale. (In *Clan MacLeod Magazine*, vol.3, no.22, 1957, pp.78-80.)
> ED/N-1 (NF.1572)

SELLAR, W. D. H.
> The lairds of Ardincaple and Darleith: Macarthurs and Macaulays. (In *Scottish Genealogist*, vol.xxi, no.2, June 1974, pp.46-53.)
> ED/N-1 (Gen.7)

THOMAS, Frederick W. L.
> Traditions of the Macaulays of Lewis. (In *Proceedings of the Society of Antiquaries of Scotland*, new series, vol.ii, 1880, pp.363-431.)
> ED/N-1 (Ref.35)

— — (Reprinted from *Proceedings of the Society of Antiquaries of Scotland*, new series, vol.ii, 1880.)
> ED/N-1 (3.2793(2))   QZ/P-1   QZ/P41   QZ/P99

Macaulay of Ardincaple

['DRAFT genealogical account of the MacAulay family of Ardincaple'. 1826?]
> ED/N-1 (Adv.MS.19.2.17,f.304)

IRVING, Joseph
> The book of Dumbartonshire. Edinburgh, 1879.
> ED/N-1 (R.286.c)

WELLES, Edward Randolph
> Ardincaple Castle and its lairds. Glasgow, 1930.
> ED/N-1 (NE.9.a.1)   GL/U-1   QZ/P49   QZ/P-1   QZ/P99

Macaulay of Inveraray

MACAULAY, Rose
> Letters to a friend from Rose Macaulay, 1950-52. [With genealogical tables.] London, 1961.
> ED/N-1 (NF.1335.d.24)

Macauslan of Calderoth

['DRAFT genealogical account of the Macauslan family of Calderoth'. 1824?]
> ED/N-1 (Adv.MS.19.2.17,f.301)

McBain *see also* **Bain**

McBain

MCBAIN, Hughston
History of Clan McBain. Cut and Shoot, Tex., 1973.
ED/N-1 (1976.272) SA/U-1 QZ/P40 (I)

— — [Reprinted]. Cut and Shoot, Tex., 1976.
ED/N-1 (HP1.79.2421)

— — Seattle, Wash., 1976.
QZ/L37

MacBane *see also* **Bain**

McBane

MCBANE, Richard L.
The McBanes: an American branch of the clan. (In
Clan Chattan, vol.iv, no.4, 1962, pp.105-7.)
ED/N-1 (Y.130)

Macbean *see also* **Bain**

Macbean

BANE, Richard L.
A history of the McBane-Mackenzie clans. [N.p.],
1955.
QZ/P40 (I)

CLAN MACBEAN ASSOCIATION IN NORTH
AMERICA
The Clan MacBean register. Vol.3, no.13- . Cut and
Shoot, Tex., 1977- .
ED/N-1 (6829 PER)

EXTRACTS from Birth, Marriage and Death records
[for Dores, Inverness, Petty, Rothimurcus] . . .
relating to the name Macbean. (Entries for
Rothimurcus parish relate to Mackintosh,
Macbean and Shaw.) [*c*. 1604-1800.] (*MSS.*)
QZ/P40

MCBAIN, Hughston
An American Scottish chief. Cut and Shoot, Texas,
1976.
ED/N-1 (HP1.83.2514)

MACBEAN, Bernie
The Clan MacBean in North America. Cut and
Shoot, Texas, 1976-82. 3v.
ED/N-1 (H8.83.477)

MORRIS, Betty
From the MacBean source file. (In *Clan MacBean
Register*, vol.4, no.4, March 1978, pp.134-6.)
ED/N-1 (6829 PER)

SMITH, Danny D.
Remarks about the early history and chiefs of the
Clan Macbean. In *Clan Macbean Register*, vol.4,
no.12, June 1980, pp.444-50.)
ED/N-1 (6829 PER)

Macbeth *see also* **Beaton** of Islay

Macbeth

MACBETH, John
Macbeth: King, Queen and clan. Edinburgh, 1921.
ED/N-1 (R.232.g) QZ/P28 QZ/P22 QZ/P40
QZ/P-7 QZ/P-1 QZ/P99

MACBETH, Malcolm
An abstract of a genealogical collection. Vol.1.
St. Louis, Mo., 1907.
QZ/P99

MACMILLAN, Somerled
A vindication of Macbeth and his claims. [With a
genealogical table.] Ipswich, Mass., 1959.
ED/N-1 (1960.8)

NICOLSON, Alexander
The McBeths: hereditary physicians of the
Highlands. (In *Transactions of the Gaelic Society of
Glasgow*, vol.v, 1958, pp.94-112.)
ED/N-1 (Q.49)

Macbrair of Almagill and Netherwood

EDGAR, Robert
An introduction to the history of Dumfries. [With
genealogical tables.] Dumfries, 1915.
ED/N-1 (R.241.b)

McBroom

MCBROOM, H. L.
The McBroom trail. [Glasgow], 1969.
ED/N-1 (H4.82.880) ED/N-2

— Supplement to the McBroom trail. [Glasgow?,
1980?]
ED/N-1 (HP3.80.2337)

McCaffer

The MCCAFFERS. 1961. (*Typescript*)
QZ/P99

McCain *see* **MacKean**

McCall

MCCALL, Hardy Bertram
Memoirs of my ancestors. Birmingham, 1884.
ED/N-1 (A.114.a) AD/U-1 QZ/L37 QZ/P-1
QZ/P99

—Some old families: a contribution to the genealogical history of Scotland. Birmingham, 1890.
ED/N-1 (A.36.a) QZ/P11 QZ/L37 ED/N-2
QZ/P-1 ED/U-1 QZ/P99

WILSON, William
Folklore and genealogies of uppermost Nithsdale. Dumfries, 1904.
ED/N-1 (R.241.h)

MacCallum, McCallum

CAMPBELL, Gavin
In the House of Lords . . . minutes of proceedings on the Breadalbane peerage claim of Gavin Campbell and of John MacCallum . . . 21st June, 25th July 1872. 2pts. [London], 1872.
ED/N-1 (Yule.146(3,4))

EAST, Sir Ronald
The Kiel family and related Scottish pioneers: Findlays, Hossacks, Gilberts, Camerons, Stewarts, McAlpins, McCallums, McDonalds. [Victoria, 1974]. (*A Family Who's Who*, vol.2.)
ED/N-1 (NE.26.d.3) ED/N-2 GL/U-1
QZ/P50

JOHNSON, I. F.
McCallum . . . family and descendants of Duncan McCallum . . . and other allied lines. 1957.
QZ/P99

McCane *see* MacKean

McClamroch

LANDSBOROUGH, Drew McClamroch
Our Galloway ancestors revisited: a genealogical and historical investigation . . . of the Laird of Lamrochton, *c.* 1400, cadet of the Cunninghames of Kilmaurs, Ayrshire, the Lords Kilmaurs and Earls of Glencairn. Thornton Heath, 1978.
ED/N-1 (HP3.80.1823) QZ/P-1 QZ/P10

MacClellan *see* MacLellan

McClelland

[GENEALOGICAL notes and pedigree of the family of McClelland. N.d.]
ED/N-1 (MS.2237,f.5)

McClure

DUNLOP, Andrew
Memorabilia of the McClures. Salisbury, Rhodesia, 1972.
ED/N-1 (NF.1375.b.10)

MacColl

MACCOLL SOCIETY
Cuairtear chloinn cholla=journal of the MacColl Society. Vol.1, no.1 (January 1932), vol.12, no.34 (September 1951). Glasgow, 1932-51.
ED/N-1 (Y.176) QZ/P-1 QZ/P99

McComb in U.S.A.

LINGENFELTER, Keith
The McCombs in America. (In *Clan Chattan*; part 1, vol.iv, no.3, 1961, pp.8-9; part 2, vol.iv, no.4, 1962, pp.113-14.)
ED/N-1 (Y.130)

MacCombie, McCombie

MACCOMBIE, Thomas
Correspondence, notes, genealogy and heraldry of the family of MacCombie, with notes on titles to property in Forfar. [N.p., n.d.]
QZ/P28

SMITH, William McCombie
Memoir of the family of McCombie. Edinburgh, 1887.
ED/N-1 (A.113.c) QZ/P30 QZ/P22 QZ/P40
AD/U-1 SA/U-1 QZ/P-1 QZ/P99

—Memoir of the families of McCombie and Thoms. New ed. Edinburgh, 1890.
ED/N-1 (A.113.c) QZ/P28 QZ/P30 ED/N-2
QZ/P22 AD/U-1 QZ/P41 SA/U-1 DN/U-1
GL/U-1 QZ/P16 QZ/P-6 QZ/L37 QZ/P49
QZ/P-1 ED/U-1 QZ/P99

McCombie of Dalkilry

FENN, Emily
The McCombies of Dalkilry. Marlow, [1953].
ED/N-1 (NE.25.f.21) QZ/L37

MacConachie of Speyside

DENOON, James W.
The McConachie bonesetters of Speyside. (In *Scots Magazine*, vol.xvii, April-September 1932, pp.24-32.)
ED/N-1 (U.424)

MacConnel

MACCONNEL, David Connor
Facts and traditions collected for a family record. Edinburgh, 1861.
ED/N-1 (S.123.f) ED/N-2 QZ/P99

McCONNEL, Ernest Whigham Jardine
James McConnel (of Carsriggan), his forbears and descendants. 1931.
QZ/P10 (Unconfirmed location)

MacConnell of Largie *see* **Macdonald** of Largie

McCorkle

McCORKLE, Louis W.
From Tomlee ruins: notes on the McCorkle family in Scotland and America. 1973.
QZ/P27

McCormick

THOMSON, David Couper
McCulloch, Turner, McCormick and Russell: [a genealogical table]. Dundee, 1943.
ED/N-1 (NE.25.a.26)   QZ/L37   QZ/P99

McCorquodale

GROVES, Joyce
The townline of West Zorra and East Nissouri, 1820-1900: the McCorquodales and their neighbours. 2nd ed. [N.p., 1973?]
QZ/P27

MACINTYRE, Peter
The Barons of Phantilands: or the MacCorquodales and their story. [N.p., n.d.]
ED/N-1 (T.283.a)   QZ/P27   ED/N-2   QZ/P-1
QZ/P99

ROSE, David Murray
The McCorquodales of Phantilans. (Reprinted from *Oban Times*, 17 February 1900.)
ED/N-1 (5.2484(42))   AD/U-1

The SONS of the baron. Edinburgh, 1932.
ED/N-1 (R.172.f)

McCoy in Kentucky, U.S.A.
McCOY, Truda Williams
The McCoys: their story. [Pikeville, Ky.], 1976.
ED/N-1 (H3.81.2451)

McCrae

The M'CRAES of Carsphairn: being a biographical sketch of the famous author of the poem "In Flanders fields", and his Galloway forebears. Dumfries, [n.d.]. (Reprinted from *Gallovidian Annual*, 1938.)
QZ/P99

McCready

MACCONNELL, Marie
The McCready clan of Scotland, Ireland and Pennsylvania. Cleveland, Ohio, [1965].
ED/N-1 (5.3485(2))

MacCrimmon

CAMPSIE, Alistair Keith
The MacCrimmon legend: the madness of Angus Mackay. Edinburgh, 1980.
ED/N-1 (Music Room)   QZ/P14   ED/S10

MACLEOD, Fred T.
The MacCrimmons of Skye, hereditary pipers to the Macleods of Dunvegan. Edinburgh, 1933.
ED/N-1 (Gen.8.M)   QZ/P27   ED/N-2   QZ/P40
AD/U-1   SA/U-1   QZ/P22   QZ/L37   QZ/P30
QZ/Q76   QZ/P13   QZ/P-1   ED/U-1   QZ/P99

POULTER, George Collingwood Brownlow
A history of the Clan MacCrimmon. 2pts. [N.p.], 1938,39.
ED/N-1 (1971.297)   QZ/L37*   QZ/P-1

POULTER, George Collingwood Brownlow *and* FISHER, Charles P.
The MacCrimmon family ... from 1500-1936. Camberley, 1936.
ED/N-1 (1935.23)   QZ/L37   ED/N-2   AD/U-1
QZ/P-1   QZ/P99

McCririck

WILSON, William
Folklore and genealogies of uppermost Nithsdale. Dumfries, 1904.
ED/N-1 (R.241.h)

McCuiston

McQUISTON, Leona Bean
The McQuiston, McCuiston and McQuesten families, 1620-1937. Louisville, Ky., 1937.
QZ/L37   QZ/P-1

McCulloch

MACDOWALL, John Kevan
Carrick Gallovidian: a historical survey ... with genealogical charts and notes. Ayr, 1947.
ED/N-1 (R.241.d)

REID, Robert Corsane
[Genealogical notes concerning the families of McCulloch, McCulloch of Myrton and McCulloch of Mochrum. N.p., n.d.]
QZ/P10 (Unconfirmed location)

THOMSON, David Couper
McCulloch, Turner, McCormick and Russell:
[a genealogical table]. Dundee, 1943.
ED/N-1 (NE.25.a.26)   QZ/L37   QZ/P99

McCulloch of Ardwall
MCCULLOCH, Walter Jameson
A history of the Galloway families of McCulloch.
Edinburgh, 1964. (*Typescript*)
QZ/P10 (Unconfirmed location)

McCulloch of Glastullich
ROSE, David Murray
The MacCullochs of Glastullich. (Reprinted from
North Star, 16 December 1897.)
ED/S10 (Unconfirmed location)

MacCullum *see* **Breadalbane,** Earldom of

Macdonald *see also* **MacAllister**

Macdonald *see also* **Macdonell**

Macdonald
BARRON, Evan Macleod
Inverness and the Macdonalds. Inverness, 1930.
ED/N-1 (R.249.g)   ED/N-2   QZ/P40   AD/U-1
QZ/P22   QZ/P-1   QZ/P99

BRADLEY, Edward
Argyll's Highlands: or, MacCailein Mor and the
Lords of Lorne; with traditional tales and legends
of . . . the Campbells and Macdonalds . . . Glasgow,
1902.
ED/N-1 (R.249.a)   QZ/P-1

BULLOCH, John Malcolm
The Macdonald ancestors of Rudyard Kipling and
Stanley Baldwin. Glasgow, 1923. (Reprinted from
the *Glasgow Herald*, 5 July 1923.)
SA/U-1

CLAN Donald Journal. Vol.1, no.1-vol.3, no.4.
Glasgow, 1896-9.
QZ/P-1

CLAN Donald Magazine. No.1- . Edinburgh, 1959- .
ED/N-1 (2668 PER)   QZ/P99

CLAN Donald roll of honour, 1914-1918; with a short
history of the clan. Glasgow, 1931.
ED/N-1 (R.35.a)   ED/N-2   GL/U-1   SA/U-1
QZ/P-1   QZ/P99

CLAN Donald Society of Edinburgh. [1951?]
QZ/99

EAST, Sir Ronald
The Kiel family and related Scottish pioneers:
Findlays, Hossacks, Gilberts, Camerons, Stewarts,
McAlpins, McCallums, McDonalds. Victoria,
1974. (*A Family Who's Who*, vol.2.)
ED/N-1 (NE.26.d.3)   ED/N-2   GL/U-1
QZ/P50

FEAR RAONUILLICH
Letters to the editor of the Inverness Journal by
"Fear Raonuillich" chiefly relating to the title of
Macranald, 1817, 1818. Edinburgh, 1818.
AD/U-1   SA/U-1   ED/U-1   QZ/L37   QZ/P-1

— — 2nd series. 1819.
ED/U-1

GRANT, Isabel Frances
The Clan Donald: a Gaelic principality as a focus of
Gaelic culture. Edinburgh, 1952.
ED/N-1 (Gen.7)   QZ/P53   QZ/P27   QZ/P26
ED/N-2   QZ/P14   QZ/P40   QZ/P22   QZ/P-6
QZ/P11   QZ/L37   SA/U-1   QZ/P30   QZ/P49
QZ/P-1   QZ/P99

— — 2nd ed. Edinburgh, 1972.
ED/U-1

— — 3rd ed. Edinburgh, 1979.
ED/N-1 (HP1.80.2914)   ED/N-2   QZ/P-1
QZ/P22   QZ/P56   QZ/P99

HISTORICAL and genealogical account of the clan or
family of Macdonald, from Somerled . . . to the
present period; more particularly as relating to . . .
the Clan Ranald. Edinburgh, 1819.
ED/N-1 (Abbot.80;R.120.c)   ED/N-2   QZ/P40
QZ/L37   QZ/P-1

LEE, Henry
History of the Clan Donald: the families of
MacDonald, McDonald and McDonnell. New
York, 1920.
ED/N-1 (NE.25.d.5)   QZ/Q41

MACDONALD SOCIETY
Yearbook of the Macdonald Society; edited by
W. H. Macdonald. Glasgow, 1899.
QZ/P27   QZ/P-1

MACDONALD, A. S.
The Clan Donald: its battles and its chiefs. Glasgow,
[1958].
ED/N-1 (6.770)   ED/N-2   QZ/P-1   QZ/P99

MACDONALD, Allan Reginald
The truth about Flora Macdonald. [Inverness], 1938.
ED/N-1 (R.232.a)   QZ/P-1

MCDONALD, Angus
The troublesome MacDonalds. [Washington], 1974.
ED/N-1 (1975.129)   SA/U-1   QZ/P-1   QZ/P99

MACDONALD, Angus J. *and* MACDONALD,
Archibald M.
The Clan Donald. Inverness, 1896-1904. 3v.
ED/N-1 (Gen.8.d)   QZ/Q17   QZ/P27   ED/N-2
QZ/P30   QZ/P40   AD/U-1   GL/U-1
QZ/L37   QZ/P-1   QZ/P99

MACDONALD, Angus R.
Letters of certification and agreement by and
between the Chief and Captain of Clan Ranald,
M'Donell of Glengarry and Macdonald of Sleat.
[N.p.], 1911.
ED/N-1 (6.58)

MACDONALD, Sir Archibald
[Estate account book, 1813-1818].
(*MS.*)
QZ/P99

MACDONALD, Donald J.
Clan Donald. Loanhead, 1978.
ED/N-1 (Gen.8.D)   SA/U-1   QZ/P40 (I, D)
QZ/P34   QZ/Q41   QZ/P14   QZ/L37   QZ/P-6
QZ/P22   QZ/P27   ED/N-2   QZ/P-1   QZ/P99

MACDONALD, Donald J. *and* REA, John
A look at Scotland and Macdonalds. [N.p.], 1975.
ED/N-2

MACDONALD, Donald M.
A genealogical MS. (In *Transactions of the Gaelic
Society of Inverness*, vol.xlii, 1958, pp.271-82.
ED/N-1 (NF.1559)

MACDONALD, Edith
Annals of the Macdonald family. London, 1928.
ED/N-1 (S.120.i)   ED/N-2   QZ/P99

MACDONALD, Hugh
History of the Macdonalds. Edinburgh, 1914. (In
Highland Papers; edited by J. R. N. MacPhail.
Vol.1 (Scottish History Society Publications, 2nd
series, vol.v), pp.1-102.)
ED/N-1 (Ref.54)   ED/N-2   QZ/P-1   QZ/P22
QZ/P27

MACDONALD, Hugh N.
Macdonald and Mackinnon families: a biographical
sketch. [N.p., 1938.]
ED/N-1 (5.857)

MACDONALD, Isobel
A family in Skye, 1908-1916. Shrewsbury,
[1977].
ED/N-1 (HP1.77.3709)

MACDONALD, Keith Norman
Macdonald bards from mediaeval times. Edinburgh,
1900.
ED/N-1 (S.145.f;Oss.291)   AD/U-1

MACDOWALL, John Kevan
Carrick Gallovidian: a historical survey . . . with
genealogical charts and notes . . . . Ayr, 1947.
ED/N-1 (R.241.d)

MCGIVERN, James S.
The MacDonalds of Red Banks, Broad Cove. In
Scottish Genealogical Helper, part 1, 1974, pp.6-9.)
ED/N-1 (P.la.6393)

MACGREGOR, Alexander
The life of Flora Macdonald and her adventures
with Prince Charles . . . . Inverness, 1882.
ED/N-1 (A.110.e)

— — 3rd ed. Inverness, 1896.
ED/N-1 (A.110.e)

MACINTYRE, James
Castles of Skye: stronghold and house of Clan
Donald. Inverness, 1938.
ED/N-1 (R.249.f)   QZ/P40   QZ/P-1   QZ/P99

MONRO, Sir Donald
Monro's Western Isles of Scotland and genealogies
of the clans. [With a genealogical table.]
Edinburgh, 1961.
ED/N-1 (NE.4.b.15)

REA, John
A look at Scotland and the Macdonalds. [McLean,
Va., 1975.]
ED/N-1 (NE.22.a.13)   ED/N-2

SELLAR, W. D. H.
The origins and ancestry of Somerled. (In *Scottish
Historical Review*, vol.45, no.140, October 1966,
pp.123-42.)
ED/N-1 (Ref.53)

TERRY, James
The pedigrees and papers of James Terry, Athlone
Herald at the Court of James II in France, 1690-1725.
Exeter, 1938.
ED/N-1 (R.172.c)

Macdonald of Achtriachtan
FRASER-MACKINTOSH, Charles
The Macdonalds of Achtriachtan. (In *Transactions of
the Gaelic Society of Inverness*, vol.xxiii, 1898-9,
pp.136-45.)
ED/N-1 (NF.1559) QZ/Q41

Macdonald of Aird and Vallay
MACDONALD, A. Grahame
The MacDonalds of Aird and Vallay in Australia
and New Zealand. (In *Clan Donald Magazine*, no.8,
1979, pp.69-73.)
ED/N-1 (2668 PER)

Macdonald of Annandale
MACDONALD, James A. D. J.
The Annandale mystery. [N.p.], 1932.
ED/N-2

Macdonald in Antrim
MACDONALD, Archibald
A fragment of an Irish MS. history of the
MacDonalds of Antrim. (In *Transactions of the Gaelic
Society of Inverness*, vol.xxxvii, 1934-6, pp.262-84.)
ED/N-1 (NF.1559)

Macdonald of Badenoch
MCALLISTER, R. I.
Macdonalds in Badenoch. (In *Clan Donald
Magazine*, no.5, 1971, pp.46-7.)
ED/N-1 (2668 PER)

Macdonald of Clanranald
CAMERON, Alexander
Reliquiae Celticae. Inverness, 1892-4. 2v.
ED/N-1 (Bk.3/3;Oss.287,288) ED/N-2

MACDONALD, Angus R.
The Chief of Clan Donald—who is he?: note, in
protest, against the finding in Clan Donald.
London, 1905.
ED/N-1 (5.511) QZ/P-1

MACDONALD, Charles
Moidart, or among the Clanranalds. Oban, 1889.
ED/N-1 (A.124.e) DN/U-1 ED/N-2 QZ/P30
QZ/P40 AD/U-1 QZ/L37 QZ/P-1 QZ/P99

MACKENZIE, Alexander
History of the MacDonalds of Clanranald.
Inverness, 1881.
ED/N-1 (Gen.8M) QZ/P27 ED/N-2 QZ/P30
QZ/P40 AD/U-1 GL/U-1 QZ/L37 QZ/P-1
QZ/P99

VINDICATION of the "Clanranald of Glengarry"
against the attacks made upon them in the Inverness
Journal and some recent printed performances with
remarks as to the descent of the family who style
themselves, "of Clanranald". Edinburgh, 1821.
ED/N-1 (A.114.c.4)

Macdonald of Dalness
MILLAR, Charles M. H.
The Macdonalds of Dalness. (In *Clan Donald
Magazine*, no.9, 1981, pp.17-20.)
ED/N-1 (2668 PER)

Macdonald of Glenalladale
MACKAY, Iain R.
The MacDonalds of Glenalladale. Inverness, [n.d.].
QZ/P40 (I) QZ/P30

Macdonald of Glengarry
MACDONALD, Norman H.
The Clan Ranald of Knoydart and Glengarry: a
history of the MacDonalds or MacDonells of
Glengarry. Edinburgh, 1979.
ED/N-1 (Gen.8.R) SA/U-1 QZ/P40 (I)
DN/U-1 QZ/Q41 QZ/P14 QZ/P22
QZ/P27 ED/N-2 ED/S10 QZ/P99

MACKENZIE, Alexander
History and genealogy of the Macdonalds of
Glengarry. Inverness, 1881.
ED/N-1 (Gen.8.M) QZ/P40 SA/U-1 AD/U-1
GL/U-1 QZ/P99 QZ/P-1

RIDDELL, John
Vindication of the "Clanronald of Glengarry"
against the attacks made upon them in the Inverness
Journal and some recent printed performances.
With remarks as to the descent of the family who
style themselves "of Clanronald". Edinburgh, 1821.
ED/N-1 (A.114.c.4) QZ/P26 ED/N-2 QZ/P40
SA/U-1 QZ/L37 ST/U-1 QZ/P-1 ED/U-1
QZ/P99

Macdonald of Glenmoriston
[MACDONALD of Glenmoriston and Glen Urquhart.
1975?] (*MS.*)
QZ/P40 (I)

Macdonald of Islay

FRASER-MACKINTOSH, Charles
The last Macdonalds of Isla. Glasgow, 1895.
ED/N-1 (A.113.a) QZ/P27 SA/U-1 QZ/P40
AD/U-1 QZ/P99 QZ/P-1 ED/U-1

MACDONALD, Donald J.
The last MacDonalds of Islay. (In *Scottish
Genealogist,* vol.vii, no.4, October 1960, pp.15-24.)
ED/N-1 (Gen.7)

SMITH, G. Gregory
The book of Islay. [With genealogical tables.]
Edinburgh, 1895.
ED/N-1 (A.58.a)

Macdonald of the Isles

EXTRACTS from the Inverness Courier relative to the
ancient Kingdom of the Isles. London, 1822.
SA/U-1 QZ/L37 QZ/P-1 QZ/P99

['A FAMILY history of the Macdonalds, Lords of the
Isles'. 17--.]
ED/N-1 (Adv.MS.20.1.10,ff.104-65.)

MACDONALD, Alice E. Bosville
The fortunes of a family: Bosville of New Hall,
Gunthwaite and Thorpe. Edinburgh, 1928.
ED/N-1 (S.121.h)

—The House of the Isles. [Edinburgh, 1925.]
ED/N-1 (R.172.g) QZ/Q41 QZ/P40 SA/U-1
QZ/L37 QZ/P-1 QZ/P99

—A romantic chapter in family history. London,
1911.
ED/N-1 (S.120.i) AD/U-1 QZ/P-1 QZ/P99

MACKENZIE, Alexander
History of the Macdonalds and Lords of the Isles.
Inverness, 1881.
ED/N-1 (Gen.8.M) SA/U-1 QZ/P26 QZ/P27
ED/N-2 QZ/P30 QZ/P40 AD/U-1 DN/U-1
GL/U-1 QZ/L37 QZ/P-1 ED/U-1 QZ/P99

STIRLING, Anna Maria D. W. Pickering
Macdonald of the Isles. London, 1913.
ED/N-1 (S.168.e) QZ/Q41 QZ/P27
QZ/P15 QZ/P40 QZ/P99 QZ/P40 AD/U-1
GL/U-1 QZ/P30 QZ/P-1 ED/U-1

Macdonald of Keppoch

MACDONALD, Angus
A family memoir of the Macdonalds of Keppoch . . .
written from 1800 to 1820. . . . London, 1885.
ED/N-1 (A.113.d) ED/N-2 SA/U-1 AD/U-1
QZ/P-1 QZ/P99

MACDONALD, Donald
Tales and traditions of the Lews. [With genealogical
tables.] Stornoway, 1967.
ED/N-1 (NE.2.d.3)

MACDONALD, John Paul
A Keppoch song . . . the origin and history of the
family . . . [Montrose], 1815.
ED/N-1 (Bk.3) QZ/P22 GL/U-1 QZ/P-1
QZ/P99

MACDONALD, Kathleen
Angus Ban of Inch. (In *Clan Donald Magazine,*
no.7, 1977, pp.92-6.)
ED/N-1 (2668 PER)

MACDONALD, Norman H.
The Clan Ranald of Lochaber: a history of the
MacDonalds or MacDonells of Keppoch.
[Edinburgh, 1972.]
ED/N-1 (6.2068) QZ/P40 (I) SA/U-1 QZ/P22
QZ/P27 QZ/L37 ED/N-2 ED/S10 QZ/P-1

Macdonald of Kingsburgh

MACDONALD, Reginald Henry
Notes on the House of MacDonald of Kingsburgh
and Castle Camus. [Pittsburg, Pa.], 1962.
ED/N-1 (NE.25.h.16) QZ/P40 (I) GL/U-1
QZ/P30 QZ/P-1 ED/U-1

Macdonald of Largie

The MACDONALDS (MacConnell) of Largie in
Kintyre. (In *Scottish Genealogist,* vol.xiv, no.4, 1967,
pp.76-80.)
ED/N-1 (Gen.7)

Macdonald of Morar

FRASER-MACKINTOSH, Charles
The Macdonalds of Morar, styled "Macdhugail".
(In *Transactions of the Gaelic Society of Inverness,*
vol.xv, 1888-9, pp.63-75.)
ED/N-1 (NF.1559) QZ/Q41

Macdonald of Ord

The DESCENDANTS of Charles Macdonald of Ord.
[N.p., 1969?]
ED/N-1 (HP3.81.830)

Macdonald of Sanda

CAMPBELL, John Macmaster
The island and house of Sanda. 2pts.
[Campbeltown], 1924.
ED/N-1 (NE.7.d.2(3))

GENEALOGICAL and historical account of the family
of Macdonald of Sanda. London, 1825.
ED/N-1 (Hall.197.a) QZ/P27 ED/N-2
QZ/P40 QZ/P-1 QZ/P99

Macdonald of Sleat *see* **Macdonald**

Macdonald of Uig
MACDONALD, Donald
Tales and traditions of the Lews. [With genealogical
tables.] Stornoway, 1967.
ED/N-1 (NE.2.d.3)

Macdonell *see also* **Macdonald**

Macdonell in Antrim
HILL, George
Historical account of the Macdonells of Antrim,
including notices of some other septs, Irish and
Scottish. Belfast, 1873.
ED/N-1 (A.28.b) DN/U-1 QZ/P27 QZ/P40
QZ/L37 QZ/P-1 QZ/P99

MACLEAN, Hector
A sketch of the Macdonells of Antrim. (In
Transactions of the Gaelic Society of Inverness, vol.xvii,
1890-91, pp.85-101.)
ED/N-1 (NF.1559)

Macdonell of Barrisdale
MACDONALD, Norman H.
The legend of Barrisdale. (In *Clan Donald Magazine*,
no.7, 1977, pp.58-70.)
ED/N-1 (2668 PER)

Macdonell of Glengarry
KELLY, Bernard W.
Fate of Glengarry, or the expatriation of the
Macdonells: an historico-biographical study.
Dublin, 1905.
ED/N-1 (Dur.266) QZ/P-1 QZ/P99

Macdonell of Insch
MACDONALD, A. Grahame
The search for the Keppoch charm stone and the
MacDonells of Insch. (In *Clan Donald Magazine*,
no.9, 1981, pp.39-44.)
ED/N-1 (2668 PER)

Macdonell of Keppoch
MACDONALD, Norman Hamilton
The Clan Ranald of Lochaber; a history of the
MacDonalds or MacDonnells of Keppoch. [N.p.,
1972.]
QZ/P-1

MACDONELL, Josephine M.
An historical record of the branch of "Clann
Domhnuill" called the MacDonells of Keppoch
and Gargavach. Glasgow, 1931.
ED/N-1 (R.172.f) SA/U-1 QZ/P-1 QZ/P99

Macdonell of Lochgarry
MACDONALD, Donald J.
The curse of Lochgarry. (In *Clan Donald Magazine*,
no.2, 1961-2, pp.25-7.)
ED/N-1 (2668 PER) QZ/P26

Macdonell of Scotos
FRASER-MACKINTOSH, Charles
The Macdonells of Scotos. (In *Transactions of the
Gaelic Society of Inverness*, vol.xvi, 1889-90,
pp.79-97.)
ED/N-1 (NF.1559)

MacDougall *see also* **Dougall**

MacDougall
DUNOLLIE CASTLE and the chiefs of the Clan
MacDougall. [N.p., 1954?]
ED/N-1 (5.2030) QZ/P99

McDOUGAL family genealogy. 1964. (*Typescript*)
QZ/P40 (I)

McDOUGAL, David B.
McDougall family genealogy. 1964. (*MS.*)
QZ/P40 (I)

MACDOUGALL, D.
MacDougall genealogy. Known descendants in the
U.S. of America of Robert McDougall of Western
Scotland; 1748-1832. [N.d.] (*Typescript*)
QZ/P40

MACDOWALL, John Kevan
Carrick Gallovidian: a historical survey . . . with
genealogical charts and notes . . . Ayr, 1947.
ED/N-1 (R.241.d)

STARFORTH, Michael
A short history of the Clan Macdougall. [N.p.,
1976.]
ED/N-1 (HP1.77.1008) QZ/P40 (D) QZ/P22
QZ/P27 ED/N-2 QZ/P42 QZ/P-1 QZ/P99

MacDougall of Lorn
The GALLEY of Lorn: historical, traditional, and
other records of the Chlann Dughaill. 7pts in 1.
Sheffield, 1909.
ED/N-1 (S.122.a) ED/N-2 QZ/L37

MacDougall of Makerston

FRASER, Sir William
Genealogical table of the families of Brisbane of Bishoptoun and Brisbane; Makdougall of Makerstoun and Hay of Alderstoun. Edinburgh, 1840. (*Xerox-copy*)
ED/N-2

Macdowall

MACDOWALL, Fergus D. H.
Macdowall. [Ottawa, 1977?]
ED/N-1 (HP3.78.1444)

Macdowall of Freuch

GOLDIE, G.
Sophia MacDowall: a genealogical note. (In *Transactions of the Dumfriesshire and Galloway Natural History and Antiquarian Society*, 3rd series, vol.xxiv, 1945-6, pp.63-7.)
ED/N-1 (J.187)

REID, Robert Corsane
Mochrum notes: calendar of Mochrum papers. [N.d.] 3v. (*MSS.*)
QZ/P10 (Unconfirmed location)

Macdowall of Garthland

[GENEALOGICAL roll of the MacDowalls of Garthland. N.p., n.d.]
QZ/P-6

Mcdowell

BOYD, Lucinda J. R.
The Irvines and their kin. [N.p.], 1908.
ED/N-2

Macduff

RAVENSCROFT,
Memorials of the antient and illustrious family of Macduff ... Aberdeen, 1848.
ED/N-1 (3.262.1(1)) ED/N-2 QZ/P-1

Macduff of Bonhard

MACDUFF, Alexander
The MacDuffs of Bonhard. (*Perth Pamphlets*, vol.10, [1883], newscutting no.69.)
QZ/P26

MacDuffie

MACPHEE, Earle Douglas
The mythology, traditions and history of MacDhubhsith-MacDuffie Clan. Vancouver, 1972- .
ED/U-1 GL/U-1* QZ/L37* QZ/P-1* QZ/P27*

MacEachern

CAMPBELL, Colin
The MacEacherns: a note. (In *Scottish Genealogist*, vol.xxiii, no.1, March 1976, pp.5-8.)
ED/N-1 (Gen.7)

MACEACHERN, N. A.
Clan MacEachern: a search for our ancestors. [1959.] (*Typescript*)
QZ/P99

TROTTER, Sally
The family of Daniel and Mary McEachern of Carroll County, Mississippi. 2pts. Greenville, Mississippi, 1969-74.
QZ/P27

McEachran of Killelan

MCKERRAL, Andrew
Two old Kintyre lawsuits, with some notes on ... McShennags of Lephenstrath; Omeys of Kilcolmkill; and McEachrans of Killelan. [N.p.], 1941.
ED/N-1 (5.969) QZ/P27 QZ/P-1

MacEwen

MACEWEN, Robert Sutherland Taylor
The Clan Ewen: some records of its history. Glasgow, 1904.
ED/N-1 (S.121.g) AD/U-1 GL/U-1 SA/U-1 QZ/P22 QZ/P27 QZ/P40 QZ/P99 QZ/Q17

SMITH, Austin Wheeler
The Dickson-McEwen and allied families genealogy. 2nd ed. Cookeville, Tenn., 1975.
ED/N-1 (H3.79.978)

McFadyen

MERRIMAN, Brenda Dougall
Research story: McFadyen of Coll in Argyll, River Denys in Cape Breton, Oakbank in Manitoba. (In *Scottish Genealogist*, vol.xxx, no.4, December 1983, pp.134-41.)
ED/N-1 (Gen.7)

MacFadzen of Ayrshire

BAILEY, William Henry
A chronicle of the family of Gairdner. Taunton, 1947.
QZ/P-1 ED/N-1 (R.159.i) SA/U-1 AD/U-1 GL/U-1 QZ/P-1 QZ/P99

Macfarlane

BAILEY, William Henry
A chronicle of the family of Gairdner. Taunton,
1947.
QZ/P-1   ED/N-1 (R.159.i)   SA/U-1   AD/U-1
GL/U-1   QZ/P-1   QZ/P99

LITTLE, C. M.
History of the Clan MacFarlane, (Macfarlane),
Macfarlan, Macfarland, Macfarlin. Tottenville,
N.Y., 1893.
ED/N-1 (A.113.c)   SA/U-1   AD/U-1   QZ/P-1
QZ/P99

MACFARLANE, James
History of Clan MacFarlane. Glasgow, 1922.
ED/N-1 (S.120.i)   QZ/P40 (D)   QZ/P27
ED/N-2   AD/U-1   ED/S10   QZ/L37   SA/U-1
ST/U-1   QZ/P49   QZ/P-1   QZ/P99

— The Red Fox: a story of the Clan Macfarlane. 1912.
QZ/P99

MACFARLANE, William Barr
The church of Clan Macfarlane. (In *Transactions of
the Scottish Ecclesiological Society*, vol.v, part 2,
1916-17, pp.143-55.)
ED/N-1 (U.436)

— — (Reprinted from *Transactions of the Scottish
Ecclesiological Society*, vol.v, 1916-17.)
ED/N-2   QZ/P-1   QZ/P99

WINCHESTER, H. S.
Traditions of Arrochar and Tarbet and the
Macfarlanes. [N.p., n.d.]
ED/N-1 (5.707)   QZ/P-1   QZ/P99

Macfarlane in Brazil

AZEVEDO, Aroldo de
Cochranes do Brasil: a vide e a obra de Thomas
Cochrane e Ignacio Cochrane. [With genealogical
tables.] São Paolo, 1965.
ED/N-1 (1966.176)

Macfarlane of Letter

MACFARLANE, Katherine Agnes
A history of MacFarlanes of Letter in Port of
Menteith. [N.p.], 1940.
ED/N-1 (HP3.82.562)   ED/N-2

Macfie

FAIRRIE, Geoffrey
The sugar refining families of Great Britain. [With
genealogical tables.] London, 1951.
ED/N-1 (NE.63.b.3)

MACFIE, John William Scott
John Macfie of Edinburgh and his family. [With
genealogical tables.] Edinburgh, 1938.
ED/N-1 (NF.1330.a.26)   QZ/P99

MACKINNON, Charles
The Clan Alpin confederation: MacGregor,
MacKinnon, MacNab, MacQuarrie, MacAulay,
Grant and MacFie. (In *The Augustan*, book 1, 1973,
pp.39-46.)
ED/N-1 (P.173)

McGhee

FAMILY records of David and Elizabeth McGhee.
[Australia], 1977.
QZ/P-6

McGhie of Berryknowe

[FAMILY history and genealogy of the descendants of
William Jarvie of Pollokshaws (d.1767) and Angus
McGhie of Berryknows, Goven [*sic*], down to
c. 1839.] (*MSS.*)
QZ/P-1

McGhie in Galloway *see* Mackay

Macgill of Oxenfoord

DALRYMPLE, Hew H.
Pedigree of the Macgills of Oxfuird, showing
descent of Stair family. [N.p.], 1893.
ED/N-1 (MS.3421,f.1)

Macgillivray

[A GENEALOGICAL account of the Macgillivray
family of Dalcrombie, then of Carolina. 1833.]
ED/N-1 (MS.9854,ff.156-9)

McGILLIVRAY, Robert
Clan McGillivray. [N.p., 1968.]
QZ/P-1

McGILLIVRAY, Robert *and* McGILLIVRAY, George B.
A history of the Clan MacGillivray. Thunder Bay,
Ont., 1973.
ED/N-1 (Gen.8.M)   QZ/P40 (I)   QZ/P99

McGILLIVRAY, William
Unto the . . . Lords of Council and Session, the
claim of William Macgillivray, eldest son now in life
of the deceas'd Farquhar Macgillivray of
Dunmaglass. [Edinburgh, 1749.]
ED/N-1 (Ry.II.b.19(42))

—Unto the . . . Lords of Council and Session, the claim of William Macgillivray [upon the estates of Midleys and Kinchyle]. [Edinburgh, 1749.]
ED/N-1 (Ry.II.b.19(43))

MILLER, Mary
From the hills and heather of Scotland. Invercargill, N.Z., 1978.
QZ/P40 (I)

WATERS, Marjory McGillivray
Ne'er forgot shall be: a genealogy of Clan McGillivray of Glenelg and Skye, Inverness-shire, 1761-1979. [Darien, Conn.], 1980.
ED/N-1 (H8.81.105) QZ/P99

Macgillivray of Dunmaglass
FRASER-MACKINTOSH, Charles
The Macgillivrays of Dunmaglass. (In *Transactions of the Gaelic Society of Inverness*, vol.xx, 1894-6, pp.29-47.)
ED/N-1 (NF.1559) QZ/Q41

[LETTERS and documents relating to the Macgillivrays of Dunmaglass. 1857.]
QZ/P40

MacGregor
BEACH, S. E. Hicks
The yesterdays behind the door. Liverpool, 1956.
ED/N-1 (NF:1180.f.15)

BURNS, David G. C.
John McGregor of Fortinghall and his descendants. (In *Scottish Genealogist*, vol.xxix, no.4, December 1982, pp.105-09.)
ED/N-1 (Gen.7)

CLAN Gregor. Edinburgh, 1825.
ED/N-2 QZ/L37

CLAN GREGOR SOCIETY
Newsletter. No.1 (February 1976)- . 1976- .
ED/N-1 (P.med.3946)

—Prospectus of a plan for the formation of the Clan Gregor Society. Edinburgh, 1823.
ED/N-2 QZ/P40 QZ/P99

COOPER, D. Aldred
MacGregor, Fergusson pedigree. [N.p., n.d.]
ED/N-2

EYRE-TODD, George
Edinchip: the seat of Captain, Sir Malcolm Macgregor of Macgregor, Bart., R.N., D.L. (In *Scottish Field*, vol.xxi, no.121, January 1913, pp.17-19.)
ED/N-1 (NJ.311) QZ/P26

— — (Reprinted from *Scottish Field*, vol.xxi, no.121, January 1913.)

GREGORY, Donald
Historical notices of the Clan Gregor. Edinburgh, 1831.
ED/N-1 (6.208(28)) ED/N-2 ED/U-1 AD/U-1
QZ/P-1 QZ/P22 QZ/P40

—Inquiry into the earlier history of the Clan Gregor, with a view to ascertain the causes which led to their proscription in 1603. (In *Archaeologia Scotica*, vol.iv, 1857, pp.130-59.)
ED/N-1 (Ref)

HISTORICAL notes of an old Scottish clan and the romance of Highland whisky. Inverness, [n.d.].
QZ/P14

HOWLETT, Hamilton
Highland constable: life and times of Rob Roy MacGregor. [With a genealogical table.] Edinburgh, 1950.
ED/N-1 (R.152.a) QZ/P-1 QZ/P14 QZ/P40

KERMACK, William Ramsay
The Clan MacGregor (Clan Gregor): the nameless clan. Edinburgh, 1953.
ED/N-1 (Gen.7) QZ/P14 QZ/P27 QZ/P26
ED/N-2 QZ/P40 QZ/P11 QZ/P15 QZ/P22
QZ/P-6 QZ/L37 SA/U-1 QZ/P30 QZ/P41
QZ/P-1 ED/U-1 QZ/P99 QZ/P16

— — [2nd ed.] Edinburgh, 1963.
ED/N-2

— — 3rd ed. Edinburgh, 1979.
ED/N-1 (HP1.80.2912) QZ/P22 QZ/P56

MACGREGOR, Grierson and Grier: chart of pedigrees. London, [1882?].
ED/N-1 (S.122.e) ED/N-2

MACGREGOR, Amelia Georgina Murray
History of the Clan Gregor from public records and private collections. Edinburgh, 1898-1901. 2v.
ED/N-1 (Gen.8.G) QZ/P27 QZ/P26 ED/N-2
QZ/P22 QZ/P40 AD/U-1 SA/U-1 GL/U-1
QZ/P-1 QZ/P99

MacGREGOR, Forbes
Clan Gregor. [N.p.], 1977.
ED/N-1 (1978.40) QZ/P40 (D) QZ/P22
QZ/P27 QZ/L37 ED/N-2 QZ/P-1 QZ/P99

MacGREGOR, John
The Macgregors of Dundurn and Balnacoull, and
Innergeldie. [N.p., n.d.]
ED/N-1 (6.224) ED/N-2 QZ/P99

MacGREGOR, Robert
Rob Roy and the Clan Macgregor. [(N.p., n.d.]
ED/N-1 (5.2051(2))

MacKINNON, Charles
The Clan Alpin confederation: MacGregor,
MacKinnon, MacNab, MacQuarrie, MacAulay,
Grant and MacFie. (In *The Augustan*, book 1, 1973,
pp.39-46.)
ED/N-1 (P.173)

MacLEAY, Kenneth
Historical memoirs of Rob Roy and the Clan
Macgregor. Glasgow, 1818.
ED/N-1 (A.110.g.10) ED/N-2 GL/U-1
QZ/P99

— — 2nd ed. Glasgow, 1919.
ED/N-1 (NE.25.c.23) QZ/P-1

— — Glasgow, 1840.
ED/N-1 (Hall.199.j) ED/N-2 GL/U-1

— — Edinburgh, 1881.
ED/N-1 (NE.25.c.27) ED/N-2 AD/U-1
QZ/P-1 QZ/P-6 QZ/P22 QZ/P99

MILLAR, Alexander Hastie
Gregarach: the strange adventures of Rob Roy's
sons. London, [n.d.].
ED/N-1 (R.233.g) QZ/P27 QZ/P26 QZ/P-1

NOTES on the immediate family and connections of
the chief of the Clan Gregor. [19--.] (*MSS.*)
QZ/P-1

[PAPERS relating to descendants of Rob Roy
MacGregor; includes family tree of MacGregor of
Glengyle and Glenorchy. N.d.]
QZ/P-1

A PROCLAMATION anent the resetters of the Clan
and name of Greigour or McGreigour, 27 August
1691. [N.p.], 1691.
ED/N-1 (H.33.a.17(66))

SCOTT, Sir Walter
The Highland clans, with a particular account of
Rob Roy and the Macgregors. Edinburgh, 1856.
QZ/P26 QZ/P22 QZ/P-1 QZ/P99

— . . . History of the Clan MacGregor, with details of
Rob Roy. Glasgow, 1893.
QZ/P27 QZ/P11 QZ/P40 QZ/P99

STEWART, D.
The life . . . of Rob Roy Macgregor, with an
historical sketch of the celebrated Clan Macregor.
Newcastle upon Tyne, [n.d.].
ED/N-1 (5.1081(12)) ED/N-2

The TRIALS of James, Duncan and Robert
McGregor, three sons of the celebrated Rob Roy,
before the High Court of Justiciary in the years
1752, '53 and '54 . . .: a memoir relating to the
Highlands with anecdotes of Rob Roy and his
family. Edinburgh, 1818.
ED/N-1 (L.C.2099) QZ/P14

MacGregor of Ardenconnel
['DRAFT genealogical account of the MacGregor
family of Ardenconnel'. 1828.]
ED/N-1 (Adv.MS.19.217,f.321)

MacGregor of Dunan
[GENEALOGICAL tree of the family of Dunan,
Perthshire.] (*MSS.*)
QZ/P22

MacGregor of Glenorchy
COOPER, Daniel A.
Genealogies of the House of Glenorchy. [N.p.],
1960.
QZ/P26

— Genealogy of the family of Glenorchy. [1960].
(*MS.*)
QZ/P22

MacGregor of Rannoch
CAMERON, R. W. D.
MacGregors of Rannoch. (In *Celtic Magazine*; part 1,
vol.xiii, no.148, February 1888, pp.175-84; part 2,
vol.xiii, no.149, March 1888, pp.219-26.)
ED/N-1 (J.183)

— — (Reprinted from *Celtic Magazine*, vol.xiii,
1888.)
QZ/P-1

McGrigor

McGRIGOR, G. D.
The family of McGrigor. 1941. (*Typescript*)
ED/N-2 QZ/L37

MacGrouther

MACGREGOR, John
The McGrouthers of Meigor in Glenartney. (In
Genealogist, new series, vol.xxxv, 1919, pp.65-81.)
ED/N-1 (Y.215)

— — (Reprinted from *Genealogist*, new series, vol.
xxxv, 1919.)
ED/N-1 (6.1504(35)) AD/U-1 ED/U-1
QZ/P26 QZ/P99

McGuffie

McGUFFIE, Isobel
A genealogical account of the McGuffie family.
[N.p.], 1972.
QZ/L37

MacHardy

ARMS, crest and tartan, with a short account of the
origin of the name MacHardy. London, [1894].
ED/N-1 (5.110(9)) ED/N-2 QZ/L37

FAMILY tree showing the descendants of John
McHardy of Braemar from *c.* 1700 A.D. to 1918.
QZ/P22

MacIan *see* MacKean

MacIlvernock *see also* Graham

MacIlvernock

MACMILLAN, Somerled
Families of Knapdale: their history and their place
names. Paisley, [1960].
ED/N-1 (1936.29) ED/N-2 QZ/P18 QZ/P27

MacIlwraith

WATERSON, Duncan
An Ayrshire family: the McIlwraiths of
Auchenflower, Ayr and Australia. (In *Ayrshire
Archaeological & Natural History Society Collections*,
vol.12, no.3, 1978, pp.101-22.)
ED/N-1 (R.241.b) GL/U-1 QZ/Q88

MacInroy

HESSLING, J. N.
The Mac Ian Ruadh of MacInroy sept: notes on its
origin and on its chieftains. [With a genealogical
table.] (In *Clan Donnachaidh Annual*; part 1, 1973,
pp.35-43; part 2, 1974, pp.42-50; part 3, 1975,
pp.21-33.)
ED/N-1 (NB.43)

LILLIE, William
A Lillie link between Setons and McInroys. (In
Scottish Genealogist, vol.xxvii, no.3, September
1980, pp.85-9.)
ED/N-1 (Gen.7)

MACINROY, J. Nicol
The MacInroys. Voorschoten, 1982.
ED/N-1 (HP3.83.410)

McIntire

McINTIRE, Robert Harry
Historical account of Micum McIntire and his
descendants. [Tuttle], 1940.
ED/N-1 (H3.79.983)

MacIntosh *see also* Mackintosh

MacIntosh

MACINTOSH, Margaret
The MacIntoshes of Georgia and Oklahoma. (In
Clan Chattan, vol.ii, no.3, February 1949, pp.140-4.)
ED/N-1 (Y.130)

MacIntosh of Borlum

ROSS, William Fraser
The family of MacIntosh of Borlum. (In *Clan
Chattan*, vol.i, no.6, March 1939, pp.180-91.)
ED/N-1 (Y.130)

McIntosh in St Andrews

G., R. W. T. *and* G., A.
Gunther family records; with notes on the families
of Nagel, Schlossberger . . . McIntosh etc. London,
1910.
ED/N-1 (S.120.h)

Macintyre

CLAN MACINTYRE ASSOCIATION
[List of members.] [Grandfather Mountain, N.C.],
1979.
ED/N-1 (7.188)

—Per ardua. Vol.1, no.1 (August 1978)- . Bethesda,
Md., 1978- .
ED/N-1 (P.la.7094)

MACINTYRE, Duncan
The MacIntyres of Glencoe and Camus-na-h-erie.
Edinburgh, 1901.
ED/N-1 (NE.26.c.2) QZ/P40 QZ/P-1 QZ/P99

MACINTYRE, Leslie D.
Clan MacIntyre: a journey to the past. Bethesda,
Md., 1977.
ED/N-1 (HP2.78.3182) ED/N-2

MacIver

CAMPBELL, Peter Colin
Account of the Clan Iver. Aberdeen, 1873.
ED/N-1 (A.114.c) ED/N-2 AD/U-1 QZ/L37
QZ/P22 QZ/P-1 QZ/P40 (W,I)

— — 1878.
QZ/P99 SA/U-1

— — Dingwall, [1910].
QZ/P53

MACIVER, Henry
Clan Iver. Liverpool, 1912.
ED/N-1 (NE.26.d.4) QZ/Q41

MacIver in North Carolina, U.S.A.

KELLY, Kenneth L.
McIver family of North Carolina. [Washington],
1964.
ED/N-1 (NF.1375.a.2)

Mack

McCRIE, James
History of the Macks of Ninewar, near Duns,
1752-1800. Lennoxtown, 1886.
QZ/P99

Mackay

CLAN MACKAY SOCIETY (COMUNN CLANN
AOIDH)
Constitution, office-bearers, list of members and
councillors . . . for session 1905-1906. Glasgow,
1907.
QZ/P27

— — 1910-11. Glasgow, 1912.
ED/N-1 (S.120.g) QZ/P-1 QZ/P99

— War memorial volume: containing a list of those
bearing the name MacKay who were killed or died
in the Great War, 1914-18, and a list of those upon
whom honours were conferred. Glasgow, 1924.
ED/N-1 (5.371) QZ/P40 QZ/P22 QZ/P-1

GAYRE, Robert
Some notes upon the MacKays of the Rhinns of
Islay: with reference to the MacKays of Kintyre,
the McGhies of Galloway, and the Irish MacGees.
Inveraray, [n.d.].
ED/N-1 (H3.81.3606) GL/U-1 QZ/L37
QZ/P27

[GENEALOGICAL account of the family of Mackay.
1824.]
ED/N-1 (MS.3742)

GENEALOGY of the Arichliney Mackays for five
centuries. [N.p., n.d.]
QZ/P40

GIBSON, John G.
Piper John Mackay and Roderick McLennan: a
tale of two immigrants and their incomplete
genealogy. (In Nova Scotia Historical Review, vol.2,
no.2, 1982, pp.69-82.)
ED/N-1 (6109 PER)

GRIMBLE, Ian
Chief of MacKay. [With a genealogical table.]
London, 1965.
ED/N-1 (NE.21.c.21) ED/U-1 GL/U-1 ST/U-1
QZ/P11 QZ/P14 QZ/P28 QZ/P30 QZ/P34
QZ/P99 ED/N-2

GUNN, Adam and MACKAY, J.
Sutherland and the Reay country. Glasgow, 1897.
ED/N-1 (A.104.g)

MACAOIDH, Garbhan
Guirme chnoc ciana. (In Gairm; part 1, aireamh
124, foghar 1983, pp.363-78; part 2, aireamh 125,
geamhradh 1983/4, pp.15-25.)
ED/N-1 (P.65)

MACDOUGALL, Margaret Oliphant
Clan Mackay: a Celtic resistance to feudal
superiority. Edinburgh, 1953.
ED/N-1 (Gen.7) QZ/P40 (D) QZ/P27
QZ/P26 QZ/P22 QZ/P-6 QZ/P11 QZ/L37
SA/U-1 QZ/P30 QZ/P49 QZ/P-1 ED/U-1
QZ/P99 QZ/P16

MACKAY, Alexander
Black Castle MS.: historical and genealogical sketch
of the noble family of Reay with an account of the
different branches. 1832. (Typescript)
ED/S10 (Unconfirmed location)

MACKAY, Angus
The book of Mackay. Edinburgh, 1906.
ED/N-1 (Gen.8.M) QZ/P22 QZ/P40 AD/U-1
SA/U-1 GL/U-1 QZ/L37 ED/U-1 QZ/P99

— Genealogy of the family of Mackay. [London],
1904.
ED/N-1 (Mf.54(12(2)) ED/N-2

MACKAY, George
Mackay regiments. 1940.
ED/N-1 (5.920)

— A Scots Brigade flag for Amsterdam in 1930: being
a narrative of some happenings, old and new,
concerning the Clan Mackay. Stirling, 1931.
ED/N-1 (1931.29) QZ/P14 ED/N-2 SA/U-1
QZ/P-1 ED/U-1 QZ/P99

MACKAY, Hugh Donald
A thumb-nail outline of notes on research of the old
royal house of Moray: a clan family of MacAedth,
later MacAod, now MacAodith of Strathnaver. (In
Scottish Genealogist, vol.xxvi, no.1, March 1979,
pp.18-21.)
ED/N-1 (Gen.7)

MACKAY, R. L.
The Clan Mackay: its origin, history and dispersal.
[Wolverhampton], 1978.
ED/N-1 (HP2.78.1211) ED/S10 SA/U-1

— The history of the Clan Mackay: its origin, history
and dispersal. [Wolverhampton, 1977.]
ED/N-1 (HP1.77.3303) ED/N-2 ED/U-1
DN/U-1 QZ/P-1 QZ/P22 QZ/P27 QZ/P40
(I,D,W) QZ/P99

— The origin of the Clan Mackay. [N.p.], 1975.
QZ/P-1

MACKAY, Robert
History of the House and Clan of Mackay.
Edinburgh, 1829.
ED/N-1 (A.114.a) QZ/P26 ED/N-2 QZ/P22
QZ/P40 SA/U-1 AD/U-1 GL/U-1 QZ/L37
QZ/P30 QZ/P-1 ED/U-1 QZ/P99

MACKAY, William
Origin of the Clan Mackay: a paper read before the
Clan Mackay Society. Inverness, 1890.
ED/N-1 (5.5858(1)) AD/U-1

WALKER, Frank
The feuding MacKays. (In Scotland's Magazine,
vol.62, no.4, April 1966, pp.18-23.)
ED/N-1 (Y.31) QZ/P22

Mackay of Achmonie
MACKAY, William
The men from whom we have come: a short history
of the Mackays of Achmonie. Inverness, 1925.
QZ/P40 QZ/P-1 ED/U-1 QZ/P99

Mackay of Bighouse
ROSE, David Murray
The Mackays of Bighouse. [N.p., 1899?]
ED/N-1 (5.2484(40)) QZ/P22

WIMBERLEY, Douglas
Selections from some family papers of the Mackays
of Bighouse. Inverness, [1896-9].
SA/U-1 QZ/P22 AD/U-1 GL/U-1 QZ/P99

Mackay of Far
MACKAY, George
Two unpublished letters from James Graham to Sir
Donald Mackay of Far. (In Juridical Review, vol.liii,
no.4, 1941, pp.298-317.)
ED/N-1 (Law)

— — (Reprinted from Juridical Review, vol.liii, 1941.)
ED/N-1 (6.773) QZ/P-1

Mackay of Strathnaver
GRIMBLE, Ian
Chief of Mackay. [With a genealogical table.]
London, 1965.
ED/N-1 (NE.21.c.21) QZ/P34 QZ/P14
GL/U-1 QZ/P30 ED/N-2 QZ/P99 QZ/P11
QZ/P28 ST/U-1 ED/U-1

MacKean
BUCHANAN, Roberdeau
Genealogy of the family of MacKean of
Pennsylvania. Lancaster, Pa., 1890.
QZ/L37

McKEAN, Frederick George
McKean historical notes, being quotations from
historical and other records, relating chiefly to the
MacIain-Macdonalds, many calling themselves
McCain, McCane, McEan, MacIan etc.
Washington, 1906.
ED/N-1 (R.172.d) GL/U-1 ED/U-1

McKee
McKEE, Raymond Walter
The book of McKee. Dublin, 1959.
ED/N-1 (NE.63.h.13) QZ/L37 SA/U-1
QZ/P99

MacKellar

The CLAN sept MacKellar. [N.p., 1972.]
ED/N-1 (6.2228)

MacKellor

SCOTT, James E.
History of the Clan Mackellor of Lochaweside in
Argyllshire. 1962. (*Typescript*)
QZ/P27

Mackenzie

ALLAN, Kenneth S.
The Mackenzie architects. [N.p., n.d.]
QZ/P26

BANE, Richard L.
A history of the McBane-Mackenzie clans. [N.p.],
1955.
QZ/P40 (I)

CLAN MACKENZIE SOCIETY
[Newsletter.] September 1962- . Edinburgh, 1962 -.
ED/N-1 (P.la.8476)

DUNLOP, Jean
The Clan Mackenzie. Wishaw, 1974.
QZ/P56

—The Clan MacKenzie: independence in the north.
Edinburgh, 1953.
ED/N-1 (Gen.7) QZ/P14 QZ/P27 QZ/P26
ED/N-2 QZ/P40 QZ/P11 SA/U-1 QZ/P22
QZ/L37 QZ/P30 QZ/P49 QZ/P-1 ED/U-1
QZ/P99

— — 2nd ed. Edinburgh, 1963.
ED/N-2 QZ/P15

[GENEALOGICAL account of the family of
Mackenzie. 1667.]
ED/N-1 (MS.657)

['GENEALOGY of the family of MacKenzie to 1661'.
17--.]
ED/N-1 (Adv.MS.49.7.12,ff.18-25)

[HISTORY of Clan Mackenzie from 1260 A.D. to *c.*
1633 A.D. N.d.] (*MS.*)
QZ/P-1

MACKENZIE genealogy. [N.d.] (*MS.*)
QZ/P99

MACKENZIE, A. Donald
Some notes. (N.p.], 1915.
AD/U-1 QZ/P99

MACKENZIE, Alexander
The family of Lochend. (Abridged from *History and
genealogies of the Clan Mackenzie.*) [Inverness, 1879.]
QZ/P99

—History of the Clan Mackenzie, with genealogies
of the principal families of that name. Inverness,
1879.
ED/N-1 (A.113.d) QZ/P30 QZ/P40 AD/U-1
GL/U-1 QZ/L37 QZ/P-1 ED/U-1 QZ/P99

— — 1894.
ED/N-1 (Gen.8.M) QZ/P27 QZ/P14 AD/U-1
SA/U-1 QZ/P22 DN/U-1 GL/U-1 QZ/L37
QZ/P-1 ED/U-1 QZ/P99

—The reputed Fitzgerald origin of the Mackenzies.
Inverness, 1892.
ED/N-1 (R.172.c.1(1)) QZ/P40 AD/U-1

MACKENZIE, Sir Alexander Muir
Memoirs of Delvine; with notes on the Clan
Mackenzie. [N.p.], 1901. (*Typescript*)
ED/N-1 (R.246.e;L.C.1110) QZ/P99

MACKENZIE, Alexander W.
Heraldry of the Clan Mackenzie. Columbus, Ohio,
1907.
QZ/P99

MACKENZIE, G.
History of the Mackenzies. [N.d.] (*MS.*)
QZ/P-1

MACKENZIE, George
Letter written by Colonel George Mackenzie with
a short account of his descendants by Alex. W.
Mackenzie. Columbus, Ohio, 1905.
ED/N-2 QZ/P99

—Proposals for printing the genealogical history
of the Fitz-Geralds and Mackenzies, (26 October
1725). [N.p., 1925.]
ED/N-1 (1.5(49))

MACKENZIE, Hector
History of the Mackenzies, written in 1710. (*MS.*)
QZ/P-1

MACKENZIE, James Dixon
Genealogical tables of the Clan Mackenzie.
Edinburgh, 1879.
ED/N-1 (R.283.b)

— — 2nd ed. Edinburgh, 1894.
QZ/P40

M'KENZIE, John
Genealogie of the Mackenzie family, preseeding ye
year 1661. Wreatin in 1669 by a Persone of Qualitie.
Ed. . . . by J. W. Mackenzie. Edinburgh, 1829.
ED/N-1 (A.113.a) QZ/P22 QZ/P40 AD/U-1
SA/U-1 QZ/P-1 QZ/P99

— — Dingwall, 1843.
ED/N-1 (R.172.c.1(2)) QZ/P40 QZ/P41
AD/U-1 QZ/L37 QZ/P-1 QZ/P99

— — (In *Highland Papers*; edited by J. R. N. MacPhail.
Vol.2 (Scottish History Society Publications, 2nd
series, vol.xii.), pp.2-68.)
ED/N-1 (Ref.54) ED/N-2 ED/U-1 QZ/P-1
QZ/P40 QZ/P41

MACKENZIE, N.
Entries in the family Bible of the Rev'd Neil
Mackenzie. 1919. (*Xerox-copy*)
QZ/P99

MACRAE, John
The brief genealogical historical account of the
origin, rise and growth of the family sirname of
Mackenzie . . . to 1678. [N.d.] (*MS.*)
QZ/P99

MATHESON, William
Traditions of the MacKenzies. (In *Transactions of the
Gaelic Society of Inverness*, vol.xxxix/xl, 1942/50,
pp.193-221.)
ED/N-1 (NF.1559) QZ/Q41

WARRAND, Duncan
Some Mackenzie pedigrees. Inverness, 1965.
ED/N-1 (Gen.8.M) QZ/P40 (I,D) SA/U-1
QZ/P41 QZ/P27 ST/U-1 QZ/P50 QZ/P-1
QZ/P99

WILSON, A. N.
MacKenzie saga. [N.p.], 1977.
QZ/P22 QZ/P50

Mackenzie in Alloa
BOASE, Edward Russell
The family of Mackenzie, Alloa. [Edinburgh, 1936.]
ED/N-1 (R.272.a.1(2))

Mackenzie of Applecross
HOLLOWAY, Edward
Clan Mackenzie: Mackenzies of Applecross,
descendants of Roderick Roy. [New York, 1950?]
ED/N-1 (6.608) QZ/L37

SINCLAIR, Alexander Maclean
The Mackenzies of Applecross. Charlottetown,
1901.
ED/N-2

Mackenzie of Ballone
MACKENZIE, Hector Hugh
The Mackenzies of Ballone, with a genealogical
account of the Tolmies of Uiginish, Skye. Inverness,
1941.
ED/N-1 (R.272.a) ED/N-2 AD/U-1 SA/U-1
QZ/L37 QZ/P-1 QZ/P22 QZ/P30 QZ/P40
QZ/P99

Mackenzie, Earl of Cromartie
FRASER, Sir William
The Earls of Cromartie: their kindred, country and
correspondence. Edinburgh, 1876. 2v.
ED/N-1 (Gen.8.M) QZ/P40 (D) ED/N-2
SA/U-1 GL/U-1 QZ/L37 QZ/P-1 ED/U-1
QZ/P99

MEMOIRS of the lives and families of the Lords
Kilmarnock, Cromartie and Balmerino. London,
1746.
ED/N-2

Mackenzie of Dailuaine
MACKENZIE, Alexander
Ancestry of Thomas Mackenzie Esq., of Dailuaine.
Inverness, 1896.
QZ/P99

Mackenzie of Delvine
TWO students at St. Andrews, 1711-1716; edited from
the Delvine papers by William Croft Dickinson.
Edinburgh, 1952.
ED/N-1 (NE.8.b.3)

Mackenzie of Dolphinton
MACKENZIE, Alice Ann
Dolphinton. [N.p.], 1888.
QZ/L37

Mackenzie of Dundonnell
MACKENZIE, Thomas
Report of the trial by jury of Thomas Mackenzie,
Esq., against Robert Roy, Esq., W.S. Edinburgh,
1830.
ED/N-1 (Law)

Mackenzie of Finegand
SMITH MACKENZIE, Margaret Scott
Some account of the M'Kenzies in Glenshee, from
their origin to the present time. Blairgowrie, 1889.
ED/N-1 (APS.1.81.94)

Mackenzie of Gairloch
BOSWELL, James
Answers for Hector Mackenzie, younger, of
Gairloch and Roderick Mackenzie of Redcastle, his
tutor . . . to the petition of Sir Alexander Mackenzie
of Gairloch, Bt. 1768.
QZ/P99

Mackenzie of Kilcoy *see* **Buchan,** Earldom of

Mackenzie of Kintail
MACKENZIE, Sir Edward Mackenzie
Cabarfeidh gu brath: a lay of the Clan Kenneth.
Melbourne, 1907.
ED/N-1 (1911.11)

Mackenzie of Redcastle
KETTLE, Rosa Mackenzie
The last Mackenzie of Redcastle. London, 1888.
ED/N-1 (Vts.57.h.23)   QZ/P99

Mackenzie of Rosehaugh
BARTY, James Webster
Ancient deeds and other writs in the Mackenzie-
Wharncliffe charter-crest; with short notices of Sir
George Mackenzie of Rosehaugh; the first Earls of
Cromartie. Edinburgh, 1906.
ED/N-1 (S.121.a)   QZ/P14   QZ/P26   SA/U-1
QZ/L37   QZ/P-1   ED/U-1   QZ/P99

Mackenzie, Earl of Seaforth *see also* **Stewart-
Mackenzie** of Seaforth

Mackenzie, Earl of Seaforth
A DEDUCTION of the family of Seaforth down to . . .
1755. (*MS.*)
QZ/P-1

MACKENZIE, Edward Mackenzie
Genealogy of the stem of the family of Mackenzie,
Marquesses and Earls of Seaforth. [Melbourne,
1904.]
QZ/P40   AD/U-1   QZ/P99

[MS. letters relating to the Mackenzies of Seaforth,
1814-1816.]
QZ/P-1

[MS. letters relating to the management of the estate
of Seaforth, 1712-1740.]
QZ/P-1

Mackerlich
CAMPBELL, Colin
Mackerlich Campbells in the Breadalbane court
books. Part 1. (In *Scottish Genealogist*, vol.xxvii,
no.1, March 1980, pp.20-1, 24-33.)
ED/N-1 (Gen.7)

MacKerlie
MCKERLIE, Emmeline Marianne H.
Two sons of Galloway: Robert McKerlie (1778-
1855) and Peter (1817-1900). Dumfries, [n.d.].
ED/N-1 (S.124.a)   QZ/P-1

Mackie
SKETCH pedigree chart, the ancestry of Mr. Maitland
Mackie of Tarves. 1957? (*MS.*)
QZ/P22

MacKillop
FEEHAN, Victor *and* MACDONELL, Ann
In search of Alexander MacKillop, 1812-1868. [With
genealogical tables.] Doncaster, Victoria, 1981.
ED/N-1 (HP4.82.176)

Mackinnon
CLAN MACKINNON SOCIETY
Annual report, 1910-11. [Glasgow, 1911.]
QZ/P-1

— — 1925-26. [Glasgow, 1926.]
QZ/P-1

— The Clan and what it stands for. [N.p., 1931.]
ED/N-2   QZ/P-1

DOWNIE, Sir Alexander Mackenzie *and*
MACKINNON, Alister Downie
Genealogical account of the family of Mackinnon.
Plymouth, 1882.
ED/N-1 (A.114.a)   QZ/L37

— — [2nd ed.] London, 1883.
ED/N-1 (A.114.a)   QZ/L37   QZ/P99   QZ/P40
QZ/P-1   QZ/P30

MACDONALD, Hugh N.
Macdonald and Mackinnon families: a biographical
sketch. [N.p., 1938.]
ED/N-1 (5.857)

MACKINNON, C. R.
The Clan MacKinnon: a short history. Coupar Angus, 1958.
ED/N-1 (5.2077) ED/N-2 GL/U-1 SA/U-1 QZ/P-1 QZ/P99 ED/U-1

MACKINNON, Charles
The Clan Alpin confederation: MacGregor, MacKinnon, MacNab, MacQuarrie, MacAulay, Grant and MacFie. (In *The Augustan*, book 1, 1973, pp.39-46.)
ED/N-1 (P.173)

—Sons of the 'Fair One': the Clan MacKinnon. (In *Scottish Genealogical Helper*, part 3, 1974, pp.38-40; part 4, 1974, pp.53-5.)
ED/N-1 (P.la.6393)

MACKINNON, Donald
The chiefs and chiefship of Clan Mackinnon. [Oban, 1931.]
ED/N-1 (5.857)

MACKINNON, Donald D.
Memoirs of the Clan Fingon. Tunbridge Wells, [1884].
ED/N-1 (A.124.c;A.57.a) QZ/L37 QZ/P99 ED/N-2 QZ/P40

— — 1899.
AD/U-1 QZ/P-1 QZ/P27

—Reply from the author of "Memoirs of the Clan Fingon" to a pamphlet entitled "The Family of Mackinnon" by Lauchlan Mackinnon. Tunbridge Wells, [n.d.].
ED/U-1 QZ/P99

Mackinnon of Kyle
MACKINNON, John
The MacKinnons of Kyle and their connections. [With genealogical tables.] Longformacus, 1981.
ED/N-1 (HP2.82.1351) QZ/L37

Mackintosh
BROOKER, J. G.
Family tree of the MacKintosh family from Wm. McIntosh of Botriphnie who died in 1856. Calcutta, 1939.
QZ/P22

BROOKER, J. S.
MacKintosh pedigree: the descendants of William MacKintosh of Botriphnie. [1960]. (*MS.*)
QZ/P22

BULLOCH, Joseph Gaston Baillie
The family of Baillie of Dunain. Green Bay, Wis., 1898.
QZ/P40 AD/U-1 QZ/L37

CLAN CHATTAN ASSOCIATION
Clan Chattan. Vol.1- . Ascot, 1934- .
ED/N-1 (Y.130) QZ/L37 QZ/P-1 QZ/P99

—[Pamphlet, containing lectures on the chiefship, etc.] Oban, 1895.
QZ/P40

DAVIDSON, C. J.
Clan Chattan and the Davidsons. Part 1. (In *Clan Chattan*, vol.viii, no.2, 1983, pp.83-7.)
ED/N-1 (Y.130)

DESCENT of Mackintosh chiefs from Shaw MacDuff. (In *Clan Chattan*, vol.iii, no.2, December 1953, pp.114-20.)
ED/N-1 (Y.130)

DUNLOP, Jean
The Clan Mackintosh: the spearhead of the Clan Chattan. Edinburgh, 1960.
ED/N-1 (Gen.7) QZ/P40 (D) QZ/P22 QZ/P27 QZ/P26 QZ/P49 QZ/P-1 ED/U-1 QZ/P99

EXTRACTS from Register of Deeds and Register of Acts and Decreets relating to the name of Mackintosh. (17th & 18th centuries.) (*MSS.*)
QZ/P40

FRASER-MACKINTOSH, Charles
Address on the history of Clan Chattan. Oban, 1895.
ED/N-1 (H.M.188(1);Ry.I.3.284)

—Confederation of Clan Chattan: its kith and kin. Glasgow, 1898.
ED/N-1 (R.172.c) QZ/P27 ED/N-2 QZ/P40 AD/U-1 GL/U-1 SA/U-1 AD/U-1 QZ/P-1 QZ/P99

—Dunachton, past and present: episodes in the history of the Mackintoshes. Inverness, 1866.
ED/N-1 (L.C.1303;S.121.g) ED/N-2 QZ/P40 GL/U-1 QZ/P-1 QZ/P99

GENEALOGY of the family of Mackintosh, from their origin until 1680. Inverness, 1865. (*MS.*)
QZ/P40

MACBAIN, Alexander
The chiefship of the Clan Chattan. Glasgow, 1896.
ED/N-1 (NE.25.f.2)

MCINTOSH, Mary
Roots and branches: the story of the Angus and
Leybourne families. [With genealogical tables.]
Newcastle, [1958].
ED/N-1 (NE.63.e.12)

MCINTOSH, Walter
Genealogical records of McIntosh families in
United States and Canada. 1984.
QZ/P99

—McIntosh, MacKintosh families of Scotland and
America. 1982.
QZ/P99

—A record of the descendants of John McIntosh of
Bedford, New Hampshire. 1980.
QZ/P99

MACKINTOSH, Alexander Mackintosh
Historical memoirs of the House and Clan of
Mackintosh, and of the Clan Chattan. London,
1880.
ED/N-1 (R.291.c;S.121.g) QZ/P26 QZ/P22
QZ/P40 AD/U-1 GL/U-1 QZ/P99 QZ/L37
SA/U-1 QZ/P36 QZ/P-1 ED/U-1

—Mackintosh families in Glenshee and Glenisla.
Nairn, 1916.
ED/N-1 (S.120.g) QZ/P26 QZ/P22 QZ/P40
QZ/P-1 AD/U-1 SA/U-1 QZ/L37 QZ/P50
ED/U-1 QZ/P99

—The Mackintoshes and Clan Chattan. Edinburgh,
1903.
ED/N-1 (Gen.8.M) DN/U-1 ED/N-2 QZ/P40
AD/U-1 GL/U-1 QZ/P99

MACKINTOSH, Margaret
The Clan Mackintosh and the Clan Chattan.
Edinburgh, 1948.
ED/N-1 (R.272.f) QZ/Q17 QZ/P53 DN/U-1
QZ/P14 QZ/P-6 QZ/P26 QZ/P56 ED/N-2
QZ/P20 QZ/P40 SA/U-1 QZ/P22 QZ/L37
GL/U-1 QZ/P30 QZ/P50 QZ/P-1 QZ/P99

— — Revised ed. Loanhead, 1982.
ED/N-1 (Gen.8.M) QZ/P22 QZ/P99

MACKINTOSH, S. F.
A collection of historical sketches and anecdotes . . .
relating to the Mackintoshes and Clan Chattan.
1835. (MS.)
QZ/P99

—Notes of a history of the origin and increase of the
Mackintoshes. [1830?]
QZ/P99

MACPHERSON, Sir Aeneas
The loyall dissuasive and other papers relating to the
affairs of Clan Chattan; edited by Alexander D.
Murdoch. Edinburgh, 1902. (Scottish History
Society Publications, vol.41.)
ED/N-1 (Ref.54) ED/N-2 DN/U-1 GL/U-1
ST/U-1 QZ/L37 QZ/P-1 QZ/P14 QZ/P20
QZ/P22 QZ/P40 QZ/P99

MACPHERSON, Alexander Cluny
Hail, Clan Chattan!: a clan ode . . . 28th October
1896. Kingussie, 1897.
AD/U-1 ED/U-1 QZ/P99

MACPHERSON, Ewan
Manuscripts in the charter-chest at Cluny Castle . . .
relative to the Clan Chattan and the Cluny of 1745.
Edinburgh, 1879.
ED/N-1 (Blk.388)

MACPHERSON, John
Notes on the names of Clan Chattan and what they
indicate. Edinburgh, 1874.
QZ/P40

[MSS. notes and newspaper cuttings relating to the
Grants, Leiths, MacKintoshes of Blervie. N.d.]
QZ/P40

[NOTES on the genealogy of the family of
Mackintosh. 1833.]
ED/N-1 (MS.9854)

PATON, Henry
The Mackintosh muniments, 1442-1820, preserved
in the Charter room at Moy Hall. Edinburgh, 1903.
ED/N-1 (S.120.b) QZ/P30 QZ/P40 AD/U-1
SA/U-1 QZ/L37 QZ/P-1 QZ/P99

SMITH, William M'Combie
Memoir of the families of M'Combie and Thoms,
originally M'Intosh and M'Thomas. New ed.
Edinburgh, 1890.
ED/N-1 (A.113.c) ED/N-2 QZ/P40 DN/U-1
GL/U-1 QZ/P-1 QZ/P99 QZ/P28 QZ/P30
QZ/P22 AD/U-1 QZ/P41 SA/U-1 QZ/P16
QZ/P-6 QZ/L37 QZ/P49 ED/U-1

—Memoir of the family of M'Combie: a branch
of the Clan M'Intosh. Edinburgh, 1887.
ED/N-1 (A.113.a) QZ/P40 QZ/P-1 QZ/P99

Mackintosh of Borlum

MACKINTOSH, Alexander Mackintosh
Brigadier MacKintosh of Borlum. Nairn, 1918.
ED/N-1 (1918.24) QZ/P-1 QZ/P40

MACLEAN, John
Historical and traditional sketches of Highland
families and of the Highlands. Inverness, 1895.
ED/N-1 (A.114.f) QZ/P-1

Mackintosh of Dalmunzie

R., M. B. H.
The Mackintoshes of Dalmunzie, Clan Ritchie. (In
Clan Chattan, vol.v, no.5, 1968, pp.250-3.)
ED/N-1 (Y.130)

Mackintosh of Kellachie

FRASER-MACKINTOSH, Charles
The Mackintoshes of Kellachie, styled "Sliochd
Alain". (In *Transactions of the Gaelic Society of
Inverness*, vol.xix, 1893-4, pp.98-115.)
ED/N-1 (NF.1559) QZ/Q41

Mackintosh in South Carolina, U.S.A.

MCINTOSH, J. Rieman
The McIntoshes of South Carolina, U.S.A. (In *Clan
Chattan*, vol.vii, no.1, 1977, pp.4-10.)
ED/N-1 (Y.130)

Maclachlan

CLAN MACLACHLAN SOCIETY
Clan Lachlan: the magazine of the Clan
MacLachlan Society, No.1, November 1979- .
[Enocdhu], 1979- .
ED/N-1 (6503 PER)

MACLACHLAN, Thomas F.
Early records of the McLachlan. (In *Scottish
Genealogist*, vol.xxiii, no.2, June 1976, pp.25-30.)
ED/N-1 (Gen.7)

Maclachlan of Kilbride

BANNERMAN, John
The Maclachlans of Kilbride and their manuscripts.
(In *Scottish Studies*, vol.21, 1977, pp.1-34.)
ED/N-1 (NH.317)

Maclagan

MACLAGAN, Sir Edward Douglas
Maclagan families. Edinburgh, 1936.
ED/N-1 (6.176) QZ/P26 QZ/L37

MACLAGAN, R. C.
The clan of the bell of St. Fillan. Edinburgh, [1879].
ED/N-1 (Cam.2.e.1(8);1879.30(14)) QZ/P26
DN/U-1 QZ/P-1 QZ/P99

McLamroch

WHYTE, Donald
The McLamroch legend. (In *Scottish Genealogist*,
vol.xxi, no.1, March 1974, pp.7-15.)
ED/N-1 (Gen.7)

McLandsborough

MCLANDSBOROUGH, John
Our Galloway ancestors: their descendants and
connections. Bradford, 1898.
ED/N-1 (NE.17.c.2) ED/N-2

Maclaren

CREAG an Tuire: Clan Maclaren journal. 1963- .
QZ/P99

MACLAREN, Margaret
The MacLarens: a history of Clan Labhran. Stirling,
1960.
ED/N-1 (NE.25.b.13) QZ/P14 QZ/P27
QZ/P26 ED/N-2 GL/U-1 SA/U-1 ST/U-1
QZ/P13 QZ/P-1 QZ/P99

— — [Edinburgh?, 1976?]
ED/N-1 (Gen.8.M.) ED/N-2

McLarty

MCLARTY, Adelaide
The McLarty family of Kintyre, Scotland and
Mecklenburg County, North Carolina, and their
descendants. [Charlotte], 1974.
ED/N-1 (H8.81.229)

Maclaurin *see* **Laurin**

McLea

MCLEA, Duncan
An account of the name of McLea, 1743.
Edinburgh, 1934. (In *Highland Papers*; edited by
J. R. N. MacPhail. Vol.4 (Scottish History Society
Publications, 3rd series, vol.xxii), pp.91-104.)
ED/N-1 (Ref.54) ED/N-2 QZ/P-1 QZ/P27

Maclean

BRISTOL, Nicholas Maclean
Building of Breacachadh and the Maclean
pedigree. (In *Notes and Queries of the Society of West
Highland & Island Historical Research*, no.xiii,
September 1980, pp.3-11.)
ED/N-1 (P.med.3574)

—Hebridean decade: Mull, Coll and Tiree, 1761-1771. [With a genealogical table.] Coll, 1982.
ED/N-1 (H.2.82.955)

CLAN MACLEAN ASSOCIATION
List of members and office-bearers . . . 1908-1909. Glasgow, [1908].
QZ/P-1

CLANN Thearlaich o Bhuidhe, or the Macleans of the North. (In *Clan Chattan*, vol.vi, no.4, 1974, pp.188-95.)
ED/N-1 (Y.130)

[GENEALOGICAL account drafted in 1716 concerning the family of Maclean. 17--.]
ED/N-1 (Adv.MS.28.3.12,f.2)

[A GENEALOGICAL account of the family of Maclean. 1807?]
ED/N-1 (MS.3018)

GENEALOGICAL notes concerning the family of Maclean. [N.p., 1916.]
QZ/P28

MACKECHNIE, John
The Clan Maclean: a Gaelic seapower. Edinburgh, 1954.
ED/N-1 (Gen.7) QZ/P26 QZ/P40 QZ/P22 QZ/P20 QZ/P-6 QZ/P11 QZ/L37 SA/U-1 QZ/P30 QZ/P49 QZ/P-1 ED/U-1 QZ/P99 QZ/P16

MACLEAN, Alexander
A breif [*sic*] genealogical account of the ffamily [*sic*] of McLean. Edinburgh, 1872.
ED/N-1 (S.120.d) ED/N-2 QZ/P99

MACLEAN, Charles Maxwell
History of Clan Tarlach o' Bui. Aberdeen, 1865.
QZ/P-1 QZ/P99

MACLEAN, J. P.
An examination into the evidences of the chiefship of Clann Ghilleain. Glasgow, 1895.
ED/N-1 (1934.14) QZ/P-1

—[Pamphlet on the chiefship of the Clan Maclean.] Glasgow, 1895.
QZ/P-1 QZ/P27 QZ/P40

MACLEAN, James Noel Mackenzie
Clan Gillean (the Macleans). London, 1955.
ED/N-1 (NE.25.c.5) SA/U-1 QZ/P40 (D) QZ/P14 QZP27 QZ/P22 QZ/L37 QZ/P-1 QZ/P99

MACLEAN, John Patterson
An account of the surname of Maclean, or Macghillean, from the MS. of 1751, and A sketch of the life and writings of Lachlan MacLean, with other information pertaining to the Clan Maclean. Xenia, Ohio, 1914.
ED/N-1 (NE.25.b.27) QZ/P27 AD/U-1 QZ/P-1 QZ/P99

—The family of Maclean, ed. from the MS. entitled "A brief general account of the family of Maclean, from its first settling in the island of Mull . . . in the year 1716", now in the Advocates Library, Edinburgh. Toronto, 1915.
AD/U-1 QZ/P-1 QZ/P99

—History of the Clan Maclean, from its first settlement at Duard Castle to the present time. Cincinnati, Ohio, 1889.
ED/N-1 (A.58.b;A.123.c) DN/U-1 QZ/P14 QZ/P27 ED/N-2 QZ/P30 QZ/P40 AD/U-1 SA/U-1 GL/U-1 QZ/P-1 QZ/P99

—A Maclean souvenir. Franklin, 1918.
ED/N-1 (NE.25.f.6) ED/N-2 QZ/P-1 QZ/P99

—Renaissance of the Clan Maclean: gathering at Duart Castle in 1912. Columbus, Ohio, 1913.
ED/N-1 (R.172.f) QZ/P27 SA/U-1 QZ/P40 AD/U-1 QZ/P-1 QZ/P99

MACLEAN, Neil
Historical and genealogical account of the Clan of Maclean from its first settlement at Castle Duart. London, 1838.
ED/N-1 (A.11.d) AD/U-1 GL/U-1 SA/U-1 QZ/P-1 QZ/P27 QZ/P40 QZ/L37 QZ/P99

SINCLAIR, Alexander Maclean
The Clan Gillean. Charlottetown, Canada, 1899.
ED/N-1 (Gen.8.g) QZ/P27 QZ/P40 AD/U-1 GL/U-1 QZ/L37 QZ/P-1 QZ/P99

—Na bàird Leathanach: the Maclean bards. Charlottetown, Canada, 1898-1900. 2v.
QZ/P-1

Maclean of Boreray
MACKENZIE, Hector Hugh
The Macleans of Boreray, with cadet families and branches. Inverness, 1946.
ED/N-1 (S.122.d) QZ/Q41 ED/N-2 QZ/P40 AD/U-1 QZ/P22 QZ/P99 QZ/L37 QZ/P30 QZ/P-1

Maclean of Coll

BRISTOL, Nicholas Maclean
The family of Coll. [N.p.], 1971.
QZ/L37

—Macleans of Coll in the lands of Lochiel. (In *Notes and Queries of the Society of West Highland & Island Historical Research*, no.xxi, August 1983, pp.3-9.)
ED/N-1 (P.med.3574)

Maclean of Dochgarroch

MACLEAN, D. A. L.
The story of the MacLeans of Dochgarroch. (In *Clan Chattan*, vol.iv, no.2, 1960, p.38.)
ED/N-1 (Y.130)

Maclean of Drimnin

MACLEAN, John
Pedigree of the Macleans of Drimnin. [Glasgow?, 1909.]
ED/N-1 (5.191) QZ/P-1

Maclean of Duart

MACLEAN, John
Genealogy of the Macleans of Dowart, 1910: chiefs of the clan. [Glasgow?, 1910.]
ED/N-1 (5.191) QZ/P-1

PAPERS relating to the Macleans of Duart, 1670-1680. Edinburgh, 1914. (In *Highland Papers*; edited by J. R. N. MacPhail. Vol.1 (Scottish History Society Publications, 2nd series, vol.v.), pp.241-337.)
ED/N-1 (Ref.54) ED/N-2 QZ/P-1 QZ/P22 QZ/P27

Maclean in Sweden

MACLEAN, James Noel Mackenzie
The Macleans of Sweden. Edinburgh, 1971.
ED/N-1 (NE.25.f.9) QZ/P-1 QZ/P99

Maclellan of Kirkcudbright

MACCLELLAN, John
Record of the House of Kirkcudbright. Dalbeattie, 1906.
QZ/L37 QZ/P-1 QZ/P99

MCLELLAN, Eric Burns
Notes on the history and genealogy, and ensigns armorial of the Clan or family of McLellan of Bombie and Kirkcudbright. [N.p.], 1968.
QZ/L37

RECORDS of the McClellands of Bombie and Kirkcudbright. [Castle Douglas, 1874.]
ED/N-2 QZ/L37

MacLennan

CLAN MacLennan Newsletter. No.8 (July 1977)- . 1977- .
ED/N-1 (P.med.1031)

GIBSON, John G.
Piper John Mackay and Roderick McLennan: a tale of two immigrants and their incomplete genealogy. (In *Nova Scotia Historical Review*, vol.2, no.2, 1982, pp.69-82.)
ED/N-1 (6109 PER)

MACLENNAN, Ronald George
The history of the MacLennans. Lochbroom, 1978.
ED/N-1 (Gen.8.M) SA/U-1 QZ/P40 (D,I)
ED/N-2 QZ/P-1

Macleod

CAMERON, Lolita Jean
The broad canvas: a history of my mother's family. Chesham, 1974.
ED/N-1 (6.2749) QZ/P-7 ED/N-2 QZ/P-1

The CLAN Macleod parliament held at Dunvegan castle, August 15th 1956. 1956. (*Typescript*)
AD/U-1

CLAN MACLEOD SOCIETY
Clan MacLeod Magazine. Vol.1, no.1- . Edinburgh, 1935- .
ED/N-1 (NE.1572) QZ/L37 QZ/P-1 QZ/P99

GRANT, Isabel Frances
Clan Macleod: with their rock-built fortress they have endured. Edinburgh, 1953.
ED/N-1 (Gen.7) QZ/P27 QZ/P26 QZ/P-6
QZ/P40 QZ/P22 QZ/P11 QZ/L37 SA/U-1
QZ/P30 QZ/P49 QZ/P-1 ED/U-1 QZ/P99
QZ/P16

— — 3rd ed. Edinburgh, 1979.
ED/N-1 (HP1.80.2913) QZ/P22 QZ/P56

—The Macleods: the history of a clan, 1200-1956. London, 1959.
ED/N-1 (Gen.8.M) QZ/P53 QZ/P-6 QZ/P22
QZ/P56 ED/N-2 QZ/L37 QZ/P40 GL/U-1
SA/U-1 QZ/P30 QZ/P15 QZ/P13 QZ/P49
ED/U-1 QZ/P99

— — Edinburgh, 1981.
ED/N-1 (Gen.8.M) QZ/P14 QZ/P22
QZ/P40 (I) QZ/P53 QZ/P56 QZ/Q41
QZ/P99

MACKENZIE, Alexander
History of the Macleods, with genealogies of the principal families of the name. Inverness, 1889.
ED/N-1 (Gen.8.M) QZ/P14 QZ/P27 ED/N-2
QZ/P30 QZ/P40 SA/U-1 AD/U-1 GL/U-1
QZ/L37 QZ/P41 QZ/P-1 QZ/P99

MACKINNON, Donald
The Macleods . . . their chiefs and cadets. Cupar, Fife, 1950.
ED/N-1 (1950.42) QZ/P-1 QZ/P99

MACKINNON, Donald *and* MORRISON, Alick
The MacLeods: the genealogy of a clan. 5pts. [Edinburgh, 1969-77.]
ED/N-1 (1970.232) QZ/L37 QZ/P22 ED/N-2
QZ/P40 (D) SA/U-1 QZ/P30 QZ/P-1
ED/U-1 QZ/P27* QZ/Q41* QZ/P99

MCLEOD, Alex C.
A bardic tradition: the clann Alasdair Ruadh. (In *Clan MacLeod Magazine*, vol.9, no.56, 1983, pp.108-11.)
ED/N-1 (NF.1572)

—The heraldry of Clan MacLeod. (In *Clan MacLeod Magazine*, vol.9, no.54, 1982, pp.6-10.)
ED/N-1 (NF.1572)

—Serendipity, sennachie and signet: an ancestral odyssey. (In *Clan MacLeod Magazine*, vol.9, no.54, 1982, pp.17-22.)
ED/N-1 (NF.1572)

MACLEOD, Anthony Macaulay
MacLeods who went to the Philippines. (In *Clan MacLeod Magazine*, vol.9, no.57, 1983, pp.164-70.)
ED/N-1 (NF.1572)

MACLEOD, C. E. Alexander
The Clan MacMhic Alasdair Ruaidh: the MacLeods of St. Kilda. [London], 1960.
ED/N-1 (6.1963)

MACLEOD, Fred T.
Notes on the relics preserved in Dunvegan Castle, Skye, and the heraldry of the family of Macleod of Macleod. (In *Proceedings of the Society of Antiquaries of Scotland*, vol.xlvii, 1912-13, pp.99-129.)
ED/N-1 (Ref.35.d)

— — (Reprinted from *Proceedings of the Society of Antiquaries of Scotland*, vol.xlvii, 1912-13.)
ED/N-1 (5.232)

MCLEOD, G. S.
Neal McLeod . . . his genealogy, 1774-1961. 1962.
QZ/P99

MACLEOD, Roderick Charles
The Macleods: a short sketch of their clan history, folk-lore, tales and biographical notices of some eminent clansmen. Edinburgh, 1906.
ED/N-1 (5.2035) QZ/P27 QZ/P22 SA/U-1
AD/U-1 QZ/P-1 ED/U-1 QZ/P99 QZ/P16

—The Macleods: their history and traditions. [Edinburgh], 1929.
ED/N-1 (S.120.i) QZ/Q41 QZ/P14 QZ/P27
ED/N-2 QZ/P22 DN/U-1 GL/U-1 SA/U-1
QZ/P30 QZ/P40 QZ/P-1 QZ/P99

—Norman Magnus Macleod of Macleod . . . a memorial of a noble life. Inverness, 1930.
ED/N-1 (5.456) QZ/P99

MACLEOD, Ruairidh H.
The heraldry of Clan MacLeod. (In *Double Tressure*, no.4, 1982, pp.22-6.)
ED/N-1 (P.sm.1445)

—Talisker, 1798-1849. (In *Clan MacLeod Magazine*, vol.8, no.49, 1979, pp.142-8.)
ED/N-1 (NF.1572)

—They tell us he drank somewhat too much. (In *Clan MacLeod Magazine*, vol.8, no.52, 1981, pp.253-8.)
ED/N-1 (NF.1572)

MATHESON, William
The ancestry of the MacLeods. (In *Transactions of the Gaelic Society of Inverness*, vol.li, 1978-80, pp.68-80.)
ED/N-1 (NF.1559) QZ/Q41

STOMOWA, Zofja M.
Jednooka Kawalkala. 1933.
QZ/P99

Macleod of Arnisdale

MACKINNON, Donald
The Macleods of Arnisdale, compiled from family and other documents. Dingwall, 1929.
ED/N-1 (R.172.d) SA/U-1 AD/U-1 QZ/L37
QZ/P-1 QZ/P99

Macleod of Drynoch

MITFORD, Brenda
The MacLeods of Drynoch. (In *Clan MacLeod Magazine*; part 1, vol.i, 1935-47, pp.144-5; part 2, vol.i, 1935-47, p.152.)
ED/N-1 (NF.1572)

Macleod of Dunvegan

The BOOK of Dunvegan: being documents from the muniment room of the MacLeods of MacLeod at Dunvegan Castle, Isle of Skye; edited by R. C. Macleod. Aberdeen, 1938,39. 2v. (3rd Spalding Club)
ED/N-1 (3rd Spald.Club.8) ED/N-2 DN/U-1
ED/U-1 GL/U-1 QZ/P-1 QZ/P14 QZ/P22
QZ/P27 QZ/P30* QZ/P40 QZ/P99
QZ/Q41

MACLEOD, Roderick Charles
The Macleods of Dunvegan from the time of Leod to the end of the 17th century. [Edinburgh], 1927.
ED/N-1 (S.121.g) ED/N-2 AD/U-1 ED/U-1
SA/U-1 QZ/L37 QZ/P-1 QZ/P22 QZ/P27
QZ/P40 QZ/P99

WHO was the tenth chief?: a critical view of the history of the chiefs of the MacLeods of Harris and Dunvegan. (In *Clan MacLeod Magazine*; part 1, vol.8, no.6, 1978, pp.18-23; part 2, vol.8, no.47, 1978, pp.56-60.)
ED/N-1 (NF.1572)

Macleod of Fascadale

MACLEOD, Rhoderick Alexander
Notes on the ancestry of Rhoderick Alexander Macleod of Fascadale, Ardnamurchan. [Fascadale, 1976.]
ED/N-1 (HP2.83.2394) ED/N-2

Macleod of Gesto

MACLEOD, Brenda
The MacLeods of Gesto. (In *Clan MacLeod Magazine*, vol.2, no.16, 1951, pp.5-7.)
ED/N-1 (NF.1572)

MACLEOD, Ruairidh H.
The lairds of Gesto. (In *Clan MacLeod Magazine*, vol.9, no.54, 1982, pp.26-31.)
ED/N-1 (NF.1572)

Macleod of Lewis

The EWILL trowbles of the Lewes, and how the Macleoid of the Lewes was with his whol trybe destroyed and put from the possession of the Lewes. Edinburgh, 1916. (In *Highland Papers*; edited by J. R. N. MacPhail. Vol.2 (Scottish History Society Publications, 2nd series, vol.xii.), pp.261-88.)
ED/N-1 (Ref.54) ED/N-2 QZ/P-1 QZ/P41
ED/U-1 QZ/P40

MACDONALD, Donald
Tales and traditions of the Lews. [With genealogical tables.] Stornoway, 1967.
ED/N-1 (NE.2.d.3)

MATHESON, William
The MacLeods of Lewis. (In *Transactions of the Gaelic Society of Inverness*, vol.li, 1978-80, pp.320-37.)
ED/N-1 (NF.1559) QZ/Q41

MITFORD, Brenda
The MacLeods of Lewis. (In *Clan MacLeod Magazine*, vol.1, 1935-47, pp.42-4.)
ED/N-1 (NF.1572)

Macleod of Raasay

MACLEOD, Loudoun
The Macleods of Raasay in Australia. (In *Clan MacLeod Magazine*, vol.8, no.52, 1981, pp.275-8.)
ED/N-1 (NF.1572)

MITFORD, Brenda
The Macleods of Raasay. (In *Clan MacLeod Magazine*, vol.1, 1935-47, pp.225-7.)
ED/N-1 (NF.1572)

Macmartin of Letterfinlay

FRASER-MACKINTOSH, Charles
The Camerons of Letterfinlay styled "Macmartin". (In *Transactions of the Gaelic Society of Inverness*, vol.xvii, 1890-1, pp.31-45.)
ED/N-1 (NF.1559)

McMath

MCMATH, Frank Mortimer
Collections for a history of the ancient family of McMath. Memphis, Tenn., 1937.
ED/N-1 (R.172.e)

WILSON, William
Folklore and genealogies of uppermost Nithsdale. Dumfries, 1904.
ED/N-1 (R.241.h)

Macmhuirich

THOMSON, Derick S.
The MacMhuirich bardic family. (In *Transactions of the Gaelic Society of Inverness*, vol.xliii, 1963, pp.276-302.)
ED/N-1 (NF.1559)

Macmillan

CLAN Macmillan Magazine; editor: Somerled MacMillan. Vol.1, nos.1-6 (July 1958-December 1966). Paisley, 1958-66.
ED/N-1 (1974.4) ED/U-1 QZ/P-1 QZ/P18

CLAN MACMILLAN SOCIETY OF NORTH AMERICA
Newsletter, 14 October 1958-Spring 1963. Ipswich,
Mass., 1958-63.
ED/N-1 (1974.4)

COOPER, James H.
The McMillans, 1750-1907: a record of the
descendants of Hugh McMillan and Jane Harvey
from Scotland through Ireland to America.
Fairborn, Ohio, [1951?].
ED/N-1 (1975.131)

MACMILLAN, George A.
Records of the clan: an address at their annual
gathering. Glasgow, 1902.
AD/U-1

MACMILLAN, Hugh
The Clan Macmillan: address given at the annual
gatherings of the clan society. London, 1901.
ED/N-1 (S.120.f) QZ/P27 QZ/P26 SA/U-1
AD/U-1 GL/U-1 QZ/P-1 QZ/P99

MACMILLAN, Somerled
Bygone Lochaber: historical and traditional.
Glasgow, 1971.
ED/N-1 (NE.12.b.15)

— The emigration of Lochaber Macmillans to
Canada in 1802. [Ipswich, Mass.], 1958.
ED/N-1 (1959.48) QZ/P18 QZ/P-6 QZ/P-1
QZ/P99

— The Macmillans and their septs. Glasgow, 1952.
ED/N-1 (Gen.12.M) QZ/Q17 QZ/P-6
QZ/P18 QZ/P27 QZ/P26 ED/N-2 QZ/P40
QZ/P22 SA/U-1 GL/U-1 QZ/P30 QZ/P-1
ED/U-1 QZ/P99

MACMILLANS. (33⅓ r.p.m. gramophone record.)
Clan Records, CLN105.)
QZ/P99

MORGAN, Charles
The House of Macmillan, 1843-1943. London,
1943.
QZ/P-1

Macmillan of Knapdale
MACMILLAN, Somerled
Families of Knapdale: their history and their place
names. Paisley, [1960].
ED/N-1 (1936.29) ED/N-2 QZ/P18 QZ/P27

MacMurtrie
MCMURTRIE, Douglas
The McMurtries in Scotland. (In *Scottish
Genealogist*, vol.xxix, no.3, September 1982,
pp.96-101.)
ED/N-1 (Gen.7)

Macnab
CAMPBELL, Colin
Some Macnabs in Argyllshire. (In *Scottish
Genealogist*, vol.ix, no.4, December 1962, pp.18-21.)
ED/N-1 (Gen.7)

— — (Reprinted from *Scottish Genealogist*, vol.ix,
no.4, 1962.)
ED/N-1 (1965.26)

CLAN MACNAB ASSOCIATION
Historic notes on the Clan Macnab. Edinburgh,
1911.
ED/N-1 (HP1.79.4683) QZ/P27 QZ/P26
QZ/P99 QZ/P-1

MCDIARMID, Garnet
The original emigrants to McNab township, upper
Canada, 1825. (In *Scottish Genealogist*, vol.xxviii,
no.3, September 1981, pp.109-21.)
ED/N-1 (Gen.7)

MACKINNON, Charles
The Clan Alpin confederation: MacGregor,
MacKinnon, MacNab, MacQuarrie, MacAulay,
Grant and MacFie. (In *The Augustan*, book 1, 1973,
pp.39-46.)
ED/N-1 (P.173)

The MACNAB of that ilk and their lands in
Glendochart. (*Perth Pamphlets*, vol.13, newscutting
no.2, 1890.)
QZ/P26

MACNAB, Alice
The Macnabs. (In *Clan MacLeod Magazine*, vol.7,
no.41, 1975, pp.111-15.)
ED/N-1 (NF.1572)

McNAB, John
The Clan McNab: a short sketch. Edinburgh, 1907.
ED/N-1 (S.120.g) QZ/P14 QZ/P22 SA/U-1
AD/U-1 GL/U-1 QZ/P-1 QZ/P99

MACNABB, Archibald Corrie
A brief outline of the story of the Clan Macnab.
[Glasgow], 1951.
ED/N-1 (1959.15) QZ/P26 QZ/P99

WILD, Roland
  Macnab, the last laird. London, 1938.
  ED/N-1 (R.187.b) QZ/P40 QZ/P-1

Macnab of Bovain
  GILLIES, William A.
  In famed Breadalbane. Perth, 1938.
  ED/N-1 (R.246.f)

  — — 2nd ed. Strathtay, 1980.
  ED/N-1 (H3.82.1269) QZ/P22

MacNachtan *see* **MacNauchtan**

MacNaghten *see* **MacNauchtan**

MacNair
  GOURLAY, James
  The Kennedys of Auchtyfardle and other papers.
  [N.p.], 1936.
  QZ/P-1 QZ/P99 ED/N-2

  MACNAIR, A. A.
  Macnair genealogies. [N.p.], 1981.
  GL/U-1

  MCNAIR, James Birtley
  McNair, McNear, and McNeir genealogies. (With
  supplement.) Chicago, Ill., 1923-8. 2v.
  ED/N-1 (NE.25.b.4) ED/N-2 QZ/P14 SA/U-1
  AD/U-1 GL/U-1 DN/U-1 QZ/L37 QZ/P-1
  ED/U-1 QZ/P99 QZ/P52 (Unconfirmed
  location)

  — — Supplement, 1955. Los Angeles, California,
  1955.
  ED/N-1 (NE.25.b.4) ED/N-2 AD/U-1
  QZ/L37 SA/U-1 QZ/P-1 ED/U-1 QZ/P99

  — — Supplement, 1960. Los Angeles, 1960.
  ED/N-1 (NE.25.b.4) ED/U-1 QZ/P99

MacNauchtan
  MACNAGHTEN, Angus
  In search of two kinsmen: a Scottish-Ulster
  chronicle. Hythe, 1979.
  ED/N-1 (H2.80.1086) SA/U-1 ED/S10
  QZ/P99

  MACNAGHTEN, Angus David Iain Jaques
  The chiefs of the Clan Macnachtan. (In *Scottish
  Genealogist*, vol.ii, no.1, January 1955, pp.10-15.)
  ED/N-1 (Gen.7)

—The chiefs of Clan Macnachtan and their
  descendants. Windsor, 1951.
  ED/N-1 (NE.25.b.2) QZ/Q17 QZ/P27
  QZ/P40 SA/U-1 AD/U-1 DN/U-1 GL/U-1
  QZ/P-6 QZ/L37 QZ/P-1 QZ/P99

—Family glimpses. [N.p., 1960.]
  ED/N-2 QZ/P99

—Family quest. [With a genealogical table.]
  Cambridge, [1958].
  ED/N-1 (NF.1312.b.28) SA/U-1 QZ/P99

—Family roundabout. Edinburgh, 1955.
  ED/N-1 (NF.1178.e.19) QZ/P99

MACNAUGHTAN of that ilk. From Crawford MSS.
  Edinburgh, 1914. (In *Highland Papers*; edited by
  J. R. N. MacPhail, Vol.1 (Scottish History Society
  Publications, 2nd series, vol.v.), pp.103-116.)
  ED/N-1 (Ref.54) ED/N-2 QZ/P-1 QZ/P22
  QZ/P27

MCNAUGHTON, Duncan
  The Clan Macnachtan. Bearsden, 1956.
  ED/N-1 (HP1.78.1470) QZ/P26 QZ/P40
  QZ/P-1 QZ/P99 QZ/P18

—The Clan McNaughton: a history. Edinburgh,
  1977.
  ED/N-1 (Gen.8.M) DN/U-1 SA/U-1 QZ/P27
  QZ/P26 QZ/P14 ED/N-2 QZ/P-1

MCNITT, Virgil V.
  The MacNauchtan saga. Palmer, Mass., 1951. 2v.
  ED/N-1 (NE.25.b.2) QZ/L37

McNaught of Kilquhanity
  MCNITT, Virgil V.
  The Macnaughts of Kilquhanitie: a historical sketch
  of the Scottish progenitors of an American family.
  New York, 1917.
  ED/N-1 (6.1076)

MacNear *see* **MacNair**

MacNeil
  CAMERON, Neil
  MacNeils of Ardnacross and Islay. (In *Scottish
  Genealogist*, vol.xxvii, no.3, September 1980,
  pp.115-17.)
  ED/N-1 (Gen.7)

MACKAY, Frank Forbes
MacNeill of Carskey: his estate journal, 1703-1743.
Edinburgh, 1955.
ED/N-1 (NE.14.a.1) QZ/P14 QZ/P27 ED/N-2
QZ/P40 ED/U-1

MACNEIL clan news. No.1 (April/May 1980)- .
[Surry Hills, N.S.W.], 1980- .
ED/N-1 (HP.1a.104)

MACNEIL, Robert Lister
The Clan Macneil: Clan Niall of Scotland. New
York, 1923.
ED/N-1 (Gen.8.M) ED/N-2 AD/U-1 GL/U-1
QZ/P-1 QZ/L37 QZ/P-1 ED/U-1 QZ/P99

MCNEILL, Donald J.
Early MacNeill history. (In *Scottish Genealogist*,
vol.xxix, no.4, December 1982, pp.123-6.)
ED/N-1 (Gen.7)

MacNeil of Ardnacross
STEWART, A. I. B.
MacNeils of Ardnacross. (In *Scottish Genealogist*,
vol.xxx, no.1, March 1983, pp.14-15.)
ED/N-1 (Gen.7)

MacNeil of Barra
CAMPBELL, John Lorne *and* EASTWICK, Constance
The MacNeils of Barra in the Forty Five. (In *Innes
Review*, vol.xvii, 1966, pp.82-90.)
ED/N-1 (Z)

— — (Reprinted from *Innes Review*, vol.xvii, 1966.)
ED/N-1 (6.1344)

MACNEIL, Robert Lister
Castle in the sea. London, 1964.
ED/N-1 (NE.4.b.24) QZ/P34 QZ/P99

— — Revised ed. New York, 1975.
ED/U-1

MACPHERSON, John
Tales of Barra. [With genealogical tables.]
Edinburgh, 1960.
ED/N-1 (5.2217)

MacNeil of Canna
ROSS, Sir Archibald
McNeills of Canna (In *Scottish Genealogist*, vol.xxx,
no.4, December 1983, pp.126-33.)
ED/N-1 (Gen.7)

MacNeil in Ireland
WESTACOTT, Margaret
The Clan Niall, or Neil in Ireland, 379 A.D.-
1030 A.D. Sydney, 1970.
ED/N-1 (NF.1372.e.6)

MacNeill
MACMILLAN, Somerled
Families of Knapdale: their history and their place
names. Paisley, [1960].
ED/N-1 (1936.29) ED/N-2 QZ/P18 QZ/P27

McNish *see* **Neish**

MacPhail
GEDDIE, Jack
The Clan Phail. (In *Clan Chattan*, vol.iv, no.3, 1961,
pp.10-13.)
ED/N-1 (Y.130)

— — (Reprinted from *Clan Chattan*, vol.iv, 1961.)
ED/N-1 (1962.22) QZ/P99

— Colfax: [history of the Geddie, M'Phail and other
families in the U.S.A.]. [N.p., 1963.]
ED/N-1 (NF.1250.b.18)

— The families Geddie and M'Phail. Fort Worth,
Tex., 1959.
ED/N-1 (NE.25.d.2) ED/N-2 SA/U-1 QZ/P-1
QZ/P18 QZ/P50 QZ/P99 QZ/P16

SINTON, Thomas
Family and genealogical sketches. Inverness, 1911.
ED/N-1 (R.172.b) AD/U-1 DN/U-1 QZ/P-1
QZ/P22 QZ/P40 QZ/P30 QZ/P99

Macpheadrain
MACINTYRE, Peter
The Macpheadrains, Macphederans or
Macphederons; to Capt. Donald M. Macphedran,
6th June, 1905 from Peter MacIntyre, Inveraray.
[N.p., n.d.]
QZ/P27

Macpherson
CLAN MACPHERSON ASSOCIATION
Clan Macpherson: a short note on a long history.
Newtonmore, [n.d.].
QZ/P40 QZ/P-1 QZ/P99

— Creag dhubh: the annual of the Clan MacPherson
Association. No.1- . 1949- .
ED/N-1* (P.sm.2233) QZ/P-1 QZ/P40
QZ/P99

MACDONALD, James
The Clan Macpherson, past and present.
Newtonmore, [1976].
ED/N-1 (HP1.77.4552)

MACPHERSON, Sir Aeneas
The loyall dissuasive and other papers relating to
the affairs of Clan Chattan; edited by Alexander D.
Murdoch. Edinburgh, 1902. (Scottish History
Society Publications, vol.41.)
ED/N-1 (Ref.54) ED/N-2 DN/U-1 GL/U-1
QZ/P-1 QZ/P14 QZ/P20 QZ/P22 QZ/P40
QZ/P99 ST/U-1 QZ/L37

MACPHERSON, Alan Gibson
The posterity of the three brethren [sic]: a short
history of the Clan Macpherson. Newmarket,
Ont., 1966.
ED/N-1 (1967.138) SA/U-1 QZ/P-1

— — Revised ed. Ontario, 1976.
ED/N-1 (HP1.77.3699)

['NOTES on the genealogy of the family of
Macpherson'. 1833.]
ED/N-1 (MS.9854,ff.172-4)

Macpherson of Barra
MACPHERSON, John
Tales of Barra. [With genealogical tables.]
Edinburgh, 1960.
ED/N-1 (5.2217)

Macpherson of Cluny Macpherson
CHEYNE-MACPHERSON, W.
The Chiefs of Clan Macpherson. Edinburgh, 1947.
ED/N-1 (Gen.8.M) QZ/P26 ED/N-2 QZ/L37
QZ/P40 QZ/P15 SA/U-1 GL/U-1 QZ/P22
AD/U-1 QZ/P30 QZ/P13 QZ/P49 QZ/P-1
QZ/P99

MACPHERSON, Duncan
Answers and defences for His Majesty's advocate . . .
to the claim of Duncan Macpherson, 27th
November 1749 [to the forfeited estate of Lauchlan
Macpherson of Cluny].
ED/N-1 (Ry.II.b.19(31))

— Unto the . . . Lords of Council and Session, the
claim of Duncan Macpherson, 13th May 1749 [to
the forfeited estate of Lauchlan Macpherson of
Cluny]. [Edinburgh, 1749.]
ED/N-1 (Ry.II.b.19(30))

MACPHERSON, Ewen Henry Davidson
The golden wedding of Cluny Macpherson, C.B.,
and Mrs. Macpherson . . . 1882. Edinburgh, 1883.
SA/U-1 QZ/P99

— The marriage of Cluny Macpherson, June 10th,
1897. (Reprinted from Scottish Highlander, 1897.)
ED/U-1

Macpherson of Skye
MACKINNON, Donald
The MacPhersons of Skye. (In Scottish Genealogist,
vol.i, no.2, April 1954, pp.26-34.)
ED/N-1 (Gen.7)

MacPike
MACPIKE, Eugene Fairfield
Pyke and MacPike families. (In Scottish Notes and
Queries, 3rd series, vol.vi, January 1928, pp.12-16.)
ED/N-1 (V.457)

— — (Reprinted from Scottish Notes and Queries,
3rd series, vol.vi, 1928.)
DN/U-1

MacQuarrie
MACKINNON, Charles
The Clan Alpin confederation: MacGregor,
MacKinnon, MacNab, MacQuarrie, MacAulay,
Grant and MacFie. (In The Augustan, book 1, 1973,
pp.39-46.)
ED/N-1 (P.173)

MacQuarrie of Ulva
MUNRO, Robert William
Lachlan MacQuarrie, XVI of Ulva, with notes on
some clansmen in India. Karachi, 1944.
ED/N-1 (1945.1) QZ/L37 QZ/P99

— The MacQuarries of Ulva. (In Scottish Genealogist,
vol.xv, no.2, 1968, pp.25-30.)
ED/N-1 (Gen.7)

MacQueen
GREGORY, Margaret Innes
A complete record of the family of George and
Jessie MacQueen-Innes, immigrants to Maine,
1873. [N.p.], 1965.
QZ/P22 QZ/P30 QZ/P40 (I)

MACELYEA, Annabella Bunting
The MacQueens of Queensdale: a biography of
Col. James MacQueen and his descendants.
[Charlotte, N.C.], 1916.
ED/N-1 (NE.25.a.6)

NYDEGGER, James Archibald
The MacQueens: a brief history of the origin of the MacQueen family, with special reference to the MacQueens of Corrybrough. Baltimore, Md., 1928.
QZ/P40   QZ/P99

MacQueen of Skye
MACKINNON, Donald
The MacQueens of Skye. (In *Clan MacLeod Magazine*; part 1, vol.2, 1948, pp.438-40; part 2, vol.2, 1949, pp.464-8.)
ED/N-1 (NF.1572)

McQuesten *see* **McCuiston**

McQuiston *see* **McCuiston**

MacRae
[GENEALOGICAL account of the MacRaes. 1849.]
ED/N-1 (MS.15927,15928)

[HISTORICAL account of the family of Macrae. N.d.] (*MS.*)
ED/N-1 (MS.3569)

MACRA, John
Genealogical account of the MacRas as written originally by Mr. John MacRa . . . 1704; transcribed 1786 by Farquhar MacRa. [Camden, Va., 1870.]
ED/N-1 (APS.1.76.18)

—Genealogy of the Macras. Edinburgh, 1914. (In *Highland Papers*; edited by J. R. N. MacPhail. Vol.1 (Scottish History Society Publications, 2nd series, vol.v.), pp.195-239.)
ED/N-1 (Ref.54)   QZ/P-1   QZ/P22   QZ/P27   ED/N-2

MACRAE, Alexander
The history of the Clan MacRae, with genealogies. Dingwall, 1899.
ED/N-1 (Gen.8.M)   QZ/P27   QZ/P40   SA/U-1   QZ/P22   GL/U-1   QZ/P-6   QZ/P99   ST/U-1   QZ/P-1

— — Dingwall, 1910.
QZ/P-1   QZ/L37

MACRAE, Donald
The Clan MacRae: the scattered children of Kintail. Edinburgh, 1970.
ED/N-1 (Gen.7)   QZ/P40 (D)   QZ/P14   QZ/L37   QZ/P99

— — Edinburgh, 1972.
QZ/P56

—From Kintail to Carolina. Glasgow, [1976].
ED/N-1 (HP1.77.442)   QZ/P-1   QZ/P99

MACRAE-GILSTRAP, Ella
The Clan MacRae, with its roll of honour and service in the Great War. Aberdeen, 1923.
ED/N-1 (R.35.a)   ED/N-2   QZ/P22   QZ/L37   QZ/P40 (I)   SA/U-1   QZ/P30   QZ/P-1   QZ/P99

MacRitchie *see* **Mackintosh** of Dalmunzie

McRobbie
BULLOCH, John Malcolm
The McRobbie family, Lumphanan, with special reference to John McRobbie Gordon, Savoy Opera director. (Cuttings taken from *Aberdeen Press & Journal*.) 1937.
QZ/P22

MANNING, Doreen Caraher
From Scotland to the U.S.A.: a civil war diary, the McRobbie/Divan migration and transition. (In *Scottish Genealogist*, vol.xxviii, no.4, December 1981, pp.177-80.)
ED/N-1 (Gen.7)

MacRobert
DODD, F. L.
Tarland and the MacRobert connection. (In *Deeside Field*, no.17, 1981, pp.67-71.)
ED/N-1 (P.1a.10,166)

MacShannon
STEVENSON, Hew Shannon
The Shannons of Lephenstrath. (In *Scottish Genealogist*, vol.xxv, no.3, September 1978, pp.77-80.)
ED/N-1 (Gen.7)

McShennag
McKERRAL, Andrew
Two old Kintyre lawsuits with some notes on . . . McShennags of Lephenstrath, etc. [N.p.], 1941.
ED/N-1 (5.969)   QZ/P27   QZ/P-1

MacSween *see also* **Sween**

MacSween
MACMILLAN, Somerled
Families of Knapdale: their history and their place names. Paisley, [1960].
ED/N-1 (1936.29)   ED/N-2   QZ/P18   QZ/P27

MacTavish

MACMILLAN, Somerled
Families of Knapdale: their history and their place names. Paisley, [1960].
ED/N-1 (1936.29) ED/N-2 QZ/P18 QZ/P27

MacThomas

CLAN MACTHOMAS SOCIETY
Clach-na-coileach: the magazine of the Clan MacThomas Society. Vol.1, 1967/74- . [Edinburgh, 1974- .]
ED/N-1 (NB.38)

PYE, Roger F.
Clan MacThomas. Part 1: The ancient chiefs. (In *Scottish Genealogist*, vol.xii, no.4, 1965, pp.87-90.)
ED/N-1 (Gen.7)

—The heraldry of Clan MacThomas. (In *Coat of Arms*, vol.x, no.76, October 1968, pp.147-55.)
ED/N-1 (NJ.689)

SMITH, William M'Combie
Memoir of the families of M'Combie and Thoms, originally M'Intosh and M'Thomas. Edinburgh, 1890.
ED/N-1 (A.113.c) ED/N-2 DN/U-1 GL/U-1 QZ/P-1 QZ/P99

MacThomas of Finegand

PYE, Roger F.
The Clan MacThomas. (In *Clan Chattan*, vol.vii, no.4, 1980, pp.230-3.)
ED/N-1 (Y.130)

MacTier

GLADSTONE, Joan
Full MacTier pedigree: Durris and Garchew, 1684-1962. [N.p.], 1962.
ED/N-1 (6.442)

MacTier in Mochrum

GLADSTONE, Joan
The MacTiers in Mochrum. (In *Transactions of the Dumfriesshire and Galloway Natural History & Antiquarian Society*, 3rd series, vol.xxxv, 1956-7, pp.131-4.)
ED/N-1 (J.187)

McVannel

CRAWFORD, Kenneth *and* CRAWFORD, Jean
The history of the McVannel clan. 2nd ed. Leek, 1981.
ED/N-1 (HP4.82.148) QZ/P-6

MacVicar

MACVICAR, Angus J.
Sons of the eagle. Oban, 1969.
ED/N-1 (5.4084) QZ/P14 GL/U-1 QZ/P-1

McWilliam

LANG, Patrick Sellar
The Langs of Selkirk, with some notes on the Sibbalds of Whitclaw. . . . Melbourne, 1910.
ED/N-2 QZ/P99 QZ/P11

McWILLIAM, John Morell
McWilliam MSS. 1955.
QZ/P10 (Unconfirmed location)

SCOTLAND'S lost royal line: the descendants of Duncan II. (Reprinted from *Dumfries & Galloway Standard*, 20 February, 23 March 1957.)
ED/N-2 QZ/P99

WILLIAMSON, A. G.
William of Scotland. Dumfries, [1970].
ED/N-1 (1970.134) QZ/P-1

Macwillie of Botriphnie

GORDON-DUFF, Archibald H.
Journals of George M'Willie. (In *Transactions of the Banffshire Field Club*, 24 January 1939, pp.29-61.)
ED/N-1 (NE.3.g.1)

Main

MAIN, Robert Hall
The House of Maine. [N.p., 1939.]
QZ/P99

Mair

MAIR, Philip Beveridge
Shared enthusiasm: the story of Lord and Lady Beveridge. [With a genealogical table.] Windlesham, 1982.
ED/N-1 (H3.83.1580)

Maitland

NISBETT, Hamilton More *and* AGNEW, Stair Carnegie
Cairnhill. Edinburgh, 1949.
ED/N-1 (R.272.f) QZ/P-3

ROGERS-HARRISON, George Harrison
Genealogical and historical account of the Maitland family. London, 1869.
ED/N-1 (S.122.f) ED/N-2 QZ/L37

Maitland of Balhalgardy
>MAITLAND, Adam
>>Family tree of the Maitlands of Balhalgardy,
>>Inverurie, Aberdeenshire. Aberdeen, 1963.
>>QZ/P30

Maitland of Dundrennan
>ROGERS-HARRISON, George Harrison
>>The pedigree of the Maitland family of
>>Dundrennan, N.B. and Otago, N.Z. London, 1905.
>>QZ/P10 (Unconfirmed location)

Maitland, Earl of Lauderdale *see also* **Lauderdale,**
Earldom of

Maitland, Earl of Lauderdale
>DALZEL, Andrew
>>A short genealogy of the family of Maitland, Earl
>>of Lauderdale. Edinburgh, 1875.
>>ED/N-1 (S.120.e) QZ/L37 QZ/P99

>ROBERTSON, D. MacKenzie
>>Two Border families. (In *History of the Berwickshire
>>Naturalists' Club*, vol.37, part 1, October 1965,
>>pp.1-5.)
>>ED/N-1 (Y.210)

Maitland in Montrose
>BONAR, Horatius
>>Notes to genealogical chart or pedigree of the
>>descendants of James Pyott, merchant, Montrose.
>>[N.p.], 1914.
>>AD/U-1 QZ/P99

Makgill
>NISBETT, Hamilton More
>>Oxenfoord and its owners. Edinburgh, 1932.
>>QZ/P-1

Makgill of Rankeilour *see* **Frendraught,** Lord

Malcolm
>[MISCELLANEOUS historical and genealogical
>material concerning the Malcolm family. 1813-30.]
>ED/N-1 (MS.6684,no.28)

Mantua, Duchess of *see* **Lennox,** Earldom of

Mar, Earldom of *see also* **Kellie,** Earldom of

Mar, Earldom of
>ACT for the restoration of John Francis Erskine of
>Mar to the dignity and title of Earl of Mar, 17
>June 1824.
>QZ/L37

BARONY of Cardross and summary of the case for
the most ancient Earldom of Mar. (In *Gentleman's
Magazine*, April 1866, pp.525-9.)
ED/N-1 (ZY(Gen))

CRAWFORD, Alexander William Crawford Lindsay,
25th Earl of
>The Earldom of Mar in sunshine and shade.
>Edinburgh, 1882. 2v.
>ED/N-1 (A.113.d) QZ/Q17 QZ/P30 QZ/P27
>ED/N-2 QZ/P15 QZ/P22 QZ/P40 GL/U-1
>QZ/L37 QZ/P14 QZ/P-1 QZ/P99

DOUBLEDAY, H. Arthur
>The Mar case, 1866-85 and after. London, 1936.
>(Reprinted from *The Complete Peerage*, vol.9.)
>ED/N-1 (Law) QZ/P15 QZ/P22

The EARLDOM of Mar. Exeter, 1886.
>QZ/P40 QZ/P99

FOSTER, Joseph
>The Scottish, or Lyon Office of Arms. London,
>[1883].
>ED/N-1 (Ry.I.3.208)

FRASER, William
>Memorial of the right of Walter Coningsby Erskine,
>Earl of Kellie . . . to the titles, honours and
>dignities of Earl of Mar and Lord Garioch in the
>peerage of Scotland. Edinburgh, 1867.
>ED/N-1 (Newb.4441)

—Memorial of Walter Coningsby Erskine, Earl of
>Kellie claiming . . . Earl of Mar. 1867.
>ED/N-1 (6.249(25)) QZ/L37

GREAT BRITAIN. Historical Manuscripts Commission
>Supplementary report on the MSS. of the Earl of
>Mar and Kellie preserved at Alloa House. London,
>1930.
>ED/N-1 (GRH.5/60)

HALLEN, Arthur W. Cornelius
>A paper on the Mar peerage read before the Alloa
>Society of Natural Science and Archaeology on
>May 4th 1875, together with the judgment of the
>Committee of Privileges, Pedigrees, etc. [Alloa],
>1875.
>ED/N-1 (A.113.d.1(1);Yule.133(4);3.2792(11))
>QZ/P14 ED/N-2 QZ/P15 QZ/P22 GL/U-1
>QZ/P-1

KELLIE, Walter Coningsby Erskine, *12th Earl of*
Case on behalf of Walter Coningsby, Earl of Kellie, on his claim to the dignity of Earl of Mar, in the peerage of Scotland. [N.d.]
QZ/P15 QZ/L37

KELLIE, Walter Henry Erskine, *13th Earl of*
Case and additional case on behalf of Walter Henry, Earl of Kellie, claiming also to be Earl of Mar, on his claim to the honour and dignity of Earl of Mar, in the peerage of Scotland. [N.d.]
QZ/L37 QZ/P-1

LINDSAY, William Alexander
Dormant and disputed peerages. Part 1: The Earldom of Mar. (In *St James Magazine*, October 1875/March 1876, pp.204-16.)
ED/N-1 (X.165-7)

— — (Reprinted from *St James Magazine*, October 1875/March 1876.)
ED/N-1 (Yule.133(6))

—A short account of the Earldom of Mar and of the recent peerage case. Edinburgh, 1875.
QZ/L37 QZ/P-1

M'KERLIE, Peter Handyside
Earldom of Marr with sketch of the times. Edinburgh, [1883].
ED/N-1 (Ry.1.3.207;A.113.c) QZ/P30 QZ/P-1
QZ/P99

MAR peerage claim, 1875. Judgment.
QZ/P-1

MAR, John Francis Erskine Goodeve-Erskine, *33rd Earl of*
Ancient and modern. [N.p.], 1875.
ED/N-1 (A.112.a;Ry.1.1.159;Yule.133(5)) ED/N-2
QZ/P15 SA/U-1 QZ/P22 GL/U-1 QZ/P40
QZ/P14 QZ/P-1 QZ/P99

—Case for John Francis ... Erskine, Earl of Mar in opposition to Walter Coningsby, Earl of Kellie, claiming the dignity of the Earl of Mar. [N.d.]
QZ/L37 QZ/P99

—[House of Lords' papers dealing with the claims of John Francis Erskine, Earl of Mar, Walter Coningsby, Earl of Kellie, and Walter Henry, Earl of Kellie, to the ancient Earldom of Mar.] London, 1868-75. 3v.
ED/N-1 (Yule.131-133(1-2))

—Letter to the Peers of Scotland from the Earl of Mar in reply to a letter from the Earl of Kellie. Edinburgh, [1879]. (Reprinted from *Edinburgh Courant*, 2 May 1879.)
QZ/L37

—Supplementary case on behalf of John Francis ... Erskine, claiming to be Earl of Mar, Baron Garioch, in opposition to the claim of the Rt. Hon. Walter Henry, Earl of Kellie ... 1873.
QZ/L37 QZ/P-1

MINUTES of evidence ... 1868-75.
QZ/L37

MINUTES of the Mar Peerage case: the case in the House of Lords; the report from the Select Committee on the Restitution Bill; minutes of evidence.
QZ/P15 QZ/L37

NUDA veritas: shall wrong prevail? With appendix of illustrative documents. London, 1888.
ED/N-1 (X.59.e.2) QZ/P26 ED/N-2 QZ/P99

PROCEEDINGS and speeches, 1873-74.
QZ/L37

REPORT of the manuscripts of the Earl of Mar and Kellie preserved at Alloa House, N.B. London, 1904. 2v.
ED/N-1 (GRH.5/60) QZ/P-1 QZ/P15

RONALD, James
The Earl of Mar's Lodging, Stirling. Stirling, 1905.
ED/N-1 (R.243.a) QZ/P14

ROUND, J. A.
Are there two Earls of Mar? 2nd ed. London, [1876].
ED/N-1 (Ry.I.3.174;Law) QZ/L37 QZ/P-1

— — London, 1883.
ED/N-1 (Ry.I.3.208) QZ/P99

The SCOTCH peerage endangered in its rights and integrity through the attack upon the old Earldom of Mar. [N.p., n.d.]
QZ/L37

[SESSION and appeal papers in the case of the Mar peerage, Walter C. Erskine, Earl of Kellie, Walter H. Erskine, Earl of Mar and Kellie, and John F. E. Goodeve-Erskine, claimants.] Edinburgh, 1867-92.
ED/N-1 (6.249(19-25))

SIMPSON, William Douglas
The Earldom of Mar. Aberdeen, 1949.
ED/N-1 (R.247.a) ED/N-2 ST/U-1

—The province of Mar. Aberdeen, 1943. (Rhind lectures.)
ED/N-1 (R.247.e) QZ/P37

SINCLAIR, Alexander
Abstract of the case for the Earl of Mar. [N.p., n.d.]
ED/N-1 (3.2417(13)) QZ/L37

—The Earldom of Mar. [N.p.], 1875.
ED/N-1 (Yule.133(7)) QZ/P-1

—Further extracts from Acts in favour of the Erle [*sic*] of Mar, 29 July 1587. [N.p., n.d.]
ED/N-1 (Newb.4849)

—Here I propose to add . . . a sketch to show the continuity of the right of female descent in the Earldom of Mar. [N.p., 1876.]
ED/N-1 (Yule.133(8))

—[Miscellaneous pamphlets concerning the Earldom of Mar.]
ED/N-1 (MS.312)

—New position of the old Earldom of Mar. [N.p., 1875.]
ED/N-1 (A.113.d.1(2); Yule.133(8))

—Observations on the inheritance and position of the most ancient Earldom of Mar. [N.d.]
ED/N-1 (MS.312) QZ/P-1 QZ/P-9

—On the question of precedence as to the old Earldom of Mar. [N.p., n.d.]
ED/N-1 (Hall.199.c.1(5)) QZ/P-9

—Remarks upon the petition of the Earl of Kellie as being in many points delusive. [N.p., n.d.]
ED/N-1 (Hall.199.e.1(6)) QZ/P-9

—Sketch of the succession of the most ancient Earldom of Mar. [N.p., n.d.]
QZ/L37

—Some of the particulars of the first restoration of the Earldom of Mar in 1565, and its confirmation in 1567 and 1787. [N.p., n.d.]
ED/N-1 (Hall.199.e.1(4)) QZ/L37 QZ/P-9

SOME observations on the two Earldoms of Mar. [N.d.] (Reprinted from *The Complete Peerage*.)
QZ/P22

SWINTON, Robert Blair
The proceedings in the case of the Earldom of Mar, 1867-85: a resumé. London, 1889.
ED/N-1 (Ry.I.3.249; 1890.27(15); A.113.d.1)
QZ/L37

The TERRITORIAL 'Earldom of Mar'. [N.p., n.d.]
QZ/L37

March, Earldom of
SINCLAIR, Alexander
Sketch of the succession of the ancient historical Earldom of March till it was confiscated in 1413. [Edinburgh, 1870.]
QZ/L37 QZ/P-9

Marchmont, Earldom of *see also* **Hume,** Earl of Marchmont

Marchmont, Earldom of
CAMPBELL, Sir Hugh Hume, of Marchmont
Case on the part of Sir Hugh Campbell of Marchmont, Bt., in relation to the claim of Francis Douglas Home, Esq., to the titles, honours and dignities of Earl of Marchmont, Viscount of Blasonberrie, Lord Polwarth of Polwarth, Rebraes and Greinlaw. 1843.
QZ/L37 QZ/P-1

HOME, Alexander
Case of Alexander Home . . . claiming the titles, honours and dignities of Earl of Marchmont, Viscount of Blazonberrie, Lord Polwarth of Polwarth, Redbraes and Greinlaw. Westminster, 1822.
QZ/L37 QZ/P-1

HOME, Francis Douglas
Additional case for Francis Douglas Home . . . son of Alexander Home, Esq., former claimant, claiming the titles, honours and dignities of Earl of Marchmont, etc. Westminster, 1842.
QZ/L37 QZ/P-1

MINUTES of evidence . . . petition of Alexander Home . . . claiming . . . Earl of Marchmont, etc. 1822.
QZ/L37

MINUTES of evidence . . . petition of Francis Home . . . claiming . . . Earl of Marchmont, etc. 1838.
ED/N-1 (Yule.144(1)) QZ/L37

Marjoribanks
BURNETT, George
Mr. Joseph Foster and the Lyon Office. [N.d.] (Reprinted from *The Genealogist*, no.44.)
QZ/P-1 QZ/P99

FOSTER, Joseph
The Lyon Office and the Marjoribanks family: a
reply to the remarks of the Lyon Clerk Depute
[R. R. Stodart] entitled "Mr Joseph Foster on the
return of Members of Parliament".... London,
[1882].
ED/N-1 (Cam.2.a.1(2)) ED/N-2 SA/U-1
GL/U-1 QZ/P40 QZ/P-1 QZ/P99

—The Lyon Office in retreat. (In *Collectanea
Genealogica*, 1881, pp.125-134.)
ED/N-1 (Biog.D.6)

— — (Reprinted from *Collectanea Genealogica*, 1881.)
QZ/P-1 QZ/P99

HISTORY of the family. 1831. (*MS.*)
ED/S10 (Unconfirmed location)

Marshall

BULLOCH, John Malcolm
William Marshall, the Scots composer, 1748-1833.
Inverness, 1933.
ED/N-1 (1933.21;1934.9)

MARSHALL, George Frederick Leycester
Marshall of Manor Cunningham: being notes on
the descendants of John Marshall. Fleet, 1931.
ED/N-1 (NF.1372.c.2)

Martin

BOASE, Edward R.
The family of Martin in Angus and Fife. [1938].
(*Typescript*)
ED/N-1 (R.172.c) QZ/Q17 QZ/L37 QZ/P-1
QZ/P99

Martin of Ross

CLARKE, Seymour Spencer Somerset
The genealogy of the Martins of Ross. Inverness,
1910.
ED/N-2

Martin of Skye

The MARTINS of Skye: a short history of a Highland
family. Glasgow, [1924].
ED/N-1 (1924.16) QZ/Q41 QZ/P22 AD/U-1
QZ/P-1 QZ/P99

Masterton

FERGUSSON, Robert Menzies
Logie: a parish history. Vol.2: Lands and landowners.
Paisley, 1905.
ED/N-1 (R.243.a) QZ/P14

MASTERTON papers, 1660-1719; edited by V. A. Noel
Paton. Edinburgh, 1893. (In *Miscellany of the Scottish
History Society*, vol.1 (Scottish History Society
Publications, vol.xv), pp.447-93.)
ED/N-1 (Ref.54) ED/N-2 QZ/P-1 QZ/P14
QZ/P15 QZ/P16

STODART, Robert Riddle
A critical examination of the genealogy of
Masterton of that ilk, Parkmill, etc. published in
'Douglas' Baronage' and 'Crawfurd's Memorials of
Alloa'. London, 1878.
ED/N-1 (S.122.f) QZ/L37 QZ/P99 QZ/P16

Masterton of West Fife

STODART, Robert Riddle
A critical examination of the genealogy of
Masterton of that ilk. London, 1878.
ED/N-1 (S.122.f) QZ/P99 QZ/P16 QZ/L37

Matheson

CLAN MATHESON SOCIETY
Newsletter. No.26 (February 1976)- . [Arbroath],
1976- .
ED/N-1 (7266 PER)

['HISTORICAL account of the family of Matheson of
Immar'. 1824.]
ED/N-1 (MS.15927,ff.49-56)

MACKENZIE, Alexander
History of the Mathesons. Inverness, 1882.
ED/N-1 (S.120.f) DN/U-1 QZ/Q41 ED/N-2
QZ/P40 AD/U-1 GL/U-1 QZ/L37 QZ/P-1
ED/U-1 QZ/P99

— — 2nd ed.; edited by A. Bain. Stirling, 1900.
ED/N-1 (Gen.8.M;I Iist.S.111.M) QZ/P27
QZ/P22 QZ/P40 QZ/P99 QZ/P14 SA/U-1
AD/U-1 GL/U-1 QZ/L37 QZ/P-1

MATHESON, William
Genealogies of Mathesons. (In *Transactions of the
Gaelic Society of Inverness*, vol.xlvii, 1971,
pp.172-206.)
ED/N-1 (NF.1559) QZ/Q41

—Traditions of the Mathesons. (In *Transactions of the
Gaelic Society of Inverness*, vol.xlii, 1956, pp.153-75.)
ED/N-1 (NF.1559) QZ/Q41

Matheson of Lochalsh

FOSTER, William Edward
Notes on the Foster family of Moulton. [With a
genealogical table.] London, 1907.
ED/N-1 (R.58.c)

—Royal descents of the [Fosters of Moreton and the] Mathesons of Shinness and Lochalsh. London, 1912.
ED/N-1 (S.121.a) ED/N-2 AD/U-2 ED/S10 GL/U-1 QZ/P-1 QZ/P99

[GENEALOGICAL material concerning the family of Matheson of Lochalsh. 1849.]
ED/N-1 (MS.15927)

MACKENZIE, Alexander
Sir James Matheson of the Lews, Baronet, and his descent from the Mathesons of Shinness. Inverness, 1882.
QZ/P-1 QZ/P99

MATHESON, Sir Torquil
Traditional sites of Matheson history in Lochalsh. [Kyle of Lochalsh], 1981.
ED/N-1 (HP2.81.3786)

Matheson of Shinness *see* Matheson of Lochalsh

Mathie

MATHIE, John
The Mathie family. [Glasgow, 1915.]
QZ/P-1

Maule

FITTIS, Robert Scott
The history of the Maules. (*Scottish Miscellanies*, vol.3, 1894-1900; newspaper cutting no. 64.)
QZ/P26

['GENEALOGY of the families of Gordon, Drummond and Maule'. 16--,17--.]
ED/N-1 (Adv.MS.23.3.24,ff.1-81)

HISTORY of the Maules. Folkestone, 1914.
ED/N-1 (NE.25.b.5) QZ/P-1

INFORMATION for George, Earl of Dalhousie, and the Honourable Mr William Ramsay-Maule against Thomas Maule. [Edinburgh, 1782.]
ED/N-1 (ABS.4.78.3) QZ/P-1 QZ/P28

Maule, Earl of Panmure

MAULE, Fox
The Panmure papers: being a selection from the correspondence of Fox Maule, second Baron Panmure; edited by Sir George Douglas and Sir George Dalhousie Ramsay. London, 1908. 2v.
ED/N-1 (X.190.a)

MAULE, Harry
Registrum de Panmure: records of the families of Maule, de Valoniis, Brechin, and Brechin-Barclay, united in the line of the Barons of Panmure; ed. by John Stuart. Edinburgh, 1874. 2v.
ED/N-1 (Gen.8.P) QZ/P28 QZ/P26 SA/U-1 AD/U-1 GL/U-1 QZ/L37 QZ/P-1 ED/U-1 QZ/P99

Maxtone

MAXTONE GRAHAM, E.
The Maxtones of Cultoquhey. Edinburgh, 1935.
ED/N-1 (R.172.e) ED/N-2 ED/U-1 GL/U-1 SA/U-1 QZ/P-1 QZ/P22 QZ/P26 QZ/P40 QZ/P99

MAXTONE GRAHAM, Robert
Rachel Townsend, 1897-1977. [Sandwich], 1981.
ED/N-1 (HP4.82.717) QZ/P99

TOWNSEND, Rachel
Aunts and great-aunts: Maxtone Grahams of Cultoquhey and Kingston-Blair-Oliphant of Ardblair. [N.p., n.d.]
QZ/P26

—Aunts and great aunts of the Maxtone Grahams of Cultoquhey. [Sandwich], 1974.
ED/N-1 (HP1.76.244)

Maxwell

[GENEALOGICAL notes on the family of Maxwell. 19--.]
ED/N-1 (MS.2113,2114)

HERRIES, D. C.
Some Maxwell family histories. (In *Transactions of the Dumfriesshire and Galloway Natural History & Antiquarian Society*, 3rd series, vol.xvi, 1929-30, pp.13-24.)
ED/N-1 (J.187)

MAXWELL, Alice Constable
Avenue of ancestors. [With genealogical tables.] Dumfries, 1965.
ED/N-1 (NE.25.e.1) ED/N-2 QZ/P-1 QZ/P14 QZ/P34 QZ/P99

Maxwell of Brediland

THOMSON, Elizabeth M.
The Maxwells of Brediland. [N.d.] (*MSS.*)
QZ/P-6

Maxwell of Calderwood
['An ACCOUNT of the history of the family of
Maxwell of Calderwood'. 1811?]
ED/N-1 (Adv.MS.6.1.17,f.151)

CAMPBELL, Colin
The arms of Maxwell of Calderwood. (In *Scottish
Genealogist*, vol.xviii, no.3, October 1966, pp.7-15.)
ED/N-1 (Gen.7)

— — (Reprinted from *Scottish Genealogist*, vol.xviii,
no.3, October 1966.)
QZ/P-1

Maxwell of Carruchan *see* **Herries,** Lord Herries of
Terregles

Maxwell of Castlemilk
REID, Robert Corsane
John Maxwell of Castlemilk. (In *Transactions of the
Dumfriesshire and Galloway Natural History &
Antiquarian Society*, 3rd series, vol.xix, 1933-5,
pp.187-204.)
ED/N-1 (J.187)

Maxwell of Hazelfield
M'CONNEL, E. W. J.
The Maxwells of Hazelfield. (In *Transactions of the
Dumfriesshire and Galloway Natural History &
Antiquarian Society*, 3rd series, vol.xxi, 1936-6,
pp.48-58.)
ED/N-1 (J.187)

Maxwell, Lord Herries *see* **Maxwell,** Earl of
Nithsdale

Maxwell of Mochrum
REID, Robert Corsane
The Maxwell family of Mochrum. [1954]. (*MSS.*)
QZ/P10 (Unconfirmed location)

Maxwell of Monreith
BORTHWICK, W. S.
The Maxwells of Monreith. [1954]. (*MSS.*)
QZ/P10 (Unconfirmed location)

REID, Robert Corsane
The Maxwell family of Monreith. [1954]. (*MSS.*)
QZ/P10

Maxwell, Earl of Nithsdale *see also* **Nithsdale,**
Earldom of

Maxwell, Earl of Nithsdale
FRASER, Sir William
The Book of Carlaverock: memoirs of the
Maxwells, Earls of Nithsdale, Lords Maxwell and
Herries. Edinburgh, 1873. 2v.
ED/N-1 (Gen.8.M) ED/N-2 SA/U-1 AD/U-1
GL/U-1 QZ/L37 QZ/P-1 ED/U-1 QZ/P99

—Inventory of the muniments of the families of
Maxwell, Herries and Nithsdale, at Terregles. 1865.
QZ/L37 QZ/P-1

TAYLER, Helen Agnes Henrietta
Lady Nithsdale and her family. [With a genealogical
table.] London, [1939].
ED/N-1 (R.195.i)

Maxwell of Pollok *see also* **Stirling** of Keir

Maxwell of Pollok
BIGGAR, J. F.
The Maxwells of Pollok, 1269-1969. [N.d.]
(*Typescript*)
QZ/P-1 QZ/P-6

FRASER, Sir William
The cartulary of Pollok Maxwell. Edinburgh, 1875.
ED/N-1 (R.291.d) QZ/P11 GL/U-1 QZ/L37
QZ/P-1 ED/U-1 QZ/P99

—Memoirs of the Maxwells of Pollok. Edinburgh,
1863. 2v.
ED/N-1 (Gen.8.M) QZ/P56 ED/N-2 AD/U-1
GL/U-1 QZ/L37 QZ/Q91 QZ/P-1 ED/U-1
QZ/P99

— — [N.p.], 1873.
QZ/P-1

—The Pollok-Maxwell baronetcy: statement of the
right of William Stirling of Keir, and now of Pollok,
to the baronetcy held by his maternal uncle the late
Sir John Maxwell of Pollok; with illustrated
documents and the opinions of counsel on the case.
Edinburgh, 1866.
SA/U-1 QZ/L37 QZ/P-1 QZ/P99

[INVENTORIES of Pollok charters and other papers.]
Glasgow, [1830?]. (Vol. commenced for the
Maitland Club and then abandoned.)
QZ/P-1

M'CALLUM, Andrew
Pollokshaws, village and burgh, 1600-1912, with
some account of the Maxwells of Pollok. Paisley,
1925.
ED/N-1 (R.290.c) QZ/P-1

Maxwell of Stroquhan
GOURLAY, James
The Kennedys of Auchtyfardle and other papers.
[N.p.], 1936.
QZ/P99

—Notes on the family of Maxwell of Stroquhan. (In
*Transactions of the Dumfriesshire and Galloway Natural
History & Antiquarian Society*, 3rd series, vol.xix,
1933-5, pp.212-30.)
ED/N-1 (J.187)

Mayne
FERGUSSON, Robert Menzies
Logie: a parish history. Vol.2: Lands and landowners.
Paisley, 1905.
ED/N-1 (R.243.a) QZ/P14

MORRISON, Alexander
The Maynes of Powis and Logie. Stirling, 1927.
QZ/P14 QZ/P99

Meikle
[GENEALOGICAL notes and a genealogical table
concerning the family of Meikle. 1933?]
ED/N-1 (MS.3574)

Mein
SIBBALD, Susan
Memoirs, 1783-1812. London, 1926.
ED/N-1 (S.130.c) QZ/P99

Meldrum
GOEBEL, Berneice Elaine
Scenes from the pioneer lives of George and Jane
(Barclay) Meldrum. Salt Lake City, 1980.
QZ/P18

THORBURN, Ian
A family history of the Thorburns. Edinburgh,
1979.
ED/N-1 (P.r.3.c.1)

Meldrum of Fyvie
STIRLING, Anna Maria D. W. Pickering
Fyvie castle: its lairds and their times. London, 1928.
ED/N-1 (R.247.e) ED/N-2 QZ/30 QZ/P49

Melville
FRASER, Sir Willam
The Leven and Melville peerages. 1857. (*MSS*)
QZ/L37

—The Melvilles, Earls of Melville, and the Leslies,
Earls of Leven. Edinburgh, 1890. 3v.
ED/N-1 (Gen.8.M) QZ/Q17 QZ/P18
QZ/P56 ED/N-2 SA/U-1 AD/U-1 GL/U-1
QZ/L37 QZ/P-9 QZ/P-1 ED/U-1 QZ/P99

LEVEN and Melville papers: letters and state papers
chiefly addressed to George, Earl of Melville,
Secretary of State for Scotland, 1689-91. Edinburgh,
1843. (Bannatyne Club.)
ED/N-1 (Bann.Club.77)

MELVILL, Eliza Jane
The Melvill family: a roll of honour of the
descendants of Capt. Philip Melvill . . . and their
immediate connections by marriage, in the years of
the world war, 1914-1918. London, 1920.
ED/N-1 (S.121.e) ED/N-2 SA/U-1

MELVILLE, Alton C.
The Melville family of Utah. [Salt Lake City], 1961.
ED/N-1 (H4.75.382) ED/N-2 QZ/P99

Melville of Strathkinnes
MELVILLE, E. W. M. Balfour
The Balfours of Pilrig and Melvilles of Strathkinnes.
(In *Scottish Genealogist*, vol.viii, no.1, February
1961, pp.17-21.)
ED/N-1 (Gen.7) QZ/P18

Menteith, Earldom of *see also* **Graham,** Earl of
Menteith

Menteith, Earldom of
COWAN, Samuel
Three Celtic earldoms: Atholl, Strathearn,
Menteith. Edinburgh, 1909.
ED/N-1 (S.120.e) QZ/P14 QZ/P22 QZ/P26
QZ/P-1

DUN, P.
Summer at the Lake of Menteith. Glasgow, 1866.
ED/N-1 (A.118.e) QZ/P14

FRASER, Sir William
The Red book of Menteith. [N.p.], 1880. 2v.
QZ/P-1 QZ/P56

GRAHAM, Elizabeth
Documents regarding the extinction of Lady
Elizabeth Graham, daughter of John Lord Kilpont,
and wife of Sir John Graham of Gartmore, and her
descendents. Edinburgh, [n.d.].
ED/N-1 (Ry.III.a.25)

HUTCHISON, Andrew F.
The Lake of Menteith ... with historical accounts
of ... the Earldom of Menteith. Stirling, 1899.
QZ/P22   QZ/L37   QZ/P14   QZ/P13   QZ/P-1

NICOLAS, Sir Nicholas Harris
History of the Earldoms of Strathern, Monteith and
Airth. London, 1842.
ED/N-1 (A.114.c)   ED/N-2   GL/U-1   QZ/L37
QZ/P26   SA/U-1   AD/U-1   QZ/P-1   QZ/P99

Menzies

DUFF, Edward Gordon
Brief notes on the Mary, Queen of Scots cabinet
from Castle Menzies, Perthshire. [N.p.], 1913.
ED/N-1 (R.291.c)   QZ/P26   QZ/P-1

FRASER, William
Report on the manuscripts of Sir Robert Menzies,
baronet of that ilk, at Castle Menzies in the county
of Perth. London, 1877. (In *Royal Commission on
Historical Manuscripts, sixth report. Part 1: Report and
appendices,* pp.688-709.)
ED/N-1 (GRH.5/5)   QZ/P-1

MENZIES CLAN SOCIETY
[Constitution, office-bearers, etc. Glasgow, 1894.]
QZ/P-1

MENZIES, David Prentice
History of the Menzies Clan Society. Glasgow,
[1901].
ED/N-1 (S.120.h)   QZ/P27   QZ/P26   QZ/P99
QZ/P40   AD/U-1   QZ/P22   GL/U-1   QZ/P-1

— The Menzies Clan Society: its history, objects,
biographies, members, etc. Glasgow, [1897].
ED/N-1 (1897.52(8,9))   QZ/P-1   QZ/P26

— The Red and White book of Menzies: the history
of Clan Menzies and its chiefs. Glasgow, 1894.
ED/N-1 (Gen.8.M)   QZ/P26   QZ/P22   QZ/P40
QZ/P11   SA/U-1   AD/U-1   GL/U-1   QZ/L37
QZ/P-6   QZ/P56   QZ/P14   QZ/P-1   QZ/P99

— — 2nd ed. 1908.
QZ/P27   QZ/P99

MENZIES, Helen
Family memorials of H.M. [N.d.]
QZ/P99

STEWART, C. Poyntz
The Red and White book of Menzies: a review.
Exeter, 1906.
QZ/P26   AD/U-1   QZ/P22   QZ/P-1

Menzies in Lanark

MENZIES, Elizabeth Bailie
The Lanark manse family: narrative found in the
repositories of the late Miss E. B. Menzies, of ...
Edinburgh; ed. by T. Reid. Lanark, 1901.
QZ/P56   QZ/Q71   ED/U-1   QZ/P99

Menzies of Pitfodels

KEITH, Alexander
The Menzies family and the Freedom lands. (In
Aberdeen Chamber of Commerce Journal, autumn
1957, pp.26-9.)
ED/N-1 (U.450)   QZ/P22

Mercer

FITTIS, Robert Scott
John Mercer: town clerk and chronicler of Perth
and his descendants, 1592-1879. [N.p., 1897.]
QZ/P26

— The Mercers of Innerpeffray and Inchbreakie from
1400 to 1513. Perth, 1877.
ED/N-1 (1932.32)

[NOTES relative to John Mercer and his son, Sir
Andrew Mercer, Admiral of Spain, c. 1377.] [N.p.,
n.d.]
QZ/P26

ROBERT Mercer and Helen Chisholm and their
descendants, 1480-1554. [N.p., n.d.]
QZ/L37

Mercer of Aldie

MERCER, Edward Smyth
The Mercer Chronicle, by an Irish seanachy.
London, 1866.
ED/N-1 (A.114.d.16)   QZ/P26   QZ/L37

MERCER, G. R.
Our seven centuries: an account of the Mercers of
Aldie and Meikleour. Perth, 1868.
ED/N-1 (L.C.228)   QZ/P26   ED/N-2   QZ/L37
QZ/P-1   QZ/P99   QZ/P16

The MERCERS of Aldie: local note: the identification
of local historical points of interest. (Perth
Pamphlets. Vol.13, 1891, newscutting no.59.)
QZ/P26

SINTON, Thomas
Family and genealogical sketches. Inverness, 1911.
ED/N-1 (R.172.b)   AD/U-1   QZ/P-1   QZ/P22
QZ/P26   QZ/P40

Meston

MESTON, Gordon
Meston genealogy. [Windsor, Ont., 1977.]
ED/N-1 (HP2.77.621)

Methven

WEMYSS ware c.1880-1930: [an exhibition] at
Sotheby's Belgravia, 17th-23rd November 1976.
[With a genealogical table.] [London, 1976.]
ED/N-1 (HP2.79.839)

Michie

The MICHIE family of Aberdeenshire. [N.d.] (*Xerox copy*)
QZ/P22

MICHIE, Charles
Notes on the family of Michie. Calcutta, 1907.
QZ/P30

MICHIES abroad. [N.p., 19--.]
ED/S10   QZ/P22   QZ/P30

PEDIGREE of Michies. (Reprinted from various
sources, incl. *Scottish Notes and Queries*, 2nd series.)
ED/N-2

Middleton

FORSTER, Mary Jane
The family of Rev. James Middleton of Bon-Accord
settlement, Elora, Ontario, who migrated from
Aberdeen in 1838. [1978.] (*MS.*)
QZ/P22

Middleton, Earl of Middleton

BISCOE, Anna Catharina
The Earls of Middleton, Lords of Clermont and
Fettercairn, and the Middleton family. London,
1876.
ED/N-1 (A.114.d)   QZ/P28   QZ/P26   QZ/P40
QZ/P99   AD/U-1   SA/U-1   GL/U-1   QZ/L37
QZ/P-1

Millar

GENEALOGICAL roll of Millar's genealogies.
[N.p., n.d.]
QZ/P-6

Miller

COUPAR, William James
The Millers of Haddington, Dunbar and
Dunfermline: a record of Scottish bookselling.
London, 1914.
ED/N-1 (X.170.f)   QZ/P34   ED/N-2   QZ/P18
QZ/P22   GL/U-1   QZ/P-6   QZ/P-9   QZ/P-1
QZ/P99   QZ/P16

Miller in Edinburgh

MILLER, William F.
Memorials of Hope Park, comprising ... particulars
of ... William Miller and ... ancestors. [N.p.], 1886.
QZ/P99

PINNEY, Maria
The Millers of Edinburgh: data contributed by an
American descendant, Maria Pinney of Los
Angeles. [N.p.], 1969.
ED/N-1 (6.1685)

Milne

CRAMOND, William
The Milnes of Banff and neighbourhood.
(Reprinted from *Banffshire Journal*, 1894.)
ED/N-1 (1893.27(12))   QZ/P-1   QZ/P22
QZ/P30   QZ/P50   QZ/Q17   QZ/P99

Milne-Home

MILNE-HOME, David
Biographical memoranda of the persons whose
portraits hang in the dining-room at Milne-Graden.
Edinburgh, 1862.
ED/N-1 (R.172.f)   QZ/P-1

Minto

ELLIOT, George Francis Stewart
The Border Elliots and the family of Minto.
Edinburgh, 1897.
ED/N-1 (Gen.8.E;A.58.a;S.122.f)   ED/U-1
GL/U-1   SA/U-1   QZ/L37   QZ/P11   QZ/P99

[GENEALOGICAL papers concerning the family of
Minto. 1700?] (*MS.*)
ED/N-1 (MS.13095)

Mitchell

[The FAMILIES of Gill ... Mitchell etc. [N.d.] (*MS.*)
QZ/P99

A FAMILY of Mitchell from 1579 to 1889 and after.
QZ/P99

HOMAN, William MacLean
Ancestors and descendants of Andrew Mitchell and
Janet Alice, his wife. [With a genealogical table.]
Glasgow, 1938.
ED/N-1 (6.231)

MITCHELL, David
Genealogy of the family of David Mitchell of
Kilmarnock, Scotland. [N.p.], 1883.
QZ/P-7

MITCHELL, Silas Weir
A brief history of two families: the Mitchells of
Ayrshire and the Symons of Cornwall. Philadelphia,
Penn., 1912.
ED/N-2

MITCHELL, Stephen
Mitchell family history. Bristol, 1923.
QZ/P-1   QZ/P99

MITCHELL, William Forbes
Genealogy of the family of William Forbes
Mitchell. [Seepore, 1881.]
ED/N-1 (R.272.g)

Mitchell in Bandeath
SOME descendants of John Mitchell in Bandeath,
Co. Stirling, and Janet Johnstone his wife, from
1579. [1888.] (*MS.*)
QZ/L37

Moffat
MOFFATANA bulletin, vol.1 (1907-9).
QZ/P99

NORTHCOTT, William Cecil
Robert Moffat: pioneer in Africa, 1817-1870. [With
a genealogical table.] London, 1961.
ED/N-1 (NF.1331.d.18)

Moffat of Craigbeck
PREVOST, W. A. J.
Moffats of Craigbeck. (In *Transactions of the
Dumfriesshire and Galloway Natural History &
Antiquarian Society*, 3rd series, vol.xxxiii, 1954,
pp.29-47.)
ED/N-1 (J.187)

— — (Reprinted from *Transactions of the Dumfriesshire
and Galloway Natural History & Antiquarian Society*,
3rd series, vol.xxxiii, 1954.)
QZ/P99

Moffat of Garwald
PREVOST, W. A. J.
Garwald and the Moffats (In *Transactions of the
Dumfriesshire and Galloway Natural History &
Antiquarian Society*, 3rd series, vol.xxix, 1950-51,
pp.143-54).
ED/N-1 (J.187)

Moffat of Moffat
MOFFAT, Robert Maxwell
A short history of the family of Moffat of that ilk,
with the genealogies of various branches in
Scotland, Ireland and England, as existing at the
present day; also passing notices of Moffats in
France, Germany and Holland. Jersey, 1908.
ED/N-2   SA/U-1   QZ/P-1

Moir
GILL, Andrew J. Mitchell
The families of Moir and Byres. Edinburgh, 1885.
ED/N-1 (A.23.c)   QZ/P30   ED/N-2   QZ/P22
SA/U-1   GL/U-1   QZ/L37   ED/U-1   QZ/P-1
QZ/P99

MOIR, Alexander L.
Moir genealogy, and collateral lines. Lowell, Mass.,
1913.
ED/N-1 (S.121.e)   QZ/P30   ED/N-2   GL/U-1
QZ/P22   AD/U-1   SA/U-1   QZ/P-1
QZ/P99

MORGAN, Patrick
Annals of Woodside and Newhill, historical and
genealogical. Aberdeen, 1886.
ED/N-1 (A.120.a)

Moir of Leckie
COOK, William B.
The Lairds of Leckie. Stirling, 1906. (Reprinted
from the *Stirling Sentinel*.)
QZ/P14   QZ/P-1   QZ/P99

MONTGOMERY-MOIR, George
George Montgomery-Moir of Leckie, appellant,
Anne, his wife and others, respondents. 1751.
QZ/P99

Moir of Otterburn
STODART, Robert Riddle
Kerr of Gateshaw, [Kerr of Corbethouse and Moir
of Otterburn]. (In *The Genealogist*, vol.iii, 1879,
pp.246-50.)
ED/N-1 (Y.215)

— — (Reprinted from *The Genealogist*, vol.iii, 1879.)
GL/U-1   QZ/L37

Moir of Stoneywood
BROWN, John
John Leech and other papers. 2nd ed. Edinburgh,
1882.
ED/N-1 (X.147.h)

—The Moirs of Stoneywood: a Jacobite family.
[N.p., n.d.]
QZ/P99

— — 5th ed. Edinburgh, 1884.
ED/N-1 (NG.1170.e.11)

Moncreiff

FAMILY records: the Moncreiffs. (Perth Pamphlets.
Vol.13, 1891, newscutting no.42.)
QZ/P26

MONCREIFF, Frederick *and* MONCREIFFE, William
The Moncreiffs and the Moncreiffes. Edinburgh,
1929. 2v.
ED/N-1 (Hist.S.112.M;Gen.8.M) QZ/P26
GL/U-1 SA/U-1 AD/U-1 QZ/L37 ED/U-1
QZ/P-1 QZ/P99

MONCREIFFE, Sir Iain
The House and family of Moncreiffe, 1957.
(Reprinted from *Perthshire Advertiser*, 30 November
1957.)
ED/N-2

SETON, George
The House of Moncreiff. Edinburgh, 1890.
ED/N-1 (Gen.8.M) QZ/P26 QZ/L37 GL/U-1
QZ/P-1 QZ/P99

Moncure

DUNCAN, Marion Moncure, and others
House of Moncure genealogy: a supplement to
Hayden's 'Virginia Genealogies', including
European and colonial ancestral background.
[Alexandria, Va.?], 1967.
ED/N-1 (NE.25.a.27)

Monfode

KERR, Robert Malcolm
Notices of the families of Ker of Kerrisland and
Monfode of that ilk. London, 1880.
QZ/L37 QZ/P-7 QZ/P-1 SA/U-1 QZ/P99

— — 1892.
QZ/P99

—Nugae antiquae. Glasgow, 1847-9.
GL/U-1

WEIR, H. F.
Monfode and the lairds of Monfode. (Reprinted
from *Ardrossan & Saltcoats Herald*, 1882.)
QZ/P-1 QZ/P99

Monro *see also* **Munro**

Monro

The MONROES in France: a history of a branch of the
the family in France, descended from the chiefs of
the clan, seated at Foulis, Ross-shire. Stirling, 1908.
ED/N-1 (1930.11;1937.16;1956.27) ED/U-1
AD/U-1 SA/U-1 GL/U-1 QZ/P-1 QZ/P14
QZ/P22 QZ/P40 QZ/P99

Monro of Allan

The MONROS of Allan. (In *Clan Munro Annual*, no.2,
1947, pp.37-41.)
ED/N-1 (P.med.1307)

Monro of Auchinbowie

GUTHRIE, Douglas James
The three Alexander Monros and the foundation of
the Edinburgh Medical School. [N.p., 1957?]
ED/N-1 (6.908)

INGLIS, John Alexander
The Monros of Auchinbowie and cognate families.
Edinburgh, 1911.
ED/N-1 (S.121.d) SA/U-1 QZ/L37 QZ/P14
QZ/P-1 QZ/P99 ED/M-1

MULLIN, W. J.
The Monro family and the Monro collection of
books and MSS. (Reprinted from *New Zealand
Medical Journal*, August 1936.)
ED/N-1 (6.336)

SAINT CLAIR, Rex E. W.
Doctors Monro: a medical saga. London, 1964.
ED/N-1 (NF.1348.a.23)

Monro of Fyrish

The MONROS of Fyrish. (In *Clan Munro Annual*,
no.3, 1951, pp.40-3.)
ED/N-1 (P.med.1307)

Monteith *see* **Menteith**

Montgomery

FRANKLYN, Charles
A genealogical history of the families of
Montgomerie of Garboldisham, Hunter of Knap
and Montgomerie of Fittleworth. Ditchling, 1967.
ED/N-1 (L.187.d) ED/N-2 GL/U-1 QZ/L37
QZ/P-1 QZ/P99

MS. notes and press cuttings on the family of
Montgomerie. [N.d.]
QZ/P99

[MATERIAL relating to the lands and lairds of
Montgomerie. N.d.]
QZ/P-6

MEMORABLES of the Montgomeries: a narrative in
rhyme.... [Edinburgh, 1770.]
ED/N-1 (Ry.I.2.69(2)) QZ/P-1

—[Edinburgh, 1822.]
ED/N-1 (H.30.c.32)

MONTGOMERY, Bo Gabriel de
Origin and history of the Montgomerys.
Edinburgh, 1948.
ED/N-1 (Gen.11.M) QZ/P27 ED/N-2 GL/U-1
QZ/L37 QZ/P-1

MONTGOMERY, Thomas Harrison
Genealogical history of the family of Montgomery.
Philadelphia, Penn., 1863.
ED/N-1 (Mf.14(13[1])) ED/N-2 QZ/L37
QZ/P99

MONTGOMERY-MOIR, George
George Montgomery-Moir of Leckie, appellant,
Anne [Montgomery] his wife and others,
respondents. London, 1751.
QZ/P99

WOOD, John Philp
Memorials of various families. [1830?] (MS.)
QZ/P99

Montgomery of the Ards
MONTGOMERY, William
The Montgomery MSS., 1603-1706; edited by Rev.
G. Hill. Belfast, 1869.
ED/N-1 (R.172.d;A.28.f) QZ/L37

Montgomery in Ballyleck, Ireland
MONTGOMERY, George S.
A history of Montgomery of Ballyleck. [With
genealogical tables.] [Belfast, 1887.]
ED/N-1 (A.34.b)

Montgomery of Bogstoun
DOBIE, James
Memoir of William Wilson of Crummock.
Edinburgh, 1894.
ED/N-1 (Hall.260.a)

Montgomery of Bridgend
ANDERSON, William
Genealogical account of the Montgomeries of
Bridgend of Doon, lineal representatives of the
families of Eglintoun and Lyle. Edinburgh, 1859.
ED/N-2 QZ/L37

Montgomery of Broomlands
INGLIS, John Alexander
The Monros of Auchinbowie and cognate families.
Edinburgh, 1911.
ED/N-1 (S.121.d) SA/U-1 QZ/L37 QZ/P-1
QZ/P14 QZ/P99

Montgomery of Easterhills
[DR Montgomerie of Eastcrhills, physician at
Penzance: a genealogical roll.]
QZ/P-6

Montgomery, Earl of Eglinton *see also* **Kilwinning,**
Lord

Montgomery, Earl of Eglinton *see also* **Winton,**
Earldom of

Montgomery, Earl of Eglinton
AIKMAN, James
Account of the tournament at Eglinton ...
biographical notice of the Eglinton family....
Edinburgh, 1839.
ED/N-1 (A.114.a.1;Dur.1890) QZ/L37

FRASER, Sir William
Memorials of the Montgomeries, Earls of Eglinton.
Edinburgh, 1859. 2v.
ED/N-1 (Gen.8.M) ED/N-2 QZ/Q78 AD/U-1
SA/U-1 GL/U-1 QZ/L37 ED/U-1 QZ/P99

FULLARTON, John
Historical memoir of the family of Eglinton and
Winton. Ardrossan, 1864.
ED/N-1 (Y.59.e.16) QZ/P-7 QZ/P-6 QZ/L37
SA/U-1 QZ/Q88 QZ/P99

MONTGOMERY, William Stephen John Fulton
Earl of Eglintoune, Lord Montgomery and
Kilwinning: the Eglintoune pedigree. [N.p., n.d.]
QZ/Q17

REILLY, E. G. S.
A genealogical history of the family of
Montgomery, comprising the lines of Eglinton and
Braidstane in Scotland. 1842.
QZ/P99

ROBERTSON, William
Ayrshire: its history and historic families.
Kilmarnock, 1908. 2v.
ED/N-1 (Hist.S.91.A)

SINCLAIR, Alexander
A succinct account of the long feud between the
Earls of Glencairn and Eglinton on account of the
bailliary of Kilwinning. [N.p., n.d.]
ED/N-1 (Hall.199.e.1(2))

Montgomerie of Fittleworth *see* **Hunter** of Knapp

Montgomerie of Garboldisham *see* **Hunter** of Knapp

Montgomery of Skelmorlie
WEIR, Hugh F.
Skerlmorlie and the Montgomeries of Skelmorlie.
[N.p.], 1881.
QZ/P-7

Montgomery of Smithton
DOUGLAS, Sir Robert
The genealogy of the family of Lind, and the
Montgomeries of Smithton. [N.p., 1795.]
ED/N-1 (A.120.a)

Montrose, Dukedom of
LINDSAY, Alexander William Crawford, *25th Earl of
Crawford and 8th Earl of Balcarres*
Report of the speeches of Counsel . . . and of the
Lord Chancellor . . . in moving the resolution upon
the claims of James, Earl of Crawford . . . to the
original Dukedom of Montrose. London, 1855.
SA/U-1 QZ/L37 QZ/P14 QZ/P18 QZ/P22
QZ/P99

LINDSAY, James, *24th Earl of Crawford and 7th Earl of
Balcarres*
Case for James, Earl of Crawford and Balcarres etc.,
claiming the honour and dignity of Duke of
Montrose. London, 1851.
ED/N-1 (Yule.34(2));49-4)

—Case of James, Earl of Crawford and Balcarres,
etc., claiming the title, honour and dignity of the
original Dukedom of Montrose created in 1488.
London, 1850.
ED/N-1 (49-4) SA/U-1 QZ/L37 QZ/P-1
QZ/P22 QZ/P99

—Case of James, Earl of Crawford and Balcarres,
with reference to the petition and alleged right of
James, Duke of Montrose. [N.p.], 1851.
ED/N-1 (A.111.a)

—Examination of the supplemental case of James,
Earl of Crawford and Balcarres, claiming the
Dukedom of Montrose, created in 1488, with a
statement of the additional evidence in support of
the original case in opposition for James, Duke of
Montrose. 1852. (*MS.*)
QZ/L37

—[Papers in the case of the] original Dukedom of
Montrose created in 1488, claimed by James, Earl of
Crawford and Balcarres. Vols 4-6. [N.p., 1851.]
ED/N-1 (Yule.149,150,151)

—[Petitions, evidence, etc., presented to the House
of Lords, 1850-53, by James, Earl of Crawford and
Balcarres, supporting his claim to the Dukedom of
Montrose]. London, [1980-3]. 2v.
ED/N-1 (Yule.182-3)

—Supplemental case of James, Earl of Crawford and
Balcarres, claiming the Dukedom of Montrose
created in 1488: including an analysis or abstract of
the claimant's original case; together with the
objections started to the claimant's arguments and
evidence by James, Duke of Montrose. [N.p., 1852.]
ED/N-1 (A.111.c.1) SA/U-1 QZ/L37 QZ/P99
QZ/P22

MINUTES of evidence . . . 1853.
QZ/L37

MONTROSE, James Graham, *4th Duke of*
Abstract of the case for James, Duke of Montrose
on his petition against James, Earl of Crawford and
Balcarres claiming the ancient Dukedom of
Montrose. Edinburgh, 1851.
ED/N-1 (Law; Yule.34(4)) SA/U-1

—Abstract of the supplemental case of James, Duke
of Montrose, in answer to the supplemental case of
James, Earl of Crawford and Balcarres, claiming the
title of Duke of Montrose. Edinburgh, 1853.
ED/N-1 (Yule.34(6)) SA/U-1

—Case for James, Duke of Montrose, petitioner upon
his right to appear and be heard against claim of the
Earl of Crawford and Balcarres to be Duke of
Montrose. 1851.
ED/N-1 (Yule.34(3)) QZ/L37

—Case of James, Duke of Montrose, in opposition
to the case of James, Earl of Crawford and Balcarres,
claiming the title, honour and dignity of the Duke
of Montrose. Edinburgh, 1853.
QZ/P22 QZ/L37

—Supplemental case of James, Duke of Montrose,
in answer to supplemental case of James, Earl of
Crawford and Balcarres, claiming . . . Duke of
Montrose. Edinburgh, 1853.
QZ/L37

RIDDELL, John
Abstract of the case of James, Earl of Crawford and
Balcarres, etc., claiming the original Dukedom of
Montrose, created in 1488. 1850.
ED/N-1 (Yule.34(1));49-4) SA/U-1

—Abstract of the supplemental case of James, Earl of
Crawford and Balcarres, etc., claiming the original
Dukedom of Montrose, created in 1488. London,
1852.
ED/N-1 (Yule.34(5))

STATEMENT of evidence for . . . Duke of Montrose in
opposition to claim of the Earl of Crawford and
Balcarres. 1850.
QZ/L37

Moodie, Mudie

MOODIE, Robert W.
Descent of the Moodie family from Clan Campbell.
(In *Orange County California Genealogical Society
Quarterly*, vol.xvii, no.3, September 1980, pp.104-5.)
ED/N-1 (P.158)

PATON, John M.
Memoranda . . . family trees of Mudie. [N.p.], 1875.
QZ/P28

RUVIGNY and RAINEVAL, M. A. H. D. H. de la C.
Massue de Ruvigny, *9th Marquis de*
The Moodie book. [N.p.], 1906.
ED/N-1 (S.120.b) ED/N-2 QZ/L37 QZ/P99

WRIGHT, Marcus Stults
Our family ties: some ancestral lines of Marcus S.
Wright, Jr. and Alice Olden Wright. [With
genealogical tables.] South River, N.J., 1960.
ED/N-1 (NF.1373.a.4) QZ/P28

Moodie, Mudie in Angus

[MATERIAL on the family history of David Mudie,
Angus. 1964.](*Xerox copy*)
QZ/P28

MUDIE, Sir Robert Francis *and* MUDIE, Ian M. N.
The Mudies of Angus. Broughty Ferry, 1959.
ED/N-1 (NE.25.h.11) QZ/P28 QZ/P99

Moodie, Mudie of Melsetter

BURROWS, Edmund H.
The Moodies of Melsetter. Cape Town, 1954.
ED/N-1 (NE.755.e.4) QZ/P99

Moray *see also* **Murray**

Moray

[PHOTOGRAPH albums of the family of Charles
Stirling Home Drummond Moray of Abercairny
and Blair-Drummond, Perthshire. N.d.] 6v.
QZ/P99

YOUNG, Robert
Notes on Burghead, ancient and modern; with an
appendix containing notices of families connected
with the place. Elgin, 1867.
ED/N-1 (Hall.197.a)

Moray, Earl of

KINNAIRD, George
Case of George, Lord Kinnaird, and other peers of
Scotland, objecting to the votes given at the late
election under the title of Moray. [With a
genealogical table.] [N.p., 1793.]
ED/N-1 (Yule.168(3))

Moray, Earl of Strathearn *see* **Strathearn**, Earldom of

More

MORE, David Fellow
History of the More family. Binghamton, N.Y.,
1893.
ED/N-2

MORE, Grace V. D.
Chronicles of the More family. Roxbury, N.Y.,
[1955].
QZ/P-1

NISBETT, Hamilton More *and* AGNEW, Stair
Carnegie
Cairnhill. Edinburgh, 1949.
ED/N-1 (R.272.f) QZ/P-3

SIMPSON, Sir Robert Russell
The Monkrigg will case. Edinburgh, 1923.
ED/N-1 (Law)

Morgan

FORBES, Alexander
Memorials of the family of Forbes of Forbesfield.
Aberdeen, 1905.
ED/N-1 (S.120.c) QZ/P22 SA/U-1 GL/U-1
QZ/P99

Morgan in Dundee

THOMS, P.
An account of the Morgan Hospital, with a sketch of the Morgans of Dundee. Dundee, 1870.
ED/N-1 (A.118.e.2)   QZ/P99

Morice, Morrice

MORICE, William C.
Aberdeen parish register extracts as supplied with index to "Morice and Morrice biographies". Aberdeen, 1937. (*Typescript*)
QZ/P22

—Collection of Morice and Morrice biographies. 1923.
QZ/P22

Morison

CARNIE, Robert Hay
Publishing in Perth before 1807. Dundee, 1960.
QZ/P26

Morison in Aberdeenshire

MORRISON, Ian Lindsay
The Morison family of Aberdeenshire. [N.p., 1970?] (*Xerox copy*)
QZ/P22

Morison of Anchorfield

MORISON, Alexander
A manuscript genealogy of the Morisons of Anchorfield, Hetland and Johnsburn: a short account of the descendants of Andrew Murison, or Morison of Anchorfield, N.B. and of the collateral representation devolving upon them. [1901.]
ED/M-1

Morison of Ness

MATHESON, William
The Morisons of Ness. (In *Transactions of the Gaelic Society of Inverness*, vol.1, 1976, pp.60-80.)
ED/N-1 (NF.1559)   QZ/Q41

Morpeth

MORPETH, Robert Scott
In search of Morpeths. [Maidstone], 1979.
ED/N-1 (H8.80.685)   ED/N-2

Morrison

CLAN MORRISON SOCIETY
Report, 1912-13. [N.p., 1914].
QZ/P-1   QZ/P99

MORISON, Alexander
The heraldry of the Clan MacGhillemhuire, or Morrison. Edinburgh, [1910].
QZ/P99

MORRISON, Alick
The Clan Morrison: heritage of the Isles. Edinburgh, 1956.
ED/N-1 (Gen.7)   QZ/P22   QZ/P26   QZ/P40
ED/U-1   QZ/P-1   QZ/P99   QZ/P11   QZ/L37
SA/U-1   QZ/P41   QZ/P49

MORRISON, Hew
Excerpts from published Scottish records and other sources relative to the family of Morrison. [N.p., 1921?]
ED/N-2   QZ/P99

—Roll of honour of the Clan Morrison (Morison, Morrison, and Gilmour). Edinburgh, [1922].
QZ/P99

MORRISON, J. Clinton
Robert W. Morrison Snr., emigrant from the Highlands, and his descendants. [Summerside], 1978.
ED/N-1 (H3.80.1601)

MORRISON, Leonard A.
History of the Morison or Morrison family. Boston, Mass., 1880.
ED/N-1 (NE.25.e.13)   ED/N-2   QZ/P99

MORRISON, Nancy Brysson
The Clan Morrison. Glasgow, 1951.
ED/N-1 (HP1.78.552)   QZ/P40   QZ/P30
ED/N-2   QZ/P-1   QZ/P99

The MORRISONS of Skinidin. (In *Clan MacLeod Magazine*, vol.2, no.17, 1952, pp.63-6.)
ED/N-1 (NF.1572)

THOMAS, Frederick W. L.
Traditions of the Morrisons (Clan MacGhillemhuire), hereditary judges of Lewis. Edinburgh, 1878.
QZ/P41

Mortimer

MACKIE, Mary
The Mortimer family in Scotland. [N.p., 1974?] (*Typescript*)
QZ/P22

Morton
> DEUCHAR, A.
> Genealogical collections relative to the family of
> Myreton or Morton. [N.d.] (*MS.*)
> QZ/P-1

Morton of Darvel
> MORTON, Jocelyn
> Three generations in a family textile firm. London,
> 1971.
> ED/N-1 (NC.293.c.4) QZ/Q88

Moubray
> [GENEALOGICAL account of the family of Moubray.
> 1830.] (*MS.*)
> ED/N-1 (MS.5271)
>
> [GENEALOGY of the families of Moubray, 1830.]
> (*MS.*)
> ED/N-1 (MS.202625,ff.7-72)

Moultray
> RUVIGNY and RAINEVAL, M. A. H. D. H. de la C.
> Massue de Ruvigny, *9th Marquis de*
> Moultray of Seafield and Roscobie. London, 1902.
> ED/N-1 (5.1570) QZ/L37 QZ/P16

Mowat
> MOUAT, Gordon Hibbins
> [Mowat. Highett, Aust., 1978?]
> ED/N-1 (H3.79.4111) QZ/P-1
>
> MOWAT, Robert Alexander
> Mowat: the family in Scotland. [N.p.], 1969.
> ED/N-1 (5.5123) QZ/P40 (I,D) QZ/P30
> QZ/P22 ED/N-2 QZ/P30 QZ/P-1 QZ/P99
>
> [ORIGINAL family papers.]
> QZ/P38 (Unconfirmed location)

Mowat of Balquholly
> BULLOCH, John Malcolm
> The Mowats of Balquholly. [N.p., 1901.]
> ED/N-1 (5.4518)

Mudie *see* **Moodie**

Muir
> MARSHALL, G. F. L.
> The Muir book; compiled . . . for the descendants of
> Sir William Muir . . ., and of Elizabeth Huntly
> Wemyss, his wife. Fleet, Hants., 1930.
> ED/N-2 QZ/P99

Muirhead
> GROSETT, Walter
> An account of the family of the Muirheads of
> Lachop, now represented by Muirhead of
> Breadisholm. [N.p., n.d.]
> ED/N-1 (1937.24(4)) ED/N-2 QZ/P99

Mundeville *see also* **De Mundeville**

Mundeville of Tinwald
> SMITH, A. Cameron
> The family of Mundeville, Lords of Tinwald. (In
> *Transactions of the Dumfriesshire and Galloway Natural
> History & Antiquarian Society*, 3rd series, vol.xxii,
> 1938-40, pp.95-129.)
> ED/N-1 (J.187)

Munro *see also* **Monro**

Munro
> BOON, J. G.
> William Munro from Forres. (In *Scottish
> Genealogist*, vol.xxix, no.3, September 1982,
> pp.86-91.)
> ED/N-1 (Gen.7)
>
> CLAN MUNRO ASSOCIATION
> Clan Munro Annual. 1939- . [N.p.], 1939- .
> ED/N-1 (P.med.1307) QZ/P-1* QZ/P99
>
> FRASER, Charles Ian
> The Clan Munro (Clann an Rothaich): a beacon
> ablaze. Edinburgh, 1954.
> ED/N-1 (Gen.7) QZ/P26 QZ/P40 QZ/P22
> QZ/P11 QZ/L37 ED/N-2 SA/U-1
> QZ/P30 QZ/P-6 QZ/P49 ED/U-1 QZ/P-1
> QZ/P99
>
> LOCKE, John Goodwin
> Munroe genealogy. [N.p.], 1853.
> ED/N-2
>
> MACLENNAN, A. F. M.
> The story of a Highland family stemming from the
> Munros of Kiltearn and Petty. 1963.
> QZ/P99
>
> MUNRO, Mary Seymour
> Appellant in the case in the House of Lords
> relating to the Munro family, George Munro, of
> Culrain and Charles, his eldest son, being
> Respondents in the case. [N.p.], 1831.
> QZ/P40

MUNROE, James Phinney
A sketch of the Munro Clan. Boston, Mass., 1900.
ED/N-1 (NE.25.a.23)

The MUNROS of Stuckghoy and Barnaline.
(In *Clan Munro Annual*, no.8, 1963/4, pp.41-6.)
ED/N-1 (P.med.1307)

Munro of Achany
MILL, H. G.
Genealogical chart of the family of Munro of
Achany. [N.p.], 1881.
QZ/L37   QZ/P99   ED/M-1

Munro of Foulis
CALENDAR of writs of Munro of Foulis, 1299-1823;
edited by C. T. McInnes. Edinburgh, 1940.
(Scottish Record Society, vol.71.)
ED/N-1 (Ref.55)   ED/N-2   QZ/P-1   QZ/P14
QZ/P99

DODDRIDGE, Philip
Life of Colonel Gardiner; [with an appendix
relating to the ancient family of the Munroes of
Fowlis.] [N.p.], 1745.
ED/N-1 (X.192.l)

— — Ayr, 1764.
ED/N-1 (X.192.l)   QZ/P-1

— — Ayr, 1813.
ED/N-1 (X.192.l)   QZ/P40   QZ/P99

['GENEALOGICAL account of the family
Munro of Foulis'. 1811?]
ED/N-1 (Adv.MS.6.1.17, f.86.)

KENNEDY, John
A letter to the Rev. P. Doddridge concerning his
life of Col. Gardiner ... and the account of the
family of Munros. [London, 1750?]
ED/N-1 (BCL.C2669)

MACKENZIE, Alexander
History of the Munros of Fowlis, with genealogies
of the principal families of the name, to which are
added those of Lexington and New England.
Inverness, 1898.
ED/N-1 (Gen.8.M)   QZ/P27   QZ/P22
QZ/P40   QZ/P14   QZ/P99   AD/U-1
GL/U-1   QZ/L37   QZ/P30   QZ/P41   QZ/P-1

MONROE, Horace
Foulis Castle and the Monroes of Lower Iveagh.
London, 1929.
ED/N-1 (S.121.g)   ED/N-2   SA/U-2   AD/U-1
QZ/P22   QZ/P99   QZ/P-1   QZ/P40

MUNRO, R. W.
The Munro tree: a genealogy and chronology of
the Munros of Foulis and other families of the clan:
a manuscript compiled in 1734: edited by
R. W. Munro. [Edinburgh], 1978.
ED/N-1 (HP2.80.262)   ED/N-2   GL/U-1
SA/U-1   ED/S10   QZ/L37   QZ/P22
QZ/P40(I)   QZ/P99

The MUNROS of Foulis.(In *Clan Munro Annual*,
no.1, 1939, pp.16-19.)
ED/N-1 (P.med.1307)

Munro in Lexington, U.S.A.
HUDSON, Charles
History of the town of Lexington, Middlesex
County, Massachusetts ... with a genealogical
register of Lexington families. Boston, Mass., 1868.
ED/N-2

MUNROE, Richard S.
History and genealogy of the Lexington,
Massachusets, Munroes. Florence, Mass., 1966.
ED/N-2

Munro of Lindertis
The MUNROS of Lindertis, formerly of
Culcraggie. (In *Clan Munro Annual*, no.4, 1952,
pp.37-41.)
ED/N-1 (P.med.1307)

Munro of Novar
The MUNROS of Novar. (In *Clan Munro Annual*,
no.5, 1955, pp.45-9.)
ED/N-1 (P.med.1307)

Munro in U.S.A.
NORTHRUP, Guilford Smith
Genealogy of Josiah Munroe ... St. Johns, Mich.,
1912.
ED/N-2

Murchison
McGOWAN, Jessie Murchison *and* FINLAYSON,
Margaret Murchison
The Murchison family. [N.p., 1951.]
ED/N-1 (5.1527)   QZ/P40(I)   QZ/P30

MURCHISON, Sir Charles Kenneth
Family notes and reminiscences. Rushden, [1940].
ED/N-1 (R.272.a)

MURCHISON, T. M.
Notes on the Murchisons. (In *Transactions of the Gaelic Society of Inverness,* vol.xxxix-xl, 1942-50, pp.262-93.)
ED/N-1(NE.1559) QZ/Q41

Murdoch

MURDOCH, Patrick
Pedigree, and his descendants 1605 downwards.
QZ/P-1

Murdoch of Cumloden

FALLOW, T. M.
A short history of the family of Murdoch of Cumloden. [1905]. (Reprinted from *The Gallovidian,* 1904.)
ED/N-1(NE.25.c.4) QZ/P-1 QZ/P99

Mure of Caldwell

SELECTIONS from the family papers preserved at Caldwell; edited by William Mure. Glasgow, 1854. 2v(in 3). [Maitland Club.]
ED/N-1(Mait.Club.71) ED/N-2 GL/U-1
QZ/P-1 QZ/P99

— Paisley, 1883-5. (New Club.)
ED/N-2 QZ/P-1

Mure of Galloway

WIGTOWNSHIRE charters; edited by R. C. Reid. Edinburgh, 1960. (Scottish History Society Publications, 3rd series, vol.51.)
ED/N-1(Ref.54)

Mure of Rowallan

MURE, Sir William
The historie and descent of the House of Rowallan; written in or prior to 1657; with a preface by William Muir. Glasgow, 1825.
ED/N-1(L.C.728; A.114.c.) ED/N-2 QZ/P40
SA/U-1 QZ/P99 GL/U-1 QZ/L37 QZ/P-7
ED/U-1 QZ/P-1 ST/U-1

Murison *see* Morison

Murray *see also* Moray

Murray

COOK, William Bowie
The chiefship of the Clan Murray. (In *Stirling Antiquary,* vol.3, 1904, pp.172-95.)
ED/N-1 (Y.59.e.12-15) QZ/P14

DUKE, Winifred
Lord George Murray and the Forty-five. [With a genealogical table.] Aberdeen, 1927.
ED/N-1 (Hist.S.115.M)

JACOBITE correspondence of the Atholl family during the Rebellion, MDCCXLV-MDCCXLVI; edited by John Hill Burton and David Laing. Edinburgh, 1984. (Abbotsford Club.)
ED/N-1(Abbot.Club.17)

JOHNSTON, George Harvey
The heraldry of the Murrays. Edinburgh, 1910.
ED/N-1(S.120.d) QZ/P11 ED/N-2 GL/U-1
QZ/P-1 QZ/P99

MURRAY CLAN SOCIETY
The Murray Clan Journal and Newsletter. No.12 (Easter 1976)- . Edinburgh, 1976- .
ED/N-1(P.1a.6363)

MURRAY, Richard Hollins
A history of certain members of the Murray, Hollins and other families. [N.p.], 1955.
QZ/P-1

N, M.
Unto children's children: lives and letters of the parents of the home at Graaf Reinet.... [N.p.], 1909.
QZ/P99

PAUL, Sir James Balfour
Murrays of Romanno, Broughton and Stanhope. [Edinburgh, 1899.]
ED/N-1(Blk.650) ED/N-2

REID, Robert Corsane
Moriquhat [Murraythwaite] charters. [1950]. (*MSS.*)
QZ/P10 (unconfirmed location)

RUTHVEN-MURRAY, Leslie
Descendants of Sir James Augustus Henry Murray, Kt. [N.p., n.d.]
QZ/L37

Murray, Earl of, Marquess of, Duke of Atholl

CHRONICLES of the Atholl and Tullibardine families; collected and arranged by John, 7th Duke of Atholl. Edinburgh, 1908. 5v.
ED/N-1(Gen.8.A) SA/U-1 QZ/P26 AD/U-1
QZ/P99

MURRAY, Elizabeth Anne
The cousin book . . . : [a genealogy of the
descendants of John, third Duke of Atholl].
London, 1935.
SA/U-1 QZ/P99

ROBERTSON, James Alexander
Comitatus de Atholis: the Earldom of Atholl. . . .
[Edinburgh], 1860.
ED/N-1(A.114.c) GL/U-1 QZ/L37 QZ/P26

—[Edinburgh], 1865.
ED/N-1(A.120.f)

—[Edinburgh], 1869.
ED/N-1(A.120.f)

Murray of Blackbarony
ELIBANK, Arthur Cecil Murray, *3rd Viscount*
Blackbarony. Edinburgh, 1960.
QZ/P11

MURRAY, Sir Digby, *11th Baronet*
Murray of Blackbarony. 1891.
QZ/P41(Unconfirmed location)

Murray of Elibank
ALLAN, John
Note on Elibank Castle. (In *History of the
Berwickshire Naturalists' Club,* vol.33, part 1, 1953,
pp.44-6.)
ED/N-1(Y.210)

ELIBANK, Arthur Cecil Murray, *3rd Viscount*
The five sons of "Bare Betty". London, 1936.
ED/N-1(R.180.b) QZ/P34 QZ/P11 ED/N-2
QZ/P99 QZ/P40 GL/U-1 QZ/P49 QZ/P-1

—Master and brother: the Murrays of Elibank.
London, 1945.
ED/N-1(R.161.b) QZ/Q88 QZ/P99 QZ/P11

—The Murrays of Elibank. Edinburgh, 1917.
ED/N-1(R.172.e) QZ/P11 QZ/P22 QZ/L37
QZ/P-1 QZ/P99

Murray, Earl of Mansfield
[HISTORICAL genealogical accounts of the family
Murray, Earls of Mansfield. 1802?]
ED/N-1(Adv.MS.33.5.9)

Murray of Mastrick
DRUMMOND-MURRAY, Peter
Family of Murray of Mastrick. [N.p.], 1963.
(*Typescript*)
QZ/P22

Murray of Murraythwaite
REID, Robert Corsane
Murray of Murraythwaite: a family history.
[N.d.] (*MSS.*)
QZ/P10 (Unconfirmed location)

Murray of Ochtertyre
[HISTORICAL account of the family of Murray of
Ochtertyre. N.d.]
ED/N-1(MS.Acc.6026)

KIPPEN, Albert D.
The Murrays of Ochtertyre. Crieff, 1893.
QZ/P26 ED/N-2 QZ/P-1

Murray of Polmaise
COOK, William B.
Genealogical chart, 1358-1907, of the Murrays of
Touchadam and Polmaise. London, 1907.
QZ/L37 ED/N-2 GL/U-1 SA/U-1 QZ/P14

Murray of Stanhope
LINEAGE and pedigree of the house of Murray of
Stanhope, Co. of Peebles-shire. [N.p., n.d.]
ED/N-2 QZ/L37

Murray of Touchadam *see* **Murray** of Polmaise

Murray, Earl of, Marquess of Tullibardine *see* **Murray,**
Earl of, Marquess of, Duke of Atholl

Muschamp of Barmoor
HODGSON, J. C.
Barmoor and the Muschamps. (In *History of the
Berwickshire Naturalists' Club,* vol.xxii, part 2, 1913,
pp.98-117.)
ED/N-1(Y.210)

Muschet
CAMPBELL, Sir Duncan
The Muschet family: an ancient Perthshire family.
(Perth Pamphlets. Vol.9 [188-], newscutting no.4.)
QZ/P26

MUSCHET, an ancient family: the Muschet family of
the parish of Kincardine in Monteith, Perthshire.
(Perth Pamphlets. Vol.11, 1886, newscutting no.14.)
QZ/P26

Mushet of Dalkeith
OSBORN, Fred M.
The story of the Mushets. London, 1952.
ED/N-1(NF.1170.f.14) GL/U-1 QZ/P-1
QZ/P99

Mutch

MUTCH, James R.
Genealogy of the Mutch family. Charlottetown, 1929.
QZ/P-1 QZ/P22

Mylne

MYLNE, Robert Scott
The master masons to the Crown of Scotland and their works. Edinburgh, 1893.
ED/N-1(L.C.1414; R.286.c) QZ/P22 QZ/P14
ED/N-2 QZ/P-1 QZ/P99

Myreton *see* Morton

Nairn

MUIR, Augustus
Nairns of Kirkcaldy: a short history of the company, 1847-1956. Cambridge, 1956.
ED/N-1(NG.1297.b.1) QZ/P18 QZ/P-1

Nairn of Dunsinane

ROUGHEAD, William
Trial of Katherine Nairn. Edinburgh, 1926.
ED/N-2 QZ/P-1

Nairne

NAIRNE, Charles Sylvester
John Nairne, 1711-1795, minister of Anstruther Easter, and his descendants. [Glasgow], 1931.
ED/N-1(R.172.d) SA/U-1 QZ/L37 GL/U-1
ED/U-1 QZ/P99

Nairne, Lord

ELPHINSTONE, Margaret Mercer
Case of Margaret Mercer Elphinstone of Aldie, Baroness Keith . . . claiming the title . . .Baroness Nairne . . . [18—.]
QZ/L37

MINUTES of evidence . . . Emily Jane Mercer Elphinstone de Flahaut, Dowager Marchioness of Lansdowne . . . entitled to the title . . . of Baroness Nairne in the peerage of Scotland. 1873.
QZ/L37

Naismith *see also* Nasmyth

Naismith

EARLY Naismith pedigree. [1911.]
QZ/P-1

GENEALOGICAL tables to 1911.
QZ/P-1 QZ/P53

NAISMITH, William Wilson
Mrs John Naismith of Drumloch . . . and other Naismith memories. Glasgow, 1911.
ED/N-1(NE.25.c.21) ED/N-2 QZ/P-1
QZ/P99

Napier *see also* Lennox, Earldom of

Napier

['GENEALOGICAL notes concerning the family of Napier'. 18—, 19—].
ED/N-1(MS.9298,ff.97-108)

HAY, George
Case of George Marquis of Tweedale, and other peers of Scotland who object to the title of the person, who voted at the late election as Lord Napier. [With a genealogical table.] [N.p., 1793.]
ED/N-1(Yule.168(2))

NAPIER, Mark
A "memorie," historical and genealogical, of my mother's maternal lineage, namely the Hamiltons of Innerwick, the Lothian Kerrs, and the Earls of Angus. . . .Edinburgh, 1872.
ED/N-1(F.7.d.3)

NAPIER, Priscilla
A difficult country: the Napiers in Scotland. London, 1972.
ED/N-1(NE.25.f.19) DN/U-1 SA/U-1
QZ/P14 QZ/P-6 QZ/P99 QZ/P22
QZ/Q88 QZ/P49 ED/S10 QZ/P-1

— Revolution and the Napier Brothers,1820-1840. London, 1973.
ED/N-1 (NE.63.e.2) DN/U-1 QZ/P22

— The sword dance: Lady Sarah Lennox and the Napiers. London, 1971.
ED/N-1(NC.269.e.11) QZ/P22 QZ/P99
QZ/Q88

RIDDELL, John
Tracts, legal and historical, etc. Edinburgh, 1835.
ED/N-1(L.C.758; A.114.c) ED/N-2 QZ/P-1
QZ/Q99

SMITH, John Guthrie
Strathendrick and its inhabitants. Glasgow, 1896.
ED/N-1(A.58.a) ED/N-2 QZ/P49 QZ/P-1

Napier of Kilmahew

[DRAFT genealogical account of the Napier family of Kilmahew. 1829.]
ED/N-1(Adv.MS.19.2.17,f.336)

IRVING, Joseph
The book of Dumbartonshire. Edinburgh, 1879.
3v.
ED/N-1 (R.286.c)

KERR, Robert Malcolm
Genealogical notices of the Napiers of Kilmahew
in Dunbartonshire. Glasgow, 1849.
ED/N-1 (S.122.e) ED/N-2 GL/U-1 QZ/L37
QZ/P-1 QZ/P99

RIDDELL, John, and others
The pedigree of Her Royal and Most Serene
Highness the Duchess of Mantua ... her descent
from ... the Houses of ... Lennox, Napier, etc. New
ed. London, 1885.
ED/N-1 (R.172.c) QZ/P99

Napier of Merchiston

HISTORY of the Napiers of Merchiston, shewing
their descent from the Earls of Lennox of auld and
their marriage into the family of the Scotts of
Thirlestane; compiled from old records. [London],
1921.
ED/N-1 (NE.25.h.5) SA/U-1 QZ/P-1

NAPIER, E. B.
Some notes on the Napiers of Merchistoun and on
the Scotts of Thirlestane. Edinburgh, [n.d.].
ED/N-1 (S.121.i) QZ/P99

NAPIER, Mark
The Lennox-legend of the House of Merchiston:
[a postscript to "The Lanox of Auld"]. [N.p., 1875.]
ED/N-1 (F.6.e.5)

— Memoirs of John Napier of Merchiston, his
lineage, life and times. Edinburgh, 1834.
ED/N-1 (L.C.1224; Fin.247) QZ/P14 GL/U-1
QZ/L37 QZ/P-1 QZ/P99 ED/M-1

Napier in U.S.A.

DOUGLASS, Hiram Kennedy
My southern families. [With genealogical tables.]
Gillingham, 1967.
ED/N-1 (NF.1372.b.18)

Nasmyth see also Naismith

Nasmyth

JOHNSON, Peter and MONEY, Ernle
The Nasmyth family of painters. Leigh-on-Sea,
1977.
ED/N-1 (H8.77.4423) QZ/P-7

Neill

MACLAREN, Moray David Shaw
The House of Neill, 1749-1949. [With a
genealogical table.] Edinburgh, 1949.
ED/N-1 (R.251.a)

Neilson see also Nelson

Neilson of Barncailzie

NIELSON, William Walter
An account of Neilson of Barnacailzie in the parish
of Kirkpatrick Durham, Stewartry of
Kirkcudbright. Leeds, 1979.
ED/N-1 (HP3.79.1129)

Neilson of Barnsoul

REID, Robert Corsane
A Barnsoul inventory. (In *Transactions of the
Dumfriesshire and Galloway Natural History &
Antiquarian Society*, 3rd series, vol.xxxiv, 1955-6,
pp.204-8.)
ED/N-1 (J.187)

Neilson of Craigcaffie

NIELSON, William Walter
An account of the family of Neilson of Craigcaffie
in the parish of Inch, Wigtownshire, Scotland.
Leeds, 1978.
ED/N-1 (HP3.79.2107) QZ/L37

— The descent of Neilson of Craigcaffie from the
ancient Earls of Carrick, together with some notes
on the latter. Leeds, 1977.
ED/N-1 (HP3.79.2108) QZ/L37

Neish

MCNISH, David and TOD, William A.
The history of the Clan Neish, or McNish of
Perthshire and Galloway. Edinburgh, 1925.
ED/N-1 (S.121.f) QZ/P27 QZ/P26 ED/N-2
QZ/P22 SA/U-1 AD/U-1 DN/U-1 GL/U-1
QZ/L37 QZ/P41 QZ/P-1 ED/U-1 QZ/P99

Nelson see also Neilson

Nelson

NELSON, William
Contributions towards a Nelson genealogy. Part 1:
Some Neilsons of Scotland. Paterson, N.J., 1904.
ED/N-1 (S.120.b)

Nesbit

HARTMAN, Blanche T.
A genealogy of the Nesbit, Ross, Porter, Taggart families of Pennsylvania. [With genealogical tables.] Pittsburgh, Pa., 1929.
ED/N-1 (H3.83.2753)

Nesbitt *see also* **Nisbet**

Nesbitt

NESBITT, Robert
History of the Nesbitt family. Belfast, 1930.
ED/N-1 (R.172.f)

Newark, Lord *see* **Anstruther**

Newburgh, Earldom of

BANDINI, Cecilia, *Marchioness*
Case on behalf of Cecilia ... Marchioness Dowager Bandini claiming ... Countess of Newburgh in the peerage of Scotland.
QZ/L37

— Supplementary case....
QZ/L37

MINUTES of evidence ... 1857-58.
QZ/L37

NICHOLLS, John
The strange succession to the Scottish Earldom of Newburgh. (In *The Augustan*, book 6, 1974, pp.810-11.)
ED/N-1 (P.173)

Nichol

SCOTT-NICHOL, John
6½ centuries in wool. [With genealogical tables.] [Leicester, 1947.]
ED/N-1 (6.330)

Nicholson

NICHOLSON, Francis
Memorials of the family of Nicholson of Blackshaw, Dumfriesshire. Kendal, 1928.
ED/N-1 (S.122.g) GL/U-1 QZ/P-1 QZ/P99

NICHOLSON, John Gibb
Clan Nicolson. [Edinburgh, 1938.]
ED/N-1 (R.172.g) QZ/P53 SA/U-1 QZ/P40
QZ/P22 QZ/Q17 AD/U-1 QZ/L37 SA/U-1
QZ/P30 ED/U-1 QZ/P-1 QZ/P99

NICHOLSON, Nettie Gove
From the Isle of Skye to P.E.I.: Armiger Nicholson's children. [Prince Edward Island, 1977?]
ED/N-1 (H8.79.568)

Nicholson of Edinbane

NICHOLSON, John S.
Nicolsons of Edinbane: a genealogy. [Borough Green], 1971.
ED/N-1 (1972.65) QZ/L37

Nicholson of Tillicoultrie

INFORMATION for Dame Helenor, Issobel and Margaret Nicolsons ... against Sir Thomas Nicolson of Tillicultrie. [Edinburgh, 1695.]
ED/N-1 (6.282(92))

Nicol of Ballogie

NICOL, W.E.
The genealogy of the Nicol family, the Kincardineshire branch. London, 1909.
ED/N-1 (NE.25.a.9) QZ/P30 SA/U-1
QZ/P22 QZ/P-1 QZ/P99

Nicol in Montrose

A LETTER concerning the Nicol family of Montrose. [N.p., 1936.]
QZ/P28

Nimmo

GENEALOGICAL tree (on the mother's side) of Mr John Tod (John Strathesk). [N.p., 1891?]
QZ/P22

Nisbet *see also* **Nesbitt**

Nisbet

DOUGLAS, William
The owners of Dirleton. (In *History of the Berwickshire Naturalists' Club*, vol.xxvii, part 1, 1929, pp.75-92.)
ED/N-1 (Y.210)

— — (Reprinted from *History of the Berwickshire Naturalists' Club*, vol.xxvii, 1929.)
QZ/P34

DOWLING, J. N.
Chart of the descent of the family of Nisbit 1926. (*MS.*)
QZ/P-1

[A GENEALOGICAL table showing the antecedents of Robert Shortreed. N.p., 1844.]
ED/N-1 (7.106(66-69))

NISBETT, Hamilton More *and* AGNEW, Stair Carnegie
Cairnhill. Edinburgh, 1949.
ED/N-1 (R.272.f) QZ/P-3 SA/U-1

Nisbet of Carfin
INGLIS, John A.
The Nisbets of Carfin. (In *Miscellanea Genealogica et Heraldica*, 5th series, vol.ii, 1916/17, pp.44-52.)
ED/N-1 (NH.296)

— — (Reprinted from *Miscellanea Genealogica et Heraldica*, 5th series, vol.ii, 1916/17.)
ED/N-1 (S.121.b) ED/N-2 QZ/P-1

Nisbet of Dean
WOOD, John Philp
Memorials of various families. [1830?] (*MS.*)
QZ/P99

Nisbet of Nisbet
MITCHELL, John Oswald
Sir Philip Nisbet. (Reprinted from *Glasgow Herald*, 25 July 1891.)
QZ/L37 QZ/P-1

NESBITT, Robert Chancellor
Nisbet of that ilk. London, 1941.
ED/N-1 (R.272.a) ED/N-2 AD/U-1 ED/U-1
GL/U-1 SA/U-1 QZ/P-1 QZ/P-3 QZ/P11
QZ/P14 QZ/P99

Nithsdale, Earldom of *see also* **Maxwell,** Earl of Nithsdale

Nithsdale, Earldom of
MAXWELL, William
Case for William Maxwell of Carruchan, Esq., claiming to be Earl of Nithsdale, Lord Maxwell, Eskdale and Carlyle and Lord Herries in the peerage of Scotland. [Edinburgh], 1857.
ED/N-1 (6.249(1)) QZ/P10 (Unconfirmed location)

Noble
NOBLE, Sir Andrew
An account of the history of the families of Noble of Ardmore and Noble of Ardkinglas, and some related families. Durham, 1964.
QZ/P27 ED/N-2

— — 2nd ed. London, 1971.
QZ/L37 QZ/P27

Noble of Ferme
IRVING, Joseph
The book of Dumbartonshire. Edinburgh, 1879. 3v.
ED/N-1 (R.286.c)

Noel-Paton
NOEL-PATON, Margaret H.
Tales of a grand-daughter. Elgin, 1970.
ED/N-1 (6.1899) ED/N-2 QZ/P11

Ochiltree
RAILEY, Clementine Brown
History of the House of Ochiltree of Ayrshire, Scotland, with the genealogy of the families of those who came to America, and of some of the allied families, 1124-1916. Sterling, Kan., 1916.
QZ/P-1

Ochterloney *see also* **Auchterloney**

Ochterloney
WATKINS, Walter Kendall
The Ochterloney family of Scotland, and Boston in New England. Boston, Mass., 1902.
QZ/P28 QZ/L37 QZ/P99

Ogilvie
BARTON, E.
The passing of the church and churchyard of Hassendean. (In *Transactions of the Hawick Archaeological Society*, 1950, pp.21-2.)
ED/N-1 (P.220)

BENZIES, Frank
A Benzies quest, 1435-1972. Coupar Angus, 1972.
QZ/P22 QZ/P26 QZ/P30

MCANDREW, Bruce
The Lion of Inchmartin. (In *Double Tressure*, no.4, 1982, pp.2-10.)
ED/N-1 (P.sm.1445)

Ogilvie of Auchiries
[PRINTED papers presented to the Court of Session in the matter of the lands of Tullibody, George Cumming of Pittulie, trustee for James Ogilvie of Auchiries, pursuer, Alexander and George Abercromby of Tullibody, defenders.] [Edinburgh], 1740-3.
ED/N-1 (X.44.h.40)

Ogilvie of Badentoul
LESLIE,
A family history: [a short account of the families of Brodie, Dunbar, Ogilvie…] [Brighton, 1891?]
ED/N-1 (6.4284)

Ogilvie of Banff

ABERCROMBY, Cavendish Douglas
The Ogilvies of Banff. [Aberdeen], 1939.
ED/N-1 (R.172.e) SA/U-1 QZ/P30 QZ/P22
SA/U-1 QZ/P99

CHRISTIE, John
Fourth and fifth Lords Banff. (In *Transactions of the
Banffshire Field Club*, 1,2 July 1910, pp.95-100.)
ED/N-1 (NE.3.g.1)

TAYLER, Alistair
The Lords Banff. (In *Transactions of the Banffshire
Field Club*, 19 March 1929, pp.19-41.)
ED/N-1 (NE.3.g.1)

Ogilvie of Barras

BARRON, Douglas Gordon
In defence of the regalia, 1651-52: selections from
the family papers of the Ogilvies of Barras.
London, 1910.
ED/N-1 (R.232.b) QZ/P30 QZ/P28 GL/U-1
QZ/P-1 QZ/P99

Ogilvie of Milton

WELSH, G. C.
Keith and its lairds. Keith, 1958.
QZ/L37 QZ/P99

Ogilvie of Ternemny

OGILVIE, Alexander John
The Ogilvies of Ternemny. Edinburgh, 1937.
ED/N-1 (1952.30) ED/N-2 QZ/P22 QZ/P30
QZ/P50 QZ/P99

Ogilvie-Grant, Earl of Seafield *see also* **Grant**

Ogilvie-Grant, Earl of Seafield

IN memoriam Ian Charles, eighth Earl of Seafield,
twenty-seventh chief of the Clan Grant.
[Inverness], 1884.
ED/N-1 (VV.2/2) QZ/P99

The RIGHT Honourable Caroline, Countess of
Seafield, born 30th June 1830, died 6th October
1911. [Banff, 1911?]
ED/N-1 (1970.18) QZ/P40

Ogilvy *see also* **Campbell** in Angus

Ogilvy

The BOOK of Ogilvy. (*MS.*)
ED/N-2 QZ/P28

RAMSAY, Sir James Henry
Ogilvys of Auchterhouse, Ogilvys of Airlie,
Ogilvys of Inverquharity and Ogilvys of Clova.
(In *The Genealogist*, new series, vol.xxxv, 1919,
pp.162-75.)
ED/N-1 (Y.215)

— — (Reprinted from *The Genealogist*, new series,
vol.xxxv, 1919.)
ED/N-2 QZ/P-1 QZ/P99

Ogilvy, Earl of Airlie *see also* **Airlie,** Earldom of

Ogilvy, Earl of Airlie

FRASER, Duncan
The land of the Ogilvys. Montrose, 1964.
ED/N-1 (NE.5.d.2) QZ/P99

— — Revised ed. Montrose, 1967.
ED/N-1 (5.4050) QZ/P14 QZ/P30

THOMASSON, Katherine
The bonnie House of Airlie. Brechin, 1963.
ED/N-1 (1974.40) QZ/P28

WILSON, William
The House of Airlie. London, 1924. 2v.
ED/N-1 (S.121.f) QZ/P53 QZ/P-3 QZ/P28
QZ/P11 AD/U-1 SA/U-1 QZ/P11 QZ/P28
QZ/P22 GL/U-1 QZ/L37 ED/N-2 QZ/P30
QZ/P99

Ogilvy of Boyne

OGILVY-BETHUNE marriage contract. 1566. [N.d.]
QZ/P-1

TAYLER, Alistair *and* TAYLER Henrietta
The Ogilvies of Boyne, Aberdeen, 1933.
ED/N-1 (R.172.e;NE.25.f.5) QZ/P30 SA/U-1
QZ/L37 AD/U-1 QZ/P50 QZ/P-1 QZ/P99

Ogilvy in Cornton

STEUART, Katherine
By Allan Water: the true story of an old house.
Edinburgh, 1901.
ED/N-1 (R.245.g) SA/U-1 QZ/P-1 QZ/P14

— — 2nd ed. Edinburgh, [n.d.]
ED/N-1 (NF.1369.b.7)

Ogilvy of Eastmiln

ROUGHEAD, William
Trial of Katherine Nairn. Edinburgh, 1926.
ED/N-2

Ogilvy, Earl of Findlater

MAIDMENT, James
Genealogical fragments relating to the families of
Findlater, Gardner, Douglas, Keith, Auchinlecks,
Veitch and Duguid. Berwick, 1855.
ED/N-1 (Y.59.f.2;Ry.II.a.51(1))   QZ/P40   GL/U-1
QZ/P99

Ogilvy, Earl of Seafield *see* **Ogilvie-Grant,** Earl of
Seafield

Ogle

OGLE, Henry Asgill
Ogle and Bothal, or history of the Baronies of
Ogle, Bothal and Hepple. Newcastle-upon-Tyne,
1902.
ED/N-1 (R.57.c)

Ogston

OGSTON, Walter Henry
Alexander Ogston, K.C.V.O.: memories and
tributes of relatives, colleagues and students.
Aberdeen, 1943.
ED/N-1 (R.164.b)

Ogstoun of Ogstoun

OGSTON, Alexander
A genealogical history of the family of Ogstoun
from . . . . c. 1200. Edinburgh, 1876.
QZ/P22   QZ/L37

— — Supplement. 1897.
SA/U-1   QZ/P30   QZ/P22   QZ/P-1   QZ/P99
ED/N-1 (NE.25.b.26)

Oliphant

ANDERSON, Joseph
The Oliphants in Scotland, with a selection of
original documents from the charter chest at Gask.
Edinburgh, 1879.
ED/N-1 (A.113.a)   QZ/P26   QZ/P40   SA/U-1
AD/U-1   QZ/P99   GL/U-1   QZ/L37   ED/N-2
ED/U-1   QZ/P-1

[A HISTORICAL account of the family of Oliphant.
1850.]
ED/N-1 (MS.2691)

MACLAGAN, Bessie
The story of Williamston: an old Jacobite home of
Strathearn. Perth, 1924.
ED/N-1 (1927.9)   QZ/P26

['PAPERS and letters on the genealogy of the family
of Oliphant'. 1741.]
ED/N-1 (Adv.MS.82.2.4; 82.1.7; 82.1.8)

TRIMBLE, William Tennant
The Trimbles and Cowens of Dalston,
Cumberland. Carlisle, 1935-7. 2v.
ED/N-1 (R.172.c)

Oliphant of Bachilton

PERTHSHIRE constitutional: the Oliphants of
Bachilton. (Perth Pamphlets. Vol. 9, 1889,
newscutting no.44.)
QZ/P26

Oliphant of Gask

FAMILY of Oliphant of Fingask, Condie, Gask,
Rossie. (*MSS.*)
QZ/P-1

GRAHAM, Ethel Maxtone
The Oliphants of Gask: records of a Jacobite
family. London, 1910.
ED/N-1 (Gen.8.0)   QZ/P26   QZ/P40   AD/U-1
QZ/P28   GL/U-1   QZ/P49   QZ/P99

['HISTORICAL and genealogical papers and a
genealogical table concerning the Oliphant family
of Gask'. 1600-1800?]
ED/N-1 (Adv.MS.82.9.1)

KINGTON-OLIPHANT, Thomas Lawrence
The Jacobite lairds of Gask. London, 1870.
(Grampian Club.)
ED/N-1 (Gramp.Club.2)   ED/N-2   DN/U-1
GL/U-1   QZ/L37   QZ/P-1   QZ/P14   QZ/P22
QZ/P26   QZ/P27   QZ/P99

ROBERTSON, James A.
History of the family of Oliphant of Gask.
1839.
ED/N-1 (Adv.MS.82.9.11)

STIRTON, John
Links with Lady Nairne and the House of Gask.
Forfar, 1930.
ED/N-1 (MS.3066)   QZ/P26

Oliver

CLAN OLIVER SOCIETY
The Clan Oliver magazine. No.1(1969)- .
Giffnock, 1969- .
ED/N-1 (3310 PER)   QZ/P-1

Omey

McKerral, Andrew
Two old Kintyre lawsuits, with some notes on . . .
Omeys of Kilcolmkill, etc. [N.p.], 1941.
ED/N-1 (5.969)   QZ/P27   QZ/P-1

Stewart, A. I. B.
The Omeys. (In *Scottish Genealogist,* vol.xxx, no.2,
June 1983, pp.47-53.)
ED/N-1 (Gen.7)

— — (In *Kintyre Antiquarian & Natural History
Society Magazine,* no.13, [1983], pp.3-10.)
ED/N-1 (7150 PER)

Orkney, Earldom of *see also* Sinclair, Earl of Orkney

Orkney, Earldom of

Records of the Earldom of Orkney, 1299-1614;
edited by J. Storer Clouston. Edinburgh, 1914.
(Scottish History Society Publications, 2nd series,
vol.vii.)
ED/N-1 (Ref.54)   ED/N-2   QZ/L37   QZ/P-1
QZ/P14

Ormiston

Ormiston, Thomas Lane
An index of Ormistons in Scotland, 1855-1933.
1937. (*Typescript*)
QZ/L37

— Ormistons in Scotland before 1854. 1936.
(*Typescript*)
QZ/L37

— The Ormistons of Teviotdale. Exeter, 1951.
ED/N-1 (S.122.c)   ED/N-2   ED/U-1   SA/U-1
QZ/L37   QZ/P99

— Registration of births, deaths and marriages of
Ormistons in Scotland, 1855-1940. 1948.
(*Typescript*)
QZ/L37

Ormiston, W. J.
Ormistons of that ilk. [N.p.], 1933.
ED/N-2   QZ/L37

Orr

McCall, Hardy Bertram
Memoirs of my ancestors. Birmingham, 1884.
ED/N-1 (A.114.a)   QZ/P99

— Some old families: a contribution to the
genealogical history of Scotland. Birmingham, 1890.
ED/N-1 (A.36.a)   QZ/P11   QZ/L37   ED/N-2
QZ/P99

[Material relating to the lands and lairds of Orr.
N.p., n.d.]
QZ/P-6

Orr of Bridgend

Family tree of Jack Orr of Bridgend at Elliston: a
genealogical roll. (*MS.*)
QZ/P-6

Orr of Kame

Hogarth-Kerr, W.
The Orrs of Kaim, Lochwinnoch parish,
Renfrewshire. (In *Scottish Genealogist,* vol.xvii,
no.2, 1970, pp.41-8.)
ED/N-1 (Gen.7)

Kerr, W. K.
The Orrs of Kame: bonnet lairds for over three
centuries. [N.p., n.d.] (*Typescript*)
QZ/P-6

Material relating to the Orrs of Kame,
Lochwinnoch parish, Renfrewshire.
[N.p., n.d.]
QZ/P-6

Orrok of Orrok

Orrok, John
Letters of John Orrock; compiled by Lady Helen
Forbes and edited by Alistair and Henrietta Tayler.
Aberdeen, 1927.
ED/N-1 (X.179.f)   QZ/P-1

Osler

Osler, James Couper
Osler tree: [chart pedigree], with some
supplementary notes on Oslers, Fentons, Spences,
Eassons, Sinclairs and Coupers by David Couper
Thomson. [Dundee], 1924.
ED/N-2   QZ/L37

Thomson, David Couper
Some supplemental notes on Oslers. . . . [Dundee],
1924.
ED/N-1 (HP1.77.4104)

Otterburn of Redhall

Inglis, John A.
Sir Adam Otterburn of Redhall, King's Advocate,
1524-1538. [With a genealogical table.] Glasgow,
1935.
ED/N-1 (R.178.e)

Ouchterlony

MORTON, Peter Douglas
The Ouchterlonys of Kelly and Guynd: an old
Forfarshire family. (Reprinted from *Arbroath Guide,*
24 June, 8 July 1922.)
QZ/P28

Paisley

PARTRIDGE, Silva Watson
Paisley and allied families. Idaho, 1972.
QZ/P-6

Panmure, Earl of *see* **Maule,** Earl of Panmure

Panter

PANTER, A. E.
The seed is for sowing. Chichester, 1972.
ED/N-1 (NE.25.c.32)   QZ/P28   QZ/P99

Papedy of Ancroft

HARDY, James
On the Border family of Papedy of Ancroft,
Dunglas, Manderston and Berwick. (In *History of
the Berwickshire Naturalists' Club,* vol.viii, 1876-8,
pp.480-90.)
ED/N-1 (Y.210)

Paplay

MAC LEAN, J.
Paplay. (In *Nederlandsche Leeuw,* jaarg.xcviii, no.1,
januari 1981, cols 12-22.)
ED/N-1 (P.1a.8434)

Park

DEUCHAR, A.
Genealogical collections relative to the family of
Park. (*MS.*)
QZ/P-1

Parker

PARKER, Donald Dean
The Graham-Patterson family history. [Includes
Parker family history.] [Brookings, S. Dakota], 1947.
ED/N-1 (5.1211)

Paterson

COPIES of typescript letters from Mrs P. M. Ffolliot
to Mr J. P. Taylor relating to the Paterson Family,
with special reference to John Paterson of Aberdeen
and Port Elizabeth, South Africa. [N.p., 1959.]
QZ/P22

DICKSON, Mora
The aunts. [With a genealogical table.] Edinburgh,
1981.
ED/N-1 (H3.81.4612)

PATERSON, James
Scottish surnames: a contribution to genealogy.
Edinburgh, 1866.
ED/N-1 (K.115.a)   QZ/P28   QZ/P22   DN/U-1

URQUHART, Edward Alexander
Castle Huntly: its development and history.
[Dundee], 1956. (Abertay Historical Society
Publications, no.4.)
ED/N-1 (P.sm.2056)   ED/N-2

Paterson of Bannockburn

CAMPBELL, J. W.
Some local Jacobite families and a plea for
Clementina Walkinshaw. Stirling, 1921.
QZ/P14

[GENEALOGICAL notes and a genealogical table on
the Paterson family of Bannockburn. 1856?]
ED/N-1 (MS.2675,f.138)

Paterson in Dumfries

PAGAN, William
The birthplace and parentage of William Paterson.
Edinburgh, 1865.
ED/N-1 (L.C.2500)   ED/N-2

Paterson of Kinhervie

REID, Robert Corsane
Paterson of Kinhervie. (In *Transactions of the
Dumfriesshire and Galloway Natural History &
Antiquarian Society,* 3rd series, vol.xxxii, 1953-4,
pp.132-7.)
ED/N-1 (J.187)

Paterson-Anstruther *see* **Polwarth,** Lord

Patillo

CROSSE, Melba C.
Patillo, Pattillo, Pattullo and Pittillo families. Fort
Worth, Tex., 1972.
ED/N-1 (NE.25.e.9)   ED/N-2

Paton

NOEL-PATON, Margaret Hamilton
Tales of a grand-daughter. Elgin, 1970.
ED/N-1 (6.1899)   ED/N-2   QZ/P11   QZ/P99

PATON, James Middleton
Memoranda by James Middleton Paton for the use of those relatives who may succeed him. Montrose, 1875.
ED/N-1 (NE.25.d.3) ED/N-2

Patrick of Roughwood
PATRICKS of Roughwood, Triarne, etc.: a genealogical roll. (*MS.*)
QZ/P-6

Patterson
PARKER, Donald Dean
The Graham-Patterson family history. [Brookings, S. Dakota], 1947.
ED/N-1 (5.1211)

RIX, Guy Scoby
Patterson genealogy: descendants of John Patterson of Argyleshire, Scotland. Concord, N.H., 1914.
ED/N-1 (1976.246) QZ/P99

Pattullo *see* **Patillo**

Paul
PAUL, Sir James Balfour
Some Pauls of Glasgow and their descendants: the scanty record of an obscure family. Edinburgh, 1912.
ED/N-1 (R.172.e) ED/N-2 QZ/P-1 QZ/P99

REID, Robert Corsane
Some relatives of John Paul Jones. (In *Transactions of the Dumfriesshire and Galloway Natural History & Antiquarian Society,* 3rd series, vol.xxiv, 1945-6, pp.79-82.)
ED/N-1 (J.187)

Pearce
PEARCE heritage of New Jersey. [N.p.], 1982. (*Typescript*)
QZ/P-6

Pearse of Holsworthy *see* **Livingston** of Callendar

Pearson, Peirson *see also* **Pierson** of Balmadies

Pearson, Pierson
BAXTER, Angus
The history of the Pearson family, 1296-1949. [1949.]
QZ/P10 (Unconfirmed location)

PEARSON, David Ritchie
A condensed account of the family of Pearson in Scotland from A.D. 1296. 1891. (*Typescript*)
ED/N-2 QZ/L37

Peile of Strathclyde
PEILE, Thomas Williamson
Annals of the Peiles of Strathclyde and of some of their kinsfolk during three centuries. London, 1899.
AD/U-1

Percy
BAIN, Joseph
The Percies in Scotland. (In *Archaeological Journal,* vol.xli, 1884, pp.335-41.)
ED/N-1 (J.187,188)

— — (Reprinted from *Archaeological Journal,* vol.xli, 1884.)
QZ/L37 QZ/P-1 QZ/P99

Perth, Earldom of *see also* **Drummond,** Earl of Perth

Perth, Earldom of
ANSWERS and defences for His Majesty's advocate on behalf of His Majesty, to the claim of Thomas Drummond of Logiealmond to the estate of Drummond and Perth. (6th July 1749.) [Edinburgh, 1749.]
ED/N-1 (Ry.II.b.19(26))

—1750.
ED/N-1 (Ry.II.b.19(51)) QZ/P-1

BANKS, Thomas Christopher
The detection of infamy earnestly recommended to the justice and deliberation of the Imperial Parliament of Great Britain by an unfortunate nobleman. (Cont. Appeal of Charles Edward, Duke of Melfort, etc., heir-male and chief representative of the house of Drummond of Perth, submitted to the two Houses of Parliament ...) London, 1816.
ED/N-1 (Ry.I.4.242) QZ/L37

CASE of Thomas Drummond of Logy-Almond, claimant [of the estate of Drummond and Perth] against His Majesty's advocate in behalf of His Majesty, respondent. 1750.
ED/N-1 (Ry.II.b.19(52)) QZ/P-1

DRUMMOND, James
Answers for His Majesty's Advocate on behalf of
His Majesty to the claim of James Lundin, Esq. of
Lundin [to the Earldom of Perth and the Lordship
of Drummond] ... (December 4, 1750).
[Edinburgh], 1750.
ED/N-1 (Ry.II.b.19(58))

DRUMMOND, John
Verbatim copies of the humble petitions,
memorial and case of John Drommond, heir to
the estate and Earldom of Perth, to his Majesty.
[N.p.], 1788.
ED/N-1 (1951.49(11))

DRUMMOND, Thomas
Earldom of Perth: case of Thomas Drummond,
of New Painshaw ... in the County of Durham,
claiming the honours and estates of the Earldom
of Perth. Newcastle upon Tyne, 1831.
ED/N-1 (Yule.84(3))

—An interesting statement of the claims of
Thomas Drummond of New Painshaw, Co.
Durham, to the .. Earldom of Perth. Newcastle
upon Tyne, 1830.
ED/N-1 (Yule.84(1))   QZ/P-1   QZ/P99

— — Newcastle upon Tyne, 1831.
QZ/P40

—In the House of Lords before the Committee of
Privileges the case of Thomas Drummond, of
Biddick, claiming the titles and dignities of Earl
of Perth, Lord Drummond, Stobhall, and
Montifex, nearest lawful heir male to the same,
and to the restored estate of the Earldom of
Perth. [Bishopwearmouth], 1831.
ED/N-1 (Yule.84(5))

—Sequel of the statement of the claims of Thomas
Drummond ... omitted in the copy of the case.
Newcastle, 1830.
ED/N-1 (Yule.84(2))

HILL, Frederick
The Pitman of Biddick and the Earldom of Perth.
[Newcastle, 1949.]
ED/N-1 (1946.20)

HISTORICAL facts and explanations regarding the
succession to the Lordships, Baronies and Regality
of Drummond and Earldom of Perth. Paris, 1866.
ED/N-1 (1945.5(6))   QZ/L37   ED/N-2   QZ/P99

INFORMATION for His Majesty's advocate on behalf
of His Majesty, respondent, against Thomas
Drummond of Logiealmond, claimant of the estate
of Drummond and Perth. 1750.
ED/N-1 (Abbot.111(30);Ry.II.b.19(53))   QZ/P-1

MELFORT, George Drummond, *Duc de*
Case on behalf of George Drummond, Duke de
Melfort in France, claiming to be Earl of Perth, in
the Peerage of Scotland. [N.p., n.d.]
QZ/P28   QZ/L37

MINUTES of evidence ... 1846.
QZ/L37

Philip

PHILIP, Peter
A Fifeshire family: the descendants of John and
Thomas Philip of Kirkcaldy. Constantia, South
Africa, 1980,82. 2v.
QZ/L37   QZ/P18*

— The story of a Fifeshire family. (In *Scottish
Genealogist,* vol.xv, no.3, September 1968,
pp.59-65.)
ED/N-1 (Gen.7)

Philipps

STEVENS, Robert A.
The path we came by. [N.p.], 1973.
QZ/P26

Philips

MACBAIN, James M.
Eminent Arbroathians: being sketches historical,
genealogical, and biographical, 1178-1894.
Arbroath, 1897.
ED/N-1 (250.a)

Pierson of Balmadies *see also* Pearson, Peirson

Pierson of Balmadies

PIERSON, John
Familien Chronik der Pierson von Balmadies.
Berlin, 1901.
QZ/L37

Pike

MACPIKE, Eugene Fairfield
Pyke and MacPike families. (In *Scottish Notes and
Queries,* 3rd series, vol.vi, January 1928, pp.12-16.)
ED/N-1 (V.457)

— — (Reprinted from *Scottish Notes and Queries,* 3rd
series, vol.vi, 1928.)
DN/U-1

Pilkington of Stanley
['A HISTORICAL account of the family Pilkington
of Stanley'. 1811?]
ED/N-1 (Adv.MS.6.1.17, f.30)

Pirie
PATTERSON, Betty
Robert and Margaret (Fyfe) Pirie and their
descendants. [Madison, Wis.,1980.]
ED/N-1 (HP3.81.1551)

PIRIE, Margaret Forbes
The story of two Aberdeenshire manses: Dyce and
Auchindoir. Aberdeen, 1967.
ED/N-1 (NE.25.f.12) AD/U-1 QZ/P30

SCOTT, Earl
Genealogy of the Pirie-Gray family, 1836-1977.
[1977.] (*Xerox-copy*)
QZ/P-1

Pitcairn
BOASE, Edward R.
The family of Pitcairn of Kinninmont and Pitcairn
of Kinnaird. Edinburgh, [1938]. (*Typescript*)
ED/N-1 (R.172.c) QZ/Q17 QZ/P-1 QZ/P99

PITCAIRN, Constance
The history of the Fife Pitcairns. Edinburgh, 1905.
ED/N-1 (S.120.e) QZ/Q17 QZ/P18 QZ/P26
QZ/P99 ED/N-2 AD/U-1 SA/U1 QZ/L37
ED/U-1 QZ/P-1 ED/M-1 QZ/P16

Pitman
PITMAN, Charles Edward
History and pedigree of the family of Pitman of
Dunchideock, Exeter, and their collaterals, and of
the Pitmans of Alphington, Norfolk, and
Edinburgh. London, 1920.
ED/N-1 (S.120.b)

PITMAN, Harry Anderson
Frederick Cobbe Pitman and his family. [London],
1930.
ED/N-1 (S.123.g) QZ/L37

Pitillo *see* **Patillo**

Playfair
PLAYFAIR, Arthur Grace
Playfair book, or notes on the Scottish family of
Playfair. Tunbridge Wells, 1906.
ED/N-1 (NE.25.c.14) SA/U-1

— — Tunbridge Wells, 1913.
ED/N-1 (S.121.e) SA/U-1 QZ/P-1

— — 4th ed. Tunbridge Wells, 1932.
ED/N-1 (R.172.f) ED/N-2 ED/U-1 GL/U-1
QZ/L37 QZ/P99

ROGER, James Cruikshank
Some account of the Rogers in Coupar-Grange,
with a synopsis ... of the family of Playfair, with
whom they intermarried. London, 1877.
ED/N-1 (R.172.f) QZ/P30 QZ/L37 QZ/P99

ROGERS, Charles
Four Perthshire families: Roger, Playfair, Constable
and Haldane of Barmony. Edinburgh, 1887.
ED/N-1 (Gramp.Club.35) QZ/Q17 QZ/P26
ED/N-2 QZ/P14 GL/U-1 SA/U-1
QZ/L37 QZ/P-1 QZ/P16

— The Scottish branch of the Norman House of
Roger, with a genealogical sketch of the family of
Playfair. London, 1872.
ED/N-1 (Gramp.Club.25) ED/N-2 QZ/P14
QZ/P16 QZ/L37

— The Scottish House of Roger, with notes
respecting the families of Playfair and Haldane of
Barmony. 2nd ed. Edinburgh, 1875.
ED/N-1 (Gramp.Club.28) ED/N-2 QZ/P-1
QZ/P99 QZ/P16 QZ/L37

Plenderleath
LANG, Patrick Sellar
The Langs of Selkirk, with some notes on the
Sibbalds of Whitelaw. ... Melbourne, 1910.
ED/N-2 QZ/P99

Pole
SANDISON, Alexander
Sandisons of Shetland. Part 1: The Delting family,
with Poles of Greenbank & Irvines of Dunsandel,
N.Z. [South Croydon], 1971.
ED/N-1 (6.1982) QZ/P41

Pollock
COCK, Edward Arthur Landslow
Pollock pedigree, 1080-1950. London, [1950].
ED/N-1 (5.1376)

POLLOCK, Walter
The Pollocks as engineers. [With genealogical
tables.] Tunbridge Wells, 1939.
ED/N-1 (NE.63.b.13)

Pollock of Stirlingshire

An AMERICAN farmer's family correspondence with Scotland, 1802-1834; edited by David Buchan Morris. Stirling, 1937.
ED/N-1 (5.752)

Pollok of Balgray

POLLOK, Selina E.
Pollok families: Pollok of Balgray: [genealogical table.] London, 1914. (*British archivist*, March 1914, pedigree no.4.)
ED/N-1 (R.292.e.1(4))

Pollok of Faside

RANKIN, John
A history of our firm: some account of the firm of Pollok, Gilmour and Co., and its offshoots and connections. Liverpool, 1908.
ED/N-1 (NG.1297.c.22)

Polwarth, Lord

ANSTRUTHER, Anne Paterson
Case of Dame Anne Paterson Anstruther ... claiming the title ... of Baroness Polewart or Polwarth.
Q2/L37

JUDGEMENT. 1835.
QZ/L37

MS. notes of the Lord Chancellor's speech. 1831, 1835.
QZ/L37

MINUTES of evidence ... 1818.
QZ/L37

SCOTT, Hugh
Case of Hugh Scott of Harden, Esq., claiming the title ... Baron Polewart or Polwarth.
QZ/L37

— Additional case for above ... [1835].
QZ/L37   QZ/S10

Porteous

DEUCHAR, A.
Genealogical collections relative to the family of Porteous. [N.d.] (*MS.*)
QZ/P-1

PORTEOUS, Barry
The Porteous story: a Scottish border family from 1439 A.D. Vol.1. [Montreal], 1980.
ED/N-1 (H4.80.1634)

Porter *see* **Ross**

Porterfield

CORBETT, Cunningham
The families of Boyds of Kilmarnock, Porterfields of Porterfield and Corbetts of Tolcross. [N.p.,n.d.]
ED/N-2

Pottinger

GREGSON, Keith
Seamanship and kinship: one Shetland family's connection with the North-east of England. (In *Northern Studies*, no.16, 1980, pp.29-37.)
ED/N-1 (5370 PER)

Preston

MS. notes and press cuttings on the family of Preston. [N.d.]
QZ/P99

Preston of Fyvie

STIRLING, Anna Maria D. W. Pickering
Fyvie Castle, its lairds and their times. London, 1928.
ED/N-1 (R.247.e)   QZ/P22   QZ/P30   QZ/P49

Primrose

ANSWERS for His Majesty's Advocate on behalf of His Majesty, to the claim of John Foulis, brother-german to the deceast Sir Archibald Primrose of Dunipace, and heir of entail in the said estate. 3rd January, 1751. [Edinburgh, 1751.]
ED/N-1 (Ry.II.b.19(61))

FOULIS, John
Unto the ... Lords of Council and Session the claim of John Foulis, brother-german to the deceast Sir Archibald Primrose of Dunnipace, and heir of entail in the said estate ... January 4, 1751. [Edinburgh, 1751.]
ED/N-1 (Ry.II.b.19(60))

GIBSON, John C.
Lands and lairds of Dunipace. Stirling, 1903.
ED/N-1 (R.243.f; 5.150)   QZ/P-1   QZ/P14   QZ/P99

— Lands and lairds of Larbert and Dunipace parishes. Glasgow, 1908.
ED/N-1 (R.243.c)   QZ/P14

Primrose, Earl of Rosebery

FORBES, J. Macbeth
History of the Primrose-Rosebery family, 1500-1900. London, 1907.
ED/N-2   QZ/L37

JAMES, Robert Rhodes
Rosebery: a biography of Archibald Philip, 5th
Earl of Rosebery. [With a genealogical table.]
London, 1963.
ED/N-1 (Hist.S.115.R)

Pringle

PRINGLE, Alexander
Records of the Pringles or Hoppringles of the
Scottish border. Edinburgh, 1933.
ED/N-1 (R.172.d) QZ/Q17 ED/N-2 GL/U-1
QZ/P11 ED/U-1 SA/U-1 QZ/P22 QZ/L37
QZ/P-1 QZ/P99

PRINGLE, Mark
Disputatio juridicia ad Tit.IV. lib.XLII. Digest.
quibus ex causis in possessionem eatur. Quam...
pro advocato munere consequendo, publicae
disquisitioni subjicit Marcus Pringle, etc.
Edinburgh, 1777.
ED/N-1 (Law)

PRINGLE, Veronica
Veronica Pringle, widow, and Robert, Andrew
and Mark Pringle...appellants; John Pringle of
Crichton, respondent. [N.p.], 1767.
QZ/P99

Pringle in South Africa

PRINGLE, Eric
Pringles of the Valleys: their history and genealogy.
Adelaide, Cape Prov., 1957.
ED/N-1 (NE.63.g.32) QZ/L37 QZ/P-1

RENNIE, John V. L.
Thomas Pringle on his ancestry. (In *Familia:
Quarterly Journal of the Genealogical Society of South
Africa*, vol.xi, no.2, 1974, pp.32-9.)
ED/N-1 (1976.91) ED/N-2

Pritty

FAMILY tree of the descendants of Lionell Pritty,
market gardener of Edinburgh: genealogical roll.
[N.p., 1973?]
QZ/P22

Proctor of Aberlour

The ABERLOUR succession: [newspaper cuttings
on the disputed succession to the estate of Margaret
G. Macpherson Grant of Aberlour. 1877-79].
ED/N-1 (Hall.210.g.3(2))

Proudfoot of Annandale

PREVOST, W.A.J.
The Proudfoots of Annandale. (In *Transactions of
the Dumfriesshire and Galloway Natural History &
Antiquarian Society*, 3rd series, vol.xxx, 1951-2,
pp.121-31.)
ED/N-1 (J.187)

Pullar

PULLAR, Laurence
Lengthening shadows: random notes of a family
history written in old age. [With a genealogical
table.] [N.p.], 1910.
ED/N-1 (NE.25.b.28) QZ/P26 QZ/P99

Purcell *see* Robertson

Purves of Purves

PURVES, Sir William
Revenue of the Scottish crown, 1681; edited by
D. Murray Rose, [with genealogy of the family of
Purves]. Edinburgh, 1897.
ED/N-1 (Hist.S.6.P) ED/N-2 QZ/P99

Pyke *see* Pike

Pyott

BONAR, Horatius
Notes to genealogical chart or pedigree of the
descendants of James Pyott, merchant, Montrose.
[N.p.], 1914.
ED/N-1 (S.122.e; Birk.183) QZ/P22 QZ/L37
QZ/P99

Queensberry, Marquessate of

CASE of Charles, Marquess and Earl of Queensberry,
etc., formerly Sir Charles Douglas of Kelhead, Bt.,
claiming to be enrolled in his due place among the
peers of Scotland and to have his right to the above
titles... recognised and established. [1812.]
QZ/L37

ROBERTS, Brian
The mad bad line: the family of Lord Alfred
Douglas. London, 1981.
ED/N-1 (H3.81.3225) QZ/P42 QZ/P99

Raleigh

SIMPSON, R. R.
Pedigree of the Linlithgowshire Simpsons,
including pedigrees of the families of Cleland of
Cleland, Jervies, Russells and Raleighs. Edinburgh,
1895.
ED/U-1

Ramsay

GIBSON, John C.
The baronies and owners of Sauchie and
Bannockburn. Stirling, 1934.
ED/N-1 (NE.25.f.24(1))   QZ/P14

RAMSAY, Sir James Henry
Notes on early Ramsay pedigrees, A.D.1200-1600.
(In *The Genealogist,* new series, vol.xxxi, 1915,
pp.1-22.)
ED/N-1 (Y.215)

— — (Reprinted from *The Genealogist,* new series,
vol.xxxi, 1915.)
QZ/P-1   QZ/P99

Ramsay of Bamff

RAMSAY, Sir James Henry
Bamff charters, 1232-1703, with introduction,
biographical summary and notes. Oxford 1915.
ED/N-1 (S.121.d)   QZ/P26   QZ/P15   QZ/P-1
QZ/P99

Ramsay, Earl of Dalhousie

INFORMATION for George, Earl of Dalhousie, and
the Honourable Mr William Ramsay-Maule
against Thomas Maule. [Edinburgh, 1782.]
ED/N-1 (ABS.4.78.3)   QZ/P-1

Ramsay of Kildalton

RAMSAY, Freda
John Ramsay of Kildalton. Toronto, [1969].
ED/N-1 (NC.268.f.1)

Ramsay of Ochtertyre

LETTERS of John Ramsay of Ochtertyre, 1799-1812;
edited by Barbara L. H. Horn. [With a
genealogical table.] Edinburgh, 1966. (Scottish
History Society Publications, 4th series, vol.3.)
ED/N-1 (Ref.54)

Ranald, Clan *see* Macdonald

Ranken of Colden

McCALL, Hardy Bertram
Some old families: a contribution to the
genealogical history of Scotland. Birmingham,
1890.
ED/N-1 (A.36.a)   QZ/P11   QZ/L37   ED/N-2
QZ/P99

Rankin

RANKIN, Paul Tory
Peter Rankin's descendants: the descendants of
Peter, 1753/4-1842, and Margaret Rankin from
Kilsyth, Scotland. Ann Arbor, Mich., 1961.
ED/N-1 (1934.26)

WHYTE, Henry
The Rankins, pipers to the Macleans of Duart,
and … Macleans of Coll. Glasgow, 1907.
ED/N-1 (1907.24)   QZ/P27   ED/N-2   QZ/P-1
QZ/P99

Reddie of Redhouse and Pratis

[GENEALOGICAL notes and genealogical tables
concerning the Reddie family of Redhouse and
Pratis. 1826,1901.]
ED/N-1 (MS.5063)

Rede

READE, Compton
A record of the Redes of Barton Court, Bucks.,
and other lines of the name. Hereford, 1899.
QZ/P40

Redford

CARR-HARRIS, G. C. M.
[Redford family: typescript and letter. N.p., 1969.]
QZ/P34

Reed

REED, Jacob W.
History of the Reed family in Europe and America.
[Boston], 1861.
ED/N-1 (AB.3.77.7)

Reid

BACKSTRÖM, Åke
"Ätten" Reeths senare led. [Helsinki, 1974.]
(*Xerox-copy*)
ED/N-1 (1976.91)

[INFORMATION concerning John Reid and his
family. N.p., n.d.] (*Xerox-copies*)
ED/N-1 (1973.271)

NEWCASTLE silversmiths. (In *Clan Donnachaidh Annual*, 1972, pp.36-7.)
ED/N-1 (NB.43)

PIRIE, Margaret Forbes
The story of two Aberdeenshire manses: Dyce and Auchindoir. Aberdeen, 1967.
ED/N-1 (NE.25.f.12)   AD/U-1   QZ/P30

REID, Herbert
The Reids of Kittochside. 2 parts. Glasgow, 1943,45.
ED/N-1 (6.270)   GL/U-1*   QZ/P-1   QZ/P53*
QZ/P99*   QZ/Q91

REID, Robert
Family records. 2nd ed. Irvine, 1912.
ED/N-1 (NE.25.h.20)   GL/U-1

Reid-Robertson

ROBERTSON, James
Historical account of the Barons Reid-Robertson of Straloch. Blairgowrie, 1887.
ED/N-1 (A.114.e)   QZ/P26   QZ/P22   GL/U-1
DN/U-1   ED/U-1   QZ/P-1   QZ/P99

Reith

BULLOCH, John Malcolm
The family of Reith. Aberdeen, 1937. (*Newspaper cuttings*)
QZ/P22

— — The Reith family. 1935.
QZ/P22

— — The riddle of the Reiths. (In *Deeside Field*, no.8, 1938, pp.17-20.)
ED/N-1 (6.589)

Rennie

[CORRESPONDENCE concerning aspects of the history of the Rennie family. N.d.]
ED/N-1 (MS.19953)

Rennie of Kilsyth

RENNIE, James E.
The Rennies of Kilsyth: the history of an agricultural family. Edinburgh, [1965].
ED/N-1 (NE.25.g.4)   ED/N-2   QZ/Q81
QZ/P14   QZ/P99

The RENNIES of Kilsyth: family tree. [1968?]
(*Xerox-copy*)
QZ/P99

Renny

RENNY, James
Papers relative to the Renny family, with particular reference to James Renny, jun. [N.d.] (*MS.*)
QZ/P28

Renton

RENTON [family history. N.p., n.d.]
ED/N-1 (S.120.i)   QZ/P99

Richardson

McMILLAN, William
Gabriel Richardson and his family. [N.p., n.d.]
QZ/P16

[MSS., and miscellaneous information.]
QZ/P10 (Unconfirmed location)

Richardson of Pitfour

BUIST, George
The steam-boat companion betwixt Perth and Dundee. [With a genealogical table.] Edinburgh, 1838.
ED/N-1 (K.157.e)

Richmond

RICHMOND, Keith *and* CRAGO, Maureen
A genealogical study: Richmond, Campbell, Cairns and Croft. [Armidale, N.S.W.], 1975.
ED/N-1 (6.2868)

Richmond and Gordon, Duke of *see* Gordon-Lennox, Duke of Richmond and Gordon

Riddell, Riddle

CARRE, Walter Riddell
Border memories. Edinburgh, 1876.
QZ/P11

McKENZIE, James
Lilliesleaf. (In *Transactions of the Hawick Archaeological Society*, 1949, pp.29-34.)
ED/N-1 (P.220)

RIDLON, G. T.
History of the ancient Ryedales ... 860 to 1884 ... Riddell, Riddle, Ridlon, Ridley, etc. Manchester, N.H., 1884.
ED/N-1 (A.113.b)   QZ/P22   QZ/P11   QZ/P99
QZ/P-1

WOOD, John Maxwell
Robert Burns and the Riddell family. Dumfries, 1922.
ED/N-1 (KR.28.a)   QZ/P-7

Riddell of Riddell

['HISTORICAL account of the Riddell family of
Riddell'. 1811?]
ED/N-1 (Adv.MS.6.1.17,f.106)

Ridpath

LE HARDY, William
History of the family of Ridpath of Redpath and
Angelraw, in the county of Berwick and
subsequently of London. [N.d.] (*Typescript*)
QZ/P99

Rig of Dumfries

EDGAR, Robert
An introduction to the history of Dumfries.
[With genealogical tables.] Dumfries, 1915.
ED/N-1 (R.241.b)

Rintoul

SPENCER, C. L.
Some notes on the Spencers, Jarvies and Rintouls in
Glasgow, comp. from family tradition and public
records. 1935. (*Typescript*)
QZ/P-1

Robertson

CLAN DONNACHAIDH SOCIETY
Clan Donnachaidh Annual. No.1(1951)- .
Edinburgh, 1951- .
ED/N-1 (NB.43) QZ/P-1 QZ/P99

['GENEALOGICAL notes concerning the family of
Robertson'. 1800?]
ED/N-1 (MS.19399,ff.9,15,25,28)

[GENEALOGICAL notes concerning the family of
Robertson and their descendants. 1890?]
ED/N-1 (MS.19403)

IN memoriam: descent of Catherine MacDiarmid,
wife of J. N. Paton, Dunfermline. [N.p., n.d.]
ED/N-2

MONCREIFFE, Iain
The Robertsons: Clan Donnachaidh of Atholl.
Edinburgh, [1954].
ED/N-1 (Gen.7) Q2/Q17 QZ/P26 QZ/P40
ED/U-1 QZ/P22 QZ/P99 QZ/P-1
QZ/P40 QZ/P11 QZ/L37 QZ/P-6
ED/N-2 SA/U-1 QZ/P30 ST/U-1 QZ/P49
ED/U-1 QZ/P16

— — 3rd ed. Edinburgh, 1979.
ED/N-1 (HP1.80.2918) QZ/P-1 QZ/P22
QZ/P56 QZ/P99

REID, James Robertson
A short history of the Clan Robertson. Stirling,
1933.
ED/N-1 (R.172.g) QZ/P27 QZ/P26 QZ/P40
QZ/P22 DN/U-1 QZ/L37 ED/N-2
QZ/P30 QZ/P99 QZ/P16

ROBERTSON, David
A brief account of the Clan Donnachaidh.
Glasgow, 1894.
ED/N-1 (A.124.c) QZ/P26 QZ/P40
AD/U-1 GL/U-1 ED/S10 QZ/L37
ED/N-2 QZ/P-1 QZ/P99 QZ/P16

ROBERTSON, H. N.
An outline of the history of Clan Donnachaidh. (In
Clan Donnachaidh Annual; part 1, 1951, pp.6-7;
part 2, 1951, p.32.)
ED/N-1 (NB.43)

ROBERTSON, Herbert
Stemmata Robertson et Durdin. London, 1895.
ED/N-1 (S.120.a) ED/N-2 QZ/L37

ROBERTSON, James
Chiefs of Clan Donnachaidh, 1275-1749, and the
Highlanders at Bannockburn. Perth, 1929.
ED/N-1 (S.121.g) SA/U-1 QZ/P27 QZ/P26
QZ/P14 AD/U-1 DN/U-1 QZ/L37
QZ/P13 QZ/P-1 QZ/P99 QZ/P16

ROBERTSON, James Alexander
Comitatus de Atholia: the Earldom of Atholl …
and their descendants, the Robertsons, with proofs.
[Edinburgh], 1860.
ED/N-1 (A.114.c) SA/U-1 QZ/P26 GL/U-1
QZ/P99 QZ/L37 ED/U-1 QZ/P-1

ROBERTSON, Laura Purcell
The Robertson, Purcell and related families.
[Missouri], 1926.
ED/N-1 (NE.63.e.13)

RODGER, Edward
Memoranda regarding the children and
descendants of William Rodger, merchant in
Glasgow, and Agnes Robertson, his wife. [N.p.],
1905.
ED/N-1 (NE.25.b.23)

Robertson of Bruar and Banvie

KERR, John
The Robertsons of Bruar and Banvie. (In *Clan
Donnachaidh Annual,* 1977/8, pp.22-7.)
ED/N-1 (NB.43)

Robertson of Cray
> WILLIAMSON, Henry McIree
>> The Robertsons of Cray. Edinburgh, 1935.
>> ED/N-1 (1936.17) QZ/P26 ED/N-2 QZ/P99

Robertson of Inshes
> FRASER-MACKINTOSH, Charles
>> The Robertsons of Inshes. Inverness, 1899.
>> QZ/P41

>> [A GENEALOGICAL account of the family of
>> Robertson of Inches. 1833.]
>> ED/N-1 (MS.9854,ff.183-7)

Robertson in Irvine
> GUTHRIE, Arthur
>> Robertson of Irvine, poet-preacher. Ardrossan,
>> 1899.
>> ED/N-1 (Hall.248.c)

Robertson of Kindeace
> AIRD, Gustavus
>> Genealogy of the families of Douglas of Mulderg
>> and Robertson of Kindeace. Dingwall, 1895.
>> ED/N-1 (A.113.c) QZ/P40 SA/U-1 QZ/P-1
>> QZ/P99

Robertson of Prenderguest
> EUSTACE, S.
>> The family of Robert Robertson of Prenderguest
>> and Brownshank and Margaret Home his wife.
>> [N.p.],1931.
>> QZ/L37

Robertson of Straloch
> NEWSPAPER cuttings relating to the Robertsons of
> Straloch in Strathardle.
>> QZ/P40

> ROBERTSON, James
>> Historical account of the Barons Reid-Robertson of
>> Straloch. Blairgowrie, 1887.
>> ED/N-1 (A.114.e) QZ/P22 QZ/P26 AD/U-1
>> DN/U-1 QZ/P99

Robertson of Strathtay
> [GENEALOGICAL notes on the Robertson family of
> Strathtay. N.d.]
>> ED/N-1 (MS.464)

Robertson of Strowan, Struan *see also* **Fergusson**
> of Dunfallandy

Robertson of Strowan, Struan
> PATON, Sir Joseph Noel
>> Genealogy of the Celtic Earls of Atholl, the
>> immediate descendants of Duncan I, King of
>> Scotland; with chart of the descendants of Conon
>> …founder of the De Atholia family, afterwards
>> known as Robertsons of Strowan, etc. [N.p.], 1873.
>> ED/N-1 (F.6.6.7(9); S.307.c) ED/N-2 AD/U-1
>> QZ/L37 QZ/P-1 QZ/P16

> ROBERTSON, Alexander
>> The history and martial achievements of the
>> Robertsons of Strowan. Edinburgh, [1785].
>> ED/N-1 (Hall.197.g) ED/N-2 GL/U-1
>> SA/U-1 QZ/P-1 QZ/P40 QZ/P99

> ROBERTSON, Hamish Neil
>> The Struan family tree. (In *Clan Donnachaidh
>> Annual*, 1956, pp.30-3.)
>> ED/N-1 (NB.43)

>> The STRUAN family tree. (In *Clan Donnachaidh
>> Annual*, 1965, pp.16-20.)
>> ED/N-1 (NB.43)

Rochead
> DEUCHAR, A.
>> Genealogical collections relative to the family of
>> Rochead. [N.d.] (*MS.*)
>> QZ/P-1

Rodger
> RODGER, Edward
>> Memoranda regarding the children and
>> descendants of William Rodger, merchant in
>> Glasgow, and Agnes Robertson, his wife.
>> [N.p.], 1905.
>> ED/N-1 (NE.25.b.23)

Roger
> ROGER, James Cruickshank
>> An historical summary of the Roger tenants of
>> Coupar. London, 1879.
>> ED/N-1 (Hall.193.d) GL/U-1 QZ/L37
>> QZ/P99

>> — Some account of the Rogers in Coupar-Grange,
>> with a synopsis of the more prominent members of
>> the family of Playfair, with whom they
>> intermarried. London, 1877.
>> ED/N-1 (R.172.f) SA/U-1 QZ/P28 QZ/L37
>> AD/U-1 QZ/P99

ROGERS, Charles
Four Perthshire families: Roger, Playfair, Constable
and Haldane of Barmony. Edinburgh, 1887.
ED/N-1 (Gramp.Club.35) QZ/Q17 QZ/P26
QZ/P14 SA/U-1 GL/U-1 QZ/L37
ED/N-2 QZ/P-1 QZ/P16

— The Scottish branch of the Norman House of
Roger, with a genealogical sketch of the family of
Playfair. London, 1872.
ED/N-1 (Gramp.Club.25) ED/N-2 QZ/P14
QZ/L37 QZ/P16

— The Scottish House of Roger. 2nd ed.
Edinburgh, 1875.
ED/N-1 (Gramp.Club.28) ED/N-2 QZ/L37
QZ/P-1 QZ/P99 QZ/P16

ROGERS, Kenneth
The family of Roger in Aberdeenshire. [N.p.], 1920.
ED/N-2

Roger of Westmeon
ROGER, Julian C.
A history of our family Rogers of Westmeon,
1451-1902. London, 1902.
ED/N-2

Rolland of Disblair
WALKER, Alexander
Disblair, 1634-1884, or, an old oak panel and
something thereon. Aberdeen, 1884.
ED/N-1 (R.286.c) ED/N-2 QZ/P-1

Rollo
NOTES on the Rollo family. [Glasgow, 1977?]
ED/N-1 (HP3.78.1445)

Romanes
GENEALOGICAL table of one of the families of
Romanes. [London], 1854.
ED/N-1 (5.794(28))

Ronald
RONALD, George
The Ronald family [of Greenock and Aberdeen.
1953]. (*MS.*)
QZ/P22

Rose
BAIN, George
History of Nairnshire. Nairn, 1893.
ED/N-1 (A.124.c)

ROSE, David Murray
Roses of Earlsmiln and Cullisse. Dingwall, [n.d.].
(Reprinted from the *North Star,* 1898.)
QZ/P40 QZ/P22 ED/U-1

ROSE, Eric Hamilton
History of the family of de Ros, de Rose, Rose of
Kilravock. Frome, 1939.
ED/N-1 (R.172.h) ED/N-2

ROSE, Mary Tweedie Stodart
Alexander Rose and his grandson Robert Traill
Rose. [With a genealogical table.] Edinburgh,
[1957].
ED/N-1 (NF.1182.h.8) QZ/P99

Rose of Holme Rose
ROSE, Henry
Genealogy of the family of Rose of Holme Rose.
Nairn, 1929.
ED/N-1 (5.433) SA/U-1 ED/N-2 QZ/P22
QZ/P40 QZ/P99 AD/U-1 DN/U-1
QZ/L37 QZ/P50 QZ/P-1

Rose of Kilravock
['GENEALOGICAL accounts of the Rose family of
Kilravock'. 1833.]
ED/N-1 (MS.9854,ff.203-7)

['PAPERS concerning the genealogy of the family
Rose of Kilravock'. 17--.]
ED/N-1 (Adv.MS.20.1.8,ff.72-91)

ROSE, Hew *and* SHAW, Lachlan
A genealogical deduction of the family of Rose of
Kilravock. Edinburgh, 1848. (Spalding Club.)
ED/N-1 (Spald.Club.18) ED/N-2 ED/U-1
GL/U-1 QZ/L37 QZ/P-1 QZ/P11
QZ/P22 QZ/P30 QZ/P40 QZ/P50
QZ/P99

SKELTON, J.
The Roses of Kilravock. 1883.
ED/N-2

Rose of Montcoffer
TAYLER, Alastair *and* TAYLER, Henrietta
The domestic papers of the Rose family. Aberdeen,
1926.
ED/N-1 (S.121.g) DN/U-1 QZ/P30 AD/U-1
QZ/P22 QZ/P99 ED/N-2 QZ/P50 QZ/P-1

Rose in U.S.A.

Rose, Christine
Rev. Charles Rose of Scotland & Westmoreland
County, Virginia: the first four generations in
America. [N.p., 1976.]
ED/N-1 (HP3.79.859)

—Rev. Robert Rose of Scotland, Essex County,
Virginia and Albemarle County, Virginia: the first
five generations in America. San Jose, 1972.
ED/N-1 (HP3.79.860)

Rosebery, Earl of *see* **Primrose,** Earl of Rosebery

Ross

Hartman, Blanche T.
A genealogy of the Nesbit, Ross, Porter, Taggart
families of Pennsylvania. [With genealogical
tables.] Pittsburgh, Pa., 1929.
ED/N-1 (H3.83.2753)

Mackinnon, Donald
The Clan Ross. Edinburgh, 1957.
ED/N-1 (Gen.7) QZ/P22 QZ/P26 QZ/P40
QZ/P11 QZ/P30 QZ/P49 ED/U-1 QZ/P-1
QZ/P99

— — 1972.
QZ/P99

Robertson, John
[The Ross Pitcruvie of Glencalvie and Ross of
Kindeace: pedigree of the families of Ross of
Kindeace and Goodsir of Pitcreivie. N.d.]
QZ/P40 (D) QZ/P99

Ross, Alan S. C.
Report on the genealogies of myself and my wife.
(With supplement.) [Birmingham?], 1967, 70.
ED/N-2

Ross, Alexander M.
History of Clan Ross, with genealogies of the
various families. Dingwall, 1932.
ED/N-1 (Gen.8.R) GL/U-1 QZ/P22 QZ/P40
SA/U-1 ED/U-1 QZ/P-1 QZ/P99

Ross, Donald
The massacre of the Rosses at Strathcarron.
Inverness, 1854.
ED/N-1 (3.2599(11))

— — Inverness, 1886.
ED/N-1 (3.2832(2)) QZ/P40

Ross, J. Bryon
The Rosses of Rossville and that ilk. [N.p.], 1978.
ED/N-1 (H3.80.2581)

Ross, John Robert *and* Ross, A. C. Gordon
The great Clan Ross. Lindsay, Canada, 1968.
ED/N-1 (NE.25.e.6) SA/U-1 QZ/P-1 QZ/P-9
QZ/P22 QZ/P26 QZ/P40 (D, I) QZ/Q41
QZ/P99

— — 2nd ed. Lindsay, Canada, 1972.
ED/N-1 (Gen.8.R) SA/U-1 QZ/L37 QZ/P34
QZ/Q41

Ross, Richard
Genealogy of R. R. [ancestor of Charles B. Boog
Watson]. [N.p., n.d.]
ED/N-1 (NE.25.h.12) QZ/P99

Watson, Charles Brodie Boog
Traditions and genealogies of some members of the
families of Boog, Heron, Leishman, Ross and
Watson. Perth, 1908.
ED/N-1 (S.120.d) QZ/P18 ED/N-2 SA/U-1
QZ/L37 QZ/P99

— — Perth, 1922.
ED/N-1 (6.102)

Ross, Earldom of
Ane Breve cronicle of the Earlis of Ross, including
notices of the Abbots of Fearn, and of the family of
Ross of Balnagowan; edited by W. R. Baillie.
Edinburgh, 1850.
ED/N-1 (A.114.d) AD/U-1 QZ/L37 QZ/P-1
QZ/P40 QZ/P99

The Earldom of Ross and lordship of Ardmanach:
MS. of memorandum by John Horne Stevenson.
1934. (*Typescript*)
QZ/L37

Reid, Francis Nevile
The Earls of Ross and their descendants.
Edinburgh, 1894.
ED/N-1 (A.124.b) QZ/P40 SA/U-1 AD/U-1
QZ/P-1 QZ/P99

Rose, David Murray
The Earldom of Ross. [N.p., n.d.]
AD/U-1

Ross of Balnagown *see* **Ross,** Earldom of

Ross of Dalton
Knowles, George Parker
A genealogical account of the Rosses of Dalton, in
the county of Dumfries. London, 1855.
ED/N-1 (R.172.d.1(2)) ED/N-2 QZ/L37

Ross of Glencalvie
ROBERTSON, John
Rosses of Glencalvie. [N.p.], 1844.
ED/N-2 QZ/P40 ST/U-1

Ross of Kindeace
ROSS of Kindeace pedigree. . . . [N.p., 1962.]
ED/N-2

SOME Kindeace letters; edited by D. Murray Rose.
[N.p., 1896.]
ED/N-1 (Ry.I.3.287) QZ/P-1

Ross in Poland
PAPERS relating to the Scots in Poland, 1576-1793;
edited by A. Francis Steuart. Edinburgh, 1915.
(Scottish History Society Publications, vol.lix.)
ED/N-1 (Ref.54)

Rosslyn, Earl of *see* **Halketh** of Pitfirrane

Row of Carnock
MAIDMENT, James
Memorials of the family of Row. Edinburgh, 1828.
ED/N-1 (A.114.d) SA/U-1 QZ/P-1 QZ/P99
QZ/P16

Roxburghe, Lord, Earl of, Duke of
KER, Sir James Innes
Additional case of Sir James Innes Ker, Bt. [N.d.]
QZ/L37

— Case of Sir James Innes Ker, Bt. 1808.
QZ/L37

— Information for . . . James, Duke of Roxburghe,
in the question of accounting between His Grace
and Mr. Archibald Swinton . . . late judicial factor
on the sequestrated estates of Roxburghe. 2 parts in 1.
Edinburgh, 1818,19.
ED/N-1 (L.C.1106(12))

KER, John
Information for the Earl of Roxburghe and
Mr. William Ker, his brother, against John Lord
Ballenden. [Edinburgh, 1800?]
ED/N-1 (MS.3584(17))

KER, John Bellenden
Case of John Bellenden Kerr and others . . . 1808.
QZ/L37

— — Tree showing propinquity of Mr. Bellenden
Ker to the family of Roxburghe. [N.p., n.d.]
QZ/P-1

KER, Walter
Case of Colonel Walter Ker of Littledean. . . .
QZ/L37

KER, William B.
[Session papers in the claims to the title and
estates of the Duke of Roxburghe made by Sir
J. N. Innes and Walter Ker. Edinburgh, 1806.]
ED/N-1 (Hall.293.f.16)

MINUTES of evidence . . . 1808.3.
QZ/L37

ROXBURGHE, James Innes Ker, *5th Duke of*
Additional appendix for James, Duke of Roxburgh
against General Walter Ker of Littledean. 1819.
QZ/L37

— — Appendix to the appellant's [James Innes Ker]
case. [N.p., n.d.]
ED/S10

— — Case of James, Duke of Roxburghe against
Walter Ker of Littledean. [N.p., 1818?]
ED/S10

— — Petition, answers, and duplies anent feu duties
of the entailed estate of Roxburghe, Jan.-Nov. 1817.
Edinburgh, 1817.
QZ/P99

Ruddiman
JOHNSTON, George Harvey
Notes on the Ruddimans, and genealogical tables.
Edinburgh, 1887.
ED/N-1 (A.38.a) QZ/L37 QZ/P-1 QZ/P99

— — The Ruddimans in Scotland: their history and
works. Edinburgh, 1901.
ED/N-1 (S.142.a: L.197.a) SA/U-1 ED/N-2
QZ/P99

JOHNSTONE and Ruddiman pedigree. [1910?]
ED/N-1 (MS.Acc.5811, no.9a)

The RUDDIMANS mentioned in this history:
[a genealogical table of the descendants of Andrew
Simson.] [N.p., 1900?]
ED/N-1 (6.2320)

Ruglen, Earl of *see* **Cassilis,** Earldom of

Runciman of Aberdeen
CRAMER, Sydney
[Inscriptions in three Bibles. Dundee, n.d.]
ED/N-1 (Mf.25(12[4]))

Russell

SIMPSON, R. R.
Pedigree of the Linlithgowshire Simpsons,
including pedigrees of the families of Cleland of
Cleland, Jervies, Russells and Raleighs. Edinburgh,
1895.
ED/U-1

THOMSON, David Couper
McCulloch, Turner, McCormick and Russell:
[a genealogical table]. Dundee, 1943.
ED/N-1 (NE.25.a.26) QZ/L37 QZ/P99

WILLSHER, Betty
The Chamberlain Russells. (In *Scottish Genealogist,*
vol.xxviii, no. 2, June 1981, pp.69-74.)
ED/N-1 (Gen.7)

Russell of Kingseat and Slipperfield

PATERSON, James
Scottish surnames: a contribution to genealogy.
Edinburgh, 1866.
ED/N-1 (K.115.a) QZ/P22 DN/U-1

Rutherford

FACTS and data relating to the Rutherford family or
clan, more especially the Rutherfords of Nisbet.
1885. (*MS.*)
SA/U-1

[GENEALOGICAL notes and a genealogical table
concerning the family of Rutherford. N.d.]
ED/N-1 (MS.1566,f.34)

Rutherfurd in Aberdeen

RUTHERFURD, James H.
The Rutherfurds in Aberdeen. [Kelso?, 1900?]
QZ/P22

Rutherfurd of Rutherfurd

COCKBURN-HOOD, Thomas H.
Rutherfurds of that ilk and their cadets. Edinburgh,
1884.
ED/N-1 (A.114.a) QZ/P11 ED/N-2 AD/U-1
GL/U-1 QZ/L27 QZ/P-1 QZ/P99

— — [Additions and corrections by C. H. E.
Carmichael and others. 5 parts in 1. Edinburgh,
1899-1903.]
ED/N-1 (6.680) SA/U-1 QZ/L37 QZ/P99

Rutherfurd, Lord Rutherfurd

RUTHERFORD, John
Case of John Rutherford, claiming the title of
Baron Rutherford of Rutherford (with pedigree).
1839.
QZ/L37

Rutherfurd, Lord Rutherfurd and Earl of Teviot

CARMICHAEL, Charles Henry Edward
Pages supplementary to Carmichael's papers,
having special reference to Andrew Rutherfurd,
Earl of Teviot. [Edinburgh?, 1884?]
ED/N-1 (5.138(4))

Ruthven

COWAN, Samuel
The Ruthven family papers. London, 1912.
ED/N-1 (R.232.f; R.232.h) QZ/Q17 QZ/P53
QZ/P26 QZ/P40 AD/U-1 QZ/P22
QZ/L37   QZ/P-6 ED/N-2 GL/U-1
QZ/P49 ED/U-1 QZ/P-1 QZ/P99

DOUGLAS, William
The owners of Dirleton. (In *History of the
Berwickshire Naturalists' Club,* vol.xxvii, 1929,
pp.75-92.)
ED/N-1 (Y.210)

— — (Reprinted from *History of the Berwickshire
Naturalists' Club,* vol.xxvii, 1929.)
QZ/P34

HARRISON, Robert
Some notices of the Stepney family. 1870.
QZ/P26

RUTHVEN, Patrick, Earl of Forth and Brentford
Ruthven correspondence: letters and papers of
Patrick Ruthven . . . and of his family, A.D.1615-
A.D.1662; edited by William Dunn Macray.
London, 1868. (Roxburghe Club.)
ED/N-1 (Rox.90) GL/U-1 QZ/P-1 QZ/P99

Ruthven, Earl of Gowrie

BRUCE, John
Papers relating to William, first Earl of Gowrie and
Patrick Ruthven, his fifth and last surviving son.
London, 1867.
ED/N-1 (A.114.d) GL/U-1 QZ/L37 QZ/P-1
QZ/P99

LANG, Andrew
The Gowrie conspiracy and the Gowrie arms. (In
The Ancestor, 2 July 1902, pp.54-7.)
ED/N-1 (Q.115)

SCOTT, James
A history of the life and death of John, Earl of
Gowrie, with preliminary dissertations.
Edinburgh, 1818.
ED/N-1 (A.114.c)

Ruthven, Lord Ruthven of Freeland
FRASER, Sir William
Memorial as to the Ruthven peerage. [N.p.], 1870.
ED/N-1 (6.1152(34))

STEVENSON, John Horne
The Ruthven of Freeland peerage and its critics.
Glasgow, 1905.
ED/N-1 (S.120.g) QZ/P53 QZ/P22 GL/U-1
QZ/L37 QZ/P-1 QZ/P99

Ryedale *see* **Riddell, Riddle**

St Clair *see also* **Sinclair**

St Clair
SAINT-CLAIR, Louis Anatole de
Histoire généalogique de la famille de Saint-Clair
et de ses alliances (France-Ecosse). Paris, 1905.
QZ/P99

SAINT CLAIR, Roland William
The Saint Clairs of the Isles; a history of the sea
Kings of Orkney and their Scottish successors of
the surname of Sinclair. Auckland, N.Z., 1898.
ED/N-1 (S.120.c) QZ/P40 SA/U-1 AD/U-1
GL/U-1 QZ/P99

St Clair of Roslin
DICKSON, John
Roslin Castle and the St. Clairs: their history.
Edinburgh, 1897.
ED/N-1 (A.104.g)

HAY, Richard Augustin
Genealogie of the Sainteclaires of Rosslyn.
Edinburgh, 1835.
ED/N-1 (A.120.c;NE.25.f.13) QZ/P18
ED/N-2 QZ/P40 SA/U-1 GL/U-1 ED/U-1
QZ/P99

['HISTORICAL account of the Saint Clair family of
Rosslyn'. 1707?]
ED/N-1 (Adv.MS.341.9.(ii),ff.121-309v)

SINCLAIR, Alexander
Sketch of the history of Roslin, and of its
possessors. Irvine, 1856.
ED/N-1 (1907.25) QZ/P-9

Sandeman
The CLAN. Vol.5, no.1 (January 1893)-vol.10, no.6
(December 1895). Hove, 1893-5.
ED/N-1 (ABS.4.79.13) QZ/P26

Continued as:

The CLAN: the Sandeman family magazine. New
series. No.1 (March 1896)-vol.3, no.4 (December
1898). Edinburgh, 1896-8.
ED/N-1 (ABS.4.79.13) QZ/P26

SANDEMAN, John Glas
The Sandeman genealogy . . . from family notes,
memoranda, and the original MS. by David Peat.
Edinburgh, 1895.
ED/N-1 (A.58.a) SA/U-1 QZ/P26 ED/N-2
QZ/L37 QZ/P-1 QZ/P99

— — Brought up to date by G. L. Sandeman.
Edinburgh, 1950.
ED/N-1 (R.272.b) QZ/P26 ED/N-2 QZ/L37
QZ/P99

SANDEMAN, Walter Albert
The Sandeman family of Perth. [N.p.], 1926.
QZ/P26 ED/N-2 AD/U-1

Sandiland
MORGAN, Patrick
Annals of Woodside and Newhill, historical and
genealogical. Aberdeen, 1886.
ED/N-1 (A.120.a)

Sandilands
MEMOIR and genealogy of the family of Sandilands
of Crabstone and Cotton in Aberdeenshire. [N.p.],
1863.
ED/N-2

TERRY, James
The pedigrees and papers of James Terry, Athlone
herald at the court of James II in France, 1690-1725.
Exeter, 1938.
ED/N-1 (R.172.c)

Sandilands of Calder
MACCALL, Hardy Bertram
The history and antiquities of the parish of Mid-
Calder with some account of the religious house of
Torphichen founded upon record. [With
genealogical tables.] Edinburgh, 1894.
ED/N-1 (R.244.a)

Sandilands, Lord Torphichen *see* **Torphichen,**
Barony of

Sandison

SANDISON, Alexander
Sandisons of Shetland. Part 1: The Delting family,
with Poles of Greenbank & Irvines of Dunsandel,
N.Z. [South Croydon], 1971.
ED/N-1 (6.1982)   QZ/P41

Sandison of Unst

CLARK, John
Index to Fordyce, Bruce and Clark families at
Uyeasound, Unst, Shetland, 2nd ed., 1902.
Prepared with some additional information from
the Unst marriage registers 1797-1863 or
concerning the Sandison family by Alexander
Sandison. Cambridge, 1955.
ED/N-1 (NE.25.f.4)   QZ/P22

Sasson

JACKSON, Samuel
The Sassons. London, [1968].
ED/N-1 (NF.1373.d.6)

Saunders

SAUNDERS, Herbert Clifford
Saunders pedigree. London, 1883.
QZ/P99

Schetky

GREENWAY, Winifred
The Scottish Schetkys. (In Scottish Genealogist,
vol.xxvi, no.4, December 1979, pp.94-7.))
ED/N-1 (Gen.7)

Scollay

MARWICK, Hugh
Some notes on an old Orkney family: the Scollays.
(In Orkney Miscellany, vol.1, 1953, pp.29-47.)
ED/N-1 (NE.1.e)   QZ/P-1

Scott

CARRE, Walter Riddell
Border memories. Edinburgh,1876.
ED/N-1 (A.118.g)   QZ/P11

DUNLOP, Jean Mary
The Scotts. Edinburgh, 1957.
ED/N-1 (Gen.7)   QZ/P22   QZ/P26   QZ/P40
QZ/P11   QZ/P99   SA/U-1   QZ/P-9   QZ/P49
ED/U-1   QZ/P-1

['A GENEALOGICAL account of the family of Scott'.
1840?]
ED/N-1 (MS.2890,ff.224-5)

['GENEALOGICAL material concerning the family of
Scott'. 1699.]
ED/N-1 (Adv.MS.20.1.66,ff.70-85)

[A GENEALOGICAL table showing the antecedents
of Robert Shortreed. N.p., 1844.]
ED/N-1 (7.106(66-9))

LEVER, Sir Tresham
Lessudden House, Sir Walter Scott and the Scotts of
Raeburn. London, 1972.
ED/N-1 (NG.1179.b.8)   ED/N-2   QZ/P-1
QZ/P11   QZ/P14

NISBETT, Hamilton More and AGNEW, Stair
Carnegie
Cairnhill. Edinburgh, 1949.
ED/N-1 (R.272.f)   QZ/P-3

SCOT, Walter
Metrical history of the honourable families of the
names of Scot and Elliot in the shires of Roxburgh
and Selkirk. Edinburgh, 1892.
ED/N-1 (F.5.d.1)   ED/N-2   QZ/P11   GL/U-1
QZ/P-1   QZ/P99

— — A true history of several honourable families of
the right honourable name of Scot. Edinburgh,
1688.
ED/N-1 (Ferg.128)   QZ/P22

— — Edinburgh, 1776.
ED/N-1 (Ry.II.b.26;A.114.c.;MS.3286)   ED/N-2
QZ/L37   QZ/P11

— — Hawick, 1786.
ED/N-1 (G.37.d)   ED/N-2

— — Edited by J. G. Winning. Hawick, 1894.
ED/N-1 (A.124.d)   ED/N-2   SA/U-1   ST/U-1
QZ/P-1   QZ/P11   QZ/P99

SCOTT, Isabella and SCOTT, Catherine
A family biography, 1662 to 1908, drawn chiefly
from old letters. [With genealogical tables.]
London, 1908.
ED/N-1 (NE.63.f.4)

SCOTT, Keith S. M.
Scott, 1118-1923, being a collection of Scott
pedigrees, containing all male descendants from
Buccleuch, Sinton, Harden, Balweary, etc.
London, 1923.
ED/N-1 (S.121.e)   QZ/P-11   SA/U-1   AD/U-1
QZ/L37   QZ/P-9   QZ/P-1   QZ/P99

SCOTT-NICHOL, John
6½ centuries in wool. [With genealogical tables.]
[Leicester, 1947.]
ED/N-1 (6.330)

SHARPE, Charles Kirkpatrick
[Scott family: some biographical notes, 1663-1723.]
1849. (*MS.*)
SA/U-1

Scott of Abbotsford
[HISTORY of the family of Thomas Scott, (younger
brother of Sir Walter Scott). 1932?]
ED/N-1 (MS.8789)

LETTERS hitherto unpublished written by members
of Sir Walter Scott's family to their own governess.
London, 1905.
ED/N-1 (T.136.f) QZ/P-1

MACKAY, Adam M.
Sir Walter Scott as a freemason: the Scott family
and Lodge St. David, No. 36. Edinburgh, [1916?].
ED/N-1 (Ry.I.2.16)

ROGERS, Charles
Genealogical memoirs of the family of Sir Walter
Scott of Abbotsford; with a reprint of his
'Memorials of the Haliburtons'. London, 1877.
(Grampian Club, 13.)
ED/N-1 (Gramp.Club.13) ED/N-2 ED/U-1
DN/U-1 QZ/L37 QZ/P-1 QZ/P-7 QZ/P11
QZ/P14 QZ/P22 QZ/P40 QZ/P99
QZ/P16

Scott of Aikwode *see* **Scott** of Wamphray

Scott of Allanhaugh
ROBSON, Michael
The Allanmouth tower and the Scotts of
Allanhaugh. (In *Transactions of the Hawick
Archaeological Society*, 1977, pp.12-22.)
ED/N-1 (P.220)

Scott of Ancrum
['GENEALOGICAL notes concerning the family of
Scott of Ancrum'. 17--.]
ED/N-1 (Adv.MS.19.1.21,ff.152-7)

Scott of Balweary
FAMILY of Scott of Balwery, Jawcraig,
Aberdeenshire, etc. [N.d.] (*MSS.*)
QZ/P-1

['GENEALOGICAL notes concerning the family of
Scott of Balwearie'. 17--.]
ED/N-1 (Adv.MS.19.1.21,ff.152-7)

Scott of Bavelaw
INGLIS, John Alexander
The Monros of Auchinbowie and cognate families.
Edinburgh, 1911.
ED/N-1 (S.121.d) SA/U-1 QZ/L37 QZ/P-1
QZ/P14 QZ/P99

WOOD, John Philp
Memorials of various families. [1830?] (*MS.*)
QZ/P99

Scott of Bowhill *see* **Scott** of Wamphray

Scott of Branxholme
LOCKHART, William Eliott
Historical notes relating to Branxholme, plates,
plan, etc. [N.p., n.d.]
QZ/L37 QZ/P-1

Scott, Earl of, Duke of Buccleuch
CRICHTON, Andrew
A short genealogical and historical account of the
noble family of Buccleuch as it appeared in the
Dumfries Weekly Journal, 18th Dec. 1827. Dumfries,
1827.
QZ/P10 (Unconfirmed location)

FRASER, Sir William
The Scotts of Buccleuch. Edinburgh, 1878. 2v.
ED/N-1 (Gen.8.S) QZ/P56 QZ/P11 SA/U-1
AD/U-1 ED/N-2 GL/U-1 QZ/L37 ED/U-1
QZ/P-1 QZ/P99

— The two heiresses of Buccleuch, Ladies Mary and
Anna Scott, and their husbands, 1647-1732.
Edinburgh, 1880. (Reprinted from his *Scotts of
Buccleuch.*)
ED/N-1 (NE.25.g.9) AD/U-1 ED/U-1
QZ/L37 QZ/P-9

GALLOWAY, George
Elegy on His Grace Henry, Duke of Buccleuch, ...
born ... 1746 ... died ... 1812. Edinburgh, 1812.
QZ/P-1 QZ/P99

— — Edinburgh, 1906.
ED/N-1 (3.937)

['HISTORICAL remarks and anecdotes concerning
the family of Buccleuch'. 17--.]
ED/N-1 (Adv.MS.31.6.20.ff.111-20)

MEMORIAL of the majority of the Earl of Dalkeith. Dalkeith, 1852.
QZ/P11 QZ/P99

OLIVER, J. Rutherford Scott
Upper Teviotdale and the Scotts of Buccleuch. Hawick, 1887.
ED/N-1 (Y.59.b.19) ED/N-2 QZ/P11
AD/U-1 QZ/P22 GL/U-1 QZ/P-6 QZ/L37
ED/U-1 QZ/P-1 QZ/P99

Scott of Ewisdale
CARLYLE, Thomas J.
The Scotts of Euisdail. Hawick, 1884.
QZ/P11 QZ/L37 QZ/P-1

Scott in Greenock
TWO centuries of shipbuilding by the Scotts at Greenock. London, 1906.
ED/N-1 (T.326.a) ED/N-2 QZ/P-1 QZ/P49
QZ/P52 (Unconfirmed location)

— — 2nd ed. London, 1920.
ED/N-1 (T.326.a; X.20.a) QZ/P-1

— — 3rd ed. Manchester, 1950.
ED/N-1 (X.88.a) QZ/P-1

TWO hundred and fifty years of shipbuilding by the Scotts at Greenock. Greenock, 1961.
ED/N-1 (NE.12.h.3) QZ/P-1

Scott of Harden *see also* **Polwarth,** Lord

Scott of Harden
BAILLIE, M. Theresa
What I have been told concerning my great grandmother and my great grandfather, and also my Grandmother, Lady Polwarth. Selkirk, [1903?].
QZ/P11

Scott of Harperrig
INGLIS, John Alexander
The Scotts of Harperrig. London, 1914.
ED/N-1 (S.121.b)

Scott of Melby
LAURENSON, James
Scott of Melby, Sandness, Shetland Islands. New Zealand, 1935.
QZ/P41

Scott of Milsington
SCOTT, William
Pedigree of the family of Scott of Stokoe, and also the pedigree of the Scotts in Milsington, etc. 2nd ed. Hawick, 1898.
ED/N-1 (NE.63.a.12) QZ/P11

Scott, Lord Polwarth *see* **Polwarth,** Lord

Scott of Raeburn
['GENEALOGICAL notes on the Scott family of Raeburn'. N.d.]
ED/N-1 (MS.1583,ff.85-90)

Scott of Scots-Hall
HANLEY, Hugh A.
Kent Archives Office U1115: Scott of Scotts Hall MSS … catalogued, title deeds calendared by Hugh A. Hanley, summer 1965. [London, 1966.]
ED/N-1 (GRH.11)

SCOTT, James R.
Memorials of the family of Scott of Scots-Hall. London, 1876.
ED/N-2 QZ/L37

Scott of Stokoe
SCOTT, William
Pedigree of the family of Scott of Stokoe. [Newcastle?, 1783?]
ED/N-1 (NI I.668.b.14(16))

— — Edinburgh, 1827.
ED/N-1 (1972.219(5))

— — London, 1852.
ED/N-1 (3.2642(4)) SA/U-1 QZ/L37 QZ/P11
QZ/P99

— — And also the pedigree of the Scotts in Milsington, etc. 2nd ed. Hawick, 1898.
ED/N-1 (NE.63.a.12) QZ/P-1 QZ/P11

Scott of Thirlestane
HAY, George
Case of George, Marquis of Tweeddale, and other peers of Scotland who object to the title of the person who voted at the late election as Lord Napier. [With a genealogical table.] [N.p., 1793.]
ED/N-1 (Yule.168(2))

HISTORY of the Napiers of Merchiston, shewing … their marriage in to the family of the Scotts of Thirlestane; compiled from old records. [London], 1921.
ED/N-1 (NE.25.h.5)

McCALL, Hardy Bertram
Memoirs of my ancestors. Birmingham, 1884.
ED/N-1 (A.114.a) QZ/P99

— Some old families: a contribution to the
genealogical history of Scotland. Birmingham,
1890.
ED/N-1 (A.36.a) ED/N-2 QZ/P11 QZ/L37
ED/N-2 QZ/P99

NAPIER, E. B.
Some notes on the Napiers of Merchistoun and on
the Scotts of Thirlestane. Edinburgh, [n.d.].
ED/N-1 (S.121.i) QZ/P99

OLIVER, James Rutherford
Border sketches, historical and biographical.
Hawick, 1904.
ED/N-1 (NE.15.a.5)

SCOTT, John
Memoirs of Scott of Thirlestane and other
families of the name of Scott. [N.p., n.d.] 2v.
(*Typescript*)
QZ/L37 QZ/P99

Scott of Wamphray
REID, Robert Corsane
Scott of Wamphray and their kinsmen. (In
*Transactions of the Dumfriesshire and Galloway
Natural History & Antiquarian Society*, 3rd series,
vol.xxxiii, 1954/5, pp.18-28.)
ED/N-1 (J.187)

— — (Reprinted from *Transactions of the
Dumfriesshire and Galloway Natural History &
Antiquarian Society*, 3rd series, vol.xxxiii, 1954/5.)
QZ/L37 QZ/P-1

Scott Moncrieff
STUART, M. M.
Ink in their veins. (In *Scottish Genealogist,* vol.xxix,
no.4, December 1982, pp.120-2.)
ED/N-1 (Gen.7)

Scrimgeour, Scrymgeour
GENEALOGICAL notes concerning the family of
Scrymgeour. [N.p., 1916.]
QZ/P28

INVENTORY of documents relating to the
Scrymgeour family estates, 1611; edited by
J. Maitland Thomson. Edinburgh, 1912. (Scottish
Record Society, vol.42.)
ED/N-1 (Ref.55) ED/N-2 GL/U-1 QZ/P-1
QZ/P14 QZ/P27 QZ/P99

MUNRO, R. W. *and* MUNRO, Jean
The Scrimgeours and their chiefs: Scotland's royal
banner bearers. [Edinburgh], 1980.
ED/N-1 (Gen.8.S) DN/U-1 ED/S10 QZ/L37
QZ/P22 QZ/P99

SCRIMGEOUR CLAN ASSOCIATION
The Skirmisher: bulletin of the Scrimgeour Clan
Association. No.1 (February 1972)- .
[Longniddry?], 1972- .
ED/N-1 (7288 PER)

WARDEN, Alexander J.
History of the Scrymgeours. 1886. (*MS.*)
ED/N-2 QZ/P99

Scrymgeour of Glassarie
WRITS relating chiefly to the lands of Glassarie and
their early possessors. Edinburgh, 1916. (In
Highland Papers; edited by J. R. N. MacPhail. Vol.2
(Scottish History Society Publications, 2nd series,
vol.xii.), pp.113-245.)
ED/N-1 (Ref.54) ED/N-2 QZ/P-1 QZ/P41
ED/U-1 QZ/P40

Scrymgeour-Wedderburn *see* **Dudhope,** Viscount

Scrymgeour-Wedderburn *see* **Dundee,** Earldom of

Seafield, Earl of *see* **Ogilvie-Grant,** Earl of Seafield

Seaforth, Earl of *see* **Mackenzie,** Earl of Seaforth

Selcraig *see* **Selkirk**

Selkirk
SELCRAIG, Thomas
Chronology of the family of John Selcraig, father
of Alexander Selcraig or Selkirk (the prototype of
Robinson Crusoe). [N.p.], 1869.
QZ/P99

Sellar
LANG, Patrick Sellar
The Langs of Selkirk, with some notes on the
Sibbalds of Whitelaw. Melbourne, 1910.
ED/N-2 QZ/P99 QZ/P11

Sempill
ARCHAEOLOGICAL and historical collections
relating to the county of Renfrew; charters and
documents relating to the parish of Lochwinnoch
and the house of Sempill. Paisley, 1885-90. 2v.
GL/U-1 QZ/P-1 QZ/P99

SEMPILL family: genealogical notes. [N.d.] (*MSS.*)
QZ/P-6

Sempill of Beltries

PATERSON, James
Poems of the Sempills of Beltrees with notes and biographical notices of their lives. Edinburgh, 1849.
ED/N-1 (Glen. 176; L.C.181; I.38/1.i) GL/U-1
QZ/P-1 QZ/P99

Sempill of Cathcart

['LETTERS and genealogical notes concerning the Sempill family of Cathcart'. 1769?]
ED/N-1 (Adv.MS.19.1.21,ff.2,32-6)

Sempill of Fulwood

['DRAFT genealogical account of the Sempill family of Fulwood'. 1828?]
ED/N-1 (Adv.MS.19.2.17,f.349)

Semple

BOOK of Middleton, or, the history of the Semples. [N.d.] (*MS.*)
QZ/P-6

SEMPLE, William Alexander
Genealogical history of the family from 1214 to 1888. Hartford, Conn., 1888.
ED/N-2

Scton

CHAMBERS, William
Story of the Setons. [Edinburgh], 1874.
ED/N-1 (3.2682(12))

['GENEALOGICAL account of the family of Seton'. 1559.]
ED/N-1 (Adv.MS.34.6.19,f.1)

GENEALOGICAL notes concerning the family of Seton. [N.p., 1916.]
QZ/P28

LILLIE, William
A Lillie link between Setons and McInroys. (In *Scottish Genealogist,* vol.xxvii, no.3, September 1980, pp.85-9.)
ED/N-1 (Gen.7)

MAITLAND, Sir Richard
The genealogy of the House and surname of Setoun; with the chronicle of the House of Setoun, compiled in metre by James Kamington, alias Peter Manye. Edinburgh, 1830.
ED/N-1 (A.114.b.16) QZ/P40 SA/U-1
QZ/P10 GL/U-1 QZ/P-1 QZ/P99

— The history of the House of Seytoun to the year MDLIX; with the continuation by Alexander, Viscount Kingston, to MDCLXXXVII. Glasgow, 1829. (Maitland Club.)
ED/N-1 (Mait.Club.1) GL/U-1 QZ/L37
QZ/P-1 QZ/P16 QZ/P26 QZ/P34 QZ/P40
QZ/P99

SETON, Sir Bruce Gordon
The House of Seton: a study of lost causes. Edinburgh, 1939-41. 2v.
ED/N-1 (R.272.a) ED/N-2 SA/U-1 AD/U-1
GL/U-1 ED/U-1 QZ/P-1 QZ/P99

SETON, Sir George
A history of the family of Seton during eight centuries. Edinburgh, 1896. 2v.
ED/N-1 (Gen.8.5) ED/N-2 QZ/P11 SA/U-1
AD/U-1 GL/U-1 QZ/L37 ED/U-1 QZ/P-1
QZ/P99 QZ/P16

SETON, Robert
An old family, or, the Setons of Scotland and America. New York, 1899.
ED/N-1 (S.123.g) ED/N-2 AD/U-1 QZ/L37
SA/U-1 QZ/P-1 QZ/P99

Seton of Abercorn *see* **Gordon,** Lord Gordon

Seton, Earl of Dunfermline

SETON, George
Memoir of Alexander Seton, Earl of Dunfermline …; with an appendix containing a list of the various presidents of the court, and genealogical tables of the legal families of Erskine, Hope, Dalrymple and Dundas. Edinburgh, 1882.
ED/N-1 (R.181.f; L.C.1915) QZ/P16 QZ/L37

Seton, Lord Fyvie

STIRLING, Anna Maria D. W. Pickering
Fyvie Castle: its lairds and their times. London, 1928.
ED/N-1 (R.247.e) QZ/P30 QZ/P49 ED/U-1

Seton of Mounie

JOHNSTON, Dorothy B.
Letters and papers of the Setons of Mounie, Aberdeenshire, including the papers of Dr. James Anderson, 1739-1808. (In *Northern Scotland*, vol.5, no.1, 1982, pp.71-9.)
ED/N-1 (HJ3.345)

Seton of Parbroath

MARSHALL, Robert Seton
The last of the Setons of Parbroath, in Fife, and their cadets, the Setons of Dumbarrow in Fife and other Setons descended therefrom, etc. Corrections, additions and notes for the hitherto printed accounts concerning this branch of the Setons. Edinburgh, 1925.
QZ/L37

SETON, Robert
Seton of Parbroath in Scotland and America. New York, 1890.
ED/N-1 (Hall.199.a) SA/U-1 QZ/P99

Seton of Touch

GIBSON, John C.
The lands and lairds of Touch. Stirling, 1929.
ED/N-1 (5.1929) QZ/P14

Seton of Urquhart

CRAMOND, William
Cramondiana. Elgin, 1965.
ED/N-1 (NE.3.a.9)

Shand

SHAND, George
Some notices of the surname of Shand, particularly of the county of Aberdeen. Norwich, 1877.
ED/N-1 (S.121.g) ED/N-2 QZ/L37 QZ/P-1
QZ/P22

Shank of Castleny

GENEALOGICAL memoranda relating to the family of Schank or Shank of Castleny in the county of Fife. [N.p., n.d.]
ED/N-2

Shank of Castlerig

STODART, R. R.
Shank of Castlerig. 1875.
QZ/P99

WEAVING, E. G.
Genealogical memoranda relating to the family of Shank, or Schank of Castlerig in the county of Fife, N.B. London, 1885.
ED/N-1 (A.113.a) QZ/P-1

Shannon *see also* **MacShannon**

Shannon

CAMERON, Lolita Jean
The broad canvas: a history of my mother's family. Chesham, 1974.
ED/N-1 (6.2749) QZ/P-7 QZ/P-1

Sharp

['GENEALOGICAL notes concerning the family of Sharp'. 17--.]
ED/N-1 (Adv.MS.19.1.21,ff.189-93)

Sharp of Hoddam

NOTES on the Sharpe family of Hoddam, Dumfriesshire.
QZ/P99

Shaw

EXTRACTS from baptism, marriage and death records for the parishes of Alvie, Croy, Inverness, Kingussie and Inch, and Petty, relating to the name of Shaw. 17th and 18th centuries. (*MSS.*)
QZ/P40

MACKINTOSH, Alexander Mackintosh
A genealogical account of the Highland families of Shaw. London, 1877.
ED/N-1 (S.121.g) QZ/L37 QZ/P-1 QZ/P99

MARSHALL, G. F. L.
The Muir book. [N.p.], 1930.
ED/N-2

SHAW, Charles John
A history of Clan Shaw. Chichester, 1983.
QZ/P99

SHAW, Margaret
Memorial for Mrs. Houston. [Edinburgh, n.d.]
ED/N-1 (Ry.III.c.35(7))

SHAW, Norman
History of the Clan Shaw. Oxford, 1951.
ED/N-1 (6.714) DN/U-1 QZ/P27 QZ/P26
QZ/P40 SA/U-1 AD/U-1 QZ/P22 GL/U-1
QZ/L37 QZ/P28 QZ/P50 ED/U-1 QZ/P-1
QZ/P99

SHAW, William G.
History and memorials of the Clan Shaw. Dundee, 1868.
GL/U-1 QZ/L37 QZ/P-1 QZ/P40

— — Appendix to "Memorials of the Shaws". No. II. [Dundee, 1868?]
ED/N-1 (1974.91(11))

—Memorials of the Clan Shaw. Forfar, 1871.
ED/N-1 (S.120.g) GL/U-1 QZ/L37 QZ/P99

Shaw in Australia

McGILLIVRAY, P.

An Australian branch of Clan Shaw. (In *Clan Chattan*, vol.vii, no.1, 1977, pp.14-15.)
ED/N-1 (233 PER)

Shaw, Baron Craigmyle

VAUGHAN-THOMPSON, Isabel

For Elspeth: memories in six reigns from Aunt Isabel (Grantabel). [London], 1974.
ED/N-1 (6.2653)

Shaw of Glenshaw, U.S.A.

SHAW, Charles John

The Shaws of Glenshaw, Pennsylvania, U.S.A. (In *Clan Chattan*, vol.vii, no.4, 1980, pp.234-5.)
ED/N-1 (233 PER)

Shaw of Rothiemurches

['NOTES on the genealogy of the Shaw family of Rothiemurches'. 1833.]
ED/N-1 (MS.9854,ff.111-13)

Shaw of Sauchie

BROWN-MORISON, John Brown

Genealogical notes anent some ancient Scottish families. Perth, 1884.
QZ/P15   ED/N-2   QZ/P-1   QZ/P16

Shaw of Tordarroch

['GENEALOGICAL account of the Shaw family of Tordarroch'. 1833.]
ED/N-1 (MS.9854,ff.123-7)

Shedden

DOBIE, James

Memoir of William Wilson of Crummock. [Edinburgh], 1854.
ED/N-1 (Hall.260.a)

Shirres

SHIRRES, Christian

Sailing ships and sheep stations. Christchurch, N.Z., 1964.
QZ/P22

Shortreed

[A GENEALOGICAL table showing the antecedents of Robert Shortreed. N.p., 1844.]
ED/N-1 (7.106(66-9))

Sibbald

SIBBALD, William

Summons of proving the tenor, Sir William Sibbald, against Officers of State, 5th August 1834. [N.p.], 1834.
QZ/P99

Sibbald of Roxburghshire

SIBBALD, Susan Mein

Memoirs (1783-1812); edited by F. P. Hett. London, 1926.
ED/N-1 (S.130.c)   QZ/P-1   QZ/P99

Sibbald of Whitelaw

LANG, Patrick Sellar

The Langs of Selkirk, with some notes on the Sibbalds of Whitelaw. Melbourne, 1910.
ED/N-2   QZ/P99

Simpson

[A GENEALOGICAL table showing the antecedents of Robert Shortreed. N.p., 1844.]
ED/N-1 (7.106(66-9))

SIMPSON, G. A. F.

Outline of the genealogical roll which was founded in Eastern Prussia, 1691, by the Scottish emigrant, William Simpson, a native of Coupar Angus, Perthshire, Scotland. (In *Scottish Genealogist*, vol.xxvii, no.4, December 1980, pp.129-45.)
ED/N-1 (Gen.7)

Simpson in Linlithgowshire

SIMPSON, R. R.

Pedigree of the Linlithgowshire Simpsons, including pedigrees of the families of Cleland of Cleland, Jervies, Russells and Raleighs. Edinburgh, 1895.
ED/U-1

Simson

COUPER, William James

The Levitical family of Simson. Glasgow, 1934.
GL/U-1

— — (In *Records of the Scottish Church History Society*, vol.iv, 1931/2, no.1, pp.119-37, no.2, pp.208-66; vol.v, 1933/5, no.2, pp.117-39.)
ED/N-1 (NE.30.f)

LANG, Patrick Sellar

The Langs of Selkirk, with some notes on the Sibbalds of Whitelaw. Melbourne, 1910.
ED/N-2   QZ/P99

The RUDDIMANS mentioned in this history: [a genealogical table of the descendants of Andrew Simson]. [N.p., 1900?]
ED/N-1 (6.2320)

SIMSON, Archibald
Annals of such patriots of the distinguished family of Fraser, Frysell, Sim-son, or Fitz-simon. . . . Edinburgh, 1795.
ED/N-1 (Ry.I.2.142(18); A.114.d.8)
QZ/P40   QZ/P99

— — 2nd edition: edited by A. Fraser. Edinburgh, 1805.
ED/N-1 (6.769(11))   QZ/P40   QZ/P11

STEVENSON, Robert
The Simsons. [N.p.], 1867.
ED/N-1 (NE.25.c.3)   SA/U-1   QZ/P-1   QZ/P99

Sinclair *see also* St Clair

Sinclair

['GENEALOGICAL notes concerning the families of Sinclair'. 17--.]
ED/N-1 (Adv.MS.81.9.9,ff.86-123)

LAURENSON, Graeme
Burrafirth. New Zealand, 1982.
QZ/P41

MORRISON, Leonard Allison
The history of the Sinclair family in Europe and America. Boston, 1896.
ED/N-2   QZ/P40

OSLER, James Couper
Osler tree: [chart pedigree], with some supplementary notes on . . . Sinclairs. . . . [Dundee], 1924.
ED/N-2   QZ/L37

['PAPERS concerning the genealogy of the family of Sinclair'. 17--.]
ED/N-1 (Adv.MS.20.1.11,ff.73-122)

SAINT-CLAIR, Roland William
The Saint-Clairs of the Isles. Auckland, N.Z., 1898.
QZ/P-1   QZ/P41

SCOTT, James E.
The Sinclairs: their history and name. [N.p.], 1962. (*Typescript*)
QZ/P27

SELDEN, Jefferson Sinclair
The Sinclair family of Virginia: descendants of Henry Sinclair, born in Aberdeen, Scotland, the second son of the Earl of Caithness and his son John Sinclair, 1755-1820, and allied families. [N.p.], 1964.
ED/N-1 (H3.79.988)

SINCLAIR, Alexander Maclean
The Sinclairs of Roslin, Caithness and Goshen. Charlottetown, 1901.
ED/N-1 (NE.25.c.34)

SINCLAIR, James
Information for James Sinclair against William Sinclair of Ratter. [N.p.], 1769.
QZ/P99

SINCLAIR, Sir John
Information [signed A. Lockhart] for Sir J. Sinclair of Stevenson, Baronet . . . against Lady D. Sinclair, Countess Fife, and James Earl Fife, her husband, for his interest. [N.p.], 1766.
SA/U-1

THOMSON, David Couper
Some supplemental notes on Oslers. . . . [Dundee], 1924.
ED/N-1 (HP1.77.4104)

— Thomson, Couper, Yule, Sinclair genealogical chart. Dundee, [1936].
QZ/L37   QZ/P20   QZ/P99

Sinclair of Brabsterdorran
ST CLAIR, Roland William
Sinclairs of Brabsterdorran, Caithness. (In *Old-Lore Miscellany of Orkney, Shetland, Caithness and Sutherland,* vol.iv, 1911, pp.194-200.)
ED/N-1 (R.250.f)   QZ/P-1

Sinclair of Brecks
CLOUSTON, John Storer
James Sinclair of Brecks. (In *Proceedings of the Orkney Antiquarian Society,* vol.xv, 1937/9, pp.61-8.)
ED/N-1 (R.250.a)

Sinclair, Earl of Caithness
KELSEY, Jeanette Garr Washburn
A diverted inheritance. [With a genealogical table.] Philadelphia, 1904.
ED/N-1 (L.187.c)

Sinclair in England
SINCLAIR, Thomas
The Sinclairs of England. London, 1887.
ED/N-1 (A.35.f)   QZ/P40   QZ/P11

Sinclair of Lybster

ST CLAIR, Roland William

Sinclairs of Lybster, Caithness. (In *Old-Lore Miscellany of Orkney, Shetland, Caithness and Sutherland*, vol.iii, 1910, pp.226-9.)
ED/N-1 (R.250.f) QZ/P-1

Sinclair of Mey

DONALDSON, John E.

Caithness in the 18th century. Edinburgh, 1938.
ED/N-1 (R.250.f) ED/N-2 QZ/P-1

SINCLAIR, James

Pedigree of the Earls of Caithness and of the descent of Sir James Sinclair of May, Baronet, asserting his right to the title of Earl of Caithness. [N.p., 1795?]
ED/N-1 (Yule.168(4,5))

Sinclair, Earl of Orkney *see also* **Orkney,** Earldom of

Sinclair, Earl of Orkney

TULLOCH, Thomas

Diploma of Thomas, Bishop of Orkney and Zetland, addressed to Eric, King of Norway, respecting the genealogy of William St. Clair, Earl of Orkney; with a translation by Dean Thomas Guild ... 1554. Edinburgh, 1855. (In *Bannatyne Miscellany*, vol.iii, 1855, pp.61-85.)
ED/N-1 (Bann.Club.19B) QZ/P-1

Sinclair of Ratter

MACDONALD, Kenneth

The Castle of Girnigoe, and the Sinclairs of Ratter. Inverness, 1889.
ED/N-1 (1890.28(13)) QZ/P40 QZ/P-1 QZ/P99

Sinclair, Lord Sinclair

ST CLAIR, Charles

The case of Charles St Clair, Esq., claiming the title and dignity of Lord Sinclair. 1782.
ED/N-1 (Yule.162(2)) QZ/P-1

Sinclar of Longformacus

CARR-HARRIS, Grant

George Sinclar, early Scottish scientist. Part 2. (In *Scottish Genealogist*, vol.xxii, no.4, December 1975, pp.87-102.)
ED/N-1 (Gen.7)

Sinton

SINTON, Thomas

Family and genealogical sketches. Inverness, 1911.
ED/N-1 (R.172.b) QZ/P26 QZ/P22 QZ/P40 AD/U-1 DN/U-1 QZ/P-1 QZ/P99

Skene

[DESCENT of the family of Skene: folding genealogical table. N.p., n.d.]
SA/U-1 QZ/L37 QZ/P-1 QZ/P22 QZ/P30 QZ/P99

The FAMILY of Skene of Auchtertool, Dyce, Rubislaw, etc. (*MSS.*)
QZ/P-1

MEMORIALS of the family of Skene of Skene from the family papers, with other illustrative documents; edited by William Forbes Skene. Aberdeen, 1887. (New Spalding Club.)
ED/N-1 (New Spald.Club.1) ED/N-2 DN/U-1 ED/U-1 GL/U-1 ST/U-1 QZ/P-1 QZ/P30 QZ/P40 QZ/P99

['PAPERS concerning the genealogy of the family of Skene'. 17--.]
ED/N-1 (Adv.MS.20.1.11,ff.19-42)

Skinner

GENEALOGICAL notes concerning the family of Skinner. [N.p., 1916.]
QZ/P28

GENEALOGICAL tree of the Scottish family of Skinner; with MSS. additions for the 20th century. [N.p., n.d.]
QZ/P22

Slemons of Dumfriesshire

SLEMONS, John A.

A short account of the Slemons family. (In *Genealogical Quarterly*, vol.i, no.2, autumn 1932, pp.206-8.)
ED/N-1 (Y.232) DN/U-1

Sloan

DICKSON, Mora

The aunts. [With a genealogical table.] Edinburgh, 1981.
ED/N-1 (H3.81.4612)

Sloan of Garroch

SLOAN, William R.
Sir Hans Sloane, founder of the British Museum: legend and lineage. [With genealogical tables.] Helen's Bay, Co. Down, 1981.
ED/N-1 (H3.81.4190)

Small

GENEALOGICAL notes concerning the family of Small. [N.p., 1916.]
QZ/P28

Smart *see* **Imrie**

Smith

GRAZEBROOK, Henry Sydney
The heraldry of Smith. London, 1870.
ED/N-1 (E.114.d.9(1)) GL/U-1 QZ/L37
QZ/P-1 QZ/P99

READE, Compton
The Smith family: a popular account of most branches of the name, however spelt, from the 14th century downwards. London, 1902.
ED/N-1 (S.120.e) QZ/P22 ED/N-2 QZ/P-1
QZ/P99

SCOTT, M. P.
[Three MS. letters on Adam Smith to Charles B. Boog Watson. Glasgow, 1935.]
QZ/P99

SMITH, Francis Montagu
The heraldry of Smith in Scotland: supplement to Grazebrook's "Heraldry of Smith". London, 1873.
ED/N-1 (E.114.d.9(2)) GL/U-1 QZ/L37
QZ/P-1 QZ/P99

Smith in Aberdeen

SMITH, James
Genealogies of an Aberdeen family, 1540-1913. Aberdeen, 1913.
ED/N-1 (S.121.d) QZ/P30 QZ/P22 ED/U-1
QZ/P99

Smith in Brechin

NOTICE of the family of Smith, Smyth or Smytht, properly Lindsay of Brechin, Co. Forfar. [With a genealogical table.] [N.p., n.d.]
ED/N-1 (S.121.g)

Smith of Cromarty

RINGEREIDE, Mabel
The flourishing tree. Ottawa, Ont., 1977.
ED/N-1 (HP1.80.478) QZ/P40 (I)

Smith of Minmore

BULLOCH, John Malcolm
The Gordons and Smiths at Minmore, Auchorachan, and Upper Drumin in Glenlivet. Huntly, 1910.
ED/N-1 (R.172.e) QZ/P22 QZ/P50

Smith of Todhills

SMITH of Todhills: a genealogical roll. (*MS.*)
QZ/P-6

Smith of Tormiston, Orkney

LEITH, Peter
The Smiths of Tormiston. (In *Proceedings of the Orkney Antiquarian Society*, vol.xiii, 1934/5, pp.9-13.)
ED/N-1 (R.250.a)

Smollet

JOHNSON, Robert
The Smollet family and their descendants. (In *Shetland Folk Book*, vol.7, 1980, pp.1-6.)
ED/N-1 (R.250.a)

WATSON, Charles Brodie Boog
Traditions and genealogies of some members of the families of Boog, Heron, Leishman, Ross, Watson. Perth, 1908.
ED/N-1 (S.120.d) SA/U-1 QZ/P99

Smollett of Bonhill

IRVING, Joseph
The book of Dumbartonshire. Edinburgh, 1879.
ED/N-1 (R.286.c)

SMOLLETT, Tobias
Some account of the family of Smollett of Bonhill; with a series of letters hitherto unpublished; . . . arranged by J. Irving. Dumbarton, 1859.
ED/N-1 (MS.3786;A.114.b.23) QZ/P-1 QZ/P99

Snodgrass

BRISTOL, Nicholas Maclean
Alexander Snodgrass, mason and indweller in Coll. (In *Notes & Queries of the Society of West Highland Historical Research*, no.1, 30 November 1972, pp.1-3; no.2, 8 May 1973, p.13.)
ED/N-1 (P.med.3574)

Sobieski-Stuart *see also* **Stewart** or **Stuart,** The Royal House of

Sobieski-Stuart

BEVERIDGE, Hugh
The Sobieski-Stuarts: their claim to be descended
from Prince Charlie. Inverness, 1909.
ED/N-1 (S.154.a) QZ/P30 QZ/P40 AD/U-1
QZ/P22 QZ/P-1 QZ/P99

CRAIG, Archibald
The Sobieski Stuarts: a short sketch of their
remarkable career. Edinburgh, 1922.
ED/N-1 (5.2078) QZ/P-1 QZ/P99

NICHOLAS, Donald
The so-called Sobieski-Stewarts. (In *The Stewarts*,
vol.ix, 1951-3, pp.305-13.)
ED/N-1 (R.172.a)

Somerled

JOHNSTONE, James
Anecdotes of Olave the Black, King of Man, and
the Hebridean princes of the Somerled family.
[Copenhagen?], 1780.
ED/N-1 (A.88.e)

Somerville

NISBETT, Hamilton More *and* AGNEW, Stair
Carnegie
Cairnhill. Edinburgh, 1949.
ED/N-1 (R.272.f) QZ/P-3

['PAPERS concerning the genealogy of the family of
Somerville'. 1761?]
ED/N-1 (Adv.MS.20.1.9,ff.85-105)

SOMERVILLE, James
The baronial house of Somerville . . . Glasgow, 1920.
ED/N-1 (R.172.g) QZ/P56 ED/N-2 QZ/P26
GL/U-1 QZ/P-1 QZ/P99

SOMERVILLE, James Somerville, *11th Baron*
Memorie of the Somervills, [1066-1677, 1679?]
(*MSS.*)
QZ/P99

—Memorie of the Somervilles; edited by Sir W. Scott.
Edinburgh, 1815. 2v.
ED/N-1 (A.114.d) QZ/P53 QZ/P28 GL/U-1
QZ/L37 QZ/P56 ST/U-1 ED/U-1 QZ/P-1
QZ/P99

Somerville of Castlehaven, Ireland

SOMERVILLE, Edith Oenone *and* SOMERVILLE,
Boyle Townshend
Records of the Somerville family of Castlehaven &
Drishane from 1174-1940.
ED/N-1 (S.130.d)

Somerville of Drum

NISBETT, Hamilton More
Drum of the Somervilles. Edinburgh, 1928.
ED/N-1 (S.121.g) QZ/P22 DN/U-1 QZ/P99

Somerville, Lord Somerville

BAIN, Joseph
The dormant barony of Somerville. (In *The
Genealogist*, new series, vol.ix, 1893, pp.1-4.)
ED/N-1 (Y.215)

— — (Reprinted from *The Genealogist*, new series,
vol.ix, 1893.)
QZ/P-1

['A GENEALOGICAL account of Somerville, the
Lords Somerville'. 17--.]
ED/N-1 (Adv.MS.20.1.11,f.61)

Soulis

M'MICHAEL, Thomas
The feudal family of de Soulis. (In *Transactions of the
Dumfriesshire and Galloway Natural History &
Antiquarian Society*, 3rd series, vol.xxvi, 1947-8,
pp.163-93.)
ED/N-1 (J.187)

Southesk, Earldom of

CARNEGIE, Sir James
An act to relieve Sir James Carnegie of Southesk,
etc., from the effect of the attainder of James, fifth
Earl of Southesk . . . 2nd July, 1855.
QZ/P28

—Case . . . [N.p.], 1855.
QZ/P28

—Case of Sir James Carnegie of Southesk, Kinnaird
and Pittarrow, Bart., on his claim to the titles,
honour and dignities of Earl of Southesk, etc. 1848.
ED/N-1 (Yule.162.(16)) QZ/P28 QZ/L37

—Supplemental case. [N.p., 1853.]
ED/N-1 (Yule.162.(17)) QZ/P28 QZ/L37

—Minutes of evidence in the petition of Sir James
Carnegie of Kinnaird, Bt., claiming the Earldom of
Southesk. 1855.
QZ/P28

Spalding

S., F.J. *and* S., M.
Notes and traditions concerning the family of
Spalding. Liverpool, 1914.
ED/N-1 (NE.63.e.9) QZ/P99

SPALDING, Eduard
Geschichtliches Urkunden, Stamm-Tafeln der
Spalding in Schottland, Deutschland und
Schweden. Greifswald, 1898.
ED/N-1 (Mf.67(14))   ED/N-2   QZ/L37

Speir of Greenock
GENEALOGICAL roll of the Greenock Speirs. [N.p.,
n.d.]
QZ/P-6

Speirs of Elderslie
MITCHELL, John Oswald
The two Elderslies. Glasgow, 1884. (Reprinted from
the *Glasgow Herald*, 13 September 1884.)
QZ/P-1

Spence
OSLER, James Couper
Osler tree: [chart pedigree], with some supple-
mentary notes on . . . Spences. . . . [Dundee], 1924.
ED/N-2   QZ/L37

THOMSON, David Couper
Some supplemental notes on Oslers. . . . [Dundee],
1924.
ED/N-1 (HP1.77.4104)

Spencer
SPENCER, C. L.
Some notes on the Spencers, Jarvies and Rintouls in
Glasgow, compiled from family tradition and public
records. 1935. (*Typescript*)
QZ/P-1

Spens of Lathallan
['PAPERS concerning the genealogy of the family of
Spens of Lathallan'. 17--.]
ED/N-1 (Adv.MS.20.1.11,ff.125-33)

Spens of Wormiston
WATSON, Harry D.
Sir James Spens of Wormiston. [N.p.], 1981.
QZ/Q17

Spittal of Blairlogie
FERGUSSON, Robert Menzies
Logie: a parish history. Vol.2: Lands and landowners.
Paisley, 1905.
ED/N-1 (R.243.a)   QZ/P14

Spottiswoode
CAMPBELL, Charles
Genealogy of the Spottiswoode family in Scotland
and Virginia. Albany, 1868.
ED/N-2

GIBSON, John C.
Lands and lairds of Dunipace. Stirling, 1903.
ED/N-1 (5.150;R.243.f;Ry.I.3.311)   QZ/P-1
QZ/P99

Spottiswoode of Spottiswoode
['GENEALOGICAL notes and a table concerning the
Spottiswoode family of Spottiswoode'. 19--.]
ED/N-1 (MS.2936,ff.168-76)

HAY, Augustin
Genealogy from the MS. collection . . . of the family
of Spottiswoode. [1844.]
GL/U-1   QZ/P-1   QZ/P99

Spreull
BUCHANAN, Leslie
Cowdonhill mansion and the Glasgow family of
Spreull, miscellaneous notes, letters, prints, etc.
[1924-27?] (*MS.*)
ED/N-2   QZ/P-1

SPREULL, J. M. *and* SPREULL, G. J.
Notes on the family of Spreull. Glasgow, 1915.
ED/N-1 (S.120.i)   ED/N-2   QZ/P-1   QZ/L37

Sprunt
CRICHTON, Anne Sprunt
Some Sprunts in Scotland. Wilmington, N.C., 1964.
ED/N-2   SA/U-1   QZ/P26   QZ/P99

Spynie, Lord Spynie *see also* **Fullarton**

Spynie, Lord Spynie
FULLARTON, William
Case of William Fullarton, Esquire, claiming the
title and dignity of Lord Spynie before the Lords
Committee of Privileges. 2 parts. [N.p., 1785.]
ED/N-1 (Yule.162(3,4))

MAIDMENT, James
Reports of claims . . . to the House of Lords . . . of
the Cassillis, Sutherland, Spynie and Glencairn
peerages, 1760-1797. Edinburgh, 1840.
ED/N-1 (Yule.94)   QZ/L37

— — Reprinted. Edinburgh, 1882.
ED/N-1 (Law)   DN/U-1   GL/U-1   QZ/P-1

The SPYNIE peerage, 1785. [Edinburgh?], 1785.
ED/N-1 (Ry.I.4.136)

Stair, Earl of *see* **Dalrymple,** Earl of Stair

Stavert
STAVERT, W. J.
A chapter in mediocrity. [N.p.], 1896.
ED/N-2

Stedman of Kinross
['MEMORANDUM books with genealogical notes
concerning the Stedman family of Kinross'.
1734-1735.]
ED/N-1 (MS.5151,f.31-8)

Steel
GENEALOGICAL notes concerning the family of Steel.
[N.p., 1916.]
QZ/P28

KERR, Robert Malcolm
Nugae antiquae. Glasgow, 1847-9.
GL/U-1

Steel of Annathill
BLACK, William George
A note on the family of Black of Over Abington . . .
with memoranda on . . . Steel of Annathill. Glasgow,
1908.
GL/U-1   QZ/L37

— — [2nd ed.] Glasgow, 1924.
ED/N-1 (S.121.e)   ED/N-2   QZ/P22   QZ/Q71
QZ/P99

Steele
STEELE, Campbell
Some Steeles in Lesmahagow and their descendants.
(In *Scottish Genealogist*, vol.xxvi, no.2, June 1979,
pp. 33-47.)
ED/N-1 (Gen.7)

STEVENSON, Robert
The Simsons. [N.p.], 1867.
ED/N-1 (NE.25.c.3)   QZ/P99

Stein
BOASE, Edward R.
The family of Stein, or Stevin, Clackmannanshire;
from notes by Miss Margaret Haig, Lochrin, 1841.
Edinburgh, 1936.
ED/N-1 (R.272.a.1(1))

Stephen
STEPHEN, Lessel P.
A history of the Stephen family in Conglass,
together with a genealogical table. [London], 1913.
ED/N-1 (R.172.g)

Stephen of Linthouse
CARVELL, John Lees
A record of two hundred years of shipbuilding,
1750-1950. [With a genealogical table.] Glasgow,
[1951].
ED/N-1 (X.88.c)

— Stephen of Linthouse: a record of two hundred
years of shipbuilding, 1750-1950. Glasgow, 1950.
ED/N-1 (X.88.c)   QZ/P-1   QZ/P28   QZ/P52
(Unconfirmed location)

A SHIPBUILDING history, 1750-1932: a record of the
business founded about 1750, by Alexander Stephen
at Burghead, and subsequently carried on at
Aberdeen, Arbroath, Dundee and Glasgow.
London, 1932.
ED/N-1 (Wordie.53;T.311.e)   QZ/P-1   QZ/P52
(Unconfirmed location)

Steuart *see also* **Stewart, Stuart**

Steuart
FITTIS, Robert Scott
Old Perthshire families. (*Miscellanea Perthensis*,
1853-61, newspaper cutting no. 76.)
QZ/P26

STEUART, Daniel Rankin
Bygone days. [With a genealogical table.]
Edinburgh, 1936.
ED/N-1 (R.182.h)

STEUART, Katherine
By Allan water: the story of an old house.
Edinburgh, 1901.
ED/N-1 (R.245.g;NE.1369.b.7)   QZ/P14   QZ/P-6
QZ/P-7   QZ/P-1

— — [N.p.], 1903.
QZ/P14   QZ/P34

STEWART, R. M.
Steuarts of Ballechin, Perthshire. (In *The Stewarts*,
vol.xii, 1964-7, pp.192-7.)
ED/N-1 (R.172.a)

Steuart of Allanbank
['GENEALOGICAL account of the Steuart family of
Allanbank'. 1790?]
ED/N-1 (Adv.MS.6.1.12.,ff.62-4)

Steuart of Allanton
[LETTERS and papers of the genealogical history of
the Steuart family of Allanton. 1817.]
ED/N-1 (Adv.MS.26.2.9)

Steuart of Annat

HENDERSON, C. Stewart
Lieutenant-General Robert Stuart of Rait. (In *The Stewarts*, vol.viii, 1946-50, pp.293-303.)
ED/N-1 (R.172.a)

Steuart of Brownlee

STEUART, W. O.
Pioneers in Australia. (In *The Stewarts*, vol.ix, 1951-3, pp.73-84.)
ED/N-1 (R.172.a)

The STEUARTS of Brownlee etc. (In *The Stewarts*, vol.iv, pp.77-94.)
ED/N-1 (R.172.a)

Steuart of Steuarthall

STEUART, George
Pedigree showing the descent of the family of Lt. Gen. George Mackenzie Steuart.... Edinburgh, 1855.
QZ/L37   QZ/P-1   QZ/P99

Stevenson

A COMPANY history [of A. & J. MacNab Ltd., Slateford, Edinburgh]. Edinburgh, 1960.
ED/N-1 (NG.1297.f.8)   QZ/P99

HAMILTON-GRIERSON, Sir Philip J.
The Kirkos of Glenesland, Bogrie, Chapel and Sundaywell (In *Transactions of the Dumfriesshire and Galloway Natural History & Antiquarian Society*, 3rd series, vol.iii, 1914-15, pp.222-41.)
ED/N-1 (J.187)

MAIR, Craig
A star for seamen: the Stevenson family of engineers. London, 1978.
ED/N-1 (H3.78.5564)   QZ/P99

STEVENSON, Hew Shannan
The Stevenson family: a record of the descendants of James Stevenson, burgess of Paisley in 1753. York, 1965.
ED/N-1 (NE.25.a.21)   GL/U-1   QZ/P-1   QZ/P-6
QZ/P53   QZ/P99

STEVENSON, Margaretha
Stevenson family history from the eastern shore of Maryland to Woodford County to Putnam County. 1966.
QZ/P99

STEVENSON, Robert
The Simsons. [N.p.], 1867.
ED/N-1 (NE.25.c.3)   ED/N-2   QZ/P-1   QZ/P99

STEVENSON, Robert Louis
Records of a family of engineers. London, 1912.
ED/N-1 (F5.e.23)   ED/N-2   QZ/P-7   QZ/P28
QZ/P-6   QZ/P41   QZ/P-1   QZ/P99

Stevin *see* **Stein**

Stewart *see also* **Steuart, Stuart**

Stewart

CARRICK, Andrew
Some account of the ancient Earldom of Carric. To which are prefixed notices of the Earldom after it came into the families of De Bruce and Stewart, by James Maidment. Edinburgh, 1857.
ED/N-1 (Ry.II.e.31)   QZ/P-1

CLAN STEWART SOCIETY
Constitution and rules. Glasgow, [n.d.].
QZ/P-1

—1st-4th annual report and list of members, 1900-1902/3; 6th annual report. Glasgow, [n.d.].
QZ/P-1

EAST, Sir Ronald
The Kiel family and related Scottish pioneers: Findlays, Hossacks, Gilberts, Camerons, Stewarts, McAlpins, McCallums, McDonalds. [Victoria, 1974.] (*A Family Who's Who*, vol.2.)
ED/N-1 (NE.26.d.3)   ED/N-2   GL/U-1   QZ/P50

[A GENEALOGICAL account and genealogical tables relating to the history of the family of Stewart. 1788-98.]
ED/N-1 (MS.5331)

[GENEALOGICAL history of the family of the Stewarts. [N.p., n.d.]
QZ/P-6

[GENEALOGICAL material on the Stuarts. 1805.]
ED/N-1 (MS.14270)

[GENEALOGICAL notes concerning the family of Stewart. 19--.]
ED/N-1 (MS.2113)

['GENEALOGICAL notes concerning the family of Stuart'. 1712.]
ED/N-1 (Adv.MS.34.6.24,ff.153-5)

[GENEALOGY of the family of Stewart. 16--, 17--.]
ED/N-1 (Adv.MS.6.1.12)

JOHNSTON, George Harvey
  The heraldry of the Stewarts, with notes on all the males of the family, etc. Edinburgh, 1906.
  ED/N-1 (S.120.c;Hall.139.c) QZ/P27 QZ/L37
  QZ/P99

NICOLL, Isobel M.
  A Stuart story, as told by some descendants for their descendants. [St Andrews], 1981.
  ED/N-1 (HP2.81.1338) ED/S10

ROBERTSON, William
  Ayrshire, its history and historic families.
  Kilmarnock, 1908. 2v.
  ED/N-1 (Hist.S.91.A)

SEAVER, J. Montgomery
  Stewart family records. Philadelphia, [1940?].
  ED/N-1 (NF.1375.a.10)

SINCLAIR, Alexander
  Miscellaneous notices of Scotch families. [N.p., n.d.]
  ED/N-1 (3.2501(8))

STEWART Clan Magazine; editor: George Thomas Edson. Vol.6, no.1 (July 1927)-vol.48, no.6 (December 1970). Minden, Nebraska, 1927-70.
  ED/N-1 (NG.730)

The STEWART possessions of old. (In *The Stewarts*, vol.vi, 1930, pp.1-9.)
  ED/N-1 (R.172.a)

STEWART SOCIETY
  Annual report and list of members. 1902-4, 1906-12, 1914, 1953-5. Edinburgh, 1906-13.
  ED/U-1* QZ/P-1

— Roll of honour. Edinburgh, 1914-16.
  QZ/P99

— The Stewarts: a historical and general magazine for the Stewart Society. Vol.i, no.1(1902)-vol.xii(1967).
  ED/N-1 (R.172.a) ED/N-2* ED/U-1*
  QZ/L37 QZ/P26* QZ/P-1* QZ/P99

STEWART, Agnes Violet Averil
  Family tapestry. London, 1961.
  ED/N-1 (NF.1332.a.16) QZ/P56

STEWART, Charles W. A.
  A short account of Clann Mhic Alastair (the children or descendants of Alexander) Cam Chasach (Cross-legged) Leonac (Lennox) Stewart.
  Perth, 1898.
  QZ/P26

STEWART, J. K.
  Address in response to the toast of "The Stewart Society" at the annual dinner, 1904.
  QZ/P-1

— The story of the Stewarts. Edinburgh, 1901.
  ED/N-1 (S.120.d) SA/U-1 QZ/P27 AD/U-1
  QZ/L37 GL/U-1 QZ/P-1 QZ/P99

STEWART, John
  An old bond of association. (In *The Stewarts*, vol.ix, 1951-3, pp.260-2.)
  ED/N-1 (R.172.a)

— The Stewarts: the highland branches of a royal name. Edinburgh, 1954.
  ED/N-1 (Gen.7) QZ/P53 QZ/Q17 QZ/P27
  QZ/P26 QZ/P40 QZ/P22 QZ/P11 QZ/L37
  QZ/P-6 ED/N-2 SA/U-1 ED/U-1 QZ/P99
  QZ/P16

— — 2nd ed. [N.p.], 1963.
  ED/N-2 QZ/P15 QZ/P40 QZ/P99

— — 4th ed. Edinburgh, 1979.
  ED/N-1 (HP1.80.2917) QZ/P-1 QZ/P22
  QZ/P56 QZ/P99

STEWART, John Alexander
  Stewart arms. (In *The Stewarts;* part 1, vol.viii, 1946-50, pp.281-92; part 2, vol.ix, 1951-3, pp.54-65.)
  ED/N-1 (R.172.a)

— Stewart arms; recent matriculations and grants.
  Glasgow, 1924.
  ED/N-1 (5.476) SA/U-1 QZ/P-1 QZ/P99

THOMSON, Elizabeth M.
  Notes re Egidia Stewart regarding the Lindsays.
  [N.d.] (*MSS.*)
  QZ/P-6

WALTER Stewart, crusader . . . and his descendants.
  [N.p., n.d.]
  QZ/P99

WORTLEY, Violet Hunter Stuart
  Highcliffe and the Stuarts. London, 1927.
  ED/N-1 (S.127.f)

Stewart in Aberdeenshire
  [STEWARTS in the shires of Aberdeen, Moray and Banff.] (In *The Stewarts*, vol.vi, 1930, pp.83-8.)
  ED/N-1 (R.172.a)

Stewart of Acholgie

STEWART, Agnes M.
Stewarts in the shires of Aberdeen, Banff and Moray.
(In *The Stewarts*, vol.vi, 1930, pp.56-61.)
ED/N-1 (R.172.a)

Stewart, Duke of Albany

FRASER, Sir William
The Dukes of Albany and their castle of Doune.
Edinburgh, 1881. (Reprinted from his *Red Book of
Menteith*. 1880.)
ED/N-1 (S.123.f) QZ/P26 SA/U-1 ED/U-1
QZ/P99

Stewart of Allanton

The COLTNESS collections. MDCVIII-
MDCCCXL; edited by James Dennistoun. [With a
genealogical table.] Edinburgh, 1842. (Maitland
Club.)
ED/N-1 (Mait.Club.58) ED/U-1 GL/U-1
QZ/L37 QZ/P-1 QZ/P40 QZ/P56 QZ/P99

['GENEALOGICAL account of the Stewart family of
Coltness'. 1790?]
ED/N-1 (Adv.MS.6.1.12,ff.47-51)

RIDDELL, John
The Salt-foot controversy as it appeared in
Blackwood's Magazine. Edinburgh, 1818.
ED/N-1 (A.114.c) QZ/P53 ED/N-2 AD/U-1
GL/U-1 QZ/L37 QZ/P-1 QZ/P99

Stewart in America

STEWART, Bradford Alan
Indian fighters with Boone. (In *The Stewarts*, vol.ix,
1951-3, pp.329-31.)
ED/N-1 (R.172.a)

Stewart of Annat

STEWART, John
The Stewarts of Annat, Ballachallan and Craigtoun.
(In *The Stewarts*, vol.xi, 1960-3, pp.149-56.)
ED/N-1 (R.172.a)

Stewart of Appin

DEWAR, John
The Dewar manuscripts: Scottish West Highland
folk tales. [With genealogical tables.] Vol.1. Glasgow,
1964.
ED/N-1 (Lit.S.62)

The REVEREND John Stirton, M.V.D., D.D., Minister
of Crathie and domestic chaplain to H.M. the King.
(In *The Stewarts*, vol.vi, 1930, pp.37-44.)
ED/N-1 (R.172.a)

STEWART, Ian M.
Clan Stewart of Appin. (In *The Stewarts*, vol.xv,
no.4, 1979, pp.285-9.)
ED/N-1 (R.172.a)

STEWART, John H. J. *and* STEWART, Duncan
The Stewarts of Appin. Edinburgh, 1880.
ED/N-1 (A.113.a;R.290.e) QZ/P27 QZ/P30
SA/U-1 AD/U-1 GL/U-1 QZ/L37 ED/U-1
QZ/P-1 QZ/P99

Stewart of Ardgowan

CAMPBELL, Colin
Inverneill and the Stewarts of Ardgowan. (In *The
Stewarts*, vol.ix, 1951-4, pp.335-40.)
ED/N-1 (R.172.a)

— — (Reprinted from *The Stewarts*, vol.ix, 1951-4.)
ED/N-1 (1965.26)

Stewart in Arran

STEWART, Gershom
Stewarts in Arran. (In *The Stewarts*, vol.xvi, no.1,
1980, pp.29-31.)
ED/N-1 (R.172.a)

Stewart of Ballachallan

STEWART, John
Stewarts of Ballachallan. (In *The Stewarts*, vol.xi,
1960-3, pp.217-21.)
ED/N-1 (R.172.a)

Stewart of Ballechin *see* **Stewart** of Kynachan

Stewart of Balloan

STEWART, Charles Poyntz
The Balloan tradition. (Reprinted from *The Stewarts*,
vol.iii, 1912-16.)
QZ/P26

— The legend of Balloan. (Reprinted from *The
Stewarts*, vol.iii, 1912-16.)
QZ/P-1 QZ/L37

Stewart of Balnakeilly

MONCREIFFE, Sir Iain
The Stewarts of Balnakeilly. (In *The Stewarts*,
vol.xvi, no.1, 1980, pp.42-52.)
ED/N-1 (R.172.a)

Stewart in Banff

STEWARTS in the shires of Aberdeen, Moray and
Banff. (In *The Stewarts*, vol.vi, 1930, pp.75-81.)
ED/N-1 (R.172.a)

Stewart, Earl of Carrick *see* **Carrick,** Earldom of

Stewart of Coltness *see* **Stewart** of Allanton

Stewart of Craigiehall
STEWART, J. K.
The Stewarts of Craigiehall: further discoveries. (In *The Stewarts*, vol.vii, 1934, pp.112-17.)
ED/N-1 (R.172.a)

STEWART, William Burton
Records of the Stewarts of Craigiehall, Newhalls and the Leuchold. Alnmouth, 1933. (*Typescript*)
ED/N-2   QZ/L37

— Sir Henry Stewart of Craigiehall: his estate and family. (In *The Stewarts*, vol.vii, 1934, pp.50-82.)
ED/N-1 (R.172.a)

Stewart of Darnley
FENWICK, Hubert
City of the Stewarts: Aubigny-sur-Nere and the Stewarts of Darnley. (In *The Stewarts*, vol.xv, no.1, 1976, pp.27-9.)
ED/N-1 (R.172.a)

STUART, Andrew
Genealogical history of the Stewarts. . . . London, 1798.
ED/N-1 (A.114.b)   ED/N-2   QZ/P40   SA/U-1   QZ/L37   QZ/P99   QZ/P49   GL/U-1   QZ/Q91   QZ/P-1

WILLIAMS, E.
Abstract of the evidence adduced to prove that Sir William Stewart of Jedworth, the paternal ancestor of the present Earl of Galloway, was the second son of Sir Alex. Stewart of Darnley. London, 1801.
SA/U-1   QZ/P-1   QZ/P99

Stewart of Drumin
BULLOCH, John Malcolm
Stewarts of Drumin and Pettyvaich. (In *Transactions of the Banffshire Field Club*, 5 December 1933, pp.76-90.)
ED/N-1 (NE.3.g.1)   QZ/P99   (*Xerox*)

STEWART, Hugh F.
Stewarts in the shires of Aberdeen, Banff, and Moray. (In *The Stewarts*, vol.vi, 1930. pp.67-75.)
ED/N-1 (R.172.a)

Stewart of Drumlin
MATHESON, W. S.
The Stewarts of Drumlin. 1933. (*MS.*)
QZ/P22

Stewart in England
STEWARD, Sir Henry
Record of a branch of the Stewart family; edited by Lady G. S. Steward. [N.p.], 1954.
QZ/L37

Stewart of Fasnacloich
HENDERSON, C. Stewart
Notes on some Fasnacloich charters. (In *The Stewarts*, vol.x, 1955-8, pp.160-61.)
ED/N-1 (R.172.a)

Stewart of Fincastle
FITTIS, Robert Scott
The auld Stewarts of Atholl. (*Miscellanea Perthensis*, 1853-61, newscutting no.55.)
QZ/P26

Stewart of Forthergill
STEWART, Charles Poyntz
Historic memorials of the Stewarts of Forthergill, Perthshire, and their male descendants. . . . Edinburgh, 1879.
ED/N-1 (A.113.a)   QZ/P26   GL/U-1   QZ/L37   SA/U-1   AD/U-1   ED/U-1   QZ/P-1   QZ/P99

— — A sequel. (Reprinted from *The Stewarts*, vols iii, iv, 1912-16.)
ED/N-1 (S.122.d)

Stewart in Galloway
STEWART, G. Macleod
The Stewart family. [N.d.].
QZ/P10 (Unconfirmed location)

— The Stewart family in Galloway. Dumfries, 1914. (*Galloway records*, vol.1.)
QZ/P99

Stewart, Earl of Galloway
DESCENT of the Earls of Galloway: a view of the evidence for proving that the present Earl of Galloway is the lineal heir-male and lawfull representative of Sir William Stewart of Jedworth. [With a genealogical table.] [N.p., 1795.]
ED/N-1 (NE.25.h.10)

Stewart of Garth *see also* **Fergusson** of Dunfallandy

Stewart of Garth
The REVEREND John Stirton, M.V.D., D.D., Minister Minister of Crathie and domestic chaplain to H.M. the King. (In *The Stewarts*, vol.vi, 1930, pp.37-44.)
ED/N-1 (R.172.a)

Stewart of Glenbucky

STEWART, John
Stewarts of Glenbucky. (In *The Stewarts*, vol.viii,
1946-50, pp.314-15.)
ED/N-1 (R.172.a)

Stewart of Glenfinglas

STEWART, J. W.
The Glenfinglas Stewarts. (In *The Stewarts*, vol.xvi,
no.1, 1980, pp.25-8.)
ED/N-1 (R.172.a)

Stewart of Goodtrees *see* **Stewart** of Allanton

Stewart of Grandtully

FRASER, Sir William
The Red book of Grandtully. Edinburgh, 1868. 2v.
ED/N-1 (Gen.8.G)   QZ/P26   SA/U-1   AD/U-1
GL/U-1   ED/N-2   QZ/P30   ED/U-1   QZ/P-1
QZ/P99

['PAPERS concerning genealogy of the Stewart
family of Grandtully'. 17--.]
ED/N-1 (Adv.MS.20.1.11,ff.45,58)

Stewart of Innerhadden

STEWART, Robert
Stewarts of Innerhadden. (In *The Stewarts*, vol.ix,
1951-3, pp.301-4.)
ED/N-1 (R.172.a)

Stewart of Invernahyle

LINNEY, D. S.
Stewarts of Invernahyle. (In *The Stewarts*, vol.x,
1955-8, pp.143-6.)
ED/N-1 (R.172.a)

Stewart in Inverness

['A GENEALOGICAL account of the Stewart family of
Inverness'. 1833.]
ED/N-1 (MS.9854,ff.100-1)

Stewart of Jedworth *see* **Stewart** of Darnley

Stewart of Kincraigie

HENDERSON, C. S.
Stewarts of Kincraigie. (In *The Stewarts*, vol.ix,
1951-3, pp.204-13.)
ED/N-1 (R.172.a)

Stewart of Kirkfield

['GENEALOGICAL accounts of the Stewart family of
Kirkfield'. 1790?]
ED/N-1 (Adv.MS.6.1.12,ff.23-51)

Stewart of Kynachan

HENDERSON, C. Stewart
The wandering Scot: Captain John Stewart of
Houston's regiment in the Dutch service, 1700-1784.
(In *The Stewarts*, vol.vii, 1934, pp.93-109.)
ED/N-1 (R.172.a)

SINTON, Thomas
Family and genealogical sketches. Inverness, 1911.
ED/N-1 (R.172.b)   AD/U-1   DN/U-1   QZ/P-1
QZ/P22   QZ/P30   QZ/P40   QZ/P99

Stewart, Earl of Lennox *see also* **Lennox,** Earldom of

Stewart, Earl of Lennox

[COLLECTION of genealogical papers concerning the
Stewart family of Lennox. 1788-9.]
ED/N-1 (MS.8320)

STUART, Andrew
Genealogical history of the Stewarts. . . . London,
1798.
ED/N-1 (A.114.b)   ED/N-2   QZ/P40   SA/U-1
GL/U-1   QZ/P49   QZ/P99

WINGFIELD-STRATFORD, Esme
The Lords of Cobham Hall. London, 1959.
ED/N-1 (NE.63.g.2)   ED/N-2   QZ/P-1

Stewart of Lorne

MACPHAIL, J. R. N.
The descent of the Stewarts of Lorne. (In *The
Stewarts*, vol.vi, 1930, pp.10-21.)
ED/N-1 (R.172.a)

Stewart of Massater, Orkney

STEWART, R. A. Clapperton
The Stewarts of Massater, Orkney. (In *Old-Lore
Miscellany of Orkney, Shetland, Caithness and
Sutherland*, vol.vi, 1913, pp.202-8.)
ED/N-1 (R.250.f)   QZ/P-1

Stewart of Menteith

BURNETT, George
The Red book of Menteith reviewed. Edinburgh,
1881.
ED/N-1 (S.122.e)   QZ/P22   SA/U-1   AD/U-1

FRASER, Sir William
The Red book of Menteith. Edinburgh, 1880. 2v.
ED/N-1 (Gen.8.G;Gen.8.M)   SA/U-1   GL/U-1
QZ/P14   AD/U-1   QZ/P49   QZ/P-1   QZ/P99

HUTCHISON, Andrew F.
The Lake of Menteith . . . with historical accounts of . . . the Earldom of Menteith. Stirling, 1899.
QZ/P22   QZ/P-1

STEWART, J. K.
The Lake of Menteith and its feudal lords. (In *The Stewarts*, vol.iv, pp.299-331.)
ED/N-1 (R.172.a)

— — (Reprinted from *The Stewarts*, vol.iv.)
ED/N-1 (NE.6.a.5)   SA/U-1   QZ/P-1   QZ/P14   QZ/P22

STEWART, John Alexander
Inchmahome and the Lake of Menteith. Edinburgh, 1933.
ED/N-1 (R.290.e)

Stewart in Moray
[STEWARTS in the Shires of Aberdeen, Banff and Moray.] (In *The Stewarts*, vol.vi, 1930, pp.56-61.)
ED/N-1 (R.172.a)

Stewart, Earl of Orkney *see* **Orkney,** Earldom of

Stewart in Orkney
STEUART, A. F.
Orkney news from the letter-bag of Mr. Charles Steuart. (In *Old-Lore Miscellany of Orkney, Shetland, Caithness and Sutherland*, vol.vi, 1913, pp.41-9, 101-9.)
ED/N-1 (R.250.f)   QZ/P-1

Stewart of Stewart Castle, Jamaica
CARDEW, Gertrude Marion
James Stewart of Stewart Castle in Jamaica, 1763-1828. (In *The Stewarts*, vol.x, 1955-8, pp.35-42.)
ED/N-1 (R.172.a)

— Stewart Castle, Jamaica. (In *The Stewarts*, vol.x, 1955-8, pp.276-8.)
ED/N-1 (R.172.a)

Stewart of Stewart Castle, N.S.W., Australia
CARDEW, Gertrude Marion
James Stewart of Stewart Castle in New South Wales, Australia, 1850. (In *The Stewarts*, vol.x, 1955-8, pp.147-59.)
ED/N-1 (R.172.a)

Stewart of Stewartfield
STEWART, J. K.
The Stewarts of Stewartfield: a tragic episode of the Borders. (In *The Stewarts*, vol.vi, 1930, pp.191-9.)
ED/N-1 (R.172.a)

Stewart in Strathdon
STEWARTS in the shires of Aberdeen, Banff and Moray. (In *The Stewarts*, vol.vi, 1930, pp.61-6.)
ED/N-1 (R.172.a)

Stewart, Earl of Strathearn *see* **Strathearn,** Earldom of

Stewart of Strathgarry
STEWART, Sir Kenneth D.
The Stewarts of Strathgarry. (In *The Stewarts*, vol.x, 1955-8, pp.238-40.)
ED/N-1 (R.172.a)

Stewart of Traquair
HENDERSON, C. Stewart
The Stuarts of Traquair. (In *The Stewarts*, vol.viii, 1947/50, pp.13-25.)
ED/N-1 (R.172.a)

— — (Reprinted from *The Stewarts*, vol.viii, 1947/50.)
QZ/P-1   QZ/P99

PINE, Leslie Gilbert
The history of the Stuarts, Earls of Traquair, Barons Linton of Cabarston and Charles Edward Traquair Stuart-Linton. [London], 1940.
ED/N-1 (1966.184)   ED/N-2   QZ/L37

STUART-LINTON, Charles E. T.
Letters to Traquair, 1773-1882. (In *The Stewarts*, vol.ix, 1951-3, pp.214-29.)
ED/N-1 (R.172.a)

Stewart of Urrard
ALSTON-STEWART, Francis Louisa
Genealogical account of the Stewarts of Urard. [N.p., 1960?]
ED/N-1 (HP4.80.33)

Stewart of Williamwood
STEWARTS in the shires of Aberdeen, Moray and Banff. (In *The Stewarts*, vol.vi, 1930, pp.81-3.)
ED/N-1 (R.172.a)

Stewart-Mackenzie of Seaforth *see also* **Mackenzie,** Earl of Seaforth

Stewart-Mackenzie of Seaforth
REPRESENTATION of the family of Seaforth in 1829. Inverness, 1867. (*MS.*)
QZ/P40

Stewart-Murray, Duke of Atholl

MONCREIFFE, Sir Iain
The Atholl arms. (In *Coat of Arms*, vol.iv, 1956-8, pp.7-12.)
ED/N-1 (NJ.689)

Stewart or Stuart, The Royal House of

ADDINGTON, Arthur Charles
The Royal House of Stuart: descendants of James VI of Scotland, James I of England. London, 1969-76. 3v.
ED/N-1 (Gen.8.S) ED/N-2 DN/U-1 QZ/P-1 QZ/P-7 QZ/P30

AENEAS and his two sons: a true portrait. London, [1746].
ED/N-1 (Ry.I.5.240)

AHAB'S evil: secret history of the family of the Stuarts. London, 1720.
QZ/P40

ARONSON, Theo
Kings over the water: the saga of the Stuart Pretenders. London, 1979.
ED/N-1 (H3.79.3343) QZ/P99

ASHLEY, Maurice
The House of Stuart: its rise and fall. London, 1980.
ED/N-1 (H3.80.3214) DN/U-1 QZ/P99

BARNARD, Percy Mordaunt
A catalogue of books, tracts, and autographs of or relating to the Stuarts and their period offered for sale by P. M. Barnard. [Tunbridge Wells, n.d.]
ED/N-1 (1959.17(16))

BROWN, John
An historical and genealogical tree of the Royal family of Scotland from the most early accounts to the present time. London, [1797].
ED/N-1 (Newb.4251;P.m.1.b.3)

BROWNE, Sir Anthony
The right of succession to the crown of England, in the family of the Stuarts, exclusive of Mary, Queen of Scots, learnedly asserted . . . by Sir Nicholas Bacon . . . against Sir A. Brown . . . published from the original MS. by Nathaniel Boothe. . . . London, 1723.
ED/N-1 (Ry.I.5.137) QZ/P99

CALENDAR of the Stuart papers belonging to His Majesty the King, preserved at Windsor Castle; [edited by F. H. Daniell]. London, 1902-23. 7v.
ED/N-1 (GRH.5/56) QZ/P14

CAMPANA, Emilia
Les derniers Stuarts à Saint-Germain en Laye. Paris, 1871. 2v.
ED/N-1 (A.112.b) ED/N-2 QZ/P-1 QZ/P99

CARTE genealogique de la Maison de Stuart dans la quelle l'on fait observer son origine, ses branches, ses armes, et ses alliances. [N.p., 1705.]
ED/N-1 (NF.1540.e.16(2))

CASSAVETTI, Eileen
The lion and the lilies: the Stuarts and France. London, 1977.
ED/N-1 (H3.78.3552) QZ/P99

[CATALOGUE of an] exhibition of the Royal House of Stuart, New Gallery, 1889. [London, 1889.]
ED/N-1 (Blk.260;K.220.a;Dur.937(1)) ED/N-2 QZ/P99

A CATALOGUE of books, MSS., and portraits relative to the Stuarts, their friends, their enemies and their times, on sale by Ellis. London, [1912].
ED/N-1 (NG.1194.d.10)

CATALOGUE of books, pamphlets, etc. in the Stuart and Jacobite collection [of the] Aberdeen University Library Macbean Collection. 1949.
ED/N-1 (T.465.b) QZ/P99

COISSAC DE CHAVREBIÈRE,
Histoire des Stuarts. Paris, 1930.
ED/N-1 (X.193.f) QZ/P-1 QZ/P99

COWAN, Samuel
The Royal House of Stuart; from its origin to the accession of the House of Hanover. London, 1908.
ED/N-1 (R.232.e) ED/N-2 QZ/P26 QZ/P99

CRAWFURD, George
. . . Genealogical history of the royal and illustrious family of the Stewarts, 1034-1710. Edinburgh, 1710.
ED/N-1 (F.5.c.22;BCL.B5606) QZ/P-6 AD/U-1 GL/U-1 QZ/P99 ED/M-1 QZ/P52 (Unconfirmed location)

— — 2nd ed., continued by W. Semple. Paisley, 1782.
ED/N-1 (A.118.g) QZ/P-6 QZ/P-1 QZ/P99

— — 3rd ed., continued to the present time by G. Robertson. Paisley, 1818.
ED/N-1 (NE.12.h.1) QZ/P-6 QZ/L37 ST/U-1 QZ/P-1 QZ/P99

DOUGLAS, Sir Robert
An historical genealogical tree of the Royal Family of Scotland, and name of Stewart for 1000 years back to the present day. Edinburgh, [1750].
ED/N-1 (S.305.c)

EDINBURGH "Royal Stuart" exhibition, 1949:
[catalogue].
QZ/P99

The EXILED Stewarts in Italy, 1717-1807; edited by
Helen Catherine Stewart. Edinburgh, 1941. (In
Miscellany of the Scottish History Society, vol.7
(Scottish History Society Publications, 3rd series,
vol.xxxv), pp.53-130.)
ED/N-1 (Ref.54) ED/N-2 QZ/P-1

FOSTER, Joshua James
The Stuarts: being illustrations of the personal
history of the family. London, 1902. 2v.
ED/N-1 (L.B) QZ/P56 QZ/P99 AD/U-1

— — London, 1907.
ED/N-1 (NE.22.a.8) ED/N-2 QZ/P-1
QZ/P99

FRANCIS, Grant R.
Scotland's royal line: the tragic House of Stuart.
London, 1928.
ED/N-1 (R.232.e) ED/N-2 QZ/P15 QZ/P26
QZ/P-3 ST/U-1 QZ/P-1 QZ/P99

[A GENEALOGICAL account and genealogical tables
relating the history of the family of Stuart.
1788-98.]
ED/N-1 (MS.5401-5404)

A GENEALOGICAL history of the royal family of
Scotland, England and Ireland . . . name of Stuart . . .
to . . . 1754. London, 1755.
QZ/P99

GRANSBY, D.
The House of Stuart. London, 1968.
ED/N-1 (GMK.7) QZ/P99

HAY, Richard Augustine
An essay on the origine of the Royal Family of the
Stewarts. Edinburgh, 1722.
ED/N-1 (2.190) QZ/P-1

— — Edinburgh, 1793.
ED/N-1 (A.114.c;Ry.I.4.161) GL/U-1 QZ/P99

LETTRE écrite au Duc de Perth . . . au sujet de la
généalogie des Stuarts dressé par . . . Mathieu
Kennedy. [Paris], 1712.
ED/N-1 (MS.6316;MS.2936,f.155)

HENDERSON, Thomas Finlayson
The Royal Stewarts. Edinburgh, 1914.
ED/N-1 (R.232.f) QZ/P40 QZ/P-3 AD/U-1
QZ/P22 ST/U-1 QZ/P-1 QZ/P99

HORTLING, Carl-Erik
The Stuarts in Sweden and the Royal House of
Scotland. (In *The Stewarts*, vol.xvi, no.4, 1983,
pp.177-95.)
ED/N-1 (R.172.a)

KENNEDY, Matthew
A chronological genealogical and historical
dissertation of the Royal Family of Stewarts. Paris,
1705.
ED/N-1 (R.232.i;Ry.I.4.161) QZ/P-6 QZ/P-1
QZ/P99

—Réponse de Mathieu Kennedy . . . à une lettre que
le père de la Haye . . . a écrite à Mylord Duc de Perth.
Paris, 1715.
ED/N-1 (Ry.II.g.16)

LINDSAY, W. A.
Pedigree of the House of Stewart. [1891.]
QZ/L37 GL/U-1 ED/N-2 QZ/P99

LINKLATER, Eric
The Royal House of Scotland. London, 1970.
ED/N-1 (Hist.S.3.L) ST/U-1 QZ/P28
QZ/P99

MACKENZIE, Agnes Mure
The passing of the Stewarts. London, 1937.
ED/N-1 (R.232.d) QZ/P-3 QZ/P41 ED/N-2
ST/U-1 QZ/P-1

— — London, 1958.
ED/N-1 (NE.20.f.7)

—The rise of the Stewarts. London, 1935.
ED/N-1 (R.232.d) QZ/P-6 QZ/P15 QZ/P-3
QZ/P41 ED/N-2 ST/U-1 QZ/P-1

— — Reprinted. Edinburgh, 1957.
ED/N-1 (NE.20.f.5)

MACKENZIE, Sir George
The antiquity of the royal line of Scotland defended.
Edinburgh, 1685.
ED/N-1 (Ferg.89;L.C.503) QZ/P-1

—The antiquity of the royal line of Scotland farther
cleared and defended. London, 1686.
ED/N-1 (R.232.i) ST/U-1 QZ/P22

MACKINNON, Archibald
The Stuart dynasty. [Kingston], 1863.
ED/N-1 (APS.1.79.31)

MARCHAND, Pierre Joseph Abel
Les Stuarts à Avignon. Avignon, 1895.
ED/N-1 (Blk.655) AD/U-1

MURDOCH, W. G. Blaikie
 The Royal Stuarts in their connection with art and
 letters. Edinburgh, 1908.
 ED/N-1 (X.170.j) GL/U-1 QZ/P22 QZ/P-1
 QZ/P99

NAPIER, Theodore
 The Royal House of Stuart: an appeal for its
 restoration. Edinburgh, 1898.
 ED/N-1 (Ry.I.3.295) QZ/P99

NICHOLAS, Donald
 Prince Rupert's children. (In *The Stewarts*, vol.10,
 1955-8, p.179-81.)
 ED/N-1 (R.172.a)

NOBLE, Mark
 A historical genealogy of the Royal House of Stuart
 .... London, 1795.
 ED/N-1 (A.114.b.18) DN-U-1 AD/U-1
 QZ/P22 QZ/P-1

PEDIGREE of Robert Barclay Allardice, heir apparent
 of the line of Prince David Stuart, Earl Palatine of
 Strathearn, etc. Edinburgh, 1892.
 ED/N-1 (S.120.a)

PETRIE, Sir Charles Alexander
 España y los Estuardo. Madrid, 1951.
 ED/N-1 (6.2064)

POTTINGER, Don
 Stewart arms. (In *The Stewarts*, vol.x, 1955-8,
 pp.57-63, 217-23.)
 ED/N-1 (R.172.a)

RAIT, Sir Robert Sangster
 Five Stuart princesses. London, 1902.
 ED/N-1 (S.149.d) GL/U-1 QZ/P-1 QZ/P99

RIDDELL, John
 Stewartiana, containing the case of Robert II and
 Elizabeth Mure and question of legitimacy of their
 issue. Edinburgh, 1843.
 ED/N-1 (R.232.e) GL/U-1 QZ/L37 QZ/P-1
 QZ/P99

 — Tracts legal and historical, etc. Edinburgh, 1835.
 ED/N-1 (L.C.758;A114.c) QZ/L37 ED/N-2
 QZ/P-1 QZ/P99

RIDLER, Alan
 Will ye no come back again? Bognor Regis, 1981.
 ED/N-1 (H2.81.1725) QZ/P99

The ROYAL House of Stuart; illustrated ... by
 William Gibb; with an introduction by John
 Skelton, and notes by W. H. St. John Hope. London,
 1890.
 ED/N-1 (NF.1538.d.2) ED/N-2 AD/U-1
 GL/U-1 QZ/P-1 QZ/P11 QZ/P22 QZ/P99

ROYAL STUART SOCIETY
 The Royalist: Bulletin of the Royal Stuart Society.
 Vol.vi, no.20 (April 1954)-vol.viii, no.47 (winter
 1961-2). London, 1954-62.
 ED/N-1 (NJ.711) QZ/P99*

SCOTTISH NATIONAL PORTRAIT GALLERY
 The Royal House of Stewart. Edinburgh, 1958.
 ED/N-1 (GMP1) ST/U-1 QZ/P99

SKEET, Francis John Angus
 Stuart papers, pictures, relics, medals and books in
 the collection of Miss Maria Widdrington. Leeds,
 1930.
 ED/N-1 (S.122.f) QZ/P22 QZ/P-1 QZ/P99

 — — Leeds, 1938.
 GL/U-1

STEUART, Sir Henry
 The genealogy of the Stewarts refuted: in a letter to
 Andrew Stuart, Esq., M.P. Edinburgh, 1799.
 ED/N-1 (A.114.b;Blk.33) AD/U-1 GL/U-1
 QZ/L37 QZ/P-1 QZ/P22 QZ/P99 QZ/Q91

STEWART, Duncan
 Short historical and genealogical account of the
 royal family of Scotland ...and of the surname of
 Stewart. Edinburgh, 1739.
 ED/N-1 (L.C.734;A.144.c) ED/N-2 QZ/P40
 GL/U-1 QZ/L37 QZ/P-1 QZ/P99

STEWART, Helen Catherine
 New light on the Royal Stewarts in Italy. Hinckley,
 [1937].
 ED/N-1 (1937.6)

STRICKLAND, Agnes
 Lives of the last four princesses of the Royal House
 of Stuart. London, 1872.
 ED/N-1 (244.c) QZ/P-1

 — Lives of the Tudor and Stuart princesses. Revised
 edition. London, 1888.
 ED/N-1 (244.e;R.4.h)

STUART, Andrew
Genealogical history of the Stuarts, from the earliest period of their authentic history. London, 1798.
ED/N-1 (A.114.b) QZ/P40 SA/U-1 GL/U-1
QZ/L37 ED/N-2 QZ/Q91 QZ/P49 QZ/P-1
QZ/P99

— — Supplement with corrections and additions, etc. London, 1799.
SA/U-1 QZ/Q91

SYMSON, David
Genealogical and historical account of the illustrious name of Stuart. Edinburgh, 1712.
ED/N-1 (R.232.h) AD/U-1 QZ/P-1 QZ/P40
QZ/P99

— — London, 1713.
ED/U-1

— — Edinburgh, 1726.
ED/N-1 (Blk.148) QZ/P52 (Unconfirmed location)

TAITT, Alexander
Right of the House of Stewart to the crown of Scotland. 2nd ed. [Edinburgh], 1746.
ED/N-1 (Ry.I.5.306;R.232.i;1974.91(8)) GL/U-1
QZ/P-1 QZ/P99

THOMPSON, Neil D. and HANSEN, Charles M.
A medieval heritage: the ancestry of Charles II, King of England. (In *Genealogist*; part 1, vol.2, no.2, fall 1981, pp.157-68; part 2, vol.3, no.1, spring 1982, pp.25-44; part 3, vol.3, no.2, fall 1982, pp.175-94.)
ED/N-1 (1309 PER)

THORNTON, Percy Melville
Stuart dynasty: short studies drawn from papers . . . at Windsor Castle. London, 1890.
ED/N-1 (Y.59.c.26) ED/N-2 QZ/L37 QZ/P-1
QZ/P99

— — London, 1891.
ED/N-1 (A.124.d)

TOWNEND, William
The descendants of the Stuarts. London, 1858.
ED/N-1 (A.110.b;C.19.d) QZ/P40 AD/U-1
GL/U-1 QZ/L37 QZ/P-1 QZ/P99

A TREWE description of the nobill race of the Stewards. Amsterdam, 1603.
ED/N-1 (L.C.1221(2)) QZ/P99

UDALL, William
The historie of the life and death of Mary Stuart, Queene of Scotland. London, 1636.
ED/N-1 (Ry.III.g.22) GL/U-1 QZ/P99

VAUGHAN, Robert
Memorials of the Stuart dynasty . . . London, 1831. 2v.
ED/N-1 (C.16.d) QZ/P-1

WALLACE, Harold Frank
A Stuart sketch book, 1542-1746. London, 1933.
ED/N-1 (R.230.a) QZ/P22 GL/U-1 QZ/P-1
QZ/P99

WASHINGTON, George Sydney Horace Lee
Pedigree of Charles Edward Stuart, Count of Roehenstart. Cambridge, 1974.
ED/N-1 (1975.6) QZ/P-1

— — [Cambridge], 1978.
ED/N-1 (HP1.78.4345)

—Prince Charlie and the Bonapartes. Cambridge, 1960.
ED/N-2

WATERHOUSE, Thomas
A genealogical account of the royal House of Stuart from 1043. Grantham, 1816.
ED/N-1 (A.114.c) AD/U-1 GL/U-1 QZ/P-1
QZ/P99

WATSON, John
Memoires of the family of the Stuarts. . . . London, 1683.
ED/N-1 (Mf.28(5[1]);RB.5.313) QZ/P-1
QZ/P99

Still of Aberdeen

MILNE, Marcus K.
The Still family of Aberdeen and U.S.A. [N.p., 1954?]
QZ/P22

Stirling

STIRLING, Alfred
Gang forward: a Stirling notebook. [N.p.], 1972.
ED/N-1 (NE.25.f.25) QZ/P14 ST/U-1
QZ/Q76

WOODWARD, W. H.
Sterlings of Stirlingshire, Ireland and London, 1500-1935. London, 1935.
ED/S10 (Unconfirmed location)

Stirling, Earldom of *see also* **Alexander,** Earl of Stirling

Stirling, Earldom of
. . . An ACCOUNT of the resumption of the titles by the present Earl of Stirling . . . with an epitome of the genealogy of . . . Alexander. London, 1826.
QZ/P99

BANKS, Sir Thomas Christopher
An analytical statement of the case of Alexander, Earl of Stirling and Dovan. . . . London, 1832.
ED/N-1 (1933.23)

—A letter to the . . . Earl of Rosebery, in relation to the proceedings at the late election of Scotch peers. [Edinburgh, 1830.]
ED/N-1 (Ry.I.3.10)

[DEFENCE and prosecution papers in the case of Alexander Humphrys, or Alexander, indicted for forgery. Edinburgh, 1839.]
ED/N-1 (6.249(75))

DEUCHAR, Alexander
Concise view of the present state of the succession, and of the proofs having reference in the case of the heirs of the line of William, first Earl of Stirling . . . [With a genealogical table.] Edinburgh, 1839.
ED/N-1 (Yule.148(1))

HUMPHRYS, Alexander
The case of Alexander, Earl and Viscount of Stirling, etc. [With genealogical tables.] [London, 1836?]
ED/N-1 (Yule.no.123)

—Narrative of the oppressive law proceedings . . . also a genealogical account of the family of Alexander. Edinburgh, 1836.
ED/N-1 (R.290.b)   GL/U-1   QZ/P14   QZ/P99
QZ/Q17

—Report of the trial of Alexander Humphrys, or Alexander, claiming the title of Earl of Stirling . . .; [edited] by Archibald Swinton. Edinburgh, 1839.
ED/N-1 (Law)   ED/N-2   GL/U-1   QZ/L37
QZ/P-1   QZ/P14   QZ/P99

—The Stirling peerage: trial of Alexander Humphrys, or Alexander, styling himself Earl of Stirling . . .; edited by W. B. D. D. Turnbull. Edinburgh, 1839.
ED/N-1 (Yule.no.95;Law)   GL/U-1   QZ/P99

—[Stirling peerage, session and other papers. N.p., n.d.]
QZ/L37   QZ/P99

—Summary of the case of Alexander, Earl of Stirling . . . Worcester, [1826?].
ED/N-1 (3.2793(13))

LOCKHART, Ephraim
Genealogical account of the family of Alexander, Earls of Stirling, etc. Edinburgh, 1836.
GL/U-1   QZ/P-1   QZ/P99

MACNEILL, Peter Grant Brass
The Stirling peerage case. (In *Juridical Review,* December 1960, pp.256-64.)
ED/N-1 (Law)

— — (Reprinted from *Juridical Review,* December 1960.)
ED/N-1 (6.148)

REMARKS on the trial of the Earl of Stirling at Edinburgh, April 29th 1839, for forgery; by an English lawyer. London, 1839.
ED/N-1 (Law)

Stirling of Cadder *see also* **Stirling** of Drumpellier

Stirling of Cadder
STIRLING, Thomas Willing
The Stirlings of Cadder: an account of the original family of that name and of the family of the Stirlings of Drumpellier, with which the representation of the ancient house of Cadder now lies. St Andrews, 1933.
ED/N-1 (NE.25.a.24)   SA/U-1   QZ/P13
QZ/P-1   QZ/P99

Stirling of Craigbernard and Glorat
BAIN, Joseph
The Stirlings of Craigbernard and Glorat. Edinburgh, 1883.
ED/N-1 (A.113.c;MS.Acc.4927)   QZ/P14
QZ/P40   SA/U-1   AD/U-1   GL/U-1   QZ/P99
QZ/L37   QZ/Q76   QZ/P13   QZ/P49   QZ/P-1

Stirling of Drumpellier *see also* **Stirling** of Cadder

Stirling of Drumpellier
ABSTRACT of the evidence submitted to a jury on behalf of Andrew Stirling, Esquire, of Drumpellier, claiming to be served heir-male in general of Robert Stirling of Bankeyr and Lettyr, or Lettyr-Stirling in the county of Stirling, who died in 1537. [With a genealogical table.] [N.p., 1818.]
ED/N-1 (6.1257(25))

STIRLING of Drumpellier. Manchester, [n.d.].
QZ/P14

Stirling of Garden
DUN, P.
Summer at the Lake of Menteith. Glasgow, 1866.
QZ/P14

Stirling of Keir *see also* **Maxwell** of Pollok

Stirling of Keir
FITTIS, Robert Scott
The Stirlings of Keir. (*Miscellanea Perthensis*,
1853-61, newspaper cutting no.74.)
QZ/P26

FRASER, Sir William
The Stirlings of Keir and their family papers.
Edinburgh, 1858.
ED/N-1 (Gen.8.5) QZ/P14 QZ/P26 AD/U-1
GL/U-1 QZ/L37 ED/N-2 SA/U-1 ED/U-1
QZ/P-1 QZ/P99

RIDDELL, John
Comments in refutation . . . of statements in "The
Stirlings of Keir and their family papers".
Edinburgh, 1860.
ED/N-1 (H.6.b) QZ/P-3 QZ/Q17 QZ/P14
QZ/P26 SA/U-1 GL/U-1 QZ/L37 ED/N-2
QZ/Q76 ED/U-1 QZ/P-1 QZ/P99

A SELECTION of original charters and papers of the
family of Stirling of Keir, commencing in the year
1338. [Edinburgh?], 1860.
QZ/P14 ED/N-2 QZ/L37

Stirton
STIRTON, John
Notes on the family of Stirton of the Stormont,
Perthshire. Aberdeen, 1920.
ED/N-1 (5.2158) QZ/P26

—Stirton of the Stormont: a brief history of the
family. Forfar, 1935.
ED/N-1 (6.246) QZ/P26 SA/U-1 AD/U-1
GL/U-1 QZ/P99

Stiven *see* **Stein**

Stivenson
[GENEALOGICAL material concerning the family of
Stivenson. 19--.]
ED/N-1 (MS.10607)

Stobo
BULLOCH, Joseph Gaston Baillie
History and genealogy of the families of Bulloch
and Stobo, and Irvine of Cults. Washington, 1911.
QZ/P22

Stodart
WYLD, Robert Stodart
Memoir of James Wyld of Gilston, and his family;
also of Robert Stodart of Kailzie and Ormiston Hill.
Edinburgh, 1889.
ED/N-1 (NF.1172.h.17)

Strachan of Glenkindie
ALLARDICE, James
The Strachans of Glenkindie, 1357-1726. Aberdeen,
1899.
ED/N-1 (S.120.f) QZ/P30 QZ/P22 QZ/L37
QZ/P-1 QZ/P99

Strachan of St Martins
CRAVEN, James Brown
Scots worthies, 1560-1688. Edinburgh, 1894.
ED/N-1 (254.c) QZ/P26

Strachan of Thornton
ROGERS, Charles
Memorials of the Scottish families of Strachan and
Wise. Edinburgh, 1877. (Grampian Club.)
ED/N-1 (Gramp.Club.31) AD/U-1 GL/U-1
SA/U-1 QZ/L37 QZ/P14 QZ/P28 QZ/P16
QZ/P99

—Memorials of the Strachans, baronets of Thornton,
Kincardineshire, and of the family of Wise of
Hillbank, formerly Wyse of Lunan in the county of
Forfar. London, [1873]. (Grampian Club.)
ED/N-1 (Gramp.Club.27) GL/U-1 SA/U-1
QZ/L37 QZ/P-1 QZ/P40 QZ/P99

THORNTON-KEMSLEY, Colin
Bonnet lairds. Montrose, 1972.
ED/N-1 (NE.25.f.17) QZ/P22 QZ/P56
QZ/P-1 ED/N-2 QZ/L37 QZ/P14

Strang of Balcaskie
MCTAGGART, William
Sketch of a history of the family of Strang or
Strange, of Balcasky, in the county of Fife in
Scotland. Edinburgh, 1798.
QZ/P99

STRANG, James Alexander
The Strang family. [196-.] 3v. (*Typescript*)
QZ/P-1

Strange

DENNISTOUN, James
Memoirs of Sir Robert Strange, Knt., engraver . . .
and of his brother-in-law, Andrew Lumisden,
private secretary to the Stuart princes. London,
1855. 2v.
ED/N-1 (X.X.4)

['A GENEALOGICAL account of the family of
Strange'. 1836.]
ED/N-1 (MS.2898,ff.x-xiii)

[GENEALOGICAL material concerning the family of
Robert Strange. 1787-1908.]
ED/N-1 (MS.14259)

STRANGE, Nora Kathleen
Jacobean tapestry. London, [1947].
ED/N-1 (R.157.d)   ED/N-2   QZ/P22   QZ/P-6
QZ/P-1   QZ/P99

Strathallan, Viscount of *see* **Drummond,** Viscount
of Strathallan

Strathearn, Earldom of

COWAN, Samuel
Three Celtic earldoms: Atholl, Strathearn,
Menteith. Edinburgh, 1909.
ED/N-1 (S.120.e)   QZ/P14   QZ/P22   QZ/P26
QZ/P-1

NICOLAS, Sir Nicholas Harris
History of the Earldoms of Strathern, Monteith and
Airth; with a report of the proceedings . . . on the
claim of Robert Barclay Allardice. . . . London, 1842.
ED/N-1 (A.114.c)   SA/U-1   AD/U-1   GL/U-1
QZ/L37   ED/N-2   QZ/P-1   QZ/P99

The PEDIGREE of Robert Barclay-Allardice, heir
apparent of the line of Prince David Stuart, Earl
Palatine of Strathearn. . . . Edinburgh, 1892.
ED/N-1 (S.120.a)

SCOT, Sir John
A true relation of William, Earle of Monteath's affair
concerning the earldome and title of Straitherne . . .
[N.p., 1834.]
ED/N-1 (6.234(10))

Strathmore, Earldom of *see also* **Bowes(-Lyon),** Earl
of Strathmore

Strathmore, Earldom of
MINUTES of evidence [and appendix] in the
Strathmore peerage claim, 1821. [N.p.], 1821.
QZ/P28

WILLIAM Ewing v. Earl of Strathmore: answers for
William Ewing. [Edinburgh, 1825.]
QZ/P99

WILLIAM Laing v. Earl of Strathmore: answers for
William Laing . . . to the petition . . . of the Rt. Hon.
Thomas Bowes designing himself Earl of
Strathmore and Kinghorn. 1821.
QZ/P99

Straton of Lauriston
[PAPERS, letters, etc. dealing with the family,
1124-1933.] 9v.
QZ/P28

STRATON, Charles Henry
The Stratons of Lauriston and their offshoots.
Exmouth, 1939.
ED/N-1 (6.233)   QZ/P28   QZ/L37

Stuart *see also* **Sobieski-Stuart**

Stuart *see also* **Steuart**

Stuart *see also* **Stewart**

Stuart of Allanbank
FORBES, Louisa Lillias
[Genealogy of the family of Stuart of Allanbank,
1643-1880.] [N.p.], 1880.
ED/N-1 (S.120.a)

Stuart of Ardsheil
STUART, Alexander
Answers for His Majesty's advocate on behalf of
His Majesty; to the claim of Alexander Stuart,
eldest son of Charles Stuart late of Ardsheil [to his
father's forfeited estate.] . . . 22nd June 1750.
[Edinburgh, 1750.]
ED/N-1 (Ry.II.b.19(46))

Stuart of Aubigny
[COLLECTION of genealogical papers concerning the
Stuart family of Aubigny. 1788-9.]
ED/N-1 (MS.8320)

CUST, Lady Elizabeth
Some account of the Stuarts of Aubigny in France.
London, 1891.
ED/N-1 (A.112.c)   QZ/P22   QZ/L37   QZ/P-1
QZ/P99

STEUART, Maria
The Stuarts of Aubigny. (In *The Stewarts*, vol.ix,
1951-3, pp.234-40.)
ED/N-1 (R.172.a)

STUART, Andrew
Genealogical history of the Stewarts . . . London,
1798.
ED/N-1 (A.114.b) ED/N-2 SA/U-1 GL/U-1
QZ/L37 QZ/P40 QZ/P49 QZ/P99

Stuart, Marquess of Bute *see* **Crichton-Stuart,**
Marquess of Bute

Stuart of Castlemilk
ANSWERS for Mrs. Rae Crawfurd of Milton, to the
petition of Sir John Stewart of Castlemilk, Bart.,
and Mrs. Stirling of Keir. 1794.
QZ/P-1

[GENEALOGICAL notes concerning the Stuart family
of Castlemilk. N.d.]
ED/N-1 (MS.8316)

. . . The PETITION of Sir John Stuart of Castlemilk,
Baronet, and of Mrs. Stirling of Keir.
QZ/P-1

STATE of the evidence for proving that the present Sir
John Stuart of Castlemilk is the lineal heir-male and
representative of Sir William Stuart of Castlemilk
who lived during part of the 14th and 15th centuries.
[N.p.], 1794.
QZ/P-1

STUART, Andrew
Genealogical history of the Stewarts. . . . London,
1798.
ED/N-1 (A.114.b) ED/N-2 QZ/P40 SA/U-1
GL/U-1 QZ/L37 QZ/P99 QZ/P49

Stuart of Castle Stuart, Ireland
STUART, Andrew Godfrey
A genealogical and historical sketch of the Stuarts of
the House of Castle Stuart, in Ireland. Edinburgh,
1854.
AD/U-1 QZ/L37 QZ/P99

Stuart in England
HUISH, Marcus Bourne
An old Stuart genealogy: a paper read before "Ye
Sette of Odd Volumes", February 5th 1897. London,
1898.
ED/N-1 (KK.7/2) QZ/P99

Stuart in Kingston
YOUNG, Archibald H.
Rev. John Stuart, D.D., of Kingston, U.C., and his
family. Kingston, Ont., 1920.
QZ/P26 AD/U-1

Stuart in Newburgh-on-Tay
STIRTON, John
An old Scottish divine: Reverend Dr Thomas
Stuart, minister of Newburgh-on-Tay, 1751-1819.
Forfar, 1910.
ED/N-1 (1910.50)

Stuart of Roehenstart
WASHINGTON, George Sydney Horace Lee
The pedigree of Charles Edward Stuart, Count of
Roehenstart. Cambridge, 1978.
ED/N-1 (HP1.78.4345) ED/N-2

Stuart of Torrance
[A GENEALOGICAL table of the Stuart family of
Torrance. 1793?]
ED/N-1 (MS.Ch.8411)

Stuart-Menteth
MENTETH, Sir James Stuart
The Stuart-Menteth pedigree not doubtful.
(In *Herald and Genealogist*, vol.5, 1870, pp.456-68.)
ED/N-1 (Q.103)

— — (Reprinted from *Herald and Genealogist*, vol.5,
1879.)
AD/U-1 QZ/P-1

Suppes in U.S.A. *see* **Hay** in U.S.A.

Sutherland
CLAN SUTHERLAND SOCIETY IN SCOTLAND
Newsletter of the Clan Sutherland Society in
Scotland. Vol.1, no.1 (March 1978)- . Golspie,
1978- .
ED/N-1 (P.1a.10,030)

EATON, Arthur Wentworth Hamilton
Families of Eaton-Sutherland, Layton-Hill. New
York, 1899.
ED/N-1 (S.120.e)

LOCH, James
Dates and documents relating to the family and
property of Sutherland. [London], 1859.
ED/N-1 (Hall.290.a) ED/N-2 QZ/L37
QZ/P50

ROSE, David Murray
Sutherlands of Duffus and Skelbo. 1900. (Reprinted
from the *Northern Times*, July 1900.)
AD/U-1 QZ/P99

YOUNG, Robert
Notes on Burghead, ancient and modern; with an appendix containing notices of families connected with the place. Elgin, 1867.
ED/N-1 (Hall.197.a)

Sutherland, Duke of *see* **Leveson-Gower,** Duke of Sutherland

Sutherland, Earldom of *see also* **Freskyn,** Earl of Sutherland

Sutherland, Earldom of
CASE of Elisabeth claiming the title . . . of Countess of Sutherland; by her guardians. 1769.
SA/U-1 QZ/L37

DALRYMPLE, Sir D.
The additional case of Elisabeth, claiming the title and dignity of Countess of Sutherland, by her guardians . . . [London, 1771.]
ED/N-1 (Yule.75(1);Yule.126) QZ/P40 GL/U-1
QZ/L37 QZ/P-1 QZ/P99 SA/U-1

FRASER, Sir William
The Sutherland book. Edinburgh, 1892. 3v.
ED/N-1 (Gen.8.5) ED/N-2 QZ/P40 SA/U-1
AD/U-1 GL/U-1 QZ/L37 ED/U-1 QZ/P-1
QZ/P99

GORDON, John
Information for the Earl of Sutherland. . . .
[Edinburgh, 1706.]
ED/N-1 (A.114.e.28(1-11))

GORDON, Robert
In the question concerning the peerage of Sutherland: brief for the Counsel of Sir Robert Gordon, Bart. claiming the title and dignity of Earl of Sutherland. [London, 1771?]
ED/N-1 (Yule.75(2)) QZ/P99

GORDON, Sir Robert
A genealogical history of the Earldom of Sutherland from its origin to the year 1630; published from the original MS. (by H. Weber). Edinburgh, 1813.
ED/N-1 (S.273.b) QZ/Q17 QZ/P40 QZ/P22
AD/U-1 GL/U-1 QZ/L37 ED/N-2 ST/U-1
QZ/P50 QZ/P-1 ED/U-1 QZ/P99

GORDON, Sir Robert, of Gordonstoun
Case of Sir Robert Gordon claiming the title . . .
Earl of Sutherland, etc. 1769.
QZ/L37 SA/U-1

—In the question concerning the peerage of Sutherland. . . . [N.p.], 1771.
ED/N-1 (Yule.127;Yule.75(2)) QZ/P40 GL/U-1
QZ/L37 QZ/P-1 QZ/P99

—Supplemental case . . . and pedigree . . . and pedigree of George Sutherland of Forss. 1770.
QZ/L37

—Sutherland: peerage case. 1769. (*MS.*)
SA/U-1 QZ/P40 QZ/P99

GOWER, Mary Caroline Leveson
Copy pamphlet printed and issued by the Dowager Duchess of Sutherland. [Trentham, 1892.]
ED/N-1 (Dur.1309)

INFORMATION for the Earl of Crawfurd and the Earl Marischall against the Earl of Sutherland. Edinburgh, 1706.
ED/N-1 (A.114.e.28(8-11))

INFORMATION for the Earl of Sutherland against the Earl of Crawfurd. Edinburgh, 1706.
ED/N-1 (A.114.e.28(1-7);A.11.e.27;Yule.17;
Ry.I.2.127(13))

MAIDMENT, James
Report of claims . . . to the House of Lords . . . of the Cassilis, Sutherland, Spynie and Glencairn peerages, 1760-1797. Edinburgh, 1840.
ED/N-1 (Yule.94) QZ/L37

— — Reprinted. Edinburgh, 1882.
ED/N-1 (Law) DN/U-1 GL/U-1 QZ/P-1
QZ/P99

[PAPERS presented to the House of Lords in support of the claims of Lady Elizabeth Leveson Gower, George Sutherland of Forss and Sir Robert Gordon, 4th Bart., of Gordonstoun, to the Earldom of Sutherland. London, 1771.]
ED/N-1 (Yule.173)

[PAPERS presented to the House of Lords in support of the claims of Sir Robert Gordon and others to the Earldom of Sutherland. London, 1771.]
ED/N-1 (Yule.173)

SINCLAIR, Alexander
Right of the Duke of Sutherland to a higher place as Earl of Sutherland than he now has on the roll of the Scottish Earls since 1606. [N.d., n.d.]
ED/N-1 (Hall.199.e.1(1)) QZ/P-9

WEMYSS, Elisabeth
Case of . . . Lady Elisabeth . . . and the Hon. James
Wemyss of Wemyss, her husband, etc.
QZ/L37

Sutherland of Dunbeath
MACEWEN, Andrew B. W.
The family connections of Alexander of Dunbeath.
(In *Genealogist*, vol.3, no.2, fall 1982, pp.131-53.)
ED/N-1 (1309 PER)

Swankie
WATSON, Harry D.
The Swankies of Arbroath and Auchmithie: an
unusual local surname. (In *Scottish Genealogist*,
vol.xxix, no.1, March 1982, pp.18-24.)
ED/N-1 (Gen.7)

Sween *see also* **MacSween**

Sween
SWEENY, R. Mingo
Sween, clan of the battle-axe: a brief history of the
MacSweenys. California, 1968.
QZ/L37   ED/N-2

Swinton
MARSHALL, R. F. L.
The Muir book. [N.p.], 1930.
ED/N-2

[NOTES on the genealogy and a genealogical table
concerning the Swinton family of Swinton.
1927-29.]
ED/N-1 (MS.350A,B)

SWINTON, A. H. C.
The Swinton family. (In *History of the Berwickshire
Naturalists' Club*, vol.xxxv, 1959/61, pp.1-9.)
ED/N-1 (Y.210)

SWINTON, Archibald Campbell
The Swintons of that ilk. (In *History of the
Berwickshire Naturalists' Club*, vol.viii, 1876/8,
pp.328-52.)
ED/N-1 (Y.210)   QZ/P-1

— The Swintons of that ilk, and their cadets.
Edinburgh, 1883.
ED/N-1 (MS.350.A: with MS. notes by George
Swinton)   QZ/P56   QZ/P11   SA/U-1   AD/U-1
GL/U-1   QZ/L37   QZ/P-1   ED/U-1   QZ/P99

SWINTON, Archibald Campbell *and* SWINTON,
J. L. Campbell
Concerning Swinton family records and portraits
at Kimmerghame. Edinburgh, 1908.
ED/N-1 (S.120.e)   QZ/P11   QZ/P-1   QZ/P99

Symes
SINNOTT, Nigel H.
Notes on the Symes family and Joseph Skurrie.
Lidcome North, 1978.
ED/N-1 (HP3.78.1259)

Symington
PATON, Henry
Genealogy of the Symington family. Edinburgh,
1908.
ED/N-1 (R.172.h)   QZ/P11   AD/U-1   QZ/L37
SA/U-1   QZ/P-1   QZ/P99

Symons
MITCHELL, Silas Weir
A brief history of two families: the Mitchells of
Ayrshire and the Symons of Cornwall. Philadelphia,
Penn., 1912.
ED/N-2

Taggart
HARTMAN, Blanche T.
A genealogy of the Nesbit, Ross, Porter, Taggart
families of Pennsylvania. [With genealogical tables.]
Pittsburgh, Pa., 1929.
ED/N-1 (H3.83.2753)

Tannahill
CORRESPONDENCE of the family of Robert
Tannahill. [N.p., n.d.]
QZ/P-6

Tarras
CORMACK, Alexander Allan
A Scoto-Swedish study: the Rev. John Gilchrist . . .
his grandsons in Sweden. Peterculter, 1969.
ED/N-1 (1970.10)   QZ/P28   QZ/P30

Taylor
DUTY, Allene B.
The Taylor family: the descendants of the Reverend
William Taylor of Stonehouse, Scotland, and St.
Lawrence County, New York. Cleveland, Ohio,
1972.
ED/N-1 (6.2459)

Tennant

CRATHORNE, Nancy
Tennant's stalk: the story of the Tennants of the
Glen. London, 1973.
ED/N-1 (NE.25.f.20) DN/U-1 SA/U-1
ED/U-1 GL/U-1 ED/S10 QZ/P11 QZ/P14
QZ/P34 QZ/Q88 QZ/P99

TENNANT, Harold John
Sir Charles Tennant, his forbears and descendants.
London, 1932.
QZ/P99 ED/S10 SA/U-1 QZ/P-1

TRIMBLE, William Tennant
The Trimbles and Cowens of Dalston,
Cumberland. Carlisle, 1935-7. 2v.
ED/N-1 (R.172.c)

Tennant, Baron Glenconner

SYMONS, A. J. A.
Essays and biographies. London, 1969.
ED/N-1 (NC.259.h.21) QZ/P-1

Terry *see* Sandilands

Thoms

SMITH, William McCombie
Memoir of the families of McCombie and Thoms.
Edinburgh, 1890.
ED/N-1 (A.113.c) ED/N-2 QZ/P22 SA/U-1
AD/U-1 DN/U-1 GL/U-1 QZ/P-6 QZ/L37
QZ/P49 QZ/P99 QZ/P16

Thomson

DEUCHAR, Alexander
Genealogical collections relative to the family of
Thomson. [183-]. (*MS. and newspaper cuttings*)
ED/N-2 QZ/P99

THOMSON, David Couper
Thomson, Couper, Yule, Sinclair genealogical
chart. Dundee, [1936].
QZ/L37 QZ/P99 QZ/P20

THOMSON, Elizabeth M.
Completed family history. [N.d.] (*MS.*)
QZ/P-6

Thomson in Aberdeenshire

TOMSON, Henry Morton *and* TOMSON,
Andrew Sherran
The Thomson family and its pedigree: descendants
and other kindred of Alexander Thomson, Greens
Marquhitter, Aberdeenshire, and Elizabeth Clark,
his wife. Norwich, 1896.
SA/U-1 QZ/P30 QZ/P99

Thomson of Corstorphine

PEDIGREE of Thomson and Forrester of
Corstorphine. [N.p., 1926.]
ED/N-1 (Portfolio II: J.138.c)

THOMSON, Theodore Radford
A history of the family of Thomson of
Corstorphine. Edinburgh, 1926.
ED/N-1 (R.172.c) SA/U-1 AD/U-1 QZ/L37
ED/U-1 QZ/P-1 QZ/P99

Thomson of Duddingston

BAIRD, William
John Thomson of Duddingston, pastor and painter:
a memoir. Edinburgh, 1895.
ED/N-1 (Ca.4/2)

— — 2nd ed. [Edinburgh], 1907.
ED/N-1 (S.153.f)

WOOD, John Philp
Memorials of various families. [1830?] (*MS.*)
QZ/P99

Thomson in Glasgow

THOMSON, G. Graham
An old Glasgow family of Thomson: a paper.
[Glasgow, 1903.]
ED/N-1 (1908.35) QZ/P-1

Thomson in Stirling

PARKHURST, Matthew S.
The John Thomson family in Stirling, Scotland.
[N.p., 1968.]
QZ/P14 QZ/P26

Thomson of Westerkirk

PORTER, William A.
A backward look at the folklore of Roy Thomson.
Edinburgh, [1962].
ED/N-1 (NE.63.h.27)

Thorburn

THORBURN, Ian
A family history of the Thorburns. [Edinburgh],
1969.
ED/N-1 (P.r.3.c.1)

—Family tree of Ian Thorburn. 1978. (*Typescript*)
QZ/P99

Thornton

THORNTON-KEMSLEY, Colin
Bonnet lairds. Montrose, 1972.
ED/N-1 (NE.25.f.17) QZ/P22 ED/N-2
QZ/P-1 QZ/L37 QZ/P14 QZ/P56

Threipland of Fingask

CHAMBERS, Robert
The Threiplands of Fingask: a family memoir.
Edinburgh, 1880.
ED/N-1(A.120.g) QZ/P26 ED/N-2 SA/U-1
QZ/P11 QZ/P40 QZ/P22 AD/U-1 DN/U-1
GL/U-1 QZ/P-6 QZ/L37 QZ/P-1 ED/M-1
QZ/P99

FITTIS, Robert Scott
Recreations of an antiquary in Perthshire history
and genealogy. Perth, 1881.
ED/N-1(A.124.e)

Thurburn

THURBURN, F. A. V.
The Thurburns; with pedigrees of Thurbrand and
Thurburn. London, 1864.
ED/N-1(A.120.c) QZ/P22 ED/N-2 QZ/L37

Tinline

BUTTON, Sylvia A.
The Tinline family in Australia. [N.p., n.d.]
(*Typescript*)
QZ/P11

Tod of Findaty

TOD, T. M.
Genealogy and its concomitant connections of the
Tod family, also other matters of varied interest in
connection with Findaty, Brackley, etc. 1947.
(*Typescript*)
QZ/P18 QZ/P26 ED/N-2

Todd of Garthy

TODD, A. H. T.
The Todds of Garthy: extracts from the family tree
of John Aiton Todd. [N.p.], 1976. (*Typescript*)
QZ/P26

Tolmie

MACKENZIE, Hector Hugh
Mackenzies of Ballone ... with genealogical
account of the Tolmies of Uiginish, Skye. Inverness,
1941.
ED/N-1(R.272.a) QZ/P40 QZ/P22 QZ/P-1
QZ/P99

Torphichen, Barony of

SANDILANDS, James
Claim for James, Lord Torphichen, to the regality
of the Barony of Torphichen. [N.p.], 1828.
ED/N-1(H.30.c.26)

Tosh

TOSH, Richard
Account of the family of Tosh. [1854?] (*MS.*)
ED/N-2

Touch

GIBSON, John C.
The lands and lairds of Touch. Stirling, 1929.
ED/N-1(1929.5) ST/U-1

TOUCHE, George A.
Some notes on the Scottish surname of Touch or
Touche. [N.p., 1906.]
AD/U-1

Trail of Aberdeen

NOTES relating to the Trail family of Old Aberdeen.
[N.p., n.d.] (*Typescript*)
QZ/P22

Traill

GUTHRIE, Charles John
Genealogy of the descendants of the Rev. Thomas
Guthrie ... connected chiefly with the families of
Chalmers and Trail. Edinburgh, 1902.
ED/N-1(S.120.a) QZ/P28 QZ/P22 SA/U-1
GL/U-1 QZ/P-1 QZ/P99

Traill in Aberdeenshire

WHYTE, Donald
The Traill family of Strichen, King Edward,
Aberdeenshire and Gamrie, Banffshire. [N.d.] (*MS.*)
QZ/P22

Traill of Blebe, Blebo

FAMILY tree of Trail of Blebe, 1390 to date-1957.
1957. (*MS.*)
QZ/P22

A SHORT account of the family of Trails of Blebe
and their descendants, copied from authentic family
manuscripts. [1836.] (*Typescript*)
ED/N-2 QZ/P22 QZ/P99

TRAILL, William
A genealogical account of the Traills of Orkney,
with a pedigree table tracing their descent from the
Traills of Blebo, in Fifeshire. Kirkwall, 1883.
ED/N-1(A.114.f) QZ/Q17 AD/U-1 SA/U-1
QZ/L37 GL/U-1 ST/U-1 QZ/P-1 QZ/P99

Traill of Elsness, Orkney
MARWICK, Hugh
Merchant lairds of long ago. 2 pts. Kirkwall,
1936,39.
ED/N-1 (6.251) QZ/P-1* QZ/P99*

[ORIGINAL family papers.]
QZ/P38 (Unconfirmed location)

Traill of Frotoft
[ORIGINAL family papers.]
QZ/P38 (Unconfirmed location)

TRAILL, Thomas W.
Genealogical sketches: the Frotoft branch of the
Orkney Traills. [N.p.], 1902.
ED/N-1 (S.120.e) ED/N-2 ED/S10

Traill in Orkney
TRAILL, William
[A genealogical account of the Traills of Orkney.
1883.]
ED/N-1 (MS.19405)

Trevor
TREVOR, Gerald
The history of the Trevor family. [N.p.], 1948.
QZ/P26

Trimble
TRIMBLE, William Tennant
The Trimbles and Cowens of Dalston,
Cumbernauld. Carlisle, 1935-7. 2v.
ED/N-1 (R.172.c)

Trotter
['GENEALOGICAL notes concerning the family of
Trotter'. 17--.]
ED/N-1 (Adv.MS.19.1.21,f.27)

HALDANE, Louisa Kathleen
Friends and kindred: memoirs of Louisa Kathleen
Haldane. [With genealogical tables.] London, 1961.
ED/N-1 (NE.1334.b.8)

KERR, Archibald
The genealogie of the Trotters of Mortoun-Hall
and Charter-Hall. 1704. (*Typescript*)
ED/N-2 QZ/P99

Troup
TROUP, J. D. Eric
Fragmentary history from the 13th century to the
present time pertaining to various branches of the
family Troup. Ontario, 1976.
QZ/P22

— The lands and family of Troup, Banffshire. [N.p.,
1972.] (*Typescript*)
QZ/P22

— Pedigree of Troop (Troup), Canada with
additional notes dated 1975. [Ontario?, 1975.]
QZ/P22

Tullibardine Earl of, Marquess of *see* **Murray,** Earl of,
Marquess of, Duke of Atholl

Turing
MCKENZIE, H.
The lay of the Turings: a sketch of the family history,
1316-1849. [N.p., 1850.]
ED/N-1 (NE.25.b.14) QZ/P22 QZ/P-1

TURING, Sir Robert Fraser
Claim for baronetcy — case of Sir Robert Fraser
Turing, Bt., with pedigrees, tables and documents.
Edinburgh, 1912.
ED/S10 (Unconfirmed location)

Turnbull
SCOTT, Richard E.
I saved the King: the story of the Turnbulls. Hawick,
1977.
ED/N-1 (HP1.77.4423) ED/N-2 QZ/P11

— — 2nd ed. Hawick, 1979.
ED/N-1 (HP2.80.3364) QZ/P11 QZ/P99

TURNBULL, John F.
History of the Turnbull family of Digby, Nova
Scotia. 1960.
QZ/P99

Turnbull of Bedrule
TURNBULLS of Bedrule. (In *Transactions of the Hawick
Archaeological Society*, 1955, pp.53-4.)
ED/N-1 (P.220)

Turnbull of Fulton
WATSON, George
Fulton Tower and some of its proprietors. (In
Transactions of the Hawick Archaeological Society, 1948,
pp.39-45.)
ED/N-1 (P.220)

Turner
THOMSON, David Couper
McCulloch, Turner, McCormick and Russell:
[a genealogical table]. Dundee, 1943.
ED/N-1 (NE.25.a.26) QZ/L37 QZ/P99

WATERS, M. M.
Our loyalist ancestors: kith and kin of Holden
Turner. 1975.
QZ/P99

Tweedie, Tweedy
TWEEDIE, Michael Forbes
The history of the Tweedie, or Tweedy, family.
London, 1902.
ED/N-1 (S.120.b) SA/U-1 QZ/L37 ED/N-2
ED/U-1 QZ/P99 QZ/P-1

Tyrie
TYRIE, Andrew
The Tyries of Drumkilbo, Perthshire, Dunnideer,
Aberdeenshire, and Lunan, Forfarshire. Glasgow,
1893.
ED/N-1 (Alex.I.6) AD/U-1 QZ/P-1 QZ/P99

Udny
GENEALOGICAL tree of the Udny family, 1350-1930.
Aberdeen, [1930].
AD/U-1

HANSEN, Mary
Family records of Dr John Udny, 1746-1849.
[N.p., n.d.] (*Typescript*)
QZ/P22

KURTEN, Love
Udnie. Helsinki, 1973. (Reprinted from *Genos,*
1973, pp.65-8.)
ED/N-1 (1976.91)

STODART, R. R.
Udny of that ilk. (In *The Genealogist*, vol.ii, 1878,
pp.33-7,87-90.)
ED/N-1 (Y.215)

— — (Reprinted from *The Genealogist*, vol.ii, 1978.)
AD/U-1 QZ/P22 QZ/P99

Umfreville
The UMFREVILLES: their ancestors and descendants,
[827-1852]. [London, n.d.]
ED/N-1 (S.122.f)

Umpherston
ALEXANDER, Helen
Passages in the lives of Helen Alexander and James
Currie of Pentland, and other papers. [With a
genealogical table.] [Belfast], 1869.
ED/N-1 (NC.272.f.8)

Ure
GENEALOGICAL notes concerning the family of Ure.
[N.p., 1916.]
QZ/P28

Urquhart
LEATHAM, Louis Salisbury
The Letham or Leatham family book . . . Robert
Letham and his wife Janet Urquhart. . . . Ann Arbor,
Mich., 1955.
ED/N-1 (NE.65.h.7) QZ/P30 QZ/P40
QZ/P-1 QZ/P99

TAYLER, Helen Agnes Henrietta
History of the family of Urquhart. Aberdeen, 1946.
ED/N-1 (Gen.8.U) ED/N-2 ED/U-1 ST/U-1
SA/U-1 QZ/P-1 QZ/P30 QZ/P50 QZ/P99

URQUHART, Beauchamp Colclough
In memoriam Beauchamp Colclough Urquhart of
Meldrum, Captain 1st Battalion Queen's Own
Cameron Highlanders . . . killed in action at the
Battle of the Atbara, Soudan, Good Friday,
April 8th 1898. [Aberdeen], 1898.
ED/U-1

URQUHART, Joseph
Mostly family matters. Aberdeen, [1978].
AD/U-1 QZ/P22

Urquhart of Cromarty
URQUHART, Sir Thomas
Tracts relating to the descent of the family of
Urquharts from the creation of the world to 1774.
Edinburgh, 1774.
ED/N-1 (Ap.5.6; L.C.578;Hall.268.h) GL/U-1
QZ/L37 QZ/P-1 QZ/P40 QZ/P99

The URQUHARTS of Cromarty. (In *Scottish
Genealogist*; part 1, vol.vi, no.2, April 1959, pp.16-18;
part 2, vol.vi, no.3, July 1959, pp.1-12.)
ED/N-1 (Gen.7)

Usher
USHER, Charles Milne
A history of the Usher family in Scotland.
Edinburgh, 1956.
ED/N-1 (NE.25.b.7) ED/U-3 SA/U-1 ED/N-2
ED/S10 QZ/P42 QZ/P-9 ED/U-1 QZ/P-1
QZ/P99

Usher of Darnick
USHER, Thomas
The Usher family of Darnick. [Edinburgh, n.d.]
ED/N-1 (1939.25) QZ/P11

Vanrenen

BLAIR-IMRIE, William
The family of General Vanrenen, with their war
services. 1902.
QZ/P28 (Unconfirmed location)

Vans *see* Vaus, Vaux

Vass

CRANNA, William H.
The surnames of Cranna and Vass. Aberdeen, 1926.
(*Typescript*)
QZ/P22

The VASSES of Lochslin: a genealogy. (In *Clan Munro
Magazine*, no.12, 1971, pp.35-9.)
ED/N-1 (P.med.1307)

Vaus, Vaux *see also* Waus

Vaus, Vaux

AGNEW, Sir Andrew
The Agnews of Lochnaw: a history of the
hereditary sheriffs of Galloway. Edinburgh, 1864.
ED/N-1 (A.113.e)   GL/U-1   SA/U-1   QZ/P-7

— — 2nd ed. Edinburgh, 1893.
ED/N-1 (Hist.S.114.L)   GL/U-1   SA/U-1
QZ/P11

AGNEW, Henry Stewart Vans
A short account of the family of De Vaux, Vaus or
Vans of Barnbarroch. 1832.
ED/N-1 (1938.6)   QZ/P99

BALBIRNIE, William
An account, historical and genealogical . . . of the
family of Vance in Ireland, Vans in Scotland,
anciently Vaux in Scotland and England, and
originally De Vaux in France. Cork, 1860.
ED/N-1 (R.172.e)

ROYAL letters and other original documents
addressed to the lairds of Barnbarroch, MDLIX-
MDCXVIII (1559-1618). [N.d.]
QZ/P10 (Unconfirmed location)

VANS AGNEW, Robert
Sketch of a genealogical and historical account of
the family of Vaux, Vaus or De Vallibus, now
represented in Scotland by Vans Agnew of
Barnbarrow. . . . Pembroke, 1800.
ED/N-1 (5.960(5))   ED/N-2

Veitch

EXTRACTS from the General Register of Sasines and
also from various parish registers (Lyne, Manor,
Peebles, etc.) and notes from the Particular Register
(Roxburgh, Selkirk and Peebles), 17th and 18th
century. (*MSS.*)
QZ/L37

MAIDMENT, James
Genealogical fragments relating to the families of . . .
Veitch. . . . Berwick, 1855.
ED/N-1 (Y.49.f.2;Ry.II.e.51(1))   QZ/P40   GL/U-1
QZ/P-1   QZ/P99

WILSON, William
Folklore and genealogies of uppermost Nithsdale.
Dumfries, 1904.
ED/N-1 (R.241.h)

Vinings

ROGERS, Julian C.
A history of our family. [N.p.], 1902.
ED/N-2

Vipont *see* De Veteripont

Walker

FAIRRIE, Geoffrey
The sugar refining families of Great Britain. [With
genealogical tables.] London, 1951.
ED/N-1 (NE.63.b.3)

[TRANSCRIPTS of writings concerning the Walker
family of Montrose between 1676-1831.]
QZ/P28

WHITE, Emma Siggins
Genealogy of the descendants of John Walker of
Wigton, Scotland, with records of a few allied
families. [Kansas City, Mo., 1902.]
QZ/P10 (Unconfirmed location)

Walker in Aberdeen

[A GENEALOGICAL deduction of the family of
Hector: descendants of George Hector, weaver in
Old Aberdeen and his wife Marjory Walker.]
(*MSS.*)
QZ/P22

GENEALOGICAL details of Walker family, shop-
keepers in Aberdeen. [N.p., n.d.]
QZ/P22

Walkinshaw *see also* Paterson of Bannockburn

Walkinshaw

WALKINSHAW papers. [N.d.] (*MSS.*)
QZ/P-6

Wallace

HARRISON-WALLACE, Charles
Notes on the Wallace family of Newton Hall in
Kennoway, Fife. (In *Scottish Genealogist*, vol.xxvii,
no.4, December 1980, pp.162-5.)
ED/N-1 (Gen.7)

WALLACE, Charles B.
Clan Wallace. 2nd edition. Dallas, Tex., 1971.
ED/N-2 QZ/P-6

WALLACE, James
Wallace-Bruce and closely related families.
Minnesota, 1930.
QZ/P14 GL/U-1

Wallace of Bathgate

CUTHBERT, Alexander A.
Genealogical chart of the Wallace family, Bathgate.
[N.p.], 1909.
ED/N-1 (1908.33;1964.75 with MS. additions)
QZ/P-1

Wallace of Elderslie

HAYDEN, H. E.
Virginia genealogies: a genealogy of the Glassell
family of Scotland and Virginia. Wilkes-Barre, Pa.,
1891.
ED/N-1 (H3.81.3660) ED/N-2 QZ/P-1

MITCHELL, John Oswald
The two Elderslies. Glasgow, 1884. (Reprinted from
Glasgow Herald, 13 September 1884.)
ED/N-2 QZ/P-1 QZ/P99

— The Wallaces of Elderslie. (In *Transactions of the
Glasgow Archaeological Society*, new series, vol.i, 1890,
pp.102-15.)
ED/N-1 (U.413)

— — (Reprinted from *Transactions of the Glasgow
Archaeological Society*, new series, vol.1, 1890.)
ED/N-2 QZ/L37 QZ/P-1 QZ/P22 QZ/P99

ROGERS, Charles
The book of Wallace: history and genealogy of the
family. Edinburgh, 1889. 2v. (Grampian Club, 22.)
ED/N-1 (Gramp.Club.22) ED/N-2 QZ/P22
QZ/P40 QZ/P14 GL/U-1 QZ/L37 QZ/P-1
QZ/P99 QZ/P16

SEAVER, J. M.
Wallace genealogical data. Texas, 1927.
ED/N-2 QZ/P99

WALLACE, Charles B.
The Clan Wallace. Texas, 1966.
ED/N-2

WALSH,
A royalist family. [N.p.], 1970.
ED/N-2

Wallace in U.S.A.

PHELPS, James A.
The Wallace family in America. New York, 1914.
ED/N-2 QZ/P99

Wardlaw

GIBSON, John C.
The Wardlaws in Scotland: a history of the
Wardlaws of Wilton and Torrie and their cadets.
Edinburgh, 1912.
ED/N-1 (S.121.d) QZ/P22 QZ/P18 AD/U-1
SA/U-1 QZ/P11 GL/U-1 QZ/L37 QZ/P14
QZ/P-1 QZ/P99 QZ/P16

Wardlaw of Pitreavie

['GENEALOGICAL account of the Wardlaw family of
Pitreavie'. 1811?]
ED/N-1 (Adv.MS.6.1.17,f.67)

Warrack of Aberdeen

WARRACK, John
Three chapters in memories, 1819-1907. [N.p., n.d.]
(*Typescript*)
QZ/P22

Waters of Caithness

WATERS, Marjory McGillivray
Waters in depth, 1648-1978: a genealogy of the
Waters family of Caithness, Scotland. . . . Decorah,
Iowa, 1978.
QZ/P13 QZ/P99

Waterston

BI-CENTENARY history: George Waterston and Sons
Ltd., 1752-1952. Edinburgh, [1953].
ED/N-1 (NE.11.b.8;1969.136) QZ/P34

WATERSTON, Robert
Random notes on long ago people . . . Waterstons,
Watherstons . . . and other spellings of the name.
[Edinburgh], 1964.
ED/N-1 (1973.205) DN/U-1 QZ/P-1 QZ/P28
QZ/P34

— Some further notes on long ago people. [N.p., 1966.]
DN/U-1

Watson

WATSON, Angus
The Angus clan, years 1588 to 1950. [With a genealogical table.] Gateshead, 1955.
ED/N-1 (NE.25.c.6)   QZ/P99

WATSON, Charles Brodie Boog
Traditions and genealogies of some members of the families of Boog, Heron, Leishman, Ross, Watson. Perth, 1908.
ED/N-1 (S.120.d)   QZ/P18   ED/N-2   SA/U-1
QZ/L37   QZ/P99

WATSON, George Oliphant
The Watson saga. London, 1974.
QZ/Q76

WATSON, Herbert A. Grant
The Grant Watsons. [N.p.], 1972.
QZ/L37

Watson of Aithernie

INGLIS, John A.
The Watsons of Aithernie, Fife. (In *Miscellanea Genealogica et Heraldica*, 5th series, vol.vi, 1926-8, pp.269-71.)
ED/N-1 (NH.296)

— — (Reprinted from *Miscellanea Genealogica et Heraldica*, 5th series, vol.vi, 1926-8.)
ED/N-1 (5.413)

Watson of Damhead

WOOD, John Philp
Memorials of various families. [1830?] (*MS.*)
QZ/P99

Watson of Saughton

WOOD, John Philp
Memorials of various families. [1830?] (*MS.*)
QZ/P99

Watt of Breckness

[ORIGINAL family papers.]
QZ/P38 (Unconfirmed location)

Watt in Edinburgh

WELLES, Albert
Watt in New York and in Edinburgh, Scotland. New York, 1898.
ED/N-1 (4.218(8))

Watt in Greenock

WILLIAMSON, George
Letters respecting the Watt family. Greenock, 1840.
ED/N-1 (S.147.e)   QZ/P-1   QZ/P52
(Unconfirmed location)

—Memorials of the lineage . . . of James Watt. Edinburgh, 1856.
ED/N-1 (Hall.226.a)   GL/U-1   QZ/P-1   QZ/P99

Wauchope

PATERSON, James
Scottish surnames: a contribution to genealogy. Edinburgh, 1866.
ED/N-1 (K.115.a)   QZ/P22   DN/U-1

WAUCHOPE, Gladys Mary
The Ulster branch of the family of Wauchope, Wanhope, Wahab, Wanghop, etc., with notes of the main Scottish family and on branches in America and Australia. London, 1929.
ED/N-1 (S.121.g)   SA/U-1   QZ/P99

Wauchope of Niddrie-Marischall

PATERSON, James
History and genealogy of the family of Wauchope of Niddrie-Marischall. Edinburgh, 1858.
ED/N-1 (A.58.a)   QZ/L37   SA/U-1   QZ/P99

Waus *see also* Vaus, Vaux

Waus of Barnbarroch

WAUS, Sir Patrick
Correspondence, 1540-1597; edited by Robert Vans Agnew. Edinburgh, 1882.
ED/N-1 (Bh.4/3)   QZ/P-1

— — Edinburgh, 1887.
ED/N-1 (R.24.a)   QZ/P-1

Wedderburn

DEUCHAR, A.
Genealogical collections relative to the family of Wedderburn. (*MS.*)
QZ/P-1

WEDDERBURN, Alexander
The Wedderburn book: a history of the Wedderburns in the counties of Berwick and Forfar. [N.p.], 1898. 2v.
ED/N-1 (S.121.a)   ED/N-2   QZ/P11   AD/U-1
SA/U-1   QZ/P28   DN/U-1   QZ/L37   GL/U-1
QZ/P-1   QZ/P99

Wedderburn of Rosslyn

['A GENEALOGICAL account concerning the Wedderburn family of Rosslyn. 1802?]
ED/N-1 (Adv.MS.33.5.9,pp.847-51)

Wellwood of Touch

MCNAUGHTON, Duncan
The descent of the Wellwoods of Touch. (In *Scottish Genealogist*, vol.xvii, no.1, March 1970, pp.7-12.)
ED/N-1 (Gen.7)

Wemyss

CUNNINGHAM, Andrew Storar
Randolph Gordon Erskine Wemyss: an appreciation. Leven, [1909].
ED/N-1 (S.158.a) QZ/P-7 QZ/P18 QZ/P-1 QZ/P16

['GENEALOGICAL account of the Wemyss family'. 1802.]
ED/N-1 (Adv.MS.34.3.21,f.7)

MCANDREW, Bruce
The Lion of Inchmartin. (In *Double Tressure*, no.4, 1982, pp.2-10.)
ED/N-1 (P.sm.1445)

MARSHALL, G. F. L.
The Muir book. [N.p.], 1930.
ED/N-2 QZ/P99

STALKER, D. M. G.
John Weemse of Lathocker: one of Scotland's early hebraists. (In *Records of the Scottish Church History Society*, vol.viii, 1944, pp.151-66.)
ED/N-1 (NE.30.f)

WEMYSS, Lady Mary Constance
Family record. London, 1932.
ED/N-1 (R.196.a) GL/U-1 QZ/P-1 QZ/P99

Wemyss of Wemyss

FRASER, Sir William
Illustrations of the memorials of the family of Wemyss of Wemyss. Edinburgh, 1888.
ED/U-1 QZ/P18 QZ/P56

— Memorials of the family of Wemyss of Wemyss. Edinburgh, 1888. 3v.
ED/N-1 (Gen.8.W) QZ/P18 QZ/P56 AD/U-1 SA/U-1 GL/U-1 QZ/L37 ED/N-2 QZ/P-1 QZ/P99 QZ/P16

['NOTES on the genealogy of the Wemyss family of Wemyss'. 17--.]
ED/N-1 (Adv.MS.49.7.3,f.35)

Wemyss, Earl of Wemyss

WOODS, David
The history of the family of Charteris-Wemyss-Douglas. [1980.] (*MSS.*)
QZ/P34

White

BENZIES, Frank
The White family, 1700-1967. Coupar Angus, 1967.
QZ/Q17

WHITE, W. R.
The White family from Donald Bain of Aberdeen, 1640-1740. [1845?] (*Typescript*)
QZ/P22

Whitefoord

PARSONS, F. M.
Anent the Whitefoords. (In *Scottish Review*, vol.xxxiv, July 1899, pp.90-101.)
ED/N-1 (NH.301) QZ/P99

Whitelaw

WHITELAW, Harry Vincent
The House of Whitelaw . . . 1400 1900. Glasgow, 1928.
ED/N-1 (S.121.e) QZ/P34 QZ/P-3 ED/N-2 QZ/L37 QZ/Q76 QZ/P-1 QZ/P99

Whitson

WITHERS, C. S.
The family of Thomas Whitson and Agnes Hogg, married 1755 at Prestonkirk, Scotland. 2nd ed. [Wellington, N.Z.], 1978.
ED/N-1 (HP1.82.156)

Whittet

WHITTET, William *and* WHITTET, Robert
Whittet: a family record, 1657-1900. Richmond, Va., 1900.
ED/N-2 QZ/P26

Whyte

GENEALOGICAL notes concerning the family of Whyte. [N.p., 1916.]
QZ/P28

MCNAUGHTON, Duncan
The Whytes of Bennochy, Kirkcaldy. (In *Scottish Genealogist*, vol.xii, no.2, 1965, pp.26-31.)
ED/N-1 (Gen.7)

WHYTE, Donald
The Whytes: a family memorial. [Kirkliston], 1961.
ED/N-1 (6.171) ED/N-2 QZ/P99

Wigtown, Earl of *see* **Fleming,** Earl of Wigtown

Wilkie of Rathobyres
McCALL, Hardy Bertram
Some old families: a contribution to the genealogical
history of Scotland. Birmingham, 1890.
ED/N-1 (A.36.a) QZ/P11 QZ/L37 ED/N-2
QZ/P99

Williamson
WILLIAMSON, Alexander G.
William of Scotland. Dumfries, [1970].
ED/N-1 (1970.134) GL/U-1

WILSON, William
Folklore and genealogies of uppermost Nithsdale.
Dumfries, 1904.
ED/N-1 (R.241.h)

Williamson of Kilrenny
HUNT, Wallis
Heirs of great adventure: the history of Balfour,
Williamson and Company Limited, 1851-1951.
[With a genealogical table.] London, 1951,60. 2v.
ED/N-1 (NG.1297.d.9)

Willison
BLACK, William George
A note on the family of Black of Over Abington ...
with memoranda on ... Willison of Redshaw. ...
Glasgow, 1908.
GL/U-1 QZ/L37

— — [2nd ed.] Glasgow, 1924.
ED/N-1 (S.121.e) ED/N-2 QZ/P22 QZ/Q71
QZ/P99

Wilson
The FAMILY of Wilson of Belltrees, Bannockburn,
etc. (*MSS.*)
QZ/P-1

WILSON, Alex.
Fragments that remain. Stroud, Glos., 1950.
QZ/P10 (Unconfirmed location)

WILSON, William
Folklore and genealogies of uppermost Nithsdale.
Dumfries, 1904.
ED/N-1 (R.241.h)

Wilson in Banffshire
BROWN, Andrew Cassels
The Wilsons: a Banffshire family of factors.
Edinburgh, 1936.
ED/N-1 (R.172.c) QZ/P30 ED/N-2 QZ/P22
AD/U-1 SA/U-1 QZ/P50 QZ/P-1 QZ/P99

Wilson of Beith
CADBURY, W. A.
Wilsons of Beith (Ayrshire). [N.p., 1933.]
QZ/P99

Wilson of Bourtrees
DOBIE, James
Memoir of William Wilson of Crummock.
[Edinburgh], 1894.
ED/N-1 (Hall.260.a)

Wilson of Croglin
REID, Robert Corsane
Wilson of Croglin. (In *Transactions of the
Dumfriesshire and Galloway Natural History &
Antiquarian Society*, 3rd series, vol.xxviii, 1949-50,
pp.135-49.)
ED/N-1 (J.187)

Wilson of Crummock
DOBIE, James
Memoir of William Wilson of Crummock.
[Edinburgh], 1894.
ED/N-1 (Hall.260.a)

Wilson in Fair Isle
WILSON, Alan T.
The Fair Isle Wilsons: a genealogical exploration.
[N.p.], 1973.
QZ/P41

Wilson in Hawick and New Zealand
WIERZBICKA, Cynthia
The story of the Wilson family: some family
documents relating to the Wilsons of Hawick, and
to James Glenny Wilson's development of Ngaio
(sheep/cattle) Station, Wellington, New Zealand.
[Ngaio], 1973.
QZ/P11

Wilsone of Murrayshall
CAMPBELL, J. W.
The story of Murrayshall. Stirling, 1925.
QZ/P14

Wimberley

WIMBERLEY, Douglas
Memorials of four old families. Inverness, 1894.
ED/N-1 (Y.59.a.23) QZ/P26 QZ/P22 QZ/P40
QZ/P-1 DN/U-1 QZ/P99

—Memorials of the family of Wimberley of South
Witham, etc. Inverness, 1893.
QZ/P30 ED/N-2 SA/U-1 AD/U-1 QZ/L37

Winton, Earldom of *see also* **Montgomery,** Earl of Eglinton

Winton, Earldom of

EGLINTOUN, Archibald William Montgomerie,
13th Earl of
Abstract of the evidence in support of the Earl's
claim.
QZ/L37

—Case for the Earl of Eglinton in his service as heir-
male general and heir-male of provision to George,
4th Earl of Winton, Lord Seaton and Tranent.
ED/N-1 (Yule.169) QZ/L37

—Claim for the Earl in the Service.
QZ/L37

INDEX to the case and abstract of evidence.
QZ/L37

PEDIGREE . . . [Edinburgh, 1840.]
QZ/L37

VERDICT of jury.
QZ/L37

Wise

ROGERS, Charles
Memorials of the Scottish families of Strachan and
Wise. Edinburgh, 1877. (Grampian Club.)
ED/N-1 (Gramp.Club.31) AD/U-1 GL/U-1
SA/U-1 QZ/L37 QZ/P14 QZ/P16 QZ/P28
QZ/P99

—Memorials of the Strachans, baronets of Thornton,
Kincardineshire, and of the family of Wise of
Hillbank, formerly Wyse of Lunan in the county of
Forfar. London, [1873]. (Grampian Club.)
ED/N-1 (Gramp.Club.27) GL/U-1 SA/U-1
QZ/L37 QZ/P-1 QZ/P40 QZ/P99

Wishart

GENEALOGICAL tree of the Wisharts of Kincardine-
shire, or the Mearns and Fifeshire, Scotland.
[N.p., 1958.]
ED/N-1 (7.56)

ROGERS, Charles
Life of George Wishart . . . and a genealogical
history of the family of Wishart. London, 1876.
(Grampian Club, 11.)
ED/N-1 (Gramp.Club.11) QZ/P40 QZ/P22
QZ/L37 QZ/P-1 QZ/P99

Wishart of Cliftonhall

WHYTE, Donald
Wishart of Cliftonhall: notes on a dormant
baronetcy. (In *Genealogists' Magazine*, vol.19, no.7,
September 1978, pp.237-41.)
ED/N-1 (Y.173)

Wishart of Pittarrow

GALBRAITH, Robert
The family of George Wishart, the martyr of
Pitarrow. (In *Deeside Field*, 2nd series, no.6, 1970,
pp.86-9.)
ED/N-1 (P.sm.590)

WISHART, D.
Genealogical history of the Wisharts of Pittarrow
and Logie Wishart. Perth, 1914.
ED/N-1 (S.121.f) ED/N-2 QZ/P-1

Wood

MONTAGU, Frances Mary
Pedigree of Colonel Sir Mark Wood. [N.d.] (*MS.*)
SA/U-1

WOOD, John Walter
William Wood, born 1656, of Earlsferry, Scotland,
and some of his descendants and their connections.
[With genealogical tables.] [New Haven], 1916.
ED/N-1 (NE.25.a.8)

Wood of Largo

MONTAGUE, Frances Mary
Memorials of the family of Wood of Largo. [N.p.],
1863.
ED/N-1 (A.114.b) QZ/Q17 QZ/P18 ED/N-2
SA/U-1 QZ/P-1 QZ/P99

Worthing

WALLACE, Joyce M. *and* WORTHING, Frank
Victorian recollections of a family and a house.
Loanhead, 1975.
ED/N-1 (H3.76.581) QZ/P-1

Wright

WRIGHT, Marcus Stults
Our family ties: some ancestral lines of Marcus S.
Wright, Jr. and Alice Olden Wright. [With
genealogical tables.] South River, N.J., 1960.
ED/N-1 (NF.1373.a.4)   QZ/P28

Wright of Auchinellan

OFFICIAL genealogy [of Wright of Auchinellan].
[N.p., n.d.] (*MS.*)
QZ/P-6

Wyld

WYLD, Robert Stodart
Memoir of James Wyld of Gilston, and his family;
also of Robert Stodart of Kailzie and Ormiston
Hill. Edinburgh, 1889.
ED/N-1 (NF.1172.h.17)

Wyllie

NOTES on the Wyllie album. [N.p., n.d.]
ED/N-1 (6.796)   ED/N-2   ED/U-1   GL/U-1
QZ/P-1   QZ/P22   QZ/P-6   QZ/P99

Wyse *see* Wise

Yellowlees

YELLOWLEES, John
The Yellowlees family. 1931.
QZ/P99

Youl *see also* Yuille

Youl

YOUL, John William
John Youl the immigrant, 1803-1882: a record of his
parents and immediate family through to eight
generations. South Yarra, Victoria, 1980.
ED/N-1 (HP1.81.888)

Young

['GENEALOGICAL collections of the Young family'.
N.d.]
ED/N-1 (MS.15481,f.35)

[HISTORICAL account of the family of Young. 1852.]
ED/N-1 (MS.15930)

JOHNSTON, Alexander
Short memoir of James Young, merchant burgess of
Aberdeen, and Rachel Cruickshank, his spouse, and
of their descendants. Aberdeen, [1861].
ED/N-1 (Hall.230.a)   ED/N-2   ED/U-1   QZ/L37
QZ/P22   QZ/P99

— — Edited by W. Johnston. Aberdeen, 1894.
ED/N-1 (A.57.a)   GL/U-1   QZ/L37   QZ/P-1
QZ/P22   QZ/P30   QZ/P99

LANG, Patrick Sellar
The Langs of Selkirk, with some notes on the
Sibbalds of Whitelaw. . . . Melbourne, 1910.
ED/N-2   QZ/P11   QZ/P99

MCCALL, Hardy Bertram
Memoirs of my ancestors. Birmingham, 1884.
ED/N-1 (A.114.a)   QZ/P99

— Some old families: a contribution to the
genealogical history of Scotland. Birmingham,
1890.
ED/N-1 (A.36.a)   QZ/P11   QZ/L37   QZ/P99

Younger of Clackmannanshire

HALLEN, Arthur Washington Cornelius
An account of the family of Younger, co. of
Clackmannan. Edinburgh, 1889.
QZ/P15   QZ/P16

Younger of Peeblesshire

HALLEN, Arthur Washington Cornelius
An account of the family of Younger, co. Peebles.
Edinburgh, 1890.
DN/U-1   QZ/P15

Yuille *see also* Youl

Yuille of Darleith

['A DRAFT genealogical account of the family Yuille
of Darleith'. 1827?]
ED/N-1 (Adv.MS.19.2.17,f.381)

WILLIAMSON, George
Old Cartsburn: a history of the estate. Appendix.
Paisley, 1894.
QZ/P-1

Yule

THOMSON, David Couper
Thomson, Couper, Yule, Sinclair genealogical
chart. Dundee, [1936].
QZ/L37   QZ/P20   QZ/P99

APPENDIX

ADAM, Frank
Clans, septs and regiments of the Scottish highlands. Edinburgh, 1908. (And later eds.)

ANDERSON, William
Genealogy and surnames, with some heraldic and biographical notices. Edinburgh, 1865.

— The Scottish nation: or, the surnames, families, literature, honours and biographical history of the people of Scotland. Edinburgh, 1860-2. 3v.

ASSOCIATION OF SCOTTISH GENEALOGISTS AND RECORD AGENTS
Newsletter. No. 1 (February 1982)- . Dunfermline, 1982- .

BAIN, Robert
The clans and tartans of Scotland. London, 1938. (And later eds.)

BAKER, Donna L.
Scottish sources in LDS [Latter-Day Saints] branch libraries. (In *Families*, vol.21, no.4, 1982, pp.251-64.)

BARROW, Geoffrey Wallis Steuart
Some problems in twelfth and thirteenth century Scottish history: a genealogical approach. (In *Scottish Genealogist*, vol.xxv, no.4, December 1978, pp.97-112.)

BEATON, Donald
Genealogical bibliography of Caithness and Sutherland. 1928. (Viking Society for Northern Research.)

BEDE, Tim
MacRoots: how to trace your Scottish ancestors. Edinburgh, 1982.

BERG, Jonas and LAGERCRANTZ, Bo
Scots in Sweden: [published for the exhibition 'Scots in Sweden' at the Royal Scottish Museum, Edinburgh, summer 1962]. [Edinburgh], 1962.

BLACK, George Fraser
Scotland's mark on America. New York, 1921.

— The surnames of Scotland: their origin, meaning and history. [New York], 1945. (And later eds.)

BLOXHAM, V. Ben
Key to the parochial registers of Scotland from earliest times through 1854. Provo, Utah, 1970.

BLUNDELL, Frederick Odo
Ancient Catholic homes of Scotland. [London], 1907.

BOLTON, Charles Knowles
Scotch Irish pioneers in Ulster and America. Boston, Mass., 1910.

BROWNE, James
A critical examination of Dr. MacCulloch's work on the Highlands and Western Islands of Scotland. Edinburgh, 1825. (And later eds.)

— A history of the Highlands and of the Highland clans. Glasgow, 1838. 4v. (And later eds.)

BRYCE, George and CAMPBELL, William Wilfred
The Scotsman in Canada. [London], 1912. 2v.

BULLOCH, Joseph Gaston Baillie
A history and genealogy of the families of Bayard, Houston of Georgia and the descent of the Bolton family from Assheton, Byron and Hulton. (With notes on some Highland families connected with them.) Washington, 1919.

BURKE, John and BURKE, Sir John Bernard
A genealogical and heraldic history of the extinct and dormant baronetcies of England, Ireland and Scotland. London, 1838. (And later eds.)

BURKE'S genealogical and heraldic history of the landed gentry. London, 1833. (And later eds.)

BURKE'S genealogical and heraldic history of the peerage, baronetage and knightage. London, 1826. (And later eds.)

CAMERON, Viola Root
Emigrants from Scotland to America, 1774-1775. Baltimore, Md., 1976.

CAMPBELL, George Douglas
Crofts and farms in the Hebrides: being an account of the management of an island estate for 130 years. [With a table of petitioners wishing to emigrate.] [Edinburgh], 1883.

CHAMBERS, William
Stories of old families. Edinburgh, 1878.

CHURCH OF JESUS CHRIST OF LATTER-DAY SAINTS
Genealogical Society Records of genealogical value for Scotland. Revised edition. Salt Lake City, Utah, 1978.

CLOUSTON, J. Storer
The origin of the Orkney chiefs. (In *Proceedings of the Orkney Antiquarian Society*, vol.xii, 1933-4, pp.29-39.)

COKAYNE, George Edward
Complete baronetage. Exeter, 1900-09. 6v.

— The complete peerage of England, Scotland, Ireland, Great Britain and the United Kingdom, extant, extinct or dormant. New edition by . . . V. Gibbs and H. A. Doubleday. London, 1910-40. 13v.

COUTTS, James
The Anglo-Norman peaceful invasion of Scotland, 1057-1200: origin of great Scottish families. Edinburgh, 1922.

CRAWFURD, George
The peerage of Scotland, etc. Edinburgh, 1716.

CUNNINGHAM, Audrey
The loyal clans. Cambridge, 1932.

DAVIDSON, Rev. John
Inverurie and the earldom of Garioch . . . with a genealogical index of Garioch families. Edinburgh, 1878.

DICKSON, R. J.
Ulster emigration to colonial America, 1718-1775. London, 1966. (*Ulster-Scot Historical Series*, vol.1.)

DOBSON, David
Directory of Scots banished to the American plantations, 1650-1775. Baltimore, Md., 1984.

— Directory of Scottish settlers in North America, 1625-1825. Vol.1. Baltimore, Md., 1984.

DODDS, James
Records of the Scotch settlers in the River Plate, and their churches. Buenos Aires, 1897.

DONALDSON, Gordon *and* MORPETH, Robert S.
Who's who in Scottish history. Oxford, 1973.

DONNER, Otto
A brief sketch of the Scottish families in Finland and Sweden. Helsingfors, 1884.

DORWARD, David
Scottish surnames. Edinburgh, 1978.

DOUGLAS, Sir Robert
The baronage of Scotland, etc. Edinburgh, 1978.

— The peerage of Scotland, etc. Edinburgh, 1764. (And later eds.)

DRUMMOND, Henry
Histories of noble British families, etc. London, 1846. 2v.

DUNAWAY, Wayland F.
The Scotch-Irish of colonial Pennysylvania. Hamden, N. Carolina, 1962.

DUNCANSON, John V.
Falmouth: a New England township in Nova Scotia, 1760-1965. [Windsor, Ont.], 1965.

DUNDEE ART EXHIBITION COMMITTEE
Old Dundee: a pictorial and historical exhibition, illustrative of the past life, social, political, municipal and industrial of the ancient burgh of Dundee, 1892-93. [Dundee, 1893.]

DUNFERMLINE CENTRAL LIBRARY
Tracing your ancestors: a guide to sources in the Central Library. Dunfermline, 1981.

EGLE, William
Pennsylvania: genealogies chiefly Scotch-Irish and German. 2nd ed., reprinted. Baltimore, 1969.

EYRE-TODD, George
The highland clans of Scotland: their history and traditions. London, 1923. 2v.

FAMILY history: a guide to Ayrshire sources; edited by Jane Jamieson. [Ayr], 1984. (Ayrshire Collections, vol.14, no.4)

FERGUSSON, Sir James
Lowland lairds. London, 1949.

FILBY, P. William
American & British genealogy & heraldry: a selected list of books. Chicago, 1970.

FISCHER, Thomas Alfred
The Scots in Eastern and Western Prussia. Edinburgh, 1903.

— The Scots in Germany. Edinburgh, 1902.

— The Scots in Sweden. Edinburgh, 1907.

FOSTER, Joseph
Members of Parliament, Scotland . . . 1357-1882; with genealogical and biographical notices. London, 1882.

FOTHERGILL, Gerald
List of emigrant ministers to America, 1690-1811. [N.p.], 1904.

— The records of naval men. [N.p.], 1910.

FRASER, Sir William
Facsimiles of Scottish charters and letters. Edinburgh, 1903.

FRASER-MACKINTOSH, Charles
Antiquarian notes, historical, genealogical and social. (2nd ser.): Inverness-shire, parish by parish. Inverness, 1897.

— Antiquarian notes. A series of papers regarding families and places in the Highlands. Inverness, 1865 etc.

GAELIC gleanings. Vol.1, no.1 (November 1981)- . Santa Ana, Calif., 1981- .

GARDNER, David E., and others
A genealogical atlas of Scotland. Salt Lake City, Utah, [1962].

GARRETT, E. M.
In search of Scottish roots. (In *Family History*, vol.12, no.95/6, March 1983, pp.318-25.)

GAYLOR, John Hamilton
New clans and grants of arms. (In *Coat of Arms*, new series, vol.iv, no.120, winter 1981/2, pp.422-9.)

The GENEALOGICAL quarterly: notes and queries dealing with British and American family and clan history and biography. Vol.I, no.1 (summer 1932)- vol.XLI, no.4 (summer 1975). London, 1932-75.

A GENEALOGIE of the barons in the Mearns of late memory deschending lineally unto the year of God 1578. (Copy of this MS. in *Misc. Third Spalding Club*, v, ii, 1940.)

GENEALOGIES in the Library of Congress: a bibliography; edited by Marion J. Kaminkow. Baltimore, Md., 1972-7. 3v.

GORDON, René
Les Ecossais en Berry: paroisse-Saint-Outrillet de Bourges. [Bourges], 1919.

GRANT, Sir Francis James
The county families of the Zetland Islands. Lerwick, 1893.

— Index to genealogies, birthbriefs and funeral escutcheons, recorded in the Lyon Office. Edinburgh, 1908.

GRIMBLE, Ian
Clans and chiefs. London, 1980.

— Scottish clans and tartans. [Feltham], 1973.

HAMILTON-EDWARDS, Gerald
In search of ancestry. Chichester, 1966. (And later eds.)

— In search of army ancestry. Chichester, 1977.

— In search of Scottish ancestry. Chichester. [1972].

— Scottish genealogical sources. (In *Family History*, vol.12, no.87/8, January 1982, pp.89-104.)

HANNA, Charles A.
The Scotch-Irish, or the Scot in north Britain, north Ireland, and North America. New York, 1902. 2v.

HARRISON, Edward Stroud
Our Scottish district checks. Edinburgh, 1968.

HARRISON, Howard Guy
A select bibliography of English genealogy; with brief lists for Wales, Scotland and Ireland. London, 1937.

HENDERSON, Alexander
Henderson's Australian families. Melbourne, 1941.

HENDERSON, John
Caithness family history. Edinburgh, 1884.

HEWLETT, William Oxenham
Notes on dignities in the peerage of Scotland, which are dormant, or which have been forefeited. London, 1882.

HIGHLAND papers; edited by J. R. N. MacPhail. Edinburgh, 1914-34. 4v. (Scottish History Society Publications, 2nd series, vols. 5, 12, 20, 3rd series, vol.22.)

HISTORY of the Highland regiments. Highland clans etc., from official and other authentic sources. Edinburgh, 1887. 2v.

A HISTORY of the Scottish Highlands, Highland clans and Highland regiments; edited by John S. Keltie. Edinburgh, 1875. 2v. (And later eds.)

INNES OF LEARNEY, Sir Thomas
The tartans of the clans and families of Scotland. Edinburgh, 1938. (And later eds.)

INSTITUTE OF HERALDIC AND GENEALOGICAL STUDIES
Family History. Vol.1, no.1 (October 1962)- . Canterbury, [1962-].

IONA CLUB
Collectanea de rebus albanicis: consisting of original papers and documents relating to the history of the Highlands and islands of Scotland. Edinburgh, 1847.

JAMES, Alwyn
Scottish roots: a step-by-step guide for ancestor-hunters in Scotland and overseas. Loanhead, 1981.

JOHNSTON, G. P.
Catalogue of heraldic, genealogical, and antiquarian books and manuscripts, which belonged to the late Alexander Sinclair, Esq. Edinburgh, 1877.

JOHNSTON, T. B. *and* ROBERTSON, James Alexander
The historical geography of the clans of Scotland. Edinburgh, 1872. (And later eds.)

JOHNSTON, Thomas
Our Scots noble families. Glasgow, 1913. (And later eds.)

JOHNSTONE, Catherine Laura
Historical families of Dumfriesshire and the Border Wars. Dumfries, 1888, etc.

KELLY'S handbook to the titled, landed and official classes. London, 1875. (And later eds.)

KNOWLES, George Parker
A genealogical and heraldic account of the Coultharts of Coulthart . . . [to which are added the pedigrees of seven other . . . families]. London, 1855.

LANCOUR, Harold
A bibliography of ship passenger lists, 1538-1825: being a guide to published lists of early immigrants to North America. 3rd ed. New York, 1963.

LANGHORNE, Rev. W. H.
Reminiscences connected chiefly with Inveresk and Musselburgh and sketches of family histories. Edinburgh, 1893.

A LOCAL index of the Dumfries and Galloway Standard and Advertiser and its predecessors over 200 years. Dumfries, 1980- .

LODGE, Edmund
The genealogy of the existing British peerage; with brief sketches of the family history of the nobility. London, 1832. (And later eds.)

MACBEAN, William M.
Biographical register of Saint Andrew's Society of the State of New York. New York, 1922.

—Register of Saint Andrew's Society of the State of New York. 2nd series: 1807-1856. [New York], 1922.

— — 3rd series: 1857-1906. [New York], 1923.

—Roster of Saint Andrew's Society of the State of New York, with biographical data. New York, 1911.

MCCALL, Henry Bertram
Some old families: a contribution to the genealogical history of Scotland. Birmingham, 1890.

MACDOUGALL, Donald
Scots and Scots' descendants in America. Vol. I. [New York, 1917.]

MACFARLANE, Margaret *and* MACFARLANE, Alastair
The Scottish radicals tried and transported to Australia for treason in 1820. Revised ed. Stevenage, 1981.

MACFARLANE, Walter
Genealogical collections concerning families in Scotland, 1750-1751; edited by James Toshach Clark. Edinburgh, 1900. 2v. (Scottish History Society Publications, vols.33,34.)

MCIAN, R. R.
The clans of the Scottish Highlands: the costumes of the clans; text by James Logan. Reprinted. London, 1983.

MCKERLIE, Peter Handyside
History of the lands and their owners in Galloway. Edinburgh, 1870-79, etc. 5v.

MACKINTOSH, John
Historic Earls and Earldoms of Scotland. Aberdeen, [1898].

MAC LEAN, J.
De huwelijksintekeningen van Schotse militairen in Nederland, 1574-1665. Zutphen, 1976. (Koninklijk Nederlandsch Genootschap voor Geslacht- en Wapenkunde Werken, vol.iv.)

MACLEAN, John Patterson
An historical account of the settlements of Scotch highlanders in America prior to the peace of 1783, together with notices of Highland regiments and biographical sketches. Cleveland, Ohio, 1900.

MACLEOD, Donald, of Garelochside
Historic families, notable people and memorabilia, of the Lennox, etc. Dumbarton, 1891.

MACVEIGH, James
   The great families of Scotland, historical and genealogical. Dumfries, 1891. 2v.

— The Scottish family history, or, the historical and genealogical account of all Scottish families and surnames. Dumfries, 1891. 3v.

MAIDMENT, James
   Collectanea genealogica. Edinburgh, 1883.

MANSON, Thomas
   Shetland's roll of honour and roll of service: [biographies and photographs of Shetlanders killed in the 1914-18 war]. Lerwick, 1920.

MARSHALL, David
   Genealogical notes anent some ancient Scottish families. Perth, 1884.

MARSHALL, George
   A catalogue of pedigrees hitherto unindexed. London, 1867.

MARSHALL, George William
   The genealogist's guide to printed pedigrees, etc. London, 1879. (And later eds.)

MARSHALL, Rosalind K.
   The Scottish National Portrait Gallery as a source for the genealogist. (In *Scottish Genealogist*, vol.xxx, no.1, March 1983, pp.5-8.)

MARTINE, Roderick
   Clan lands of Scotland: a guide to territories and locations of historic interest connected with the clans and major families of Scotland. [Edinburgh], 1981.

— Clans and tartans. Edinburgh, 1982.

— A guide to the clans and major families of Scotland. Perth, 1977. (*Scottish Field*, vol.cxxiii, souvenir supplement.)

— — Homelands of the Scots: a guide to territories and locations of historic interest connected with the clans and major families of Scotland. Edinburgh, 1981.

MEYER, Duane
   The Highland Scots of North Carolina, 1732-1776. Chapel Hill, N. Carolina, 1961.

MILLER, Thomas
   Historical and genealogical record of the first settlers of Colchester County down to the present time. Halifax, Nova Scotia, 1873.

MINUTE book kept by the War Committee of the Covenanters in the Stewartry of Kirkcudbright in 1640 and 1641. Kirkcudbright, 1855.

MITCHELL, Alison
   Monumental inscriptions. (In *Scottish Genealogist*, vol.xxv, no.4, December 1978, pp.133-6.)

MONCRIEFFE, Sir Iain
   The Highland clans: the dynastic origins, chiefs and background of the clans connected with highland history, and of some other families. London, 1967. (And later eds.)

MOWLE, P. C.
   A genealogical history of pioneer families of Australia. Sydney, 1939. (And later eds.)

MUNRO, Robert William
   Highland clans and tartans. [London], 1977.

— Kinsmen and clansmen. [Edinburgh], 1971.

MUNRO, Robert William *and* MUNRO, Ian
   Highland genealogy in local publications. (In *Scottish Genealogist*, vol.xi, no.1, May 1964.)

NEW ENGLAND HISTORIC GENEALOGICAL SOCIETY
   The Greenlaw Index of the New England Historic Genealogical Society. Boston, Mass., 1979. 2v.

NICOLSON, Alexander
   History of Skye . . . a record of the families . . . illustrated with genealogical tables. Glasgow, 1930.

NISBET, Alexander
   Alexander Nisbet's heraldic plates originally intended for his "System of heraldry". Edinburgh, 1892.

— A system of heraldry speculative and practical: illustrated with suitable examples of armorial figures, and achievements of the most considerable surnames and families in Scotland. Edinburgh, 1722,42. 2v. (And later eds.)

The ORIGINAL lists of persons of quality: emigrants, religious exiles, political rebels . . . who went from Great Britain to the American plantations, 1600-1700; edited by John Camden Hotten. London, 1874.

PAPERS relating to the Scots in Poland, 1576-1793; edited by A. Francis Steuart. Edinburgh, 1915. (Scottish History Society Publications, vol.59.)

PASSENGER and immigration lists index: a guide to published arrival records of about 500,000 passengers who came to the United States and Canada in the seventeenth, eighteenth, and nineteenth centuries; edited by P. William Filby with Mary K. Meyer. Detroit, Mich., 1981. 3v.

PATCH, Guthrie Shaw
Highland brotherhoods. New York, 1939.

PATERSON, James
Scottish surnames: a contribution to genealogy. Edinburgh, 1866.

—History of the County of Ayr, with a genealogical account of the families of Ayrshire. Ayr, 1847-52. 2v.

PAUL, Sir James Balfour
The Scots peerage. Edinburgh, 1904-14. 9v.

The PEDIGREE register; edited by George Sherwood. Vols. 1-2 (1907-13).

The PEERAGE of Scotland, including the dormant, attained and extinct titles, with the descent, marriage, issue etc. Edinburgh, 1834.

PHILIP, Peter
British residents of the Cape, 1795-1819: biographical records of 4,800 pioneers. Cape Town, 1981.

PINE, Leslie G.
The Highland clans. [Newton Abbot], 1972.

—Your family tree: a guide to genealogical sources. London, 1962.

PLAYFAIR, William
British family antiquity illustrative of the origin and progress of the rank, honours and personal merit of the nobility of the United Kingdom. Vol.8: The Baronetage of Scotand. London, 1811.

PRITCHARD, M. F. Lloyd
Scots in New Zealand before 1852. (In *Scottish Genealogist*, vol.xxv, no.3, September 1978, pp.81-4.)

REID, John Eaton
History of the county of Bute and families connected therewith. Glasgow, 1864.

ROBERTSON, George
A genealogical account of the principal families in Ayrshire, more particularly in Cunninghame. Irvine, 1823-7. 4v. (3v+Suppl.)

ROBERTSON, William
Proceedings relating to the peerage of Scotland from January 16th 1707 to April 29th 1788. Edinburgh, 1790.

ROGERS, Charles
Estimate of the Scottish nobility during the minority of James the Sixth, with preliminary observations. London, 1873. (Grampian Club)

ROSS, Peter
The Scot in America. New York, 1896.

RUVIGNY AND RAINEVAL, Melville Amadeus Henry Douglas Heddle de la Caillemotte de Massue de, *Marquis de*
The Jacobite peerage, baronetage, knightage and grants of honour. Edinburgh, 1904.

SAINTY, Malcolm R. *and* JOHNSON, Keith A.
Index to birth, marriage, death & funeral notices in the Sydney Herald, 18 April 1831-30 September 1853. Sydney, 1972-5. 4v.

SANDISON, Alexander
A list of some residents of Northmavine and Delting, Shetland, 1808-15 and 1825-35, also an index to MS. merchants account books in the County Library. [N.p.], 1957.

—Some inhabitants of Delting (Shetland) 1706-1732: an index to a MS. rent book. [N.p.], 1961.

—Tracing ancestors in Shetland. London, 1978.

SCARLETT, James Desmond
The tartans of the Scottish clans. Glasgow, 1975.

The SCOTS compendium, or pocket peerage of Scotland. Edinburgh, 1826. 2v.

SCOTTISH GENEALOGY SOCIETY
The Scottish Genealogist: the quarterly journal of the Scottish Genealogical Society. Vol.I, no.1 (January 1954)- . Edinburgh, 1954- .

SIMS, Clifford Stanley
The origin and signification of Scottish surnames, with a vocabulary of Christian names. Baltimore, 1968.

SINCLAIR, Alexander
Historical, genealogical and miscellaneous tracts. 22 parts. [Edinburgh, 1860?]

SKENE, William Forbes
History of the Highlanders of Scotland. Edinburgh, 1837. 2v. (And later eds.)

SOCIETY OF WEST HIGHLAND HISTORICAL RESEARCH
Notes & Queries of the Society of West Highland Historical Research. No.1 (30 November 1972)- . [Coll], 1972- .

SOME names of persons and places in Dalmellington Parish and neighbourhood, (Dalmellington, Straiton, and Carsphairn), 1565-1800. Stirling, 1904.

STEEL, Donald J.
National index of parish registers. Vol.12: Sources for Scottish genealogy and family history. [London], 1970.

STEPHENSON, Jean
Scotch-Irish migration to South Carolina, 1772: Rev. William Martin and his five shiploads of settlers. Washington, 1971.

The STIRLING Journal & Advertiser: a local index. Stirling, 1978-81. 3v.

STODART, Richard Riddle
Scottish arms: being a collection of armorial bearings, A.D.1370-1678. Edinburgh, 1881. 2v.

STUART, Margaret *and* PAUL, Sir James Balfour
Scottish family history: a guide to works of reference on the history and genealogy of Scottish families. Edinburgh, 1930.

TANCRED, George
The annals of a border club (the Jedforest) and biographical notices of the families connected therewith. Jedburgh, 1899. (And later eds.)

TAYLER, Alistair *and* TAYLER, Henrietta
Jacobites of Aberdeenshire and Banffshire in the Forty-Five. Aberdeen, 1928.

TAYLOR, James
The great historic families of Scotland. London, 1887. 2v. (And later eds.)

TEMPLE, Rev. William
The thanage of Fermartyn . . . its proprietors with genealogical deductions, etc. Aberdeen, 1894.

THOMSON, Theodore Radford
A catalogue of British family histories. London, 1928. (And later eds.)

TORRANCE, D. R.
List of graveyards for which transcriptions exist. (In *Scottish Genealogist*, vol.xxviii, no.1, March 1981, pp.19-32.)

TROTTER, Robert
Derwentwater, or the adherents of King James: a tale of the first rebellion; with an appendix containing notices of several ancient families. Edinburgh, 1825.

TURNBULL, William Barclay David Donald
Catalogue of the manuscripts relating to genealogy and heraldry, preserved in the library of the Faculty of Advocates at Edinburgh. London, 1852.

VESTIARIUM Scoticum: from the manuscript formerly in the library of the Scots College at Douay; with an introduction and notes by John Sobieski Stuart. Edinburgh, 1842.

WALFORD, Edward
County families of the United Kingdom. London, 1860. (And later eds.)

WALLACE, George
The nature and descent of ancient peerages connected with the State of Scotland, the origin of tenures, the succession of fiefs and the constitution of parliament in that country. Edinburgh, 1783. (And later eds.)

WARDEN, Alex. J.
Angus or Forfarshire. Dundee, 1880-1. 3v.

WARNER, Gerald
Homelands of the clans. London, 1980.

WHITMORE, J. B.
A genealogical guide: [an index to British pedigrees in continuation of Marshall's genealogist's guide]. London, 1947-50. 3v. (Publications of the Harleian Society, vols. xcix,ci,cii.)

WHYTE, Donald
A dictionary of Scottish emigrants to the U.S.A. Baltimore, Md., 1972.

—Genealogical studies in Scotland. (In *Families*, vol.21, no.4, 1982, pp.235-44.)

—Introducing Scottish genealogical research. Edinburgh, [1977]. (And later eds.)

—St Andrew's Church, Toronto, and its memorials. (In *Scottish Genealogist*, vol.xxx, no.1, March 1983, pp.18-23.)

Appendix

—Scottish ancestry research: a brief guide. Scotpress, Morgantown, , West Virginia, 1984.

—Scottish collections of family papers. (In *Genealogy Club of America Magazine*, vol.2, no.3, October 1971, pp.6-7.)

—Scottish emigration: a select bibliography. (In *Scottish Genealogist*, vol.xxi, no.3, August 1974, pp.65-86.)

—Source material for the Scottish Highlands and islands. (In *Genealogical Magazine*, vol.20, no.9, March 1982, pp.289-91.)

WIGTOWN Free Press index: a local index to the Galloway Advertiser and Wigtownshire Free Press newspaper. Dumfries, 1982-3. 2v.

Printed in Scotland for HMSO by Holmes McDougall Limited, Edinburgh.
Dd 8687818 H.F.6239. 8/86